WELCOME TO AMERICA'S TEST KITCHEN

THIS BOOK HAS BEEN TESTED, WRITTEN, AND edited by the folks at America's Test Kitchen, a very real 2,500-square-foot kitchen located just outside of Boston. It is the home of *Cook's Illustrated* magazine and *Cook's Country* magazine and is the Monday-through-Friday destination for more than three dozen test cooks, editors, food scientists, tasters, and cookware specialists. Our mission is to test recipes over and over again until we understand how and why they work and until we arrive at the "best" version.

We start the process of testing a recipe with a complete lack of conviction, which means that we accept no claim, no theory, no technique, and no recipe at face value. We simply assemble as many variations as possible, test a half dozen of the most promising, and taste the results blind. We then construct our own hybrid recipe and continue to test it, varying ingredients, techniques, and cooking times until we reach a consensus. The result, we hope, is the best version of a particular recipe, but we realize that only you can be the final judge of our success (or failure). As we like to say in the test kitchen, "We make the mistakes, so you don't have to."

All of this would not be possible without a belief that good cooking, much like good music, is indeed based on a foundation of objective technique. Some people like spicy foods and others don't, but there is a right way to sauté, there is a best way to cook a pot roast, and there are measurable scientific principles involved in producing perfectly beaten, stable egg whites. This is our ultimate goal: to investigate the fundamental principles of cooking so that you become a better cook. It is as simple as that.

You can watch us work (in our actual test kitchen) by tuning in to *America's Test Kitchen* (www.americastestkitchentv.com) or *Cook's Country from America's Test Kitchen* (www.cookscountrytv.com) on public television, or by subscribing to *Cook's Illustrated* magazine (www.cooksillustrated.com) or *Cook's Country* magazine (www.cookscountry.com). We welcome you into our kitchen, where you can stand by our side as we test our way to the "best" recipes in America.

SOUPS, STEWS & CHILIS

A BEST RECIPE CLASSIC

SOUPS, STEWS & CHILIS

A BEST RECIPE CLASSIC

BY THE EDITORS OF

COOK'S ILLUSTRATED

PHOTOGRAPHY

KELLER + KELLER, CARL TREMBLAY, AND DANIEL J. VAN ACKERE

ILLUSTRATIONS

JOHN BURGOYNE

America's
TEST KITCHEN

BROOKLINE, MASSACHUSETTS

America's Test Kitchen
17 Station Street
Brookline, MA 02445

ISBN-13: 978-1-933615-62-2
ISBN-10: 1-933615-62-1

Library of Congress Cataloging-in-Publication Data
The Editors of *Cook's Illustrated*

Soups, Stews & Chilis: Tired of bland broth, dry, stringy meat, and vegetables that turn to mush? We were. We simmered more than 4,000 soups, stews, and chilis to bring you 200 foolproof recipes that won't let you down.

1st Edition
ISBN-13: 978-1-933615-62-2
ISBN-10: 1-933615-62-1
(hardcover): U.S. $35
1. Cooking. I. Title
2010

Manufactured in the United States of America

10 9 8 7 6 5 4 3 2 1

Distributed by America's Test Kitchen, 17 Station Street, Brookline, MA 02445

Editorial Director: Jack Bishop
Executive Editor: Elizabeth Carduff
Executive Food Editor: Julia Collin Davison
Senior Editor: Lori Galvin
Associate Editors: Kate Hartke and Dan Zuccarello
Test Cooks: Jennifer Lalime, Christie Morrison, Adelaide Parker, and Dan Souza
Design Director: Amy Klee
Art Director: Greg Galvan
Designer: Beverly Hsu
Staff Photographer: Daniel J. van Ackere
Additional Photography: Keller + Keller and Carl Tremblay
Food Styling: Marie Piraino and Mary Jane Sawyer
Illustrator: John Burgoyne
Production Director: Guy Rochford
Senior Production Manager: Jessica Lindheimer Quirk
Senior Project Manager: Alice Carpenter
Traffic and Production Coordinator: Kate Hux
Asset and Workflow Manager: Andrew Mannone
Production and Imaging Specialists: Judy Blomquist, Heather Dube, and Lauren Pettapiece
Copyeditor: Cheryl Redmond
Proofreader: Debra Hudak
Indexer: Elizabeth Parson

Pictured on front of jacket: Tortilla Soup (page 45)

CONTENTS

PREFACE

SOME VERMONTERS GET UP EVERY MORNING and do things exactly the same way, day in and day out. The horse feeders are top-heavy so they tip over, the chickens have to be to shut in each night after supper, and the fences aren't checked so the horses and cattle get out. Others, however, fix the feeders, install an automatic, electric door in the henhouse, and check the fencing every spring. That's a smarter way of doing business.

This stubborn acceptance of less-than-ideal circumstances is well told in this old Vermont story about a special meeting at which the town selectmen were being questioned about the dangerous, icy roads. Some of the newer residents were particularly vocal and, after much back and forth, the first selectman finally admitted that the town did, indeed, have a good supply of both sand and salt.

"Why don't you use them more freely?" asked an angry local.

"Can't," replied the selectman.

"Why not?" responded the now-angrier local man.

"Just can't," said the old-timer. "Sometime we're bound to be needing 'em."

Even at a test kitchen where we are committed to finding the "best" recipe, we still get up every morning searching for a better way. From time to time, we change our minds about the best way to make, say, chicken broth, or perhaps the best brand of store-bought beef broth, or we come up with a new idea for bean cookery—brining the beans first to improve their texture and flavor. And, so, even for a book on soups and stews, a category of recipes that most folks would regard as being well-researched, we have gone back to the kitchen many times over the years to see if we could do better, to improve existing recipes, update older ones, invent or develop all-new soups and stews, and to bring you the latest in tastings, testings, and techniques.

Some of these recipes are among my all-time favorites, including Tortilla Soup (my go-to recipe on a Sunday night), White Chicken Chili, a great Old-Fashioned Chicken Noodle Soup, and Classic French Onion Soup, a stripped-down, delicious version of the real thing that depends on caramelizing the onions for flavor instead of simply floating a raft of melted cheese on top. Plus, we bring you spectacular recipes from our most recent test kitchen work, including Creamy Gazpacho Andaluz, which I think is a marked improvement over the bare-bones V8 juice recipe more familiar to Americans; a hearty Kentucky Burgoo that sounds, well, a bit dubious but turns out to be one of my favorite recipes of all time; Callaloo, a lively, pesto-green stew from the Caribbean with butternut squash and Swiss chard; and a delicious Cajun Chicken, Sausage, and Corn Stew.

We also offer three special chapters including "Speedy Soups" (not all soups require a long simmer), "Big-Batch Favorites" (scaling up is a lot harder than just multiplying amounts), and "Slow-Cooker Favorites" (plenty of new tricks here including how to build flavor without browning meat and foolproof work-arounds to avoid overcooking chicken).

Back in the 1960s in Vermont, a friend of mine, Dave Trachte, was driving by the Yellow Farmhouse, where the food was prepared on a Kalamazoo wood cookstove. He noticed a pile of burning logs in the driveway, stopped, and inquired. He discovered that Herbie, one of the farmhands, had tried to dry out wet wood by sticking it into the hot cast-iron oven with predictably disastrous results. (Herbie was also famous for sitting in front of the cookstove in the winter, the firebox door wide open, with a much-too-long log sticking out. Every few minutes he would give it a kick and push it an inch or two farther into the coals. He was too unorganized to cut the wood to size in the fall.)

Herbie reminds me a lot of the principles of good cooking. If you have the right well-tested recipes and if you do a bit of advance planning, you can depend on good results. Woe to the cook who shows up unprepared and in a mad rush!

So, enjoy *Soups, Stews & Chilis*. Enjoy the cooking, the recipes, and the everyday success you will experience with the backing of our test kitchen. It's nice to know that a collection of recipes is dependable, just like a good neighbor.

Christopher Kimball
Founder and Editor,
Cook's Illustrated and *Cook's Country*
Host, *America's Test Kitchen* and
Cook's Country from America's Test Kitchen

SOUPS AND STEWS 101

SOUPS AND STEWS 101

MAKING A GREAT POT OF SOUP, STEW, OR chili isn't hard, but it does require attention to detail, the right ingredients, well-made equipment, and a good recipe. Skimp on any of these things and you're bound to be disappointed with the results of your efforts. Whether you are making a company-worthy beef stew, a homey chicken noodle soup from scratch, or an elegant pureed vegetable soup, you'll likely build a flavorful base the same way, and need a good broth, fragrant herbs and spices, and a solid, sturdy pot that can take the heat (and go from the stovetop to the oven, in some cases). So if you plan on adding soups, stews, and chilis to your regular repertoire, it's worth starting out right. In this section, you'll find our guide to essential kitchen equipment and tools, along with tips and techniques for successful soup and stew making.

STOCKING YOUR KITCHEN

You don't need a host of equipment to make good soups and stews. A good chef's knife and a sturdy, heavy-bottomed Dutch oven will go a long way. But that's not to say that there aren't many other tools that will more than come in handy, especially as you work your way through the wide variety of recipes you'll encounter in this book.

DUTCH OVEN

When making soups and stews, a good Dutch oven, with at least a 6-quart capacity, is essential. Any smaller, and you'll have a hard time squeezing in the contents of the recipes in this book. The pot's bottom should be thick so that it conducts heat evenly and prevents food from scorching, and the lid should fit tightly to prevent excessive moisture loss—especially important when we simmer soup or stew covered. Our favorite Dutch ovens are the Le Creuset French Oven ($269) and the All-Clad Stainless 8-Quart Stockpot ($294.95). For a cheaper option, our best buy is the Tramontina 6.5-Quart Cast Iron Dutch Oven, which is $54.95.

LE CREUSET

CHEF'S KNIFE

With a good chef's knife in hand—the ultimate kitchen workhorse—you can accomplish any cutting task. You can prep vegetables for soups, hack up chicken for broth, and cube roasts for stews and chilis. Our favorite is the Victorinox (formerly Victorinox Forschner) Fibrox 8-Inch Chef's Knife ($24.95), which is lightweight, has a blade that's just the right length (8 inches), and has a comfortable grip and nonslip handle (useful for cutting up messy chicken parts).

VICTORINOX

WOODEN SPOON

For a tool as simple as a wooden spoon, any model will do, right? Wrong. We found wooden spoons that were just too big, with hulking handles that made stirring thicker stews tiresome. Spoons can also be too light; you don't want it to snap in half when you're stirring chili. Ultimately, a good wooden spoon should have a broad bowl that covers a lot of surface area, thin edges (thin edges scrape more effectively than thick edges), and a handle that's strong but not bulky or awkward to hold. Our winner, the Mario Batali 13-Inch Wooden Spoon ($5.95), has a form-fitting handle, a broad bowl, and is sturdy yet lightweight.

MARIO BATALI

PARING KNIFE

A paring knife isn't just useful for peeling fruits and vegetables; the small, sharp blade provides incredible dexterity and precision for a variety of jobs. We like a blade size between 3½ and 4 inches long, which makes the knife nimble enough to comfortably core tomatoes, devein shrimp, and get into the nooks and crannies of a chicken thigh, and any other tight corners. Our favorite paring knife is the Victorinox Fibrox 4-Inch Paring Knife ($4.95).

VICTORINOX

MEAT CLEAVER

A cleaver comes in handy when chopping up bones for broth, but it's also useful for other difficult tasks, such as cutting up lobster for bisque or halving butternut squash. The best meat cleavers feature a razor-sharp blade and perfectly balanced design. The test kitchen favorite is the Global 6-Inch Meat Cleaver ($145). For the more reasonable price of $43.99, the LamsonSharp 7¼-Inch Meat Cleaver has a comfortable handle and a sharp blade.

GLOBAL

KITCHEN SHEARS

Whether you're cutting the backbone out of a chicken or mincing chives for a garnish, kitchen shears are your best bet. No matter the job, you need a pair that's sturdy, strong, and sharp. Our favorite pair is the Messermeister Take-Apart Kitchen Shears ($19.95), which are precise, super-sharp, and have a slip-resistant handle. The only downside is a definite right-hand bias. For left-handed users, we recommend Wüsthof's Come-Apart Kitchen Shears ($19.95), which also perform well.

MESSERMEISTER

VEGETABLE PEELER

A vegetable peeler should make quick work of peeling potatoes, carrots, and any other ingredients that require peeling before being added to a pot. In the test kitchen, we rely on the Messermeister Pro-Touch Swivel Peeler ($6.95). This peeler passed every peeling test we could throw at it with flying colors and had a comfortable grip, even after we'd peeled piles of potatoes.

MESSERMEISTER

LARGE SAUCEPAN

When we're reheating leftovers, we reach for a large (4-quart) saucepan. We like the All-Clad Stainless Saucepan ($194.99) and the Cuisinart MultiClad Unlimited Saucepan ($69.99), which is our best buy. Both have tight-fitting lids, heavy bottoms, and rounded corners that whisks and spoons can reach into easily.

ALL-CLAD

MEASURING CUPS

Both dry and liquid measuring cups are essential in every kitchen. Dry ingredients, such as pasta, should always be measured in dry measuring cups; wet ingredients require a liquid measuring cup, so you can easily read the bottom of the concave arc at the liquid's surface, ensuring an exact measurement. Our favorite dry measuring cups are the Amco Basic Ingredient 4-Piece Measuring Cup Set ($11.50); these cups are hefty and durable and evenly weighted between handle and cup. Liquid measuring cups are usually clear plastic or glass, which makes it easy to get an accurate reading. We like the Cuisipro Deluxe, which comes in multiple sizes ($10.95 for a 2-cup measure; $14.95 for a 4-cup measure).

AMCO   CUISIPRO

LADLE

A ladle makes serving soups and stews easy and mess-free. We like a ladle with a handle about 9 to 10 inches in length; ladles with shorter handles will sink into deeper pots, and ladles with longer handles are too cumbersome to maneuver easily. The handle should be slightly offset; without this slight bend in the handle, cleanly transferring the ladle's contents into a bowl is nearly impossible. Our favorite ladle is the Rösle Ladle with Pouring Rim ($29.95), which, as its name implies, has a drip-prevention pouring rim that keeps even wiggly noodles in place all the way to your bowl.

RÖSLE

TONGS

Tongs aren't just useful for flipping steaks and burgers; we use ours to stir aromatics and vegetables and lift the lids of pots (especially when the pot is right out of the oven and the lid is ripping hot). We like tongs that have slightly concave pincers to grip the food and scalloped edges on the pincers; we've found that tongs with serrated edges can nick and tear food. Our favorite pair is the OXO Good Grips 12-Inch Locking Tongs ($12.95), which are just the right length to keep our hands away from the heat.

OXO

WHISK

When you need to reach into the corner of a pot to incorporate broth into a roux, a long, narrow whisk is your best choice. The tight radius of the tines can dig flour out of the corner, and the long, relatively straight wires can scrape a sauce from the sides of a pan. When tilted on its side, this whisk covers a wide swath of pan for efficient deglazing. We recommend a whisk measuring between 10 and 12 inches—too long to be lost to the bottom of a Dutch oven but too short to tilt out of most small pans. We like the Best Manufacturers 12-Inch Standard French Whip ($10.50).

BEST MANUFACTURERS

GARLIC PRESS

Garlic makes an appearance in most of our soups and stews—but mincing it can be a sticky, annoying task. To make it easier, we use a garlic press, which operates quite simply. It comprises two handles connected by a hinge. At the end of one handle is a small perforated hopper; at the other end is a plunger that fits snugly inside the hopper. The garlic cloves in the hopper get crushed by the descending plunger when you squeeze the handles together and the puree is extruded through the perforations in the hopper. Our favorite press is the Kuhn Rikon Easy-Squeeze Garlic Press ($20). It has curving plastic handles that are very easy to squeeze together. Also, it makes pressing garlic a practically effortless task, thanks to a longer handle and a shorter distance between the pivot point and the plunger. For a best buy, we like the Trudeau Garlic Press ($11.99), which produces uniform pieces of garlic and is easy to clean.

KUHN RIKON

FINE-MESH STRAINER

From draining canned tomatoes to removing meat and spent vegetables from broth, strainers are a soup-making essential. While a standard coarse-mesh strainer or even a colander may be perfectly adequate for separating solid ingredients from liquid, a fine-mesh strainer is essential for filtering out all the tiny bits so that broth is perfectly clear. Our favorite is the CIA Masters Collection 6¾-Inch Fine Mesh Strainer ($27.49), which is sturdily constructed and has a wide bowl rest.

CIA

FAT SEPARATOR

Before broth can be used or many braises can be served, the fat must be removed. The fastest way to do this is by using a fat separator. We keep the test kitchen stocked with the Trudeau Gravy Separator ($9.95), which is our favorite because of its large (4-cup) capacity, integrated strainer, and wide mouth that makes for easy filling.

TRUDEAU

BLENDER

When we want smooth, velvety pureed soups, we use a blender. The blender is the best tool for this job because the blade pulls ingredients down from the top of the container and the tall jar forces food down into the vortex so that no stray bits go untouched by the blade. We like the powerful KitchenAid 5-Speed Blender ($119.95), which has a 6½-cup capacity and is dishwasher safe. Our best buy is the ultra-quiet Kalorik BL Blender ($45).

KITCHENAID

FOOD PROCESSOR

A food processor is a great all-around appliance and makes quick work out of chopping and slicing vegetables and breaking down tomatoes, chiles, and other ingredients when we need a potent paste to infuse a soup or chili with concentrated flavor. Our favorite food processor is the KitchenAid KFP750 12-Cup Food Processor ($179.99), which has sharp, sturdy blades and a large feed tube.

KITCHENAID

SLOW COOKER

Slow cookers are the perfect tool for simmering soups, stews, and chilis—that's why we've devoted a whole chapter to slow-cooker recipes. Our favorite slow cooker is the Crock-Pot Touchscreen Slow Cooker ($129.99), which has a 6.5-quart capacity and an easy-to-use, intuitive control panel that clearly indicates the slow cooker is programmed and ready to go. The clear glass lid makes it easy to see the food as it is cooking. Also, the insert has handles, which make it easy to remove the insert from the cooker.

CROCK-POT

Store-Bought Broth 101

Homemade broth adds unequaled depth and flavor to soups and stews, which is why you'll find recipes for broth in this book (see pages 11–22). But it's not always essential or practical to use homemade. When selecting store-bought broth, it's important to choose wisely since what you use can have a big impact on your final recipe.

CHICKEN BROTH

While searching for the best commercial chicken broth, we discovered a few critical characteristics. First, we like broth with a lower sodium content— less than 700 milligrams per serving— because, when simmered, evaporation loss concentrates the broth's saltiness. Also, we like broth with a short ingredient list that includes flavor-boosting vegetables like carrots, celery, and onions. Our favorite chicken broth is Swanson Certified Organic Free Range Chicken Broth. If you can't find it, Swanson's "Natural Goodness" Chicken Broth rated almost as highly in our tasting.

VEGETABLE BROTH

We turn to store-bought vegetable broth for vegetarian soups or for vegetable soups that might be overwhelmed by the flavor of chicken broth alone. In fact, because commercial vegetable broths tend to be sweet, we'll often mix vegetable broth with chicken broth for the best flavor. To determine the best broth, we tested 10 brands, finding that those with a higher sodium level and higher vegetable content performed the best. Our favorite is Swanson Vegetarian Vegetable Broth.

CLAM JUICE

When we need clam juice for seafood stews or chowders, we reach for commercially prepared juice, made by briefly steaming fresh clams in salted water and filtering the resulting broth before bottling. We tested three brands, and only one tasted "too strong" and "too clammy," perhaps because its sodium was more than double that of the other two. Our winner, Bar Harbor Clam Juice, hails from the shores of clam country in Maine and is available nationwide. It brings a "bright" and "mineral-y" flavor to seafood dishes.

BEEF BROTH

Historically we've found beef broths short on beefy flavor, but with a few flavor additives, beef broth can pull off a deeply flavored beef soup or stew. We tasted 13 different beef broths, stocks, and bases to find out which one would suitably stand in for homemade. Generally, you should note the ingredients on the label; we found the best broths had flavor-amplifying ingredients, such as yeast extract and tomato paste, near the top of the list and included concentrated beef stock. Our winner, Rachael Ray Stock-in-a-Box All-Natural Beef Flavored Stock, elicited consistent praise from tasters, who found it to have "steak-y," "rich" flavor.

FREEZING BROTH EFFICIENTLY

Whether we're using homemade or store-bought broth, we frequently have some extras left after cooking. To save the leftover amount, we either store it in an airtight container in the refrigerator for up to four days or freeze it using one of the methods below.

A. Ladle the broth into nonstick muffin tins (each muffin cup will hold about one cup) and freeze. When the broth is frozen, twist the muffin tin as you would twist an ice cube tray. Transfer the frozen blocks to a plastic zipper-lock bag and store in the freezer.

B1. An alternative is to pour the broth into coffee mugs lined with quart-size plastic zipper-lock bags.

B2. Place the filled bags flat in a large, shallow baking pan and freeze. Once the broth is solidly frozen, the bags can be removed from the pan and stored in the freezer.

The Test Kitchen's Top Tips for Better Soups

Soup might seem easy enough to make—but it's hard to hide mistakes in a pot (or bowl) of soup. To make sure every spoonful of soup is richly flavored, with juicy meat and tender (but not mushy) vegetables, follow these tips.

I. USE A STURDY POT
Flimsy pots with thin bottoms cook unevenly and are prone to scorching, which can impart a burnt flavor to your soup. Instead, invest in a pot with a thick, heavy bottom, which will transfer heat evenly. See our top-rated brands of Dutch ovens on page 2.

2. SAUTÉ YOUR AROMATICS AND SPICES
The first step in making many of our soups (as well as stews, chilis, and other dishes) is to sauté aromatics, such as onion and garlic, to enhance their savory flavor, which in turn makes for a more complex, fuller-flavored soup. Medium heat ensures that the aromatics just begin to soften (they will cook through when the broth is added); we cook onions about 5 minutes but the small pieces of minced garlic require just 30 seconds of sauté time. By comparison, skipping this step and simply adding raw onions and garlic to simmering broth will result in flat-tasting, weak, watery soup.

3. START WITH GOOD BROTH
Broth forms the flavor background for any soup. So whether it's homemade broth or store-bought broth that's been enhanced with aromatic vegetables and herbs, starting with a good base is essential. See pages 11 to 22 for our recipes for homemade broths and page 5 for our recommended brands of store-bought broths.

4. CUT VEGETABLES THE RIGHT SIZE
Improperly cut vegetables can result in unevenly cooked vegetables—some may be mushy while others are crunchy. For perfectly cooked, tender vegetables, cut the vegetables to the size specified in the recipe.

5. STAGGER THE COOKING OF YOUR VEGETABLES
When a soup contains a variety of vegetables, their additions to the pot must often be staggered to account for their varying cooking times. Hardy vegetables like potatoes and winter squash can usually be added to the pot early on, whereas delicate vegetables like asparagus and green beans cook through much more quickly and should be added later in the cooking process.

6. SIMMER, DON'T BOIL
There is a fine line between simmering and boiling, and it can make all the difference in your soups. A boil refers to a rapidly bubbling and reducing liquid. Water, for example, boils at 212 degrees (at sea level). A simmer is a restrained version of a boil; fewer bubbles break the surface and do so with less vigor. We have found that a boil can break down vegetables (like potatoes) and toughen meat. A hard boil can also cause fat droplets to become more finely dispersed in broth, making the soup more difficult to defat and thus resulting in a greasy soup.

7. SEASON BEFORE SERVING
In general, we add salt (and other select seasonings) at the end of cooking. Many ingredients, such as store-bought broth, canned tomatoes, and canned beans, are heavily seasoned. Even though we may suggest rinsing some ingredients (such as beans), a small amount of salt may linger. That's why it's best to add salt at the end, after tasting the finished soup first. We also often reserve some additional flavorings, such as fresh herbs or lemon juice, to add freshness and brightness at the end of cooking.

The Test Kitchen's Top Tips for Better Stews

While stews generally require a moderate amount of preparation and effort, time and gentle simmering really do most of the work. That said, we've all had (or made) stews with tough meat, listless vegetables, and dull, watery broth. Follow these tips for producing superior stew.

1. CUT YOUR OWN MEAT

Packaged stew meat is often made up of irregularly shaped scraps that cook at varying rates. Cut your own stew meat to guarantee same-size chunks that share the same flavor and cooking time. Use fatty, flavorful cuts (we like chuck eye roast and pork butt) that will stay moist with extended cooking.

2. SKIP THE FLOUR BEFORE BROWNING

Contrary to popular belief, dusting meat with flour before searing it doesn't help it brown better. In fact, we have found just the opposite. The flour itself darkens a little, but the meat remains pale and doesn't develop the intense flavor compounds that are the goal of browning. Instead of flouring, pat stew meat dry and season it with salt and pepper before browning.

3. BROWN MEAT PROPERLY

Crowding the pan with too much meat or using inadequate heat can cause meat to steam (rather than brown) and ultimately lose flavor. To avoid this problem, add the meat only after the oil begins to smoke and leave plenty of space (about ½ inch) between pieces (this may mean browning in batches). Turn only when the first side is well seared and brown.

4. IF THE FOND BURNS, REMOVE IT

Browning meat in more than two batches can lead to a pan covered by burnt (rather than browned) fond that can impart a bitter flavor to the stew. If the fond is blackening, add a little water to the empty pot and scrape the fond to loosen it. Discard burnt bits and water and wipe the pot clean. Add fresh oil and proceed with the next batch of meat.

5. SAUTÉ AROMATICS TO ENHANCE FLAVOR

Recipes that call for dumping spices and aromatics, such as garlic and onion, into the pot at the same time as the liquid fail to maximize their flavor. So hold the liquid and sauté these flavor-enhancing ingredients first.

6. FLOUR AROMATICS TO THICKEN STEW

Many recipes call for thickening a stew by simmering with the lid off, but this method risks overcooking. Thicken stew at the beginning of cooking by sprinkling flour over the sautéed aromatics. Then cook the flour for a minute to remove any raw taste.

7. STAGGER THE ADDITION OF VEGETABLES

When vegetables are dumped indiscriminately into the pot at the outset of cooking, they not only lose flavor and turn mushy, but also water down the stew. Take into account the cooking time of individual vegetables and add them at the appropriate time.

8. SIMMER THE STEW IN THE OVEN

To ensure a steady, gentle simmer that allows the internal temperature of the meat to rise slowly and eliminates the risk of scorching the pot bottom, cook the stew in a covered Dutch oven at 300 degrees (for chicken) or 325 degrees (for beef and pork). This will keep the temperature of the stewing liquid below the boiling point (212 degrees) and ensure meat that is tender.

9. COOK MEAT UNTIL FALL-APART TENDER

When meat is undercooked, its fat and connective tissue have not had the chance to break down sufficiently, and it will taste rubbery and tough. Cook meat to the point where the collagen has melted down. This yields tender meat that separates easily when pulled apart with two forks.

10. DEFAT BEFORE SERVING

Let the stew settle, then skim away the fat with a wide, shallow spoon or ladle, or pour the stew liquid into a tall, narrow container, which creates a thicker layer of fat that's easier to remove. If you have one, a fat separator make this step incredibly easy. Or, if there's time, refrigerate the stew overnight; when the fat solidifies, it can be lifted right off. For more information on defatting, see page 18.

Storing and Reheating 101

Soups, stews, and chilis make a generous number of servings—perfect if you have six to eight at your dinner table, but not so great if you're cooking for two and wondering what to do with the leftovers. Luckily, it's easy enough to stock your freezer (or refrigerator) with last night's leftovers, so you can pull them out and reheat them whenever you like. In general, we recommend refrigerating delicate soups, including vegetable or brothy soups, for no more than two days but we find that heartier stews and chilis will keep refrigerated for up to three days. As for freezing, we don't recommend freezing broths, soups, or stews for longer than one month (see below for additional information). Here are the steps you need to follow to properly cool, store, and thaw your soups and stews so they heat up just as flavorful as freshly made.

COOLING AND STORING

For safety reasons, the U.S. Food and Drug Administration (FDA) recommends cooling liquids to 70 degrees within the first two hours after cooking and 40 degrees within four hours after that. As tempting as it might seem, avoid transferring hot soup straight to the refrigerator. You may speed up the cooling process, but you'll also increase the fridge's internal temperature to unsafe levels, which is dangerous for all the other food stored in the fridge. We found that letting the soup cool on the countertop for an hour helps it drop to about 85 degrees; then the soup can be transferred to the fridge and it will come down to 40 degrees in about four hours and 30 minutes (well within the FDA's recommended range).

We like to refrigerate or freeze soup in airtight plastic storage containers; remember to leave a little room at the top of the container(s) to prevent the lid(s) from popping off. Here are some other tips that will help you cool and freeze soups and stews quickly and efficiently.

COOLING SOUPS AND STEWS QUICKLY

If you don't have an hour to cool your soup or stew at room temperature, you can divide the hot dish into a number of storage containers, which allows the heat to dissipate more quickly than letting the entire batch of soup or stew cool down in the pot. Or try this method, which requires some advance planning: Fill a large plastic beverage bottle almost to the top and freeze it, then use the frozen bottle to stir the contents of the pot. The ice will cool the soup or stew down rapidly so it can be transferred to storage containers.

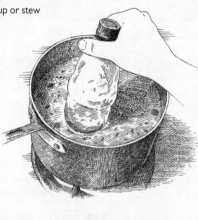

FREEZING SINGLE-SERVE PORTIONS

Freezing soups and stews in small amounts is handy when you only need one or two servings. Here's an easy way to freeze convenient single servings.

Set out a number of 10- or 12-ounce paper cups for hot beverages and fill each with a portion of cooled soup or stew (but not all the way to the top). Label, wrap well in plastic wrap, and freeze each cup. Reheat by microwaving each cup (or squeeze out the contents into a bowl and microwave) until hot.

FREEZING SOUPS WITH DAIRY OR PASTA

Creamy soups and soups that have a pasta component simply don't freeze very well. The dairy curdles as it freezes and the pasta turns bloated and mushy. Instead, make and freeze the soup without the dairy or pasta component included. After you have thawed the soup and it has been heated through, either stir in the uncooked pasta and simmer until just tender or stir in the dairy and continue to heat gently until hot (do not let it boil).

THAWING

For safety reasons, we recommend thawing frozen soups and stews in the refrigerator, never at room temperature, for 24 to 48 hours. (That said, if you've forgotten to plan ahead, you can heat frozen soups or stews directly in the microwave or on the stovetop, but note that the texture of meat and vegetables may suffer slightly.)

REHEATING

To reheat soups and stews, we prefer to gently simmer them on the stovetop; however, a spin in the microwave works, too. To reheat on the stovetop, use a Dutch oven or large heavy-bottomed saucepan with a tight-fitting lid. These sturdy pots will conduct heat evenly and are not apt to scorch during a long simmer, as could happen with a flimsy, thin-bottomed pot. If using the microwave, avoid reheating in the same container used to refrigerate or freeze the soup or stew. Not all storage containers are microwave-safe and the space inside the container will be too tight for you to comfortably stir the food during the heating process. Instead, we recommend that you transfer the food to a microwave-safe dish that's somewhat larger than the storage container. Just be sure to cover the dish with plastic wrap (or a plate) to prevent a mess in your microwave.

1

TAKING STOCK

Taking Stock

CHICKEN BROTH

IN THE CULINARY WORLD, WHEN IT COMES to broth, chicken is king. No other broth is quite as versatile or as fundamental. But we know that not every home cook has the time to make their own chicken broth for soup, so it's important to distinguish when homemade chicken broth is truly necessary. Generally, we find that store-bought broth works fine when the flavor of the broth is overshadowed by other, more potent ingredients. But for soups where the pure, clean flavor of the broth is a major player, homemade broth is essential. So we set out to make a broth that really tasted like chicken and could become the costar of many great soups. We also wanted to see if we could stray from the conventional method for making broth— simmering chicken parts and aromatics, such as onions, carrots, and celery, in water for hours— so we could create a flavorful broth in less time.

A number of recipes that we came across promoted roasting chicken bones or parts and then using them to make broth. The theory, at least, is that roasted parts will flavor broth in minutes, not hours. We gave it a try several times, roasting chicken backs, necks, and bones—with and without vegetables. We preferred the broth made with roasted chicken parts and vegetables, but the actual chicken flavor was too tame.

Next, we tried a method we had read about in our research, which calls for hacking chicken backs and necks into small pieces, browning the pieces (which helps a fond form on the bottom of the pot), and then sautéing them with an onion. The pot is then covered and the chicken pieces and onion are cooked over low heat until they release their rich, flavorful juice, which takes about 20 minutes. Only at that point is the water added, and the broth is simmered for just 20 minutes longer.

We knew we were onto something as we smelled the chicken and onion sautéing, and the finished broth confirmed what our noses had detected. The broth tasted pleasantly sautéed, not boiled. We realized that exposing more of the chicken parts' surface area made it easier for the chicken flavor to seep into the water in a short period of time. Hacking the parts into pieces also exposed the bone marrow, which is crucial for both the flavor and consistency of the broth.

Reviewing our ingredients again, we got stuck on the chicken backs. While chicken backs are an inexpensive way to make broth for soup (our local grocery store usually sells them for almost nothing), they may be difficult to find. In yet another test, we substituted relatively inexpensive whole legs and found that they also make a full-flavored broth for soup.

We made the broth twice more—once with onion and once with onion, celery, and carrot. The onion added a flavor dimension and complexity we liked; the extra vegetables neither added nor detracted from the final broth, so we left them out, not wanting to add an unnecessary step.

While the broth tasted great, after five minutes of sautéing, 20 minutes of sweating, and another 20 minutes of simmering, the meat was completely void of flavor. So, for a recipe that provides both broth and a good amount of usable meat, we created a variation using a whole chicken. (After hacking up the chicken, the breasts are browned and simmered, then the meat is shredded and reserved for soup.)

After much trial and error, we had a recipe that delivered liquid gold in about an hour. While this recipe requires more hands-on work (hacking chicken parts or a whole chicken, browning the pieces, then browning an onion), it is ready in a fraction of the time required to make broth by more traditional methods.

Simple Chicken Broth
MAKES ABOUT 8 CUPS

Any chicken meat left over after straining the broth will be very dry and flavorless; it should not be eaten. Chicken thighs can be substituted for the legs, backs, and wings in a pinch. If you'd like to make a chicken broth that also produces edible shredded meat, see the recipe for Simple Chicken Broth with Shredded Breast Meat (page 13).

SECRETS TO GREAT CHICKEN BROTH

You don't need to simmer a huge pot filled with pounds of roasted chicken bones and vegetables in order to make a good chicken broth. Our Simple Chicken Broth (page 11) delivers a rich, golden broth in about 1 hour using just water, an onion, and roughly one chicken, using the following key steps.

1. Hack Up the Chicken Parts

Many recipes simply simmer a whole chicken in water. But we've found that it is important to cut chicken parts into small pieces to release their flavorful juice in a short period of time. The increased surface area makes it easier for the chicken flavor to seep into the water, and also it exposes the bone marrow, which is crucial for the flavor and consistency of the broth. A meat cleaver makes this task easy; simply grasp the handle and use a hammering motion to drive through the bones.

2. Sauté Onion

We tested all sorts of vegetables in the chicken broth, including onion, carrot, and celery, but found only the flavor of the onion to be crucial. Browning the chicken first encourages the formation of a rich fond, which also contributes to the overall flavor of the broth. Sautéing the onion before adding the chicken and water helps to release its flavor more quickly and efficiently.

3. Sweat the Chicken Pieces for 20 Minutes

After sautéing the onion, add the hacked-up chicken pieces to the pot, cover, and let them cook for 20 minutes before adding the water. This step, known as sweating, is the key to the broth's overall short simmering time. During this 20-minute period, the chicken easily releases all of its juice and flavor into the pot, along with the onion. If the water is added to the pot too soon, the chicken will take longer to release its flavor.

4. Add Water and Simmer for Just 20 Minutes

With the flavor of the onion and chicken now released into the pot (you should see puddles of liquid in the pot), add the water and simmer everything for just 20 minutes to infuse the water with flavor. No extra flavor is gained by simmering the broth for longer than 20 minutes. After this amount of time, the chicken and onion will taste spent and flavorless.

1 tablespoon vegetable oil

3 pounds whole chicken legs, backs, and/or wings (see note), hacked with a meat cleaver into 2-inch pieces (see the illustration on page 12)

1 medium onion, chopped medium

8 cups water

2 teaspoons salt

2 bay leaves

1. Heat the oil in a large stockpot or Dutch oven over medium-high heat until just smoking. Add half of the chicken pieces and brown lightly, about 5 minutes; transfer the chicken pieces to a large bowl. Repeat with the remaining chicken pieces; transfer to the bowl.

2. Add the onion to the fat left in the pot and cook until softened, about 3 minutes. Return the chicken pieces to the pot, along with any accumulated juice, cover, and reduce the heat to low. Cook, stirring occasionally, until the chicken has released its juice, about 20 minutes.

3. Add the water, salt, and bay leaves and bring to a boil. Cover, reduce to a gentle simmer, and cook, skimming as needed, until the broth tastes rich and flavorful, about 20 minutes longer.

4. Strain the broth through a fine-mesh strainer, then defat the broth (see page 18). (The broth can be refrigerated in an airtight container for up to 4 days or frozen for up to 1 month; see page 5 for more information on freezing broth.)

➤ VARIATION

Simple Chicken Broth with Shredded Breast Meat

MAKES ABOUT 8 CUPS BROTH WITH 2 CUPS SHREDDED MEAT

Choose this broth when you want to have some breast meat in your soup.

1 (3½- to 4-pound) whole chicken

1 tablespoon vegetable oil

1 medium onion, chopped medium

8 cups water

2 teaspoons salt

2 bay leaves

1. Following the illustrations on page 14, cut the chicken into 7 pieces (2 split breasts, 2 legs, 2 wings, and a backbone). Set the split breasts aside, then hack the remaining chicken into 2-inch pieces with a meat cleaver following the illustration on page 12.

2. Heat the oil in a large stockpot or Dutch oven over medium-high heat until just smoking. Add the chicken breasts and brown lightly, about 5 minutes, then transfer to a plate and set aside.

3. Add half of the chicken pieces and brown lightly, about 5 minutes; transfer the chicken pieces to a large bowl. Repeat with the remaining chicken pieces; transfer to the bowl.

4. Add the onion to the fat left in the pot and cook until softened, about 3 minutes. Return the chicken pieces (not the breasts) to the pot, along with any accumulated juice, cover, and reduce the heat to low. Cook, stirring occasionally, until the chicken has released its juice, about 20 minutes.

5. Add the reserved chicken breasts, water, salt, and bay leaves and bring to a boil. Cover, reduce to a gentle simmer, and cook, skimming as needed, until the chicken breasts register 160 to 165 degrees on an instant-read thermometer, about 20 minutes.

6. Remove the chicken breasts from the pot, let cool slightly, then remove and discard the skin and bones and shred the meat into bite-size pieces (see the illustration on page 43). Strain the broth through a fine-mesh strainer, then defat the broth (see page 18). (The broth and the chicken can be refrigerated separately in airtight containers; the broth can be refrigerated for up to 4 days or frozen for up to 1 month and the chicken can be refrigerated for up to 2 days. See page 5 for more information on freezing broth.)

Butchering a Chicken 101

CUTTING UP A WHOLE CHICKEN FOR BROTH

Cutting up a whole chicken may seem like an intimidating process, but it's a handy technique to learn, especially if you want to make our Simple Chicken Broth with Shredded Breast Meat (page 13). After cutting the chicken into parts, hack each part into pieces (see the illustration on page 12) to extract maximum flavor.

1. With a sharp chef's knife, cut through the skin around the leg where it attaches to the breast.

2. Using both hands, pop the leg joint out of its socket.

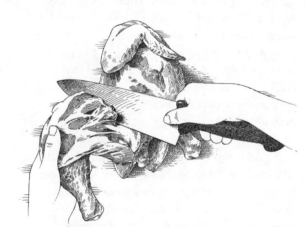

3. Use a chef's knife to cut through the flesh and skin to detach the leg from the body.

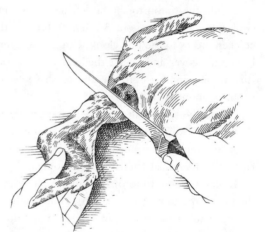

4. Bend the wing out from the breast and use a boning knife to cut through the joint. Repeat with the other wing.

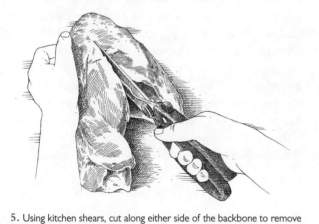

5. Using kitchen shears, cut along either side of the backbone to remove it from the chicken.

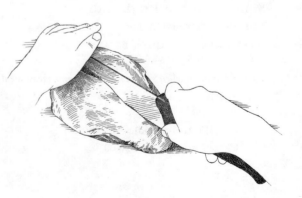

6. Using a chef's knife, firmly cut down the center of the breastbone to split the breast in half; set the split breasts aside.

TURKEY BROTH

UNLIKE CHICKEN BROTH, TURKEY BROTH usually starts out with the remnants of a fully roasted bird. Home cooks tend to think the lack of meat on the bones requires them to throw piles of vegetables into the stockpot with the carcass so the broth has some flavor. But this misstep tends to overwhelm any remaining turkey flavor. Other cooks think the bird must be simmered endlessly to draw out any flavor; this doesn't work either. We wanted to find the best way to make a turkey broth that had big, rich flavor—and we didn't want to spend all day doing it.

The first thing we learned was that turkey broth tastes best if there is a fair amount of meat clinging to the carcass; a barren carcass will provide little flavor. When carving the bird, it's best to leave a thin layer of meat on the bones for maximum flavor. Turkey skin will also enhance the flavor profile of the broth, so it shouldn't be removed when packing up the carcass for the fridge.

We began by identifying which vegetables to use in our broth; they had to contribute flavor, but not so much so that they overwhelmed the turkey flavor. We tested a variety of vegetable combinations, including mushrooms, fennel, and tomato in some, but ultimately stuck with the standard onion, carrot, and celery. Adding them at the start of cooking, along with enough water to cover the bones, complemented the turkey flavor nicely. Garlic contributed depth and was added as well. Another classic trio, parsley, thyme, and bay leaves, added a pleasant, aromatic quality tasters liked.

At this point, our broth had decent flavor but it was a little stodgy. We wondered if adding an acid might brighten it. We began by adding a modest amount (½ cup) of white wine to the pot with the water, and tasters noticed a subtle improvement. Ultimately, we settled on 2 cups of wine to balance the broth's flavors.

Now we wondered how long we'd have to simmer our broth. Unlike our Simple Chicken Broth (page 11), which relies on a substantial amount of meat to flavor the broth, we were working with mostly bones and just a small amount of meat. Would we have to simmer our broth for hours to extract maximum flavor from the bones and meat?

Thankfully, no. After experimenting with cooking times, we determined that our broth had to simmer for four hours to be fully flavored. Any longer than that and the broth was too gelatinous; any shorter, and the broth was too watery. We found that simmering the broth uncovered helped the liquid reduce and concentrated its flavor. Our broth was now fully flavored in a reasonable amount of time.

So the next time you roast a turkey, leave some meat and skin on the carcass, wrap it well, then store it in the refrigerator (it will hold for a day or two) and use it to make broth. (Properly wrapped bones can also be frozen for up to 1 month.) Nothing could be more economical or delicious.

Turkey Broth

MAKES ABOUT 12 CUPS

This broth tastes best made with a carcass that has a good amount of meat and skin still clinging to it.

1	carcass from a (12- to 14-pound) roasted turkey, cut into 4 or 5 rough pieces to fit into the pot
18	cups water
2	cups dry white wine
1	large onion, halved
1	large carrot, peeled and chopped coarse
1	large celery rib, chopped coarse
3	medium garlic cloves, smashed and peeled (see the illustration on page 299)
2	bay leaves
5	sprigs fresh parsley
3	sprigs fresh thyme

1. Bring the turkey carcass, water, wine, onion, carrot, celery, garlic, and bay leaves to a boil in a large stockpot or Dutch oven. Reduce to a gentle simmer and cook, skimming as needed, for 2 hours.

2. Add the parsley and thyme and continue to simmer gently until the broth tastes rich and flavorful, about 2 hours longer. Strain the broth through a fine-mesh strainer, then defat the broth (see page 18). (The broth can be refrigerated in an airtight container for up to 4 days or frozen for up to 1 month; see page 5 for more information on freezing broth.)

Rich Beef Broth

BEEF BROTH SHOULD TASTE LIKE BEEF—almost as intense and rich as pot roast jus—and be flavorful enough to need only a few vegetables and a handful of noodles or barley to make a good soup. When you think about the traditional method for making beef broth, which requires at least two pots and what seems like days of prep work and cooking, it's easy to see where all the flavor comes from. Beef bones and aromatics are roasted, the pan is deglazed with red wine, the whole mass is then dumped into a stockpot and covered with cold water, and (finally) the broth is simmered, along with some herbs and seasonings, for up to 16 hours. After all of this, the broth is strained and defatted before being used in soup. We wanted to streamline this laborious method as much as possible without compromising flavor; ideally, we wanted to complete the whole process, start to finish, in just a few hours. Also, we sought to use a cut of beef that could be easily located at any supermarket, so we could make lush, meaty beef broth any time we wanted.

Our first order of business was to determine the cut of beef. Using just beef bones, though traditional, wouldn't be possible if we wanted to keep the whole process to a few hours because the bones require hours of simmering to release their beefy flavor and gelatin, which contributes body to homemade broth. We knew we'd have to use more meat than bones if we wanted intense beef flavor in a relatively short amount of time.

We tried making several basic broths using different cuts of meat, including chuck, shank, round, oxtail, and short ribs. After simmering each cut with aromatics and water for only about two hours, we had intensely flavorful broths, but shank broth was the best one overall. However, the broth required 6 pounds of shank—a hefty amount for only a couple quarts of broth. Moreover, it resulted in too much meat for a soup or stew and we didn't want to eat the leftovers for days. The runner-up was the broth made with boneless chuck; this broth had significant flavor but no body. We decided to try cutting our chuck into smaller pieces (we'd been trimming it to 2-inch chunks) prior to simmering to see if we could eke more flavor out of it. Exposing more surface area, as we did in our

Simple Chicken Broth (page 11), worked wonders toward adding more complexity and deeper flavor. As a bonus, this broth required just 2 pounds of meat. We liked where this was going.

Brainstorming ways to get our chunks of chuck even smaller, we hit on pulsing the small pieces in the food processor. We simmered our home-ground chuck in 8 cups of water (covered, to preserve the yield) and crossed our fingers. The ground beef gave up its flavor so readily that we had good flavor in just 30 minutes. This broth also had substantial body, which was an unexpected but welcome result. At this point, we wondered why we were bothering with the food processor when ground beef is a staple at every supermarket. One more test confirmed it—ground beef was in.

Before we determined simmering time, we set out to establish a balanced flavor profile. Onion, carrot, and celery reinforced the hearty flavor of the broth without tasting overly vegetal. Tomato paste added color and acidity. Deglazing the pot with red wine fortified the broth even further.

Though not yet perfect, this broth was well on its way to being bold and velvety in record time. Unfortunately, it was still lacking some of the richness found in simmered-all-day broths. Considering additional ingredients that might add flavor and body, we hit upon mushrooms, which are high in glutamates, naturally occurring compounds that make food taste richer and meatier. We decided to try to capitalize on the chemistry of this vegetable. In the next test, we browned some mushrooms with the onion, which led to the development of a nice, brown fond on the bottom of the pot. This fond went far towards enhancing the beefy richness of our broth. Mushrooms were definitely here to stay.

Looking for another ingredient to up the richness and meatiness of our shortcut broth, we decided to add soy sauce (just 2 tablespoons). Now we needed just a moderate amount of salt (2 teaspoons) to bring out the flavors of our broth without making it taste salty.

With the flavor profile on track, we sought to determine the optimal simmering time and the right amount of ground beef. Our working recipe simmered 2 pounds of ground beef for half an hour; maybe a longer simmering time would mean we could get away with less meat. We compared our baseline broth to broths made with 1 pound and 1½ pounds of meat. We tasted the broths after 30 minutes, 1 hour, 1½ hours, and 2 hours. We were surprised by our findings. The first thing we learned was that more beef doesn't necessarily translate into more beef flavor. In fact, tasters found minimal flavor differences between the broth made with 1 pound of ground beef and the broth made with 2 pounds. What did matter was simmering time. The longer the beef simmered, the more flavor it imparted—but only up to a point. The broth that had simmered for 1 hour was too mild in flavor, but the broth that had simmered for 2 hours had a livery, metallic flavor that tasters disliked. Ultimately, tasters preferred the broth that had simmered for 1½ hours, which had the cleanest, beefiest flavor; also, we found that 1 pound of ground beef would be ample.

In less than three hours (including prep time), our broth was full-flavored, rich, and meaty.

SECRETS TO GREAT BEEF BROTH

Our goal was to create a flavorful, full-bodied beef broth without the hassle of having to buy and roast pounds of big, heavy, and expensive beef bones. We found that just a pound of ground beef, a few vegetables, water, and wine (along with a few other enhancements) produced a rich, velvety beef broth in less than 3 hours.

1. Sauté Mushrooms
We wanted to omit the long hours required for roasting beef bones, but found that we missed the roasted flavor in the broth. Many recipes build a flavor base by sautéing onions. We went one step further and added mushrooms and sautéed them until they left a golden brown fond on the bottom of the pot, which adds a roasted flavor (and some color) to the broth. Mushrooms are the best pick to create this fond because they are high in glutamates, naturally occurring compounds that make food taste richer and meatier.

2. Add Ground Beef
In early testing, we found that chuck roast, rather than bones, imparted great beefy flavor to our broth. And when we chopped the meat fine in a food processor, the flavor got even better. But why bother finely chopping beef when the supermarket already does it for you? In the end, we found that 1 pound of ground beef gave us the most bang for our buck. Not only is it easy to find and relatively inexpensive, but the meat breaks apart into tiny pieces as it simmers, releasing its flavor quickly.

3. Add Tomato Paste and Soy Sauce
To get big beefy flavor in a short amount of time, we found it important to add a few more flavor-enhancing ingredients to the broth. Like mushrooms, tomato paste and soy sauce are also high in glutamates and help to drive the beefy flavor home in our broth.

4. Cover and Simmer for 1½ Hours
To eke out as much flavor as possible from the ground beef and vegetables, it's crucial to simmer the broth for 1½ hours. But don't let the broth simmer for much longer, or the meat will give off an overcooked, livery flavor. Also, the pot should be covered at this point; it prevents the broth from overreducing during the long simmering time.

Defatting 101

Defatting a broth, soup, stew, or braise is important if you don't want your final dish to look and taste greasy. Below we've compiled four different ways to defat a liquid. The method you choose will depend on the dish you are making and the equipment you have on hand. For the first three methods, it is important to let the liquid settle for 5 to 10 minutes before defatting; this allows all of the fat to separate out and float to the top.

SKIM WITH A LADLE OR WIDE SPOON

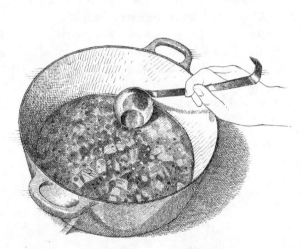

This is the simplest way to defat a liquid, and it works with broths, soups, stews, and braises. Let the liquid settle in the pot for 5 to 10 minutes, then skim the fat away with a ladle or wide spoon. The advantages of this method are that it's very easy and it doesn't dirty any extra dishes; however, some fat will remain in the broth.

USE A TALL, NARROW CONTAINER

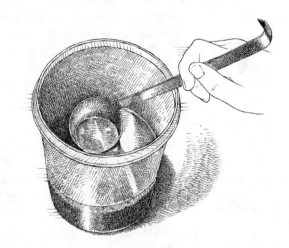

If you are using a large pot or have a large quantity of fat to skim, pour the broth into a tall, narrow container before defatting. This will create a deeper layer of fat that is easier to skim and remove. After letting the broth settle for 5 to 10 minutes, skim with a ladle or wide spoon. (Although some fat will remain behind, there will be less than if you simply defat the broth right in the pot.) This method also works with all kinds of broths, soups, and stews.

USE A FAT SEPARATOR

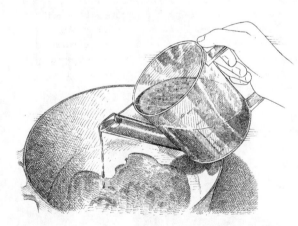

This technique works best with broths and braises that don't have much in the way of vegetables or garnishes taking up space in the pot. It requires a fat separator (as for size, we recommend buying the largest fat separator you can find). To use, simply pour the liquid into the fat separator and let it settle for 5 to 10 minutes. Then pour it back into your pot through the spout, leaving the fat behind in the separator.

REFRIGERATE OVERNIGHT

If you are making a stew or braise, you can simply refrigerate it without defatting—the fat will collect and solidify on the top as it chills. Upon removing it from the refrigerator, you can simply scrape the large solid pieces of fat right off the top before reheating and using. This also works for broths.

Rich Beef Broth

MAKES ABOUT 8 CUPS

We prefer to use 85 percent lean ground beef in this recipe; 93 percent lean ground beef will also work, but it will be less flavorful. Be sure to let the fond form on the bottom of the pot in step 1 because it is important for the flavor and color of the broth.

1	teaspoon vegetable oil
1	pound white mushrooms, wiped clean, trimmed, and quartered
1	large onion, chopped medium
1	pound 85 percent lean ground beef
2	tablespoons tomato paste
½	cup dry red wine
8	cups water
1	large carrot, peeled and chopped medium
1	large celery rib, chopped medium
2	tablespoons soy sauce
2	teaspoons salt
2	bay leaves

1. Heat the oil in a large stockpot or Dutch oven over medium-high heat until just smoking. Add the mushrooms and onion and cook, stirring often, until the onion is browned and a golden brown fond has formed on the bottom of the pot, 8 to 12 minutes.

2. Stir in the ground beef and cook, breaking up the meat with a wooden spoon, until no longer pink, about 3 minutes. Stir in the tomato paste and cook until fragrant, about 30 seconds. Stir in the red wine, scraping up any browned bits, and cook until nearly evaporated, 1 to 2 minutes.

3. Stir in the water, carrot, celery, soy sauce, salt, and bay leaves and bring to a boil. Cover, reduce to a gentle simmer, and cook, skimming as needed, until the broth tastes rich and flavorful, about 1½ hours.

4. Strain the broth through a fine-mesh strainer, then defat the broth (see page 18). (The broth can be refrigerated in an airtight container for up to 4 days or frozen for up to 1 month; see page 5 for more information on freezing broth.)

FISH STOCK

FISH STOCK, ALSO CALLED FISH FUMET, IS the basis for many fish soups and stews. Since most fish and seafood cooks in a matter of minutes, it can't really be relied upon to flavor the rest of the soup or stew. Therefore, the fish stock must be rich and flavorful. Good fish stock also gives a soup or stew some viscosity, which comes from the gelatin released by the fish bones.

Most recipes for fish stock follow the traditional method for making chicken broth. Fish frames (what's left over once the fillets have been removed—that is, the head, bones, and tail) are simmered in water along with some aromatic vegetables for up to an hour. We tried several classic fish stock recipes and were unimpressed. They were clear and thin and not nearly flavorful enough. Increasing the amount of fish frames improved the flavor, but developing a recipe that called for several pounds of frames to produce a couple quarts of stock seemed absurd.

Looking back at our Simple Chicken Broth (page 11), we recalled that sautéing the chicken and onion prior to simmering helped us coax more flavor out of both the meat and the bones. We decided to give this method a try and cooked some chopped aromatic vegetables along with the fish frames in some melted butter, thinking that the fat would bring out the flavor of the vegetables and fish frames. Since our goal was to draw out liquid that would contribute flavor to the stock (not to develop a fond on the bottom of the pot), we kept the pot covered while we did this. Then we added the white wine followed by the water.

After just half an hour, the flavors of the fish and vegetables were much deeper than in any fish stock we had tasted. Just as important, our stock had an excellent lushness. Clearly, this cooking process had unlocked the gelatin in those fish bones. The opaque, almost whitish color was another indication of the stock's body and richness.

We tinkered with the proportions, then ran a few more tests. White wine gave the stock a pleasing acidic edge. As for the vegetables and herbs, we liked the usual suspects—onions, celery, garlic, parsley, thyme, peppercorns, and a bay leaf. We found that carrots added too much sweetness and were best left out. We had one surprise addition to the stock—mushrooms. As in our Rich Beef Broth (page 19), white mushrooms, as well as a few dried mushrooms, gave the stock a fuller flavor.

Our updated method helped us cut down on overall simmering time—just half an hour—while still maximizing flavor.

Fish Stock

MAKES ABOUT 8 CUPS

You can often buy fish frames cheaply at your local fish market, or ask for them at the fish counter of your local supermarket. Note that the type of fish bones you use can make a big difference in the flavor of the stock; see below for more information.

2 tablespoons unsalted butter
3 pounds fish frames, cleaned (see the illustrations on page 21)
2 medium onions, chopped medium
1 large celery rib, chopped coarse
5 ounces white mushrooms, wiped clean, trimmed, and quartered
½ ounce dried porcini mushrooms, rinsed (optional)
5 medium garlic cloves, smashed and peeled (see the illustration on page 299)
1¾ cups dry white wine
8 cups water
6 sprigs fresh parsley
5 sprigs fresh thyme
2 teaspoons salt
8 black peppercorns
2 bay leaves

1. Melt the butter in a large stockpot or Dutch oven over high heat. Add the fish frames, onions, celery, white mushrooms, porcini mushrooms (if using), and garlic, cover, and cook, stirring occasionally, until the fish frames have begun to release some liquid, 6 to 8 minutes.

2. Reduce the heat to medium; continue to cook, covered, stirring often to break apart the fish frames with a wooden spoon, until the vegetables and bones are soft and aromatic, 6 to 8 minutes longer.

INGREDIENTS: **Fish for Stock**

We tested more than a dozen fish when developing our stock recipe and found that bones from mild white fish generally make the best stock. Within this group, we found a few that make especially gelatinous stock. Other white fish were perfectly acceptable and made good stock, although it was a tad thinner. As expected, our tasters did not like stock made with oily fish, such as salmon or bluefish. The flavors of those fish were much too strong.

Consequently, we have divided fish into three categories—highly recommended, recommended, and not recommended. Feel free to mix and match, using several kinds of fish in the same pot of stock.

There was a time when fishmongers would gladly give away bones, heads, and tails. But no longer, unless perhaps you're an especially good customer. And don't expect the fishmonger to have bones on hand whenever you show up at the market. It's advisable to call one day ahead and reserve what you need.

If freezer space permits, you can pack away fish bones each time you buy seafood. (If the fishmonger fillets some red snapper for you, ask for the bones.) But don't freeze fish frames for more than three or four months; after that amount of time, it is best to go ahead and make the stock, even if you subsequently freeze it.

HIGHLY RECOMMENDED	RECOMMENDED	NOT RECOMMENDED
Blackfish	Cod	Bluefish
Monkfish (especially the heads)	Flatfish (such as sole or flounder)	Mackerel
Red Snapper	Haddock	Pompano
Sea Bass	Pacific Pollock	Salmon
	Rockfish	Smelt
	Skate	

CLEANING FISH FRAMES FOR STOCK

1. Lift the gill cover and detach the gills with shears.

2. Remove and discard the gills. Rinse the fish frame under cool running water to flush out any blood.

3. Cut the fish frame into small pieces that will fit easily into the stockpot.

3. Add the wine, cover, and simmer gently for 10 minutes. Add the water, parsley, thyme, salt, peppercorns, and bay leaves. Return to a gentle simmer and cook, uncovered, skimming as needed, until the stock tastes rich and flavorful, about 30 minutes longer.

4. Strain the stock through a fine-mesh strainer, then defat the broth (see page 18). (The stock can be refrigerated in an airtight container for up to 4 days or frozen for up to 1 month; see page 5 for more information on freezing broth.)

VEGETABLE BROTH

VEGETARIAN SOUPS DON'T HAVE THE LUXURY of meat or bones to impart rich flavor, so a flavor-packed base is essential. Store-bought vegetable broth is often unbalanced, with sweet flavors dominating; certain soups, such as our Hearty Vegetable Soup (page 97), benefit hugely from the clean, vegetal flavor that only homemade vegetable broth can provide. Beyond soups, we reach for homemade vegetable broth when we want a flavorful cooking liquid that isn't meat-based, such as when preparing a simple risotto. In creating our own vegetable broth, we knew that this clean flavor depended on using a precise mix of vegetables—one variety too many (or one too few), and the overall flavor could be thrown off. We knew we might end up with a long and complex ingredient list, but we believed we could come up with a truly good vegetable broth that boasted balanced vegetable flavor.

To kick off our testing, we made several broths, using different techniques and vegetable combinations. In quick-simmered broth, on the stove for less than an hour, most of the flavor was left locked in the vegetables. Simmering for longer periods of time also resulted in a spiritless broth. Roasting vegetables in the oven first did deepen the broth's color and flavor, but deglazing the roasting pan and transferring the vegetables to a pot was a nuisance. The best option we found was sautéing aromatics in a little oil before adding water and the remaining ingredients and simmering for a good chunk of time. This broth had rich flavor, only slightly compromised clarity, and minimal oily residue.

We decided to begin testing potential ingredients, one by one. We started with different mixes of onions, shallots, garlic, scallions, and leeks. Onions, scallions, and garlic worked best. The onions offered strong, pure onion presence, the scallions were soft and bright, and a hefty amount of garlic (15 cloves) added complexity.

We moved on to the carrots and celery, both of which tended to dominate most vegetable broths. We found they were essential when used in moderation (just two of each) to prevent a broth that was overly vegetal or too sweet.

Now we began testing other vegetables. Mushrooms, although essential to our Rich Beef Broth (page 19) and Fish Stock (page 20), simply took up space in the pot and added nothing in the way of flavor to our vegetable broth. Bell peppers (both red and green) were dismissed as tasters found the resulting broth to be distinctly unpleasant. Fennel was also nixed almost immediately for the unappealing flavor it contributed.

We went through a few more misses when we finally got one hit—cauliflower. One medium head, cut into florets and added with the water, added a nice earthiness and nuttiness.

At this point, we had a pleasing vegetable broth but we wanted to improve it further. Examining the method again, we wondered if we could add deeper flavor by letting the aromatics cook longer, until they had developed a rich fond on the bottom of the pot. We found that cooking the onions, scallions, garlic, celery, and carrots, covered, for at least 20 minutes pulled more flavor out of the vegetables and guaranteed a richer vegetable broth.

Though we were mostly happy with our broth, it was now bordering on slightly sweet. We looked for an acid to counter the sweetness and tested lemon juice, but it was too potent. In the end, we found that a single plum tomato lent the right amount of acidity and brightness to balance out the sweetness.

INGREDIENTS: Stock versus Broth

The terms stock and broth have become synonymous in recent years. However, technically, there are differences between them.

According to classic culinary reference books, broth is something that can be served on its own. Broth is made with meat (and sometimes bones) or a whole chicken and simmered until the meat or chicken is done. The meat or chicken is then used in the soup or reserved for sandwiches or salads.

In contrast, stock is always destined to be a component in another dish, such as a soup, sauce, gravy, or risotto. Stock is made from meaty bones, usually from the leg if making beef stock or from the back, neck, and wings if making chicken stock. The bones are simmered until they are spent, having given every ounce of their flavor to the liquid. The bones (and any meat attached to them) are discarded once the stock is strained.

Still, these are technical distinctions. While home cooks might be likely to categorize soup liquid as either a stock or a broth depending on whether it is homemade or commercial, we have opted to use the more common term broth throughout this book, regardless of whether it is homemade or store-bought. The only exception we have made, which satisfies our culinary school instinct, is for fish stock, which is made with fish bones only (and no meat).

It was time to nail down the finishing flavors. Fresh thyme, bay leaves, and peppercorns went into the pot with the water. Although simple, our vegetable broth was richly flavored, and a great addition to any number of vegetarian soups and stews.

Vegetable Broth

MAKES ABOUT 8 CUPS

Be sure to let the fond form on the bottom of the pot in step 1 because it is important for the flavor and color of the broth. To prevent the broth from looking cloudy, be sure to simmer it gently (do not boil), and do not press on the solids when straining.

3	medium onions, chopped medium
2	celery ribs, chopped medium
2	carrots, peeled and chopped medium
1	bunch scallions, chopped
15	medium garlic cloves, smashed and peeled (see the illustration on page 299)
1	teaspoon olive oil
1	teaspoon salt
12	cups water
1	medium head cauliflower (about 2½ pounds), trimmed, cored, and cut into 1-inch florets (see the illustrations on page 281)
1	plum tomato, cored and chopped medium
8	sprigs fresh thyme
3	bay leaves
1	teaspoon black peppercorns

1. Combine the onions, celery, carrots, scallions, garlic, oil, and salt in a large stockpot or Dutch oven. Cover and cook over medium-low heat, stirring often, until a golden brown fond has formed on the bottom of the pot, 20 to 30 minutes.

2. Stir in the water, cauliflower, tomato, thyme, bay leaves, and peppercorns and bring to a simmer. Partially cover, reduce to a gentle simmer, and cook until the broth tastes rich and flavorful, about 1½ hours.

3. Strain the broth gently through a fine-mesh strainer, without pressing on the solids. (The broth can be refrigerated in an airtight container for up to 4 days or frozen for up to 1 month; see page 5 for more information on freezing broth.)

2

CHICKEN AND TURKEY SOUPS

CHICKEN AND TURKEY SOUPS

OLD-FASHIONED CHICKEN NOODLE SOUP

THE ROBUST, RICH FLAVOR OF OLD-FASHIONED chicken noodle soup can never start with a can—homemade broth is a must. We knew that with our Simple Chicken Broth with Shredded Breast Meat (page 13) as a foundation, a truly great bowl of soup would not be far away. But there were still questions to be answered. Which vegetables would be best added to this soup? Could they be simply diced and added raw or should they be sautéed first? As for the pasta, which kind of noodles worked best? Should they be cooked in a pot of boiling water or simmered right in the soup? Our goal was a richly flavored chicken soup boasting moist chunks of chicken, lots of vegetables, and tender noodles. With a master recipe in hand, we'd then be able to move on and create a few interesting variations on this classic.

To start, we tested a wide range of vegetables, including onions, carrots, celery, leeks, zucchini, tomatoes, cauliflower, and mushrooms. We concluded that the classic mirepoix ingredients (onions, carrots, and celery) should be part of a traditional chicken noodle soup. Tasters liked the other vegetables as well, but we decided that they were more appropriate for variations. For instance, tomatoes and zucchini worked well together and gave the soup a distinctly Italian character, while leeks and fennel were a good match with orzo and fresh tarragon.

To settle the issue of how to cook the vegetables, we prepared two batches of soup. For the first batch, we sautéed the onions, carrots, and celery in a little vegetable oil until softened and then added the chicken broth. For the second batch, we simply simmered the sliced vegetables in broth. As might be expected, we found that sautéing brought out the flavors of the vegetables and made a big difference in the finished soup.

We saw a few recipes that suggested saving the chicken fat skimmed from the homemade broth and using this fat as a cooking medium for the vegetables. We tested this and found that chicken fat does in fact add another level of chicken flavor to the soup. Although not essential, it makes sense to use chicken fat if you have planned ahead and saved what you skimmed from the surface of your broth.

In addition to the vegetables, we found that a bit of thyme and parsley brightened the flavors. We added thyme (fresh or dried) early on in the cooking to give it time to soften and permeate the broth. To preserve its grassy freshness, the parsley was best added just before serving.

The noodles were the last (and the most important) element that we needed to investigate. Dried egg noodles are the most common choice, but we also came across recipes that called for fresh pasta. Before we determined the kind of pasta, we decided to clarify the issue of how to actually cook it. We simmered dried egg noodles in the soup as well as in a separate pot of salted water. The noodles cooked in the soup pot shed some starch, which made the soup somewhat cloudy. In contrast, noodles cooked in a separate pot and then added to the broth left the finished soup completely clear.

Looks aside, we picked up our spoons to taste the noodles. The differences were dramatic. Noodles cooked separately tasted bland and did not meld with the soup. The noodles cooked in the soup absorbed some of the chicken broth, giving the pasta a rich, well-rounded flavor. We concluded that you must cook the noodles in the soup.

We identified several possible noodle choices: dried egg noodles (both thin and wide), dried linguine, dried spaghetti, fresh linguine, and fresh spaghetti. We cooked 2 cups of each in a pot of chicken soup. Tasters preferred the two styles of egg noodles over the dried and fresh spaghetti and linguine. The longer pastas were just too unwieldy when it came to scooping them out of the bowl, even when the pasta was trimmed to shorter lengths. They also had less-than-stellar textures; the dried spaghetti and linguine were deemed chewy, while the fresh pasta was too soft when cooked. The egg noodles, on the other hand, cooked up perfectly tender. Also, tasters liked that the bulkiness of the egg noodles made the soup feel heartier and more substantial.

With our classic soup down, we could focus on a few variations. To start, we wanted a soup starring wild rice; we found that leeks and mushrooms enhanced this variation. Next, we swapped the egg noodles for orzo and paired the pasta with fennel, leek, and fresh tarragon. To round out our Italian-style chicken soup (with zucchini and plum tomatoes), we added pasta shells and fresh basil. And, finally, cauliflower and curry are a natural match, so we used these flavors in a more exotic spin on chicken noodle soup.

One last note: While the recipes that follow are adaptable, we have carefully timed the addition of vegetables, noodles, and other ingredients to make sure that each item is perfectly cooked—not overcooked. You can make adjustments if you keep in mind general cooking times for additional ingredients or substitutions.

Old-Fashioned Chicken Noodle Soup

SERVES 6 TO 8

The flavor of this soup depends on homemade broth; do not substitute store-bought broth. If desired, substitute chicken fat (reserved from making the broth) for the vegetable oil.

1	tablespoon vegetable oil (see note)
1	medium onion, minced
1	carrot, peeled and sliced ¼ inch thick
1	celery rib, sliced ¼ inch thick
1	teaspoon minced fresh thyme leaves or ¼ teaspoon dried
8	cups Simple Chicken Broth with Shredded Breast Meat (page 13)
2	cups (3 ounces) wide egg noodles
2	tablespoons minced fresh parsley leaves Salt and ground black pepper

1. Heat the oil in a large Dutch oven over medium heat until shimmering. Add the onion, carrot, and celery and cook until softened, 5 to 7 minutes. Stir in the thyme and cook until fragrant, about 30 seconds. Stir in the broth and bring to a boil. Reduce to a simmer and cook until the vegetables are nearly tender, 6 to 8 minutes.

2. Stir in the noodles and simmer until tender, 10 to 15 minutes. Stir in the shredded chicken and let it heat through, about 2 minutes. Off the heat, stir in the parsley, season with salt and pepper to taste, and serve.

➤ VARIATIONS

Chicken Soup with Wild Rice, Leeks, and Mushrooms

The flavor of this soup depends on homemade broth; do not substitute store-bought broth. If desired, substitute chicken fat (reserved from making the broth) for the vegetable oil.

1	tablespoon vegetable oil (see note)
2	medium leeks, white and light green parts only, halved lengthwise, sliced ¼ inch thick, and rinsed thoroughly (see the illustrations on page 103)
8	ounces cremini mushrooms, wiped clean, trimmed, and sliced ¼ inch thick
1	carrot, peeled and sliced ¼ inch thick
1	teaspoon minced fresh thyme leaves or ¼ teaspoon dried
½	ounce dried porcini mushrooms, rinsed and minced
8	cups Simple Chicken Broth with Shredded Breast Meat (page 13)
1	cup water
½	cup wild rice
2	tablespoons minced fresh parsley leaves Salt and ground black pepper

1. Heat the oil in a large Dutch oven over medium heat until shimmering. Add the leeks, cremini mushrooms, and carrot and cook until softened and lightly browned, 10 to 15 minutes. Stir in the thyme and porcini mushrooms and cook until fragrant, about 30 seconds. Stir in the broth and water and bring to a boil. Reduce to a simmer and cook until the vegetables are nearly tender, 6 to 8 minutes.

2. Stir in the wild rice, cover, and simmer gently until the rice is tender, about 1 hour. Stir in the shredded chicken and let it heat through, about 2 minutes. Off the heat, stir in the parsley, season with salt and pepper to taste, and serve.

Chicken Soup with Orzo, Fennel, and Leeks

The flavor of this soup depends on homemade broth; do not substitute store-bought broth. If desired, substitute chicken fat (reserved from making the broth) for the vegetable oil.

- 1 tablespoon vegetable oil (see note)
- 1 medium leek, white and light green parts only, halved lengthwise, sliced ¼ inch thick, and rinsed thoroughly (see the illustrations on page 103)
- 1 medium fennel bulb (about 12 ounces), trimmed of stalks, cored, and chopped fine (see the illustrations below)
- 1 teaspoon minced fresh thyme leaves or ¼ teaspoon dried
- 1 teaspoon ground coriander
- 8 cups Simple Chicken Broth with Shredded Breast Meat (page 13)
- ¾ cup orzo
- 1 tablespoon minced fresh tarragon leaves
  Salt and ground black pepper

1. Heat the oil in a large Dutch oven over medium heat until shimmering. Add the leek and fennel and cook until softened, 5 to 7 minutes. Stir in the thyme and coriander and cook until fragrant, about 30 seconds. Stir in the broth and bring to a boil. Reduce to a simmer and cook until the vegetables are nearly tender, 6 to 8 minutes.

2. Stir in the orzo and simmer until tender, 10 to 15 minutes. Stir in the shredded chicken and let it heat through, about 2 minutes. Off the heat, stir in the tarragon, season with salt and pepper to taste, and serve.

PREPARING FENNEL

1. Cut off the stems and feathery fronds. (The fronds can be minced and used for a garnish.)

2. Trim a very thin slice from the base and remove any tough or blemished outer layers from the bulb.

3. Cut the bulb in half through the base. Use a small, sharp knife to remove the pyramid-shaped core.

4. Then slice each bulb half into thin strips.

5. If necessary, cut the strips into small pieces as directed in the recipe.

Chicken Soup with Shells, Zucchini, Tomatoes, and Basil

The flavor of this soup depends on homemade broth; do not substitute store-bought broth. If desired, substitute chicken fat (reserved from making the broth) for the vegetable oil.

1	tablespoon vegetable oil (see note)
1	medium onion, minced
4	medium garlic cloves, minced or pressed through a garlic press (about 4 teaspoons)
1	teaspoon minced fresh thyme leaves or ¼ teaspoon dried
8	cups Simple Chicken Broth with Shredded Breast Meat (page 13)
1	cup medium pasta shells
3	plum tomatoes, cored and cut into ½-inch pieces
1	medium zucchini (about 8 ounces), halved lengthwise, seeded, and cut into ½-inch pieces
2	tablespoons chopped fresh basil leaves
	Salt and ground black pepper
	Freshly grated Parmesan cheese, for serving

1. Heat the oil in a large Dutch oven over medium heat until shimmering. Add the onion and cook until softened, 5 to 7 minutes. Stir in the garlic and thyme and cook until fragrant, about 30 seconds. Stir in the broth and bring to a boil.

2. Stir in the pasta and simmer for 5 minutes. Stir in the tomatoes and zucchini and simmer until the pasta and vegetables are tender, 5 to 10 minutes longer. Stir in the shredded chicken and let it heat through, about 2 minutes. Off the heat, stir in the basil, season with salt and pepper to taste, and serve with freshly grated Parmesan cheese.

Chicken Noodle Soup with Curried Cauliflower and Cilantro

The flavor of this soup depends on homemade broth; do not substitute store-bought broth. If desired, substitute chicken fat (reserved from making the broth) for the vegetable oil.

1	tablespoon vegetable oil (see note)
1	medium onion, minced
1	carrot, peeled and sliced ¼ inch thick
1	tablespoon curry powder
3	medium garlic cloves, minced or pressed through a garlic press (about 1 tablespoon)
1	teaspoon minced fresh thyme leaves or ¼ teaspoon dried
8	cups Simple Chicken Broth with Shredded Breast Meat (page 13)
2	cups (3 ounces) wide egg noodles
½	medium head cauliflower, trimmed, cored, and cut into ½-inch pieces (about 3 cups; see the illustrations on page 281)
½	cup frozen peas
2	tablespoons minced fresh cilantro leaves
	Salt and ground black pepper

1. Heat the oil in a large Dutch oven over medium heat until shimmering. Add the onion and carrot and cook until softened, 5 to 7 minutes. Stir in the curry powder, garlic, and thyme and cook until fragrant, about 30 seconds. Stir in the broth and bring to a boil. Reduce to a simmer and cook until the vegetables are nearly tender, 6 to 8 minutes.

2. Stir in the noodles and cauliflower and simmer until both are tender, 10 to 15 minutes. Stir in the shredded chicken and peas and let them heat through, about 2 minutes. Off the heat, stir in the cilantro, season with salt and pepper to taste, and serve.

HEARTY CHICKEN AND VEGETABLE SOUP

GREAT CHICKEN AND VEGETABLE SOUP IS A marriage of intensely flavored chicken broth, tender bites of chicken, complementary vegetables, and heady herbs. But too often, this soup is little more than a jumble of improperly cooked vegetables (some are crunchy while others are mushy) playing second fiddle to the chicken (which is usually overcooked and dry). We were after a hearty chicken and vegetable soup that gave equal billing to tender, moist chicken and well-cooked vegetables and also featured a full-bodied broth. With this goal in mind, we headed into the test kitchen.

Our first order of business was the broth. Most of the recipes we tested took for granted that in a bowl overflowing with chicken and vegetables, no one would notice the flavor (or lack thereof) of the broth. However, after tasting our way through a half-dozen recipes using store-bought broth, we can say with certainty that a homemade broth is absolutely crucial to this recipe, where the flavor of chicken provides the backbone of the soup. Since our soup needed cooked chicken, we began testing using our Simple Chicken Broth with Shredded Breast Meat (page 13). In about an hour, this recipe yields flavorful broth and tender, shredded meat. With our base in place, we shifted our attention to the veggies.

We started by sautéing some minced onion and garlic, then focused on the vegetables that would define the soup. We knew root vegetables, with their earthy flavor and hearty texture, would be key to a successful chicken and vegetable soup. We really liked the sweet, vegetal flavor of parsnips, celery root, and turnips (any of the three will work fine), as well as the more traditional carrots and potatoes. Cut into tidy ½-inch pieces and added at the same time, the root vegetables and potatoes all cooked in 20 to 25 minutes. Next, we looked for another vegetable that would provide some contrast to the starchy ones. We wanted a hearty soup, so delicate greens like spinach and assertive spring vegetables like peas, asparagus, and fennel seemed out of place. After cooking our way through most of the produce aisle, we landed on zucchini, which proved to be the perfect counterpoint to our starchy vegetables. Added toward the end of cooking, the zucchini kept a bit of crunch and added a welcome freshness and mild flavor.

Simple Drop Biscuits

MAKES 12 BISCUITS

The tender, flaky texture of these biscuits depends on the melted butter clumping into small bits as it is combined with the chilled buttermilk. A ¼-cup spring-loaded ice cream scoop makes portioning these biscuits very easy. You will need about 2 tablespoons melted butter for brushing the tops of the biscuits.

2	cups (10 ounces) unbleached all-purpose flour
2	teaspoons baking powder
1	teaspoon sugar
¾	teaspoon salt
½	teaspoon baking soda
1	cup buttermilk, chilled
8	tablespoons (1 stick) unsalted butter, melted and warm, plus extra for brushing (see note)

1. Adjust an oven rack to the middle position and heat the oven to 475 degrees. Line a rimmed baking sheet with parchment paper.

2. Whisk the flour, baking powder, sugar, salt, and baking soda together in a large bowl. In a medium bowl, stir the buttermilk and warm melted butter together until the butter forms small clumps. Stir the buttermilk mixture into the flour mixture with a rubber spatula until just incorporated and the dough pulls away from the sides of the bowl.

3. Using a greased ¼-cup measure, scoop out and drop mounds of dough onto the prepared baking sheet, spacing them about 1½ inches apart. Bake until the tops are golden brown and crisp, 12 to 14 minutes, rotating the baking sheet halfway through baking.

4. Brush the baked biscuits with extra melted butter, transfer to a wire rack, and let cool for 5 minutes. Serve warm.

➤ VARIATION

Rosemary and Parmesan Drop Biscuits
Follow the recipe for Simple Drop Biscuits, adding 1½ ounces Parmesan cheese, grated (about ¾ cup), and ½ teaspoon finely minced fresh rosemary leaves to the flour mixture in step 2.

Up to this point, tasters had been pleased with the broth and vegetables, but complained that the finished product tasted more like a brothy chicken soup with some vegetables than a cohesive, hearty chicken and vegetable soup. Determined to add real vegetable depth and body, we headed back to the produce aisle.

Mushrooms, with their assertive, earthy flavor and texture, seemed like a good place to start. Cremini mushrooms, sliced thin and well browned before we sautéed the aromatics, provided great depth of flavor (slightly more flavor than white mushrooms in this application) and a pleasing texture. Still, tasters wanted a bolder, more complex bowl of soup. In the test kitchen, we often turn to tomato paste to add meatiness and heartiness to dishes. Tomato paste, like mushrooms and soy sauce, is high in glutamates, a class of amino acids that lends foods a meaty flavor. We added a tablespoon of tomato paste to our aromatics and let it cook for a minute; as we had hoped, the rich flavor of the tomato paste bloomed and infused the broth. We also took this opportunity to add a little flour to the pot in hopes of giving the soup more body, as some tasters complained it was too thin. Worried we'd create a stew not a soup, we started low, eventually settling on just 2 tablespoons of flour, for a broth with more substantial body. Satisfied with our mix of properly cooked vegetables, tender shredded chicken, and flavorful, balanced chicken and vegetable broth, we turned to the finishing touches.

With such a deep, unctuous broth, tasters wanted some acidity. White wine, added after the tomato paste and cooked until it had almost evaporated, worked great, offering a more nuanced acidity than lemon juice or vinegar. For complex herbal notes, we selected thyme and parsley. Adding the thyme early allowed the woodsy herb to soften and slowly infuse the soup, while a shower of parsley at the very end served to liven things up. Finally, we had arrived at our ideal bowl of Hearty Chicken and Vegetable Soup: rich, satisfying, and complex, with great chicken and vegetable flavor in every bite.

Hearty Chicken and Vegetable Soup
SERVES 8

The flavor of this soup depends on homemade broth; do not substitute store-bought broth. If desired, substitute chicken fat (reserved from making the broth) for the vegetable oil. White mushrooms can be substituted for the cremini mushrooms. Serve with Simple Drop Biscuits (page 29) if desired.

2   tablespoons vegetable oil (see note)
8   ounces cremini mushrooms, wiped clean, trimmed, and sliced ¼ inch thick (see note)
    Salt and ground black pepper
1   medium onion, minced
3   medium garlic cloves, minced or pressed through a garlic press (about 1 tablespoon)
1   teaspoon minced fresh thyme leaves or ¼ teaspoon dried
2   tablespoons unbleached all-purpose flour
1   tablespoon tomato paste
½   cup dry white wine
8   cups Simple Chicken Broth with Shredded Breast Meat (page 13)
1   pound parsnips, celery root, and/or turnips, peeled and cut into ½-inch pieces
8   ounces red potatoes (about 2 medium), scrubbed and cut into ½-inch pieces
2   carrots, peeled and cut into ½-inch pieces
1   medium zucchini (about 8 ounces), halved lengthwise, seeded, and cut into ½-inch pieces
2   tablespoons minced fresh parsley leaves

1. Heat 1 tablespoon of the oil in a large Dutch oven over medium heat until shimmering. Add the cremini mushrooms and ¼ teaspoon salt, cover, and cook until the mushrooms have released their liquid, about 5 minutes. Uncover and continue to cook until the mushrooms are dry and browned, 5 to 10 minutes.

2. Stir in the remaining 1 tablespoon oil and onion and cook until softened, 5 to 7 minutes. Stir

in the garlic and thyme and cook until fragrant, about 30 seconds. Stir in the flour and tomato paste and cook for 1 minute. Stir in the wine, scraping up any browned bits, and cook until almost completely evaporated, about 1 minute.

3. Gradually whisk in the broth, smoothing out any lumps. Stir in the parsnips, potatoes, and carrots and bring to a boil. Partially cover, reduce to a gentle simmer, and cook until the vegetables are just tender, 20 to 25 minutes.

4. Stir in the zucchini and continue to simmer gently until just tender, 5 to 10 minutes. Stir in the shredded chicken and let it heat through, about 2 minutes. Off the heat, stir in the parsley, season with salt and pepper to taste, and serve.

MATZO BALL SOUP

PICTURE A STEAMING BOWL OF TENDER, light dumplings floating in rich chicken broth, and you'll have a good sense of what matzo ball soup is. An essential part of Jewish culinary history, matzo balls are made with ground matzo (matzo meal), chicken fat or oil, eggs, and water. Yet even with this most traditional recipe, there are many variations in the size and texture of matzo balls. Some people like fluffy, light matzo balls; others prefer something denser and chewier. Flavor variations involving bitter herbs, especially dill or parsley, are also popular, as are matzo balls flavored with ground spices, including ginger, nutmeg, and cinnamon. We decided to create a simple, foolproof matzo ball recipe that could be easily varied in terms of texture and seasonings.

Our initial tests focused on the ratio of ingredients and its effect on texture. We started with 1 cup of matzo meal (a basic measure in most recipes) and tried varying amounts of eggs, fat, and liquid. Testers preferred matzo balls made with four eggs for 1 cup of meal. With five eggs, the matzo balls tasted eggy. With three eggs, the matzo balls were heavy and dense. Four eggs produced matzo balls that were noticeably lighter but not overly eggy.

When it comes to the fat used in matzo balls, chicken fat is the traditional choice, although vegetable oil can be substituted. As might be expected,

we found that chicken fat (we suggest keeping the fat skimmed from making our Simple Chicken Broth, page 11) does in fact make tastier and more tender matzo balls. We saw recipes that called for as little as 2 tablespoons and as much as ½ cup of fat for every cup of matzo meal. We found that ¼ cup made tasty matzo balls that weren't overly rich.

Water was the final component to examine. In some respects, this proved the most perplexing element in our testing. Adding too much water makes the matzo meal mixture too soft to shape. However, too little water makes the matzo balls dense. To complicate matters, it seems that different brands of matzo meal absorb water at different rates. After running more than a dozen tests, we found it necessary to rest the matzo ball mixture for a few moments to let it set up before adjusting the amount of water or matzo meal to achieve our desired texture. Right after the batter was mixed, it was too loose to form into matzo balls; its texture at this point resembled pancake batter—when we ran a wooden spoon through the middle of the batter to divide it in half, the two sides ran back together. But after a few minutes of resting, when separated at the bottom of the bowl, the mixture slowly came back together and the texture of the batter was now similar to soft mashed potatoes. We found this was the ideal consistency for fluffy, light matzo balls. If your batter is too runny or too stiff at this point, the consistency can be adjusted with more matzo meal or water (be sure to let the batter rest for 2 to 3 minutes after each addition) until it reaches the desired texture.

With the batter mixed, we now considered chilling time. All the recipes we consulted suggested chilling it to make it easier to handle and shape. Recommended times in the refrigerator ranged from 15 minutes to 24 hours. We found that chilling the batter for at least one hour, or up to four hours, definitely makes it easier to handle. We next moved on to cooking the matzo balls. Traditionally, this soup is crystal-clear, so rather than clouding it up by cooking the matzo balls in the broth (we used our Simple Chicken Broth on page 11), we simmered them in a pot of water separately, then transferred them to the chicken broth just before serving.

As for the actual cooking, we found that a modest simmer and using a wide pot was best. Also, distributing the matzo balls evenly across the bottom of the pot ensured even cooking. Once the matzo balls were cooked through (we checked by cutting one in half to make sure the center was not dark or raw-looking), we transferred them directly to our simmering chicken broth.

We now had light and airy matzo balls floating in a rich chicken broth, but we felt something was missing. Carrots and dill are traditional additions, so we sliced a few carrots and minced some dill, then added them to the pot. For a simple herb variation, we mixed fresh dill (parsley works, too) right into the matzo ball mixture; for spiced matzo balls, we added in cinnamon, ginger, and nutmeg.

Matzo Ball Soup

SERVES 6 TO 8

The flavor of this soup depends on homemade broth; do not substitute store-bought broth. We prefer the flavor of matzo balls made with chicken fat, but vegetable oil can be substituted. If you make the matzo balls larger, they may require a longer cooking time. The flavor and texture of the matzo balls will vary widely depending on the brand of matzo meal you use; more finely ground matzo meal will produce fluffier matzo balls.

4	large eggs, lightly beaten
¼	cup chicken fat or vegetable oil (see note)
6	tablespoons water, plus extra as needed
I	cup matzo meal, plus extra as needed
	Salt and ground black pepper
8	cups Simple Chicken Broth (page 11)
3	carrots, peeled and sliced ⅛ inch thick
2	tablespoons minced fresh dill or parsley leaves

1. Whisk the eggs, chicken fat, and water together in a medium bowl. In a separate bowl, whisk together the matzo meal, 1½ teaspoons salt, and ¼ teaspoon pepper. Stir the matzo mixture into the egg mixture until just combined and let sit for 2 minutes.

2. Adjust the consistency of the matzo mixture as needed with additional matzo meal or water,

until it resembles the texture of soft mashed potatoes (when a wooden spoon is run through the mixture to divide it in two, the two sides do not run back together). Cover and refrigerate for at least 1 hour or up to 4 hours.

3. Bring 4 quarts water and 2 teaspoons salt to a boil in a large Dutch oven. Following the illustration below, use moistened hands to shape 1 tablespoon of the matzo mixture into a 1-inch ball; repeat with the remaining matzo mixture. Drop the balls into the boiling water, cover, reduce to a gentle simmer, and cook until the matzo balls are cooked through and firm, about 20 minutes.

4. Meanwhile, bring the broth to a simmer in a large Dutch oven. Add the carrots and simmer gently until tender, 10 to 15 minutes. Using a slotted spoon, transfer the cooked matzo balls to the soup. Off the heat, stir in the dill, season with salt and pepper to taste, and serve.

➤ VARIATIONS

Herbed Matzo Ball Soup

Follow the recipe for Matzo Ball Soup, adding ¼ cup minced fresh dill or parsley leaves to the egg mixture in step 1.

Spiced Matzo Ball Soup

Follow the recipe for Matzo Ball Soup, adding ½ teaspoon ground nutmeg, ½ teaspoon ground ginger, and ½ teaspoon ground cinnamon to the matzo mixture in step 1.

SHAPING MATZO BALLS

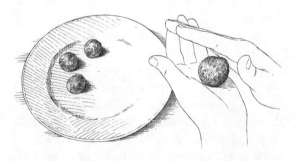

After lightly moistening your hands, use your palms to quickly and gently shape 1 tablespoon of the matzo mixture into a 1-inch ball.

PENNSYLVANIA DUTCH CHICKEN SOUP

THE FOOD OF THE PENNSYLVANIA DUTCH has long been enjoyed for its seamless melding of German flavors and techniques with New World sensibilities. Chicken, corn, and rivel soup is a great example of how successful this marriage can be. The highlight of this soup is the rivels, which are a cross between soft and doughy American-style dumplings and pasta-like German spaetzle. The tender rivels are paired with sweet corn and moist chicken in a velvety chicken broth to create a simple, yet satisfying, soup. Wishing to pay homage to this quaint soup, we set about developing a recipe that would properly balance these elements so they all contributed equally to the flavor and texture of the dish.

We began by researching and testing recipes from various Pennsylvania Dutch cookbooks. While the resulting soups often differed dramatically from one another, each was assembled in much the same way. First, simple aromatics are sautéed in butter. Then either store-bought or homemade chicken broth is added and brought to a simmer. Then the rivels—small pinches of a crumbly dough made from flour, egg, salt, and sometimes melted butter or milk—are added to the broth and simmered gently until tender. Finally corn and chicken are stirred in until cooked through. With such a short list of ingredients, we knew we needed to pay close attention to each one.

Focusing first on the broth, we quickly settled on homemade. While we find store-bought broth to be perfectly acceptable in heavily spiced or thickened soups, we felt it would lack the body and bold chicken flavor needed for this simple recipe in which each of the few ingredients really need to shine. Since chicken flavor provides the foundation of this soup, and we wished to have bites of tender white meat mixing with the corn and rivels, we started testing using our Simple Chicken Broth with Shredded Breast Meat (page 13), which yields both broth and shredded breast meat in just under an hour. We focused on the next key component, the corn.

Because corn is one of the main ingredients of this soup, we knew it had to have a definite presence. The corn had to be sweet, tender, and retain some crispness, even after cooking. We suspected fresh corn was the way to go, but for the sake of experimentation, we tested both frozen corn and fresh corn in our soup. We made two batches of soup (without rivels at this point) with 2 cups of each and compared. The fresh corn was sweet and remained pleasantly crisp as it simmered, while the frozen corn tasted dull and turned slightly soggy. As we had guessed, fresh corn contributed more to the overall flavor profile of the soup and would also add some textural contrast with the tender rivels.

With frozen corn out of the picture, we could focus on getting the most flavor possible out of the fresh corn. While the corn itself had good flavor and bite, tasters wanted the corn flavor to permeate the broth as well. We first tried increasing the amount of corn from two ears (2 cups kernels) to three ears (3 cups kernels). While tasters appreciated the extra bites of corn, this step didn't improve the overall corn flavor in the broth. Borrowing a technique we often use in corn chowder, we tried scraping the milk and pulp from the spent cobs and adding it to the broth. The result of this simple technique was dramatic, adding big corn flavor as well as creaminess to the broth. With two of the pieces in place, we turned to the keystone of this soup, the rivels.

As with most beloved foods, there seem to be as many ways to make rivels as there are people who make them. While most versions we found were a mix of just flour, egg, and salt, many also included melted butter or milk. At the most rustic end of the spectrum, egg and flour were mixed in a bowl with a fork to create dough crumbs. The contents of the bowl (extra flour and all) were then dumped into simmering broth. The result of this technique was a soup akin to lumpy gravy. At the other end of the spectrum were more refined rivels that closely resembled noodles (one dough actually required a pasta roller). We tried a variety of styles and ended up preferring rivels that combined the best aspects of both extremes; they had a soft, feathery exterior and slightly firm center. We found we also preferred rivels that were just flour, egg, and salt—no melted butter or milk—because they had a cleaner flavor.

Having settled on the style of rivel, we tested ratios of flour and egg until we hit upon a winning combination. Dry doughs (generally two eggs to 2 cups of flour) were easy to work with, but produced dense, leaden rivels. By decreasing the flour to 1½ cups, we got a moist, sticky dough that yielded delicate dumplings with a satisfying chew. To achieve a rustic look, we used our fingertips to pinch off small rivels and then dropped them directly into the simmering broth. Cooked gently over low heat for 30 minutes, these rivels became tender as they absorbed the rich chicken and corn broth, all the while releasing some starch and providing the soup with additional body.

With the chicken, corn, and rivels in balance, all our soup needed was a fresh touch. We sprinkled some minced parsley over the top and tucked into one truly great American soup.

Pennsylvania Dutch Chicken, Corn, and Rivel Soup

SERVES 6 TO 8

The flavor of this soup depends on homemade broth; do not substitute store-bought broth. Do not substitute frozen corn for the fresh corn here; fresh corn is crucial to the flavor of this soup. The rivel dough is quite soft and sticky; dip your fingers in cool water as needed to prevent it from sticking to your hands when shaping.

1	tablespoon unsalted butter
1	medium onion, minced
3	medium garlic cloves, minced or pressed through a garlic press (about 1 tablespoon)
1	teaspoon minced fresh thyme leaves or ¼ teaspoon dried
8	cups Simple Chicken Broth with Shredded Breast Meat (page 13)
2	cups plus 3 tablespoons water
3	ears corn, husks and silk removed, kernels and cob pulp removed and reserved separately (see the illustrations on page 108)

1½	cups unbleached all-purpose flour
2	large eggs, lightly beaten
	Salt and ground black pepper
2	tablespoons minced fresh parsley leaves

1. Melt the butter in a large Dutch oven over medium heat. Add the onion and cook until softened, 5 to 7 minutes. Stir in the garlic and thyme and cook until fragrant, about 30 seconds. Stir in the broth, 2 cups of the water, and corn cob pulp and bring to a simmer.

2. Combine the flour, eggs, and ¼ teaspoon salt in a large bowl with a rubber spatula until a sticky dough forms. If the dough does not come together easily, add the remaining 3 tablespoons water, 1 tablespoon at a time, until it forms a sticky, cohesive mass.

3. Following the illustration below, use moistened fingers to pinch the dough into ½-inch rivels and drop them into the simmering soup. Cover and simmer gently, stirring occasionally, until the rivels are tender, about 30 minutes.

4. Stir in the corn kernels and simmer gently until tender, 5 to 7 minutes. Stir in the shredded chicken and let it heat through, about 2 minutes. Off the heat, stir in the parsley, season with salt and pepper to taste, and serve.

MAKING RIVELS

Using lightly moistened fingers, pinch small pieces of the dough to form ½-inch rivels, then drop them into the gently simmering soup to cook.

FARMHOUSE CHICKEN CHOWDER

TO MOST COASTAL DWELLERS, CHOWDER means one thing: seafood (usually clams). However, for much of landlocked, rural America, up until the last hundred years, seafood wasn't part of the average diet. In the center of the country, hearty farmhouse chowders were the status quo. These chowders made use of locally available foods, especially corn, potatoes, and, of course, chicken. Farmhouse chicken chowder is a classic example of one of these lesser-known chowders. With the exception of the poultry, the ingredient list looks like that of a seafood chowder: pork (salt pork or bacon), potatoes, and milk or cream. Unfortunately, this chowder can also suffer the same fate as seafood chowders—a bland bowl of mushy spuds and rubbery meat suspended in a gravy-like soup. With the hope of bringing this soup out of the shadows and into the limelight, we set out to create the ultimate bowl of farmhouse chicken chowder.

The best chicken chowder recipes rely on a time-honored technique that builds layers of flavor by first rendering either salt pork or bacon, then cooking aromatics in this flavorful fat. Next, chicken broth is added along with chicken, potatoes, and additional vegetables. Once everything is tender, dairy—usually milk or cream—is stirred in to add richness. We decided to first test the pork, then the chicken, chicken broth, and potatoes, and finally the dairy and any extra vegetables, determining additional seasonings along the way.

Since pork provides the flavor foundation for any chowder, this is where we began our testing. Pork is most often found in chowders in one of its cured forms: salt pork or bacon. While both products come from the pig's belly and are salt-cured, bacon is also smoked and sometimes highly seasoned. Salt pork is the fattier choice of the two and the more traditional choice for chowder. However, bacon has become more popular in recent decades, no doubt because it is more readily available than salt pork. We decided to test both in chicken chowder recipes that we uncovered in our research. While tasters liked both chowders, there

was a nice smoky flavor in the bacon-studded version. With our pork product of choice in hand, we tested using different amounts until we hit upon just the right level of meatiness and smoke (which we achieved with four slices of bacon). Next, we tackled the broth.

After softening some minced onion, garlic, and a bit of thyme in the rendered bacon fat, we had to make a decision about the broth. We wanted big, rich chicken flavor that would reflect this soup's farmhouse heritage, and so homemade broth seemed like the obvious choice. We tested a batch made with store-bought broth next to one made with our Simple Chicken Broth with Shredded Breast Meat (page 13), and tasters confirmed that we were right, rallying wholeheartedly behind homemade broth. Our chicken broth also took care of the chicken, providing 2 cups of gently poached, shredded white meat, which tasters preferred to chicken that was first cut and then cooked. With our foundation in place, we could concentrate on the potatoes.

Many of the chicken chowder recipes we uncovered relied solely on potatoes to thicken the broth, mashing them right in the soup itself for thickness. While this technique certainly worked, we found the resulting texture to be rather mealy and the flavor muddled. Ideally, we wanted our simmering potatoes to both absorb the flavor of the broth and give off some starch. Ultimately, they should provide satisfying, creamy bites in the final soup, but not necessarily thicken it. With this goal in mind, we tested all the varieties of potatoes available at our local market. Russet potatoes, which are high in starch and low in moisture, went from tender to crumbly and mushy in a matter of minutes. High-moisture, low-starch red potatoes were plagued with the opposite problems: they stayed too firm, absorbed little of the broth's flavor, and contributed almost no starch to the soup. In the end, Yukon Gold potatoes proved the perfect spud. With a moderate level of moisture and starch, these potatoes provided a small amount of starch and also absorbed some of the rich flavors of the broth. Tasters found that ½-inch pieces were the right size for our chowder.

While the potatoes did give up some starch to the chowder, they didn't thicken the soup so we knew we had to look elsewhere to achieve our desired consistency. Based on our experience with other chowders, we knew that flour, when cooked with fat, produces smooth, velvety soups. Wary of tripping over the line into gravy territory, we began with just a few tablespoons of flour, slowly increasing the amount until we hit ⅓ cup, at which point our chowder was substantial but not overly thickened. Finally, it was time to consider the vegetables, dairy, and finishing touches.

We found a range of vegetables included in the recipes we uncovered, everything from green beans and snap peas to rutabagas and turnips. While none of these vegetables ruined the chowder, some were much more successful than others. A single carrot, sliced thin, proved to be all the root vegetable our chowder could handle; any more, and the soup was heavy and stew-like. At the other end of the spectrum, spring vegetables, such as asparagus and spinach, seemed too light and subtle for this rustic chowder. Red bell pepper, with its sweetness and light crunch, proved to be a winner, offering freshness and visual appeal. At this point, with the shredded chicken, carrot, potatoes, and bell pepper in place, our chowder needed no other vegetables.

As for the dairy, tasters preferred the richness of cream to both half-and-half and milk. Added at the end of cooking along with the shredded chicken (which just needed to warm through), a single cup of cream filled out the soup and balanced its flavors. While this chowder felt like a winner, tasters were still asking for something more.

While brainstorming about different garnishes that might make our chowder really sing, one taster recalled a clam chowder he had enjoyed that was adorned with small bites of crunchy bacon. Up to this point, we had been leaving the crisped bacon in the pot and building the soup right on top of it. Guessing that crispy bacon might provide a welcome contrast to the soft textures of our chowder, we removed half of the cooked bacon and sprinkled it on as a garnish at the end. This simple step provided the perfect finish to our Farmhouse Chicken Chowder, now ready to assume its rightful place in the chowder hall of fame.

Farmhouse Chicken Chowder
SERVES 8

The flavor of this soup depends on homemade broth; do not substitute store-bought broth.

4	ounces (about 4 slices) bacon, chopped medium
1	medium onion, minced
3	medium garlic cloves, minced or pressed through a garlic press (about 1 tablespoon)
1	teaspoon minced fresh thyme leaves or ¼ teaspoon dried
⅓	cup unbleached all-purpose flour
8	cups Simple Chicken Broth with Shredded Breast Meat (page 13)
2	pounds Yukon Gold potatoes (about 4 medium), peeled and cut into ½-inch pieces
1	carrot, peeled and sliced ¼ inch thick
1	red bell pepper, stemmed, seeded, and cut into ½-inch pieces
1	cup heavy cream
2	tablespoons minced fresh parsley leaves Salt and ground black pepper

1. Cook the bacon in a large Dutch oven over medium heat until crisp and rendered, 5 to 7 minutes. Using a slotted spoon, transfer half of the bacon to a paper towel–lined plate; set aside.

2. Add the onion to the bacon left in the pot and cook until softened, 5 to 7 minutes. Stir in the garlic and thyme and cook until fragrant, about 30 seconds. Stir in the flour and cook for 1 minute.

3. Gradually whisk in the broth, scraping up any browned bits and smoothing out any lumps. Stir in the potatoes and carrot and bring to a boil. Reduce to a gentle simmer and cook until the vegetables are nearly tender, about 10 minutes. Stir in the bell pepper and continue to simmer gently until all of the vegetables are tender, 10 to 15 minutes longer.

4. Stir in the cream and bring to a simmer. Stir in the shredded chicken and let it heat through, about 2 minutes. Off the heat, stir in the parsley and season with salt and pepper to taste. Sprinkle individual portions with the reserved bacon before serving.

➤ VARIATION

Farmhouse Chicken Chowder with Corn, Poblano Chile, and Cilantro

If desired, you can substitute 1 cup frozen corn, thawed, for the fresh corn.

Follow the recipe for Farmhouse Chicken Chowder, substituting 1 poblano chile, stemmed, seeded, and chopped medium, for the bell pepper. Add 1 ear corn, husk and silk removed, kernels cut from the cob (see the illustration on page 108), to the soup with the chile in step 3. Substitute 2 tablespoons minced fresh cilantro leaves for the parsley.

COCK-A-LEEKIE

RUMORED TO BE A FAVORITE OF MARY QUEEN of Scots, cock-a-leekie (chicken and leek soup) is a soup with some serious pedigree—the first recorded version of this recipe dates back to the late 1500s. While it is eaten throughout the year, cock-a-leekie tends to show up on the menu at "Burns suppers," which are held in late January to commemorate the birthday of the beloved Scottish poet Robert Burns. Given its proud history, we felt it was time to give Scottish-style chicken and leek soup its due on this side of the pond.

All of the recipes we uncovered in our research called for chicken, chicken broth, and leeks, but that's where the similarities ended. Many recipes disagreed about how much of a role the leeks should play. Some recipes called for simmering an entire bunch of leeks with the bird, resulting in a bitter soup, while other recipes treated the ingredient as a garnish, adding just a smattering at the end. Also, some recipes called for the use of a grain, such as barley, oats, or rice, for thickness, while others added prunes for sweetness. After tasting and enjoying some rather laborious renditions, we decided a little American modernization would go a long way toward making an authentic-tasting yet streamlined cock-a-leekie.

The first step in many traditional recipes is stewing a rooster for up to 8 hours. Searching for an easier path, we bucked tradition and turned to our Simple Chicken Broth with Shredded Breast Meat (page 13), which produces a broth with a pronounced, meaty chicken flavor and a good amount of shredded breast meat. It was now time to consider the other starring ingredient, the leeks.

We knew we didn't want a bitter, overly leek-y soup, but we also didn't want to relegate the allium to a simple garnish. We wanted a soup somewhere in the middle: the leek flavor had to be persistent but pleasant, and the leeks themselves had to contribute some texture. To start, we sliced a few leeks and sautéed them in butter before adding the broth. After just 10 minutes of sautéing, our leeks had released a great deal of flavor, and the resulting soup was rich, with a subtle sweetness that tasters appreciated. However, there was no leek texture in the final soup. Wishing to have our leeks and eat them too, we added a few more sliced leeks to the pot after we added the broth. These leeks didn't have as much time to soften, so they provided the texture we were looking for, as well as an additional burst of fresh leek flavor. Now we turned our attention to the final details.

Many older recipes from our research included barley, oats, or rice to thicken the soup. While we generally appreciate the texture and heartiness that grains add to brothy soups, we found that in this recipe they muddied the clean leek flavor we had worked so hard to achieve. Cloves also featured heavily in a number of recipes, but tasters found that too much overpowered the leek flavor. A pinch, added with a couple cloves of minced garlic, provided just the right amount of warm spice flavor.

Prunes, another common addition, originally served the purpose of disguising the often-gamey flavor of the rooster. While gaminess was clearly not a problem for us, tasters actually preferred soup that included prunes; they found the soup to be more balanced and complex. Just as with the leeks, some recipes cooked the prunes for hours, while others chopped them fine and added them as a garnish. Again, we settled in the middle, preferring to cut the prunes into larger pieces (small pieces just disintegrated) and adding them to the soup with the shredded chicken to simmer for just a few minutes. This technique allowed the prunes to soften slightly but still maintain their shape, ensuring rich, sweet bites of prune throughout.

With a full, rich leek flavor, sweetened by a handful of prunes, and a hearty texture from two additions of the namesake allium, our cock-a-leekie soup was perfect, and certainly destined for another five centuries of popularity.

Cock-a-Leekie

SERVES 6 TO 8

The flavor of this soup depends on homemade broth; do not substitute store-bought broth. Look for leeks with large white and light green parts. If your leeks are small, you may need a few extra for this recipe.

2	tablespoons unsalted butter
6	medium leeks, white and light green parts only, halved lengthwise, sliced ¼ inch thick, and rinsed thoroughly (about 6 cups; see the illustrations on page 103)
	Salt and ground black pepper
2	medium garlic cloves, minced or pressed through a garlic press (about 2 teaspoons)
	Pinch ground cloves
8	cups Simple Chicken Broth with Shredded Breast Meat (page 13)
10	pitted prunes, cut into ½-inch pieces
2	tablespoons minced fresh parsley leaves

1. Melt the butter in a large Dutch oven over medium heat. Add half of the leeks and ¼ teaspoon salt and cook until very soft, 8 to 10 minutes. Stir in the garlic and cloves and cook until fragrant, about 30 seconds. Stir in the broth, scraping up any browned bits, and bring to a boil.

2. Stir in the remaining leeks, reduce to a gentle simmer, and cook until the leeks are just tender, 5 to 7 minutes. Stir in the shredded chicken and prunes and let them heat through, about 2 minutes. Off the heat, stir in the parsley, season with salt and pepper to taste, and serve.

MULLIGATAWNY

MULLIGATAWNY IS A SILKY, ELEGANT PUREED vegetable soup that is often enriched with chicken (or lamb) and lentils. The flavor profile, a nod to the soup's Anglo-Indian origin, comes from coconut, which contributes some sweetness, and curry and other spices, which add a pungent flavor and aroma. But occasionally, this soup falls short of expectations, with poorly incorporated, raw-tasting spices and a texture that is neither completely smooth nor chunky. We wanted to reclaim this soup's deep, complex flavor and keep the texture velvety.

We decided to start with the liquid for the broth. We knew that chicken broth was the ideal base for the wide range of spices and vegetables and we thought the spices and aromatics would hide any flaws in store-bought chicken broth, so we decided against homemade. Unfortunately, this left us with no cooked chicken to stir in. We decided to poach two chicken breasts in the broth once we established our spice mix.

Moving on to the spices, we knew that curry was essential and debated whether to use a prepackaged curry powder (which is a blend of spices to begin with) or to make our own. After experimenting with store-bought curry powders, we found the end product to be muted, so we decided to make our own. We found great results with a blend of garam masala, cumin, coriander, and turmeric, especially when we bloomed the spices in butter.

We focused next on the aromatics, garlic and ginger, and on the coconut. After testing various amounts of garlic and ginger, we noted that we liked equal amounts of both. Testing coconut ingredients next, we found coconut milk gave the soup a silky consistency, but the coconut flavor tended to dominate the dish. Fresh coconut was too troublesome to prepare. Dried coconut, in the form of sweetened shredded coconut, was the best option, adding enough flavor and sweetness to the soup without taking it over. We cooked the coconut with the onions to allow it to soften and develop in flavor before the rest of the ingredients were added.

With our aromatics and spices under control, it was time to test the vegetables and legumes, which would give the soup flavor, bulk, and color when pureed. We tested onions, carrots, celery, cauliflower, spinach, and peas. Not surprisingly, we found that onions were a must. Carrots added color and sweetness, and the celery provided a cool flavor that contrasted nicely with the hot spices. Cauliflower was rejected for the cabbage-like flavor it contributed; spinach and peas did little to enhance the soup's flavor. In addition, they imparted an undesirable color when pureed.

Several recipes suggested using pureed rice or lentils to thicken the soup, and while tasters didn't oppose these flavors, they didn't like the thick, porridge-like texture they produced when pureed. After a bit more testing, we found that sprinkling a little flour over the sautéed aromatics gave the soup a thickened yet velvety consistency. Although a few sources said that pureeing the soup was optional, we think that mulligatawny must be mostly smooth, just punctuated by a small amount of lentils and shredded chicken.

Returning to the idea of adding lentils to the soup (but leaving them whole), we experimented with adding them after the soup was pureed and tested a few varieties. Red lentils all but disintegrated in the soup, but standard brown lentils (or French green lentils) held their shape nicely when cooked and readily absorbed the surrounding flavors. A dollop of yogurt and some cilantro was all that we needed to finish this flavorful soup.

Mulligatawny

SERVES 6

French green lentils (lentilles du Puy) will also work well here; the cooking time will remain the same. Garam masala is a flavorful spice blend popular in Indian cooking; it is available in the spice aisle of most supermarkets. See page 121 for more information on pureeing.

1½	pounds bone-in, split chicken breasts (about 2 breasts), trimmed
	Salt and ground black pepper
1	tablespoon vegetable oil
2	tablespoons unsalted butter
2½	teaspoons garam masala
1½	teaspoons ground cumin
1½	teaspoons ground coriander
1	teaspoon ground turmeric

2	medium onions, minced
2	carrots, peeled and chopped medium
1	celery rib, chopped medium
½	cup sweetened shredded or flaked coconut
4	medium garlic cloves, minced or pressed through a garlic press (about 4 teaspoons)
4	teaspoons minced or grated fresh ginger (see the illustrations on page 89)
¼	cup unbleached all-purpose flour
1	teaspoon tomato paste
7	cups low-sodium chicken broth
½	cup dried brown lentils, picked over and rinsed
2	tablespoons minced fresh cilantro leaves
1	cup plain yogurt, for serving

1. Pat the chicken dry with paper towels and season with salt and pepper. Heat the oil in a large Dutch oven over medium-high heat until just smoking. Brown the chicken lightly on both sides, about 5 minutes, then transfer to a plate.

2. Melt the butter in a large Dutch oven over medium heat. Stir in the garam masala, cumin, coriander, and turmeric and cook until fragrant, about 30 seconds. Stir in the onions, carrots, celery, and coconut and cook until softened, 5 to 7 minutes. Stir in the garlic and ginger and cook until fragrant, about 30 seconds. Stir in the flour and tomato paste and cook for 1 minute. Gradually whisk in the broth, scraping up any browned bits and smoothing out any lumps, and bring to a boil.

3. Add the browned chicken, cover, and simmer gently until the chicken registers 160 to 165 degrees on an instant-read thermometer, 15 to 20 minutes. Remove the chicken from the pot, let cool slightly, then shred the meat into bite-size pieces (see the illustration on page 43), discarding the skin and bones.

4. Working in batches, puree the soup until smooth, return to a clean pot, and simmer. Stir in the lentils, cover, and simmer gently until the lentils are tender, 35 to 45 minutes.

5. Stir in the shredded chicken and let it heat through, about 2 minutes. Off the heat, stir in the cilantro and season with salt and pepper to taste. Dollop individual portions with yogurt before serving.

Chef's Knives 101

Your chef's knife is a kitchen workhorse—with a little know-how you can use it for 90 percent of your kitchen cutting jobs, from chopping onions to mincing herbs to butchering chicken. In the test kitchen, our favorite chef's knife is the inexpensive, lightweight Victorinox Fibrox (formerly Victorinox Forschner) 8-Inch Chef's Knife ($24.95). For more information, see page 2.

ANATOMY OF A CHEF'S KNIFE

BLADE CURVE
A good chef's knife's blade should have a long, gently sloping curve suited to the rocking motion of mincing and chopping.

BLADE LENGTH
An 8-inch blade provides plenty of power without being unwieldy.

BLADE MATERIAL
We prefer knives made with high-carbon stainless steel because, once sharpened, they stay that way. Some purists prefer carbon steel knives, which may take a sharper edge but don't retain it for as long. Expensive ceramic blades are ultra-sharp but equally fragile.

FORGED VS. STAMPED BLADES
Forged blades—made by hammering or forming a heated steel blank between dies—are weightier than stamped blades, which are punched out of steel. Both perform equally well. The blade above is stamped.

HANDLE
The knife handle helps balance the blade's weight. A good handle should virtually disappear in your grip, making the knife the oft-cited "extension of your hand." When choosing a knife, try gripping it before making your choice. The handle should be comfortable and resist slipping, even when your hand is wet or greasy.

BLADE MAINTENANCE

A KNIFE'S LIFE CYCLE
A sharp blade tapers down to a thin edge (see below). However, even a few minutes of cutting can make that edge roll over and cause the blade to feel slightly dull. A quick steeling will remove the folded edge and restore sharpness. After the sharp angles become rounded and very dull, the knife needs a new edge, achievable only through true sharpening, not steeling.

Very Sharp   Slightly Dull   Very Dull

MAKE IT SHARP
To reshape the edge of a dull knife, you have three choices: You can send it out, you can use a whetstone (tricky for anyone but a professional), or—the most convenient option—you can use an electric or manual sharpener. In the test kitchen, our favorite electric model is the Chef'sChoice Model 130 Professional Sharpening Station ($149.95) and our preferred manual tool is the AccuSharp Knife and Tool Sharpener ($11.99), a simple plastic handheld device with a single tungsten carbide V-shaped blade.

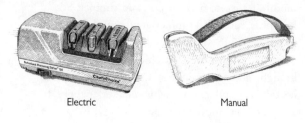

Electric   Manual

IS IT SHARP?
Even the best knives dull quickly with regular use. To determine if your knife needs sharpening, put it to the paper test. Hold a folded, but not creased, sheet of newspaper by one end. Lay the blade against the top edge at an angle and slice outward. If the knife fails to slice cleanly, try steeling it. If it still fails, it needs sharpening.

DULL AND DANGEROUS
A dull knife is a dangerous knife. Here's why: The duller the blade, the more force it takes to do the job—and the easier it is for the blade to slip and miss the mark (slippery ingredients like onions are the worst offenders), quickly sending the knife toward your hand. With a sharp knife, the blade does the work—and the razor-like edge is far less likely to slip. To protect your knife from dulling, avoid hard cutting surfaces such as glass or acrylic and keep it out of the dishwasher, where getting knocked around might damage its edge.

WHEN TO USE A SHARPENING STEEL

A so-called sharpening steel, the metal rod sold with most knife sets, doesn't sharpen at all: It's a tune-up device. As you cut with a sharp knife, the edge of the blade can actually get knocked out of alignment. The knife may seem dull, but its edge is simply misaligned. Running the knife blade over the steel repositions that edge. But it can't reshape a blade that's rounded and worn down—that's when you need a sharpener to cut away metal and restore the standard 20-degree angle of each side of the edge.

CUTTING CORRECTLY

Different cuts make use of different parts of the blade. Here's how to utilize all parts of the blade safely and efficiently.

GRIP

Most people tend to hold a chef's knife by keeping their fingers entirely on the handle. For added control, choke up on the knife, with the thumb and index finger actually gripping the heel of the blade.

Less Control

More Control

WHOLE BLADE

To make fast work of mincing fresh herbs, garlic, and the like, place one hand on the handle and rest the fingers of the other hand lightly on the knife tip. This lighter two-handed grip facilitates the up-and-down rocking motion needed for quick mincing. To make sure the food is evenly minced, pivot the knife as you chop.

TIP

We rarely use a cutting motion that brings the blade toward the body. However, when using the tip, drawing the knife inward is unavoidable.

1. To use this technique safely, place the knife into the food with the tip facing slightly down. Pivot the blade so the tip slices through the ingredient and rests on the board.

2. Drag the knife toward you, making sure to keep the tip against the board as you pull.

HEEL

The heel is the sturdiest part of the blade, offering a flat cutting edge for hacking up chicken bones, divvying up a large piece of hard Parmesan, or splitting winter squash. To apply a lot of force using the heel, hold the handle and place the flat palm of your other hand over the top of the blade (use a towel to cushion your hand) and cut straight down on the item. Use utmost caution and make sure your knife, hands, and cutting surface are completely dry (to avoid slippage).

MIDDLE

While using the blade's curve to guide the knife through a series of smooth cutting strokes, push the blade forward and down. If the food is small enough (e.g., celery or scallions), the tip of the blade should touch the cutting board at all times. However, for large ingredients such as eggplant or sweet potatoes, the tip of the blade should come off the board while making smooth cutting strokes through the ingredient.

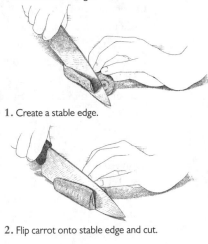

MOROCCAN-STYLE CHICKEN SOUP

HARIRA IS AN INTENSELY FLAVORED Moroccan soup of lentils, tomatoes, chickpeas, and often chicken or lamb. It's best known as a dish with which to break fast during the holy month of Ramadan, but it's also served at other celebrations and get-togethers. While harira is commonly thought of as a bean soup, it is the heavy presence of classic North African spices, notably ginger, cumin, and cinnamon, that give this soup its character. As enthusiasts of other Moroccan specialties (think tagines and couscous) we had a good feeling about harira and thought the interplay created by such flavors could be exciting.

However, after gathering and testing a number of recipes, our excitement started to wane. Most authentic versions contained a laundry list of ingredients, many obscure and hard to find. Beyond the long list of ingredients, there were few similarities in the recipes we encountered—regional and even household traditions seemed to dictate the norm. We found versions chock-full of lentils, chickpeas, and even rice, while others were sparsely dotted with just lentils. While we considered all of the soups to be brothy, some were slightly thickened by the rice or lentils as they broke down. Regardless of personal touches, all of the soups we tried were finished with minced fresh cilantro and served with harissa (a spicy paste of olive oil, spices, and garlic) for stirring in. We had our work cut out for us.

We started with the mix of spices, which are usually bloomed in oil to create a flavorful base for the soup. After sautéing some onion in extra-virgin olive oil, we followed the lead of one recipe and added a teaspoon each of ground ginger, cumin, and cinnamon before pouring in our homemade chicken broth. The resulting broth, while certainly bold, was completely out of balance. The cinnamon was overpowering, making the broth taste sweet rather than savory, while the ground ginger provided none of the brightness we expect from ginger. Dialing the cinnamon back to just ¼ teaspoon and swapping in freshly grated ginger for the ground ginger was a big step in the right direction. The soup now seemed balanced, if a little

uninspired. Taking cues from recipes that incorporated a good deal of spice in the form of hot dried chiles and black pepper, we returned to the spice rack. Paprika and cayenne provided the sweet and hot combination usually derived from the chiles, while a full ¼ teaspoon of freshly ground black pepper added both richness and heat. For added depth and roundness, as well as to enhance this soup's characteristic orange hue, we crumbled in a pinch of saffron threads. The soup now tasted so rich and flavorful that we wondered whether homemade chicken broth was even necessary.

A test with store-brought chicken broth confirmed what we suspected—the generous mix of spices easily made up for the store-bought broth's shortcomings. A tablespoon of flour, added after the spices, ensured our broth had plenty of body. The switch from homemade to store-bought broth cut about an hour from our cooking time, but it also meant that we wouldn't have shredded breast meat from our homemade broth recipe. Although some recipes got by on chickpeas and lentils alone, tasters were in favor of keeping meat in the soup to make it a more filling dinner. We solved the problem by poaching two chicken breasts (which we had already browned) in the simmering soup. Once shredded and stirred back in, the tender meat absorbed the broth's rich spiciness.

Next, we experimented with a variety of ingredients to mix in. Tasters loved the flavor and texture of both lentils and chickpeas but found white rice to be out of place. While authentic recipes called for dried chickpeas that need to be soaked overnight and then simmered in the broth for upwards of two hours, we had excellent luck with canned chickpeas. Red lentils disintegrated and thickened the soup, but brown lentils held their shape and provided great texture. While we loved canned chickpeas, tomatoes were a different story. Following a few recipes, we tried adding a can of diced tomatoes to the soup with the lentils, giving them almost an hour to cook and blend with the broth. Even with this extended cooking time, tasters disliked the canned tomato flavor and argued that it made the broth taste like a watery tomato sauce. Instead we switched to a full pound of fresh plum tomatoes; cut into large pieces and simmered for just 10 minutes, they provided just the right amount of tomato flavor and acidity.

With a satisfying, flavorful soup in the pot, we looked to the final and arguably most important component: the harissa. Usually made from hot chiles, cumin, coriander, garlic, and olive oil, this super-spicy paste is a ubiquitous tabletop condiment in the Middle East. That popularity, unfortunately, doesn't translate into availability stateside. While we managed to track down two brands at a local Middle Eastern market, they had widely different heat levels and, given their relative scarcity, were quite pricey. Since omitting harissa entirely was not an option, we knew we would have to make our own. While authentic recipes called for up to three different kinds of dried chiles, we got great results from 1½ tablespoons of sweet paprika mixed with ¼ teaspoon cayenne pepper. We then added extra-virgin olive oil, garlic, coriander, cumin, and salt to this paprika mix. A quick spin in the microwave served to bloom and intensify the spices. Spooned over individual bowls of soup, our homemade paste added great spice, heat, and depth of flavor. In fact, tasters liked the harissa addition so much that we chose to stir ¼ cup of it directly into the soup with the minced cilantro, reserving just a few tablespoons of harissa for passing at the table.

Finally, we had a lively, spicy soup that delivered all the rich flavors, colors, and aromas of Morocco.

SHREDDING CHICKEN

Using two forks, shred the cooked chicken meat into bite-size pieces.

Spicy Moroccan–Style Chicken and Lentil Soup
SERVES 8

You can substitute store-bought harissa if you wish, though spiciness can vary greatly by brand. French green lentils (lentilles du Puy) will also work well here; the cooking time will remain the same.

HARISSA

5	tablespoons extra-virgin olive oil
1½	tablespoons sweet paprika
4	medium garlic cloves, minced or pressed through a garlic press (about 4 teaspoons)
2	teaspoons ground coriander
¾	teaspoon ground cumin
¼	teaspoon cayenne pepper
⅛	teaspoon salt

SOUP

1½	pounds bone-in, split chicken breasts (about 2 breasts), trimmed
	Salt and ground black pepper
1	tablespoon extra-virgin olive oil
1	medium onion, minced
1	teaspoon minced or grated fresh ginger (see the illustrations on page 89)
1	teaspoon ground cumin
½	teaspoon sweet paprika
¼	teaspoon ground cinnamon
¼	teaspoon cayenne pepper
	Pinch saffron threads, crumbled
1	tablespoon unbleached all-purpose flour
10	cups low-sodium chicken broth
¾	cup dried brown lentils, picked over and rinsed
4	plum tomatoes (about 1 pound), cored and cut into ¾-inch pieces
1	(15-ounce) can chickpeas, drained and rinsed
⅓	cup minced fresh cilantro leaves

1. FOR THE HARISSA: Combine all the ingredients in a medium bowl; microwave on high until bubbling and fragrant, 15 to 30 seconds. Set aside to cool.

2. FOR THE SOUP: Pat the chicken dry with paper towels and season with salt and pepper. Heat the oil in a large Dutch oven over medium-high heat until just smoking. Brown the chicken lightly on both sides, about 5 minutes; transfer to a plate.

3. Add the onion to the fat left in the pot and cook until softened, 5 to 7 minutes. Stir in the ginger, cumin, paprika, cinnamon, cayenne, saffron, and ¼ teaspoon black pepper and cook until fragrant, about 30 seconds. Stir in the flour and cook for 1 minute. Gradually whisk in the broth, scraping up any browned bits and smoothing out any lumps, and bring to a boil.

4. Add the lentils and browned chicken; bring to a boil. Cover, reduce to a gentle simmer, and cook until the chicken registers 160 to 165 degrees on an instant-read thermometer, 15 to 20 minutes.

5. Remove the chicken from the pot, let cool slightly, then shred the meat into bite-size pieces (see the illustration on page 43), discarding the skin and bones. Meanwhile, continue to simmer the lentils, covered, for 15 minutes.

6. Stir in the tomatoes and chickpeas and continue to simmer until the lentils are tender, 10 to 15 minutes longer. Stir in the shredded chicken and let it heat through, about 2 minutes. Stir in the cilantro and ¼ cup of the harissa and season with salt and pepper to taste. Serve, passing the remaining harissa separately.

TORTILLA SOUP

WITH A SPICY, GARLICKY, TOMATOEY BROTH, chunks of chicken, and garnishes galore, not to mention a buried treasure of crispy tortilla strips underneath it all, tortilla soup aims to please. But for all the flavor and variety it provides, one thing it does not offer is free time. In fact, making tortilla soup is often a day-long saga involving at least one, if not several, uniquely Mexican ingredients, none of which are easy to find in your average supermarket. While the truly authentic recipes taste great, we wanted to find a streamlined recipe that didn't require homemade broth (with so much action in one bowl, we were certain no one would notice if we used store-bought broth), frying tortillas, or traveling south of the border for a handful of ingredients.

We started our research by reviewing recipes and looking for commonalities. We were able to break the soup down into its three classic components: a flavor base made with fresh tomatoes, garlic, onion, and chiles; chicken broth; and an array of garnishes, including fried tortilla strips. We tested a number of recipes, zeroing in on the flavor base first.

A number of recipes called for charring the vegetables on a griddle before pureeing and frying the mixture to create a paste to flavor the soup. We decided to substitute a cast-iron skillet for the griddle—we weren't looking for a recipe that required any extra equipment. While our substitution

PITTING AN AVOCADO

1. Start by slicing around the pit and through both ends with a chef's knife. With your hands, twist the avocado to separate both halves.

2. Stick the blade of the chef's knife sharply into the pit. Lift the knife, twisting the blade to loosen and remove the pit.

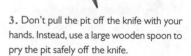

3. Don't pull the pit off the knife with your hands. Instead, use a large wooden spoon to pry the pit safely off the knife.

paid off (the results were superb) the downside was that this task took half an hour. We wondered if we could use chipotle chiles (smoked jalapeños) instead. Canned in a vinegary tomato mixture called adobo sauce, chipotles pack heat, roasted smoky flavor, and, more important, convenience. After processing, we cooked the mixture over high heat, which concentrated its flavor.

With the flavor base settled, we moved on to the chicken broth. We had already decided to capitalize on the convenience of store-bought chicken broth, especially since this soup is overflowing with so many other vibrant flavors. While store-bought broth would work fine, we felt it could still use some enhancement. We decided to cook our chicken in the broth with onion and garlic, reasoning that the chicken would release and take on flavor while it poached. We used bone-in breasts because they have more flavor than boneless breasts (chicken thighs can be used but they must be trimmed of excess fat). After just 20 minutes, our chicken breasts were poached and ready to be shredded and reserved until we were ready to stir it in. This method ensured that the chicken stayed tender and it helped the broth take on nice flavor.

Every authentic recipe for tortilla soup calls for fresh epazote, a common Mexican herb that imparts a heady, distinctive flavor to the broth. Unfortunately, this herb is impossible to find at our local supermarket. Looking for stand-ins that would mimic the citrusy, slightly bitter, and floral flavor of epazote, we settled on a combination of strong, warm oregano with pungent cilantro. Our soup was now starting to taste like the real thing.

We were ready to figure out our garnishes and started with the tortillas. In tortilla soup, the crispy tortillas are placed on the bottom of the soup bowl, then the soup is ladled on top. We began our testing with flour tortillas. Whether fried or oven-baked, flour tortillas quickly disintegrated in the hot soup. Corn tortillas, which we fried, were great, but the results were a bit greasy. We decided to simply toast the tortilla strips, which we had lightly oiled, in the oven. These strips were just as crisp and less greasy.

As for the remaining garnishes, we worked through the traditional list one ingredient at a time. Lime added sharp, fresh notes to an already complex bowl, as did cilantro leaves and minced jalapeño. Avocado was another essential topping. Thick, tart Mexican *crema* (a mildly tangy, cultured cream) is normally swirled into individual soup bowls, too. If it's unavailable, sour cream is a natural stand-in. Crumbled Cotija is sharp and rich, but may be hard to find; Monterey Jack, which melts nicely, works well too.

Tortilla Soup
SERVES 6 TO 8

For more heat, include the jalapeño seeds. Look for thin corn tortillas—we found that thicker tortillas baked up chewy rather than crisp.

SOUP

8	cups low-sodium chicken broth
2	medium onions, quartered
4	medium garlic cloves, peeled
8	sprigs fresh cilantro
1	sprig fresh oregano
	Salt and ground black pepper
1½	pounds bone-in, split chicken breasts (about 2 breasts) or 1¼ pounds bone-in chicken thighs (about 4 thighs), trimmed
8	(6-inch) corn tortillas, cut into ½-inch-wide strips
3	tablespoons vegetable oil
2	medium tomatoes (6 ounces each), cored and quartered
1	jalapeño chile, stemmed and seeded (see note)
1½–4	teaspoons minced chipotle chile in adobo sauce

GARNISHES

8	ounces Cotija, crumbled, or Monterey Jack cheese, shredded
1	medium, ripe avocado, pitted, peeled, and diced (see the illustrations on pages 44 and 46)
½	cup Mexican crema or sour cream
½	cup fresh cilantro leaves
	Lime wedges
1	jalapeño chile, stemmed, seeded, and minced (see note)

1. Bring the broth, 1 of the onions, 2 of the garlic cloves, cilantro, oregano, and ½ teaspoon salt to a boil in a large Dutch over medium-high heat. Add the chicken, cover, and simmer gently until the chicken registers 160 to 165 degrees on an instant-read thermometer, 15 to 20 minutes.

2. Remove the chicken from the pot, let cool slightly, then shred the meat into bite-size pieces (see the illustration on page 43), discarding the skin and bones. Strain the broth through a fine-mesh strainer, then defat the broth (see page 18). (The broth and the chicken can be refrigerated separately in airtight containers for up to 2 days.)

3. Meanwhile, adjust an oven rack to the middle position and heat the oven to 425 degrees. Toss the tortilla strips with 2 tablespoons of the oil, spread them out over a rimmed baking sheet and bake, stirring occasionally, until crisp and dark golden, 10 to 15 minutes. Season with salt and transfer to a paper towel–lined plate.

DICING AN AVOCADO

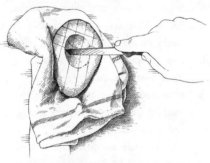

1. Use a dish towel to hold the avocado steady. Make ½-inch cross-hatch incisions in the flesh of each avocado half with a dinner knife.

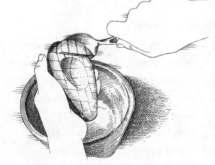

2. Using a spoon inserted between the skin and the flesh, separate the diced flesh from the skin and gently scoop out the avocado cubes.

4. Process the tomatoes, remaining onion, jalapeño, remaining 2 garlic cloves, 1½ teaspoons of the chipotles, and ⅛ teaspoon salt in a food processor until smooth. Heat the remaining 1 tablespoon oil in a large Dutch oven over medium-high heat until shimmering. Add the pureed mixture and cook, stirring frequently, until fragrant and darkened, about 10 minutes.

5. Stir in the strained broth, bring to a simmer, and cook until the flavors blend, about 15 minutes. Stir in the remaining chipotles to taste. Stir in the shredded chicken and let it heat through, about 2 minutes. Off the heat, season with salt and pepper to taste. Place some tortilla strips in the bottom of individual bowls, ladle the soup over the top, and serve, passing the garnishes separately.

MEXICAN–STYLE CHICKEN SOUP

CALDO TLALPEÑO IS A SMOKY, SPICY MEXICAN soup of chicken, chickpeas, and chipotle chiles. While the exact origin of the soup's name is unknown—some insist it references the smoky barbecue popular in the Mexico City suburb of Tlalpan—its flavor, spice, and spirit are unmistakably Mexican. Dipping your spoon into a bowl of Tlalpeño reveals tender pieces of shredded chicken, meaty chickpeas, and savory bites of avocado united in a rich chicken broth laced with the smoky flavor and spice of chipotle chiles. Unfortunately, much of this soup's magic is lost in many of the "Americanized" versions we have sampled this side of Mexico City. While it's true that Mexican food derives much of its complexity from slow-cooking and hard-to-find ingredients, we knew that with some thoughtful testing we could bring an authentic, but still manageable, version of this Mexican *caldo* north of the border.

In the most authentic recipes we found, this soup is started with a rich foundation of aromatics, softened and browned in either lard or vegetable oil. Chicken broth, chickpeas, and epazote, a citrusy, bitter herb common in Mexican cooking, are then added to the mix. Finally, a puree of dried chipotle chiles (first seeded and soaked) is stirred into the broth, adding spice, smoke, and richness. While Mexican soups are infamous for their multitude of garnishes, most of the recipes for this soup were quite minimalist, calling for just diced avocado. Before we could start building our soup, we needed to figure out how to handle a few of the soup's hard-to-find Mexican ingredients.

Caldo Tlalpeño could rightfully be called chipotle soup, as it is the flavor, smoke, and spice of this chile that gives it personality. While many traditional recipes called for charring, seeding, and soaking dried chipotle chiles (which are hard to find outside of Mexico or the American Southwest), we were happily surprised to see that just as many used the canned alternative. Packed in a sharp tomato mixture called adobo sauce, canned chipotles offer impressive smoky flavor, heat, and depth. Confident that we could put canned chipotle chile to work in our soup, we turned our attention to another Mexican ingredient: epazote. While available in some parts of the country, for most, epazote is quite difficult to find. As with our Tortilla Soup (page 45), we found that a mix of cilantro and oregano provided a good approximation. With a handle on the more exotic ingredients, we started building our soup.

Since chicken is an important part of this soup, it seemed like a logical place to begin. We started by browning two bone-in, skin-on chicken breasts (many traditional recipes call for white meat, which tasters preferred to dark), developing flavorful fond and rendering some chicken fat. After removing the browned breasts to a plate, we added a minced onion and a sliced carrot. Once these had softened, we stirred in a teaspoon of minced chipotle chile in adobo sauce and a few minced cloves of garlic. To this base we added store-bought chicken broth (we knew the heady spice and smoke of this soup would overwhelm the nuances of homemade broth), our epazote equivalent of eight sprigs of cilantro and one sprig of oregano, one can of chickpeas, and the browned chicken breasts. Once it was cooked through, we shredded the breast meat and returned it to the soup along with a diced avocado. For a first attempt, we had to admit

this soup tasted pretty good, if a little incomplete. Taking cues from tasters' comments, we set about making adjustments.

While tasters felt the broth was rich in chicken flavor (thanks to the rendered fat and the poaching step), some felt it needed more body and complexity. For body, we borrowed a technique from many of our other soups and stirred a little flour into the pot after the garlic and chipotles had become fragrant. This seemingly small adjustment made a big difference, producing a broth with great substance. For more complexity we increased the amount of onion and carrot to two each, increased the garlic to five cloves, and added some thyme (fresh and dried both worked well) to the mix. The added aromatics lent sweetness and earthiness, while the thyme provided a subtle background note. Finally, we doubled the minced chipotle chile to two full teaspoons. This broth was rich, deep, and complex—exactly what tasters had wanted. Unfortunately, we now had a new problem; with so many deep flavors (including chicken, chickpeas, chipotles, and caramelized onions and carrots) and so little brightness, the soup seemed out of balance. It was time to freshen things up.

Looking for an additional vegetable that could serve as contrast to the substantial chickpeas, we did some more digging and found that zucchini showed up in a number of recipes. From other soups, we have learned that zucchini provides the best texture when seeded (when cooked, the translucent seeds can have a slimy texture) and cooked briefly. Simmered for less than 10 minutes, zucchini provided a slightly crisp counterpoint to the richness of the soup. Next, we looked to the herbs. Up to this point, we had been steeping the cilantro and oregano in the soup, as traditional recipes dictate. Wishing for a fresh flourish to finish our soup, we instead tried mincing these herbs and sprinkling them in just before serving. This break from tradition provided just the right burst of freshness that the soup needed.

Served with lime wedges, our chicken and chickpea soup, though thousands of miles from Mexico, now radiated with all of its birthplace's character, flavor, and spice.

Mexican-Style Chicken and Chickpea Soup with Chipotle Chiles

SERVES 6 TO 8

Look for small to medium zucchini, as these have a better ratio of flesh to seeds.

1½	pounds bone-in, split chicken breasts (about 2 breasts), trimmed
	Salt and ground black pepper
1	tablespoon vegetable oil
2	medium onions, minced
2	carrots, peeled and sliced ½ inch thick
5	medium garlic cloves, minced or pressed through a garlic press (about 5 teaspoons)
2	teaspoons minced chipotle chile in adobo sauce
1½	teaspoons minced fresh thyme leaves or ½ teaspoon dried
2	tablespoons unbleached all-purpose flour
8	cups low-sodium chicken broth
2	medium zucchini (about 1 pound), halved lengthwise, seeded, and cut into ½-inch pieces
1	(15-ounce) can chickpeas, drained and rinsed
3	tablespoons minced fresh cilantro leaves
1	teaspoon minced fresh oregano leaves
1	medium, ripe avocado, pitted, peeled, and diced (see the illustrations on pages 44 and 46), for serving
	Lime wedges, for serving

1. Pat the chicken dry with paper towels and season with salt and pepper. Heat the oil in a large Dutch oven over medium-high heat until just smoking. Brown the chicken lightly on both sides, about 5 minutes, then transfer to a plate.

2. Add the onions and carrots to the fat left in the pot and cook until softened and browned, 8 to 10 minutes. Stir in the garlic, chipotles, and thyme and cook until fragrant, about 30 seconds. Stir in the flour and cook for 1 minute. Gradually whisk in the broth, scraping up any browned bits and smoothing out any lumps, and bring to a boil.

3. Add the browned chicken, cover, and simmer gently over low heat until the chicken registers 160 to 165 degrees on an instant-read thermometer, 15 to 20 minutes. Remove the chicken breasts from the pot, let cool slightly, then shred the meat into bite-size pieces (see the illustration on page 43), discarding the skin and bones.

4. Return the broth to a simmer, stir in the zucchini and chickpeas, and cook until the zucchini is just tender, 5 to 10 minutes. Stir in the shredded chicken and let it heat through, about 2 minutes. Off the heat, stir in the cilantro and oregano and season with salt and pepper to taste. Serve, passing the avocado and lime wedges separately.

SPANISH-STYLE MEATBALL SOUP

SOUPS FULL OF TENDER MEATBALLS FLOATING in a light broth make a nice alternative to typical chicken soups with shredded meat—and recipes for meatball soups can be found the world over. One of our favorites is a Spanish meatball soup infused with a generous amount of heady saffron. True to Spanish form, the broth effortlessly blends a few simple ingredients—saffron, paprika, aromatics, and extra-virgin olive oil—into a subtle yet complex whole. Continuing the minimalist theme, tiny meatballs and a smattering of vegetables dot the broth, which has been slightly thickened with a *picada*, a mixture of finely ground almonds, bread crumbs, and olive oil. The texture of the picada is so fine that it practically disappears into the sunset-colored broth. Eager to recreate this unique soup for the American table, we gathered several recipes and started cooking.

Based on the recipes we uncovered, making Spanish meatball soup is a relatively straightforward endeavor. It begins with a sofrito of onion, red bell pepper, and garlic, which are cooked until softened; saffron and paprika then join this trio to form a distinctly Spanish flavor base. Chicken broth and dry white wine are added to the pot to form the backbone of the soup. Next, bite-size meatballs are stirred in and simmered until just cooked through. Just before serving, the soup is finished with the picada and fresh herbs. While the recipe steps and ingredients seemed easy enough to master, we knew it would take just the right amount of spices and picada to keep the flavors balanced. We decided to work our way up and start with the broth.

In simple, brothy soups, such as our Matzo Ball Soup (page 32) and Old-Fashioned Chicken Noodle Soup (page 26), in which chicken is the main flavor element, we believe homemade broth is essential. However, in more complex soups where spices and aromatics are the star, homemade broth is often overshadowed. We had a hunch that Spanish meatball soup would fall into this latter category. To the traditional sofrito of onion, red bell pepper, and garlic, we added our saffron—¼ teaspoon saffron threads seemed a good jumping-off point—along with both sweet paprika and red pepper flakes to boost both pepper flavor and heat. After deglazing the pot with a cup of white wine (in subsequent tests, we found that more than this made our soup taste too winey), we split this sofrito in half, adding homemade broth to one half and store-bought broth to the other. A side-by-side tasting of these two soup bases confirmed our suspicion: homemade broth was virtually undetectable under the complex layers of spices and aromatics. With store-bought broth as our clear winner, we took a step back and tweaked the spice amounts.

We decided to reexamine the amount of saffron first. Because saffron is the star of the broth, we wanted the spice to have plenty of presence, but it couldn't be the singular flavor in our soup. We tested ⅛ teaspoon and ½ teaspoon saffron threads, crumbled, and felt that our original amount of ¼ teaspoon provided the right balance of potent but not overwhelming saffron flavor. As for the paprika, ½ teaspoon wasn't providing enough sweetness for tasters, so we bumped it up to 1 teaspoon, which also helped reinforce the orange hue of the broth. Finally, revisiting the red pepper flakes, we felt the soup should have a little heat but it shouldn't be spicy; ⅛ teaspoon was perfect. Now we could focus on the meatballs.

After consulting several recipes, we noticed that the meatballs usually found in this soup aren't very different from Italian meatballs. The basics are the same: a combination of ground meat—traditionally either beef or pork—bread mixed with milk to form a paste (for tenderness), and seasonings like salt, pepper, and parsley. As meatballs are the other major component of this soup (after the broth), we vowed to leave no stone unturned in our testing. While beef and pork seemed like the obvious choices, we also tested meatballs made with veal, lamb, chicken, and turkey. To our surprise, tasters almost unanimously preferred the meatballs made with ground turkey. Simmered in the rich broth, these meatballs absorbed and complemented the flavor of the soup, whereas their beef, pork, veal, and lamb counterparts overwhelmed it, while the chicken meatballs' flavor was too mild.

To improve the flavor of our turkey meatballs, we added a little grated cheese; we used Manchego, the sharp sheep's milk cheese, to keep with the Spanish theme, but Parmesan or Asiago work well too. For freshness and some texture, we added minced shallot (garlic was overpowering) and a generous amount of minced fresh parsley. Finally, for more richness and flavor, we added a full 2 tablespoons of extra-virgin olive oil. Because the meatballs had to fit on a spoon, we made them quite small, about ½ inch around, then chilled them briefly so they could firm up. We then dropped them into the soup to simmer. After 10 minutes, tasters sampled and were pleased; these meatballs won rave reviews for their delicate texture and complex flavor. Last but not least, we tackled the picada.

Many of the picada recipes we tried were heavily spiced with garlic and herbs, effectively dominating the flavor of the soup and the meatballs. We decided to follow a simpler, cleaner path, relying on a combination of almonds, bread crumbs, extra-virgin olive oil, and salt and pepper. When we stirred this picada into the hot broth, the heady aroma of toasted almonds and extra-virgin olive oil bloomed and filled the air, while the bread crumbs absorbed and slightly thickened the rich broth. A sprinkle of fresh parsley was the crowning touch on this golden-hued, richly flavored Spanish soup.

Spanish-Style Meatball Soup with Saffron

SERVES 6 TO 8

The picada (a toasted mixture of ground almonds, bread crumbs, and olive oil) is very important for the flavor and texture of this soup. Do not use ground turkey breast here (also labeled 99 percent lean) or the meatballs will be very dry. Parmesan or Asiago cheese can be substituted for the Manchego.

MEATBALLS

2	slices high-quality white sandwich bread, torn into quarters
⅓	cup whole milk
I	pound 93 percent lean ground turkey (see note)
I	ounce Manchego cheese, grated (½ cup)
3	tablespoons minced fresh parsley leaves
I	medium shallot, minced (about 3 tablespoons)
2	tablespoons extra-virgin olive oil
½	teaspoon salt
½	teaspoon ground black pepper

SOUP

I	tablespoon extra-virgin olive oil
I	medium onion, minced
I	red bell pepper, stemmed, seeded, and cut into ¾-inch pieces
2	medium garlic cloves, minced or pressed through a garlic press (about 2 teaspoons)
I	teaspoon sweet paprika
¼	teaspoon saffron threads, crumbled
⅛	teaspoon red pepper flakes
I	cup dry white wine
8	cups low-sodium chicken broth
I	recipe Picada (page 178)
2	tablespoons minced fresh parsley leaves
	Salt and ground black pepper

1. FOR THE MEATBALLS: Mash the bread and milk together into a paste in a large bowl. Add the ground turkey, Manchego, parsley, shallot, oil, salt, and pepper and mix thoroughly to combine. Pinch off 2-teaspoon-sized pieces of the mixture, roll firmly into balls, and arrange on a rimmed baking sheet; you should have 30 to 35 meatballs. Cover with plastic wrap and refrigerate until firm, at least 30 minutes.

2. FOR THE SOUP: Heat the oil in a large Dutch oven over medium-high heat until shimmering. Add the onion and bell pepper and cook until softened and lightly browned, 8 to 10 minutes. Stir in the garlic, paprika, saffron, and red pepper flakes and cook until fragrant, about 30 seconds. Stir in the wine, scraping up any browned bits, and cook until almost completely evaporated, about 1 minute.

3. Stir in the broth and bring to a simmer. Gently add the meatballs and simmer until they are cooked through, 10 to 12 minutes. Off the heat, stir in the picada and parsley, season with salt and pepper to taste, and serve.

➤ VARIATION

Spanish-Style Meatball Soup with Saffron and Kale

Follow the recipe for Spanish-Style Meatball Soup with Saffron, adding ½ bunch kale (about 8 ounces), stemmed, leaves chopped into 1-inch pieces (see the illustrations on page 56), to the soup with the meatballs in step 3.

TURKEY SOUPS

BLACK FRIDAY BRINGS A FEW THINGS TO mind: crowds at the mall, televisions on sale, and turkey soup in a pot on the stove. Good turkey soup is one of the great things about the day after Thanksgiving—while the pecan pie might be gone, you can still savor the flavor of the holiday bird as it simmers away with herbs and vegetables. But sometimes, turkey soup is a slapdash affair, boasting none of the good meaty, roasted flavor of the bird from just a day earlier. Bad turkey soup is easy to identify—a few pieces of turkey meat, slices of mushy carrot, and waterlogged noodles floating aimlessly around a broth that has no more flavor than water. We wanted to revitalize this soup—while still keeping it a speedy recipe—and bring back the big, rich turkey flavor.

We knew having a great broth was key and so chose to employ our Turkey Broth (page 15), which is made from the carcass of a holiday bird that still has some meat and skin clinging to it. The meat and skin are essential parts of the recipe, as they contribute substantial flavor. The bones themselves provide body and gelatin when simmered, but the flavor is really dependent on having some meat and skin in the pot, too. In addition to the turkey carcass, the broth uses the classic trio of onion, carrot, and celery for vegetal flavor, garlic for an aromatic baseline, and some white wine for brightness. Fresh parsley and thyme, added halfway through the simmering time, infuse the broth with plenty of herb flavor. And for the meat, we turned to cooked turkey meat reserved from our roasted bird. Two cups of meat proved ample for 12 cups of broth.

With the turkey and turkey broth in hand, sorting out the other elements of our soup was easy. We started with the basic mirepoix of onion, carrot, and celery. Tasters liked this vegetable combination but also wanted a little more flavor and depth. A full two teaspoons of minced fresh thyme leaves provided great depth, while three tablespoons of minced fresh parsley was just the right finish. Next, we looked at various types of pasta and noodles. We settled on medium pasta shells, which cooked up tender and flavorful, with just enough bite to add some texture and interest to the soup. Since sometimes we want a turkey soup with a little more gusto, we also developed two soup variations with bold, ethnic flavors.

Turkey and Pasta Soup

SERVES 8 TO 10

This soup is made using the leftovers from a roast turkey; you will use the turkey carcass to make the broth (page 15), and will need 2 cups of leftover meat for the soup.

1   tablespoon vegetable oil
2   carrots, peeled and sliced ¼ inch thick
1   medium onion, minced
1   celery rib, sliced ¼ inch thick
2   teaspoons minced fresh thyme leaves or
      ¾ teaspoon dried

12   cups Turkey Broth (page 15)
3   cups medium pasta shells
2   cups cooked turkey meat, shredded
      (see note)
3   tablespoons minced fresh parsley leaves
      Salt and ground black pepper

1. Heat the oil in a large Dutch oven over medium-high heat until shimmering. Add the carrots, onion, and celery and cook until softened, 5 to 7 minutes. Stir in the thyme and cook until fragrant, about 30 seconds. Stir in the broth and bring to a boil. Reduce to a simmer, and cook until the vegetables are nearly tender, 10 to 15 minutes.

2. Stir in the pasta and simmer until just tender, 10 to 15 minutes. Stir in the shredded turkey meat and let it heat through, about 2 minutes. Stir in the parsley, season with salt and pepper to taste, and serve.

➤ VARIATIONS

Turkey Soup with Potatoes, Linguiça, and Kale

This soup is made using the leftovers from a roast turkey; you will use the turkey carcass to make the broth (page 15) and will need 2 cups of leftover meat for the soup. Chorizo sausage can be used in place of the linguiça.

1   tablespoon vegetable oil
12   ounces linguiça sausage, sliced ¼ inch thick
1   medium onion, minced
3   medium garlic cloves, minced or pressed
      through a garlic press (about 1 tablespoon)
2   teaspoons minced fresh thyme leaves or
      ¾ teaspoon dried
12   cups Turkey Broth (page 15)
1½   pounds red potatoes, scrubbed and cut into
      ½-inch pieces
1   bunch kale (about 1 pound), stemmed
      and leaves chopped into 1-inch pieces
      (see the illustrations on page 56)
2   cups cooked turkey meat, shredded
      (see note)
      Salt and ground black pepper
      Extra-virgin olive oil, for serving

1. Heat the oil in a large Dutch oven over medium heat until shimmering. Brown the linguiça lightly, 3 to 5 minutes, then transfer to a plate.

2. Add the onion to the fat left in the pot and cook until softened, 5 to 7 minutes. Stir in the garlic and thyme and cook until fragrant, about 30 seconds. Stir in the broth and potatoes and bring to a boil. Reduce to a simmer and cook until the potatoes are nearly tender, 10 to 15 minutes.

3. Stir in the kale and simmer until just tender, 10 to 15 minutes. Stir in the shredded turkey and browned sausage and let them heat through, about 2 minutes. Season with salt and pepper to taste and drizzle individual portions with olive oil before serving.

Spicy Turkey Soup with Jasmine Rice and Lemon Grass

This soup is made using the leftovers from a roast turkey; you will use the turkey carcass to make the broth (page 15), and will need 2 cups of leftover meat for the soup. Long-grain white rice or basmati rice can be substituted for the jasmine rice. Don't be tempted to use jarred or dried lemon grass—their flavor is characterless.

I	tablespoon vegetable oil
I	medium onion, minced
2	jalapeño chiles, sliced thin
4	medium garlic cloves, minced or pressed through a garlic press (about 4 teaspoons)
I	tablespoon minced fresh ginger (see the illustrations on page 89)
I	stalk lemon grass, bruised (see the illustration at right)
12	cups Turkey Broth (page 15)
I	cup jasmine rice (see note)
2	cups cooked turkey meat, shredded (see note)
¼	cup fish sauce
2	tablespoons light brown sugar
2	tablespoons minced fresh cilantro or basil leaves
	Lime wedges, for serving

1. Heat the oil in a large Dutch oven over medium-high heat until shimmering. Add the onion and cook until softened, 5 to 7 minutes. Stir in the jalapeños, garlic, ginger, and lemon grass and cook until fragrant, about 30 seconds. Stir in the broth and bring to a boil. Reduce to a simmer and cook until the broth is flavorful, 10 to 15 minutes.

2. Stir in the rice and simmer until just tender, 15 to 20 minutes. Stir in the shredded turkey, fish sauce, and brown sugar and let the turkey heat through, about 2 minutes. Remove and discard the lemon grass, stir in the cilantro, and serve with the lime wedges.

BRUISING LEMON GRASS

To bruise lemon grass, smack the stalk with the back of a large chef's knife.

3

BEEF SOUPS

Beef Soups

〜〜〜

OLD-FASHIONED BEEF SOUPS

BEEF AND VEGETABLE SOUP SHOULD BE A meal in a bowl. It should taste undeniably rich and be chock-full of tender pieces of beef and lots of vegetables. Too often, however, this soup has a pallid broth, chewy bits of beef, and mushy vegetables. We felt we had a leg up on the broth front. Using our velvety Rich Beef Broth (page 19) as a base, we knew that truly meaty, rich versions of our favorite old-fashioned beef soups—beef and vegetable, beef noodle, and beef barley—would not be difficult to achieve. Along the way, we also wanted to see if we could streamline the soups' preparation since beef often requires hours of simmering to turn tender. After all, a big bowl of chunky beef soup makes a great weeknight supper.

We started with beef and vegetable soup. To get our bearings, we prepared several traditional recipes along with a handful of quick recipes. While every single classic recipe yielded intense flavor, the quick soups were uniformly disappointing and lacked any real beef flavor. Most used either cubes of "stew meat"—a butcher's catchall term for any relatively chunky scrap of beef—or more tender cuts like strip steak or rib eye. Although stew meat contributed a pleasant beefy flavor, it was barely chewable after simmering for half an hour. The strip and rib eye, though more tender, tasted livery and had a chalky, dry texture. Our first and most important goal was to find a cut of meat that could give quick beef and vegetable soup the same texture and flavor as one that cooked for hours.

Tasters praised the fall-apart tenderness of the shin meat in our working recipe, but it took hours to break down those tougher muscle fibers into anything remotely tender. After pulling out our diagrams for beef cuts, we tried to find a cut of meat that had the same textural characteristics of the shin meat but would cook in a quarter of the time. We cooked through various cuts and discovered that those with a loose, open grain—

including hangar steak, flank steak, sirloin tip steak (or flap meat), and blade steak—had a shreddy texture that fooled tasters into thinking we had cooked the meat for hours. Of these four cuts, sirloin steak tips offered the best balance between meaty flavor and tenderness.

On to the vegetables. Several of the quick soup recipes we uncovered took an "everything but the kitchen sink" approach to the vegetables. While these soups had flavor, it didn't always enhance the beef flavor of the soup. We had better luck sticking to the basics: onions, carrots, and celery—flavorful, yes; exciting, not very. Then we remembered that many recipes for French onion soup rely on mountains of caramelized onions to up the meaty flavor of the broth. The liquid and sugars released from the onions leave a rich brown coating on the pan, contributing a depth of flavor that onions simply simmered in the broth can't attain. When we tested this idea, tasters praised the added depth and sweetness. Caramelized onions were in.

It was time do some research into exactly what complements beefy flavor. What we discovered was that beef flavor is accentuated by foods high in glutamates, a class of amino acids. Like salt, glutamate-rich ingredients, such as mushrooms, tomato paste, and soy sauce, make food taste richer and meatier. Thinking mushrooms, which are commonly paired with beef, would make for an even meatier-tasting bowl, we prepared soups with white, portobello, cremini, and porcini mushrooms. Portobellos imparted an overly murky flavor, and earthy porcinis overwhelmed any beef flavor we had already developed. Utilitarian white mushrooms were OK but a bit bland. Cremini mushrooms were perfect, providing mushroom intensity without being obtrusive. We also liked red wine in the soup—it complemented the soup's beefy flavor and added its own complexity.

We had now replicated the beef flavor of long-simmered soups but not the mouth-coating richness. This can only be created when collagen, the tough protein in the meat and bones, breaks down into gelatin. Could we cheat and just add a little flour to thicken the soup? Two tablespoons of flour, added to the pot right before we deglazed it with red wine, provided the viscosity of traditional broths.

With beef and vegetable soup down, we created a variation with sweet parsnips and hearty kale.

Next, beef barley soup required a bit more tinkering. First up was the choice of barley. We settled on pearl barley because it has had its tough outer hulls removed, making it a fairly quick-cooking grain. After some experimenting, we found that ½ cup was the ideal amount; it lent a pleasing texture to the soup without overwhelming it with swollen grains. Tasters also asked for an additional herb to accentuate the rustic feel of the soup. We discovered that thyme worked best and found that it was important to add it early in the process so that its robust flavor could infuse the broth evenly. Many beef and barley soups contain some diced canned tomatoes and we followed suit. The tomatoes added complexity and some acidity, which helped balance the heartiness of the barley.

Lastly, we turned to beef noodle soup, which turned out to be a cinch. Tasters liked the richness and hearty heft of wide egg noodles simmered right in the broth.

Now we had a host of old-fashioned beef soups with extraordinarily deep beef flavor and, once we had the broth ready, any of them could be on the table in less than an hour.

Old-Fashioned Beef and Vegetable Soup

SERVES 6 TO 8

Look for whole sirloin steak tips, rather than those that have been cut into small pieces for stir-fries. If sirloin steak tips are unavailable, you can substitute flank steak or blade steak well trimmed of gristle and fat. White mushrooms can be substituted for the cremini mushrooms. If you're tight on time, you can use store-bought broth; substitute 4 cups beef broth and 2 cups low-sodium chicken broth for the homemade broth.

I	pound beef sirloin steak tips, trimmed and cut into ½-inch pieces
	Salt and ground black pepper
2	tablespoons vegetable oil
½	pound cremini mushrooms, wiped clean, trimmed, and sliced ½ inch thick
I	medium onion, chopped medium
I	medium garlic clove, minced or pressed through a garlic press (about I teaspoon)
2	tablespoons unbleached all-purpose flour
¼	cup dry red wine
6	cups Rich Beef Broth (page 19)
3	carrots, peeled and cut into ½-inch pieces
2	celery ribs, cut into ½-inch pieces
2	bay leaves
I	pound red potatoes (about 3 medium), peeled and cut into ½-inch pieces
2	tablespoons minced fresh parsley leaves

PREPARING KALE, SWISS CHARD, OR BOK CHOY

1. Cut away the leafy green portion from either side of the stalk or stem using a chef's knife.

2. Stack several leaves on top of one another, and either slice the leaves crosswise or chop into pieces (as directed in the recipe). Wash and dry the leaves after they are cut, using a salad spinner.

3. If including the stalks or stems, wash them thoroughly, then trim and cut them into small pieces as directed in the recipe.

1. Pat the beef dry with paper towels and season with salt and pepper. Heat 2 teaspoons of the oil in a large Dutch oven over medium-high heat until just smoking. Add half of the meat and cook, stirring occasionally, until well browned, 5 to 7 minutes, reducing the heat if the pot begins to scorch. Transfer the browned beef to a medium bowl. Repeat with 2 teaspoons more oil and the remaining beef; transfer to the bowl.

2. Add the remaining 2 teaspoons oil to the pot and place over medium heat until shimmering. Add the mushrooms and onion and cook until softened, 7 to 10 minutes. Stir in the garlic and cook until fragrant, about 30 seconds. Stir in the flour and cook for 1 minute. Whisk in the wine, scraping up any browned bits, and cook until nearly evaporated, about 1 minute.

3. Stir in the broth, carrots, celery, bay leaves, and browned meat with any accumulated juice. Bring to a boil, then cover, reduce to a gentle simmer, and cook for 10 minutes. Stir in the potatoes and continue to cook until the meat and vegetables are tender, 20 to 30 minutes longer.

4. Off the heat, remove the bay leaves. Stir in the parsley, season with salt and pepper to taste, and serve.

➤ VARIATIONS

Old-Fashioned Beef and Vegetable Soup with Parsnips and Kale

Follow the recipe for Old-Fashioned Beef and Vegetable Soup, omitting the carrots, celery, and potatoes. In step 3, add 4 parsnips, peeled and cut into ½-inch pieces, with the broth, bay leaves, and browned meat and simmer for 15 minutes. Stir in ½ bunch kale (about 8 ounces), stemmed and leaves chopped into 1-inch pieces, and continue to simmer until the meat and vegetables are tender, 15 to 25 minutes longer. Continue with step 4 as directed.

Old-Fashioned Beef and Barley Soup

Follow the recipe for Old-Fashioned Beef and Vegetable Soup, omitting the potatoes. Stir in 1½ teaspoons minced fresh thyme leaves or ½ teaspoon dried thyme with the garlic in step 2. Add 1 (14.5-ounce) can diced tomatoes, drained, and

INGREDIENTS: Vegetable Oil

Vegetable oil is a workhorse of the kitchen—used in almost any recipe that calls for sautéing. Vegetable oil, unlike other fats such as butter or olive oil, has a neutral taste that doesn't compete with other ingredients. That unobtrusive flavor profile makes it ideal not only for sautéing and frying, but also for some baked goods that need more moisture than butter alone can offer, and salad dressings where the stronger presence of olive oil is not preferred. But when picking out vegetable oil at the grocery store, you're likely to encounter more than a dozen kinds, from canola to corn to soybean, and blends of one or more oils. We decided to test the most common vegetable oils with the hopes that we'd find an oil that we could use in any application.

We focused on widely available brands (Crisco, Mazola, and Wesson) and selected 10 oils, testing them first in homemade mayonnaise, in which any off-flavors would stand out. Canola oil and canola blends performed best here, receiving praise for their "light" and "clean" taste; corn oils were at the bottom of the pack, disliked by many tasters for the "pungent" or "sour" flavors they imparted. In the next test, using the oils to fry french fries, the canola oils flopped, tasting "fishy" or metallic. The corn oils, on the other hand enhanced the fries' potato flavor and yielding crisp, sweet spuds with little to no oily aftertaste.

While these findings might seem contradictory, they actually make sense from a scientific point of view: As oil is heated, chemical changes take place, and new flavor compounds are created that literally change its taste. So certain flavors exist in uncooked corn oil that don't exist in cooked corn oil, and vice versa. With our top- and bottom-ranked oils in hand, we performed two more tests, trying the oils in white layer cakes and basic vinaigrettes. Here, most tasters couldn't detect any differences whatsoever.

In the end, we had a winning oil, although the margin was slim. Our top-ranking oil was Crisco Natural Blend, a mix of canola and soybean oils with an unusual addition: sunflower oil. It ranked first in mayonnaise and second in our french fry test, and is the only oil in the lineup to include sunflower oil, which resists oxidation well, giving it better shelf stability.

THE BEST VEGETABLE OIL

Crisco Natural Blend Oil came in on top, praised for its "very clean" taste in mayonnaise and "neutral and balanced" flavor in fries.

CRISCO

½ cup pearl barley with the broth in step 3 and cook as directed.

Old-Fashioned Beef Noodle Soup

Follow the recipe for Old-Fashioned Beef and Vegetable Soup, omitting the potatoes. Before removing the soup from the heat in step 4, add 2 cups (3 ounces) wide egg noodles and continue to simmer until the noodles are tender, about 8 minutes longer; continue with step 4 as directed.

HEARTY MEXICAN BEEF SOUP

IN CUISINES AROUND THE WORLD, BEEF AND vegetable soup is a meal in a bowl. One popular version, Mexico's *caldo de res,* consists of an aromatic broth, rich with spices and overflowing with tender chunks of meat and vegetables like tomatoes, corn, and squash. Authentic recipes we sampled demanded a major investment of time, often requiring a slow simmer of beef shanks or short ribs to develop a flavorful broth and achieve tender pieces of meat to incorporate into the soup. Our goal for this recipe was to develop a soup that kept the authentic flavors of a caldo but eliminated most of the fuss.

Starting with the beef itself, we hoped to avoid the long simmering of bone-in cuts and focused on boneless cuts. We were confident we could obtain flavorful broth and tender meat by simmering chunks of beef in broth, but we would still need to determine the proper cut for our hearty soup. Following our standard method of making a beef soup, we tried a variety of boneless beef cuts, browning and reserving the meat, then sautéing garlic and onion. We then returned the beef to the pot along with the broth (we used a combination of beef broth and chicken broth) and brought the mixture to a simmer until the meat was tender. In the end, chuck proved to be our cut of choice—flavorful, tender, and juicy, with a meaty richness.

The names given to different cuts of chuck vary, but the most commonly used names for retail chuck cuts include boneless chuck eye roast, cross rib roast, blade steak and roast, shoulder steak and roast, and arm steak and roast. We particularly liked chuck eye roast, but all chuck cuts worked well. Trying various sizes for the chunks of meat, tasters preferred larger 1-inch pieces, which contributed to the hearty nature of the soup.

We focused on the spices next. Cumin was quickly voted in by tasters. Most everyone liked the addition of some fragrant oregano but tasters were divided about cayenne—some liked a little heat, but others did not. We decided to make this spice optional.

Although some sources suggested tossing the meat with the spices before browning it, we found that this caused the spices to burn. Other recipes added the spices with the liquid, but rather than permeating the soup, they tasted raw. Instead, we found that sautéing the spices in a little oil, a technique called blooming, helped to bring out their flavor. Added to the sautéed onion and garlic, the spices quickly created a coating on the pan bottom. Therefore, we found it essential to scrape the pan bottom when the broth was added to incorporate the spices into the soup and develop their flavor.

Confident about our soup base, we were ready to consider which vegetables to add. Every authentic recipe we found called for chayote, a gourd-like fruit similar to a summer squash that is often used in Mexican cooking. Unfortunately, while chayote is widely available in the American Southwest, it is virtually nonexistent in other parts of the country. Still, we managed to track some down for testing purposes. Surprisingly, its mild flavor was a disappointment and tasters encouraged using a more flavorful squash. After several tastings, we found zucchini was an appropriate substitute, lending a texture similar to the chayote but with much more flavor.

Tomatoes and corn are another constant in most caldos. We found that canned diced tomatoes provided a more reliable flavor than fresh, and while frozen corn worked well, tasters enjoyed the more authentic versions including sections of whole corn on the cob. To finish out the selection, we also included carrots and red potatoes, which contributed an earthiness that tasters felt enriched the overall flavor of the soup. To maintain the rustic feel of the soup, we also decided to cut the zucchini, corn, and potatoes into large pieces. Testing various sizes, we found 1-inch pieces were perfect; anything larger and our soup became hard to eat with a spoon.

As for the garnishes, we decided to reexamine the typical ingredients and test out a few new ones. Lime added sharp, fresh notes to an already complex bowl, as did cilantro, contributing a pleasant floral flavor. Tasters also enjoyed the heat of minced jalapeño. Taking the suggestion of a fellow test cook, we also tried sliced radishes and were pleased with their contrasting crunch. With a host of complex flavors and contrasting textures our soup was now much less work than the original, but still just as hearty and delicious.

Hearty Mexican Beef Soup

SERVES 6 TO 8

For a spicier soup, include a pinch of cayenne or dash of hot sauce near the end of cooking.

1   (1-pound) boneless beef chuck eye roast, trimmed and cut into 1-inch pieces (see the illustrations on page 221)
    Salt and ground black pepper
4   teaspoons vegetable oil
1   medium onion, chopped medium
5   medium garlic cloves, minced or pressed through a garlic press (about 5 teaspoons)
1   tablespoon minced fresh oregano leaves or 1 teaspoon dried
½   teaspoon ground cumin
4   cups beef broth
2   cups low-sodium chicken broth

1   (14.5-ounce) can diced tomatoes, drained
2   bay leaves
2   carrots, peeled and cut into ½-inch pieces
2   medium red potatoes (about 10 ounces), scrubbed and cut into 1-inch chunks
1   medium zucchini (about 8 ounces), halved lengthwise, seeded, and cut into 1-inch pieces
2   ears fresh corn, husks and silk removed, sliced crosswise into 1-inch-thick rounds
2   tablespoons minced fresh cilantro leaves

GARNISHES
Fresh cilantro leaves
Minced jalapeño chiles
Thinly sliced radishes
Lime wedges

1. Pat the beef dry with paper towels and season with salt and pepper. Heat 2 teaspoons of the oil in a large Dutch oven over medium-high heat until just smoking. Add the meat and cook, stirring occasionally, until well browned, 5 to 7 minutes, reducing the heat if the pot begins to scorch. Transfer the browned beef to a medium bowl.

2. Add the remaining 2 teaspoons oil to the pot and place over medium heat until shimmering. Add the onion and cook until softened, 5 to 7 minutes. Stir in the garlic, oregano, and cumin and cook until fragrant, about 30 seconds.

3. Stir in the beef broth and chicken broth, scraping up any browned bits. Stir in the tomatoes, bay leaves, and browned meat with any accumulated juice. Bring to a boil, then cover, reduce to a gentle simmer, and cook for 30 minutes.

4. Stir in the carrots and potatoes and continue to simmer, uncovered, until the beef and vegetables are just tender, 20 to 25 minutes. Stir in the zucchini and corn and continue to simmer until the corn is tender, 5 to 10 minutes longer.

5. Off the heat, remove the bay leaves. Stir in the cilantro, season with salt and pepper to taste, and serve, passing the garnishes at the table.

BEEF AND CABBAGE SOUP

BEEF AND CABBAGE SOUP MIGHT NOT BE typical of the American table, but that doesn't mean it's any less delicious. Crisp, tangy cabbage makes the perfect counterpoint to rich chunks of tender beef. Popular in Eastern Europe and Russia, this bold, flavorful soup most often includes beef brisket along with hearty chunks of root vegetables and cabbage enhanced with a splash of tangy vinegar. Topped with a dollop of sour cream and a sprinkling of dill, this beef soup is comfort food with an Eastern European accent.

After trying several classic recipes, we identified a number of issues at the outset. How should we make the broth and cook the meat for the soup? Should the cabbage be chopped or shredded? What other vegetables would be utilized in this soup and how should they be incorporated? Finally, since beef and cabbage soup is often characterized by a pronounced sour flavor, what acid should be used to add these tangy notes?

We started our testing with the broth and meat. Several traditional sources suggested simmering a large piece of beef brisket in water for several hours until it turned tender. The cooked meat was then removed, diced, and added back to the cooking liquid along with cabbage and other vegetables. We tried this method as well as a variation in which we browned the meat first, but in both cases, tasters found the broth to be weak in flavor and color.

More contemporary recipes we found recommended making a traditional beef broth—we used our Rich Beef Broth (page 19)—and then utilized the broth to simmer the brisket. This method produced far superior flavor, but while we were pleased with the results, we wondered if there was a shorter (and easier) way to create great beef and cabbage soup. After all, the soup contained so many other distinct flavors—cabbage, a sour component (we were using white vinegar at this point), and some dill—that it might be possible to start with store-bought beef broth.

With that in mind, we tried a third approach. We began by first browning chunks of beef brisket— the small pieces would enable us to reduce the overall cooking time—in a little oil, then added the broth. Once the beef had simmered for 30 minutes, we added the cabbage to the pot and allowed the soup to continue simmering until the meat and cabbage were tender. This soup tasted rich and was much less work, but some tasters found that the store-bought beef broth was now overpowering the other flavors of the soup. Cutting the beef broth with some water only diluted the flavors of the soup, but using store-bought chicken broth balanced the flavors nicely.

With our stock and meat elements under control, we were ready to focus on the vegetables. Cabbage was obvious, but most recipes also included carrots and onion. Other possible choices included potato, celery, parsnip, celery root, turnip, and leek. To start, we focused on vegetables that were essential—the cabbage, carrot, and onion— and then moved on to other possible additions.

Cabbage played an integral role in our soup, adding substance and flavor, and with several varieties to choose from, we tried them all. Shredded cabbage was preferred to chopped, and, surprisingly, tasters preferred the more delicate flavor and texture of savoy cabbage over other harsher tasting varieties. The standard green cabbage was a close second and offered a slightly more aggressive flavor and chew. It's fine to use green cabbage if you have some on hand, but if shopping specifically for this recipe, buy savoy cabbage.

Carrots and onion both added a familiar earthy flavor to the soup. Dicing the carrots and onion (rather than grating or slicing them) provided a nice textural contrast with the shredded cabbage. We tried adding raw onion to the beef stock with the carrots as well as sautéing it first and then adding the stock. Sautéing the onion extracted more flavor and the addition of a little garlic enriched the stock even more. As for the laundry list of other vegetables, we found tasters were indifferent. The soup had not suffered from their inclusion, nor had it been much improved. In the end, we stuck with the basics and avoided including any additional vegetables.

We had one last area to explore: the sour element that gives this soup its distinctive character. In our research, we uncovered several options including vinegar (usually white wine or red wine), lemon juice, and sauerkraut (fermented cabbage). We prepared three batches of the soup and tested each choice. Lemon juice was too citrusy, while the vinegars were one-dimensional. Sauerkraut was the hands-down winner. Its sharp and assertive taste was perfect in this soup. We found it best to add the sauerkraut with the fresh cabbage so it had time to blend with the other flavors. As a final flourish, a dollop of sour cream, along with the traditional fresh dill, completed the dish.

Russian Beef and Cabbage Soup

SERVES 4 TO 6

If savoy cabbage is unavailable, you can substitute regular green cabbage; however, it has a less delicate texture. We prefer the flavor of sauerkraut that has been packaged in plastic bags, rather than those packaged in cans and jars.

I	(1-pound) beef brisket, trimmed and cut into ½-inch pieces
	Salt and ground black pepper
2	tablespoons vegetable oil
I	medium onion, chopped medium
3	medium garlic cloves, minced or pressed through a garlic press (about I tablespoon)
4	cups beef broth
4	cups low-sodium chicken broth
2	bay leaves
2	carrots, peeled and cut into ½-inch pieces
½	small head savoy cabbage (about 5 ounces), cored and shredded into ¼-inch-thick pieces (see the illustrations below)
½	cup sauerkraut, rinsed (see note)
2	tablespoons minced fresh dill
	Sour cream, for serving

1. Pat the beef dry with paper towels and season with salt and pepper. Heat 2 teaspoons of the oil in a large Dutch oven over medium-high heat until just smoking. Add half of the meat and cook, stirring occasionally, until well browned, 5 to 7 minutes, reducing the heat if the pot begins to scorch. Transfer the browned beef to a medium bowl. Repeat with 2 teaspoons more oil and the remaining beef; transfer to the bowl.

2. Add the remaining 2 teaspoons oil to the pot and place over medium heat until shimmering. Add the onion and cook until softened, 5 to 7 minutes. Stir in the garlic and cook until fragrant, about 30 seconds.

3. Stir in the beef broth and chicken broth, scraping up any browned bits. Stir in the bay leaves and browned meat with any accumulated juice. Bring to a boil, then cover, reduce to a gentle simmer, and cook for 30 minutes.

4. Stir in the carrots, cabbage, and sauerkraut, cover partially (leaving about 1 inch of the pot open), and simmer gently until the beef and vegetables are tender, 30 to 40 minutes longer.

5. Off the heat, remove the bay leaves. Stir in the dill, season with salt and pepper to taste, and serve with the sour cream.

SHREDDING CABBAGE

1. Cut the cabbage into quarters and cut away the hard piece of core attached to each quarter.

2. Separate the cored cabbage into stacks of leaves that flatten when pressed lightly.

3. Use a chef's knife to cut each stack diagonally (this ensures long pieces) into thin shreds.

OXTAIL SOUP

FOR MANY PEOPLE, OXTAIL SOUP CONJURES up images of medicinal broths used by ancient ancestors to bring forth strength and healing. For others, oxtail soup means fine restaurant dining from an age long gone by. Either way, the qualities that make oxtail soup so appealing are the same. Oxtails are prized for their richly flavored marrow—perfect for soup. The beef flavor in this soup is deep and rich; the body is thick, almost unctuous; and the color is an intense reddish golden brown.

After consulting a dozen or so sources, we soon realized why most cooks (both at home and in restaurants) don't make oxtail soup. Many recipes require 12 hours of simmering. Even though most of this time is unattended, few modern cooks are willing to make a recipe with such a long cooking time. Our goal was clear—figure out how to make great oxtail soup in a reasonable amount of time.

We started our testing by preparing two classic recipes. The first began by roasting oxtails in a 500-degree oven until nicely browned. The oxtails were then placed in a stockpot and covered with water. The roasting pan was deglazed with more water, which was then added to the stockpot. The stock was simmered until the oxtails were tender, about three hours. At this point, the oxtails were fished out of the pot and cooled. The meat was removed and the picked-over bones were added back to the pot. The stock and bones simmered another eight hours before being strained, cooled, and defatted. This broth was intensely delicious. It jelled to a solid mass in the refrigerator and when heated had a gorgeous deep golden brown color, heady aroma, and rich beef flavor.

Our second recipe began with homemade beef broth—we used our Rich Beef Broth (page 19). The oxtails were then browned in a large Dutch oven, as were carrots and onions. Once the oxtails and vegetables were browned, the pot was deglazed with some red wine. A bouquet garni (herbs tied together for easy retrieval) was then added along with the homemade broth. The broth, oxtails, and aromatics were simmered for about three hours. This broth was just as rich as the first recipe but with herbal and vegetal flavors in the background. Most tasters liked the onion flavor, while others felt that the carrots made the broth too sweet. No one found an abundance of herbs to be necessary; a small amount for fragrance was sufficient. Although quicker to make than the first broth, it wasn't a significant enough improvement since this version, which included making a beef broth, took almost eight hours to prepare.

So what had we learned up to this point? First, it takes a long time to extract flavor from oxtail bones. Second, you can shortcut the process slightly by making a double stock—that is, by covering the oxtail bones with beef broth rather than water.

We were now ready to start testing a quicker method. Working with the previously tested oxtail broth recipe that used beef broth rather than water, we wondered if we could cut off a significant amount of time by using store-bought rather than homemade broth. Following this basic recipe, we prepared three batches—one with store-bought beef broth, one with store-bought chicken broth, and a third with an equal blend of store-bought beef and chicken broths.

Tasters immediately dismissed the recipe made with store-bought beef broth, citing an overly concentrated beef flavor. The recipe made with chicken broth had excellent body, but it lacked the clarity and rich beef flavor that defines good oxtail soup. The third recipe was the most promising. The color was appealing and the clarity issue faded with the use of less chicken broth. The flavor was decent but needed some help.

We tried a few new approaches—adding vegetables for more complexity and simmering tomato paste and/or dried porcini mushrooms with the broth to improve flavors. The vegetables detracted from the beef flavor, the tomato paste produced a sour flavor, and the porcini were too strong tasting and easy to identify. We had struck out.

Since no ingredient changes seemed to improve our recipe, we turned to the cooking method. At this point we had been simmering the oxtails for three hours, but thought more time might be required. We increased the simmering time to three and a half hours and noticed some improvement, but when we went to four hours, the results were dramatic. The beef flavor was incredibly rich and the body was perfect.

We tried another batch, increasing the simmering time to six hours. Thankfully, tasters detected no improvement. We had successfully taken a recipe that was thought to require eight to 12 hours of stovetop cooking and reduced that time to about four hours. Not exactly fast food, but most of that cooking time is unattended.

The heavy lifting was done. Our broth was delicious, and we could focus on the garnishes that would transform it into oxtail soup. While many of the traditional recipes we found called for a small amount of garnishes, tasters liked the heartier versions best. With that in mind, we tried carrots, leeks, turnips, parsnips, and potatoes, all diced small so that they would cook relatively quickly. Tasters found that turnips were too bitter and detracted from the oxtail flavor. Leeks provided an interesting textural component but caused too much emphasis on the onion flavor already in the stock, so we chose to omit them. Carrots and parsnips added some mild sweetness and red potatoes contributed some depth.

Sherry is a classic addition to many oxtail soup recipes. In fact, sherry even makes it into the recipe name in some of the sources we consulted. Sherried oxtail consommé is a classic, straight from the menu of the Titanic. We found that a medium-dry sherry blended nicely with the broth, adding complexity to the final dish. (Don't use sweet sherry or cooking sherry, both of which are more jarring than pleasing.) A final garnish with parsley and our soup was ready to be served.

BUYING OXTAILS

Depending on which part of the tail they come from, oxtail pieces can vary in diameter from ¾ inch to 4 inches. (Thicker pieces are cut close to the body; thinner pieces come from the end of the tail.) Try to buy oxtail packages with thicker pieces that will yield some meat for the soup. Thicker pieces also lend more flavor to the broth. It's fine to use a few small pieces—just don't rely on them exclusively.

Oxtail Soup
SERVES 6 TO 8

Oxtails can often be found in the freezer section of the grocery store; if using frozen oxtails, be sure to thaw them completely before using. Oxtails are very fatty, so to prevent a greasy soup, be sure to defat the broth.

6   pounds oxtails (see below)
    Salt and ground black pepper
1   tablespoon vegetable oil
1   medium onion, chopped medium
2   medium garlic cloves, minced or pressed
    through a garlic press (about 2 teaspoons)
1   tablespoon minced fresh thyme leaves or
    1 teaspoon dried
½   cup dry red wine
4   cups beef broth
4   cups low-sodium chicken broth
2   bay leaves
2   carrots, peeled and cut into ½-inch pieces
2   parsnips, peeled and cut into ½-inch pieces
3   tablespoons dry sherry
2   medium red potatoes (about 10 ounces),
    scrubbed and cut into ½-inch pieces
2   tablespoons minced fresh parsley leaves

1. Pat the oxtails dry with paper towels and season with salt and pepper. Heat the oil in a large Dutch oven over medium-high heat until just smoking. Add half of the oxtails and brown well on all sides, 7 to 10 minutes, reducing the heat if the pot begins to scorch. Transfer the oxtails to a large bowl. Using the fat left in the pot, repeat with the remaining oxtails; transfer to the bowl.

2. Pour off all but 2 teaspoons of the fat left in the pot, add the onion, and cook over medium heat until softened, 5 to 7 minutes. Stir in the garlic and thyme and cook until fragrant, about 30 seconds. Stir in the red wine, scraping up any browned bits, and cook until nearly evaporated, 1 to 2 minutes.

3. Stir in the beef broth, chicken broth, bay leaves, and browned oxtails with any accumulated juice. Bring to a boil, then cover, reduce to a gentle simmer, and cook until the meat is very tender and a fork poked into it meets little resistance, about 4 hours.

4. Transfer the oxtails to a large bowl, let cool slightly, then shred the meat into bite-size pieces, discarding the fat and bones (you should have about 4 cups of meat). Strain the soup through a fine mesh strainer, then defat the strained broth (see page 18). (The strained broth and shredded meat can be refrigerated in separate airtight containers for up to 3 days before assembling the soup.)

5. Return the broth to a clean pot and bring to a simmer over medium-low heat. Add the shredded meat, carrots, parsnips, and sherry and simmer for 10 minutes. Stir in the potatoes and continue to simmer until the meat and vegetables are tender, 20 to 30 minutes longer.

6. Off the heat, stir in the parsley, season with salt and pepper to taste, and serve.

➤ VARIATIONS

Asian-Style Oxtail Soup

Warm spices like star anise, cinnamon, and ginger give oxtail soup a whole new character.

Follow the recipe for Oxtail Soup, omitting the thyme and adding 2 star anise pods and 1 small cinnamon stick to the pot with the broths in step 3. Omit the potatoes and add 1 (8-ounce) can bamboo shoots, drained, and 1 tablespoon minced or grated fresh ginger (see the illustrations on page 89) to the soup with the shredded beef in step 5. Substitute 2 scallions, sliced thin, for the parsley.

Jamaican-Style Oxtail Soup

Allspice and a jalapeño infuse this soup with warm, spicy flavor.

Follow the recipe for Oxtail Soup, adding 1 teaspoon ground allspice to the pot with the garlic and thyme in step 2. Omit the parsnips and add 1 (15-ounce) can butter beans, drained and rinsed, and 1 jalapeño chile, sliced thin, to the soup with the shredded meat in step 5. Substitute 1 green bell pepper, stemmed, seeded, and cut into ½-inch pieces, for the potatoes.

PITTSBURGH WEDDING SOUP

PITTSBURGH WEDDING SOUP (ALSO CALLED Italian wedding soup) has an interesting history that actually has nothing to do with matrimony. The recipe is based on a centuries-old southern Italian meat and vegetable soup called *minestra maritata*; the "marriage" is of flavors and ingredients—in this case, meatballs and greens. Nowhere is it more popular than in Pittsburgh, where it appears on menus at high-end and fast food restaurants alike. And of course it's a staple at wedding receptions. Our goal was to develop a recipe for this classic soup—with a flavorful broth, tender meatballs, hearty pasta, and earthy greens.

Wedding soup is traditionally made with a slow-simmered homemade chicken broth. Since it takes time to make the meatballs, we decided to streamline our recipe by using store-bought broth instead. Our first step was to improve the flavor of the broth. Cooking garlic and red pepper flakes in extra-virgin olive oil before adding the broth was an obvious way to build better flavor. And while some recipes suggest browning meatballs and then adding them to the soup, we found that poaching the raw meatballs directly in the broth added more depth and richness to the broth, and it saved time.

Our next focus was the meatballs. Usually the meat varies from ground beef to pork, but we found that using ground meatloaf mix (which is a combination of ground beef, pork, and veal) gave us the most well-rounded flavor and delicate texture. We then simply boosted the flavor of this meat mixture with some basic seasonings including garlic, parsley, and oregano. To keep the meatballs tender, we mashed two slices of white bread with ½ cup whole milk into a paste and mixed it in with the meat. We also found it best to add an egg yolk to help bind the filling ingredients and add richness. While cheese isn't completely necessary in these meatballs, tasters felt that the addition provided extra richness that not only contributed to the flavor but also helped to protect the meatballs from drying out while they poached. Because these meatballs are meant to be eaten in just one bite from a spoon, we made them quite small—just 2 teaspoons of the meat mixture per meatball.

Next, we moved on to the greens. Most recipes call for stirring chopped spinach or escarole into the soup just before serving. But our tasters found these greens too bland and too delicate (they dissolved in the soup). After testing several different types of hearty greens, we settled on earthy-tasting chopped kale. It added great flavor and texture and was hearty enough to withstand the hot broth. If you are unable to find kale, collard greens are a reliable substitute.

The last area of investigation was pasta and we found our pasta choices were small—literally. Testing showed that smaller shapes worked best in this soup. Larger shapes only crowded out the other ingredients and soaked up too much liquid. Ditalini (small tubes), tubettini (very small tubes), or orzo (rice-shaped pasta) were all popular options. All three worked fine, but tasters preferred the slender, elegant pieces of orzo, which easily fit on a soupspoon. Some recipes we found called for cooking the pasta separately, but we found that cooking the orzo in the soup helped flavor the orzo—plus, we had one less pot to clean.

Lastly, for a complete, authentic experience, we found it was important to garnish the soup with grated Parmesan and a splash of fruity extra-virgin olive oil just before serving; the cheese's nuttiness and the oil's fruitiness bring out and heighten the flavors in this Italian-style soup.

Pittsburgh Wedding Soup

SERVES 8 TO 10

You can substitute a combination of ground pork and ground beef for the meatloaf mix if necessary. The kale may seem like a lot at first, but it wilts down substantially. Collard greens can be substituted for the kale. We like to serve this soup with a drizzle of extra-virgin olive oil and a grating of Parmesan cheese.

MEATBALLS

2 slices high-quality white sandwich bread, torn into quarters
½ cup whole milk

1 pound meatloaf mix (see note)
1 ounce Parmesan cheese, grated (½ cup)
3 tablespoons minced fresh parsley leaves
1 large egg yolk
3 medium garlic cloves, minced or pressed through a garlic press (about 1 tablespoon)
¾ teaspoon salt
½ teaspoon ground black pepper
½ teaspoon dried oregano

SOUP

1 tablespoon extra-virgin olive oil, plus extra for serving
2 medium garlic cloves, minced or pressed through a garlic press (about 2 teaspoons)
¼ teaspoon red pepper flakes
12 cups low-sodium chicken broth
1 bunch kale (about 1 pound), stemmed and leaves chopped into 1-inch pieces (see note)
1 cup orzo
3 tablespoons minced fresh parsley leaves
Salt and ground black pepper
Freshly grated Parmesan cheese, for serving

1. FOR THE MEATBALLS: Mash the bread and milk together into a paste in a large bowl. Add the meatloaf mix, Parmesan, parsley, egg yolk, garlic, salt, pepper, and oregano and mix thoroughly to combine. Pinch off 2-teaspoon-sized pieces of the meat mixture, roll firmly into balls, and arrange on a rimmed baking sheet; you should have 30 to 35 meatballs. Cover with plastic wrap and refrigerate until firm, at least 30 minutes.

2. FOR THE SOUP: Heat the oil in a large Dutch oven over medium heat until shimmering. Add the garlic and red pepper flakes and cook until fragrant, about 30 seconds. Stir in the broth and bring to a simmer.

3. Stir in the kale and simmer until softened, 10 to 15 minutes. Stir in the orzo, then gently add the meatballs and continue to simmer until the pasta is tender and the meatballs are cooked through, about 10 minutes longer.

4. Off the heat, stir in the parsley and season with salt and pepper to taste. Serve, passing the olive oil and Parmesan separately.

TOMATO AND MEATBALL SOUP

TOMATO SOUP ENRICHED WITH MEATBALLS is our idea of a great soup supper. We envisioned a garlicky tomato soup with tender, well-seasoned meatballs. Inspired by one of our favorites—spaghetti and meatballs—we set out to create a soup version.

We started by focusing on the soup base. Overall we wanted a tomato soup that was easy, but still had bold, fresh tomato flavor with a hint of acidity. To accomplish this, we immediately decided upon using canned diced tomatoes, which provided the necessary ease of preparation— no need for blanching and peeling skins off fresh tomatoes—as well as reliable flavor. Other questions then came to mind. Which type of broth would complement the tomato flavor without becoming overwhelming? How could we include aromatics without causing a distraction? Did we need tomato paste to boost tomato flavor? Is sugar necessary for added sweetness?

To get a better sense of what we wanted in the tomato base, we went into the kitchen and cooked up several basic versions, all containing a relatively concise list of ingredients—tomatoes, broth, onion, garlic, and seasonings. To our surprise, there was considerable agreement among tasters as to what worked and what didn't. Beef broth tended to blur the bright, slightly acidic flavor of the tomatoes, while chicken broth added a pleasant meaty background. Tasters liked onion and garlic, but thought the tomato paste made the tomato flavor too intense. Some recipes include carrots, and tasters liked the double-duty role carrots played—lending the soup a complementary vegetal flavor as well as a subtle sweetness. With carrots in, sugar was out.

With these observations, we compiled a master recipe. We began by sautéing the onion, carrots, and garlic, then added the broth and tomatoes and simmered until the vegetables were tender. Once the vegetables were tender, we processed the soup in a blender until smooth and returned it to a clean pot. We were now ready for the meatballs and pasta.

Having created a reliable meatball recipe for our Pittsburgh Wedding Soup (page 65), we decided to start there. With the smaller amount of meat in this recipe, we omitted the egg and simply bound together the meat with the bread and milk mixture and seasoned it with garlic, basil, oregano, and salt and pepper. Parmesan cheese rounded out the flavors and after portioning the meatballs out on a sheet pan, we allowed them to set up in the refrigerator for 30 minutes. Poached in the soup, the meatballs cooked up tender and full of flavor.

Ready to move on to the pasta, we began by testing spaghetti, broken into smaller pieces, but we found that even small pieces of spaghetti were awkward to scoop up with a spoon. After several additional tests, we concluded that small pasta shapes were best in this soup. Ditalini, a small tubular pasta, was the favorite among tasters, although small shells or elbow macaroni also worked. We also found that it was important to serve the soup immediately. When left sitting too long, the pasta absorbed the excess liquid and turned mushy, while at the same time making the soup too thick.

All our tomato and meatball soup needed now was a sprinkle of Parmesan cheese and a drizzle of extra-virgin olive oil and we had a soup that was simple yet completely satisfying, just like the dish that inspired it.

Tomato and Meatball Soup with Ditalini

SERVES 4

You can substitute a combination of ground pork and ground beef for the meatloaf mix if necessary. Also, you can substitute 1 cup small pasta shells or elbow macaroni for the ditalini. Serve with a drizzle of extra-virgin olive oil and crusty bread. See page 121 for more information on pureeing.

MEATBALLS

1	slice high-quality white sandwich bread, torn into quarters
¼	cup whole milk
8	ounces meatloaf mix (see note)
¼	cup Parmesan cheese, grated
2	tablespoons chopped fresh basil leaves
1	medium garlic clove, minced or pressed through a garlic press (about 1 teaspoon)

½   teaspoon salt
¼   teaspoon ground black pepper
¼   teaspoon dried oregano

SOUP
I   tablespoon olive oil
I   medium onion, chopped medium
I   carrot, peeled and chopped medium
I   celery rib, chopped coarse
3   medium garlic cloves, minced or pressed
    through a garlic press (about I tablespoon)
3½ cups low-sodium chicken broth
I   (28-ounce) can diced tomatoes
I   cup ditalini pasta (see note)
    Salt and ground black pepper
    Freshly grated Parmesan cheese,
    for serving

1. FOR THE MEATBALLS: Mash the bread and milk together into a paste in a large bowl. Add the meatloaf mix, Parmesan, basil, garlic, salt, pepper, and oregano and mix thoroughly to combine. Pinch off 2-teaspoon-sized pieces of the meat mixture, roll firmly into balls, and arrange on a rimmed baking sheet; you should have roughly 16 meatballs. Cover with plastic wrap and refrigerate until firm, at least 30 minutes.

2. FOR THE SOUP: Heat the oil in a large Dutch oven over medium heat until shimmering. Add the onion, carrot, and celery and cook until the vegetables are softened, 5 to 7 minutes. Stir in the garlic and cook until fragrant, about 30 seconds. Stir in the broth and diced tomatoes with their juice, bring to a simmer, and cook until the vegetables are tender, about 20 minutes.

3. Working in batches, puree the soup until smooth and return to a clean pot. Cover and bring the soup to a simmer.

4. Stir in the pasta, then gently add the meatballs, and continue to simmer, uncovered, until the pasta is tender and the meatballs are cooked through, 12 to 15 minutes. Off the heat, season with salt and pepper to taste and serve, passing the Parmesan separately.

KENTUCKY BURGOO

LIKE BOURBON AND BARBECUE, BURGOO is another Kentucky favorite, albeit a little-known one outside of state lines. A chunky soup of tomatoes, corn, potatoes, chicken, and mutton, it boasts a warming, slow heat and a compelling tangy quality. In traditional recipes we found in our research, whole chickens (and sometimes beef or pork stewing meat) are boiled to make broth. In a second pot, mutton is boiled until tender and then the meat is removed from both pots, shredded and combined into one pot with the broth and vegetables are added. The whole mixture simmers until the vegetables are cooked through and the flavors meld. Burgoo draws crowds at barbecue joints, church suppers, and other community gatherings. We set out to find out what was so special about this bluegrass state specialty.

We peeled, chopped, shredded, and simmered, hoping to re-create a reasonable approximation. Many hours later, we had many gallons of burgoo. It tasted pretty good, too, but it had been a project and a half to make. For this recipe to work at home, we needed to streamline the ingredients, cut back the cooking time, and find new ways to build flavor.

The test kitchen typically relies on a basic method when making soup: Brown the meat first. Add aromatic vegetables. Sprinkle in flour as a thickener, if necessary. Deglaze the pan and simmer everything with broth, herbs, and spices until tender. If you're adding more vegetables, do it in stages so that the delicate ones don't overcook. We thought if we followed these rules, we might get away with using store-bought broth, precut frozen or canned for some of the vegetables, and small pieces of chicken and beef for a tasty, reasonably quick burgoo.

Off the bat, we needed to settle on the meat. Mutton was out, but beef and chicken were in. Starting with the beef, we hit our first stumbling block. Shanks and short ribs gave great flavor, but made the burgoo greasy, plus they came with the added requirement of removing the meat from the bones. Chuck, however, was completely bone-less and still tasted great—the meat was flavorful, tender, and juicy, with a meaty richness that tasters enjoyed. Tasters preferred chicken thigh meat to breasts, which dried out and got lost in the busy stew. As for vegetables, the ease of using canned tomatoes, frozen corn, and frozen lima beans made up for the onions, garlic, and potatoes we had to chop by hand.

The burgoo was now thick and tasted pretty good, but it lacked the rich meatiness and heat that makes this stew so memorable. Adding more meat to our already full pot was not an option. We thought long and hard and realized that the flavor that had eluded us in the burgoos we'd tasted must be a missing ingredient. We went back to the recipes we'd collected, and a light went on—Worcestershire sauce! Astonishingly, it took a full ¼ cup to give the stew the richness it lacked. Adding ¾ teaspoon of black pepper at the end of cooking rather than at the beginning restored a pleasant, spicy heat. To brighten the burgoo, we tried both vinegar and lemon juice. Lemon won hands down.

Kentucky Burgoo

SERVES 8 TO 10

We like to use the rendered chicken fat (left over after browning the chicken in step 1) to brown the meat and sauté the vegetables; substitute vegetable oil if you don't have enough rendered fat.

2	pounds bone-in, skin-on chicken thighs (5 to 6 thighs), trimmed
1	(1-pound) boneless beef chuck eye roast, trimmed and cut into ½-inch pieces (see the illustrations on page 221) Salt and ground black pepper
1	tablespoon vegetable oil
2	medium onions, chopped medium
2	garlic cloves, minced or pressed through a garlic press (about 2 teaspoons)
2	tablespoons unbleached all-purpose flour
6	cups low-sodium chicken broth
1	(14.5-ounce) can diced tomatoes
¼	cup Worcestershire sauce
2	medium Yukon Gold potatoes (about 1 pound), peeled and cut into ½-inch pieces
1½	cups frozen corn
1½	cups frozen baby lima beans
2	tablespoons juice from 1 lemon

1. Pat the chicken and beef dry with paper towels and season with salt and pepper. Heat the oil in a large Dutch oven over medium-high heat until just smoking. Add the chicken to the pot and brown well, 5 to 8 minutes. Transfer the browned chicken to a medium bowl, let cool slightly, then remove and discard the skin.

2. Meanwhile, pour off and reserve the rendered chicken fat (see note). Return 2 teaspoons of the reserved fat to the pot and place over medium-high heat until just smoking. Add the beef and cook, stirring occasionally, until well browned, 5 to 7 minutes, reducing the heat if the pot begins to scorch. Transfer the browned meat to the bowl with the chicken.

3. Add 2 teaspoons more reserved fat to the pot and place over medium heat until shimmering. Add the onions and cook until softened, 5 to 7 minutes. Stir in the garlic and cook until fragrant, about 30 seconds. Stir in the flour and cook until golden, about 1 minute.

4. Gradually whisk in the broth, scraping up any browned bits and smoothing out any lumps. Stir in the tomatoes, Worcestershire sauce, chicken, and beef with any accumulated juice. Bring to a boil, then cover, reduce to a gentle simmer, and cook for 30 minutes. Stir in the potatoes and continue to simmer, uncovered, until the meat, chicken, and potatoes are completely tender, 20 to 30 minutes longer.

5. Remove the chicken from the pot, let cool slightly, then remove and discard the bones and shred the meat into bite-size pieces (see the illustrations on page 43). Return the shredded chicken to the pot, stir in the corn and lima beans, and continue to simmer until everything is heated through, 2 to 5 minutes. Off the heat, stir in the lemon juice, season with salt to taste and ¾ teaspoon pepper, and serve.

4
ASIAN SOUPS

Asian Soups

HOT AND SOUR SOUP

THE HOT AND SOUR SOUP WE EAT IN Chinese-American restaurants today isn't much different from the Sichuan original. Named for its potent peppery and vinegary flavors, the lightly thickened soup contains strips of pork, cubes of tofu, and wisps of egg. According to the cookbooks and Chinese cooking experts we consulted, hot and sour soup encapsulates the Taoist principle central to Chinese culture: yin and yang, the notion of balancing the universe's opposing yet complementary forces. Balancing universal forces we'd have to leave to the philosophers. (All we were after was a good soup.) But balancing flavors, textures, and temperatures? That was familiar territory. At the very least, we figured, the yin-yang principle left us some leeway to explore stand-ins for hard-to-find ingredients that show up in some authentic versions—for instance, mustard pickle, pig's-foot tendon, and dried sea cucumber—without sacrificing the spirit of authenticity. So we headed to the test kitchen to work on a balanced and (philosophically) authentic take on hot and sour soup.

The heat in hot and sour soup traditionally comes not from fresh chiles but from ground white (or sometimes black) peppercorns. Unlike chiles, pepper delivers direct spiciness but doesn't leave a lingering burn in its wake. An all-black-pepper soup was sharp but one-dimensional. Better still was a version made with distinctive, penetrating white pepper. Nice, but we suspected that a second heat source might deliver yet another layer of complexity. Sure enough, chili oil—a bit unconventional for this recipe—supported the white-hot heat of the pepper, laying the groundwork for the opposing flavor of vinegar.

But the vinegar in this dish tripped us up. Made from toasted rice, Chinese black vinegar (the traditional sour component) has an elusive flavor that almost defies description. Because it can be difficult to find, we needed to identify a substitute—but it wasn't so easy. Emboldened by the success of our first improvisation, we raided the test kitchen pantry and assembled 14 bottles of

vinegar. Sadly, every concoction was exceedingly harsh. Resting our weary palates, we reexamined the black vinegar label and noticed an acidity level of 1.18 percent. Most American vinegars measure in the 5 to 7 percent range, so we would have to use a lot less of our substitute vinegars. After several more rounds, we finally settled on a tablespoon each of dark, fruity balsamic and robust red wine vinegar as a workable substitute for 5 tablespoons of black vinegar. (That said, black vinegar is so distinctive that we recommend seeking it out.)

Next, we turned our focus to texture. Cornstarch is the standard thickener, but a heavy hand resulted in a goopy gravy instead of a silky broth. We found that just 3 tablespoons yielded an agreeable, not-too-thick consistency that would gently support the other textures in the soup. In addition to its role as thickener, cornstarch is believed by many Chinese cooks to play the part of meat (or protein) tenderizer. To test what seemed to us a dubious theory, we prepared two batches of soup, adding cornstarch to a simple soy sauce marinade for one julienned pork chop and omitting it in the marinade for another. The cornstarch-marinated pork was noticeably more tender. The cornstarch created a protective sheath that bought us the few extra minutes we needed to finish the soup without overcooking the pork.

After the pork is cooked and the soup thickened, beaten egg is drizzled in to create yet another complementary texture: fine, feathery shreds. The problem is if the egg doesn't set immediately, it can blend into the soup and muddy the appearance of the broth. Wanting to make this step foolproof, we tried mixing the egg with vinegar and cornstarch. The vinegar instantly coagulated the egg, whereas the cornstarch, once again, was the miracle worker: The cornstarch molecules stabilized the liquid proteins, preventing them from contracting excessively when they hit the hot liquid. The result? Lighter, softer eggs.

Spicy, bracing, pungent, tender, fluffy—this soup was already replete with pleasing balances of flavor and texture. But we weren't quite done yet. Almost all authentic hot and sour soup recipes start with reconstituted dried wood ear mushrooms and lily buds. Wood ear mushrooms, also known as tree ear or cloud ear, offer snappy texture but little else. We swapped in commonly available dried porcini, but their woodsy notes overwhelmed the broth. Fresh, mild shiitake mushrooms were a better choice. Lily buds, or golden needles, are the dried buds of the tiger lily flower. Tangy, mildly crunchy canned bamboo shoots closely approximated the musky, sour flavor of lily buds and added textural variety (a crisp foil for the fluffy wisps of egg).

As for the tofu, we had one basic question: Must it be pressed? The answer was a simple yes. Using extra-firm tofu and weighting it beneath a heavy plate yielded very firm, clean-tasting cubes that are appropriate in this soup. Many recipes call for passing potent toasted sesame oil at the table, but a generous pour overwhelmed the other flavors. We took a low-risk approach and added a measured amount to the marinade for the pork. A sprinkling of raw, crisp green scallions on the cooked soup completed the dish.

HOW TO JULIENNE A PORK CHOP

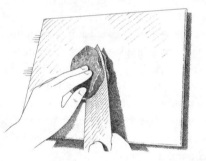

1. Holding the knife so that the blade is parallel to the cutting board, carefully slice the pork chop into 2 thin cutlets.

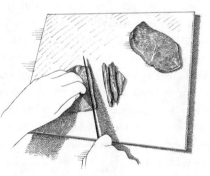

2. Press each cutlet flat with your hand, then slice it crosswise into thin strips.

Hot and Sour Soup

SERVES 6 TO 8

To make cutting the pork chop easier, freeze it for 15 minutes. The distinctive flavor of the Chinese black vinegar is important here (you can find it in Asian supermarkets); if you can't find it, substitute a mixture of 1 tablespoon red wine vinegar and 1 tablespoon balsamic vinegar. This soup is very spicy; for a less spicy soup, use the lower amount of chili oil or omit it altogether.

TOFU AND PORK

7	ounces (½ block) extra-firm tofu
I	tablespoon soy sauce
I	teaspoon toasted sesame oil
I	teaspoon cornstarch
I	(6-ounce) boneless center-cut pork chop, trimmed and julienned (see the illustrations at left)

SOUP

6	cups low-sodium chicken broth
I	(5-ounce) can bamboo shoots, drained and sliced into ⅛-inch-thick matchsticks
4	ounces shiitake mushrooms, wiped clean, stemmed, and sliced thin
5	tablespoons Chinese black vinegar (see note)
3	tablespoons soy sauce
3	tablespoons water
3	tablespoons cornstarch
I–2	teaspoons chili oil (see note)
½	teaspoon ground white pepper

EGG AND SCALLIONS

I	teaspoon water
½	teaspoon cornstarch
I	large egg
3	scallions, sliced thin on the bias (see the illustration below)

1. For the tofu and pork: Place the tofu in a pie plate, top with a heavy plate, and weigh down with 2 heavy cans. Set the tofu aside until it releases roughly ½ cup liquid, about 15 minutes. Drain the tofu, pat dry with paper towels, and cut into ½-inch cubes. Meanwhile, whisk the soy sauce, sesame oil, and cornstarch together in a medium bowl, then stir in the pork and let it marinate for at least 10 minutes, or up to 30 minutes. (Do not overmarinate.)

2. For the soup: Bring the broth to a boil in a large saucepan over high heat. Reduce the heat to medium, add the bamboo shoots and mushrooms, and simmer until the mushrooms are just tender, 2 to 3 minutes.

3. Stir in the diced tofu and pork with marinade. Whisk the vinegar, soy sauce, water, cornstarch, chili oil, and pepper together to dissolve the cornstarch, then whisk into the soup. Continue to simmer the soup, stirring constantly, until it thickens and turns translucent, about 1 minute. Remove the soup from the heat (do not let it cool off).

4. For the egg and scallions: Whisk the water and cornstarch together in a small bowl, then whisk in the egg until combined. Following the illustrations at right, use a spoon to slowly drizzle very thin streams of the egg mixture into the hot soup in a circular motion. Without stirring the soup, let it continue to sit off the heat for 1 minute.

5. Briefly return the soup to a simmer over medium-high heat without stirring, then remove it from the heat immediately. Gently stir the soup to evenly distribute the egg. Serve, sprinkling individual portions with the scallions.

GETTING THE WISPED EGG JUST RIGHT

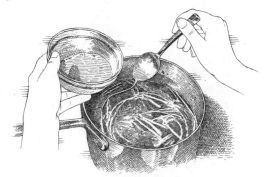

1. In order to achieve wispy, delicate ribbons of egg in the soup, you must first turn off the heat so that the surface of soup is still. Then, using a soupspoon, drizzle thin streams of egg in a circular motion over the surface.

2. Let the egg set in the soup off the heat for 1 minute, then briefly return the soup to a gentle boil to cook the egg through. Once the soup reaches a gentle boil, remove it from the heat immediately to prevent the egg from overcooking. Gently stir the soup to evenly redistribute the egg.

SLICING SCALLIONS ON THE BIAS

Slicing the scallions on the bias makes for an attractive presentation. Simply hold the scallion at an angle, then slice the scallion thin.

Asian Ingredients 101

With the increased interest in authentic Asian cooking, many supermarkets are now carrying a wider array of Asian ingredients—look for them in the international foods aisle. The following list includes some of the Asian ingredients that you'll find in our recipes.

ASIAN CHILI SAUCES

Used both in cooking and as a condiment, these sauces come in a variety of styles. Sriracha contains garlic and is made from chiles that are ground into a smooth paste. Chili-garlic sauce also contains garlic and is similar to sriracha except that the chiles are coarsely ground. Sambal oelek differs in that it is made purely from ground chiles without the addition of garlic or other spices, thus adding heat but not additional flavor. Once opened these sauces will keep for several months in the refrigerator.

| SRIRACHA SAUCE | CHILI-GARLIC SAUCE | SAMBAL OELEK CHILI PASTE |

MISO

Miso is the Japanese word for "bean paste." Commonly found in Asian—most notably Japanese—cuisines, miso is a fermented paste of soybeans and rice, barley, or rye. Miso is incredibly versatile, suitable for use in soups, braises, dressings, and sauces as well as for topping grilled foods. This salty, deep-flavored paste ranges in strength and color from a mild, pale yellow (referred to as white) to stronger-flavored red or brownish-black, depending on the fermentation method and ingredients. Avoid miso labeled "light," as this is an American low-sodium product whose flavor pales in comparison to the real thing. Miso can be found in well-stocked grocery stores and Japanese or Asian markets. It will keep for up to a year in the refrigerator.

SOY SAUCE

Soy sauce is a fermented liquid made from soybeans and roasted grain, usually wheat, but sometimes barley or rice. This Asian condiment should enhance flavor and contribute complexity to food—not just make it salty. It can offer nearly as much variety, complexity, and flavor as wine or olive oil. In general, lower-sodium soy sauces are preferred for dipping and higher-sodium soy sauces hold up better to heat in cooked applications.

COCONUT MILK

Widely available in cans, coconut milk adds rich flavor and body to soups, curries, and stir-fries. Coconut milk is made by steeping shredded coconut meat in warm milk or water. The meat is then pressed or mashed to release as much liquid as possible, the mixture is strained, and the result is coconut milk. Do not confuse coconut milk with cream of coconut, which contains added sugar and is thus much sweeter.

MIRIN

This Japanese rice wine has a subtle salty-sweet flavor prized in Asian marinades and glazes. The most traditional method for creating mirin uses glutinous rice, malted rice, and distilled alcohol. Many supermarket brands in this country, however, combine sake or another type of alcohol with salt, corn syrup, other sweeteners, and sometimes caramel coloring and flavoring. We use mirin to brighten the flavor of stir-fries, teriyaki, and other Asian dishes. If you cannot find mirin, substitute 1 tablespoon dry white wine and ½ teaspoon sugar for every 1 tablespoon of mirin.

SESAME OIL

Raw sesame oil, which is very mild and light in color, is used mostly for cooking, while toasted sesame oil, which has a deep amber color, is primarily used for seasoning because of its intense, nutty flavor. For the biggest hit of sesame flavor, we prefer to use toasted sesame oil. Just a few drops will give dishes a deep, rich flavor. Sesame oil stored at room temperature will turn rancid if not used within a few months. Refrigeration will extend its shelf life.

FISH SAUCE

Fish sauce is a salty amber-colored liquid made from fermented fish. It is used both as an ingredient and a condiment in certain Asian cuisines, most commonly in the foods of Southeast Asia. Fish sauce has a very concentrated flavor and, like anchovy paste, when used in very small amounts it lends dishes a salty complexity that is impossible to replicate. Color correlates with flavor in fish sauce; the lighter the sauce, the lighter the flavor. Fish sauce will keep indefinitely without refrigeration.

WONTON SOUP

WITH ONLY A SPRINKLING OF GARNISH TO distract, a good wonton soup needs great dumplings and a great broth in which to float them. Even a cursory review of recipes raises a plethora of questions about wonton wrappers (do you need to make your own?), filling ingredients, how to shape the wontons, and how best to cook them. On top of all that is the issue of the broth: it needs to be savory enough to hold its own but not so rich that it distracts from the wontons. Our goals were clear: We wanted to find the best method for making wonton soup at home, but we didn't want it to be an all-day affair with an endless ingredient list.

We started by making wonton wrappers from scratch and pitted them against store-bought. Just as we would with other pastas, we made a dough from flour and eggs, then rolled it into thin sheets through a hand-cranked pasta machine. The process was tedious, so we were relieved to find that store-bought wrappers delivered better results than homemade. Commercial wrappers are moisture-free and much easier to work with than homemade pasta wrappers, which stuck to pots and cooked up gummy in our tests. Plus, commercial wrappers would allow us to focus our attention on the filling and the broth.

We tested seven different dumpling fillings, including those made with shrimp, vegetables, and pork, and the rich pork filling was deemed the most authentic. For seasonings, tasters preferred just a few classics—a little garlic, soy sauce, sesame oil, black pepper, and some minced scallion.

The flavor of our filling was good, but texture was a different story. Ground pork has a tendency to form a dense, solid mass when it's shaped and cooked, a phenomenon test kitchen staffers dubbed "the meatball effect." One bite into the dumpling and the small, dense "meatball" hidden inside would fall out of the wonton. The scallions folded into the pork helped to mitigate this problem by providing moisture and textural variety but it wasn't enough; tasters complained that the filling seemed a bit hard and dense.

To solve this problem, we borrowed a trick from meatloaf cookery and added 1 tablespoon of lightly beaten egg whites to the pork mixture. As the meat mixture cooked, the egg whites puffed up almost like a soufflé, making the otherwise compact ground meat filling light and tender.

The traditional wonton shape is a triangle with the two corners brought together. We found we had no trouble with leaking as long as we were careful to brush the edges of the wrappers with water to create a tight seal. When properly cooked, this shape allows for a large part of the wrapper to turn silky smooth, just as great noodles do in broth.

With our wontons ready, we addressed the broth. Wontons are classically poached in water before being drained and served in a delicate, flavorful chicken broth, studded with a few garnishes. Wonton soup is not a quickly prepared meal, for sure, but we thought the bulk of the labor should be shaping the wontons, and so we sought a streamlined approach by enhancing store-bought chicken broth, rather than using homemade. Simmering the broth with some aromatics—chopped onion, garlic, and ginger—brightened it, but it wasn't enough; tasters felt it was too thin and flavorless. Adding more aromatics only gave it a vegetal muddiness. What the broth was lacking was meatiness. Augmenting the broth with chicken meat was one solution, but rather than have to purchase and prepare an additional ingredient, what if we used some of the ground pork from the filling? Because of its maximum surface area, ground meat gives up flavor quickly.

We wanted richness in the broth but we didn't want it to taste identifiably "pork-y" or overwhelm the wontons, so we sautéed a small amount of pork—2 ounces—with the minced onion, a couple of smashed garlic cloves, and a few slices of fresh ginger, to encourage the release of flavor from the pork and vegetables. When the pork was no longer pink, we added the chicken broth and brought it to a simmer. The results were dramatic. In only 25 minutes, the broth had gained a rich (but balanced) meaty depth.

So far we had been following the conventional wisdom espoused by many recipes and boiling the wontons in water before adding them to the broth. Would cooking the wontons directly in the broth turn them mushy and slimy and cloud the broth? We're not ones to take anything for granted (and who wants to clean an extra pot?), so we decided to take on this issue and test both methods side by side. For one batch, we boiled the wontons in salted water, drained them, then stirred them into the soup. For the other batch, we dropped the raw wontons directly into the simmering broth and cooked them until tender. The results were surprising. Not only was the texture of the wontons identical in both soups, tasters had a clear preference for the soup with the wontons cooked in the broth. The wontons both added and absorbed flavor from the broth as they cooked, and starch released from the pasta slightly thickened the soup. The starch may have made the soup a touch cloudier, but not a single taster minded.

For garnishing the soup, we liked the simple addition of a grated carrot and sliced scallions. And, rather than serve them raw, we found it best to simmer them with the wontons to soften and mellow their flavor.

Wonton Soup
SERVES 6 TO 8

The uncooked wontons can be frozen for up to 1 month; freeze them on a baking sheet until firm, then transfer to a large zipper-lock bag for easy storage. Do not thaw the frozen wontons before cooking, but add them directly to the boiling soup and cook until tender, 6 to 9 minutes.

WONTONS
6 ounces ground pork
1 tablespoon egg white (about ½ large egg white), lightly beaten
2 medium scallions, minced
⅛ teaspoon ground black pepper
1 tablespoon soy sauce
1 teaspoon toasted sesame oil

1 small garlic clove, minced or pressed through a garlic press (about ½ teaspoon)
25 square wonton wrappers

SOUP
1 tablespoon vegetable oil
2 ounces ground pork
1 medium onion, chopped medium
2 medium garlic cloves, smashed and peeled (see the illustration on page 299)
1 (1-inch) piece fresh ginger, sliced thin and smashed (see the illustration on page 79)
8 cups low-sodium chicken broth
1 small carrot, peeled and grated over the large holes of a box grater
3 scallions, sliced thin on the bias (see the illustration on page 73)

1. FOR THE WONTONS: Combine all the ingredients in a medium bowl; mix thoroughly. Cover the bowl with plastic wrap and freeze until the mixture is cold, about 10 minutes. Meanwhile, line a large, rimmed baking sheet with parchment paper.

2. Lay three of the wonton wrappers on a dry counter (keep the remaining wrappers covered with plastic wrap). Place 1 slightly rounded teaspoon of the cold filling in the center of each wrapper, brush the edges lightly with water, and fold the wrapper into a wonton following the illustrations on page 77.

3. Place the wontons on the prepared baking sheet and repeat with the remaining filling and wrappers. Cover the wontons loosely with plastic wrap and refrigerate for at least 20 minutes or up to 4 hours.

4. FOR THE SOUP: Heat the oil in a large Dutch oven over medium heat until shimmering. Add the ground pork, onion, garlic, and ginger and cook, breaking up the meat with a wooden spoon, until the pork is no longer pink, 3 to 5 minutes.

5. Stir in the broth and bring to a boil. Reduce to a gentle simmer, cover partially (leaving about 1 inch of the pot open), and cook until the broth is flavorful, about 25 minutes. Strain the broth

through a fine-mesh strainer. (The broth can be refrigerated in an airtight container for up to 1 day.)

6. Return the strained broth to a clean saucepan and bring to a boil. Carefully add the wontons, carrot, and scallions, and simmer until the wontons are tender, 4 to 6 minutes. Serve immediately.

SHAPING WONTONS

1. Working with 3 wonton wrappers at a time (keeping the others covered to prevent them from drying out), lay them on a dry counter. Place 1 slightly rounded teaspoon of the cold filling in the center of each wrapper and brush the edges lightly with water.

2. Fold the wrapper over the filling to form a triangle. Pinch the edges of the wrapper together firmly to seal, pressing out any air pockets.

3. Lightly moisten the 2 farthest corners with water, fold them over your finger, and pinch together to seal.

RAMEN SOUP

INSTANT RAMEN NOODLES HAVE THE reputation of being a mainstay on college campuses across the country. Ramen is the go-to meal for many college students, who sometimes even forgo the troublesome task of boiling the noodles and instead eat them raw like giant wavy potato chips. However, in Japan, ramen (or ramen soup) is a much more serious endeavor, with ramen shops on almost every street corner, where the noodles are served in a variety of broths. Our favorite among these is a rich, meaty broth made from long-simmered pork bones. This version of ramen is commonly garnished with thinly sliced pieces of tender pork, scallions, and toasted sesame seeds. We set out to duplicate this hearty bowl of noodles in our test kitchen with the goal of keeping it accessible to the home cook, but without compromising flavor. Good ramen starts with a great broth, so we began there.

The pork broth starts with pounds of meaty bones, so off the bat we sought out a more practical alternative method. We've had good results with store-bought chicken broth, so we decided to use that as a base and looked for ways to boost its meaty flavor. We looked at several cuts of pork, noting that we wanted one cut to provide both flavor for the broth and meat for the garnish. For testing purposes, we chose boneless shoulder (also called pork butt), pork tenderloin, bone-in ribs, and boneless country-style ribs.

To start, we cut the shoulder, tenderloin, and boneless ribs into 1-inch chunks and placed them into their respective pots with an onion and 8 cups of chicken broth. The bone-in ribs were separated from one another to increase their surface area and added to another pot.

After an hour, we gathered around for a tasting. The pork butt came across as too ham-like while the tenderloin offered little in the flavor department, and the bone-in ribs made the broth excessively greasy. The boneless country-style ribs passed muster, delivering a strong meaty flavor without coming across as too "gamey." Overall, however, tasters still commented that the finished broth needed a stronger, more complex meat flavor to win their approval. So back to the stove we went to try and eke out more flavor from our pork ribs.

Again, we started by cutting the meat into 1-inch chunks, but then transferred them to the food processor and pulsed them until coarsely ground. This increased the surface area of the meat, allowing more pork flavor to infuse the broth. Our next move was to thoroughly brown the meat before adding the chicken broth. The browned meat and browned bits in the pot (called fond) gave our broth a solid base of flavor and, once simmered in the broth, mimicked a long, slow cooking process. At this point, we revisited our cooking time of 1 hour and found that by browning the meat before adding the broth, we were able to reduce the simmering time to 40 minutes.

To give the broth a sweet and smoky flavor we incorporated a small amount of red miso (a salty, savory fermented bean paste; see page 74 for more information). The finished broth was strained and now its deep flavor could fool even some of our more experienced tasters. Our broth was coming together and the addition of garlic and ginger rounded it out nicely.

With our broth in place, we turned our attention to the meat garnish. Boneless country-style ribs, which we were already using for our broth, fit the bill. They come in a long rectangular shape that is ideal for slicing into bite-size pieces. To help with getting the slices as thin as possible, we put the meat in the freezer to firm up for 15 minutes while we prepared the broth. Initially we experimented with marinating the meat in soy sauce, mirin, and sesame oil, but we found that the amount of flavor that the marinade provided was negated when the meat was added to the broth. Instead, after the broth had been strained, we added the soy sauce, mirin, and sesame oil along with the sliced pork and allowed the meat to steep off the heat for 3 minutes. This technique resulted in flavorful meat that was also extremely tender.

When it came to the noodles, we were admittedly a little hesitant to use the dried ramen noodles that flood grocery store shelves. For com-parison, we sought out dried ramen from an Asian market, but when we tasted them, they were indistinguishable from their supermarket counterparts.

In the end, each soupy bowl of noodles needed little more than some thinly sliced scallions and a sprinkling of toasted sesame seeds. The finished product was a rich, meaty concoction that elevated a college staple to a true Japanese treat.

Ramen Soup
SERVES 6 TO 8

To make processing and slicing the pork easier, freeze it for 15 minutes. If you can't find red miso, you can simply omit it but the soup will have a less rich flavor; see page 74 for more information on miso. Be ready to serve the soup immediately after cooking the pork in step 6; if the pork sits in the hot broth for too long it will overcook and become tough.

BROTH

1½	pounds boneless country-style pork ribs, trimmed
1	tablespoon vegetable oil
1	medium onion, chopped medium
6	medium garlic cloves, smashed and peeled (see the illustration on page 299)
1	(1-inch) piece fresh ginger, sliced thin and smashed (see the illustration on page 79)
8	cups low-sodium chicken broth

SOUP

4	(3-ounce) packages ramen noodles, flavoring packets discarded
	Salt
3	tablespoons red miso (see note) (optional)
2	tablespoons soy sauce
1	tablespoon mirin (see page 74)
½	teaspoon toasted sesame oil
2	scallions, sliced thin on the bias (see the illustration on page 73)
1	tablespoon sesame seeds, toasted

1. FOR THE BROTH: Slice ½ pound of the pork ribs crosswise into ⅛-inch-thick slices (see note)

and refrigerate until needed. Cut the remaining 1 pound pork ribs into 1-inch chunks, then pulse in a food processor to a coarse chopped texture, 10 to 12 pulses.

2. Heat the oil in a large Dutch oven over medium heat until shimmering. Add the processed pork and cook, breaking up the meat with a wooden spoon, until well browned, about 10 minutes. Stir in the onion, garlic, and ginger and cook until fragrant and the onion begins to soften, about 2 minutes.

3. Stir in the broth; bring to a boil. Reduce to a gentle simmer, cover partially (leaving about 1 inch of the pot open), and cook until the broth is flavorful, about 40 minutes. Strain the broth through a fine-mesh strainer. (The broth can be refrigerated in an airtight container for up to 1 day.)

4. FOR THE SOUP: Bring 4 quarts water to a boil in a large pot. Stir in the noodles and 1 tablespoon salt and cook until just tender, about 2 minutes. Drain the noodles and portion them into individual serving bowls.

5. Return the strained broth to a clean saucepan and bring to a boil. Whisk ½ cup of the hot broth into the miso until dissolved and smooth, then whisk the mixture back into the saucepan. Return the soup to a brief simmer, then remove from the heat.

6. Stir in the sliced pork, soy sauce, mirin, and sesame oil, cover, and let stand off the heat until the pork is cooked through, 2 to 3 minutes. Ladle the soup into the prepared bowls, sprinkle with the scallions and sesame seeds, and serve immediately.

➤ VARIATIONS

Spicy Ramen Soup with Shiitakes and Corn

Follow the recipe for Ramen Soup, adding 8 ounces shiitake mushrooms, wiped clean, stemmed, and sliced thin, to the strained boiling broth before adding the miso in step 5; cover, reduce the heat, and simmer gently until the mushrooms are tender, 5 to 7 minutes. Uncover the soup and continue to incorporate the miso as directed. Add 1 cup frozen corn, thawed, and 2 teaspoons sambal oelek chili paste (see page 74) to the soup with the pork in step 6.

Sesame Ramen Soup with Asparagus and Carrot

Follow the recipe for Ramen Soup, adding 8 ounces asparagus (about ½ bunch), tough ends trimmed (see the illustration on page 120), and sliced on the bias into 2-inch lengths, and 1 carrot, peeled and cut into matchsticks, to the strained boiling broth before adding the miso in step 5; cover, reduce the heat, and simmer gently until the vegetables are crisp-tender, 2 to 3 minutes. Uncover the soup and continue to incorporate the miso as directed. Increase the amount of toasted sesame oil to 1 tablespoon.

SMASHING SLICED GINGER

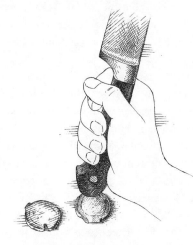

To release flavorful oils from fresh ginger, thinly slice an unpeeled knob and then use the end of a chef's knife to smash each piece. This technique works best when you want to infuse the flavor of ginger into a liquid, especially broth.

JAPANESE SOBA NOODLE SOUP

SOBA NOODLES, MADE WITH BUCKWHEAT, can be served hot or cold, with hot soba more widespread in the winter and cold soba more predominant in the summer months. Hot soba noodles are served in a light broth flavored with soy sauce and mirin and garnished with a few vegetables, offering a delicate balance of key Japanese flavors. Although the most common broth is a seafood broth made from a simple combination of water, kombu (kelp), and bonito flakes (dried, smoked fish flakes), we were intrigued by the idea of mushroom broth, and thought it would pair well with nutty soba noodles for an accessible but refined Japanese noodle soup.

The mushroom broth is traditionally made by soaking or simmering dried shiitakes in water. While dried shiitakes are widespread in Japan and in fact are more common than fresh, they are difficult to get in the U.S. aside from specialty Asian markets. We could use fresh shiitakes or stick to dried mushrooms and use a more readily available type. Both options had some serious drawbacks; drying shiitakes concentrates and intensifies their flavor, so it only takes a few ounces to make a broth, whereas it would take a large quantity of fresh shiitakes to approach this depth of flavor. Using another variety of dried mushroom would avoid this problem, but the broth would lack the characteristic shiitake flavor. While neither was an appealing option on its own, a compromise seemed promising. We often use dried porcinis in the test kitchen to enhance the flavor of fresh mushrooms. What if we supplemented a moderate quantity of fresh shiitakes with a small amount of dried porcinis?

Back in the kitchen, we simmered fresh shiitakes and dried porcinis in water for 1 hour, then strained the liquid and discarded the mushrooms, which were limp and lifeless (dried porcinis, unlike dried shiitakes, aren't typically sold as whole caps, so reserving them after simmering to add back to the soup wasn't an option). One taste and we'd knew we'd hit upon a winning technique; the fresh mushrooms infused the broth with a bright, distinctively shiitake flavor, while the porcinis fell into the background, providing a deep, rich base. In fact, tasters preferred this broth overall, finding it to be more balanced and clean-tasting than the one made with dried shiitakes, which some thought was overly musky.

All that was left was to work out the details of the broth—starting with 6 cups of water, we settled on 7 ounces fresh shiitakes (including the stems in the broth) and ½ ounce of dried porcinis. Chopping the mushrooms increased their surface area and encouraged them to give up their flavor more quickly, allowing us to reduce the simmering time to 40 minutes. Tasters also liked the addition of a few tablespoons each of soy sauce and mirin, which rounded out the broth and gave it complexity.

With our broth in place, we addressed the soba noodles. Buckwheat contains no gluten, so a binder, such as wheat, is added to give the noodles structure and hold them together under cooking. That said, in Japan, soba noodles must contain a minimum of 30 percent buckwheat flour to be labeled soba. To cook soba, they must be boiled, then rinsed under hot, warm, or cold water to wash away the excess starch. When we rinsed the noodles under hot water, we found that they softened further and became mushy. This makes sense—the noodles were continuing to cook. Rinsing the noodles under cold water was fine, but the noodles sometimes cooled down too much and were too chilled when covered with broth. Warm water washed away the starch without further cooking. It also kept the noodles at the right temperature for use in soups.

As for vegetables, we thinly sliced some additional fresh shiitake caps and gently poached them in the strained broth until they were just softened. Earthy spinach complemented the mushroom flavor and added freshness and color to the soup. We found it best to stir the spinach in at the last minute of cooking until it had just wilted.

To compose the soup, we portioned the noodles before ladling the hot broth and vegetables into each bowl. A final garnish of thinly sliced scallions and toasted sesame seeds completed the soup by providing textural and visual contrast.

Japanese Soba Noodle Soup with Mushrooms and Spinach

SERVES 6

Make sure to include the shiitake stems when preparing the broth. Look for soba noodles in Asian markets or the international foods aisle of supermarkets. When rinsing the cooked noodles in step 2, be sure to use warm water; do not use either hot or cold water.

MUSHROOM BROTH

- 6 cups water
- 7 ounces shiitake mushrooms, wiped clean, trimmed, and chopped coarse (see note)
- ½ ounce dried porcini mushrooms, rinsed and minced
- 3 tablespoons soy sauce
- 3 tablespoons mirin

SOUP

- 8 ounces soba noodles
- Salt
- 5 ounces shiitake mushrooms, wiped clean, stemmed, and sliced thin
- 3 ounces (about 3 cups) baby spinach
- 2 scallions, sliced thin on the bias (see the illustration on page 73)
- I tablespoon sesame seeds, toasted

1. **FOR THE MUSHROOM BROTH:** Bring the water, chopped shiitake mushrooms, and porcini mushrooms to a boil in a medium saucepan. Cover, reduce to a gentle simmer, and cook until the broth is flavorful, about 40 minutes. Strain the broth through a fine-mesh strainer, then stir in the soy sauce and mirin. (The broth can be refrigerated in an airtight container for up to 1 day.)

2. **FOR THE SOUP:** Bring 4 quarts water to a boil in a large pot. Stir in the noodles and 1 tablespoon salt and cook until tender, about 4 minutes. Drain the noodles, then rinse them under warm running water to remove the excess starch. Portion them into individual serving bowls.

3. Return the strained broth to a clean saucepan and bring to a simmer. Stir in the sliced shiitake mushrooms and simmer gently until tender, 5 to 7 minutes.

4. Stir in the spinach and continue to simmer, uncovered, until just wilted, about 1 minute. Season with salt to taste. Ladle the soup into the prepared bowls, sprinkle with the scallions and sesame seeds, and serve.

VIETNAMESE RICE NOODLE SOUP

PHO (PRONOUNCED "FUH") IS PERHAPS THE best-recognized rice noodle soup from Southeast Asia. It begins with a broth made from beef bones, which is then flavored with Asian spices and sauces. The broth is rich but not heavy and is poured over wide rice noodles, meat (which can be anything from thinly sliced beef and chicken to organ meats), scallion slices, crisp bean sprouts, and an abundance of fresh herbs such as Thai basil and cilantro leaves. This mix of raw and cooked, hot and cold creates a unique and satisfying soup. We wanted to prepare this soup at home, but we didn't want it to take hours.

To start, we decided to forgo homemade broth and punch up the otherwise mild flavor of store-bought broth with extra aromatics. We began to build our base by sautéing onions, garlic, and lemon grass, then adding a combination of beef and chicken broth and some water and simmering the mixture briefly to allow the flavors to meld. (After testing with both beef and chicken broths, tasters preferred a mix of the two.) This was a good start, but we thought we could further enhance our broth. Soy and fish sauces added much-needed body and depth of flavor. Soy sauce lent a meatiness that homemade beef broth would normally contribute, while fish sauce added just the right combination of salt and musky sweetness. Cloves and star anise are common components of this soup and tasters unanimously welcomed their addition, as they permeated the broth with their spicy warmth. Lastly, we added a pinch of sugar, which balanced the salt and acidity from the sauces.

Satisfied with the broth, we turned our attention to the noodles. We found that boiled rice noodles had a tendency to turn mushy, and if left in the hot soup for any length of time, they break apart. Ultimately, we settled on soaking the noodles in water that had been brought to a boil and then removed from the heat; the slightly cooler temperature did not overcook them. We drained the noodles when they had softened to the point that they were tender but still had a little chew and then let them finish cooking in the hot broth until they softened through.

We next looked at what meat to add and how it should be cooked. While tripe and tendons are common additions, we decided to focus on two meats that would be the simplest to prepare and find: thinly sliced beef and shredded chicken. Traditionally, for the beef soup, the beef is sliced paper-thin and is added to the individual soup bowls raw (the idea is that it cooks directly in the broth). We had trouble getting the broth to cook the beef fully every time, so we opted for letting the beef steep in the pot of hot broth before serving it. We tested a variety of steaks and concluded that beef tenderloin—the authentic choice for this soup—was indeed the best because it was naturally lean yet extremely tender and flavorful. As for the chicken soup, we chose to use boneless, skinless chicken breasts because they were so easy to poach in the broth then shred into bite-size pieces. The finishing touch for this soup is a generous garnish of bean sprouts, fresh herbs, lime, and some sliced chile for heat.

Vietnamese Rice Noodle Soup with Beef

SERVES 6 TO 8

To make slicing the beef easier, freeze it for 15 minutes. This soup is very well seasoned; be sure to use low-sodium chicken broth and soy sauce or it will taste too salty. If you are salt sensitive, hold back on the fish sauce in the broth and add it to taste before serving. Be ready to serve the soup immediately after cooking the beef in step 3; if the beef sits in the hot broth for too long it will overcook and become tough.

BROTH

2	teaspoons vegetable oil
2	medium onions, minced
4	medium garlic cloves, minced or pressed through a garlic press (about 4 teaspoons)
I	stalk lemon grass, bottom 5 inches only, minced (see the illustrations on page 85)
⅓	cup fish sauce (see page 74)
4	cups low-sodium chicken broth
4	cups beef broth
2	cups water
2	tablespoons low-sodium soy sauce
2	tablespoons sugar
4	star anise pods
4	whole cloves

NOODLES, MEAT, AND GARNISH

8	ounces (¼-inch-wide) dried flat rice noodles
2	cups bean sprouts
I	cup loosely packed fresh Thai basil or regular basil leaves
I	cup loosely packed fresh cilantro leaves
2	scallions, sliced thin on the bias (see the illustration on page 73)
I	fresh Thai, serrano, or jalapeño chile, stemmed, seeded, and sliced thin Lime wedges
12	ounces beef tenderloin, sliced in half lengthwise, then sliced crosswise into ¼-inch-thick pieces (see note)

1. FOR THE BROTH: Heat the oil in large saucepan over medium heat until just shimmering. Add the onions, garlic, lemon grass, and 1 tablespoon of the fish sauce and cook, stirring frequently, until the vegetables are softened but not browned, 2 to 5 minutes.

2. Stir in the chicken broth, beef broth, water, soy sauce, sugar, star anise, cloves, and remaining fish sauce, and bring to a boil. Cover, reduce to a gentle simmer, and cook until the flavors have blended, about 10 minutes. Strain the broth through a fine-mesh strainer. (The broth can be refrigerated in an airtight container for up to 1 day.)

3. FOR THE NOODLES, MEAT, AND GARNISH: Bring 4 quarts water to a boil in a large pot. Remove the pot from the heat, add the rice noodles, and let stand, stirring occasionally, until the noodles are tender but still slightly firm, about 10 minutes.

4. Drain the noodles, portion them into individual serving bowls, and top with the bean sprouts. Arrange the basil, cilantro, scallions, chile, and lime wedges attractively on a large serving platter.

5. Return the strained broth to a clean saucepan, bring to a brief simmer, then remove from the heat. Stir in the beef, cover, and let stand off the heat until the meat is cooked through, 2 to 3 minutes. Ladle the soup into the prepared bowls and serve immediately, passing the platter of garnishes separately.

➤ VARIATION

Vietnamese Rice Noodle Soup with Chicken

Follow the recipe for Vietnamese Rice Noodle Soup with Beef, substituting 2 boneless, skinless chicken breasts (about 12 ounces), trimmed, for the beef tenderloin. Add the chicken breasts to the saucepan with the broths and seasonings in step 2, cover, and simmer gently until the chicken registers 160 to 165 degrees on an instant-read thermometer, 10 to 15 minutes. Remove the breasts from the broth, let cool slightly, then shred the meat into bite-size pieces (see the illustration on page 43); strain the broth as directed. Before ladling the soup into the bowls, simmer the shredded chicken in the broth for 1 minute to reheat.

THAI CHICKEN SOUP

ONE OF OUR FAVORITE WAYS TO BEGIN A meal at a Thai restaurant is with a bowl of *tom kha gai*, or the easier-to-pronounce translation: Thai chicken soup. It doesn't look like much—a creamy, pale broth laced with chicken slices, mushrooms, and cilantro—but what it lacks in looks it makes up for in flavor. Sweet and sour components balance the richness of lemon grass-and-lime-infused coconut milk, which, in turn, tempers a slow-building chili burn.

This classic Thai soup is relatively easy to make if you can find all of the proper ingredients, which not all of us can. Its complex flavor is largely derived from such exotica as galangal, kaffir lime leaves, and lemon grass. We'd be hard pressed to find most of these ingredients at our local market. Instead we aimed to make the most authentic version possible with widely available ingredients. We found a handful of "simplified" or "Americanized" Thai chicken soup recipes that, while largely informative regarding substitutions, mostly missed the mark. Each lacked the taut balancing of hot, sour, salty, and sweet components that makes Thai cooking so compelling. (Appropriately enough, that balance, in Thai, is called *yum*.) So, for the time being at least, we stuck with the classic recipes. We'd address substitutions once we knew how best to prepare the soup.

Variation in Thai chicken soup recipes tends to center on two basic components: broth and garnishes. Traditional recipes typically prepare the broth using one of two methods. The first involves poaching a whole chicken in water with aromatics, after which the broth is blended with coconut milk and further seasoned. The chicken is then shredded and stirred in with mushrooms. In the second approach, chicken broth and coconut milk are simmered with the aromatics, after which thin-sliced raw chicken and the remaining ingredients and seasonings are added. Both methods have their merits, but we much preferred the latter, which took half the effort and time without any apparent injury to flavor. The richness of the coconut milk and assertive seasonings added big flavor fast.

How long did the broth and aromatics need to simmer for the best results? We used broth ingredients from the best recipes we had tried—a blend of chicken broth, coconut milk, lemon grass, shallots, galangal, and cilantro. After sautéing the aromatics for a few minutes to bring out and deepen their flavors, we added the broth and noted that a scant 10 minutes of simmering proved perfect. Much longer and the broth tasted bitter and vegetal.

After preparing a few more batches with varying ratios of chicken broth and coconut milk, we settled on a combination of the two. Rich-tasting without being cloying, and definitely chicken-flavored, the blend was perfectly balanced. We also tried a technique we had come across in a couple of recipes. We added the coconut milk in two parts: half at the beginning and the remainder just before serving. What seemed fussy made a big difference, allowing the coconut flavor to come through clearly.

Now came the hard part: making substitutions. Most of the "simplified" recipes we tried or reviewed replaced the lemon grass with lemon zest, but we found the swap objectionable. Lemon zest—in conjunction with the sweet coconut milk—made for a broth with an odd, candy-like flavor. Dried lemon grass also failed to impress, as it lacked any of the depth of the fresh stuff. In any case, fresh lemon grass is often available in the produce section of well-stocked supermarkets.

Galangal is a knotty, peppery-flavored rhizome distantly related to ginger, which most food writers suggest is the perfect substitute. While it wasn't perfect to us—ginger lacks the depth of flavor and piney finish of galangal—we decided it would do.

Kaffir lime leaves, the fresh or dried leaves from a potent variety of tropical lime, lend the broth a particularly floral, deep flavor and alluring aroma. Lime zest is the usual substitute, but one we felt lacked the intensity of the leaves. Once again, the substitute felt like a distant second. This was a bad

trend. Replacing the authentic ingredients was not working as well as we hoped and the soup didn't taste nearly as good as we expected. Perhaps authentic flavor really wasn't possible without the proper ingredients.

Then we found our magic bullet. After one taste test, a colleague suggested red curry paste, an ingredient we hadn't considered to that point. While it is never added to traditional Thai chicken soup, the curry paste did include all the exotic ingredients for which we were trying so hard to find acceptable substitutions. We whisked a small spoonful of the paste into the soup in front of us and were struck by the surprising transformation from boring to—dare we say?—authentic.

Curry paste is usually added early on in cooking to mellow its potent flavor, but we found this flattened the flavor too much. Adding a dollop at the very end of cooking—whisked together with pungent fish sauce and tart lime juice—allowed the sharpness of the galangal, the fragrance of the kaffir lime leaves, and the bright heat of the chiles to come through loud and clear. Out went the mediocre ginger and lime zest and in went 2 teaspoons of easy-to-find red curry paste.

With the broth tasting great, we could finally tackle the chicken and mushrooms. We initially thought that rich-tasting thigh meat would be the best choice to stand up to the full-flavored broth, but it was too fatty; boneless, skinless breast meat was better.

As for the mushrooms, oyster mushrooms are traditional but hard to find and expensive. Supermarket options like cremini, shiitake, and white mushrooms each had their merits, but the latter proved to be the closest match to the mild flavor and chewy texture of oyster mushrooms. Sliced thin and submerged in the broth, they quickly softened and absorbed the soup's flavors like a sponge.

A sprinkle of cilantro usually suffices as a finishing touch, but tasters wanted more. The clean, bright heat of thin-sliced Thai chiles and sharp bite of scallions did the trick. With twenty-odd minutes of cooking and a minimum of hands-on effort, we had a rich, authentic-tasting Thai chicken soup.

Thai Chicken Soup

SERVES 6

To make the chicken easier to slice, freeze it for 15 minutes. Although we prefer the deeper, richer flavor of regular coconut milk, light coconut milk can be substituted for one or both cans. Don't be tempted to use jarred or dried lemon grass—their flavor is characterless. For a spicier soup, add additional red curry paste to taste. Cremini mushrooms can be substituted for the white mushrooms.

1	teaspoon vegetable oil
3	stalks lemon grass, bottom 5 inches only, minced (see the illustrations at right)
3	large shallots, chopped coarse
8	sprigs fresh cilantro, chopped coarse
3	tablespoons fish sauce (see page 74)
4	cups low-sodium chicken broth
2	(14-ounce) cans coconut milk
1	tablespoon sugar
8	ounces white mushrooms, wiped clean, trimmed, and sliced thin
1	pound boneless, skinless chicken breasts, halved lengthwise and sliced on the bias into ⅛-inch-thick pieces (see note)
3	tablespoons juice from 2 limes
2	teaspoons Thai red curry paste

GARNISH

½	cup loosely packed fresh cilantro leaves
2	fresh Thai, serrano, or jalapeño chiles, stemmed, seeded, and sliced thin
2	scallions, sliced thin on the bias (see the illustration on page 73)
	Lime wedges

1. Heat the oil in a large saucepan over medium heat until just shimmering. Add the lemon grass, shallots, chopped cilantro sprigs, and 1 tablespoon of the fish sauce and cook, stirring frequently, until just softened but not browned, 2 to 5 minutes.

2. Stir in the broth and 1 can of the coconut milk and bring to a simmer. Cover, reduce to a gentle simmer, and cook until the flavors have blended, about 10 minutes. Strain the broth through a fine-mesh strainer. (The broth can be refrigerated in an airtight container for up to 1 day.)

3. Return the strained broth to a clean saucepan, stir in the remaining can of coconut milk and sugar, and bring to a simmer. Stir in the mushrooms and cook until just tender, 2 to 3 minutes. Stir in the chicken; cook until no longer pink, 1 to 3 minutes.

4. Remove the soup from the heat. Whisk the lime juice, curry paste, and remaining 2 tablespoons fish sauce together to dissolve the curry, then stir the mixture into the soup. Serve immediately, garnishing individual portions with the cilantro leaves, chiles, scallions, and lime wedges.

MINCING LEMON GRASS

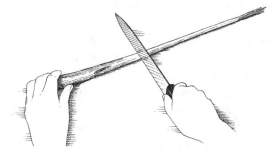

1. Trim and discard all but the bottom 5 inches of the lemon grass stalk.

2. Remove the tough outer sheath from the trimmed lemon grass. If the lemon grass is particularly thick or tough, you may need to remove several layers to reveal the tender inner portion of the stalk.

3. Cut the trimmed and peeled lemon grass in half lengthwise, then slice it thin crosswise.

KOREAN SPICY BEEF SOUP

THE KEY COMPONENTS OF THE KOREAN SOUP called *yukgaejang* are as follows: fall-apart-tender beef brisket, lots of hot red pepper, and an ample dose of green onions. This intensely spicy soup exemplifies the philosophy of "fight fire with fire"; it is served in the winter to combat the cold and it also encourages sweating to cool off on the hottest summer days. Although recipes we found varied in ingredient lists, some calling for obscure additions such as fernbrake (an edible fern), sweet potato noodles, and tripe, as well as more familiar Asian ingredients such as bean sprouts, egg, and soy sauce, we thought it would be simple enough to recreate this fiery soup in the test kitchen.

We soon came across a few roadblocks. First of all, most of the recipes simmered the brisket by itself for several hours before shredding it and continuing to cook the soup for an additional half hour or so. While we weren't demanding a quick soup (brisket takes some time to get tender), we also didn't want to be standing over a pot all day. Secondly, although not all recipes called for tripe and fernbrake, they all relied on Korean red pepper powder, a specialty product that not everyone can find easily. We set out to see if we could come up with a streamlined version of this fiery Korean soup that would cook in little over an hour and rely— if possible—solely on supermarket ingredients.

We first addressed the cooking liquid and the beef. Some recipes start by making a homemade broth, others start with water, but either way, the brisket is then simmered in the liquid for a few hours before being removed, shredded, and returned to the pot to cook with the other ingredients. The water method was appealingly easy, but the resulting broth was weak and, not surprisingly, watery. Clearly water was not a sufficient cooking liquid for this recipe; however, making a broth from scratch was contrary to our timesaving mission. Plus, for a soup with such bold heat and seasonings, a homemade broth seemed unnecessary.

Therefore, we started with store-bought broth, focused on boosting its flavor. We knew that sautéed aromatics would help, but to get deep flavor, we decided to depart from the traditional recipes for this soup and brown the brisket in oil before adding any liquid to the pot. This step only took a few minutes, but the resulting fond, or flavorful browned bits, packed the broth with rich, slow-cooked flavor. To further save time, we opted to forgo cooking the brisket whole in favor of cutting it into thin strips that would replicate the shape of the shredded beef in the original dish. In addition to cooking much faster, the increased surface area of these small pieces would maximize browning and therefore flavor.

After browning the beef in a Dutch oven, we set it aside and sautéed some onion and a generous amount of garlic—six cloves. We then added the store-bought broth (a combination of chicken and beef broth produced the most balanced flavor) and brought it to a simmer before returning the beef back to the pot. With this method, we had tender, perfectly cooked brisket in only an hour. Plus, we could skip the step of fishing the meat out of the hot broth to shred it into bite-size pieces.

When it came to seasoning, it was paramount that we find a substitute for Korean red pepper powder. Although referred to as "powder," the type of Korean red pepper powder that is commonly used for cooking actually has a consistency somewhere between cayenne powder and red pepper flakes. It doesn't contain the seeds of the peppers and has a more mild heat and sweet pepper flavor than either cayenne pepper or red pepper flakes. Most recipes that we found for this soup used several tablespoons of the powder. Using a lesser amount of cayenne or red pepper flakes gave us a soup with comparable heat, but it lacked the pepper flavor and deep color. After some experimentation, we settled upon a combination of 1 tablespoon red pepper flakes (for heat) with 3 tablespoons of sweet paprika (for pepper flavor and color). In addition to a tablespoon of soy sauce, 2 tablespoons of toasted sesame oil rounded out the flavors. We found it best to add the seasonings to the soup during the last 20 minutes of cooking. This way their flavors had time to meld but their brightness wasn't dulled.

The major components of our soup decided, we looked at other ingredients we'd come across in our research. After some testing, we decided that the slightly exotic additions of fernbrake, sweet potato noodles, and Korean radish were unnecessary, but a generous quantity (two bunches) of scallions was crucial, providing a sweet earthiness that offset the heat of the soup. We found it best to cut the scallions into 2-inch lengths and add them to the soup with the seasonings. Many recipes included bean sprouts and wisped egg; we tried them and liked both. To incorporate the egg, we borrowed the method we had hit upon for our Hot and Sour Soup (page 72), mixing the egg with a small amount of cornstarch to stabilize the proteins before stirring the mixture into the hot soup, resulting in wispy, soft ribbons. The bean sprouts were best added just before serving to maintain their crunchy texture.

Our soup had the bracing heat, deep red brick color, and distinct pepper flavor of the real thing, and tasters were surprised to learn it contained no Korean red pepper or other specialty ingredients. Although this soup may be meant for extreme weather, our recipe is easy and flavorful enough that we would want to make it year-round.

Korean Spicy Beef Soup
SERVES 6 TO 8

To make slicing the beef easier, freeze it for 15 minutes. This soup is very spicy; for a less spicy soup, reduce the quantity of red pepper flakes. Serve with steamed white rice, if desired.

SOUP

1	pound beef brisket, trimmed and julienned (see the illustrations on page 88)
	Salt and ground black pepper
2	tablespoons vegetable oil
1	medium onion, chopped medium
6	medium garlic cloves, minced or pressed through a garlic press (about 2 tablespoons)
4	cups low-sodium chicken broth
4	cups beef broth
3	tablespoons sweet paprika
1	tablespoon red pepper flakes (see note)
2	tablespoons toasted sesame oil
1	tablespoon soy sauce
2	bunches scallions, cut into 2-inch lengths

EGG AND BEAN SPROUTS

1	teaspoon water
½	teaspoon cornstarch
1	large egg
2	cups bean sprouts

1. FOR THE SOUP: Pat the beef dry with paper towels and season with salt and pepper. Heat 2 teaspoons of the oil in a large Dutch oven over medium-high heat until just smoking. Add half of the meat and cook, stirring occasionally, until well browned, 5 to 7 minutes, reducing the heat if the pot begins to scorch. Transfer the browned beef to a medium bowl. Repeat with 2 teaspoons more oil and the remaining beef; transfer to the bowl.

2. Add the remaining 2 teaspoons oil to the pot and place over medium heat until shimmering. Add the onion and cook until softened, 5 to 7 minutes. Stir in the garlic and cook until fragrant, about 30 seconds. Stir in the chicken broth, beef broth, and browned meat with any accumulated juice. Bring to a boil, then cover, reduce to a gentle simmer, and cook for 45 minutes.

3. Stir in the paprika, red pepper flakes, sesame oil, soy sauce, and scallions, cover partially (leaving about 1 inch of the pot open), and simmer gently until the beef is tender, 15 to 25 minutes. Remove the soup from the heat (do not let it cool off) and season with salt to taste.

4. FOR THE EGG AND BEAN SPROUTS: Whisk the water and cornstarch together in a small bowl, then whisk in the egg until combined. Following the illustrations on page 73, use a spoon to slowly drizzle very thin streams of the egg mixture into

the hot soup in a circular motion. Without stirring the soup, let it continue to sit off heat for 1 minute.

5. Briefly return the soup to a simmer over medium-high heat without stirring, then remove it from the heat immediately. Gently stir in the bean sprouts and serve immediately.

HOW TO JULIENNE A BRISKET

1. Cut the brisket, against the grain, into 1½-inch-wide strips.

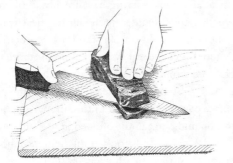

2. Holding the knife parallel to the cutting board, slice each strip of meat into 2 thin pieces.

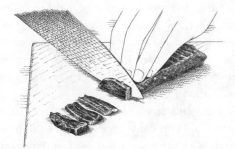

3. Slice each thin strip crosswise into thin strips.

KIMCHI SOUP

KIMCHI, A COMBINATION OF PICKLED vegetables (typically cabbage, scallions, garlic, and ground chiles), is present at nearly every Korean meal as a condiment/side dish as well as an ingredient in a variety of other dishes, such as kimchi soup. This homey, nourishing soup features bite-size pieces of kimchi, pork, and tofu and is often served at the table simmering in the stone pot in which it's cooked. Because the kimchi and its pickling liquid give this soup its intense flavor—and kimchi is easy enough to purchase premade and jarred—most recipes don't require complicated broths or extended cooking time to eke out flavor, We set out to develop our own recipe.

Recipes we researched seemed straightforward, consisting of kimchi, scallions, tofu, a few aromatics, and some type of pork simmered briefly in kimchi liquid that is thinned with water or a simple broth. Because these recipes were fairly similar, the two main points of divergence were the type of cooking liquid and the pork (what cut to use and how to incorporate it). We'd tackle these two issues first and then address seasoning, tofu, and other additions.

Right away we eliminated the idea of making a broth from scratch. First of all, we wanted this to be a quick-cooking, streamlined soup. Plus, kimchi is so flavor-packed, a homemade broth wouldn't be necessary. Instead we focused on water and store-bought broth. We made batches of soup by briefly simmering chopped-up kimchi with water, store-bought chicken broth, store-bought beef broth, and a combination of the latter two before tasting them side by side. Not surprisingly, tasters thought the soup made with water tasted thin. The best cooking liquid turned out to be a combination of the broths. Using half chicken broth and half beef broth resulted in a soup that was rich but balanced.

Most recipes we found called for small, bite-size pieces of pork belly, but this fat-streaked meat from the underside of the pig is also the cut of choice for most bacon made in this country, and we could only find it smoked or cured. The most sensible option was boneless country-style pork ribs. Though fatty, these meaty ribs from the upper side of the rib cage have rich flavor and are naturally tender. After some experimentation we found that it was best to treat the ribs with the same technique that we'd hit upon when developing our Ramen Soup (page 78): we sliced the pork into thin, bite-size pieces (15 minutes in the freezer made this job easy) that we steeped in the soup off the heat for three minutes. Poaching the pork in the hot soup off the heat ensured that it was tender and perfectly cooked.

For seasonings, we settled on a generous six cloves of garlic, a teaspoon of fresh ginger, and some thinly sliced scallion whites (we reserved the greens to add later to the soup), sautéing them briefly in oil to bring out their flavor. A tablespoon each of soy sauce and sesame oil went in the pot next, along with 2 cups chopped kimchi and its liquid, which we simmered to intensify their flavor before adding the other soup ingredients. A few recipes we found called for a Korean semisweet rice wine called cheongju. Looking for a more readily available substitute, we tried mirin, a sweet Japanese cooking wine, and found that 2 tablespoons (in addition to a tablespoon of sugar) tamed the edges of the other flavors and brought the soup into balance.

In the past we've preferred extra-firm tofu in soup, which we pressed between two plates to extract as much water as possible in order to achieve clean, firm bites of tofu. However, for this soup we were after a more supple, tender bite of tofu, so we chose to use firm tofu, which we cut into ½-inch cubes. We found that the additional step of pressing the tofu was unnecessary; simply draining the cubed tofu on several layers of paper towels was sufficient to remove excess moisture. For the scallion greens, we cut them into ½-inch pieces and stirred them into the soup with the pork, giving them time to soften but not turn limp.

GRATING AND MINCING GINGER

The goal is a fine mince of ginger that will evenly distribute throughout a dish.

TO GRATE GINGER:

Peel a small section of a large piece of ginger. Grate the peeled portion, using the rest of the ginger as a handle to keep fingers safely away from the grater.

TO MINCE GINGER:

1. Slice the peeled knob of ginger into thin rounds, then fan the rounds out and cut them into thin, matchstick-like strips.

2. Chop the matchsticks crosswise into a fine mince.

Kimchi Soup

SERVES 4 TO 6

To make the pork easier to slice, freeze it for 15 minutes. Look for kimchi packed in jars in the refrigerated section of Asian markets and well-stocked supermarkets. Do not drain the kimchi before measuring it; the pickling liquid is quite flavorful. Note that the flavor and spiciness of cabbage kimchi can vary from brand to brand and will slightly affect the flavor of the soup. Be ready to serve the soup immediately after cooking the pork in step 4; if the pork sits in the hot broth for too long it will overcook and become tough.

7	ounces (½ block) firm tofu, drained, and sliced into ½-inch cubes
2	tablespoons mirin (see page 74)
1	tablespoon soy sauce
1	tablespoon sugar
1	tablespoon toasted sesame oil
1	tablespoon vegetable oil
6	medium garlic cloves, minced or pressed through a garlic press (about 2 tablespoons)
1	teaspoon minced or grated fresh ginger (see the illustrations on page 89)
4	scallions, white and green parts separated, whites sliced thin and greens cut into ½-inch pieces
2	cups cabbage kimchi (about 14 ounces), cut into 1-inch pieces (see note)
2½	cups low-sodium chicken broth
2½	cups beef broth
8	ounces boneless country-style pork ribs, trimmed and sliced crosswise into ⅛-inch-thick pieces (see note)

1. Spread the tofu out over several layers of paper towels and let drain for 20 minutes. Whisk the mirin, soy sauce, sugar, and sesame oil together in a small bowl.

2. Heat the vegetable oil in a large saucepan over medium-high heat until shimmering. Add the garlic, ginger, and scallion whites and cook until fragrant, about 1 minute. Stir in the mirin mixture and kimchi with its juice and cook until the liquid has nearly evaporated, 5 to 7 minutes.

3. Stir in the chicken and beef broths, bring to a simmer, and cook for 5 minutes. Stir in the tofu and simmer until it is warmed through, about 2 minutes.

4. Remove the soup from the heat. Stir in the pork and scallion greens, cover, and let stand off the heat until the pork is cooked through, 2 to 3 minutes. Serve immediately.

INGREDIENTS: Tofu

Popular across Asia, tofu is made from the curds of soy milk, which are pressed into blocks and sold either fresh or vacuum-packed in water. Tofu is an ideal canvas for bold or aromatic flavors, such as those found in spicy soups and curries. You can find tofu in a variety of textures, such as silken, soft, medium-firm, firm, and extra-firm. Generally, we prefer firm or extra-firm, as these varieties hold their shape after simmering or stir-frying.

We prefer to use tofu within a few days of opening. If you want to keep an open package of tofu fresh for several days, cover the tofu with fresh water and store it in the refrigerator in an airtight container, changing the water daily. Any hint of sourness means the tofu is past its prime.

5

VEGETABLE SOUPS AND CHOWDERS

VEGETABLE SOUPS AND CHOWDERS

Classic Gazpacho

OF ALL THE WAYS TO SHOWCASE THE GLORIOUS fresh vegetables found at our local farmers' market in August, our favorite is making gazpacho. While gazpacho comes in a variety of styles in Spain (see Creamy Gazpacho Andaluz on page 96), we wanted to develop a foolproof recipe for the most popular version stateside—a classic, chunky gazpacho, one with clearly flavored, distinct pieces of vegetable in a bracing tomato broth. With our goal clearly established, we had to figure out the best method for preparing the vegetables and seasoning this refreshing classic.

We began by testing the various tools at our disposal. Although it was a breeze to use, the blender broke the vegetables down beyond recognition. The food processor performed somewhat better, especially when we processed each vegetable separately. This method had distinct pros and cons. On the pro side were ease and the fact that the vegetables released some juice as they broke down, which helped flavor the soup. The con was that no matter how we finessed the pulse feature, the vegetable pieces were neither neatly chopped nor consistently sized. This was especially true of the tomatoes, which broke down to a pulp. The texture of the resulting soup was more along the lines of vegetable slush—not ideal.

In the end, we preferred the old-fashioned, purist method of hand chopping the vegetables. It does involve some extra work, but it went much more swiftly than we'd imagined, and the benefits to the gazpacho's texture were unmistakable. Because the pieces were consistent in size and shape, they not only retained their individual flavors but also set off the tomato broth beautifully, adding immeasurably to the whole. This was just what we were after.

One last procedural issue we investigated was the resting time. Gazpacho is best served ice-cold, and the chilling time also allows the flavors to develop and meld. We found that four hours was the minimum time required for the soup to chill and the flavors to blossom.

Several of the key ingredients and seasonings also bore some exploration. Tomatoes are a star player here, and we preferred beefsteak to plum because they are larger, juicier, and easier to chop.

Gazpacho is truly a dish to make only when local tomatoes are plentiful. We made several batches using handsome supermarket tomatoes, but the flavor paled in comparison to those batches made with perfectly ripe, local farm-stand tomatoes. We considered skinning and seeding them, but not a single taster complained when we didn't, so we skipped the extra steps.

When it came to peppers, we preferred red to green for their sweeter flavor. But red was less popular in the onion department; tasters preferred sweet onions, such as Vidalia, and shallots over red onions, which were too sharp when consumed in big pieces. Also, any onion was overpowering if used in the quantities recommended in most recipes (especially in the leftovers the next day), and the same was true of garlic, so we dramatically reduced the quantity of both. To ensure thorough seasoning of the whole mixture, we marinated the vegetables briefly in garlic, salt, pepper, and vinegar before adding the bulk of the liquid. These batches had more balanced flavors than the batches that were seasoned after all the ingredients were combined.

The liquid component was also critical. Most recipes called for tomato juice, which we sampled both straight and mixed in various amounts with water. The winning blend was 2½ cups of tomato juice thinned with ½ cup of water. The water cut the viscosity of the juice just enough to make it brothy and light, but not downright thin. Given our preference for ice-cold gazpacho, we decided to add ice cubes instead of straight water. The ice cubes helped to chill the soup while providing water as they melted.

Finally, we turned to the two primary seasonings, vinegar and olive oil. Spain is a noted producer of sherry, so it follows that sherry vinegar is a popular choice for gazpacho. When we tasted it, along with champagne, red wine, and white wine vinegars, the sherry vinegar was our favorite by far, adding not only acidity but also richness and depth. (However, in a pinch, white wine vinegar can be substituted.) The olive oil contributes both flavor and richness to this simple soup. We found that just a splash of extra-virgin olive oil on each bowl provided some lushness that nicely countered the fresh, bright flavors of the vegetables.

93

Classic Gazpacho

SERVES 6

This recipe can easily be doubled if desired. Serve with Garlic Croutons (page 116), chopped black olives, chopped hard-cooked eggs, and finely diced avocado. White wine vinegar can be substituted for the sherry vinegar.

12 ounces tomatoes (about 2 medium), cored and cut into ¼-inch pieces (see the illustrations below)

1 red bell pepper, stemmed, seeded, and cut into ¼-inch pieces (see the illustrations below)

1 small cucumber, halved lengthwise, seeded, and cut into ¼-inch pieces (see the illustrations below)

¼ cup minced shallot or sweet onion (such as Vidalia, Maui, or Walla Walla)

2 tablespoons sherry vinegar, plus extra to taste (see note)

1 medium garlic clove, minced or pressed through a garlic press (about 1 teaspoon)
   Salt and ground black pepper

2½ cups tomato juice

½ teaspoon hot sauce (optional)

4 ice cubes
   Extra-virgin olive oil, for serving

1. Combine the tomatoes, bell pepper, cucumber, shallot, 2 tablespoons of the vinegar, garlic, 1 teaspoon salt, and black pepper to taste in a large (at least 2-quart) nonreactive bowl. Let stand until the vegetables just begin to release their juice, about 5 minutes.

2. Stir in the tomato juice, hot sauce (if using), and ice cubes. Cover tightly and refrigerate to blend the flavors, at least 4 hours or up to 2 days.

3. Remove and discard any unmelted ice cubes. Season with vinegar, salt, and pepper to taste. Serve cold, drizzling each portion with about 1 teaspoon extra-virgin olive oil.

DICING VEGETABLES FOR CLASSIC GAZPACHO

TOMATO

1. Core the tomatoes, halve them pole to pole, and, working over a bowl to catch all the juice, scoop out (and reserve) the inner pulp and seeds with a spoon. Cut the pulp into ¼-inch pieces.

2. Cut the empty tomato halves into ¼-inch slices. Turn the slices 90 degrees and cut into even ¼-inch pieces.

PEPPER

1. Slice a ¾-inch section off both ends of the pepper. Make one slice through the wall of the pepper, lay the pepper skin side down on a board, and open the flesh, exposing the seeds and membranes.

2. Cut away and discard the seeds and membranes. Cut the flesh into ¼-inch strips. Turn the strips 90 degrees and cut them into even ¼-inch pieces. Cut the tip and top into even ¼-inch pieces.

CUCUMBER

1. Trim the ends of the cucumber. Halve the cucumber lengthwise and scoop out the seeds with a spoon; discard the seeds. Cut each seeded half lengthwise into ¼-inch strips.

2. Turn the strips 90 degrees and cut into even ¼-inch pieces.

➤ VARIATIONS

Classic Gazpacho with Shrimp

Follow the recipe for Classic Gazpacho, adding 1 pound small shrimp (51 to 60 per pound), peeled, deveined (see the illustration on page 169), and cooked, to the soup before serving.

Spicy Gazpacho with Chipotle Chiles and Lime

We recommend garnishing bowls of this spicy soup with finely diced avocado. If desired, reduce the amount of chipotles to make the soup less spicy.

Follow the recipe for Classic Gazpacho, omitting the hot sauce. Add 2 tablespoons minced fresh cilantro leaves, 1 tablespoon minced chipotle chile in adobo sauce, 1 teaspoon grated zest from 1 lime, and 3 tablespoons juice from 2 limes to the soup with the tomato juice and ice cubes in step 2.

CREAMY GAZPACHO

AMERICAN COOKS KNOW GAZPACHO AS A chilled raw-vegetable soup, a sort of "liquid salad," with diced cucumber, bell pepper, and onion floating in a tomato-juice broth (see Classic Gazpacho on page 94). But in Spain, the birthplace of gazpacho, a variety of styles abound. Versions of this Spanish classic include everything from almonds to grapes, but the most popular type comes from Andalusia, the southernmost region of the country. It starts with the same vegetables as its chunky cousin, but is blended with bread for body. The result is a creamy, refreshing, complex soup—a soup, we felt, that belonged in our lineup.

To begin, we prepared a typical recipe, gathering several tomatoes along with a cucumber, a red bell pepper, and a red onion (since the bulk of it would be pureed, we wouldn't have to worry about big bites of pungent onion turning us off). We finely diced a portion of each vegetable, setting the cubes aside to use as a colorful garnish, and then roughly chopped and pureed the rest with two cloves of garlic, a slice of bread softened in water, and 2 tablespoons of sherry vinegar (which also hails from Spain). We then drizzled in ½ cup of extra-virgin olive oil until the soup was smooth

and emulsified. After seasoning and chilling our concoction, we tasted samples. Unfortunately, the soup tasted so bland, it might as well have been made with just bread. The reason we were so disappointed, we suspected, was our off-season supermarket tomatoes—not exactly ripe and juicy. There had to be some way we could utilize even winter tomatoes to make a flavorful gazpacho.

Before we addressed the problematic tomatoes, we made some refinements to the other vegetables. While the red pepper made the soup an attractive, bright red, its distinct sweetness was distracting, so we swapped it for a green pepper. For a touch of heat, we added a single serrano chile.

Now the tough part: the tomatoes. We had selected tomatoes that looked ripe and full, but were ultimately light on flavor. In the past, we've salted tomatoes in an attempt to rid them of excess water and ensure undiluted tomato flavor. We wondered if salting would help in this application and tossed some chopped tomatoes with salt. An hour later, the tomatoes were swimming in juice. We then pureed these salted specimens along with their exuded liquid. As a control, we also pureed unsalted tomatoes, stirring in the same amount of salt after blending. We crossed our fingers as tasters evaluated the samples. To our surprise, the salted puree boasted a deep, full flavor while the control paled in comparison. Figuring the same process could only improve the cucumbers, onions, and bell peppers, we salted them as well, yielding our finest soup yet. It turns out salt pulls out water-soluble flavor compounds as it makes the cell walls of the vegetables more prone to breaking down, releasing even more flavor.

Then we thought of one more way to maximize flavor. We'd been soaking the bread in water. Wouldn't it make better sense to use the exuded vegetable liquid? After salting the vegetables, we put half of them in a strainer set over a bowl to collect their juices, which we then reserved to soak the bread. Sure enough, this soup tasted even better.

In addition to the vegetable garnish, we gussied up each bowl with fresh herbs, ground black pepper, and more extra-virgin olive oil and sherry vinegar. Summer (or winter) in a bowl never looked—or tasted—so good.

Creamy Gazpacho Andaluz

SERVES 4 TO 6

The flavor of this soup depends on high-quality extra-virgin olive oil; for information on our winning brand, see page 149. We prefer to use kosher salt in this soup; however, half the amount of table salt can be substituted. A blender is essential to the proper texture of this soup (see page 121); do not use an immersion blender or food processor, as neither will result in the desired texture.

3	pounds ripe tomatoes (about 6 large), cored
I	small cucumber, peeled, halved lengthwise, and seeded
I	green bell pepper, stemmed and seeded
I	small red onion, peeled and halved
I	small serrano chile, stemmed and halved lengthwise
2	medium garlic cloves, peeled and quartered
	Kosher salt (see note)
I	slice high-quality white sandwich bread, crust removed, torn into 1-inch pieces
½	cup extra-virgin olive oil, plus extra for serving
2	tablespoons sherry vinegar or red wine vinegar, plus extra for serving
2	tablespoons finely minced parsley, chives, or basil leaves
	Ground black pepper

1. Roughly chop 2 pounds of the tomatoes, half of the cucumber, half of the pepper, and half of the onion and place in a large bowl. Add the chile, garlic, and 1½ teaspoons salt and toss to combine.

2. Dice the remaining 1 pound tomatoes, half cucumber, and half pepper into ¼-inch pieces and mince the remaining half onion. Toss these vegetables with ½ teaspoon salt, then transfer to a fine-mesh strainer and let drain over a medium bowl for 1 hour, reserving the juice. Once drained, return the vegetables to a medium bowl. (You should have about ¼ cup reserved juice.)

3. Add the bread to the bowl of reserved vegetable juice and let soak for 1 minute. Toss the soaked bread mixture with the roughly chopped vegetables to combine.

4. Puree half of the bread-vegetable mixture in a blender for 30 seconds. With the blender running, slowly add ¼ cup of the olive oil, then continue to process until completely smooth, about 2 minutes. Strain the soup through a fine-mesh strainer into a large serving bowl, pressing on the solids to release as much liquid as possible. Repeat with the remaining bread-vegetable mixture and ¼ cup olive oil.

5. Stir in 2 tablespoons of the vinegar, parsley, and half of the drained, diced vegetables. Season with salt and pepper to taste. Cover and refrigerate until well chilled and the flavors have melded, at least 2 hours or up to 12 hours. Serve, passing the remaining diced vegetables, olive oil, vinegar, and black pepper separately.

HEARTY VEGETABLE SOUP

MOST HOME COOKS THINK THAT VEGETABLE soup is made by dumping the entire contents of the crisper drawer into a pot with some broth and letting the whole mass simmer away. Sadly, though, this method drives out all of the vegetables' desirable qualities, resulting in soup with a bland, watery broth and dull, flabby, and waterlogged vegetables. Great vegetable soup should be just the opposite—a hearty, satisfying soup packed with fresh, tender vegetables that are lightly accentuated by a modest amount of herbs. Although the method is fairly straightforward (sauté aromatics, add broth and vegetables, then simmer), the challenge lies in winnowing down the pool of vegetables to a small but precise selection that will play nicely together but still let each other's natural flavors and sweetness shine through. Of course, there's cooking time to consider, too; some veggies need but a few minutes in the hot broth, while others require almost half an hour to become tender. We decided to work our way up—starting with the broth and then picking out the starring ingredients—in search of the perfect bowl of hearty vegetable soup.

In some soups, potently flavored ingredients like chiles and assertive herbs and spices dominate. In these cases, store-bought broth works just fine. But as with our Old-Fashioned Chicken Noodle Soup (page 26) and Old-Fashioned Beef and Vegetable Soup (page 56), we felt that the flavor of homemade broth contributed a clean, pure flavor that was unmatched by store-bought broth. Our Vegetable Broth (page 22) draws major vegetal flavor out of carrots, onions, celery, garlic, a tomato, and a head of cauliflower in about two hours. We thought this flavorful broth would provide the perfect backbone for this soup.

With the broth ready to go, it was time to move on to the vegetables. Our preliminary list included carrots, potatoes, tomatoes, and leeks (which we found added a more sophisticated note than common onions). For the potatoes, we chose high-starch russets, which we thought would break down somewhat and provide a bit of body to the broth; for the tomatoes, canned were our preference so we could make this soup any time of year. After a few tests, tasters confessed they were unimpressed with this combination of vegetables, so we thought we'd add more interesting choices. Root vegetables like parsnips and turnips proved too potent, as did cruciferous broccoli and Brussels sprouts. Green beans and peas were right for a spring or summer soup, but we needed something more substantial for our hearty soup. After a few more tests, we hit on lima beans, which were just right. (But because some tasters disliked limas, we made them optional.) Celery was too flimsy and disappeared, but its starchy, heartier cousin, celery root, was perfect. For visual and textural contrast, we wanted to add leafy greens. Among the greens we tried, bitter, quick-cooking escarole came out on top, adding bright color and flavor.

To ensure that our vegetables cooked through at the same rate, we cut them the same size (½-inch pieces) and staggered their additions to the pot. The first veggies to go in were the heartier vegetables, including the potatoes, celery root, and carrots. We also added the tomatoes at this point so their flavor could permeate the broth. After about 25 minutes, we added the escarole (cut into bigger 1-inch pieces) and lima beans, then let the soup simmer a few more minutes.

Our soup was pretty good at this point, but we felt it could use more body. We decided to capitalize on the starchiness of the potatoes and mashed some of them against the side of the pot to thicken our soup. This move worked like a charm; now we had both big bites of tender potato and a slightly thickened broth.

Our soup was so packed with great vegetable flavor, we decided to take a simple approach with the herbs—about 2 tablespoons of chopped parsley was all the soup needed. Now we had a soup with great body, multidimensional flavor, and tender chunks of vegetables throughout.

Hearty Vegetable Soup
SERVES 6 TO 8

The flavor of this soup depends on homemade broth; do not substitute store-bought broth. Serve with Cheese Toasties (page 98) or crusty bread.

1	tablespoon extra-virgin olive oil
2	medium leeks, white and light green parts only, halved lengthwise, sliced ¼ inch thick, and rinsed thoroughly (see the illustrations on page 103)
	Salt and ground black pepper
3	medium garlic cloves, minced or pressed through a garlic press (about 1 tablespoon)
6	cups Vegetable Broth (page 22)
1	(14.5-ounce) can diced tomatoes, drained and chopped coarse
12	ounces russet potatoes (about 2 small), peeled and cut into ½-inch pieces
½	medium head celery root (about 12 ounces), peeled and cut into ½-inch pieces
2	carrots, peeled and cut into ½-inch pieces
1	small head escarole (about 12 ounces), trimmed and cut into 1-inch pieces
1	cup frozen baby lima beans, thawed (optional)
2	tablespoons minced fresh parsley leaves

1. Heat the oil in a large Dutch oven over medium-low heat until shimmering. Stir in the leeks and ½ teaspoon salt, cover, and cook, stirring occasionally, until the leeks are softened, 8 to 10 minutes.

2. Stir in the garlic and cook until fragrant, about 30 seconds. Stir in the broth, tomatoes, potatoes, celery root, and carrots and bring to a boil. Cover, reduce to a gentle simmer, and cook until the vegetables are tender, about 25 minutes.

3. Using the back of a wooden spoon, mash some of the potatoes against the side of the pot to thicken the soup. Stir in the escarole and lima beans (if using) and cook until the escarole is wilted and the beans are heated through, about 5 minutes longer.

4. Off the heat, stir in the parsley, season with salt and pepper to taste, and serve.

~

Cheese Toasties

MAKES ABOUT 12 SMALL TOASTS

You can use any flavorful shredded, semisoft cheese in place of the cheddar in this recipe, including Gruyère, Swiss, Gouda, Colby, Havarti, or Monterey Jack.

1   small baguette, cut on the bias into ½-inch-thick slices
2   ounces cheddar cheese, shredded (½ cup)

Adjust an oven rack to the middle position and heat the oven to 400 degrees. Lay the baguette slices on a rimmed baking sheet and sprinkle evenly with the cheese. Bake until the bread is crisp and golden at the edges and the cheese is melted, 6 to 10 minutes.

PROVENÇAL VEGETABLE SOUP

DURING THE SUMMER MONTHS IN THE SOUTH of France, there is one soup that reigns supreme and it is *soupe au pistou*—a summer vegetable soup with a delicate broth that is intensified by a dollop of garlicky pistou—the French equivalent of Italy's pesto. This soup makes the most of late summer's harvest; it includes basil, garlic, haricots verts (slim green beans), zucchini, and white beans. This soup should taste like summer in a bowl—but we've had some bad versions of it. Vegetables that are overcooked and in the wrong proportions, as well as too much garlic in the pistou, can ruin not only the flavor of this soup, but its texture as well. Our goal was to develop a recipe that would guarantee the perfect balance of all the soup's elements.

To make a good summer soup, these tender vegetables would need the support of a broth that was rich and multidimensional, so we started our testing using our homemade Vegetable Broth (page 22). The resulting soup had the pleasant flavor of fresh vegetables, but once we swirled in the pistou, the delicate flavors became overwhelmed by the pistou's heady garlic, basil, and cheese. We quickly decided that we could forgo the homemade broth in favor of store-bought broth. We decided to mix the vegetable broth with water (in a 1–1 ratio) to tone down its sweetness; finally, we had achieved an excellent balance of flavors.

Now we could focus on the stars of this soup: summer vegetables. Not wanting to clutter the soup with any vegetables that weren't essential, we steered toward a simple, clean soup filled only with vegetables of the season. Leeks, green beans, and zucchini all made the cut quickly. Their tender flavors, different shapes, and varying shades of green made for a balanced summer mix.

Next we turned to traditional white beans to give the soup some heft. Typically, fresh white beans are used, but fresh beans can be difficult to find. Instead we tested both canned and dried white beans (cannellini or navy beans). Both canned and dried were great in this dish, but the canned white beans won out for sheer convenience. Pasta is also a traditional accompaniment to the summer vegetables, and we chose orecchiette for its easy-to-spoon shape. We added carrot, celery, and garlic to give the soup an aromatic quality. Finally, a tomato was included as a final nod to summer; it added a hit of bright acidity as well as a dash of color.

With our vegetables chosen, we turned to perfecting the technique. For this recipe, timing is everything. Ideally, all the vegetables and pasta should be finished cooking at once, then served immediately before any of them can overcook. To do that we staggered the addition of the vegetables based on their required cooking times.

We started by cooking the leek, carrot, and celery slowly over medium heat. Once they were soft, we added the garlic for 30 seconds, just long enough to bloom the flavor. To this we added the liquid (3 cups each of broth and water) and brought the soup to a simmer. Now it was time to add the pasta and vegetables. Since the pasta needs the longest amount of time to cook, we added that first. After a few minutes we added the haricots verts. Last, we tossed in the white beans, zucchini, and tomato, all of which needed only a couple of minutes to heat through and turn tender.

Now it was time to tackle the pistou. Although it's traditionally made by mashing fresh basil, garlic, and olive oil together in a mortar and pestle, our first task was to update this technique for modern kitchens. Turning to the food processor, we made the pistou in seconds, tossing in the cheese as well.

At last, we ladled the soup into individual serving bowls, then topped each with a dollop of pistou. This soup looked just like summer— and tasted like it too.

Provençal Vegetable Soup
SERVES 6

If you cannot find haricots verts (thin green beans), substitute regular green beans and cook them for an extra minute or two. You can substitute small shells or ditalini for the orecchiette (the cooking times might alter slightly). Serve with Garlic Toasts (page 138) or crusty bread.

PISTOU

½	cup packed fresh basil leaves
1	ounce Parmesan cheese, grated (½ cup)
⅓	cup olive oil
1	medium garlic clove, minced or pressed through a garlic press (about 1 teaspoon)

SOUP

1	tablespoon olive oil
1	medium leek, white and light green parts only, halved lengthwise, sliced ½ inch thick, and rinsed thoroughly (see the illustrations on page 103)
1	celery rib, cut into ½-inch pieces
1	carrot, peeled and sliced ¼ inch thick Salt and ground black pepper
2	medium garlic cloves, minced or pressed through a garlic press (about 2 teaspoons)
3	cups vegetable broth
3	cups water
½	cup orecchiette
8	ounces haricots verts, trimmed and cut into ½-inch lengths (see note)
1	(15-ounce) can cannellini or navy beans, drained and rinsed
1	small zucchini (about 6 ounces), halved lengthwise, seeded, and cut into ¼-inch pieces
1	large tomato, cored, seeded, and chopped medium

1. FOR THE PISTOU: Process all the ingredients together in a food processor until smooth, stopping to scrape down the sides of the bowl as needed, about 15 seconds; set aside. (The pistou can be refrigerated in an airtight container for up to 4 hours before serving.)

2. FOR THE SOUP: Heat the oil in a large Dutch oven over medium heat until shimmering. Add the leek, celery, carrot, and ½ teaspoon salt and cook until the vegetables are softened, 8 to 10 minutes. Stir in the garlic and cook until fragrant, about 30 seconds. Stir in the broth and water and bring to a simmer.

3. Stir in the pasta and simmer until slightly softened, about 5 minutes. Stir in the haricots verts

and simmer until bright green but still crunchy, about 3 minutes. Stir in the beans, zucchini, and tomato and continue to simmer until the pasta and all of the vegetables are tender, about 3 minutes.

4. Season with salt and pepper to taste. Serve, topping individual portions with a generous tablespoon of the pistou.

ARTICHOKE SOUP À LA BARIGOULE

BARIGOULE IS A FRENCH DISH OF BRAISED artichokes, mushrooms, onions, and garlic, cooked in a rich wine-laced broth. While artichokes aren't commonly the subject of soups, we liked the combination of delicate yet earthy artichokes and meaty mushrooms, so we decided to translate this French gem into a satisfying and flavorful soup.

On the way to a finished soup, we knew we'd have several obstacles to overcome. Our primary concern was about the artichokes—they're available fresh, canned, jarred, and frozen, but which option would provide the most flavor while still retaining some texture? Additionally, we had to consider the supporting roles the other vegetables would play. In the original French braise, onions, carrots, and garlic were essential. Would these complement the artichokes sufficiently or would we need to look elsewhere to complete our soup? Finally, we had to balance the overall flavors of the various components—the broth had to be robust yet understated so as not to overpower the delicate artichoke flavor. Could we achieve our goal with a single type of broth or would we need to experiment with different broths? With a long list of questions at the ready, we hit the test kitchen, starting with the namesake ingredient: the artichokes.

After just a few tests, we were able to scratch two options off the list—fresh and jarred artichokes. Although they taste great, fresh artichokes simply take too much time to prepare and cook.

Jarred artichokes are usually marinated in an Italian-style vinaigrette; we found that even when we rinsed the artichokes well, this unappealing flavor still dominated the soup.

Next up were canned artichokes. Packed in a watery liquid, canned artichokes were very wet even after we drained them well and patted them dry. Even sautéing them briefly didn't rid them completely of their excess moisture. Taking this test one step further, we simmered the sautéed artichokes briefly with the aromatics and chicken broth to see how they would be in the finished soup. This only made matters worse—the artichokes were now broken down and their texture was slimy and unpleasant.

Moving on to frozen artichokes, we kept our optimism intact. These were readily available and ready to go—the only precooking required was thawing them. After quickly thawing them in the microwave, we patted the artichokes dry and browned them. This intensified their flavor and evaporated excess moisture. After a brief simmer, the frozen artichokes retained more texture than the canned artichokes, but tasters still demanded more bite. We solved the problem by cooking half of the artichokes in the soup to impart flavor, then stirring in the remaining half at the end, which allowed this batch to retain their texture.

With the artichokes selected and our basic cooking method established, we considered additional ingredients. As with our Hearty Vegetable Soup (page 97), we found we preferred leeks to onions for their elegance and delicate flavor. We considered carrots initially, but found that their sweetness overpowered the flavor of the artichokes; we turned to parsnips instead, which added a more subdued sweetness. As for the garlic, a hefty four cloves offered some pungency. Next, we considered the mushrooms. Typically the artichokes are paired with wild mushrooms, but we set our sights on commonly available white mushrooms. To intensify their flavor and expel excess moisture, we sautéed them first until they released their juice, then browned them. This worked well.

Our soup tasted good at this point but was still lacking depth. Some recipes we found in our research contained anchovies. We gave it a shot and they did indeed contribute a rich, meaty, but not fishy, flavor that complemented the artichoke flavor nicely. Tasters raved about the improved flavor of the soup and did not detect that anchovies were behind it.

Finally, we had to address the soup's broth. Up until now, we'd been using chicken broth, but now that the other flavors had been ironed out, we thought the chicken broth was muddling the delicate balance we'd worked so hard to achieve. We tried using all vegetable broth, but on its own, it was too vegetal and sweet. In the end, we found that equal parts chicken broth and vegetable broth proved best. In keeping with tradition, and to add a bright, acidic touch, we added a small amount of white wine. The broth was flavorful, but slightly thin, so we added a small amount of flour for some body.

For a finishing touch, and to add some richness, we stirred in a small amount of cream. A sprinkling of tarragon amplified the French tone of our elegant, rich ode to the artichoke.

Artichoke Soup à la Barigoule
SERVES 4 TO 6

To thaw the frozen artichokes quickly, microwave them on high, covered, for 3 to 5 minutes. Frozen artichokes are generally packaged already quartered; if yours are not, cut the artichoke hearts into quarters before using.

2   tablespoons olive oil
2   (9-ounce) boxes frozen artichokes, thawed and patted dry (see note)
12 ounces white mushrooms, wiped clean, trimmed, and sliced thin
1   medium leek, white and light green parts only, halved lengthwise, sliced ¼ inch thick, and rinsed thoroughly (see the illustrations on page 103)
2   tablespoons unsalted butter
4   medium garlic cloves, minced or pressed through a garlic press (about 4 teaspoons)
2   anchovy fillets, rinsed and minced
1   teaspoon minced fresh thyme leaves or ¼ teaspoon dried
3   tablespoons unbleached all-purpose flour
¼   cup dry white wine
3   cups low-sodium chicken broth
3   cups vegetable broth
2   parsnips, peeled and cut into ½-inch pieces
2   bay leaves
⅓   cup heavy cream
2   tablespoons minced fresh tarragon or basil leaves
    Salt and ground black pepper

1. Heat 1 tablespoon of the oil in a large Dutch oven over medium heat until shimmering. Lightly brown the artichokes, 8 to 10 minutes, then transfer to a plate.

2. Heat the remaining 1 tablespoon oil over medium heat until shimmering. Add the mushrooms, cover, and cook until they have released their liquid, about 5 minutes. Uncover and cook until the mushrooms are dry and browned, about 5 minutes longer.

3. Stir in the leek and butter and cook until the leek is softened, 8 to 10 minutes. Stir in the garlic, anchovies, and thyme and cook until fragrant, about 30 seconds. Stir in the flour and cook for 1 minute. Stir in the wine, scraping up any browned bits, and cook until nearly evaporated, about 1 minute.

4. Gradually whisk in the chicken broth and vegetable broth, smoothing out any lumps. Stir in the parsnips, bay leaves, and half of the browned artichokes and bring to a boil. Cover, reduce to a gentle simmer, and cook until the parsnips are tender, 30 to 40 minutes.

5. Off the heat, remove the bay leaves. Stir in the remaining browned artichokes, cream, and tarragon, and let stand off the heat until the artichokes are heated through, about 1 minute. Season with salt and pepper to taste and serve.

Aromatics Prep 101

The primary aromatics in any cook's arsenal are garlic, onions, shallots, leeks, carrots, and celery. These core vegetables provide the flavor base for many dishes, including soups, stews, chilis, and braises. Here's how to avoid common mistakes in buying, storing, and prepping them to ensure you're making the most of these indispensable staples.

GARLIC

BUYING

DO go for the loose garlic, not the heads sold packaged in little cellophane-wrapped boxes that don't allow for close inspection.

DON'T buy heads that feel spongy or have skins where cloves used to reside. Also avoid garlic that smells unusually fragrant or fermented or has spots of mold—all signs of spoilage.

STORING

DO keep unpeeled garlic heads and cloves in a dry, breathable pantry space away from direct sunlight.

DON'T store garlic in the refrigerator. In tests we've found it softens and deteriorates far more quickly.

NEVER store raw garlic cloves in oil; this can result in botulism.

PREPPING

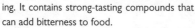

DO remove the green sprout from the center of the clove before cooking. It contains strong-tasting compounds that can add bitterness to food.

DO use a garlic press to mince cloves. In the test kitchen we've found a good press can break down the cloves more finely and evenly (and far faster) than the average cook wielding a knife, which means better distribution of garlic flavor throughout any given dish.

THE ONLY WAY TO SKIN A CLOVE

Forget trying to painstakingly pick skin off garlic. Crush the cloves with the side of a large chef's knife. The skin will loosen for easy removal.

MAKE A PASTE

Here's an easy way to turn minced garlic into a smooth puree for applications such as salad dressings, where you want the garlic's texture to be as unobtrusive as possible.

1. Sprinkle minced garlic with a coarse salt such as kosher.

2. Repeatedly drag the side of a chef's knife over the mixture until all the garlic turns into a smooth paste.

ONIONS

STORING

DO store onions at cool room temperature and away from light.

DON'T store in the fridge—their odors can permeate other foods.

SLICE IT RIGHT

The way in which onions are sliced makes no difference in flavor, but we find it does affect appearance, especially in soups, stews, and braises. Cooked in liquid, onions sliced against the grain (parallel with the root end) turn lifeless and wormy-looking. Sliced with the grain (pole to pole), the onions retain more shape and become a more significant component of the dish.

DICING AND MINCING

A sharp knife and a good technique make chopping onions a quick, easy, and even tear-free task.

1. Using a chef's knife, halve the onion pole to pole. Lop off the tops of each half, leaving the root end intact, and peel the onion.

2. With the knife blade parallel to the work surface, make horizontal cuts, starting with the heel of the knife and carefully pulling the knife toward you, without cutting through the root end. The number of cuts will depend on the size of the onion and the desired size of the dice.

3. Using the tip of the knife, make several vertical cuts, dragging the knife toward you and making sure to keep the tip against the board as you pull.

4. Slice across the lengthwise cuts, using your knuckles as a guide for the knife while holding the onions with your fingertips.

KNOW YOUR CUTS

MINCED	⅛-inch pieces or smaller
CHOPPED FINE	⅛- to ¼-inch pieces
CHOPPED MEDIUM	¼- to ½-inch pieces
CHOPPED COARSE	½- to ¾-inch pieces
CUT INTO CHUNKS	¾-inch pieces or larger
SLICED	Cut into flat, thin pieces (the thickness of the slices will depend on the recipe).
DICED	Cut into uniform cubes (the size of the dice will depend on the recipe).
CUT ON THE BIAS	Food is cut at an angle (the length will depend on the recipe).

SHALLOTS

WHEN TO USE

Shallots have a more mild and delicate flavor than that of onions—a difference accentuated by cooking. A finely minced shallot will also melt away until its texture is all but indiscernible. Choose shallots when you want onion flavor to meld into the mix or when silky texture is important.

SUBSTITUTES

Green onion (white part only) or red onion.

MINCING

1. Place the peeled shallot flat side down on a work surface and make a number of closely spaced parallel cuts through it, leaving the root end intact.

2. Make 2 or 3 cuts lengthwise through the shallot.

3. Thinly slice the shallot crosswise, creating a fine mince.

LEEKS

WHEN TO USE

We turn to leeks in place of onions when we want a milder, sweeter flavor and a texture that turns tender and silky when cooked. We love leeks in soups, but they're also delicious braised and served hot or cold with a vinaigrette.

STORING

Store leeks in a partially open plastic bag in your refrigerator's crisper. The crisper provides a humid environment that helps keep the leeks—which have a high water content—from shriveling and rotting.

BUYING

DO buy leeks with sprightly, unblemished leaves and long white stems, as this white part is the only edible portion of the vegetable. In tests, we found the size of the leek has no impact on taste or texture.

DON'T buy leeks that have been trimmed down to the lighter base—we've found the purpose of this procedure is to trim away aging leaves and make old leeks look fresher.

SLICE IT RIGHT

1. Trim and discard the roots and the dark green leaves.

2. Slice the trimmed leek in half lengthwise, then cut into thick or thin pieces as directed in the recipe.

CLEANING

Because leeks are often quite gritty and dirty, a thorough cleaning is a must. After trimming the leek and cutting it into small pieces, rinse the cut leek thoroughly in a salad spinner to remove the dirt and sand, then lift the spinner out to drain away the dirt and water.

CARROTS

BUYING

DO look for sturdy, hard carrots—a sign of freshness.

DON'T buy extra-large carrots, which are often woody and bitter.

STORING

To prevent carrots from shriveling, store them in the crisper, wrapped in their original plastic bag or in a partially open plastic bag.

DICING

Trying to cut wobbly, tapered carrots can be a dangerous proposition. The best way is to first create a stable edge.

1. Remove a thin slice from one side of the carrot to form a flat, stable edge. Place the carrot on that edge and slice it lengthwise into planks of even thickness.

2. Make two stacks and cut each evenly, lengthwise.

3. Turn the stacks 90 degrees and cut horizontally to complete the dice.

CELERY

BUYING

DO look for tightly packed, crisp green stalks.

DON'T buy bunches with brown spots or blemishes and anything that's begun to shrivel from age.

STORING

Like carrots, celery should be stored in the crisper in its original plastic wrapping or a partially open plastic bag. Note: In a pinch, you can revive tired celery stalks by trimming off roughly an inch from each end and submerging the stalks in a bowl of ice water for 30 minutes.

DICING

To yield an even dice, start by slicing a rib of celery in half crosswise. Then, cut each half lengthwise into strips of equal width. Cut across the strips to form an even dice.

CLASSIC FRENCH ONION SOUP

THE IDEAL FRENCH ONION SOUP COMBINES A satisfying broth redolent of sweet caramelized onions with a slice of toasted baguette and melted cheese. But the reality is that most of the onion soup you find isn't very good. Once you manage to dig through the layer of congealed cheese to unearth a spoonful of broth, it just doesn't taste like onions. We discovered the source of these watery, weak broths when we looked up some recipes. One called for barely half a pound of onions to make soup for six. Even more disturbing were those recipes that advised sautéing the onions for only five or six minutes—not nearly enough time for them to caramelize.

The good news is that we really didn't need these lackluster recipes. We know of a terrific one introduced to the test kitchen by a visitor from France, Henri Pinon. Henri patiently cooked 3 pounds of onions in butter over very low heat until they were golden brown (this took about 90 minutes), then deglazed the pot with water. Nothing unusual there—deglazing is common in onion soup recipes. What followed, however, was something entirely new. Henri allowed the onions to recaramelize, and then he deglazed the pan again. And again. He repeated this process several more times over the course of another hour, finally finishing the soup by simmering the onions with water, white wine, and a sprig of thyme. He garnished the soup in the traditional way, with a slice of crusty toasted baguette and a very modest amount of shredded Gruyère, passing the crocks under the broiler to melt the cheese. How did it taste? Beyond compare—the broth was impossibly rich, with deep onion flavor that burst through the tanginess of the Gruyère and bread.

Having watched Henri make his soup, we couldn't wait to give the recipe a try. But before we started cooking, we thought about his technique. When onions caramelize, a complex series of chemical reactions takes place. Heat causes water molecules to separate from the onions' sugar molecules. As they cook, the dehydrated sugar molecules react with each other to form new molecules that produce new colors, flavors, and aromas. (This is the same series of reactions that occurs when granulated sugar is heated to make caramel.) Each time Henri deglazed the pan and allowed the onions to recaramelize, he was ratcheting up the flavor of the soup in a big way.

Back in the test kitchen with Henri's recipe in hand, we started cooking, and a long while later, the soup was on. It was as delicious as when Henri had made it, but after standing at the stove for more than two hours, who had the energy to enjoy it? Was there a way to borrow Henri's technique while cutting down on the active cooking time?

We cranked the heat from low to high to hurry the onions along, and our risk taking was rewarded with burnt onions. We needed steady heat that wouldn't cause scorching—the stovetop was concentrating too much heat at the bottom of the pot. Why not use the oven? We spread oiled sliced onions on a baking sheet and roasted them at 450 degrees. Instead of caramelizing, however, they simply dried out. Lower temperatures caused the onions to steam. Next, we cooked as many sliced onions as we could squeeze into a Dutch oven (4 pounds), with far more promising results— the onions cooked slowly and evenly, building flavor all the while. After some trial and error, we finally settled on a method by which we cooked the onions, covered, in a 400-degree oven for an hour, then continued cooking with the lid ajar for another hour and a half. With our new hands-off method, the onions emerged from the oven golden, soft, and sweet, and a nice fond had begun to collect on the bottom of the pot. Even better, we'd had to tend to them only twice in 2½ hours. Next, we continued the caramelization process on the stovetop. Because of their head start in the oven, deglazing only three or four times was sufficient (the process still took nearly an hour—but this was far better than the two-plus hours Henri spent on his dozens of deglazings). Once the onions were as dark as possible, we poured in a few splashes of dry sherry.

Settling on a type of onion from standard supermarket varieties was a snap. We quickly dismissed red onions—they bled color and produced a dingy-looking soup. White onions were too mild, and Vidalia onions made the broth candy-sweet.

Yellow onions, on the other hand, offered just the sweet and savory notes we were after.

Henri had used only water for his soup, but after making batches with water, chicken broth, and beef broth, alone and in combination, we decided the soup was best with all three. The broths added complexity, and our goal was to build as many layers of flavor as possible.

At last, we could focus on the soup's crowning glory: bread and cheese. So as not to obscure the lovely broth, we dialed back the hefty amounts that have come to define the topping. Toasting the bread before floating a slice on the soup warded off sogginess. With a sprinkling of nutty Gruyère, we had a grand, gooey finish to a great soup.

Classic French Onion Soup

SERVES 6

Don't use sweet onions, such as Vidalia, Maui, or Walla Walla, in this soup or it will taste overly sweet. Be patient when caramelizing the onions in steps 3 and 4; the entire process takes 45 to 60 minutes. If you don't have broiler-safe crocks for serving, broil the bread and cheese on a baking sheet until the cheese melts, then float the bread on top of bowls of hot soup.

SOUP

4	pounds yellow onions, halved and sliced pole to pole into ¼-inch-thick pieces (see note) (see the illustration below)
3	tablespoons unsalted butter, cut into 3 pieces
	Salt and ground black pepper
	Water
½	cup dry sherry
4	cups low-sodium chicken broth
2	cups beef broth
6	sprigs fresh thyme, tied with kitchen twine
I	bay leaf

CROUTONS

I	small baguette, cut on the bias into ½-inch-thick slices
8	ounces Gruyère cheese, shredded (2 cups)

1. **FOR THE SOUP:** Adjust an oven rack to the lower-middle position and heat the oven to 400 degrees. Generously spray the inside of a large Dutch oven with vegetable oil spray, then stir in the onions, butter, and 1 teaspoon salt. Cover and bake until the onions wilt slightly and look moist, about 1 hour.

2. Stir the onions thoroughly, scraping the bottom and sides of the pot. Cover partially (leaving about 1 inch of the pot open) and continue to cook in the oven until the onions are very soft and golden brown, 1½ to 1¾ hours longer, stirring the onions thoroughly after 1 hour. (At this point, the pot of onions can be cooled, covered, and refrigerated for up to 3 days before continuing with step 3.)

3. Carefully remove the pot from the oven and place over medium-high heat. Using oven mitts to handle the pot, continue to cook the onions, stirring and scraping the pot often, until the liquid evaporates, the onions brown, and the bottom of the pot is coated with a dark crust 20 to 25 minutes. (If the onions begin to brown too quickly, reduce the heat to medium. Also, be sure to scrape any of the browned bits that collect on the spoon back into the onions.)

4. Stir in ¼ cup water, thoroughly scraping up the browned crust. Continue to cook until the water evaporates and the pot bottom has formed another dark crust, 6 to 8 minutes. Repeat this process of deglazing 2 or 3 more times, until the onions are very dark brown.

5. Stir in the sherry and cook until it evaporates, about 5 minutes. Stir in the chicken broth, beef

SLICING ONIONS

When slicing onions for soup or stew, be sure to slice them with the grain, from pole to pole. When sliced the opposite way, against the grain, the onions will have a stringy texture.

broth, 2 cups more water, thyme bundle, bay leaf, and ½ teaspoon salt, scraping up any remaining browned bits. Bring to a simmer, cover, and cook for 30 minutes. Remove the thyme bundle and bay leaf and season with salt and pepper to taste.

6. FOR THE CROUTONS: Adjust an oven rack to the middle position and heat the oven to 400 degrees. Lay the baguette slices on a rimmed baking sheet and bake until dry, crisp, and lightly golden, about 10 minutes, flipping the slices over halfway through baking.

7. TO SERVE: Position an oven rack 6 inches from the broiler element and heat the broiler. Set individual broiler-safe crocks on the baking sheet and fill each with about 1½ cups soup. Top each bowl with 1 or 2 baguette slices (do not overlap the slices) and sprinkle evenly with the cheese. Broil until the cheese is melted and bubbly around the edges, 3 to 5 minutes. Let cool for 5 minutes before serving.

HEARTY CABBAGE SOUP

THE DIFFERENCE BETWEEN RAW AND COOKED cabbage is like night and day—raw cabbage can taste harsh and astringent, whereas cooked cabbage has a flavor profile that's almost sweet and delicate. We wanted to make the most of the inherent qualities of cooked cabbage and decided to create a rich soup around it. Cabbage soup, when done right, can be incredibly satisfying. But, more often than not, cabbage soup is just that—a bowl of wilted, sad cabbage and watery broth. We set out to make an exciting soup, full of crisp-tender cabbage and chunks of potato (a classic pairing) floating in a rich, flavorful broth.

We knew we'd need to determine what type of cabbage to use as well as how long to cook it so it didn't completely disintegrate (some recipes we encountered suggested up to two hours). As a starting point, we scanned the cabbage section at the supermarket to choose the most appropriate variety for a hearty soup. Though we like the milder flavor of napa and savoy cabbages, tasters preferred the more assertive flavor of green cabbage. We decided to chop the cabbage into 1-inch pieces as our starting point.

Now we had to nail down the right cooking time. After sautéing some aromatics (onion, garlic, and thyme), we stirred in a combination of vegetable broth and chicken broth—either one alone proved too dominating in this soup—along with the cabbage and a bay leaf. Then we covered the pot and simmered the cabbage for 45 minutes. After so much time, the cabbage was a bit slimy and flavorless. We repeated this test, cutting down on time in five-minute increments. Ultimately, the cabbage was sweetest in flavor and best in texture after 30 minutes. We decided to cut the cabbage smaller so the pieces would be easier to scoop up with a spoon. We also tried sautéing the cabbage with the aromatics, but this did nothing for its texture so we decided to skip this additional step.

Our next consideration was what to add to bulk up the soup. Potatoes were a definite, but what kind? Low-starch red potatoes beat out other varieties because they held their shape after a period of simmering. Root vegetables were next on our list; we found we preferred the sweetness of carrots to earthier parsnips. We also tested peas and bell peppers, but neither of these options felt authentic. We decided to experiment with other ingredients that might punch up the flavor and feel of our soup.

All along, we had been sautéing the aromatics in butter, but we thought some bacon (and bacon fat) would add depth and smokiness. We sautéed a few slices of bacon until rendered, then used the fat to sauté the onion. This improved the flavor hugely. Many Eastern European cabbage soups add caraway seeds; tasters were in favor of this, praising the seeds' delicate anise flavor, which brought out the sweetness of the cabbage. A small amount of white wine brightened up the flavor of the broth and made the cabbage flavor cleaner.

Looking for one last ingredient to make our soup a standout, we thought back to other common Eastern European flavorings. In recipes for cabbage soup, one ingredient came up time and again: sour cream. We thought this would add a rich counterpoint to the sweetness of the soup. Since sour cream can curdle and create unattractive lumps when added directly to hot soup, it was important to properly incorporate it. Adding a little hot broth to the sour cream (a technique known as tempering) raises its temperature and helps stabilize it so it can be slowly stirred into the soup without fear of curdling. Following this method, we added ½ cup sour cream to start. While the tangy, rich sour cream complemented the mildly sweet, slightly sharp flavor of the cabbage, tasters demanded more creaminess. In the end, we increased the sour cream to 1 cup. Our soup was now rich and velvety. The only thing missing was a bright touch at the end, which we easily remedied with a sprinkling of fresh dill.

Hearty Cabbage Soup

SERVES 8

Do not boil the soup after adding the sour cream or it will curdle.

4	ounces (about 4 slices) bacon, cut into ¼-inch pieces
I	medium onion, minced
I	tablespoon unsalted butter
4	medium garlic cloves, minced or pressed through a garlic press (about 4 teaspoons)
I	teaspoon caraway seeds
I	teaspoon minced fresh thyme leaves or ¼ teaspoon dried
¼	cup dry white wine
3	cups low-sodium chicken broth
3	cups vegetable broth
2	pounds green cabbage (I medium head), cored and cut into ¾-inch pieces
12	ounces red potatoes (2 to 3 medium), scrubbed and cut into ¾-inch pieces
3	carrots, peeled and cut into ½-inch pieces
I	bay leaf
I	cup sour cream
	Salt and ground black pepper
I	tablespoon minced fresh dill

1. Cook the bacon in a large Dutch oven over medium heat until crisp and rendered, 5 to 7 minutes. Stir in the onion and butter and cook until the onion is softened, 5 to 7 minutes. Stir in the garlic, caraway seeds, and thyme and cook until fragrant, about 30 seconds longer.

2. Stir in the wine, scraping up any browned bits, and simmer until nearly evaporated, about 1 minute. Stir in the chicken broth, vegetable broth, cabbage, potatoes, carrots, and bay leaf and bring to a boil. Cover, reduce to a gentle simmer, and cook until the vegetables are tender, 25 to 30 minutes.

3. Off the heat, remove the bay leaf. Stir about ½ cup of the hot soup into the sour cream to temper, then stir the sour cream mixture into the pot. Season with salt and pepper to taste, sprinkle with the dill, and serve.

CORN CHOWDER

WHILE IT IS MOST EASILY APPRECIATED ON the cob, fresh corn also lends itself well to another American favorite: corn chowder. The ingredients in most corn chowder recipes are relatively standard: corn and other vegetables, usually at least potatoes and onions; liquids such as water or chicken broth enriched with some sort of dairy; and some sort of fat, be it butter, oil, or the traditional favorite, salt pork. Most recipes also have in common a reliance on the time-honored technique of first cooking the onions in fat to develop flavor and then adding the liquids and vegetables. Comfortable with this basic approach, we decided to build our recipe from the ground up.

We knew from the outset that we wanted our chowder to be loaded with fresh corn flavor. What became apparent after testing a few recipes is that the texture and flavor of the base (the dairy-enriched liquid) are also critical to a great chowder. The first contributor to that flavor is fat. Because salt pork is an ingredient some people aren't familiar with, we were hoping that butter or oil would prove to be adequate substitutes. But tests proved otherwise, with neither adding ample complexity.

While salt pork, the traditional type of fat used in chowders, served the chowder well, bacon has become the more popular option in recent years, no doubt owing to its availability, so we decided to give it a shot. We grabbed a few slices of bacon from the fridge, cut them into small pieces, and added them to the pot. Tasters were just as pleased with this chowder; in fact, they actually preferred the smoky flavor of the bacon-enriched chowder to the one without bacon. It looked like we would have to balk tradition this time around.

Bacon was a definite, but how to add it to the pot was up for debate. In our early tests, we cut the slices into 1-inch pieces and left these bits in the pot for the duration of cooking. But some testers complained about the flabbiness of the pieces in the finished dish—after simmering in the soup, the bacon had lost any sort of texture. In our next test, we decided to remove the bacon after it crisped in the pot; we could still use the fat to cook the aromatics, but we would wait to add the bacon back later on, so it retained some texture.

Sadly, this chowder had just an inkling of the smoky flavor and richness that tasters felt defined the earlier soup. In the end, we found that chopping the bacon finely and leaving it in the pot, not only to provide the fat for sautéing the aromatics but also to permeate the chowder as it simmered, guaranteed the best flavor. By the end of

simmering, the bacon had practically disintegrated into the chowder so there was no longer a concern that any tasters would encounter flabby, flimsy bites of bacon. While the bacon did provide some richness, we found that adding a tablespoon of butter with the onions provided a clean richness that played off the smokiness of the bacon.

With this first important building block of flavor in place, we could go on to consider how best to infuse the chowder base with the flavor of corn. Corn broth, corn juice, and corn pulp were all possibilities.

We made two quick broths with corncobs and husks, using water in one and chicken broth in the other. Although both brews had some corn flavor, their overall effect on the chowder was minimal; making corn broth was clearly not worth the effort. We did learn, though, that water diluted the flavor of the chowder, while chicken broth improved it; this would be our liquid of choice for the base.

In the past, we have identified grating the corncobs and then scraping off their pulp as a good means of extracting flavor from corn. We decided to revisit this method. The pulp, which is thick, lush, smooth-textured, and full of corn flavor, improved both the flavor and texture of our chowder dramatically.

Our next concern was the dairy and, as it turned out, the thickener to be used. A problem with the

PREPARING FRESH CORN FOR SOUP

 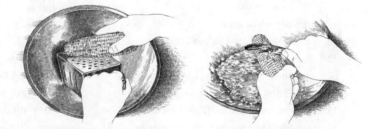

1. To cut the kernels off an ear of corn without having them fly all over the kitchen counter, hold the ear on its end inside a large wide bowl and use a paring knife to cut off the kernels.

2. To grate the kernels off an ear, simply hold a box grater over a large wide bowl and use the large grating holes.

3. To scrape the milk and pulp from a corncob, firmly scrape the cob using the back of a butter knife.

dairy component of chowder is its tendency to curdle when heated, with lower-fat products more likely to curdle than higher-fat products. But we thought relying entirely on higher-fat dairy, such as heavy cream, would make for an overly rich chowder. While some heavy cream was needed to give the base some depth of character, whole milk, which is neutral and therefore capable of being infused with corn flavor, would make up the larger part of the dairy. This composition gave us some concern about curdling, which is where the thickening factor came in. We realized that the most practical thickener to use would be flour, which is known to help stabilize dairy proteins and so prevent curdling. To prevent the curdling, though, the flour has to be in the pot before the dairy is added. So we decided to make a roux, stirring the flour into the fat and onions at the beginning of the cooking process.

Finally, we could address the vegetables, aromatics, and herbs. Onions, potatoes, and corn kernels were a given. The favorite potatoes were red potatoes, which remained firm and looked great with their skins left on. Whole corn kernels added authenticity to the chowder, and we learned that adding the kernels after the potatoes have been cooked till tender, then cooking the kernels just briefly, results in a fresh-from-the-cob corn flavor. A bit of garlic added some depth and fullness, while thyme, parsley, and a bay leaf helped to round out the flavors.

With our foolproof corn chowder recipe established, we took the time to develop a few interesting variations. So many kinds of pork and sausage work well with the sweet flavor of fresh corn that we decided to capitalize on this harmonious relationship and create recipes using ham, chorizo, and andouille sausage. For a seafood-based variation, we paired our corn chowder with crabmeat and Old Bay seasoning.

Corn Chowder

SERVES 8

This soup tastes best with sweet corn from the height of the season; do not substitute frozen corn.

10	ears corn, husks and silk removed (see note)
3	ounces (about 3 slices) bacon, chopped fine
2	medium onions, chopped fine
1	tablespoon unsalted butter
2	medium garlic cloves, minced or pressed through a garlic press (about 2 teaspoons)
1	teaspoon minced fresh thyme leaves or ¼ teaspoon dried
3	tablespoons unbleached all-purpose flour
3	cups low-sodium chicken broth
2	cups whole milk
12	ounces red potatoes (2 to 3 medium), scrubbed and cut into ¼-inch pieces
1	bay leaf
1	cup heavy cream
2	tablespoons minced fresh parsley leaves Salt and ground black pepper

1. Following the illustrations on page 108, cut the kernels from 4 of the ears of corn into a large bowl, reserving the cobs. In a separate bowl, grate the remaining 6 ears of corn over the large holes of a box grater. Using the back of a butter knife, scrape the pulp from all of the cobs into the bowl of grated corn.

2. Cook the bacon in a large Dutch oven over medium heat until crisp and rendered, 5 to 7 minutes. Stir in the onions and butter and cook until the onions are softened, 5 to 7 minutes. Stir in the garlic and thyme and cook until fragrant, about 30 seconds. Stir in the flour and cook for 1 minute.

3. Gradually whisk in the broth, scraping up any browned bits and smoothing out any lumps. Stir in the milk, potatoes, bay leaf, grated corn and pulp,

and bring to a boil. Reduce to a gentle simmer and cook until the potatoes are nearly tender, 8 to 10 minutes.

4. Stir in the heavy cream and corn kernels and simmer until the corn kernels are tender yet still slightly crunchy, about 5 minutes. Off the heat, remove the bay leaf and stir in the parsley. Season with salt and pepper to taste and serve.

➤ VARIATIONS

New Orleans–Style Corn Chowder

Follow the recipe for Corn Chowder, substituting 8 ounces andouille sausage, cut into ¼-inch pieces, for the bacon and reducing the browning time to 3 minutes in step 2. Remove the sausage from the pot. Add 1 celery rib, chopped fine, and 1 green bell pepper, stemmed, seeded, and chopped fine, to the pot with the onions in step 2. Return the browned sausage to the pot with the heavy cream in step 4.

Maryland-Style Corn Chowder with Crabmeat

For a hearty presence of crab, double the amount of crabmeat.

Follow the recipe for Corn Chowder, adding 2 tablespoons Old Bay seasoning to the pot with the garlic and thyme in step 2. Substitute 2 tablespoons minced fresh chives for the parsley and add 8 ounces fresh crabmeat, picked over for shells, before seasoning the soup with salt and pepper to taste.

Corn Chowder with Ham and Sweet Potatoes

Follow the recipe for Corn Chowder, substituting 8 ounces thick-cut ham steak, cut into ¼-inch pieces, for the bacon; add 2 teaspoons vegetable oil to the pot with the ham in step 2 and reduce the browning time to 3 minutes. Add ½ teaspoon ground coriander and a pinch ground allspice to the pot with the garlic in step 2. Substitute 1 medium sweet potato, peeled and cut into ¼-inch pieces, for the red potatoes.

Corn Chowder with Chorizo and Chiles

For more heat, include the jalapeño seeds and ribs when mincing.

Follow the recipe for Corn Chowder, substituting 8 ounces chorizo sausage, cut into ¼-inch pieces, for the bacon and reducing the browning time to 3 minutes in step 2. Remove the chorizo from the pot before adding the onions. Add 2 jalapeño chiles, stemmed, seeded, and minced, to the pot with the onions in step 2. Add 1 tablespoon chili powder and ½ teaspoon ground cumin to the pot with the garlic. Return the browned sausage to the pot with the heavy cream in step 4 and substitute ¼ cup minced fresh cilantro leaves for the parsley.

WINTER SQUASH CHOWDER

VEGETABLE CHOWDERS AREN'T LIMITED TO corn. Take winter squash: Its sweet, subtle flavor pairs well with many ingredients, especially smoky bacon and sweet, nutty spices. Though squash can take a relatively long time to cook when roasted whole, small, bite-size pieces cook more quickly, making it perfect for a soup.

Our main concern was how to best accentuate the mild, sweet flavor of the squash without overpowering it. We'd also have to carefully consider the aromatics and other ingredients to be incorporated; while we worried that a heavy hand with any one spice would negate the flavor of the squash, we were also aware that the squash's sweetness could easily take over. The success of our chowder rested on properly balancing the sweet and savory elements.

We tackled the squash first, narrowing down the kinds that would be suitable for chowder. Butternut and acorn squash are the most commonly available varieties, but acorn squash can be sour and stringy, so it was nixed. Accessible butternut, with its smooth, buttery flavor, would work fine, but we expanded our horizons to consider carnival and delicata squashes, which are starting to gain in popularity. Carnival squash is creamy, delicate, buttery, and sweet and would make a delicious soup, too, as would delicata, which is also sweet and has a pleasant flavor reminiscent of corn. Other varieties, such as sugar pumpkin and spaghetti, were cut from the running, as they can be too fibrous.

Armed with our squash, we set out to select our aromatics and provide the proper backdrop of flavor for the squash. For a meaty flavor base, we first cooked a small amount of bacon to render its fat. Then we sautéed onion, garlic, and a moderate amount of thyme before stirring in a combination of chicken broth and vegetable broth; we found that slightly more chicken broth balanced the sweetness of the vegetable broth. At this point, we added the squash—cut into small pieces—and let it simmer until tender.

Evaluating the flavor profile of our trial run, tasters commented that they appreciated the smokiness contributed by the bacon, but thought it was starting to take over the chowder. Looking for a more subtle inclusion, we hit on pancetta, an unsmoked Italian bacon, which provided the same meaty, salty undertones. By this point, we had deemed our teaspoon of thyme, along with a single bay leaf, as essential, but we wanted to look beyond these for additional spices and herbs that would pair well with the squash. Warm, spicy nutmeg and slightly bitter sage provided just the right savory notes we were looking for. We also found that a small amount of dark brown sugar added some rich, caramel notes that worked well with the squash's natural sweetness.

Now we needed to address the broth's consistency. We had been making the soup with vegetable broth and chicken broth, which made for a soup too thin to be considered a chowder. We weren't sure how much of the squash's natural starch would thicken the soup. As it turned out, not at all. To thicken the base, we had to stir in some flour; we started with just 1 tablespoon. We worked our way up in single-tablespoon increments until we achieved the right consistency. A third of a cup gave the chowder a thick, but not gloppy, consistency, and tasters approved. As for the requisite dairy, a modest amount of heavy cream imparted richness and lent a velvety texture.

Tasters were mostly happy with the chowder now but felt it could use a vegetable to round out the mix of ingredients in the pot. Specifically, they wanted a hearty green that would provide a nice foil to the sweetness of the soup. Bitter kale was the answer. It held up well to simmering, getting tender and nicely wilted without completely melting away.

A sprinkling of some nutty, salty grated Parmesan made the perfect garnish. At last, our new chowder was a wonderful balance of hearty and rich, sweet and savory.

Winter Squash Chowder
SERVES 6 TO 8

If you can't find pancetta, substitute 4 ounces of bacon (about 4 slices). We prefer to use squash that is smaller in size because it has a more concentrated flavor and finer texture than larger squash does. Delicata or carnival squash can be substituted for the butternut squash.

4	ounces pancetta, cut into ¼-inch pieces (see note)
I	medium onion, minced
I	tablespoon unsalted butter
3	medium garlic cloves, minced or pressed through a garlic press (about I tablespoon)
I	teaspoon minced fresh thyme leaves or ¼ teaspoon dried
	Pinch freshly grated nutmeg, plus extra to taste
⅓	cup unbleached all-purpose flour
4	cups low-sodium chicken broth
3	cups vegetable broth
3	pounds butternut squash, peeled and cut into ½-inch pieces (see note) (see the illustrations on page 112)
I	bay leaf

½   bunch kale (about 8 ounces), stemmed and leaves sliced ¼ inch thick (see the illustrations on page 56)

½   cup heavy cream

I   tablespoon minced fresh sage leaves

I   teaspoon dark brown sugar

    Salt and ground black pepper

    Grated Parmesan cheese, for serving

1. Cook the pancetta in a large Dutch oven over medium heat until crisp, 5 to 7 minutes. Stir in the onion and butter and cook until the onion is softened, 5 to 7 minutes. Stir in the garlic, thyme, and a pinch of nutmeg and cook until fragrant, about 30 seconds. Stir in the flour and cook for 2 minutes.

2. Gradually whisk in the chicken broth and vegetable broth, scraping up any browned bits and smoothing out any lumps. Stir in the squash and bay leaf and bring to a boil. Cover, reduce to a gentle simmer, and cook until the squash begins to soften, 10 to 15 minutes.

3. Stir in the kale and continue to simmer, covered, until the squash and kale are tender, about 10 minutes longer.

4. Off the heat, remove the bay leaf and stir in the heavy cream, sage, and sugar. Season with salt, pepper, and nutmeg to taste. Serve, sprinkling individual portions with the cheese.

PREPPING BUTTERNUT SQUASH

With its tough outer skin, bulbous base filled with seeds and fibers, and long, skinny neck, preparing butternut squash can be a formidable task. Follow these key steps, however, and you'll be ready to cut the squash into evenly sized pieces.

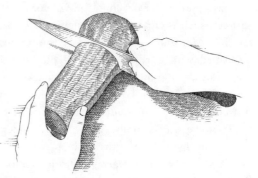

1. Cut off both ends of the squash, remove the skin with a vegetable peeler, and cut the squash in half, separating the bulb from the neck.

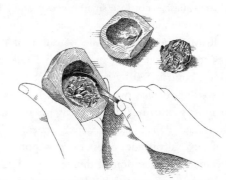

2. Cut the bulb in half through the base and remove the seeds with a spoon. Cut the peeled and seeded squash as directed in the recipe.

6
PUREED SOUPS

PUREED SOUPS

CREAMLESS CREAMY TOMATO SOUP

TOMATO SOUP SHOULD HAVE IT ALL: GOOD looks, velvety smoothness, and a bright tomato taste balanced by the fruit's natural sweetness. But poor versions are the norm, featuring either an acidic, watery broth or an overdose of cream. Though cream is meant to tame tartness and lend body, it can sometimes mute flavor. We wanted soup with rich tomato taste and a satisfying texture. Could we get there without the cream?

The first step in the process was to pass over fresh tomatoes for canned, which we find are almost always far better than your average supermarket tomato, boasting more consistently rich and concentrated flavor. Working with whole tomatoes, we then developed a simple working recipe, sautéing onions and garlic in butter, stirring in the tomatoes and a can of chicken broth, and then giving the whole thing a quick spin in the blender. The results were decent, but dull.

If cream subdues tomato flavor, could the milk solids in the butter be tamping it down as well? We substituted extra-virgin olive oil for the butter and found that the soup was brighter as a result. A few more small changes—a pinch of red pepper flakes sautéed with the onions and the addition of a bay leaf with the tomatoes—upped the flavor significantly. To compensate for the flavor the oil lost as it cooked, we drizzled a little more over the soup before it went into the blender. Most tasters also welcomed a couple tablespoons of brandy.

Now that we had our flavor profile nailed down, we moved on to the soup's tartness and thin texture. Sugar is often used as a means to combat tartness. We preferred brown sugar to one-dimensional white sugar, but sweetness only took us so far.

Next, we needed a thickener that would also help temper the acid. Flavor-dulling dairy ingredients were definitely out, but what about a starch? Adding flour made for a thicker soup, but the texture turned slimy instead of creamy and the flour did nothing for flavor. Cornstarch produced similar results. We scoured our cookbook library before finding inspiration in another tomato-based soup, gazpacho. At its most basic, this Spanish soup is classically made from tomatoes, olive oil, and garlic, along with a wholly unexpected element for thickening—bread. But gazpacho is served cold. Would bread work as a thickener for hot soup?

We tore several slices of sandwich bread into pieces and stirred them into the pot with the tomatoes and chicken broth as they simmered. When we processed the mixture in the blender, we ended up with bread chunks that swam in a sea of broth and resisted being sucked down into the blender's spinning blades. To cut back on the amount of liquid in the blender, we decided to try leaving out the broth until the very end. For our next batch of soup, we pureed the tomatoes with the aromatics and bread before returning the mixture to the pan and whisking in the broth. One taste and we knew we'd hit on just the right solution. Our tomato soup had the same velvety texture as the creamy kind, but with bright, fresh flavor. None of the tasters even guessed our soup contained a secret ingredient. And if the empty pot left on the table was any indication, they'd never need to.

~

Creamless Creamy Tomato Soup

SERVES 8

For an even smoother soup, pass the pureed mixture though a fine-mesh strainer before stirring in the chicken broth in step 4. Serve with Butter Croutons (page 116). See page 121 for more information on pureeing soup.

3	tablespoons extra-virgin olive oil, plus extra for serving
I	medium onion, chopped medium
3	medium garlic cloves, minced or pressed through a garlic press (about I tablespoon)
	Pinch red pepper flakes (optional)
2	(28-ounce) cans whole peeled tomatoes
3	slices high-quality white sandwich bread, crusts removed, torn into I-inch pieces
I	tablespoon light brown sugar
I	bay leaf
2	cups low-sodium chicken broth
2	tablespoons brandy (optional)
	Salt and ground black pepper
¼	cup minced fresh chives

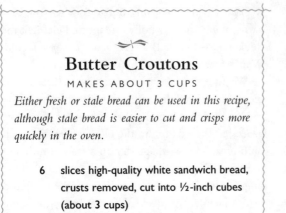

Butter Croutons

MAKES ABOUT 3 CUPS

Either fresh or stale bread can be used in this recipe, although stale bread is easier to cut and crisps more quickly in the oven.

6   slices high-quality white sandwich bread, crusts removed, cut into ½-inch cubes (about 3 cups)

3   tablespoons unsalted butter, melted
    Salt and ground black pepper

Adjust an oven rack to the middle position and heat the oven to 350 degrees. Toss the bread cubes and butter together in a medium bowl and season with salt and pepper to taste. Spread the croutons onto a rimmed baking sheet and bake until golden brown and crisp, 20 to 25 minutes, tossing them halfway through baking. Let cool and serve. (The croutons can be stored in an airtight container for up to 3 days.)

➤ VARIATIONS

Garlic Croutons

Follow the recipe for Butter Croutons, whisking 1 garlic clove, minced or pressed through a garlic press (about 1 teaspoon), into the melted butter before tossing with the bread cubes.

Cinnamon-Sugar Croutons

Follow the recipe for Butter Croutons, tossing the buttered bread cubes with a mixture of 6 teaspoons sugar and 1½ teaspoons ground cinnamon before baking.

1. Heat 1 tablespoon of the oil in a large Dutch oven over medium heat until shimmering. Add the onion and cook until softened, 5 to 7 minutes. Stir in the garlic and red pepper flakes (if using) and cook until fragrant, about 30 seconds. Stir in the tomatoes with their juice. Using a potato masher, mash the tomatoes until there are no pieces larger than 2 inches.

2. Stir in the bread, sugar, and bay leaf and bring to a boil. Reduce to a simmer and cook, stirring occasionally, until the bread is saturated and starts to break down, about 5 minutes.

3. Remove the bay leaf. Working in batches, puree the soup with the remaining 2 tablespoons oil until smooth, 1 to 2 minutes. Return the soup to a clean pot.

4. Stir in the chicken broth and brandy (if using), bring to a brief simmer, and season with salt and pepper to taste. Serve, sprinkling individual portions with the chives and drizzling with olive oil.

SIMPLE CREAM OF VEGETABLE SOUPS

IT'S EASY TO UNDERSTAND THE APPEAL OF creamy vegetable soups. We think they rank right up there with classic comfort foods like macaroni and cheese and lasagna. They are rich, silky tasting, and when done well, bursting with vegetable flavor. Add a few croutons or a dollop of something creamy, and you have a soul satisfying meal in a bowl. Too often, however, these soups are overly rich from a heavy hand with cream and/or butter, which dilutes the vegetable's flavor and dulls its color.

Our challenge, therefore, would lie in developing a host of cream of vegetable soups in which the richness of the cream wouldn't overtake the flavor of the vegetables. We also wanted to choose vegetables that could all be prepared similiarily so that once we determined our method, prepearing these soups would be almost as easy as swapping in one vegetable for another.

Typically, cream soups start out by sautéing aromatics, such as onion and garlic. Once the aromatics are softened, flour is added and cooked to make a roux, which aids in thickening the soup and creating a velvety texture. Next, broth (usually chicken) is whisked in and brought to a boil in order for the liquid to thicken and the flavors to meld. The vegetables are then added and simmered until tender, at which point the soup is pureed and finished with heavy cream.

Following this basic technique, we set out to make a batch of soup with broccoli. After simmering the broccoli in the soup until tender, we pureed the mixture, then substituted an equal amount of whole milk for the heavy cream the recipe usually includes. We reasoned that the less rich dairy wouldn't mute the broccoli flavor. But the soup was a disappointment. It lacked body, tasted lean, and the color was drab.

We regrouped and went back to the beginning. Vegetable flavor was a big problem. And broccoli is a tricky vegetable. Because it has two parts—the hardy stems and the delicate florets—it clearly requires two different approaches. We made another batch of soup and put the longer-cooking stems in first and then towards the end of cooking, we dropped in the florets. The color was brighter and the flavor was improved. But we wondered if we could go one better. In another batch, we sautéed the stems with the aromatics, then simmered the florets as we had done before. Bingo. The broccoli flavor in this batch was deep and well-rounded. Now we had to tackle the broth. We wondered if vegetable broth, rather than chicken broth would highlight the vegetable flavor more. A batch made with vegetable broth was pleasant but a little lean-tasting. In the end we used half of each, but you could certainly use all vegetable broth for a vegetarian soup.

Next we moved on to the dairy. Clearly, whole milk was too lean—we needed a richer alternative. We found some recipes in our research that offered up evaporated milk as a substitute for heavy cream—we thought we'd give it a shot. Evaporated milk is whole milk that has been cooked to evaporate as much as half of its water content; the result is a creamier product with, cup for cup,

higher amounts of sugar, protein, and calcium. Though many tasters like the flavor and texture evaporated milk imparted, others complained that it was "too sweet" with an "off-flavor." Running out of dairy alternatives, we had one choice left: half-and-half.

We tried substituting an equal amount of half-and-half for the heavy cream, but the soup was just as rich-tasting and the dairy flavor masked the vegetable flavor. We reduced the amount to ¾ cup, but the dairy was still overpowering. We settled on ½ cup—it provided the right amount of dairy flavor and richness, giving the soup a smooth and creamy body without eclipsing the vegetable. And as a final touch, we cut the creaminess with a little acidity in the form of white wine. The wine brought out the brightness of the vegetables and added a bit of depth to the soup.

We were pretty pleased at how our tests were proceeding. We started swapping in other vegetables for the broccoli, first asparagus, then cauliflower. Both were great. But trouble started when we tried adding peas to our one-size-fits-all soup. We realized that if we wanted to showcase this vegetable in its best light, we would have to tailor the recipe around it.

We started by choosing frozen peas over fresh for their reliable flavor and year-round availability. Our initial batch of pea soup made following our working recipe was disappointing—by the time the peas released considerable flavor into the broth, they were overcooked and produced a murky-looking and -tasting soup. Looking for a way to incorporate pea flavor into the broth faster, it occurred to us that if we processed the peas before putting them into the soup, we could accelerate their ability to impart their flavor and avoid any overcooking. With this in mind, we coarsely chopped partially frozen peas in a food processor and simmered them briefly in the soup base to release their starch and flavor. The result was a vast improvement over our earlier effort—the resulting soup had a bright, sweet pea flavor and vibrant green color.

Though it wasn't as easy as we had thought it would be, we finally achieved success with four rich and creamy soups with great vegetable flavor.

Cream of Broccoli Soup

SERVES 4 TO 6

Be sure to use fresh broccoli in this soup; do not substitute frozen broccoli. Serve with Cheese Toasties (page 98), if desired. See page 121 for more information on pureeing soup.

1	tablespoon vegetable oil
1	medium onion, chopped medium
1½	pounds broccoli (1 large bunch), florets cut into 1-inch pieces, stems trimmed and sliced thin (see the illustrations at right)
3	medium garlic cloves, minced or pressed through a garlic press (about 1 tablespoon)
1	tablespoon unbleached all-purpose flour
¼	cup dry white wine
2	cups low-sodium chicken broth, plus extra as needed
2	cups vegetable broth
1	bay leaf
½	cup half-and-half
	Salt and ground black pepper

1. Heat the oil in a large Dutch oven over medium heat until shimmering. Add the onion and broccoli stems and cook until the vegetables are softened, 5 to 7 minutes. Stir in the garlic and cook until fragrant, about 30 seconds. Stir in the flour and cook for 1 minute. Stir in the wine, scraping up any browned bits, and cook until almost completely evaporated, about 1 minute.

2. Gradually whisk in the chicken broth and vegetable broth, smoothing out any lumps, and bring to a simmer. Stir in the broccoli florets and bay leaf, reduce to a simmer, and cook until the florets are tender, 7 to 10 minutes.

3. Remove the bay leaf. Working in batches, puree the soup until smooth, 1 to 2 minutes. Return the soup to a clean pot.

4. Stir in the half-and-half and additional chicken broth as needed to adjust the soup's consistency. Heat the soup gently over low heat until hot (do not boil). Season with salt and pepper to taste and serve.

> VARIATION
Garlicky Cream of Broccoli Soup

Follow the recipe for Cream of Broccoli Soup, increasing the amount of oil to 2 tablespoons and the amount of minced garlic to 12 garlic cloves (about 3 tablespoons). Before starting step 1, cook all the garlic and oil together in the pot over low heat, stirring constantly, until the garlic is foamy, sticky, and straw-colored, 8 to 10 minutes. Continue to add the onions and broccoli stems and cook as directed.

PREPARING BROCCOLI

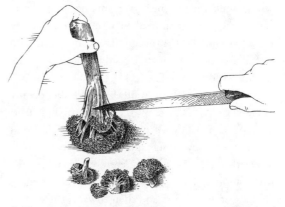

1. Place the head of broccoli upside down on a cutting board and with a large knife trim off the florets very close to their heads. Cut the florets into 1-inch pieces.

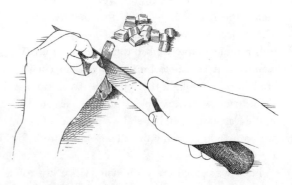

2. Stand each stalk up on the cutting board and square it off with a large knife. This will remove the outer ⅛-inch from the stalk, which is quite tough. Continue to cut the squared stalk into pieces as directed in the recipe.

Cream of Cauliflower Soup

SERVES 4 TO 6

See page 121 for more information on pureeing soup.

- 1 tablespoon vegetable oil
- 1 medium onion, chopped medium
- 3 medium garlic cloves, minced or pressed through a garlic press (about 1 tablespoon)
- 1 tablespoon unbleached all-purpose flour
- ¼ cup dry white wine
- 2 cups low-sodium chicken broth, plus extra as needed
- 2 cups vegetable broth
- 1 medium head cauliflower (about 2½ pounds), trimmed, cored, and cut into 1-inch pieces (see the illustrations on page 281)
- 1 bay leaf
- ½ cup half-and-half
    Salt and ground black pepper

1. Heat the oil in a large Dutch oven over medium heat until shimmering. Add the onion and cook until softened, 5 to 7 minutes. Stir in the garlic and cook until fragrant, about 30 seconds. Stir in the flour and cook for 1 minute. Stir in the wine, scraping up any browned bits, and cook until almost completely evaporated, about 1 minute.

2. Gradually whisk in the chicken broth and vegetable broth, smoothing out any lumps, and bring to a simmer. Stir in the cauliflower and bay leaf, reduce to a simmer, and cook until the cauliflower is tender, 15 to 20 minutes.

3. Remove the bay leaf. Working in batches, puree the soup until smooth, 1 to 2 minutes. Return the soup to a clean pot.

4. Stir in the half-and-half and additional chicken broth as needed to adjust the soup's consistency. Heat the soup gently over low heat until hot (do not boil). Season with salt and pepper to taste and serve.

➤ VARIATION

Curried Cream of Cauliflower Soup

We prefer the flavor of whole milk yogurt or Greek yogurt as well as whole milk in this soup. You can substitute low-fat yogurt or low-fat milk, but do not use nonfat yogurt or skim milk.

Follow the recipe for Cream of Cauliflower Soup, adding 1 teaspoon minced or grated fresh ginger (see the illustrations on page 89) and 2 teaspoons curry powder to the pot with the garlic. Substitute ½ cup plain yogurt and ½ cup whole milk for the half-and-half. Stir 1 tablespoon minced fresh cilantro leaves and 1 teaspoon sugar into the soup before serving.

Cream of Green Pea Soup

SERVES 4 TO 6

Remove the peas from the freezer just before you begin to cook the soup so they will be partially thawed for processing in step 2. See page 121 for more information on pureeing soup.

- 1 tablespoon vegetable oil
- 1 medium onion, chopped medium
- 3 medium garlic cloves, minced or pressed through a garlic press (about 1 tablespoon)
- 1 tablespoon unbleached all-purpose flour
- ¼ cup dry white wine
- 2 cups low-sodium chicken broth, plus extra as needed
- 2 cups vegetable broth
- 1 bay leaf
- 4 cups frozen peas, partially thawed at room temperature for 10 minutes (see note)
- ½ cup half-and-half
    Salt and ground black pepper

1. Heat the oil in a large Dutch oven over medium heat until shimmering. Add the onion and cook until softened, 5 to 7 minutes. Stir in the garlic and cook until fragrant, about 30 seconds. Stir in the flour and cook for 1 minute. Stir in the wine, scraping up any browned bits, and cook until almost completely evaporated, about 1 minute.

2. Gradually whisk in the chicken broth and vegetable broth, smoothing out any lumps. Add the bay leaf and bring to a simmer. Pulse the peas in a food processor until coarsely chopped, about 10 pulses. Stir the chopped peas into the soup and simmer until tender, 2 to 5 minutes.

3. Remove the bay leaf. Working in batches, puree the soup until smooth, 1 to 2 minutes. Return the soup to a clean pot.

4. Stir in the half-and-half and additional chicken broth as needed to adjust the soup's consistency. Heat the soup gently over low heat until hot (do not boil). Season with salt and pepper to taste and serve.

➤ VARIATION

Cream of Green Pea Soup with Prosciutto and Parmesan

Follow the recipe for Cream of Green Pea Soup, cooking 2 ounces thinly sliced prosciutto, chopped coarse, in the shimmering oil in step 1 until crisp, 5 to 7 minutes. Transfer the crisp prosciutto to a paper towel–lined plate; set aside. Add the onion to the fat left in the pot and continue to cook as directed. Substitute 2 ounces Parmesan cheese, grated (1 cup), for the half-and-half. Sprinkle individual portions with the crisp prosciutto and additional grated Parmesan before serving.

Cream of Asparagus Soup

SERVES 4 TO 6

Be sure to use fresh asparagus in this soup. Serve with Butter Croutons (page 116) or blanched asparagus tips. To blanch asparagus tips, cook them in boiling salted water until just tender, about 2 minutes. Immediately drain the tips and plunge them into ice water to stop the cooking.

1	tablespoon vegetable oil
1	medium onion, chopped medium
3	medium garlic cloves, minced or pressed through a garlic press (about 1 tablespoon)
1	tablespoon unbleached all-purpose flour
¼	cup dry white wine
2	cups low-sodium chicken broth, plus extra as needed
2	cups vegetable broth
1½	pounds asparagus (about 1½ bunches), tough ends trimmed (see the illustration at right), and cut into ½-inch lengths
1	bay leaf
½	cup half-and-half
	Salt and ground black pepper

1. Heat the oil in a large Dutch oven over medium heat until shimmering. Add the onion and cook until softened, 5 to 7 minutes. Stir in the garlic and cook until fragrant, about 30 seconds. Stir in the flour and cook for 1 minute. Stir in the wine, scraping up any browned bits, and cook until almost completely evaporated, about 1 minute.

2. Gradually whisk in the chicken broth and vegetable broth, smoothing out any lumps, and bring to a simmer. Stir in the asparagus and bay leaf, reduce to a simmer, and cook until the asparagus is tender, 7 to 10 minutes

3. Remove the bay leaf. Working in batches, puree the soup until smooth, 1 to 2 minutes. Return the soup to a clean pot.

4. Stir in the half-and-half and additional chicken broth as needed to adjust the soup's consistency. Heat the soup gently over low heat until hot (do not boil). Season with salt and pepper to taste and serve.

➤ VARIATION

Cream of Asparagus Soup with Leeks and Tarragon

Follow the recipe for Cream of Asparagus Soup, substituting 1 medium leek, white and light green part only, halved lengthwise, sliced ¼ inch thick, and rinsed thoroughly (see the illustrations on page 103), for the onion. Stir 2 teaspoons minced fresh tarragon leaves into the soup before serving.

TRIMMING TOUGH ENDS FROM ASPARAGUS

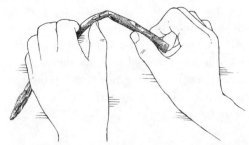

In our tests, we found that the tough, woody part of the stem will break off in just the right place if you hold the spear the right way. With one hand, hold the asparagus about halfway down the stalk; with the thumb and index fingers of the other hand, hold the spear about an inch up from the bottom. Bend the stalk until it snaps.

Pureed Soups 101

Pureed soups offer a smooth, velvety texture that seems very sophisticated. In reality, the method is quite simple and straightforward. Here's what you need to know.

CHOOSING EQUIPMENT

FOOD PROCESSOR

The food processor does a decent job of pureeing, but some small bits of vegetables can get trapped under the blade. Also, if you fill your workbowl too much, liquid can leak through the blade hole. Remember to fill the workbowl no more than a third full, so that the liquid doesn't leak out.

IMMERSION BLENDER

The immersion blender has appeal because it can be brought to the pot, eliminating the need to ladle hot ingredients from one vessel to another. However, we found that this kind of blender can leave unblended bits of food behind, and can make a mess if you're not careful. When using an immersion blender, tip the pot to one side to collect the soup, and make sure the blade of the blender is fully immersed before using.

STANDARD BLENDER
The Test Kitchen Favorite

We found that a standard blender turns out the smoothest pureed soups. The blade on the blender does an excellent job with soups because it pulls ingredients down from the top of the container. No stray bits go untouched by the blade. And as long as plenty of headroom is left at the top of the blender, there is no leakage. To prevent a mess, make sure the blender is filled only two-thirds full (or less) and hold the lid in place with a kitchen towel. Pulse a couple times before blending continuously.

CLEANING THE EQUIPMENT

Cleaning dirty blenders can be frustrating and dangerous. Fortunately, we have a few tricks up our sleeve. To clean an immersion blender, we recommend placing the dirty blender blade in a bowl of hot soapy water in the sink. Then turn on the blender to whirl away stuck-on food and rinse it with hot water. To clean a regular blender, the idea is the same—simply fill the blender with warm soapy water, then blend until the blades and jar are mostly clean. Finally, rinse out the blender. There are no special instructions for cleaning a food processor—since the blade detaches, the bowl is easy to clean—just take care when handling the sharp blade.

HOW TO MAKE PUREED SOUPS

With just a few minor exceptions, nearly all pureed vegetable soups are made the same way. Once you learn the basic method, you can easily add other flavors to suit your own tastes.

1. Sauté the Aromatics

As with most soups, you need to start with a few basic aromatics, like onion and sometimes garlic. Sautéing the aromatics before simmering enhances and deepens their flavors.

2. Add Vegetables and Broth and Simmer

Add the vegetables and broth and simmer gently until the vegetables are tender. Don't be tempted to overcook the vegetables to make them more tender for easier pureeing, or to deepen the flavor—this doesn't work. You want the vegetables to be tender, but still taste fresh for a soup with great flavor.

3. Puree the Soup

Working in batches, puree the soup until it is completely smooth. Depending on what you use to puree the soup (blender, immersion blender, or food processor), this can take a few minutes, so be patient.

4. Return to a Clean Pot and Stir in Dairy, if Necessary

Return the soup to a clean pot and gently reheat until it is hot before serving. If your soup has dairy, stir it in before reheating. But note that lean dairy products, such as milk and half-and-half, have a tendency to curdle when boiled, so these soups should be heated gently—simply heat over low heat until hot. This is also a good time to adjust the soup's consistency with additional broth if it looks too thick.

CARROT-GINGER SOUP

SWEET, SUNNY CARROTS SOFTEN AND mellow once cooked, making them a perfect candidate for a creamy soup. But so often we've found carrot soups miss the mark, from lean, brothy concoctions marred by tiny bits of unpureed carrot to creamy ultrarich versions that taste more of butter and cream than carrot. We've also been faced with nearly inedible versions that turn out thick and bland. Because the flavor of carrots can be somewhat quiet, ginger is often added to provide additional depth, but too often the ginger is out of whack. What's the secret to really great carrot soup—one with a bright, sweet flavor and rich, creamy body? We set out to find the answers.

To get the lay of the land, we reviewed several pureed carrot soup recipes. The use of a thickener stood out in a number of them. Carrots are already fairly starchy—once pureed into a soup, do they even require a thickener? Flour was used in some recipes (and we use it often as a thickener when working with more watery vegetables such as asparagus and broccoli). We gave it a whirl and weren't surprised by the thick and gummy results. Other recipes used potatoes or rice as thickeners, usually cooked right along with the carrots in the broth. We tried this and found that the potatoes and rice detracted from the carrot flavor and caused the color of the soup to fade. Where did that leave us for our next test? Using no thickener at all. This was our best soup yet—the texture had lost the gumminess and the flavor was definitely more vibrant.

Next, we looked at the ratios of carrots to broth. Most seemed to use a fairly modest amount of carrots—around ¾ pound for 4 cups broth—resulting in weak flavor in the end. We played around with the ratios until we made a soup that pleased everyone—a whopping 1½ pounds of carrots for 4 cups of broth. For broth, tasters unanimously chose chicken broth. For vegetarians, our Vegetable Broth (page 22) can be used, but tasters found store-bought vegetable broth detracted from the carrot flavor. We also found that as we did for the longer-cooking stems in our Cream of Broccoli Soup (page 118), it was important to start the carrots early by sautéing them with the aromatics—this extracted maximum flavor from the vegetable.

Increasing the amount of carrots in the soup not only resulted in better flavor, but a thicker body as well. After we pureed the soup, we returned it to a pot to add some cream. We used about one cup of cream to get the right consistency, but this was too much dairy fat for our taste. Lesser amounts yielded better flavor but an overly thick consistency. We tried substituting half-and-half as well as whole milk. Half-and-half was good, but still a little too rich for the carrot flavor. Whole milk did the trick, giving the soup a smooth and creamy texture without overwhelming the carrot flavor.

Finally we were ready to examine the ginger component of the soup. Ginger's warm, spicy flavor works especially well with mild, sweet carrots. Off the bat we dismissed ground ginger—its flavor is at home in some baked goods but in soup, it simply gets lost in the mix. Four teaspoons of grated fresh ginger, sautéed just after the aromatics, infused the soup with a spicy punch while keeping the carrot flavor intact. In addition, we found that supplementing the milk with a little orange juice lent the soup a bright, citrusy freshness. Anything but boring, our carrot-ginger soup is a velvety mix of warm flavors.

Carrot-Ginger Soup

SERVES 4 TO 6

Do not substitute ground ginger for the fresh ginger here. Serve with Butter Croutons (page 116). See page 121 for more information on pureeing soup.

2	tablespoons vegetable oil
1½	pounds carrots (about 9 medium), peeled and chopped medium
1	medium onion, chopped medium
4	teaspoons minced or grated fresh ginger (see note) (see the illustrations on page 89)
4	cups low-sodium chicken broth, plus extra as needed
¾	cup whole milk
¼	cup orange juice
	Salt and ground black pepper
1	tablespoon minced fresh chives

1. Heat the oil in a large Dutch oven over medium heat until shimmering. Add the carrots and onion and cook until the vegetables are softened, 7 to 10 minutes. Stir in the ginger and cook until fragrant, about 30 seconds.

2. Stir in the chicken broth and bring to a boil. Reduce to a simmer and cook until carrots are tender, 20 to 30 minutes.

3. Working in batches, puree the soup until smooth, 1 to 2 minutes. Return the soup to a clean pot.

4. Stir in the milk, orange juice, and additional broth as needed to adjust the soup's consistency. Heat the soup gently over low heat until hot (do not boil). Season with salt and pepper to taste and serve, sprinkling individual portions with the chives.

ROASTED RED PEPPER SOUP

WE LOVE THE RAW, SWEET CRUNCH OF RED bell peppers tossed into a salad or swiped into a creamy dip. But roasting red bell peppers really makes them shine by transforming their character into something smoky and rich. With a host of pureed vegetable soups behind us, we turned to creating a soup that showcases the intense, vibrant flavor of red bell peppers.

To start, we reviewed several recipes found in our research for pureed roasted red pepper soup. At its foundation, the soup is little more than aromatics like onion and garlic, roasted peppers, and broth simmered together to blend the flavors, then pureed to a velvety consistency.

We began from the ground up and started our testing with the aromatics. While we normally reach for standard yellow onions when beginning to build a soup, we favored red onions in this instance for their intense sweetness and red color, which intensified the soup's hue once pureed. For

richness, olive oil won out over butter and vegetable oil as the cooking medium, providing the best flavor and fruitiness to the soup.

Garlic and broth were the next ingredients to try. We wanted a distinct garlic bite to the soup to accent the sweetness of the peppers, but we did not want the garlic to overpower them. Quickly sautéed minced garlic—the fastest and easiest method—delivered the best flavor. For broth, chicken broth was favored over both beef and vegetable broth. Its mild, rich flavor took a back seat to the peppers but provided much-needed body. Beef broth was overwhelming and vegetable broth lacked presence.

With the basics settled, we moved on to the star of the soup: the peppers. Although many modern recipes we found for roasted red pepper soup call for jarred roasted red peppers, we found they made for a nasty soup. No matter how well we rinsed and dried the jarred peppers, the undesirable acrid flavor from the packing liquid always found its way into the broth and ruined it. Freshly roasted sweet red bell peppers, on the other hand, had a clean, complex, smoky flavor that tasters could not get enough of.

After some trial and error, we found that the best way to roast bell peppers was to cut them and then broil them on a rack set about 3 inches from the broiler element for eight to 10 minutes. The peppers consistently achieved a meaty texture and rich flavor. In addition, peppers that have been cut open and roasted under the broiler are easier to peel than peppers roasted by any other method. The skin blackens and swells up like a balloon and lifts off in large sections.

Unless you have asbestos fingers, roasted peppers need time to cool before handling, and covering them so they steam as they cool makes the charred skin a bit easier to peel off. The ideal cooling time is 10 minutes—any less and the peppers are still too hot to work with comfortably. Also, seeding the peppers before roasting makes it possible to peel the peppers without having to rinse them to wash away the seeds. If you are still tempted to rinse, notice the rich oils that cling to the peppers as you peel them. It seems silly to rinse away those oils since they add so much flavor to the soup. Coarsely chopping the peppers allowed them to soften quickly and blend into the soup easier.

Once pureed, the soup tasted bold and sweet, but tasters found the consistency to be lacking in body. Looking for a solution, we tried adding a little flour and tomato paste—a technique that we had found worked well in creating body quickly in our beef soups. Tasting the results, we instantly knew we had hit our mark; the flour had thickened the soup perfectly, while the tomato paste provided the necessary body. We also decided to stir in a little half-and-half and a splash of sherry once the soup was pureed, which added a richness and sweetness that balanced the flavor of the peppers.

With a basic recipe mastered, we were ready to tackle additional seasonings. We wanted to keep them simple and nonintrusive—just zippy enough to highlight the peppers. While we had been using quickly sautéed garlic in the basic soup, we felt garlic sautéed slowly until just straw-colored would have a nuttier, sweeter flavor that would complement the smoky flavors already in the soup. Minced and pressed garlic tends to burn quickly, so we made sure to cook it over low heat, which allowed for slower, more easily controlled cooking. Sautéing the garlic this way brought out its sweet, nutty edge as we had hoped and tasters praised the additional flavor it contributed to the soup.

Our soup was on its way, but we still wanted to include some additional warm flavors. A little ground cumin helped, but it wasn't until we added some smoked paprika that the soup's flavors really came alive. The smoky flavor is strong, not subtle—just ½ teaspoon was all it took to impart its flavor throughout the soup.

For a final garnish, we found the fresh bite of cilantro worked best. We also created a simple sour cream sauce enriched with a little lime juice and lime zest for a burst of bright flavor. Drizzled over each portion before serving, it was the perfect complement to the soup.

Roasted Red Pepper Soup with Smoked Paprika and Cilantro Cream
SERVES 8

The flavor of this soup depends on homemade roasted red peppers; do not substitute jarred red peppers. Be sure to keep your eye on the peppers as they broil in step 2; the broiling time may vary depending on the intensity of your broiler. Sweet paprika can be substituted for the smoked paprika if necessary. See page 121 for more information on pureeing soup.

CILANTRO CREAM

¾	cup sour cream
¼	cup whole milk
1	tablespoon minced fresh cilantro leaves
1	tablespoon juice from 1 lime
½	teaspoon grated zest from 1 lime
	Salt and ground black pepper

SOUP

8	red bell peppers, trimmed, cored, and flattened (see the illustrations on page 125)
1	tablespoon olive oil
2	medium garlic cloves, minced or pressed through a garlic press (about 2 teaspoons)
1	medium red onion, chopped medium
½	teaspoon ground cumin
½	teaspoon smoked paprika
2	tablespoons tomato paste
1	tablespoon unbleached all-purpose flour
4	cups low-sodium chicken broth, plus extra as needed
1	bay leaf
½	cup half-and-half
2	tablespoons dry sherry
2	tablespoons minced fresh cilantro leaves
	Salt and ground black pepper

1. FOR THE CILANTRO CREAM: Whisk all the ingredients together in a small bowl and season with salt and pepper to taste. Cover with plastic wrap and refrigerate until needed.

2. For the soup: Position an oven rack 3 inches from the broiler element and heat the broiler. Following the illustrations below, spread half of the peppers out over a foil-lined baking sheet and broil until the skin is charred and puffed but the flesh is still firm, 8 to 10 minutes, rotating the pan halfway through broiling.

3. Transfer the broiled peppers to a bowl, cover with aluminum foil, and let steam until the skins peel off easily, 10 to 15 minutes. Repeat with the remaining peppers. Peel all of the broiled peppers, discard the skins, and chop coarse.

4. Cook the oil and garlic together in a large Dutch oven over low heat, stirring constantly, until the garlic is foamy, sticky, and straw-colored, 8 to 10 minutes. Stir in the onion, increase the heat to medium, and cook until softened, 5 to 7 minutes.

5. Stir in the cumin and smoked paprika and cook until fragrant, about 30 seconds. Stir in the tomato paste and flour and cook for 1 minute. Gradually whisk in the chicken broth, smoothing out any lumps. Stir in the bay leaf and chopped roasted peppers, bring to a simmer, and cook until the peppers are very tender, 5 to 7 minutes.

6. Remove the bay leaf. Working in batches, puree the soup until smooth, 1 to 2 minutes. Return the soup to a clean pot.

7. Stir in the half-and-half, sherry, and additional broth as needed to adjust the soup's consistency. Heat the soup gently over low heat until hot (do not boil). Stir in the cilantro and season with salt and pepper to taste. Serve, drizzling individual portions with the cilantro cream.

ROASTING BELL PEPPERS

1. Slice ¼ inch from the top and bottom of the bell pepper, then gently remove the stem from the top slice.

2. Pull the core out of the pepper.

3. Make a slit down one side of the pepper, then lay it flat, skin side down, in one long strip. Slide a sharp knife along the inside of the pepper and remove all ribs and seeds.

4. Arrange the strips of peppers and the tops and bottoms skin side up on a foil-lined baking sheet. Flatten the strips with the palm of your hand.

5. Broil the peppers about 3 inches below the broiler element until the skin of the peppers is charred and puffed up but the flesh is still firm. If you can't get the rack close enough to the broiler element, use an overturned rimmed baking sheet to elevate the tray of peppers closer to the broiler.

6. Transfer the broiled peppers to a bowl, cover with foil, and let steam until the skins loosen, 10 to 15 minutes. The skin should then peel off easily in large strips.

CREAMY MUSHROOM SOUP

MUSHROOMS ARE ONE OF THE MEATIEST OF vegetables: substantial, distinctive, and rich. But cream of mushroom soups can be a gamble. Some are creamy and rich—but short on mushroom flavor. Others taste inherently of mushrooms, but these soups often rely on expensive wild mushrooms. We wanted a cream of mushroom soup that had it all—a creamy, rich base with earthy mushrooom flavor at the fore. And we wanted to rely on the humble white mushroom to get there. Their flavor is somewhat elusive, so our goal was clear—find a way to coax the rich, meaty flavor from everyday white mushrooms.

In the past, we have sautéed sliced mushrooms in butter to soften them up and release their juice. But we were also interested in exploring roasting. Roasting mushrooms appealed to us not only because roasting intensifies flavor, but also because we saw it as a way of streamlining the mushroom prep. Roasting causes mushrooms to shrink considerably. We hoped that roasted mushrooms could simply be simmered whole in broth and then be pureed.

To start, we roasted mushrooms for one batch of soup and sliced and sautéed mushrooms for a second batch. Both batches were simmered in beef broth (chosen over chicken for its heartier flavor), pureed, finished with cream, and tasted. To our surprise, the roasted mushroom soup was less flavorful than the soup made with sautéed mushrooms. Juice released during the roasting process had browned on the sheet pan and was, for all intents and purposes, irretrievable. While it was a little extra work, we decided to stick with slicing our mushrooms.

Butter was the obvious fat to go with here, earning high marks for its creamy rich flavor. Four tablespoons did the trick and allowing it to brown before adding the mushrooms lent extra complexity to the soup. Leeks were more delicate tasting and more supportive of the mushroom flavor than onions and four minced garlic cloves provided an extra layer of flavor. Fragrant thyme was also included since it pairs so well with the woodsy flavor of mushrooms. After we sautéed the mixture, we added broth and simmered away until the mushrooms were tender and the flavors melded. Pureed and then finished with cream, this soup wasn't bad, but it wasn't very good either.

Taking a step back, we rifled through some French mushroom soup recipes that call for sweating the mushrooms—cooking them covered—then uncovering the pot to evaporate the excess liquid and brown the mushrooms. Could the French be on to something? We gave it a try, sweating not only the mushrooms, but the leeks, garlic, and thyme as well. After five minutes of covered cooking, we uncovered the pot and inhaled the fragrance of the mushrooms and aromatics. Things were looking good. We then continued cooking the mixture, uncovered, and watched as the mushrooms softened and turned brown. After adding the broth, we began to simmer the soup. Twenty minutes of measured simmering drained every last bit of fiber and flavor from the mushrooms and fused the small family of flavors together.

Once run through the blender and enriched with some heavy cream, the soup took on a beautiful light body with deep color. Tasters approved, but felt some contrasting texture in the smooth soup would be beneficial, so we chopped and reserved some of the cooked mushrooms before adding the broth and returned them to the soup with the cream. As a final touch some lemon juice and a splash of Madeira rounded out the flavors and added just the right touch of sweetness. Great mushroom soup, using supermarket mushrooms, wasn't as elusive as we'd thought.

Creamy Mushroom Soup

SERVES 6 TO 8

You can substitute brandy or dry sherry for the Madeira here. Serve with Garlic Croutons (page 116). See page 121 for more information on pureeing soup.

4	tablespoons (½ stick) unsalted butter
3	pounds white mushrooms, wiped clean, trimmed, and sliced thin
2	medium leeks, white and light green parts only, halved lengthwise, sliced ¼ inch thick, and rinsed thoroughly (see the illustrations on page 103)
4	medium garlic cloves, minced or pressed through a garlic press (about 4 teaspoons)
2	teaspoons minced fresh thyme leaves or ½ teaspoon dried
	Salt and ground black pepper
5	cups beef broth, plus extra as needed
½	cup Madeira, plus extra for serving
1	cup heavy cream
2	tablespoons juice from 1 lemon

1. Melt the butter in a large Dutch oven over medium-high heat and cook, stirring constantly, until it is dark golden brown and has a nutty aroma, 1 to 3 minutes. Stir in the mushrooms, leeks, garlic, thyme, ½ teaspoon salt, and ¼ teaspoon pepper, cover, and cook until the mushrooms release their liquid, about 5 minutes.

2. Uncover and continue to cook, stirring occasionally, until the liquid has evaporated and the mushrooms begin to brown, about 15 minutes longer. Remove ⅔ cup of the mushroom mixture, let it cool slightly, then chop fine; reserve separately.

3. Stir in the beef broth and Madeira, scraping up any browned bits, and bring to a boil. Reduce to a simmer and cook until the mushrooms and leeks are tender, about 20 minutes.

4. Working in batches, puree the soup until smooth, 1 to 2 minutes. Return the soup to a clean pot.

5. Stir in the heavy cream, lemon juice, reserved chopped mushrooms, and additional broth as needed to adjust the soup's consistency. Heat the soup gently over low heat until hot (do not boil). Season with salt and pepper to taste. Serve, drizzling individual portions with Madeira.

BUTTERNUT SQUASH SOUP

BUTTERNUT SQUASH SOUP IS ESSENTIALLY A simple soup. Little more than squash, cooking liquid, and a few aromatic ingredients, this soup can come together fairly easily, yet is creamy and deeply flavorful. But many squash soups fail to live up to their potential. Rather than being lustrous, slightly creamy, and intensely "squashy" in flavor, they are vegetal or porridge-like, and sometimes taste more like a sweet squash pie than a squash soup.

Knowing that our basic method would be to cook the squash and then puree it with a liquid, our first test focused on how to cook the squash for the soup. Some recipes suggest boiling the squash in a cooking liquid, others roasting it in the oven, others sautéing it on the stovetop.

We tried boiling the squash, but having to peel the tough skin away before dicing it seemed unnecessarily tedious. We eliminated the sauté technique for the same reason. While the roasting was infinitely easier than our attempts at boiling or sautéing (all we had to do was slice the squash in half, scoop out the seeds, and roast it on a rimmed baking sheet), it produced a caramel-flavored soup with a gritty texture. Roasting also took at least one hour—too long for what should be a quick, no-nonsense soup.

In an effort to conserve time without sacrificing the quick preparation we liked from the roasting test, we decided to try steaming the squash. In a large Dutch oven, we sautéed shallots in butter (we tried garlic and onion but found them too overpowering and acrid with the sweet squash), then added water to the sautéed shallots and brought the mixture to a simmer. We seeded and quartered the squash and placed it into a collapsible steaming insert, then added the squash and insert to the Dutch oven. We covered the pot and let the squash steam for about 40 minutes until it was tender. This method proved to be successful. We liked it because all of the cooking took place in just one pot and, as a bonus, we ended up with a squash-infused cooking liquid that we could use in the soup.

But there was a downside. Essentially, steaming had the opposite effect of roasting: whereas roasting concentrated the sugars and eliminated the liquid in the squash (which is what made the roasted squash soup gritty), steaming added liquid to the squash and diluted its flavor.

As we were preparing squash one morning, it occurred to us that we were throwing away the answer to more squash flavor—the seeds and fibers. Instead of trashing the scooped-out remnants, we added them to the sautéed shallots and butter. In a matter of minutes, the room became fragrant with an earthy, sweet squash aroma, and the butter in our Dutch oven turned a brilliant shade of saffron. We added the water to the pan and proceeded with the steaming preparation. After the squash was cooked through, we strained the liquid of seeds, fibers, and spent shallot, then blended the soup.

To intensify the sweetness of the squash (but not make the soup sweet), we added a teaspoon of dark brown sugar. Not only was this batch of squash soup brighter in flavor, it was more intense in color as well. To round out the flavor and introduce some richness to the soup we added ½ cup of heavy cream. Now the soup was thick, rich, and redolent of pure squash flavor.

As is true with many creamed soups, texture is almost as important as flavor. We found blending the squash in batches worked best—making it easier for the blender to smooth out any lumps or remaining squash fibers. Once all the squash was pureed to a silken texture, we transferred the soup to a clean pot and stirred in the cream and brown sugar to combine. We heated the soup briefly over low heat and stirred in a little freshly grated nutmeg. In under one hour and with only one pot, we made a squash soup that offered nothing less than autumn in a bowl.

Butternut Squash Soup
SERVES 4 TO 6

If you are short on steaming liquid after straining in step 4, add more water as needed. Serve with Cinnamon-Sugar Croutons (see page 116). See page 121 for more information on pureeing soup.

4 tablespoons (½ stick) unsalted butter, cut into ½-inch pieces

I large shallot, chopped medium (about 4 tablespoons)

3 pounds butternut squash (about I large squash), cut in half lengthwise (see the illustrations on page 129), each half cut in half widthwise; seeds and strings scraped out and reserved

6 cups water
   Salt and ground black pepper

½ cup heavy cream

I teaspoon dark brown sugar
   Pinch ground nutmeg

1. Melt 2 tablespoons of the butter in a large Dutch oven over medium heat. Add the shallot and cook until softened, 2 to 3 minutes. Add the squash seeds and strings and cook, stirring occasionally, until the butter turns orange, about 4 minutes.

2. Stir in the water and 1 teaspoon salt and bring to a boil. Reduce to a simmer, place the squash cut side down in a steamer basket, and lower the basket into the pot. Cover and steam the squash until it is completely tender, 30 to 40 minutes.

3. Using tongs, transfer the cooked squash to a rimmed baking sheet. When cool enough to handle, use a large spoon to scrape the cooked squash from the skin. Reserve the flesh and discard the skin.

4. Strain the steaming broth through a fine-mesh strainer into a large liquid measuring cup. (You should have at least 3 cups of broth; see note). Working in batches, puree the cooked squash with 3 cups of the strained broth until smooth, 1 to 2 minutes. Return the puree to a clean pot.

5. Stir in the heavy cream, brown sugar, nutmeg, and remaining 2 tablespoons butter. Return to a

brief simmer, adding additional strained squash broth as needed to adjust the soup's consistency. Season with salt and pepper to taste and serve.

➤ VARIATIONS

Butternut Squash Soup with Fennel

Follow the recipe for Butternut Squash Soup, reducing the amount of squash to 2 pounds and adding 1 teaspoon fennel seeds to the pot with the squash seeds and strings. Add 1 large fennel bulb (about 1 pound), trimmed of stalks, cored, and cut into 1-inch-thick strips (see the illustrations on page 27) to the pot with the squash.

CUTTING UP BUTTERNUT SQUASH

With its thick skin and odd shape, butternut squash is notoriously difficult to cut, even with the best chef's knife. We prefer to use a cleaver and mallet.

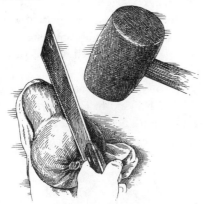

1. Set the squash on a damp kitchen towel to hold it in place. Position the cleaver on the skin of the squash.

2. Strike the back of the cleaver with a mallet to drive the cleaver deep into the squash. Continue to hit the cleaver with the mallet until the cleaver cuts completely through the squash.

Curried Butternut Squash and Apple Soup

A tart apple, such as a Granny Smith, adds a nice contrast to the sweet squash, but any type of apple may be used.

Follow the recipe for Butternut Squash Soup, reducing the amount of squash to 2½ pounds. Add 1 large apple (about 8 ounces), peeled, cored, and quartered to the pot with the squash. Substitute 2 teaspoons curry powder for the nutmeg.

Southwestern Butternut Squash Soup

To make this soup spicier, increase the amount of chipotles to taste.

Follow the recipe for Butternut Squash Soup, substituting 1 tablespoon honey for the brown sugar and ½ teaspoon ground cumin for the nutmeg. Stir 2 tablespoons minced fresh cilantro and 2 teaspoons minced chipotle chile in adobo sauce into the soup before serving.

HEARTY GARLIC-POTATO SOUP

IN THE MIDDLE OF THE 18TH CENTURY, France's wheat crop failed and baguettes could no longer be found at the local boulangerie. When the country was on the verge of crisis, the Academy of Besançon held a competition to find a food "capable of reducing the calamities of famine." Enter Antoine-Augustin Parmentier, an entrepreneurial young soldier, who won the contest by championing the humble potato. He went on to open numerous potato soup kitchens in Paris, ladling out bowls of *potage Parmentier* to hungry Frenchmen. The rustic potato soup became a classic and is still the pinnacle of simple, economical fare. Pair the potatoes with heady garlic and what the duo lacks in glamour it makes up for with rich flavor and satisfying texture.

And yet an afternoon at the stove established that the stars of this soup can also ruin it. Take, for example, a recipe culled from the Internet that called for boiling 2 pounds of potatoes and a single clove of garlic in copious amounts of water. With zero flavor and a thin, gray broth, this potion was unfit for sampling. Then there was the concoction containing five whole heads of garlic, which obliterated any hint of potato. An ideal garlic-potato soup recipe should have discernible garlic and potato flavors along with an agreeable (not-too-thick, not-too-thin) consistency.

Working with a stripped-down recipe containing a spoonful of minced garlic, chicken broth, and a splash of cream (a common enrichment), we tested batches prepared with each of the three most common potato varieties, both peeled and unpeeled. From highest to lowest starch content, they are: russet, Yukon Gold, and Red Bliss. While the hearty flavor of unpeeled Red Bliss potatoes was appealing, tasters generally leaned toward soups made with peeled russets, praising the starchy spuds for the way they broke down and thickened the broth.

With our potato decision made, we moved on to the garlic. The few cloves of minced sautéed garlic in our working recipe added pleasant background notes, but we sought more complexity. It was not surprising that increasing the amount of garlic simply fortified the soup with overpowering flavor. Looking to temper the harshness, we turned to a few different methods for mellower garlic flavor. A whole head or two of oven-roasted garlic added gentle sweetness to the soup, as did heads of garlic poached in water or milk. A more direct approach, poaching the garlic in the soup, worked just as well without requiring a second cooking vessel. The soup now tasted OK but wasn't really redolent of garlic. Maybe we'd dampened the flavor too much.

We were stuck. Sautéed garlic was too harsh and poached was too mild. We regrouped and attempted a hybrid approach, finding that, for this recipe, two methods were better than one. Combining sautéed minced garlic with whole poached garlic heads lent the complexity we were after. However, now that we were satisfied with the layers of garlic flavor in the soup, we realized that we'd thrown off the overall balance, and the potato presence was meager.

Then we remembered the earlier test where we liked the earthy flavor of Red Bliss potatoes but rejected them in favor of starchier russets.

After more tests, we found that keeping the russets but adding some Red Bliss ramped up the potato flavor nicely.

In the lexicon of French cookery, there are three classifications for soup: *consommé* describes a clear, brothy soup; *soupe* refers to a thick, chunky, stew-like mixture; and *potage* is a hybrid of consommé and soupe, being at once partly chunky and partly smooth. For our country-style soup, we followed the lead of Parmentier, adopting the texture of a potage. We pureed a portion of the soup into a creamy, smooth consistency and left the remaining chunks untouched.

The framework of the soup was now complete, and it was time for refinements. We often start our soups with sautéed aromatics, so we added the classic trio of diced carrots, onion, and celery (called mirepoix) to our recipe. The mirepoix added flavor, but not the right kind: Tasters criticized the soup for being too vegetal. Leaving the carrots and celery in the refrigerator, we prepared a batch of soup using onions alone. This was better, but not as good as the soup we prepared with leeks, a natural partner for potatoes.

For the dairy component, cream was favored over milk and half-and-half. Finally, bay leaves and fresh thyme contributed a bright herbal dimension. At this point, the soup tasted great but looked a bit

Garlic Chips

MAKES ABOUT ¼ CUP

3   tablespoons olive oil
6   medium garlic cloves, sliced thin
     lengthwise
     Salt

Heat the oil and garlic in a 10-inch skillet over medium-high heat. Cook, turning frequently, until light golden brown, about 3 minutes. Using a slotted spoon, transfer the garlic to a paper towel–lined plate; discard the oil. Season lightly with salt.

drab and pale. Our first instinct was to add a sprinkling of chives, and then we also added garlic chips. Garlic chips, fried in olive oil, really hit the mark: Their toasty, pleasantly bitter flavor and crunchy texture pushed the soup over the top. We now had a peasant's soup fit for a king.

Hearty Garlic-Potato Soup

SERVES 6

We find a garnish is essential to add crunch and flavor to this soup; we prefer Garlic Chips, but Garlic Croutons (page 116) or crisp fried bacon pieces taste good, too.

3	tablespoons unsalted butter
1	medium leek, white and light green part only, halved lengthwise, sliced ¼ inch thick, and rinsed thoroughly (see the illustrations on page 103)
3	medium garlic cloves, minced or pressed through a garlic press (about 1 tablespoon)
6	cups low-sodium chicken broth, plus extra as needed
2	bay leaves
2	large garlic heads, rinsed, outer papery skins removed, and top third of stem end sliced off to expose the garlic cloves inside
1½	pounds russet potatoes (about 3 medium), peeled and cut into ½-inch pieces
1	pound Red Bliss potatoes (about 3 medium), scrubbed and cut into ½-inch pieces
½	cup heavy cream
1½	teaspoons minced fresh thyme leaves
	Salt and ground black pepper
¼	cup minced fresh chives
	1 recipe Garlic Chips (page 130)

1. Melt the butter in a Dutch oven over low heat. Add the leek, cover, and cook, stirring occasionally, until softened, 8 to 10 minutes. Uncover, stir in the minced garlic and cook until fragrant, about 30 seconds. Stir in the chicken broth and bay leaves and bring to a boil.

2. Stir in the garlic heads, reduce to a simmer, and cover partially (leaving about 1 inch of the pot open). Cook until the garlic is very tender when pierced with the tip of a knife, 30 to 40 minutes.

3. Stir in the potatoes and continue to simmer, partially covered, until the potatoes are tender, 15 to 20 minutes.

4. Remove the bay leaves. Remove the garlic heads; using tongs or paper towels, squeeze the garlic heads at the root end until the cloves slip out of their skins. Using a fork, mash the garlic to a smooth paste in a bowl.

5. Puree 1½ cups of the potatoes and 1 cup of the broth until smooth, 1 to 2 minutes, and return to the pot.

6. Stir in the heavy cream, thyme, and half of the mashed garlic. Return to a brief simmer, adding additional broth as needed to adjust the soup's consistency. Season with the remaining garlic paste, salt, and pepper to taste. Serve, sprinkling individual portions with the chives and garlic chips before serving.

CREAMY LEEK AND POTATO SOUP

COOKS HAVE BEEN MAKING LEEK AND potato soup for centuries, but we're not sure why the recipe has persisted. The versions we've encountered inevitably fall short, turning out stodgy and gluey, or blending in so much cream or butter it's hard to detect the leek—or the potato. So we were puzzled when flipping through Julia Child's *Mastering the Art of French Cooking* we noticed that leek and potato soup opens the book. Clearly Julia Child thought highly of the soup. What were we missing?

To find out, we decided to give her recipe a closer look. Like many other cooks, she simmers equal parts potatoes and chopped leeks in water until tender. The only notable difference: Instead of pureeing the vegetables in a blender, as virtually all contemporary recipes call for, Child passes them through a food mill. Wondering if this rarely used tool made a difference, we hunted down the test kitchen's model and gave it a try. The result? A consistency that, while strewn with a few stray bits of leek, was remarkably creamy—even with just 2 tablespoons of cream. Thanks to this judicious amount of dairy, an unprecedented clear vegetable flavor came through.

That left the blender as the culprit, which we realized made some sense. When overwhipped (as in a blender), potatoes leach too much starch and turn gluey, which some recipes remedy with gobs of flavor-dulling cream—as much as a cup per pound of potato. For such a simple soup, we weren't about to require a food mill; most home cooks don't even own one. As for the cream, we wanted to keep it to 2 tablespoons to preserve the taste of the vegetables.

Putting the glueyness problem on hold, we drew up a basic recipe to evaluate potato types: Sweat the white parts of four leeks in butter, then add a quart of water and a pound of potatoes. Yukon Golds tasted too distinct, and waxy Red Bliss potatoes failed to break down; russets fared best. A 15-minute simmer followed by a stint in the blender with a swirl of cream and our soup was ready. As expected, the consistency of this near-creamless version was gluey and the leek flavor was barely discernible.

More leeks didn't help; their flavor became sulfurous. Caramelizing them lent an off-putting browned-vegetable aroma to the soup, and sugar was too cloying. But one onion ramped up the sweetness just enough. Next, we replaced half the water with chicken broth, dropped in a bay leaf and a sprig of thyme (for grassy notes), and simmered the potent dark-green leek tops that we'd been throwing away in the broth. These steps infused the broth with a great base of bright leek flavor.

Now back to that gummy texture. The only thing left to tinker with was the potato. The correlation was obvious: Less potato would mean less starch; less starch would mean less glueyness. To make any impact, we actually had to drop down from a pound to just 5 ounces. As tasters slurped away, it wasn't the flavor of the potatoes they missed most (the leeks provided plenty) but their thickening power. This version was brothy.

Brainstorming for a cream- and potato-free way to thicken the soup, we recalled our recipe for Creamless Creamy Tomato Soup (page 115). There, we added sandwich bread to the mix, which seamlessly added body without disturbing flavor.

Following suit, we added a slice of torn bread to the soup, but it turned out a bit gluey. On our next test, we toasted a slice to remove moisture, tore it into pieces, tossed it into our latest batch, and pureed the whole assembly. Simple, smooth, and deeply flavorful, this soup had it all.

Creamy Leek and Potato Soup
SERVES 4 TO 6

Use the lowest setting on your toaster to dry out the bread without browning it too much. Garlic Chips (page 130) or Garlic Croutons (page 116) work well with this soup. See page 121 for more information on pureeing soup.

4	medium leeks, dark green leaves cut into 2-inch pieces and washed, white and light green parts halved lengthwise, sliced ¼ inch thick, and rinsed thoroughly (about 6 cups) (see the illustrations on page 103)
2	cups low-sodium chicken broth, plus extra as needed
2	cups water
4	tablespoons (½ stick) unsalted butter
1	medium onion, chopped medium
	Salt and ground black pepper
1	bay leaf
1	sprig fresh thyme or tarragon
1	small russet potato (about 5 ounces), peeled and cut into ½-inch pieces
1	slice high-quality white sandwich bread, lightly toasted and torn into ½-inch pieces

1. Bring the dark green leek leaves, chicken broth, and water to a boil in a large Dutch oven. Reduce the heat to low, cover, and simmer for 20 minutes. Strain the broth through a fine-mesh strainer, pressing on the solids to release as much liquid as possible.

2. Melt the butter in the pot over low heat. Add the white and light green leeks, onion, and 1 teaspoon salt, cover, and cook, stirring occasionally, until the vegetables are softened, 8 to 10 minutes. Stir in the strained broth, bay leaf, and thyme and bring to a boil.

3. Stir in the potato, reduce to a gentle simmer, and cook until tender, 20 to 25 minutes. Stir in

the toasted bread and continue to simmer until the bread is saturated and starts to break down, about 5 minutes.

4. Working in batches, puree the soup until smooth, 1 to 2 minutes. Return the soup to a clean pot and return to a brief simmer, adding additional broth as needed to adjust the soup's consistency. Season with salt and pepper to taste and serve.

CHEDDAR CHEESE SOUP

WHEN MADE WELL, CHEDDAR CHEESE SOUP IS a rich, elegant dish. It should burst with cheese flavor, but the dairy element should not be overpowering. The color should be an inviting, warm yellow, not shocking orange. Using white cheddar instead of orange cheddar seemed a good start, but we knew the recipe would be more complicated to develop than simply choosing a cheese.

For our first tests we tried three recipes. The first was very simple, using a basic béchamel sauce that was finished with some cheese. Butter and flour were cooked to create a roux, milk was added to form the béchamel, and shredded cheese was stirred in at the end. The second recipe was essentially the same except that cream was used in place of the milk and some onions were sautéed in the butter. The third recipe was more complex. It began by sautéing mirepoix (diced onions, carrots, and celery) in butter. Flour was added to form a roux, but the liquid was a blend of milk and chicken broth. Aromatics were simmered to add flavor to the soup, which was processed until smooth and then finished with cheese just before serving.

The results were as expected. This simple soup of béchamel with cheese had little flavor. The second version with cream and onions had better flavor, but still didn't score high marks. The third soup was the best of the lot. The combination of the mirepoix, chicken broth, and bay leaf made this soup taste more interesting than the others, but it was not without problems. It lacked a good cheddar punch.

We came away from this initial round of testing with these observations. Cheddar cheese soup needs both sautéed vegetables (mirepoix) and chicken broth. Without both, the soup has a one-dimensional, lactose-heavy flavor that's hard to distinguish from good-quality nacho sauce.

We made our third recipe (made with the mirepoix) our working recipe and started some experiments. We tried half-and-half in place of the milk and the soup improved greatly. The extra fat made the soup rich and luxurious, but not too much so. Cheddar cheese is the focal point of this soup and we fussed with the amount of cheese until we dared go no higher. We ended up with 12 ounces of cheese for 5 cups of liquid. Our recipe calls for more cheese than any recipe we uncovered in our research.

We tried a variety of white American cheddars in our recipe and, although there were differences, they all worked. Aged, crumbly English (or farmhouse) cheddars didn't work as well, however, because they were too dry, difficult to melt, and made the soup taste grainy. As for the differences between mild, sharp, and extra-sharp, we found that an extra-sharp cheddar makes the soup piquant, while mild cheddar produces a bland soup. We decided to steer a middle course and use sharp cheddar cheese. Owing to the amount of cheese used, the soup does reflect the flavor of the cheese, whatever its quality or degree of sharpness.

Up until this point in our testing, we had based all of the soups on a roux. However, we had uncovered several recipes without any flour or a roux. Most of these recipes called for reducing half-and-half to thicken the soup. We were intrigued by these recipes and tried several. While this method does work, we found that it produces a soup that is much less stable. The roux, on the other hand, provides a stable, starchy base into which we could easily load a lot of cheese without worrying about the soup separating, or curdling. So we experimented with the amount of flour and found that 2 tablespoons of flour and 3 tablespoons of butter make enough roux to thicken and stabilize 6 cups of soup without making it gummy.

After testing several seasonings, we decided to include a pinch of cayenne, a drizzle of dry sherry, and a sprinkling of fresh thyme. The cayenne added a touch of heat and helped balance the richness in this soup. The dry sherry brought the various flavors together and gave the soup a more refined taste. The fresh thyme was a nice complement to the cheddar. No one really liked Worcestershire sauce or dry mustard, common additions in other recipes.

As for the cooking process, it is very easy to sauté the vegetables in butter, add flour to make a roux, then whisk in the broth and half-and-half, add a bay leaf, and simmer until the vegetables are tender. The real trick to making this soup is in how you add the cheese. Even with a roux, this soup can easily separate because so much cheese is used. We found that it was best to puree the soup base first before incorporating the cheese. Brought to a simmer, then taken off the heat, the soup was able to accommodate the cheese without a problem.

The final soup is fantastic. It is elegant and has a great cheddar punch without being too thick or chalky. It's perfect on a winter's day. Best of all, it can be made—start to finish—in about 30 minutes.

Cheddar Cheese Soup

SERVES 4 TO 6

For the best flavor, use a sharp cheddar here. Also, be sure to choose a cheddar that is firm and shreds; do not use crumbly, aged English (or farmhouse) cheddars here. See page 121 for more information on pureeing soup.

3	tablespoons unsalted butter
1	medium onion, chopped medium
1	carrot, chopped medium
1	celery rib, chopped medium
1	small shallot, chopped medium (about 2 tablespoons)
1	medium garlic clove, minced or pressed through a garlic press (about 1 teaspoon)
1	tablespoon minced fresh thyme leaves or 1 teaspoon dried
2	tablespoons unbleached all-purpose flour
2½	cups low-sodium chicken broth
2½	cups half-and-half
1	bay leaf

3	tablespoons dry sherry Pinch cayenne pepper
12	ounces sharp cheddar cheese, shredded (3 cups) Salt and ground black pepper

1. Melt the butter in a large Dutch oven over medium heat. Add the onion, carrot, celery, and shallot and cook until the vegetables are softened, 7 to 10 minutes. Stir in the garlic and thyme and cook until fragrant, about 30 seconds. Stir in the flour and cook for 1 minute.

2. Gradually whisk in the chicken broth and half-and-half, smoothing out any lumps. Add the bay leaf, bring to a simmer, and cook until the vegetables are tender, 20 to 25 minutes.

3. Remove the bay leaf. Working in batches, puree the soup until smooth, 1 to 2 minutes. Return the soup to a clean pot and return to a simmer.

4. Off the heat, stir in the sherry and cayenne. Slowly whisk in the cheese, one handful at a time, until smooth. Season with salt and pepper to taste and serve.

➤ VARIATIONS

Cheddar Cheese and Ale Soup with Potato

We find that inexpensive, light-colored ales work best here. Heartier ales can be used, however they will produce a darker, more potent-tasting soup.

Follow the recipe for Cheddar Cheese Soup, reducing the amount of chicken broth to 1 cup and whisking 1½ cups ale into the pot with the broth and half-and-half. Add 1 medium Yukon Gold potato (about 8 ounces), peeled and cut into ½-inch pieces, to the pot with the bay leaf. Reduce the amount of sherry to 2 tablespoons.

Cheddar Cheese and Broccoli Soup

Follow the recipe for Cheddar Cheese Soup, adding 8 ounces broccoli florets, chopped fine (about 2 cups) to the pureed soup after returning to a simmer in step 3; continue to simmer the soup until the broccoli is tender, about 10 minutes, before continuing with step 4.

7

BEAN SOUPS

Bean Soups

~~~~~~

Hearty Tuscan White Bean Soup

WHITE BEANS PLAY A STARRING ROLE IN innumerable soups, but one of our favorites is Tuscan white bean soup, which boasts creamy, tender beans in a light, velvety broth. Cannellini (white kidney beans) are the region's most famous legume, and Tuscan cooks go to great extremes to ensure that these beans cook up incredibly tender every time. Simmering the cannellini in rainwater to produce an almost buttery texture is not uncommon. And putting the beans in an empty wine bottle to slow-cook overnight in a fire's dying embers is not unheard of. We set out to make a hearty version of classic Tuscan white bean soup that was just as good as what we'd find in Italy, but we hoped to ditch the fire and rainwater in favor of a more practical approach.

The first task was to sort through all the contradictory advice given for dried-bean cookery. We began with the most hotly contested issue: how long to soak the beans before cooking. Some recipes swear that a lengthy soak leads to beans with a more tender, uniform texture. Others insist that a quick soak—an hour-long rest off the stove covered with just-boiled water—is best. In the past, our own research has shown that no soak at all can be the way to go.

To judge for ourselves, we cooked up batches of beans using all three approaches. To our surprise, we found relatively minor differences. The biggest difference was in the cooking time: The no-soak beans took 45 minutes longer to soften fully than the beans soaked by the other two methods. Since the beans soaked overnight were, in fact, the most tender and evenly cooked of the bunch and had the least number of exploded beans, that's the method we settled on.

But while the beans' interiors were creamy, their skins remained tough. Like length of soaking, when to add salt is another much-debated topic in bean cookery. We decided to investigate the matter.

The conventional wisdom is that salt added to beans at the beginning of cooking will prevent them from ever fully softening, so they remain gritty. Paradoxically, other advice maintains that salting beans too early can create a mushy texture. When we added salt to a batch of beans at the outset of cooking, we found that it made some of the beans mealy. We checked with our science editor and learned that the salt effect may be a matter of semantics. As beans cook, their starch granules swell with water, softening to a creamy texture and eventually bursting. The presence of salt in the cooking water causes the starch granules to swell less, so that fewer reach the point of bursting. The result: beans that have a lot of starch granules still intact. To us, the texture of such beans is mealy; others may call the same effect gritty.

Though the texture of the beans was now inferior, their skins were exactly what we wanted: soft and pliable. Was there a different way to use salt to get the same effect? Our thoughts turned to brining, which we use in the test kitchen to help meat trap water and remain moist during cooking. Over the years, we've brined everything from poultry and pork to beef and even shrimp. We had a hunch it might work with beans too, so we made a brine by dissolving a few tablespoons of salt in water and left the beans to soak overnight in the solution. The next day, we rinsed the beans before proceeding with the recipe. Our experiment was a success: The cannellini now boasted tender, almost imperceptible skins with interiors that were buttery soft. As it turns out, when beans are soaked in salted water, rather than being cooked in it, not as much salt enters the beans. Its impact is confined mainly to the skins, where sodium ions interact with the cells to create a softer texture. (See page 145 for more information.)

Although tasters were impressed with this technique, we were getting snide comments about the number of exploded beans in the pot. Usually the culprit is vigorously bubbling cooking liquid, which causes the beans to blow out and disintegrate. We would need to simmer the beans very gently. Thinking back to the Tuscan technique of cooking beans overnight in a dying fire, we wondered if we might simply try cooking our beans in the oven. In our next test, we brought the beans and water to a simmer on the stovetop, then covered the pot and placed it in a 250-degree oven. This method required a little more time, but it worked beautifully, producing perfectly cooked beans that stayed intact.

With tender, creamy beans in our pot, it was time to work on the soup's other flavors. Salt-cured Italian bacon, or pancetta, is traditional in Tuscan white bean soup, lending depth and flavor. Earthy-tasting kale, another Tuscan favorite, made the soup more substantial; canned diced tomatoes, carrots, celery, onion, and lots of garlic contributed a pungent, vegetal aroma. For extra richness, we replaced some of the water in the soup with chicken broth (low-sodium, to compensate for the additional salt from brining); the long simmering time in the oven infused the broth with loads of flavor, so we decided store-bought broth would work well in this recipe. We sautéed the onion and celery (reserving the carrots, kale, and tomatoes) with the pancetta, added the beans and liquid, and placed the soup in the oven. The acid in tomatoes can toughen beans, so we rinsed the tomatoes and waited until the beans were sufficiently softened, about 45 minutes, before adding them to the pot, along with the kale and carrots (so they wouldn't overcook). The final touch: a sprig of rosemary,

steeped in the soup just before serving, which infused the broth with a delicate herbal aroma.

To make our soup even more substantial, we made garlic toasts and served them on the side. But watching tasters lustily dip their bread in the broth gave us an even better idea—setting the toasts in the bowls first, then ladling the soup on top, which slowly "melted" the bread and slightly thickened the broth. Drizzled with fruity extra-virgin olive oil, this hearty soup was pure comfort food.

Hearty Tuscan White Bean Soup

SERVES 8

If you can't find pancetta, substitute 4 ounces of bacon (about 4 slices). The garlic toasts, which are optional, will turn this soup into a more substantial dish.

6	ounces pancetta, chopped fine (see note)
1	tablespoon extra-virgin olive oil, plus extra for serving
1	large onion, chopped medium
2	celery ribs, chopped medium
8	medium garlic cloves, minced or pressed through a garlic press (about 8 teaspoons)
5	cups low-sodium chicken broth
3	cups water
1	pound dried cannellini beans, picked over, salt-soaked (see page 145), and rinsed
2	bay leaves
1	(14.5-ounce) can diced tomatoes, drained and rinsed
½	bunch kale or collard greens (about 8 ounces), stemmed, and leaves chopped into 1-inch pieces (see the illustrations on page 56)
2	carrots, peeled and cut into ½-inch pieces
1	sprig fresh rosemary
	Salt and ground black pepper
1	recipe Garlic Toasts (optional)

1. Adjust an oven rack to the lower-middle position and heat the oven to 250 degrees. Cook the pancetta and oil together in a large Dutch oven over medium heat until the pancetta is rendered and lightly browned, about 8 minutes. Stir in the

---

Garlic Toasts

MAKES 8 SLICES

Be sure to use a high-quality crusty bread, such as a baguette; do not use sliced sandwich bread.

8	(1-inch-thick) slices of rustic bread
1	large garlic clove, peeled
3	tablespoons extra-virgin olive oil
	Salt and ground black pepper

Position an oven rack 6 inches from the broiler element and heat the broiler. Spread the bread out over a rimmed baking sheet and broil until golden brown on both sides, about 2 minutes per side. Briefly rub one side of each toast with the garlic. Drizzle the toasts with the oil, season with salt and pepper to taste, and serve.

onion and celery and cook until the vegetables are softened and lightly browned, 12 to 15 minutes.

2. Stir in the garlic and cook until fragrant, about 30 seconds. Stir in the broth, water, soaked beans, and bay leaves and bring to a boil. Cover the pot, transfer to the oven, and cook until the beans are almost tender, 45 to 60 minutes.

3. Stir in the tomatoes, kale, and carrots and continue to cook, covered, in the oven until the beans and vegetables are fully tender, 30 to 40 minutes longer.

4. Remove the pot from the oven. Submerge the rosemary sprig in the soup, cover, and let it steep off the heat for 15 minutes. Remove the bay leaves and rosemary sprig and season with salt and pepper to taste. If desired, use the back of a spoon to mash some beans against the side of the pot to thicken the soup. To serve, place the garlic toasts (if using) into individual bowls, ladle the soup over the top, and drizzle lightly with additional olive oil.

➤ VARIATION

Hearty Vegetarian Tuscan White Bean Soup

Follow the recipe for Hearty Tuscan White Bean Soup, omitting the pancetta and adding ½ ounce dried porcini mushrooms, rinsed and minced, to the pot with the onion. Substitute 4 cups Vegetable Broth (page 22) for the chicken broth and increase the amount of water to 4 cups.

HEARTY 15-BEAN AND VEGETABLE SOUP

DRY BEAN SOUP MIXES, BOTH THE EVERYDAY supermarket type and the boutique versions that are a mainstay of craft fairs and gourmet food shops, promise a short-cut route to a flavorful bean soup. The idea is that you get your soup ingredients in one package (seasonings, vegetables, an array of beans); the shopping, measuring, and prep work is done for you. The cooking method couldn't be easier—simply dump everything into a pot, add some water, turn on the burner, and an hour or two later you have a hearty, homemade soup. With the

exception of a few stray ingredients—a chopped onion or a ham hock, perhaps—there is nothing else to purchase or prepare. Whether the packaging is fancy or no-frills, however, the soup produced by these mixes is invariably disappointing. Different beans cook at different rates, leaving some of the beans blown-out and disintegrated while others are still rock-hard; the dried seasonings (often a dubious envelope of powder ominously labeled "flavoring packet") offer zero flavor, instead making the soup taste dusty and stale; and the petrified bits of vegetables that resemble astronaut food belong in a museum, not in a soup bowl.

Still, we didn't want to give up on the idea of a hearty bean and vegetable soup made from a bean mix. After all, those mixes do offer convenience and value and most contain a tempting mix of legumes such as white beans, cranberry beans, black-eyed peas, baby limas, and pintos along with various kinds of lentils and split peas. Bean mix in hand, we ditched the flavor packet and instead opted to focus on building our own flavor from scratch with fresh vegetables and a savory broth.

Putting aside the other components of the soup for the time being, we focused on the beans. Different beans, of course, have different cooking times, and since we would be cooking 15 in one pot, the challenge would be to get them to cook evenly. We suspected that brining the beans (soaking them in salt water) before cooking might be the first step on the path to a foolproof recipe. Brining is something we've done a lot with meat—it helps the meat trap water and remain moist while cooking. When applied to beans, we found that brining softens the bean skins and evens out the cooking time, so that fewer beans burst during cooking. Following the soak, we borrowed the cooking technique we employed in our Hearty Tuscan White Bean Soup (page 138). After bringing the beans to a simmer on the stovetop, we transferred them to a 250-degree oven, where the low, constant heat of the oven cooked them as gently and evenly as possible. With these two techniques in our arsenal, we were able to achieve uniformly cooked, tender beans with mostly intact skins.

With the beans figured out, we addressed the other elements. The first step to building flavor in soup is sautéing aromatics. We chose onion, carrot, thyme, and garlic and sautéed them in oil to draw out their flavor. Next we added the soaked beans, a couple of bay leaves, and the cooking liquid, water cut with store-bought chicken broth (we'd tweak the ratio later). Most of the bean mixes we found incorporated pork (such as smoked sausage or a ham hock). We thought the soup would benefit from something meaty and rich so we followed suit. We tried ham steak, ham hock, and sausage, but they all had too distinct a presence in the soup and stole the spotlight. Bacon, in addition to being convenient, added a savory depth and a touch of smokiness without drawing too much attention to itself. To get the most flavor from the bacon, we cut it into small pieces and rendered its fat to sauté the aromatics (instead of using the oil).

Next we considered what vegetables to add to the soup. Mushrooms added an appealing meaty texture and held up to the long cooking time of the beans. For convenience, we used the supermarket standard, white mushrooms. Tasters were happy with their texture but wanted the soup to have more mushroom flavor overall. In the test kitchen we often use a small amount of dried porcini to enhance the flavor of fresh mushrooms. One ounce of rinsed, minced porcini added to the pot with the aromatics made the soup taste muddy, but ½ ounce was just right. As they cooked, the minced porcini broke down and infused the soup with their rich, earthy flavor.

Looking at our bowls of soup, we thought something green was missing. Swiss chard added a fresh, bright element and some textural interest. Chard stems and leaves have different cooking times, so it's best to separate them. We chopped the stems fine and added them to the aromatics while they sautéed; the leaves we sliced into larger pieces and set aside to add to the soup later on.

Most of the bean mixes incorporated tomato, either as a dehydrated powder in the seasoning packet or by calling for tomato paste or canned tomatoes in the recipe. After testing a few options, we liked the addition of a chopped fresh tomato, which provided a bright, slightly acidic counterpoint to the richness of the bacon and the earthiness of the mushrooms. We added the tomato toward the end of cooking (with the chard leaves) so the acid wouldn't interfere with the cooking of the beans.

Our soup was nearly there, but it was a bit thin (even having been slightly thickened by the lentils and split peas breaking down) and the flavors were not quite in harmony. We decided to revisit the issue of cooking liquid. We've learned with other soups that swapping out some of the water for store-bought chicken broth gives the soup depth. While the exact ratio depends on the other ingredients in the soup, we usually find that some water is necessary; otherwise the chicken broth is overwhelming. Starting with 5 cups water and 3 cups broth (the ratio we'd been using), we gradually increased the broth by the cup to see when tasters would protest. Surprisingly, they never did, and the soup made with all broth was by far the richest and most balanced. The broth provided a deeper backdrop and some much-needed cohesion, bringing the flavors of the beans, bacon, and vegetables into unison.

Finally, we had a recipe for 15-bean and vegetable soup that was worth making.

Hearty 15-Bean and Vegetable Soup

SERVES 8 TO 10

You can find 15-bean soup mix alongside the other bagged dried beans in the supermarket; 15-bean mix is the most common, but any 1-pound bag of multiple varieties of beans will work in this recipe. The different varieties of beans cook at different rates, so be sure to taste several beans to ensure they are all tender before serving.

4	ounces (about 4 slices) bacon, chopped fine
1	small onion, chopped medium
1	carrot, peeled and chopped fine
1	large bunch Swiss chard (about 1 pound), stems and leaves separated, stems chopped medium, and leaves sliced ½ inch thick (see the illustrations on page 56)
½	ounce dried porcini mushrooms, rinsed and minced
12	ounces white mushrooms, wiped clean, stemmed, and quartered

6   medium garlic cloves, minced or pressed
    through a garlic press (about 2 tablespoons)
2   teaspoons minced fresh thyme leaves or
    ½ teaspoon dried
8   cups low-sodium chicken broth
1   pound 15-bean soup mix, flavoring pack
    discarded, picked over, salt-soaked
    (see page 145), and rinsed
2   bay leaves
1   large tomato (about 8 ounces), cored and
    chopped medium
    Salt and ground black pepper

1. Adjust an oven rack to the lower-middle position and heat the oven to 250 degrees. Cook the bacon in a large Dutch oven over medium heat until rendered and crisp, about 8 minutes. Stir in the onion, carrot, chard stems, and porcini mushrooms and cook until the vegetables are softened, 7 to 10 minutes.

2. Stir in the white mushrooms, cover, and cook until the mushrooms have released their liquid, about 5 minutes. Uncover and continue to cook until the mushrooms are dry and browned, 5 to 10 minutes.

3. Stir in the garlic and thyme and cook until fragrant, about 30 seconds. Stir in the broth, soaked beans, and bay leaves and bring to a boil. Cover the pot, transfer to the oven, and cook until the beans are almost tender, 1 to 1¼ hours.

4. Stir in the chard leaves and tomato and continue to cook, covered, in the oven until the beans and vegetables are fully tender, 30 to 40 minutes longer. Remove the pot from the oven and remove the bay leaves. Season with salt and pepper to taste and serve.

➤ VARIATION

Hearty Vegetarian 15–Bean and Vegetable Soup

In this soup, we prefer the pure flavor of homemade Vegetable Broth (page 22) to store-bought vegetable broth.

Follow the recipe for Hearty 15-Bean and Vegetable Soup, omitting the bacon and cooking the vegetables in 2 tablespoons olive oil in step 1. Substitute 8 cups Vegetable Broth for the chicken broth.

BLACK BEAN SOUP

THE BEST BLACK BEAN SOUPS CAREFULLY balance sweet, spicy, and smoky flavors, and are full of tender beans floating in a slightly thickened, incredibly dark broth. Bad black bean soups are a completely different story—watery, thin, and bland or overspiced, bitter, and gray are the two camps that horrible black bean soups tend to fall into. We set out to create a foolproof, flavorful black bean soup with beans that were tender, not mushy, and we also wanted it to be attractive, dark, and thick.

We started out with our dried beans in hand. Usually we prefer beans that have been soaked in a saltwater solution (or brined) prior to cooking, as this step softens the tough bean skins and evens out the cooking time, so that fewer beans burst open. In this case, however, a few broken beans wouldn't be a bad thing; we wanted a somewhat thickened soup and a portion of burst beans would only contribute to our desired texture. We opted to forgo the salt-soaking, but now we found that our unbrined beans would need to be seasoned at some point. We determined that 1 teaspoon of salt was a good amount for 1 pound of black beans, but the question was when to add it. We tested beans salted at the end of cooking against those salted at the beginning. In a blind taste test, we couldn't tell the difference between the textures, but only the beans salted from the beginning were seasoned enough for our taste. In addition to salt, we found a couple of aromatic bay leaves contributed to a deeper flavor in our beans.

Considering the broth next, we knew we'd be adding so much flavor in the way of spices and aromatics that the nuances of homemade broth would be missed, so we opted to utilize store-bought broth. We tried beef broth first, but it seemed out of place. Chicken broth, cut with the cooking liquid from the beans, fit the bill perfectly. For more meaty flavor, we turned to pork. Our first thought was adding a ham hock. While tasters liked the meaty flavor offered by the hock, it also made them want more—not just more meat flavor (hocks are mostly bone) but real meat. We tried various cured pork products: salt pork, slab bacon, and ham steak. Ham steak contributed some pork flavor and decidedly more meat than any of the other options, making it our top pick. That said, we didn't want the ham to take over the soup, so we limited the amount to just 4 ounces.

Aside from the ham flavor, the soup tasted rather hollow. We found improvement with a sofrito, a Spanish preparation in which aromatic vegetables and herbs (we used green pepper, onion, garlic, and oregano) are sautéed until softened and lightly browned. But our sofrito needed refinement. Fragrant oregano was replaced with more traditional cumin. We slowly incorporated the ground spice, working our way up to 1½ tablespoons. It was a lot, but we were after big flavor, and when the cumin was toasted along with the aromatics, its pungency was tempered. We also replaced the green pepper with minced carrot and celery for a sweeter, fresher flavor. Tasters urged us not to be shy with the minced garlic and red pepper flakes: we added six cloves and ½ teaspoon, respectively.

We found that some recipes added the sofrito at the start of cooking, when the beans went into the pot, but in our tests, this resulted in the flavors of the spices and aromatics becoming seriously muted. Adding the sofrito partway through cooking, so its freshness and brightness remained intact, worked much better. Our soup was a hit, layered with sweet, spicy, smoky, and fresh vegetable flavors.

However, now the consistency—somewhat thin, with the beans, aromatics, and ham dotting the landscape—needed a fix. For a soup that was somewhere between smooth and chunky, we opted to puree some of the beans and liquid. Even after pureeing, though, a thickener seemed necessary. Simply using less liquid in the soup improved the texture somewhat, but the soup still lacked body. Cornstarch, mixed with water to create a slurry and stirred in at the end of cooking, worked well.

We were finally satisfied, save for the soup's unappealing gray color. We had heard that changes in pH would affect the color of our beans. One test confirmed it: A more alkaline broth made them darker, and a more acidic broth made them lighter. We experimented by adding various amounts of baking soda to the beans both during and after cooking. The winning quantity was a mere ⅛ teaspoon, which produced a great-tasting soup (there was no soapy aftertaste, as was the case with

larger quantities) with a darker, more appetizing color than unadulterated beans.

Classic additions to black bean soup include Madeira, rum, sherry, or Scotch from the liquor cabinet and lemon, lime, or orange juice from the citrus bin. Given the other flavors in the soup, lime juice seemed the best fit. Because it is acidic, too much lime juice can push the color of the soup toward pink. Two tablespoons added flavor without marring the color.

While our soup was potently flavored, we found it benefited from at least a few of the traditional garnishes. Sour cream, minced red onion, and diced avocado all played off various aspects of the flavor profile. For a super-spicy soup, we created a variation amped up with a generous amount of chipotle chiles. If you're looking for a meatless option, there's also a brightly flavored vegetarian variation.

Black Bean Soup

SERVES 6

We recommend serving this soup with a few garnishes. Common garnishes include lime wedges, minced fresh cilantro leaves, minced red onion, diced avocado, and sour cream. See page 121 for more information on pureeing soup.

BEANS

1	pound dried black beans, picked over and rinsed
5	cups water, plus extra as needed
4	ounces ham steak, patted dry
2	bay leaves
1	teaspoon salt
⅛	teaspoon baking soda

SOUP

3	tablespoons olive oil
2	large onions, minced
3	celery ribs, chopped fine
1	large carrot, peeled and chopped fine
6	medium garlic cloves, minced or pressed through a garlic press (about 2 tablespoons)
1½	tablespoons ground cumin
½	teaspoon red pepper flakes
6	cups low-sodium chicken broth
2	tablespoons cornstarch

2 tablespoons water
2 tablespoons juice from I lime
   Salt and ground black pepper

1. FOR THE BEANS: Combine the beans, water, ham, bay leaves, salt, and baking soda in a large saucepan. Bring to a boil, skimming any impurities that rise to the surface. Cover, reduce the heat to low, and simmer gently until the beans are tender, 1¼ to 1½ hours. (If after 1½ hours the beans are not tender, add 1 cup more water and continue to simmer until the beans are tender). Remove the bay leaves. Transfer the ham steak to a carving board and cut into ¼-inch pieces; set aside. (Do not drain the beans.)

2. FOR THE SOUP: Heat the oil in a large Dutch oven over medium heat until shimmering. Add the onions, celery, and carrot and cook until the vegetables are softened and lightly browned, 12 to 15 minutes.

3. Stir in the garlic, cumin, and red pepper flakes and cook until fragrant, about 1 minute. Stir in the broth and cooked beans with their cooking liquid and bring to a boil. Reduce to a simmer over medium-low and cook, uncovered and stirring occasionally, until the flavors have blended, about 30 minutes.

4. Puree 1½ cups of the beans and 2 cups of the liquid until smooth, then return to the pot. Whisk the cornstarch and water together in a small bowl, then gradually stir half of the cornstarch mixture into the simmering soup. Continue to simmer the soup, stirring occasionally, until slightly thickened, 3 to 5 minutes. (If at this point the soup is thinner than desired, repeat with the remaining cornstarch mixture.) Off the heat, stir in the lime juice and reserved ham, season with salt and pepper to taste, and serve.

➤ VARIATIONS

Black Bean Soup with Chipotle Chiles
Chipotle chiles are spicy; for a spicier soup, use the greater amount of chipotles given.
Follow the recipe for Black Bean Soup, omitting the red pepper flakes and adding 1 to 2 tablespoons minced chipotle chile in adobo sauce to the pot with the chicken broth in step 3.

Vegetarian Black Bean Soup
In this soup, we prefer the pure flavor of homemade Vegetable Broth (page 22) to store-bought vegetable broth.
Follow the recipe for Black Bean Soup, omitting the ham steak. Add 1 ounce dried porcini mushrooms, rinsed and minced, to the pot with the beans in step 1. Substitute 6 cups Vegetable Broth for the chicken broth in step 3.

U.S. SENATE NAVY BEAN SOUP

A CLASSIC AMERICAN BEAN SOUP, U.S. SENATE navy bean soup has supposedly been on the menu in the Senate restaurant since 1901. Legend has it that Senator Fred Dubois of Idaho, who served from 1901 to 1907, demanded that navy bean soup be on the restaurant menu in perpetuity. The mandate has been attributed to other epicurean senators as well, but all that really matters is that it has been on the menu for a very, very long time.

The authentic Senate version contains nothing more than dried beans and ham hocks simmered in water until the beans are tender and the ham has transformed the water into a smoky broth. A stray carrot or onion provides a bit more flavor, but that's about it. While we appreciate the government-sanctioned thrift behind this recipe, we were in the mood for a heartier navy bean soup, one with serious chunks of ham.

Knowing that we wanted both smoky flavor and bites of meat in our soup, we started by swapping out one of the ham hocks in favor of a ham steak, which we diced. While the steak provided nice chunks of meat, after simmering in the soup for an hour (with the hock), the ham was now lacking in flavor and the soup was overly salty.

To improve the flavor of the ham, we tried first sautéing it before simmering it in the soup; this gave it a deeper, caramelized flavor. While one problem was fixed, the soup was still too salty. Patting the ham steak dry before dicing it and rinsing the ham hock prior to cooking both helped, but these steps weren't enough. We been using low-sodium chicken broth for the liquid, but decided to switch to water. Unfortunately, the resulting soup tasted flat. Ultimately, using slightly more water than broth (4 cups and 3 cups, respectively) provided good flavor while keeping the saltiness in check.

Now we could focus on properly cooking the beans. Following our established soaking method, we brined the beans overnight so their skins would be less likely to burst during cooking. To further ensure intact beans, once the soup was simmering, we transferred it to a 250-degree oven. Cooking the beans in the low and gentle heat of the oven produced evenly cooked beans that were mostly intact.

For the vegetables, we sautéed onion, celery, and garlic with the ham, which gave them the same deep, caramelized flavor. Fresh thyme added a welcome herbal note and ground black pepper added a touch of pungency. Tasters also liked bits of carrots, which we added to the soup later to preserve their texture. At this point the soup needed something to brighten and balance the robust flavors. A teaspoon of red wine vinegar, preferred over cider and white wine vinegars, provided the acidity the soup needed.

Our soup was almost there, but it was a bit thin. To thicken the soup, we opted for the simplest method—mashing some of the beans right in the soup pot using the back of a spoon—which gave our Senate soup a rustic look and texture. Now the broth was thick and creamy—perfect for suspending the tender beans, ham, and carrots.

U.S. Senate Navy Bean Soup
SERVES 8

This soup can easily turn overly salty because of the ham; be sure to use low-sodium broth and taste the soup carefully before seasoning with any salt.

2 tablespoons vegetable oil
1 pound ham steak, patted dry and cut into ½-inch pieces
1 medium onion, chopped medium
2 celery ribs, chopped fine
6 medium garlic cloves, minced or pressed through a garlic press (about 2 tablespoons)
2 teaspoons minced fresh thyme leaves or ½ teaspoon dried
   Salt and ground black pepper
4 cups water
3 cups low-sodium chicken broth
1 pound dried navy beans, picked over, salt-soaked (see page 145), and rinsed
1 smoked ham hock, rinsed
2 bay leaves
3 carrots, peeled and cut into ½-inch pieces
1 teaspoon red wine vinegar, plus extra for seasoning

1. Adjust an oven rack to the lower-middle position and heat the oven to 250 degrees. Heat the oil in a large Dutch oven over medium heat until just smoking. Brown the ham on all sides, about 5 minutes. Stir in the onion and celery and cook until the vegetables are softened, 5 to 7 minutes.

2. Stir in the garlic, thyme, and ½ teaspoon pepper and cook until fragrant, about 30 seconds. Stir in the water, broth, soaked beans, ham hock, and bay leaves and bring to a boil. Cover the pot, transfer to the oven, and cook until the beans are almost tender, 45 to 60 minutes.

3. Stir in the carrots and 1 teaspoon of the vinegar and continue to cook, covered, in the oven until the beans and vegetables are fully tender, 30 to 40 minutes longer.

4. Remove the pot from the oven and remove the bay leaves. Transfer the ham hock to a cutting board, let cool slightly, then shred the meat, discarding the bone and skin.

5. Return the ham hock meat to the soup and heat over medium heat until the soup is hot, about 2 minutes. Off the heat, use the back of a spoon to press some beans against the side of the pot to thicken the soup. Season with salt, pepper, and additional vinegar to taste and serve.

Beans and Lentils 101

Dried beans and lentils can make especially hearty soups, but you need to know a few things about them—such as how to prepare beans for cooking and the best lentils to use in various applications—before you get started.

SORTING DRIED BEANS AND LENTILS

Before cooking, it is important to rinse and pick over dried beans and lentils to remove any stones or debris. To make the task easier, sort the beans on a large white plate or a rimmed white cutting board. The neutral background makes any unwanted matter a cinch to spot and discard.

BUYING AND STORING DRIED BEANS

When you go shopping, it's imperative to buy the freshest beans you can find. Be sure to shop at a supermarket with high turnover (dusty bags of beans are a sure sign the beans are past their prime). If buying beans in bulk, choose those that are uniform in size and have a smooth exterior. Dried beans should be stored in a cool, dry place in a sealed plastic or glass container.

DIFFERENT KINDS OF LENTILS

Lentils come in dozens of sizes and colors (and from many parts of the world), and the differences in flavor and color are considerable. Because they are thin-skinned, they require no soaking, which makes them a most versatile legume. Below you'll find the most commonly available types of lentils.

BROWN AND GREEN LENTILS

These larger lentils are what you'll find in every supermarket. They are a uniform drab brown or green. Tasters found these to exhibit a "mild yet light and earthy flavor." These lentils hold their shape and are tender inside when cooked. These are an all-purpose lentil; beyond soups, we like them in salads or simply tossed with olive oil and herbs.

LENTILLES DU PUY

These French lentils from the city of Le Puy are smaller than the more common brown and green varieties. They are a dark olive green, almost black. Tasters praised these for their "rich, earthy, complex flavor" and "firm yet tender texture." These lentils keep their shape, making them perfect for soup.

RED AND YELLOW LENTILS

Split, very colorful, and skinless, these small orange-red or golden-yellow lentils completely disintegrate when cooked. If you are looking for lentils that will quickly break down, these are the ones to use. These lentils are commonly used in Indian cuisine.

SALT-SOAKING BEANS

We've found that brining dried beans (soaking them in salt water) before cooking them evens out the bean cooking time so that fewer burst open, while the salt softens the tough bean skins and makes them more palatable (see below). Don't worry if you don't have time to soak the beans (or forgot)—we've come up with a "quick salt-soak" method that works nearly as well (we still slightly prefer the overnight soak if given a choice). Be sure, however, to rinse the salt-soaked beans thoroughly before using, or your dish may taste too salty. Note also that soaking is not necessary for lentils.

SCIENCE: The Effect of Salting on Beans

Why does soaking dried beans in salted water make them cook up with softer skins? It has to do with how the sodium ions in salt interact with the cells of the bean skins. As the beans soak, the sodium ions replace some of the calcium and magnesium ions in the skins. Because sodium ions are weaker than mineral ions, they allow more water to penetrate into the skins, leading to a softer texture. During soaking, the sodium ions will filter only partway into the beans, so their greatest effect is on the cells in the outermost part of the beans.

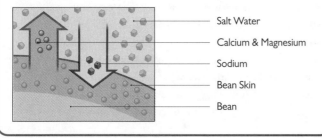

Salt Water
Calcium & Magnesium
Sodium
Bean Skin
Bean

OVERNIGHT SALT-SOAKING METHOD

Dissolve 3 tablespoons table salt in 16 cups cold water in a large container or pot. Stir in 1 pound beans and soak at room temperature for at least 8 hours, or up to 24 hours. Drain and rinse the beans thoroughly before proceeding with the recipe.

QUICK SALT-SOAKING METHOD

Combine 16 cups water, 3 tablespoons table salt, and 1 pound beans in a large Dutch oven and bring to a boil over high heat. Remove the pot from the heat, cover, and let stand for 1 hour. Drain and rinse the beans thoroughly before proceeding with the recipe.

PASTA E FAGIOLI

"PASTA FAZOOL," THE ITALIAN-AMERICAN version of Italy's *pasta e fagioli* (pasta and bean soup) is hearty, thick, almost stew-like, and always orange-red in color from the presence of tomatoes. Each spoonful is laden with pasta and beans, and the soup is full of harmonious flavors, with no one taste standing out or interrupting the consonance. The vegetables are cut small and used as accents to the pasta. Typically, in mediocre pasta e fagioli, the beans have no flavor, the pasta is mushy, the broth is too tomatoey, and the soup is bland. We wanted to make a pasta e fagioli that would make any Italian-American family proud.

We began by preparing a half-dozen recipes, most of which followed a similar procedure. First the aromatics (vegetables and often some pork product) were sautéed in olive oil. Then the tomatoes and broth went into the pot, followed by the beans and, finally, the pasta. Almost all of these recipes produced bland soups with mushy pasta. The soup with the best flavor took more than four hours to prepare and used dried beans. Although the long hours at the stove paid off, the speed and ease with which some other recipes came together were certainly appealing. We decided to follow suit and use canned beans (not dried) to create a really good pasta e fagioli that was streamlined and speedy.

Many recipes for pasta e fagioli contain pancetta (unsmoked Italian bacon), while completely Americanized recipes call for regular bacon. The simplest recipes avoid the pork and use only olive oil. Our first test showed that even a small amount of a pork product added much flavor to the soup, so we began by sautéing some diced pancetta in olive oil.

Next, we turned to the aromatics. Most Italian recipes use the same quartet of onions, celery, carrots, and garlic. Tasters liked the onions, celery, and garlic but were divided over the sweetness of the carrots, so we decided to omit them.

In many recipes, the aromatics are sautéed, and then the pan is deglazed with either tomatoes or broth. For the tomatoes, we tried crushed and diced. The crushed tomatoes were overpowering, but the diced tomatoes worked well, helping to intensify the flavors of the aromatics. We also tested chicken broth, a close second to the tomatoes (we would add the broth later), and white wine, which simply turned the soup sour.

Cranberry beans, a beautiful pink-and-white mottled variety, are popular in Italy but in this country, it's tough enough to find the dried version outside of farmers' markets or online at various retailers let alone finding them canned. We tested two common substitutes, pinto and red kidney beans. Neither had the sweet, delicate flavor of a cranberry bean, so we tried canned cannellini beans. Tasters found these oval-shaped beans to be sweet and creamy (great Northern beans work well, too).

Although our canned beans were good, we wanted to find a way to boost their flavor. Our first thought was to add the beans to the tomato mixture while it simmered, a step that might infuse them with the flavors of the pancetta, oil, and vegetables. We prepared two batches of soup— one with beans and broth added simultaneously and one with beans added to the tomatoes and cooked for 10 minutes prior to adding the broth. The results were black and white. The beans added to the tomato mixture adopted its flavors readily, easily beating out the bland beans added later in the recipe.

The makeup of the broth was also critical. Although chicken broth is standard in many recipes, tasters felt that the resulting pasta e fagioli tasted like chicken soup. We tried water instead of chicken broth, adding some Parmesan rind to boost the flavor. This test was a success, but we went on to try a combination of broth and water, retaining the cheese rind. This soup was the winner, with good body and even better flavor.

For additional flavorings, we added oregano and red pepper flakes to the pot with the aromatic vegetables; tasters approved. Parsley is typically added at the end of cooking, and it took just one test to show that it brightened the flavor and color of the soup. The last flavor-enhancing idea—a long shot, perhaps—was a teaspoon of minced anchovy fillet. Tasters could not identify what was different about the batch with anchovy, but everyone agreed that it was more complex and fuller in flavor.

Our tests showed that pastas with relatively small shapes, such as small shells, are best in this soup. Larger shapes, like elbows and medium shells, crowded out the other ingredients and soaked up too much broth. Tiny pastas, such as stars and pastina, were lost next to the more sizable beans and tomatoes.

Pasta e Fagioli

SERVES 8 TO 10

You can substitute the same amount of ditalini, tubettini, or orzo pasta for the small shells if desired. If you can't find pancetta, substitute 3 ounces of bacon (about 3 slices). Parmesan rind is added for flavor, but it can be replaced with a 2-inch chunk of the cheese.

3	ounces pancetta, chopped fine (see note)
1	tablespoon extra-virgin olive oil, plus extra for serving
1	medium onion, chopped fine
1	celery rib, chopped fine
4	medium garlic cloves, minced or pressed through a garlic press (about 4 teaspoons)
1	tablespoon minced fresh oregano leaves or 1 teaspoon dried
¼	teaspoon red pepper flakes
3	anchovy fillets, minced
2	(15.5-ounce) cans cannellini beans, drained and rinsed
1	(28-ounce) can diced tomatoes
1	(5-inch-long) piece Parmesan cheese rind (see note)
3½	cups low-sodium chicken broth
2½	cups water
	Salt and ground black pepper
2	cups small pasta shells (see note)
¼	cup minced fresh parsley leaves
3	ounces Parmesan cheese, grated (about 1½ cups)

1. Cook the pancetta and oil together in a large Dutch oven over medium heat until the pancetta is rendered and lightly browned, about 8 minutes. Stir in the onion and celery and cook until the vegetables are softened, 5 to 7 minutes.

2. Stir in the garlic, oregano, red pepper flakes, and anchovies and cook until fragrant, about 30 seconds. Stir in the beans, tomatoes with their juice, and Parmesan rind and bring to a boil. Reduce to a simmer and cook until the flavors have blended, about 10 minutes.

3. Stir in the broth, water, and 1 teaspoon salt and return to a boil. Stir in the pasta and cook until tender, 8 to 12 minutes.

4. Off the heat, remove the Parmesan rind (scraping off any cheese that has melted and adding it back to the pot). Stir in the parsley and season with salt and pepper to taste. Sprinkle individual portions with the grated Parmesan and drizzle lightly with additional olive oil before serving.

INGREDIENTS:
Supermarket Parmesan Cheese

The buttery, nutty, slightly fruity taste and crystalline crunch of genuine Parmigiano-Reggiano cheese is a one-of-a-kind experience. Produced using traditional methods for the past 800 years in one government-designated area of northern Italy, this hard cow's-milk cheese has a distinctive flavor that is touted as coming as much from the region's geography as from the production process. But is all of this regional emphasis for real, or can really good Parmesan be made anywhere?

Recently, many more brands of shrink-wrapped, wedge-style, American-made Parmesan have been appearing in supermarkets. They're sold at a fraction of the price of authentic stuff, which can cost up to $33 a pound. To see how they stacked up, we bought eight nationally distributed brands at the supermarket: six domestic Parmesans and two imported Parmigiano-Reggianos. The wedges ranged from $9 to almost $20 per pound. Twenty testers tasted the eight brands of Parmesan cheese three ways: broken into chunks, grated, and cooked in polenta. Boar's Head Parmigiano-Reggiano, about $17 a pound, was the tasters' favorite, with a pleasingly nutty flavor.

THE BEST SUPERMARKET PARMESAN CHEESE
Tasters like the tangy, nutty flavor of this rich, complex cheese.   **BOAR'S HEAD**

SICILIAN CHICKPEA AND ESCAROLE SOUP

WHILE MOST PEOPLE ARE FAMILIAR WITH Italian soups that feature cannellini beans, in Sicily, chickpeas (*ceci*) are the favored legume and the most common bean to use in soup. We found dozens of soup recipes starring chickpeas but were most interested in versions in which the mild bean shared the stage with escarole, a bitter green frequently paired with chickpeas in southern Italian cooking. Borrowing from several recipes, we set out to create our own chickpea and escarole soup.

From the outset, we knew that dried beans were the way to go for our traditional soup. While we like the flavor of canned chickpeas in salads and some soups, we were in search of a homestyle soup that had rich, deep flavor. Using dried chickpeas meant we were starting with a blank slate and could infuse the chickpeas with lots of flavor as they cooked. Since chickpeas rarely break apart, even when cooked beyond the point of tenderness, we knew we could cook them as long as necessary to properly flavor them.

Being that chickpeas are so sturdy, we wondered if we could skip the step of brining (or soaking the beans overnight in salt water) before cooking—a technique we use to prevent the beans from bursting during cooking. After tasting two batches of cooked beans (one unbrined and one brined) we found that the unbrined chickpeas were chalky and took almost two hours longer to cook, while the brined beans were tender, creamy, and cooked quickly. Brining was here to stay.

As for cooking method, we briefly considered utilizing the low, slow heat of the oven, which is our preferred way to cook more delicate beans. But for our chickpeas, which are so robust and hardy, the stovetop worked fine. Simmering didn't cause the chickpeas to burst, and since they take a little longer to cook than most beans we had no interest in slowing down the process. Brined and then simmered on the stove in a mixture of chicken broth and water, the chickpeas achieved their ideal texture: soft and creamy, with just a bit of chew.

While some recipes simmer the escarole for quite a long time, our tasters agreed that this made the vegetable slimy. A quick simmer was preferable; when stirred in the last five minutes of cooking, the escarole leaves wilted and were velvety and the stems retained the faintest crunch.

For aromatics, we started with the classic flavors of the region: onion, garlic, oregano, and red pepper flakes. To enhance the authenticity of our soup, we also added fennel, which grows wild throughout much of the Mediterranean; its mild anise bite complemented the nutty chickpeas. Diced fresh tomato added brightness and color.

Looking about the test kitchen for an additional ingredient to continue the Sicilian tones and also punch up the flavor, we hit upon leftover Parmesan rind, a traditional flavoring agent for many Italian soups. The rind added a nutty richness and complexity that bolstered the chickpeas' flavor.

Our soup was nearly finished when a colleague suggested a few last additions that seemed intriguing: anchovy and orange peel. These ingredients, along with fennel, are a classic combination in southern Italian cooking. The briny richness of the minced anchovy and the citrus punch of the orange peel brought the soup to another level, providing just the right final accent.

Many Sicilian soups are served with bread of some sort, such as toasted slices of country bread rubbed with garlic. Although the soup is fantastic on its own, we included the option of garlic toasts to make it a more substantial dinner.

REMOVING LARGE STRIPS OF CITRUS ZEST

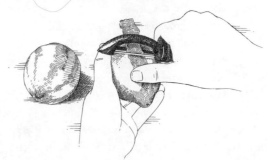

To remove long, wide strips of zest from a lemon, orange, or any other citrus fruit, run a vegetable peeler on the surface from pole to pole. Be careful not to remove the white pith, which has a bitter flavor.

Sicilian Chickpea and Escarole Soup

SERVES 8 TO 10

Parmesan rind is added for flavor, but can be replaced with a 2-inch chunk of the cheese. The optional garlic toasts will turn this soup into a more substantial dish.

2	tablespoons extra-virgin olive oil, plus extra for serving
2	medium fennel bulbs (about 1½ pounds), trimmed of stalks, cored, and chopped fine (see the illustrations on page 27)
1	small onion, chopped medium
3	medium garlic cloves, minced or pressed through a garlic press (about 1 tablespoon)
2	teaspoons minced fresh oregano leaves or ½ teaspoon dried
2	anchovy fillets, minced
¼	teaspoon red pepper flakes
7	cups water
5	cups low-sodium chicken broth
1	pound dried chickpeas, picked over, salt-soaked (see page 145), and rinsed
1	(5-inch-long) piece Parmesan cheese rind (see note)
2	bay leaves
1	(3-inch-long) strip zest from 1 orange (see the illustration on page 148), trimmed of white pith
1	large tomato (about 8 ounces), cored and chopped medium
1	head escarole (about 1 pound), trimmed and cut into 1-inch pieces Salt and ground black pepper
1	recipe Garlic Toasts (page 138) (optional)
2	ounces Parmesan cheese, grated (about 1 cup)

1. Heat the oil in a large Dutch oven over medium heat until shimmering. Add the fennel and onion and cook until the vegetables are softened, 7 to 10 minutes. Stir in the garlic, oregano, anchovies, and red pepper flakes and cook until fragrant, about 30 seconds.

2. Stir in the water, broth, soaked chickpeas, Parmesan rind, bay leaves, and zest and bring to a boil. Reduce the heat to a gentle simmer and cook until the chickpeas are tender, 1 to 1½ hours.

3. Stir in the tomato and continue to simmer for 20 minutes longer. Stir in the escarole and cook until wilted, 5 to 10 minutes.

4. Off the heat, remove the bay leaves and Parmesan rind (scraping off any cheese that has melted and adding it back to the pot). Season with salt and pepper to taste. To serve, place the garlic toasts (if using) into individual bowls, ladle the soup over the top, sprinkle with the grated Parmesan, and drizzle lightly with additional olive oil.

INGREDIENTS:
Extra-Virgin Olive Oil

On today's supermarket shelves you will find row upon row of different olive oils. But given the cost—an average of $18.99 per liter for the oils in our lineup—we wondered if we could just go with the cheapest supermarket variety or if we needed to find something better from a gourmet shop or online seller.

To find out if there were any extra-virgin olive oils truly worth bringing home from the supermarket, we chose 10 of the top-selling brands and conducted a blind taste test—first plain, and then warmed and tossed with pasta. While a few oils passed muster, most ranged from plain-Jane to distinctly unpleasant.

However, we did find two acceptable products. Perhaps not surprisingly, origin did make a difference—both are made from all-Italian olives. Price was a factor, too: Our top picks were the two most expensive oils. Our front-runner was Lucini Italia Premium Select Extra Virgin Olive Oil ($32 for a 750-milliliter bottle), which tasters described as "fruity, with a slightly peppery finish," and "buttery undertones." A close second was Colavita Extra Virgin Olive Oil ($16.49 for a 1-liter bottle). Tasters found it "round and buttery," with a "briny and fruity" flavor.

But both were bested in a second tasting that included our favorite premium brand, Columela, available in high-end supermarkets. Tasters found it exceptionally fruity and well-balanced. At about $36 per liter, it's actually cheaper than Lucini.

THE BEST SUPERMARKET EXTRA-VIRGIN OLIVE OIL
Tasters described our winning supermarket brand Columela as "buttery," "with a peppery finish."   **COLUMELA**

CAJUN RED BEAN AND RICE SOUP

THOUGH BEANS AND RICE ARE HARDLY A unique combination, the Cajun spin is revelatory: smoky, spicy andouille sausage and peppery tasso ham provide a piquant backdrop for creamy red beans and buttery white rice, all married together in a rich, thick sauce built on herbs, spices, and aromatics. We thought this dish would be the perfect basis for a hearty, spicy soup, so we set out to create a recipe that incorporated all the great flavors of this Louisiana staple.

We started by surveying classic red beans and rice recipes to get our bearings. After cooking up several recipes, we learned one thing quickly: If you're on the prowl for ways to ruin a pot of beans, there's no need to look far. Even recipes from Cajun-cuisine luminaries (whom we won't name here) had serious issues, including dried spice overkill and crazy pork-fest ingredient lists (six ham hocks for a single pot of beans!). Plus, when it came to texture, the beans ran the gamut from mushy and blown-out to way too firm. We decided to start with a stripped-down recipe and build it up as we saw fit, taking on the elements of the soup one by one.

First up: the legumes. While New Orleans cooks prefer local dried red kidney beans, citing their tender skins and ultra-creamy interiors, this was supposed to be a simple, down-home supper, so we decided to look for a bean that could be found easily (without a plane trip). We began by testing dried kidney beans and, on the suggestion of a few fellow test cooks, the small red beans used in Caribbean and Latin American cooking. We prepared two batches of beans, one kidney and one small red, soaking them in salted water overnight, then simmering them in the slow, gentle heat of the oven with sautéed chopped onion, celery, and green bell pepper. Hands down, tasters preferred the batch made with small red beans, praising their creamy flavor and smooth interior.

Now that we had figured out the beans, we addressed the rice. In the past we have found that rice tastes best when cooked directly in soup rather than a separate pot. As we suspected, however, adding the rice at the beginning (so it was in the oven for more than an hour) resulted in overcooked rice. The obvious solution seemed to be to add the rice later on. But no matter when we stirred it in, we found that the rice wasn't just crunchy (underdone) or blown-out (overdone), it was both crunchy *and* blown-out; it seemed that the exterior of the rice was absorbing too much moisture and becoming bloated before the interior could cook through. Clearly the low oven heat was good for our beans but terrible for the rice. The solution was to finish cooking the soup at a simmer on the stovetop, where the heat could be easily adjusted and the rice closely monitored.

The next major ingredient to sort out was the pork. True Cajun red beans can include as many as three different pork products, among them sausage, ham, and tasso. We were determined to get a similar depth of meaty flavor into our beans with less fuss.

The sausage was easy—andouille is the usual choice and a single tasting confirmed that this heavily smoked link, seasoned with garlic and spices, provided the right depth and complexity. Sliced into half-moons, the andouille could cook with the rice to release its flavor into the broth.

Many authentic recipes call for tasso ham, which is pork coated thickly with spices, onion powder, and granulated garlic, then hot-smoked until it resembles jerky. Diced and browned, it lends a peppery kick to the dish. Since it's difficult to find outside Louisiana, we searched for a stand-in. Ultimately, we found that we already had our hands on a suitable replacement—the andouille sausage. To replicate the tasso flavor, all we had to do was sauté some additional andouille (finely chopped) with the onion, celery, and bell pepper and then add some paprika, black pepper, and cayenne. Now we had the smoky, spicy flavor and aroma we were looking for.

Finally, some Cajun recipes include pickled pork shoulder, which adds a nice acidic respite from the barrage of earthy, porky flavors. However, we had no hope of finding this obscure product outside Louisiana, and making some on our own—pickling diced pork shoulder in vinegar for three days—was absurd. On a whim, we replaced the acidity of the pickled pork with plain vinegar. This simple solution worked: Just 1 teaspoon of red wine vinegar, plus a few splashes added right before serving, cut through the richness of the pork and provided some much-needed brightness.

Now we were down to a few final refinements. Tasters felt the pot could use a noticeable vegetal element (beyond the aromatics), so we decided to cut the bell pepper into larger, bite-size pieces and add it to the pot after the beans had cooked in the oven. This way, the big bites of pepper could provide some contrast to the richness of the beans and meat. The cooking liquid also needed tweaking. While the older recipes we found called for plain water, many modern recipes used chicken broth. Store-bought broth did add complexity to the beans, but it also lent too much chicken flavor that competed with the andouille sausage. Eventually we settled on a combination of broth and water.

With a final sprinkling of sliced scallions for color, our Cajun-inspired soup was now complete, boasting all the smoky, spicy flavors you'd find down on the Bayou.

Spicy Cajun Red Bean and Rice Soup with Sausage

SERVES 6 TO 8

This soup is fairly spicy due to the andouille sausage and cayenne pepper. To make it less spicy, choose a mild andouille or use less cayenne. Kielbasa can be substituted for the andouille.

12	ounces andouille sausage (see note)
1	tablespoon vegetable oil
1	medium onion, chopped medium
1	celery rib, chopped fine
3	medium garlic cloves, minced or pressed through a garlic press (about 1 tablespoon)
1	teaspoon sweet paprika
1	teaspoon minced fresh thyme leaves or ¼ teaspoon dried
¼	teaspoon cayenne pepper (see note) Salt and ground black pepper
5	cups low-sodium chicken broth
2	cups water
8	ounces (about 1 cup) dried small red beans, picked over, salt-soaked (see page 145), and rinsed
2	bay leaves
2	green bell peppers, stemmed, seeded, and chopped medium
½	cup long-grain white rice
1	teaspoon red wine vinegar, plus extra for seasoning
3	scallions, sliced thin

1. Adjust an oven rack to the lower-middle position and heat the oven to 250 degrees. Slice 8 ounces of the sausage in half lengthwise, then crosswise into ¼-inch-thick slices; refrigerate until needed. Finely chop the remaining 4 ounces sausage.

2. Cook the finely chopped sausage and oil together in a large Dutch oven over medium heat until the sausage is rendered and lightly browned, about 8 minutes. Stir in the onion and celery and cook until the vegetables are softened, 5 to 7 minutes.

3. Stir in the garlic, paprika, thyme, cayenne, and ¼ teaspoon black pepper and cook until fragrant, about 30 seconds. Stir in the broth, water, soaked beans, and bay leaves and bring to a boil. Cover the pot, transfer to the oven, and cook until the beans are almost tender, 1 to 1¼ hours.

4. Remove the pot from the oven. Stir in the reserved sliced sausage, peppers, rice, and 1 teaspoon of the vinegar and bring to a simmer. Cover, reduce to a gentle simmer, and cook until the beans and rice are fully tender, 15 to 20 minutes longer.

5. Off the heat, remove the bay leaves and season with salt, pepper, and additional vinegar to taste. Sprinkle individual portions with the scallions and serve.

SPLIT PEA SOUP

OLD-FASHIONED RECIPES FOR SPLIT PEA SOUP usually start with the bone from a large roast ham that has been picked almost (but not quite) clean. The bone is thrown in a pot with some water and cooked until the little meat that's left is nearly falling off the bone, about two hours, before the split peas are stirred in. By the time the ham is fully tender, the fat has discreetly melted into the liquid, and the peas have become creamy enough to thicken the soup. While soup prepared in this manner is delicious, times have changed, and it's the rare occasion when the home cook is blessed with a leftover ham bone begging to be thrown into a soup pot. Our goal, then, would be to duplicate this wonderful soup without having to buy, and simmer for hours, a huge ham.

In some recipes, ham hocks are used in place of a meaty ham bone, but they still require a long simmering time to give up their flavor and become tender. In addition, the hocks offer little in the way of meat, and we wanted soup with chunks of meat in every bite. A ham steak, which is sold precooked, seemed an easy way to get plenty of meat. To improve the flavor of the ham, we cut it into ½-inch pieces and browned the pieces in oil before adding the split peas and water and simmering. The browning gave the soup some of the flavor that comes from long cooking times and cutting the ham into small pieces ensured that the flavor permeated the soup.

We now had plenty of chunks of ham, which added flavor to the cooking liquid, but it didn't approach the deep flavor of a broth made with ham bone. Switching from water to store-bought chicken broth helped the flavor but created another problem: ham steak is quite salty, and although we were using low-sodium chicken broth, the combination made our soup too salty. Two steps helped bring our soup back into balance. First, before browning the ham steak, we patted it dry with paper towels (to absorb excess salt on the surface of the ham). Second, we cut the broth with some water;

4½ cups broth to 4 cups water kept the savory flavor intact while also cutting down on saltiness. (But because this soup can easily turn too salty, it's important to taste it before seasoning with salt.)

As for the split peas, we found that it was important to thoroughly check over the dried split peas before adding them to the soup. Dried beans often contain tiny pebbles that can be a real surprise if you're unlucky enough to bite down on one.

In reviewing the other ingredients in a typical recipe, we found garlic and bay leaves, as well as onions and carrots, to be subtle but necessary flavor boosters. But most of the other ingredients—like potatoes, celery, leeks, thyme, and red pepper flakes—were unnecessary, masking the flavor of the ham and split peas rather than enhancing them. In our early tests, we treated the carrots as an aromatic, allowing them to break down and flavor the soup, but tasters wanted this vegetable to have more presence in the soup. Cutting two carrots into ½-inch pieces and stirring them in later on ensured they kept their shape. The carrots added a light sweetness, but we felt a pinch of sugar was necessary to balance the saltiness of the ham.

Our soup wasn't bad, but it still didn't taste quite as rich as the traditional soup made with ham bone or ham hock, owing to the lack of both fat and the flavorful marrow-filled bone. Taking another look back at the traditional recipes, we noticed that some called for smoked ham instead of fresh. This made us think of another smoked pork product—bacon, which might have seemed an odd ingredient in a split pea soup, but now made sense. The addition of some bacon, which we chopped fine and sautéed with the ham, added depth, fat, and a touch of smokiness, which tasters agreed lent the soup a more complex flavor. Adding a slice of bacon at a time, we ultimately settled on three slices, which enhanced the flavor of the soup without overwhelming it.

At last, we had arrived at a simple yet delicious split pea soup—made without the ham bone and without the hassle.

Split Pea and Ham Soup

SERVES 8

This soup can easily turn overly salty because of the bacon and ham; be sure to use low-sodium broth and taste the soup carefully before seasoning with any salt.

3	ounces (about 3 slices) bacon, chopped fine
1	pound ham steak, patted dry and cut into ½-inch pieces
1	medium onion, minced
5	medium garlic cloves, minced or pressed through a garlic press (about 5 teaspoons)
4½	cups low-sodium chicken broth (see note)
4	cups water
1	pound dried split peas, picked over and rinsed
2	bay leaves
	Pinch sugar
2	carrots, peeled and cut into ½-inch pieces
	Salt and ground black pepper

1. Cook the bacon in a large Dutch oven over medium heat until rendered and crisp, about 8 minutes. Add the ham and cook until well browned, about 5 minutes. Add the onion and cook until softened, 5 to 7 minutes. Stir in the garlic and cook until fragrant, about 30 seconds.

2. Stir in the broth, water, split peas, bay leaves, and sugar. Bring to a boil, then reduce to a gentle simmer and cook for 10 minutes. Stir in the carrots and continue to simmer until the carrots are soft and the peas are tender and no longer hold their shape, 30 to 40 minutes longer.

3. Off the heat, remove the bay leaves. Season with salt and pepper to taste and serve.

HEARTY LENTIL SOUP

LENTIL SOUP IS CHEAP TO MAKE, COMES together quickly and, when made well, tastes great. We were determined to develop a recipe for our cold weather repertoire that would be a keeper. We wanted a hearty lentil soup worthy of a second bowl—not the tasteless variety we have so often encountered.

We started by preparing five representative recipes, and two discoveries came quickly to light. First, garlic, herbs, onions, and tomatoes are common denominators. Second, texture is a big issue. None of our tasters liked the soup that was brothy or, at the other extreme, the one that was as thick as oatmeal. They also gave a big thumbs-down to those that looked like brown split pea soup. Consequently, recipes that included carrots, tomatoes, and herbs were rewarded for their brighter colors (and flavors). There was also a clear preference for the subtle, smoky depth meat provides. With the pros and cons weighed (and our likes clearly identified), the next step was to determine which lentils to buy and how to cook them.

Brown, green, and red lentils are the most common choices on supermarket shelves. At specialty markets and high-end supermarkets, you can also find yellow lentils and French green lentils (lentilles du Puy). We decided to test all these kinds. Red and yellow lentils, traditionally used in Indian cooking, were out—they disintegrated when simmered. All the remaining choices produced an acceptable texture, but tasters preferred, as expected, the earthy flavor and firm texture of the lentilles du Puy. However, the larger green and brown lentils fared reasonably well.

Next, we set out to test cooking methods. Some lentils, including the large brown and green varieties, can fall apart if overcooked or cooked too vigorously. Searching for a way to avoid this problem, we employed a common culinary trick: sweating the lentils in a covered pan with the aromatics prior to adding the liquid. Using brown lentils, we cooked up two batches and, bingo, we had solved the problem! The sweated lentils remained intact, while the unsweated lentils had broken down. And we discovered that sweating the lentils with canned tomatoes and salt (as well as aromatics) not only ensured an ideal texture but boosted the flavor of the legumes as well.

One issue concerning texture remained. Tasters wanted a chunkier soup and did not like the brothy base. We tried pureeing a few cups of the soup and then adding it back to the pot. Tasters praised the contrast of the now-creamy base with the whole lentils and found the entire soup more interesting.

Pork was the meat of choice in all the recipes we examined. We found that the lentils cooked too quickly to extract the smoky flavor that a ham bone or hock can impart. Prosciutto and pancetta were too mild. Tasters preferred the smoky flavor of bacon and liked the textural addition of the bacon bits. Another advantage bacon offered was rendered fat. We used it to sauté the aromatics, which further infused the soup with smoky flavor. A touch of white wine, bay leaves, thyme, and parsley rounded out the other flavors.

Last, but not least, was the question of liquid. We prepared two batches, one with water and one with chicken broth. Neither was ideal. Water produced a soup that was not as rich in flavor as desired, while the broth-only version tasted too much like chicken soup. After several more tests, we concluded that a mix of 3 parts broth to 1 part water produced a hearty depth of flavor without being overpowering.

Many recipes called for the addition of vinegar or lemon juice just before the soup is served. We stirred a touch of balsamic vinegar into the pot at completion, and tasters gave this soup a perfect 10.

Hearty Lentil Soup
SERVES 4 TO 6

Lentilles du Puy, sometimes called French green lentils, are our first choice for this recipe, but brown, black, or regular green lentils are fine, too. Note that cooking times may vary depending on the type of lentils used. See page 121 for more information on pureeing soup.

3	ounces (about 3 slices) bacon, chopped fine
1	large onion, minced
3	medium garlic cloves, minced or pressed through a garlic press (about 1 tablespoon)
1	teaspoon minced fresh thyme leaves or ¼ teaspoon dried
1	(14.5-ounce) can diced tomatoes, drained
1	cup (about 7 ounces) dried lentils, picked over and rinsed
	Salt and ground black pepper
2	bay leaves
½	cup dry white wine

4½	cups low-sodium chicken broth
1½	cups water
2	carrots, peeled and cut into ½-inch pieces
3	tablespoons minced fresh parsley leaves
1½	teaspoons balsamic vinegar

1. Cook the bacon in a large Dutch oven over medium heat until rendered and crisp, about 8 minutes. Stir in the onion and cook until beginning to soften, about 2 minutes. Stir in the garlic and thyme and cook until fragrant, about 30 seconds. Stir in the tomatoes and cook for 30 seconds.

2. Stir in the lentils, 1 teaspoon salt, and bay leaves. Cover, reduce the heat to medium-low, and cook until the vegetables are fully softened and the lentils have darkened, 8 to 10 minutes.

3. Uncover, stir in the wine, and cook until nearly evaporated, about 30 seconds. Stir in the broth, water, and carrots and bring to a boil. Reduce to a simmer, cover partially (leaving about 1 inch of the pot open), and cook until the lentils are tender but still hold their shape, 30 to 35 minutes.

4. Off the heat, remove the bay leaves. Puree 3 cups of the soup until smooth, then return to the pot. Stir in the parsley and vinegar, season with salt and pepper to taste, and serve.

➤ VARIATIONS

Hearty Lentil Soup with Fragrant Spices
Follow the recipe for Hearty Lentil Soup, adding 1 teaspoon ground cumin, 1 teaspoon ground coriander, 1 teaspoon ground cinnamon, and ¼ teaspoon cayenne pepper to the pot with the garlic in step 1. Substitute 3 tablespoons minced fresh cilantro leaves for the parsley and 1½ teaspoons juice from 1 lemon for the balsamic vinegar in step 4.

Hearty Curried Vegetarian Lentil Soup
In this soup, we prefer the pure flavor of homemade Vegetable Broth (page 22) to store-bought vegetable broth.

Follow the recipe for Hearty Lentil Soup, omitting the bacon and balsamic vinegar. Add 1 teaspoon curry powder to the pot with the onion in step 1 and substitute 4½ cups Vegetable Broth for the chicken broth in step 3.

8

SEAFOOD CHOWDERS, BISQUES, AND STEWS

Seafood Chowders, Bisques, and Stews

New England Clam Chowder

WE LOVE HOMEMADE CLAM CHOWDER ABOUT as much as we love good chicken soup. But we must confess that many cooks (including some who work in our test kitchen) don't make their own chowder. While they might never buy chicken soup, they seem willing to make this compromise with chowder. We wondered why.

Time certainly isn't the reason. You can actually prepare clam chowder much more quickly than you can a pot of good chicken soup. The reason why many cooks don't bother making their own clam chowder is the clams. First of all, clams can be expensive. Second, clams are not terribly forgiving—you must cook them soon after their purchase (chickens can be frozen), and then the soup itself must be quickly consumed (again, chicken soup can be frozen or at least refrigerated for another day). Last, chowders are more fragile (and thus more fickle) than other soups. Unless the dairy in the chowder is stabilized in some way, it can curdle, especially if the soup is brought to a boil. Our goals for this soup, then, were multiple but quite clear. We wanted to develop a delicious traditional chowder that was economical, would not curdle, and could be prepared quickly.

Before testing chowder recipes, we explored our clam options. Chowders are typically made with hard-shell clams, so we purchased (from smallest to largest) cockles, littlenecks, cherrystones, and chowder clams, often called quahogs (pronounced ko-hogs). Although they made delicious chowders, we eliminated littlenecks and cockles. Since we needed 6 pounds to serve six people, both these clams were deemed just too expensive. Chowders made with the cheapest clams, however, weren't really satisfactory, either. The quahogs we purchased for testing were too large (4 to 5 inches in diameter), tough, and strong-flavored. Though only a little more expensive than quahogs, cherrystones offered good value and flavor. The chowder made from these slightly smaller clams was distinctly clam-flavored, without an inky aftertaste. Because there are no industry sizing standards for each clam variety, you may find some small quahogs labeled as cherrystones or large cherrystones labeled as quahogs. Regardless of designation, clams much over 4 inches in diameter will deliver a distinctly metallic, inky-flavored chowder.

Some recipes suggest shucking raw clams and then adding the raw clam bellies to the soup pot. Other recipes steam the clams open. We tested both methods and found that steaming clams open is far easier than shucking them. After seven to 10 minutes over simmering water, giving the clams a stir halfway through, they open as naturally as budding flowers. Ours did not toughen up as long as we pulled them from the pot as soon as they opened and didn't let them cook too long in the finished chowder.

With almost 5 cups of intensely flavored homemade clam broth on hand, we figured it would be easy to turn out a great clam chowder. However, to our frustration, chowders made using all of the homemade broth were far too salty. But diluting it with water, the obvious choice, made for chowders that lacked great clam flavor. Looking for a way to keep the flavor, but lose some of the saltiness, we turned to bottled clam juice. With good clam flavor, but far less sodium than our homemade broth, bottled clam juice proved the perfect compromise. We tested ratios of homemade broth to clam juice until we hit upon a winner: 2 cups homemade broth to 3 cups bottled clam juice. With our broth in place, we turned our attention to texture.

We wanted a chowder that was thick but still a soup, rather than a stew. Older recipes call for thickening clam chowder with crumbled biscuits; bread crumbs and crackers are modern stand-ins. Bread crumb–thickened chowders failed to impress. We wanted a smooth, creamy soup base for the potatoes, onions, and clams, but no matter how long the chowder was simmered, bread crumbs or crackers never completely dissolved into the cooking liquid. Heavy cream alone, by contrast, did not give the chowder enough body. We discovered fairly quickly that flour was necessary, not only as a thickener but as a stabilizer, because unthickened chowders separate and curdle.

For potatoes, we found that Yukon Golds, with their moderate levels of starch and moisture, blended seamlessly with this creamy chowder.

PREPARING CLAMS FOR CHOWDER

1. Before cooking, use a soft brush (sometimes sold as a vegetable brush) to scrub away any bits of sand trapped in the shell.

2. Steam clams until they just open, as seen on the left, rather than completely open, as shown on the right.

3. Carefully use a paring knife to open the clams.

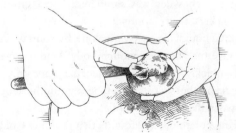

4. Once open, discard the top shell and use the knife to cut the clam from the bottom shell.

They released a small amount of body-giving starch, while staying firm but creamy as they simmered. We now had two final questions to answer about New England clam chowder. First, should it include salt pork or bacon and, if the latter, did the bacon need to be blanched, as suggested in some recipes? Second, should the chowder be enriched with milk or cream?

Salt pork is the more traditional choice in chowder recipes, although bacon has become popular in recent decades. We made clam chowder with both and, in the end, tasters slightly preferred the smokiness of the chowder made with bacon. As for the cream versus milk issue, we found that milk simply made the chowder milky, rather than creamy. Finishing the stew with a cup of cream gave us what we were looking for—a rich, creamy chowder that tasted distinctly of clams.

New England Clam Chowder

SERVES 6

Be sure to use fresh clams for this chowder; for a quick version using canned clams, see Quick Clam Chowder (page 320). This chowder uses a combination of the clam steaming liquid and bottled clam juice; a chowder made entirely from the clam steaming liquid will taste unpalatably salty. Serve with oyster crackers.

3	cups water
6	pounds medium hard-shell clams, such as cherrystones, scrubbed (see the illustration at left)
2	ounces (about 2 slices) bacon, chopped fine
2	medium onions, minced
2	celery ribs, chopped fine
I	teaspoon minced fresh thyme leaves or ¼ teaspoon dried
⅓	cup unbleached all-purpose flour
3	(8-ounce) bottles clam juice
I½	pounds Yukon Gold potatoes (about 3 medium), peeled and cut into ½-inch pieces
I	bay leaf
I	cup heavy cream
2	tablespoons minced fresh parsley leaves
	Salt and ground black pepper

1. Bring the water to a boil in a large Dutch oven. Add the clams, cover, and cook for 5 minutes. Stir the clams thoroughly, cover, and continue to cook until they just begin to open following the illustrations on page 158, 2 to 5 minutes. As the clams open, transfer them to a large bowl and let cool slightly. Discard any unopened clams.

2. Measure out and reserve 2 cups of the clam steaming liquid, avoiding any gritty sediment that has settled on the bottom of the pot. Following the illustrations on page 158, remove the clam meat from the shells and chop coarse.

3. In a clean Dutch oven, cook the bacon over medium heat until rendered and crisp, 5 to 7 minutes. Stir in the onions and celery and cook until the vegetables are softened, 5 to 7 minutes. Stir in the thyme and cook until fragrant, about 30 seconds. Stir in the flour and cook for 1 minute.

4. Gradually whisk in the bottled clam juice and reserved clam steaming liquid, scraping up any browned bits and smoothing out any lumps. Stir in the potatoes and bay leaf and bring to a boil. Reduce to a gentle simmer and cook until the potatoes are tender, 20 to 25 minutes.

5. Stir in the cream and return to a brief simmer. Off the heat, remove the bay leaf, stir in the parsley, and season with salt and pepper to taste. Stir in the chopped clams, cover, and let stand until the clams are warmed through, about 1 minute. Serve.

Rhode Island Red Clam Chowder

WHILE CLAM CHOWDER AFICIONADOS DEBATE the relative merits of New England versus Manhattan-style, we'd like to add a third chowder to the mix—one that we find especially intriguing— Rhode Island red clam chowder. Consisting of chopped fresh clams, tender chunks of potato, and a creamy-tasting, rich-flavored tomato and clam broth, this clam chowder is a minimalist expression of where the sea meets the land. Our research into the origins of this chowder brought us to the small coastal Rhode Island town of Warwick. It was there, in the Rocky Point Shore Dinner Hall

(publicized as the world's largest shore dinner hall) that generations of sun-baked seaside visitors were first introduced to this unique bowl of soup. And while the dinner hall and adjacent amusement park closed a few years ago, locals' love for the chowder remains as strong as ever. Wishing to share this small-town soup with a wider audience and give chowder partisans a new topic for debate, we set about creating our ultimate bowl of Rhode Island red clam chowder.

Most of the recipes touted as "authentic" and "original" turned out a simple, if not particularly inspiring, chowder. Many start by cooking salt pork in a large pot until the fat is rendered. To this fat, onions are added and cooked until softened, then tomato puree, clam juice, and water go into the pot to form the base of the soup. Next up are the diced potatoes, which are simmered until tender, followed, finally, by chopped clams. Served with crumbled pilot crackers (an unsalted cracker similar to hardtack), these chowders, while certainly edible, tasted thin and sharp; a far cry from the creamy-tasting, rich, tomatoey clam soup that Rhode Islanders hold so dear. Since this chowder is composed of a few simple ingredients, we decided to tackle each one in our effort to make a better bowl. We started with the clams.

While most of the recipes we found called rather ambiguously for chopped clams, we knew that starting with fresh, live clams would be key to getting great flavor. From our experience in developing classic New England Clam Chowder (page 158), we had some firm and tested opinions about clams. Our favorite chowder clam, the cherrystone, offers great flavor and value and would be our clam of choice here. We found that steaming the clams in water and stirring them halfway through cooking ensured evenly cooked clams. Also important is checking the pot every few minutes to remove clams as they open—otherwise a portion of the batch will overcook and turn tough and chewy.

In tasting our way through a multitude of recipes, we found that what separates a good bowl of Rhode Island red clam chowder from a great one is the broth. It should look and taste creamy (while containing no cream) and perfectly balance the flavor of clams and tomatoes. All the recipes we tested were imbalanced in one direction or the other, producing either a tomato soup with clams or a clam-rich broth with just a hint of tomato. With the goal of letting each element shine, we looked first at the clam flavor. As we had learned in prior testing, using all the steaming liquid from the clams produces an unpalatably salty base. Instead, we found a combination of 2 cups of homemade broth and 3 cups of bottled clam juice yielded a chowder base with great clam flavor minus the salt lick. Without an equally obvious source for getting great tomato flavor into our chowder, we tested a multitude of options.

While most of the recipes we uncovered called for tomato puree, we found that it produced a sharp, harsh-tasting chowder, with little tomato richness. Resigned to the fact that we were going to need to break out the blender to create our own smooth tomato puree, we rounded up all of our tomato options: fresh, diced, crushed, and whole. We pureed them until smooth and then added each to a batch of our clam broth. Tasters unanimously preferred the batch made with whole canned tomatoes, praising it for its true tomato flavor. Still, tasters felt that the chowder needed more tomato presence and complexity. In addition, it had little of the requisite creaminess that defines Rhode Island red clam chowder.

Looking for ways to bump up the tomato flavor and add creaminess, we looked to a few tomato soup recipes. One perennial tomato soup ingredient, which we had overlooked up to this point, was tomato paste. One recipe called for cooking the tomato paste, tomatoes, and some onion in butter until dry and browned in order to concentrate their flavors. We gave this method a shot, adding our clam broth to the browned tomato mixture before pureeing it a blender until completely smooth. Not only did this chowder base have incredible tomato flavor, it was also surprisingly creamy. Puzzled by this rapid transformation from a thin tomato broth to a creamy, viscous soup, we did a little research. It turns out that our broth tasted creamy for the same reason that jams and jellies are thick and spreadable: pectin. Since tomatoes are a natural source of

pectin, and tomato paste is a highly concentrated form of tomatoes, we had unknowingly boosted our soup's pectin content and subsequent creaminess. With our flavors in balance, we moved on to the chowder's last few ingredients.

As with most of our chowders, when it came to potatoes, we found Yukon Golds to be our favorite, besting both super-starchy russets (which crumbled into mashed potatoes once tender) and high-moisture red potatoes (which absorbed little of the chowder's flavor as they cooked). With moderate levels of both starch and moisture, Yukon Golds absorbed flavor while maintaining their shape. While salt pork is the more traditional choice for Rhode Island red clam chowder, tasters preferred the gentle smokiness of bacon. Since crisping the bacon and then pureeing it with the rest of broth ingredients left us with an odd grainy texture, we had to find a new way incorporate it. On a whim, we tried adding whole slices of bacon to the chowder as it simmered, removing them, as we would bay leaves, prior to serving. This unusual method did the trick, providing just the right amount of smoky bacon flavor and aroma. And although untraditional in the ocean state, we added a splash of sherry to our chowder for brightness and complexity. Finally, we had arrived our at ultimate bowl of creamy, tomatoey Rhode Island red clam chowder.

Rhode Island
Red Clam Chowder

SERVES 6

Be sure to use fresh clams for this soup. For more information on pureeing soup, see page 121. This soup is classically served with oyster crackers; however, it also tastes great with Garlic Toasts (page 138).

3	cups water
6	pounds medium hard-shell clams, such as cherrystones, scrubbed (see the illustration on page 158)
2	tablespoons unsalted butter
I	(28-ounce) can whole tomatoes, drained with juice reserved

1   medium onion, minced
1   tablespoon tomato paste
2   medium garlic cloves, minced or pressed
     through a garlic press (about 2 teaspoons)
3   (8-ounce) bottles clam juice
1½   pounds Yukon Gold potatoes
     (about 3 medium), peeled and
     cut into ½-inch pieces
2   ounces (about 2 slices) bacon
1   bay leaf
2   tablespoons minced fresh parsley leaves
2   teaspoons dry sherry
     Salt and ground black pepper

1. Bring the water to a boil in a large Dutch oven. Add the clams, cover, and cook for 5 minutes. Stir the clams thoroughly, cover, and continue to cook until they just begin to open following the illustrations on page 158, 2 to 5 minutes. As the clams open, transfer them to a large bowl and let cool slightly. Discard any unopened clams.

2. Measure out and reserve 2 cups of the clam steaming liquid, avoiding any gritty sediment that has settled on the bottom of the pot. Following the illustrations on page 158, remove the clam meat from the shells and chop coarse.

3. In a clean Dutch oven, melt the butter over medium heat. Add the tomatoes, onion, and tomato paste and cook until dry and beginning to brown, 11 to 13 minutes. Stir in the garlic and cook until fragrant, about 30 seconds. Stir in the bottled clam juice and reserved clam steaming liquid, scraping up any browned bits.

4. Working in batches, puree the soup until smooth, 1 to 2 minutes. Return the soup to a clean pot. Stir in the potatoes, bacon slices, and bay leaf and bring to a boil. Reduce to a gentle simmer and cook until the potatoes are tender, 20 to 25 minutes.

5. Off the heat, remove the bacon slices and bay leaf. Stir in the parsley and sherry and season with salt and pepper to taste. Stir in the chopped clams, cover, and let stand until warmed through, about 1 minute. Serve.

New England Fish Chowder

LOADED WITH MOIST PIECES OF FISH AND tender chunks of potatoes in a creamy, briny broth, New England fish chowder isn't so different from New England clam chowder. Still, there are some minor, but important, differences. Clams shed so much juice that they produce their own broth. The firm, meaty white fish used in this hearty soup (typically haddock or cod) sheds much less liquid, so fish stock is often used instead. Fish chowder is also often thinner than clam chowder and commonly finished with milk instead of cream. We decided to sort through these details to produce an accessible New England fish chowder recipe that would be as popular as its clammy cousin.

After preparing several versions of this chowder, we noticed two problems that would need to be addressed. The first issue was the fish—in many recipes the fish fell apart into masses of small flakes. Some flaking was fine, but we wanted the fish to remain in large chunks when cooked. The second problem was the seasonings. Too many recipes added ingredients that had no place in this spartan chowder. This was easy enough to fix. We jettisoned tomatoes, cayenne, and any other ingredients that just didn't feel right.

Given the importance of the fish, we decided to work on this question next. We had read several tips for keeping the fish from falling apart in the chowder. One recipe suggested laying whole fillets on top of the liquid and letting the fish naturally fall apart into large chunks as it cooked. We found that cutting each fillet into 3- to 4-inch pieces yielded the best results. The pieces were small enough to sink down into the chowder liquid but large enough to hold their shape, making for only a minimum of flaking.

With the fish issue resolved, we moved on to the seasonings. We found recipes with salt pork as well as those with bacon. We prepared pots with each pork product and tasters favored the smoky flavor of the bacon. Once the bacon had been fried, we followed the lead of one traditional recipe and removed the crisp bits so that we could swirl them into the finished soup. Adding them to the chowder just before serving maximized their flavor and crunch. The bacon fat stayed in the pan, though; we found that this fat was the best medium for cooking the onions, giving the stew a smoky flavor that vegetable oil could not match. Once the onions softened, the liquid and potatoes went into the pot.

While we loved this chowder with Fish Stock (page 20) we wanted to offer an easier, quicker option. We turned to readily available bottled clam juice, and while certainly different than fish stock, it offered some of the same briny ocean flavor. We tested whole milk (the most traditional dairy product), but were disappointed with the results. The liquid was too thin, in terms of both consistency and flavor. Cream, on the other hand, added just the right amount of richness. In addition to cream and our clam juice mixture, we noticed that white wine was used in several recipes. Tasters agreed that the acidity of the white wine balanced the richness of the cream, so wine became part of our working recipe. We found that a mix of 5 cups clam juice, ¾ cup cream, and ½ cup wine provided the ideal balance of flavors.

But there was a problem—the liquid was a bit thin. We tried using more cream, but then the dairy overwhelmed the other flavors. At this point, we decided to pick up a technique from our New England Clam Chowder and stir some flour into the pot once the onions had softened. The flour did the trick, improving the texture of the stew liquid and stabilizing it.

Our recipe was nearly done, with only the potatoes and herbs to test. Yukon Gold potatoes were our top choice for this dish, and they performed admirably when cut into ½-inch pieces. As for the herbs, we limited ourselves to bay leaves, thyme, and a bit of parsley for freshness, stirred in just before serving. Our finished chowder was restrained and dignified, just as you would expect, given its Yankee roots. But it was not austere. The combination of fish, onions, potatoes, bacon, and cream is hearty and satisfying, no matter where you live.

New England Fish Chowder
SERVES 6 TO 8

Five cups of Fish Stock (page 20) can be substituted for the clam juice. Cod, halibut, striped bass, and hake make good alternatives to haddock.

4	ounces (about 4 slices) bacon, chopped medium
2	medium onions, minced
1	teaspoon minced fresh thyme leaves or ¼ teaspoon dried
⅓	cup unbleached all-purpose flour
½	cup dry white wine
5	(8-ounce) bottles clam juice (see note)
1½	pounds Yukon Gold potatoes (about 3 medium), peeled and cut into ½-inch pieces
1	bay leaf
3	pounds skinless haddock fillets (¾ to 1 inch thick), cut into 3- to 4-inch pieces Salt and ground black pepper
¾	cup heavy cream
2	tablespoons minced fresh parsley leaves

1. Cook the bacon in a large Dutch oven over medium heat until rendered and crisp, 5 to 7 minutes. Using a slotted spoon, transfer the bacon to a paper towel–lined plate and reserve for serving.

2. Add the onions to the fat left in the pot and cook until softened, 5 to 7 minutes. Stir in the thyme and cook until fragrant, about 30 seconds. Stir in the flour and cook for 1 minute. Stir in the wine, scraping up any browned bits, and cook until nearly evaporated, about 1 minute.

3. Gradually whisk in the clam juice, smoothing out any lumps. Stir in the potatoes and bay leaf and bring to a boil. Reduce to a gentle simmer and cook until the potatoes are nearly tender, 15 to 20 minutes.

4. Pat the fish dry with paper towels and season with salt and pepper. Add the fish to the pot, cover, and simmer gently until the fish is just cooked through and the potatoes are tender, 5 to 7 minutes.

5. Gently stir in the cream and bring to a brief simmer. Off the heat, remove the bay leaf and stir in the parsley. Season with salt and pepper to taste and break up any remaining large pieces of fish. Sprinkle individual portions with the reserved bacon before serving.

LOBSTER AND CORN CHOWDER

FOR ANYONE WHO HAS SPENT A SUMMER'S day along the shores of New England, the combination of succulent lobster and sweet summer corn is hard to resist. Lobster and corn chowder, both rustic and delicate, is perhaps our favorite way to enjoy this natural pairing. At its finest, this chowder features tender, rich bites of perfectly cooked lobster meat, sweet kernels of summer corn, and creamy potatoes, all enveloped in a rich, cream-infused lobster and corn broth. However, when the mark is missed (which is often), this soup is better described as corn chowder strewn with a few obligatory pieces of chewy lobster. Given the high probability of this unfortunate outcome, the cost of lobster, and the often-arduous work involved in making a lobster broth, most home cooks leave lobster and corn chowder to the professionals. Wishing to enjoy this chowder at home, we set about developing a foolproof, accessible recipe that would deliver all of the sweet richness we have come to expect from this summertime treat.

The recipes we found in our research fell into two very different camps. The first was the shortcut method, which often employed the use of frozen or canned corn and called for cooked lobster meat to be stirred in toward the end of cooking. These renditions were, at best, plain and lifeless and, at worst, a complete waste of time (and lobster meat). We found the majority of recipes at the other extreme, calling for myriad restaurant-style ingredients and techniques to get great lobster flavor. Some of the more esoteric recipes suggested using extra lobster bodies (something only seafood restaurants have

lying around), roasting and grinding lobster shells, and making a finishing butter out of the lobster roe. While many of these versions were tasty, the work and expense involved made them nonstarters. We decided to use a classic chowder approach and determine the best way to get great lobster and corn flavor without breaking our backs or the bank. We started with the lobster broth.

Ask a dozen chefs how to make good lobster broth, and you are likely to get just as many variations on the recipe. But while professionals may disagree on the proper ratios, aromatics, and simmering time, they all seem to align on one point: for big lobster flavor, the shells must first be exposed to dry heat (think: roasting, sautéing, or grilling). When lobster shells are cooked with dry heat they start to brown and undergo changes much like chicken, fish, shrimp, and beef do. This process, known as the Maillard reaction, develops new and enticing flavor and aroma compounds.

To find the best way to take advantage of this flavor boon, we broke down two 1¼-pound lobsters (enough to serve four to six people) into their three main components: claws (with arms), body, and tail. Since we planned on using the claws and tail for their meat, and not necessarily to flavor the broth, we set them aside for now. Following the advice of most recipes we found, we split the bodies in half and removed the innards (brain sac, tomalley, and roe) before proceeding. We then roasted one of the bodies at 400 degrees until very aromatic and brittle, and sautéed the other for a few minutes in vegetable oil until bright red and lightly browned. Simmered in equal amounts of water for 30 minutes, both bodies produced a broth with subtle lobster flavor. The roasted broth, though, had a harsh, almost bitter undercurrent. Wondering if shorter roasting would improve matters, we removed the lobster from the oven once it had turned bright red. This second broth wasn't bitter, but it also had little lobster flavor. Pleased that sautéing, the decidedly easier method of cooking the shells had prevailed, we began the broth.

To start, we killed and cut up the lobsters just as before, and browned the split bodies in a couple tablespoons of vegetable oil (since fats readily absorb flavors, we found using a substantial amount of oil produced a more flavorful broth). Once the shells turned bright red and lightly browned, we added the classic mirepoix of onion, carrot, and celery and continued to cook until softened. Finally, we added water and simmered the broth for 30 minutes (most recipes discourage simmering for longer than half an hour, lest off-flavors be pulled from the shells). This broth smelled great but tasted a little flat. Thinking that some acidity might brighten things up, we added some fresh diced tomato and white wine to the mix. This

broth was much improved, but tasters still wanted more potent lobster flavor. Bucking conventional wisdom, we tried simmering batches of the broth for 45 minutes and 60 minutes. While both broths were a big improvement over the 30-minute broth (with no detectable off-flavors), tasters noticed little difference between the 45- and 60-minute versions. Happy to cut 15 minutes from our cooking time, we strained the 45-minute broth and started to put together our chowder.

We first cooked bacon (which tasters preferred over salt pork) in a large Dutch oven, before adding onion and celery to help reinforce the aromatics in

INGREDIENTS: Lobsters

As with most seafood, knowing how to shop for lobster is just as important as knowing how to cook it. Lobsters must be purchased alive. Choose lobsters that are active in the tank; avoid listless specimens that may have been in the tank too long. Maine lobsters, with their large claws, are meatier and sweeter than clawless rock or spiny lobsters, and they are our first and only choice.

When serving whole lobsters, size is really a matter of preference and budget. For soups and stews, we recommend buying small lobsters (about one pound is fine) because they are so reasonably priced. These so-called "chicken lobsters" have plenty of meat for bisques and soups. You might even consider buying "cull" lobsters, which are missing a claw. There will be enough meat in the tail and remaining claw. And remember that the shells are the main source of flavor for the soup base, not the meat.

Before working on this topic in the test kitchen, the terms "hard-shell" and "soft-shell" lobster meant nothing to us. Unlike crabs, there's certainly no distinction between the two at the retail level. Of course, we knew from past experience that some lobster claws rip open as easily as a can of soda, while others require shop tools to crack. We also noticed the small, limp claw meat of some lobsters and the full, packed meat of others. We attributed these differences to how long the lobsters had been stored in tanks. It seems we were wrong. These variations are caused by the particular stage of molting a lobster is in at the time it is caught.

As it turns out, most of the lobsters we eat during the summer and fall are in some phase of molting. During the late spring, as waters begin to warm, lobsters start to form new shell tissue

underneath their old shells. As early as June off the shores of New Jersey and in July or August in colder Maine and Canadian waters, lobsters shed their hard exterior shell. Because the most difficult task in molting is pulling the claw muscle through the old shell, the lobster dehydrates its claw (hence the smaller claw meat).

Once a lobster molts, it emerges with nothing but a wrinkled, soft covering, much like that on a soft-shell crab. Within 15 minutes, the lobster inflates itself with water, increasing its length by 15 percent and its weight by 50 percent. This extra water expands the wrinkled, soft covering, allowing the lobster room to grow long after the shell starts to harden. The newly molted lobster immediately eats its old shell, digesting the crucial shell-hardening calcium.

Understanding the molt phase clarifies the deficiencies of soft-shell summer lobster. It explains why it is so waterlogged, why its claw meat is so shriveled and scrawny, and why its tail meat is so underdeveloped and chewy. There is also far less meat in a one-pound soft-shell lobster than in a hard-shell lobster that weighs the same.

During the fall, the lobster shell continues to harden, and the meat expands to fill the new shell. By spring, lobsters are at their peak, packed with meat and relatively inexpensive, since it is easier for fishermen to check their traps than it is during the winter. As the tail grows, it becomes firmer and meatier and cooks up tender, not tough. The shells are also more flavorful. For these reasons, ask at the fish counter if you can give the lobsters a squeeze and buy only those with hard shells. As a rule of thumb, hard-shell lobsters are reasonably priced from Mother's Day through the Fourth of July.

our broth. Next, we stirred in a little flour for body and thickening and then our homemade lobster broth and some diced Yukon Gold potatoes. In testing, we found that Yukon Golds, which have moderate amounts of both moisture and starch, kept their shape better than russets and lent more starch to the broth than red potatoes. Once the chowder came to a simmer, we added the reserved lobster claws and tails and gently poached them until just cooked through. After the claws and tails had cooled slightly, we removed the meat from the shells and reserved it for stirring in at the end. Meanwhile, we continued to simmer the soup until the potatoes were almost cooked through. Finally, we added two ears' worth of corn kernels (about 2 cups) and cooked the chowder for another five to seven minutes. Finished with a swirl of cream and the reserved cooked meat, this chowder tasted good, but lacked corn essence.

Taking a page from our corn chowder recipes, we tried grating an ear of corn on a box grater and scraping the milk and pulp from the two spent ears of corn. We added this mash of grated corn and pulp to the chowder with the broth, giving it plenty of time to infuse into, and thicken, the soup. To our surprise, this chowder actually over-shot our target, boasting an overwhelming amount of corn flavor. In the hope of bringing things into balance, we ditched the grated cob, choosing to only milk the spent cobs. This small adjustment resulted in a bowl of chowder with the perfect interplay of lobster and corn flavor. With our ideal bowl of lobster and corn chowder visible on the horizon, we turned our attention to a few final adjustments.

For freshness, we added a splash of dry sherry and a sprinkle of minced fresh parsley just before serving. Finally, after testing our way through countless pounds of lobster and corn, we had arrived at a rich, luxurious lobster and corn chowder recipe that brought to mind all the warmth and pleasure of a day at the beach.

PREPARING A LOBSTER FOR SOUP

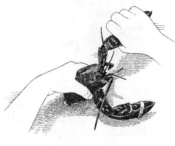

1. Holding the partially frozen lobster firmly with a kitchen towel, firmly drive the tip of a large heavy-duty chef's knife through the back of the upper portion of the lobster's head, then swing the knife down through the head to sever.

2. Using your hands, twist the tail free from the body.

3. Using your hands, twist the claws (with arm) free from the body.

4. Turn the lobster body over and split it in half lengthwise with a heavy knife.

5. Use a spoon to remove and discard the innards (the brain sac, the green colored tomalley, and roe).

6. Remove and discard the feathery gills.

Lobster and Corn Chowder

SERVES 4 TO 6

Do not be tempted to substitute frozen corn for the fresh corn here; fresh corn is crucial to the flavor of this soup.

BROTH

2	(1- to 1¼-pound) live lobsters
3	tablespoons vegetable oil
1	medium onion, chopped medium
1	carrot, peeled and chopped medium
1	celery rib, chopped medium
2	plum tomatoes, cored and cut into ½-inch pieces
⅓	cup dry white wine
7	cups water
1	bay leaf

CHOWDER

2	ounces (about 2 slices) bacon, chopped fine
1	medium onion, minced
1	celery rib, chopped fine
1	teaspoon minced fresh thyme leaves or ¼ teaspoon dried
¼	cup unbleached all-purpose flour
1	large Yukon Gold potato (10 to 12 ounces), peeled and cut into ½-inch pieces
2	ears corn, husk and silk removed, kernels cut off the cobs, and cobs scraped clean of pulp (see the illustrations on page 108)
¾	cup heavy cream
2	tablespoons minced fresh parsley leaves
2	teaspoons dry sherry
	Salt and ground black pepper

REMOVING MEAT FROM COOKED LOBSTERS

1. Twist the tail to separate it from the body. Then, working at the end of the tail, twist off the tail flippers.

2. Use a fork or your finger to push the tail meat up and out through the wide end of the tail.

3. Twist the claw appendages off the body, then twist the claw free from the arm.

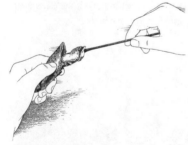  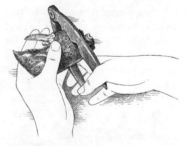

4. Crack open the arm and remove the meat with a cocktail fork.

5. Remove the small, pincer half of the claw. Use a gentle motion: the meat will often stay attached to the rest of the claw. Otherwise, use a cocktail fork to pick out the meat.

6. Use a lobster cracker to break open the claw and, if possible, remove the meat in a single piece.

1. FOR THE BROTH: Freeze the lobsters for 10 to 15 minutes to sedate them (do not overfreeze). Following the illustrations on page 165, kill the lobsters, then remove claws (with arms) and tails. Slice the bodies in half and discard the innards and gills.

2. Heat the oil in a large Dutch oven over medium-high heat until just smoking. Add the cleaned lobster bodies and cook until bright red and lightly browned, 3 to 5 minutes. Stir in the onion, carrot, celery, and tomatoes and cook until the vegetables are softened, 5 to 7 minutes. Stir in the wine and cook until nearly evaporated, about 1 minute.

3. Stir in the water and bay leaf and bring to a boil. Add the lobster claws and tails, reduce to a gentle simmer, and cook for 4 minutes. Remove the claws and tails from the pot and let cool slightly. Following the illustrations on page 166, remove the lobster meat from the shells, cut into ½-inch pieces, and refrigerate until needed.

4. Meanwhile, continue to simmer the lobster broth until it is rich and flavorful, about 45 minutes. Strain the broth through a fine-mesh strainer, pressing on the solids to release as much liquid as possible.

5. FOR THE CHOWDER: Cook the bacon in a large Dutch oven over medium heat until rendered and crisp, 5 to 7 minutes. Stir in the onion and celery and cook until the vegetables are softened, 5 to 7 minutes. Stir in the thyme and cook until fragrant, about 30 seconds. Stir in the flour and cook for 1 minute.

6. Gradually whisk in the strained lobster broth, scraping up any browned bits and smoothing out any lumps. Stir in the potato and corn cob pulp and bring to a boil. Reduce to a gentle simmer and cook until the potato is nearly tender, 15 to 20 minutes.

7. Stir in the corn kernels and continue to simmer until tender, 5 to 7 minutes. Stir in the cream and bring to a brief simmer. Off the heat, remove the bay leaf, stir in the parsley and sherry, and season with salt and pepper to taste. Stir in the lobster meat, cover, and let stand until warmed through, about 1 minute. Serve.

SHRIMP BISQUE

THOUGH A BISQUE IS BY IMPLICATION ANY soup that is rich, velvety, and smooth, by definition it contains shellfish, cream, and the classic French aromatic trio of celery, carrot, and onion known as mirepoix. Shrimp bisque, in particular, should be a rich, blushing pastel color—delicate in character but deeply intense—with an almost sweet shrimp essence and an elusive interplay of supporting flavors. Its texture must run unfettered and silky over the tongue. If you are very lucky, there will be tender pieces of poached shrimp and crisp, buttery croutons.

To start, we gathered together several shrimp bisque recipes found in our research and headed into the test kitchen. The fundamental challenge in making a shrimp bisque is extracting flavor from the shrimp and shells. The recipes we tested did this in a couple ways. Some pureed the shrimp meat into the base and left it there, others simmered the shrimp in the base until spent and then strained them out. The bisques made with pureed shrimp were grainy with shrimp curds; the ones in which the shrimp were strained out achieved the velvety texture properly associated with a bisque.

Because the shrimp flavor resides more in the shells than in the meat, a bisque made with shrimp alone is weak and unsatisfying. But trying to deal with shells and meat to the advantage of each tends

INGREDIENTS: Shrimp

We're often asked whether it's better to cook with fresh or frozen shrimp. It's somewhat of a trick question—almost all shrimp are frozen after being harvested, so the "fresh" shrimp you see at the market have very likely been frozen and then thawed by your fishmonger. Since there's no way to know for certain when these "fresh" shrimp were defrosted, quality varies dramatically. In the test kitchen, we find that buying frozen shrimp and defrosting them at home yields superior results. To defrost shrimp, place them in a colander under cold running water; they will be thawed and ready to cook in a few minutes (always thoroughly dry them first). Make sure to buy frozen shrimp with their shells on; shelled shrimp don't survive the freezing and thawing process very well and will surely be mush.

to induce procedural overkill. The recipes that we tested got carried away by having several pots and pans active at once (here a little pot of simmering aromatics, here fish stock simmering with shells and rice, there a pan to sauté shrimp) rather than proceeding one step at a time in sequence. One recipe, for example, sautéed shell-on shrimp to start and later simmered them in wine, broth, and previously sautéed aromatics. At that point the shrimp were peeled. Because the flavor from the shells had not been sufficiently extracted, a shrimp butter was advised. That involved crushing the shells to a paste, using them to make a butter infusion, and straining them out. The resulting resolidified butter was stirred into the bisque at the end. Though arguably authentic, the technique was absurdly complicated and rendered the finished bisque far too rich for our tastes.

We talked strategy in the test kitchen and established our priorities. The shrimp were key; other ingredients must add background depth and nuance. We began by taking 2 pounds of shrimp, shelling 1 pound of them and putting those aside to use later as a garnish. We then heated a splash of oil in a heavy Dutch oven and sautéed the remaining shell-on shrimp and shrimp shells until they reached a blistering pink. To wring every drop of flavor from the shells, we then flambéed the shrimp and shells in brandy. Next we took the sautéed shrimp and shells, dumped them into a food processor, and ground them to a pulp. Because we knew the shrimp and the shells were destined to be strained from the bisque, a food processor was the fastest way to cut the shrimp into small pieces and to unlock its flavor potential.

Our next step was to sauté the shrimp pulp with a mirepoix and, since we were going to dirty the food processor with the shrimp anyway, we decided to save some chopping and process the mirepoix as well. After five minutes, we stirred in some flour, preferring its convenience to the rice or bread suggested for thickening in some recipes. Next came white wine, diced tomatoes, and some clam juice. After 20 minutes or so we strained the fragrant base through a fine-mesh strainer, pressing to extract every drop.

Back on the stove we offered the soup base a bit of cream, a little lemon juice, a sprig of fresh tarragon, cayenne, and then the remaining shrimp, cut into pieces. A brief simmer poached the shrimp garnish and harmonized the flavors. We removed the tarragon sprig and added a splash of sherry. This bisque possessed everything we demanded of it: flavor in spades and a peerless texture and color. And so it seemed we had a one-pot wonder. But we had to admit, a skillet would beat a Dutch oven at sautéing the shrimp and make the flambéing more manageable. OK, so now it was a two-pot wonder, but a very quick one—and a very good one. And for those occasions when you are craving more than just shrimp in your bisque, we developed an easy seafood bisque variation that features lobster and scallops.

TWO WAYS TO FLAMBÉ SHRIMP

A. To flambé on a gas stove, tilt the pan of shrimp, shells, and brandy toward the flame to ignite it and then shake the skillet.

B. To flambé on an electric stove, wave a lit match over the pan of shrimp, shells, and brandy until the brandy ignites and then shake the skillet.

Shrimp Bisque

SERVES 6

In this soup, half the shrimp are used just to flavor the broth (they are ground, simmered, then strained out), while the other half are added at the last minute as garnish. Before flambéing the shrimp, be sure to tie back any loose hair and roll up your sleeves.

2 pounds large shrimp (31 to 40 per pound)
2 tablespoons vegetable oil
⅓ cup brandy or cognac
1 medium onion, chopped coarse
1 carrot, peeled and chopped coarse
1 celery rib, chopped coarse
1 medium garlic clove, peeled
2 tablespoons unsalted butter
½ cup unbleached all-purpose flour
1½ cups dry white wine
4 (8-ounce) bottles clam juice
1 (14.5-ounce) can diced tomatoes, drained
1 cup heavy cream
1 tablespoon juice from 1 lemon
1 small sprig fresh tarragon
Pinch ground cayenne
2 tablespoons dry sherry or Madeira
Salt and ground black pepper
2 tablespoons minced fresh chives
1 recipe Butter Croutons (page 116)

1. Following the illustration at right, peel and devein 1 pound of the shrimp, reserving the shells, and cut each shrimp into 3 pieces; refrigerate until needed.

2. Heat the oil in a 12-inch skillet over medium-high heat until just smoking. Add the remaining 1 pound shrimp and reserved shrimp shells and cook until lightly browned, 3 to 5 minutes. Add the brandy, let it warm through for a minute, then following the illustrations on page 168, flambé, shaking the pan until the flames subside.

3. Transfer the flambéed shrimp mixture to a food processor and process until the mixture resembles fine meal, 10 to 20 seconds. Transfer to a bowl. Process the onion, carrot, celery, and garlic in the food processor until finely chopped, about 5 pulses.

DEVEINING SHRIMP

Hold the peeled shrimp between your thumb and forefinger and cut down the length of its back, about ⅛ to ¼ inch deep, with a sharp paring knife. If the shrimp has a vein, it will be exposed and can be pulled out easily. Once you have freed the vein with the tip of a paring knife, just touch the knife to a paper towel and the vein will slip off the knife and stick to the towel.

4. Melt the butter in a large Dutch oven over medium heat. Add the processed shrimp and vegetables, cover, and cook until softened and fragrant, 5 to 7 minutes. Stir in the flour and cook for 1 minute.

5. Gradually stir in the wine and clam juice, scraping up any browned bits and smoothing out any lumps. Stir in the tomatoes and bring to a boil. Reduce to a gentle simmer and cook until thickened and the flavors meld, about 20 minutes.

6. Strain the broth through a fine-mesh strainer, pressing on the solids to release as much liquid as possible. Clean the pot and return it to the stove.

7. Add the strained broth, cream, lemon juice, tarragon sprig, and cayenne to the pot and bring to a simmer. Stir in the reserved shrimp pieces and gently simmer until the shrimp are bright pink, 1 to 2 minutes. Off the heat, discard the tarragon, stir in the sherry, and season with salt and pepper to taste. Sprinkle individual portions with the chives and croutons before serving.

➤ VARIATION

Seafood Bisque

Follow the recipe for Shrimp Bisque, reducing the amount of peeled and deveined shrimp in step 1 to 8 ounces. Add 8 ounces large sea scallops, tendons removed (see the illustration on page 176), cut into quarters, to the soup with the reserved shrimp pieces in step 7. Add 8 ounces cooked lobster meat, cut into ½-inch pieces, to the soup with the sherry in step 7; cover, and let heat through before serving.

GUMBO

PEEK INTO A POT OF GUMBO AND YOU'LL SEE the influence of the many groups who have settled in New Orleans. The base, a roux, arrived with the French; smoked sausage was brought by Germans and Acadians (from northeastern Canada); and the peppers that give gumbo its kick tagged along with the Spanish. Okra came from Africa and ground sassafras (filé powder) was used by Native Americans. Many Louisiana natives fondly remember waking up to the smell of cooking roux (usually flour and lard), which the cook would stir over low heat until it was chocolate-colored. Aromatic vegetables were stirred in, then homemade fish or meat stock, and finally the meat: Poultry, sausage, game, and seafood are all traditional. The process takes the better part of an afternoon—but time is not gumbo's only problem. There's also what New Orleans chef Paul Prudhomme refers to as "Cajun napalm."

To understand Prudhomme's comment, it helps to know how roux is prepared. It's made by cooking equal parts fat and flour until colored. Light roux is the base of many cheese sauces and gravies, but dark roux is used almost exclusively in Cajun and Creole cooking. To achieve the requisite deep, dark brown color and toasted flavor, the flour and fat (usually vegetable oil today) are cooked over low heat for a bare minimum of 30 minutes. But dark roux not only requires time, it practically requires a hazmat suit. To avoid burning the flour, the cook needs to stir constantly, and even over low heat, temperatures in the pot can reach 500 degrees—one splatter and you're reaching for the burn cream. Worse, after a steady hour of slow stirring, the roux can go from toasty brown to burnt in seconds. Is it any wonder some cooks avoid making gumbo? We wanted to find an easier, safer, quicker way to make gumbo at home.

Our testing started with a handful of recipes for "faster" roux. Those that didn't give the roux time to darken made for insipid gumbo. Others, like Prudhomme's version, turned up the heat to accelerate the process, with explosive and scary results. We did find one recipe, though, that offered the promise of both ease and safety. Three-quarters cup each of flour and vegetable oil were mixed together in a large pot and moved to a 350-degree oven to cook—sans stirring—for just under two hours. This hands-off roux sounded too good to be true. The same recipe called for homemade shrimp stock, so before getting started on the gumbo, we painstakingly peeled a pound of shrimp and simmered the shells with onion and peppercorns. When it was time to check on the roux, we were delighted to discover that it looked (and smelled) perfect. The closed lid and gentle heat had provided the perfect no-stir environment for the roux to brown. How would it hold up in the gumbo?

Traditional gumbos start with sautéing chopped onion, celery, green bell pepper, and garlic in the dark roux, and ours would be no exception. Thyme and cayenne pepper were essential seasonings. We prefer dark-meat chicken thighs to breasts in stews because the thighs have more flavor. Simmering them in the gumbo for about 40 minutes before chopping the meat and returning it to the pot ensured that the meat stayed moist. Tomatoes and okra are controversial additions to gumbo in Louisiana—gumbo lovers are passionately for or against. We included both on the basis of the "more is more" theory. Finally, stirring in the spicy andouille sausage, okra, and shrimp at the end kept them from overcooking. When the gumbo was done, tasters were amazed at the rich, toasty, silky taste. The only downside: It wasn't as speedy as we'd hoped.

Cranking up the oven temperature shortened the cooking time, but at a cost: The roux required stirring or it scorched. Jump-starting the roux on the stovetop before transferring it to the oven would require high heat and constant stirring, so we ruled it out. What about toasting just the flour in a dry pot on the stove? After five minutes (yes, we had to stir) the flour began to brown, so we added the oil and put the pot in the oven. Forty-five minutes later, the roux was beautifully dark brown—but how would it taste? We added everything to the pot and waited anxiously. Success at last! Our gumbo had the toasted, smoky flavor of a long-cooked roux and, at just 45 minutes, gave us time to prepare the other ingredients. We fine-tuned the roux, which was a tad thin and greasy, by cutting back the oil by ¼ cup and adding an extra tablespoon of flour with the vegetables.

One sticking point remained: the stock. Though we had been making our own shrimp stock, peeling a pound of shrimp and then simmering and straining stock were neither fast nor easy. We switched to store-bought chicken broth, but tasters complained that it lacked the rich, briny depth of the shrimp stock. Would mixing the broth with clam juice do the trick? Nope—the resulting liquid also lacked complexity and punch. We sometimes add a little soy or Worcestershire sauce to add depth and richness to stew and sauces, so we made two gumbos and added each in turn. These improved the taste, but it still wasn't quite right. We needed something to enhance the shrimp flavor. And then we had an idea we hoped just might be crazy enough to work: adding Asian fish sauce, which is complex, intensely flavored, and made from fish. We snuck some into our next batch without telling tasters, and they unanimously agreed that this gumbo was the best yet; the fish sauce added briny depth without being identifiable. Sure, some may view it as heretical to authentic gumbo. We prefer to look at it as yet another culture stirred in to an already diverse pot.

Creole-Style Gumbo
SERVES 6 TO 8

Fish sauce is an important flavoring in this stew; don't omit it. The roux cooking time in step 2 may be longer depending on the type of pot you use; the color of the finished roux should be that of an old, dark copper penny.

¾   cup plus 1 tablespoon unbleached all-purpose flour
½   cup vegetable oil
1   medium onion, minced
1   green bell pepper, stemmed, seeded, and chopped medium
1   celery rib, chopped fine
5   medium garlic cloves, minced or pressed through a garlic press (about 5 teaspoons)
1   teaspoon minced fresh thyme or ¼ teaspoon dried
¼   teaspoon cayenne pepper
1   (14.5-ounce) can diced tomatoes, drained
3¾   cups low-sodium chicken broth
¼   cup fish sauce (see note) (see page 74)
2   pounds bone-in chicken thighs (about 5 thighs), skin removed and trimmed
     Salt and ground black pepper
8   ounces andouille sausage, halved lengthwise and sliced ¼-inch thick
2   cups frozen okra, thawed (optional)
2   pounds extra-large shrimp (21 to 25 per pound), peeled and deveined (see the illustration on page 169)

1. Adjust an oven rack to the lowest position and heat the oven to 350 degrees. Toast ¾ cup of the flour in a large Dutch oven over medium heat, stirring constantly, until it just begins to brown, about 5 minutes.

2. Off the heat, whisk in the oil until smooth. Cover the pot, transfer it to the oven, and cook until the mixture is deep brown and fragrant, about 45 minutes. Remove the pot from the oven and whisk the roux to combine. (The roux can be cooled, transferred to an airtight container, and refrigerated for up to 1 week. Return the roux to the pot and reheat over medium-high heat, whisking constantly, until just smoking before continuing.)

3. Stir the onion, bell pepper, and celery into the hot roux and cook over medium heat, stirring often, until the vegetables are softened, about 10 minutes. Stir in the remaining 1 tablespoon flour, garlic, thyme, and cayenne and cook until fragrant, about 1 minute. Stir in the tomatoes and cook until they look dry, about 1 minute. Gradually stir in the broth and fish sauce, scraping up any browned bits and smoothing out any lumps.

4. Season the chicken with pepper, add it to the pot, and bring to a boil. Cover, reduce to a gentle simmer, and cook until chicken is cooked through and tender, about 40 minutes.

5. Skim any fat that has collected on the top. Transfer the chicken to a plate, let cool slightly, then shred into bite-size pieces, discarding the bones. Stir the shredded chicken, sausage, and okra (if using) into the stew, return to a simmer, and allow to heat through, about 5 minutes.

6. Stir in the shrimp and continue to simmer until cooked through, about 5 minutes. Season the gumbo with salt and pepper and serve. (The gumbo can be refrigerated in an airtight container for up to 3 days; reheat over medium-low heat, stirring often.)

BOUILLABAISSE

BOUILLABAISSE IS A CLASSIC PROVENÇAL dish with humble origins. But what may have begun as a fisherman's cost-effective family meal has evolved into a renowned and fashionable fish stew. Authentic bouillabaisse relies on a deeply flavored fish stock (or fumet) made from scratch. After simmering for hours, the briny sweet broth is strained and the supporting flavors are added—tomato, wine, fennel, olive oil, and saffron. When the broth portion of the stew is fully assembled, a variety of fish, crustaceans, and mollusks are added and poached in the complex broth. It is always served with thick slices of French bread or garlic croutons to sop up the flavorful broth, and with rouille, a luxuriant roasted red pepper and garlic mayonnaise. Our goal was to create a simpler adaptation of this classic that was still authentic in flavor, without being overly time-consuming.

First, we focused on the medley of seafood that would be the heart of the stew. Nearly all bouillabaisse recipes emphasize that a variety of fish and shellfish are essential to bringing character to the stew. They caution against using fish that are too delicate in texture or too strong in flavor. Certain fish have no place in bouillabaisse, among them bluefish and mackerel, which are too oily and intrusive. In our tests, other fish fell out of play early on for the simple reason that their cooking times were too dissimilar. In a traditional bouillabaisse, upward of six different aquatic species are layered into the pot, with longer-cooking varieties going in first, while the more delicate varieties top the stack. In the interest of time and expense, we wanted to limit the variety to three or four diverse but widely available species. Shrimp and scallops fit the bill for our first two choices. To round out our selection, we tested a variety of fish: haddock, cod, sea bass, and halibut were our favorites. But overall, we preferred the halibut for its sweet, firm flesh that retained its shape during cooking. Finally, we tested both clams and mussels, wishing to have at least one shell-on mollusk in the mix. Mussels, with their more delicate flavor and shorter cooking time, proved the best option.

Next we focused on the broth. While we liked the idea of using our homemade Fish Stock (page 20), we wondered if, with everything else going on in the pot, we could get away with bottled clam juice. We started with the aromatics and sautéed fresh fennel, carrot, onion, and lots of garlic in olive oil. We started with 2 cups of white wine and two bottles of clam juice and crossed our fingers. The clam juice scored high marks, but the wine was sour and acidic. We pulled back on the wine, opting to simmer it briefly to eliminate the raw alcohol aftertaste. Perfumed with undertones of licorice from the fresh fennel, the white wine, and the generous amount of garlic, this broth gave us a solid foundation on which to build the rest of our dish. Next we added diced tomatoes with their juice and the illustrious saffron. We found that a mere ¼ teaspoon was enough to perfume the broth with its distinctive flavor, color, and aroma.

We added fresh thyme and bay leaves and briefly simmered the mixture down to what we thought

INGREDIENTS: Scallops

Scallops are naturally ivory or pinkish tan; processing (dipping them in a phosphate and water mixture to extend shelf life) turns them bright white. Processed scallops are slippery and swollen and are usually sitting in a milky white liquid at the store. You should look for unprocessed scallops (also called dry scallops), which are sticky and flabby; they will taste fresher than processed scallops and if you are pan-searing them, they will develop a nice crust when browned because they are not pumped full of water.

was the proper amount for cooking the fish. It turned out that the fish exuded such a copious quantity of liquid during cooking that our base became diluted and thin. We tried reducing the sauce by roughly half, which took about seven minutes, before adding the seafood. As the shrimp, scallops, haddock, and mussels cooked, their juices combined with the saffron-infused tomato base to produce the ideal amount of flavorful liquid. The generous quantity was ideal for steaming the fish to perfection, with plenty left to serve in a soup plate. As a final touch, a sprinkling of fresh tarragon added a clean anise-like flavor and a brightness that gave the stew distinction. At last, we had a richly scented broth with complex flavors and the

right combination of perfectly cooked fish. Served with our Garlic Toasts (page 138) and Red Pepper Rouille (page 174), this upscale seafood stew is easy to shop for, quick to prepare, and will bring the flavors and aromas of the French seaside into your kitchen.

Bouillabaisse
SERVES 6 TO 8

Haddock, cod, striped bass, and hake make good alternatives to the halibut. You can substitute 2 cups Fish Stock (page 20) for the clam juice. Note that this stew comes together rather quickly, so be sure to have all the ingredients prepped and ready to go before you begin cooking.

¼	cup olive oil
I	small fennel bulb (about 9 ounces), trimmed of stalks, cored, and chopped fine (see the illustrations on page 27)
I	medium onion, minced
8	medium garlic cloves, minced or pressed through a garlic press (about 8 teaspoons)
I	teaspoon minced fresh thyme leaves or ¼ teaspoon dried
⅛	teaspoon red pepper flakes
¼	teaspoon saffron threads, crumbled
¾	cup dry white wine or dry vermouth
2	(8-ounce) bottles clam juice
I	(14.5-ounce) can whole tomatoes, chopped medium and juice reserved
2	bay leaves
I	pound skinless halibut fillets (¾ to I inch thick), cut into 3- to 4-inch pieces Salt and ground black pepper
24	mussels (about 12 ounces), scrubbed and debearded if necessary (see the illustration on page 177)
I	pound large sea scallops (10 to 12 scallops), tendons removed (see the illustration on page 176)
8	ounces large shrimp (31 to 40 per pound), peeled and deveined (see the illustration on page 169)
2	tablespoons minced fresh tarragon leaves
I	recipe Garlic Toasts (page 138)
I	recipe Red Pepper Rouille (page 174)

INGREDIENTS: Saffron

Sometimes known as "red gold," saffron is the world's most expensive spice. It's made from the dried stigmas of *Crocus sativus* flowers; the stigmas are so delicate they must be harvested by hand in a painstaking process. (It takes about 200 hours to pick enough stigmas to produce just I pound of saffron, which typically sells for thousands of dollars.) Luckily, a little saffron goes a long way, adding a distinct reddish-gold color, notes of honey and grass, and a slight hint of bitterness to dishes like bouillabaisse, paella, and risotto. You can find it as powder or threads, but we've found threads are more common. The major producers are Iran and Spain; the saffron you find in the supermarket is usually Spanish. Look for bottles that contain dark red threads—saffron is graded, and the richly hued, high-grade threads from the top of the stigma yield more flavor than the lighter, lesser-grade threads from the base.

With double-digit prices for amounts as tiny as one 100th of an ounce, we wondered how much brand matters. To find out, we chose four brands of high-grade red Spanish saffron—two national supermarket brands (all we could find) and two mail-order options. To our surprise, when we tasted the saffron in garlicky mayonnaise, we couldn't distinguish one brand from another. Only when we sampled the spice in plain chicken broth, without competing flavors, did the floral, grassy taste of our winner, Morton & Basset Saffron Threads ($10.99 for .01 ounce), stand out. Despite being sold in the supermarket, this brand was the most expensive in the lineup. Our conclusion: Unless saffron is the main flavoring in your recipe, you'll likely be fine with any brand of dark red threads.

1. Heat the oil in a large Dutch oven over medium-high heat until shimmering. Add the fennel and onion and cook until softened, 5 to 7 minutes. Stir in the garlic, thyme, red pepper flakes, and saffron and cook until fragrant, about 30 seconds. Stir in the wine and cook until slightly reduced, about 30 seconds.

2. Stir in the clam juice, tomatoes with their juice, and bay leaves and bring to a boil. Reduce to a gentle simmer and cook until the amount of liquid has reduced by about half, 7 to 9 minutes.

3. Pat the fish dry with paper towels and season with salt and pepper. Add the fish to the pot, cover, and gently simmer for 2 minutes. Add the mussels and scallops and continue to simmer gently until the fish is almost cooked through, about 3 minutes. Add the shrimp, cover, and continue to cook until the shrimp are bright pink, the scallops are milky white, and the mussels have opened, 1 to 2 minutes longer.

4. Off the heat, remove the bay leaves, discard any unopened mussels, stir in the tarragon, and season with salt and pepper to taste. Serve in wide, shallow bowls with the Garlic Toasts and Red Pepper Rouille.

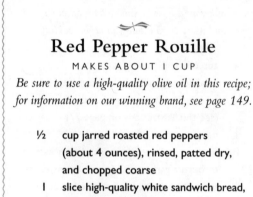

Red Pepper Rouille

MAKES ABOUT 1 CUP

Be sure to use a high-quality olive oil in this recipe; for information on our winning brand, see page 149.

½	cup jarred roasted red peppers (about 4 ounces), rinsed, patted dry, and chopped coarse
1	slice high-quality white sandwich bread, torn into 1-inch pieces
1	large egg yolk
2	medium garlic cloves, minced or pressed through a garlic press (about 2 teaspoons)
⅛	teaspoon cayenne pepper
¼	cup vegetable oil
2	tablespoons extra-virgin olive oil
	Salt and ground black pepper

Process the roasted red peppers, bread, egg yolk, garlic, and cayenne in a food processor until smooth, about 1 minute, scraping down the sides of the bowl as needed. With the machine running, gradually add the oils through the feed tube in a slow, steady stream and process until the rouille has a thick, mayonnaise-like consistency, 1 to 2 minutes. Season with salt and pepper to taste. (The rouille can be refrigerated in an airtight container for up to 24 hours.)

CIOPPINO

CIOPPINO IS A SAN FRANCISCO SEAFOOD stew with roots that stretch to the shores of northern Italian fishing communities, where tomato and seafood stew was known as *ciuppin*. Bay Area lore is brimming with tales of Italian fishermen simmering the rich, red stew aboard small fishing boats as they headed back through the Golden Gate. On shore, cioppino was among the first signature dishes served in the city's earliest restaurants at Fisherman's Wharf.

As with many region-specific dishes, there is no one recipe for cioppino. Ingredients and technique vary radically from recipe to recipe. In fact, the stew is more a concept than a combination of specific ingredients. In our research, only one common thread surfaced—the stewing liquid is based on tomatoes. The rest of the ingredients seem to have depended entirely on the sea's daily bounty and the personal taste of the recipe's author. Thus armed with a collection of extremely different recipes, we set out to develop a streamlined cioppino recipe that seafood lovers could enjoy.

Initially, it became clear that many of the recipes for cioppino, especially those from popular cookbooks, were unnecessarily complicated. Most of them boasted long lists of fish, shellfish, and aromatics, and had intricate and somewhat troublesome techniques for a stew that was said to have been "thrown together" on fishing boats and piers. Digging further and into more obscure territory, we turned up simpler, more straightforward recipes. These recipes were more appealing to us. We decided to make cioppino as simple as possible, in part to offer a recipe that would be less exacting than many we had come across. Consequently, we decided to eliminate fish stock and fillets from our cioppino and concentrate on quick-cooking shellfish.

The simpler, more homespun recipes we uncovered had their own problems—a handful called for every dried herb imaginable and some were nothing more than tomatoes and fish. We knew we wanted something fresher-tasting and more complex than fish in tomato sauce. But we found four recipes that looked promising. They were similar enough to compare but different enough for experimentation.

Three of the four contenders were universally panned. The procedures, while not difficult, proved to be time-consuming. And with thick, gloppy sauces, it was nearly impossible to submerge and evenly cook the seafood. Tasters commented that these stews contained too many ingredients; they had to "fight their way" through them. And the extraneous ingredients—such as green peppers, leeks, carrots, and celery—competed entirely too much with the stew's tomato and seafood flavors. The taste of green pepper was especially forward.

These three recipes also called for native San Francisco Dungeness crabs. Fine if you are firing up the stove in Noe Valley, but not quite so easy for the rest of us. We did secure some of these crabs by mail order, but tasters actually found them extremely hard to eat in a stew (especially for those not accustomed or willing to pick meat from the crabs) and voted them out. For our shellfish, then, we settled on clams, mussels, shrimp, and scallops.

Of the four initial test recipes, one stood at the fore. It was a simple recipe that yielded a buttery, sweet tomato broth that was studded with a bounty of seafood—and no excessive or unwanted embellishments. Aromatics included only garlic (of which tasters wanted more), onions, and parsley (which tasters thought too pedestrian).

The surprise ingredient in this test recipe was butter. The broth was finished with a pat, and it added a luxurious richness to the flavor and texture. With more testing, we found that butter is best incorporated at the outset so it has time to emulsify and blend with other ingredients, so we decided to sauté the aromatic vegetables in a combination of butter and oil. Another interesting finding from this round of tests concerned chicken broth. We had been using store-bought chicken broth along with clam juice and canned tomatoes, to make the liquid for the stew. While the liquid was no doubt tasty, the chicken broth seemed like the odd man out. We wanted to see if its inclusion was really necessary.

The base, tomatoes, was a done deal, but we wondered if tasters would be able to detect any difference in stews made with all clam juice or all chicken broth in addition to the tomatoes. In the end, the differences were minimal, but most tasters favored the clam juice—the broth was sweeter, somewhat "fresher," and more fish-like. A simple combination of tomatoes and bottled clam juice tasted best. But with a relatively small amount of liquid in the pot, we were still having a hard time properly cooking the seafood. We decided to try steaming open the clams and mussels in a combination of water and white wine, before building the soup, so we could use their juices as part of the broth. This preemptive step did the trick. On the other hand, it seemed best to cook the shrimp and scallops at the last minute, right in the cioppino broth.

Next we concentrated on the garlic, the heat, and the herbs. Tasters wanted more of everything. We played with the amount of garlic, eventually settling on six cloves. We upped the heat by adding red pepper flakes to the sautéing onions and garlic in small increments until the tasters cried uncle. As for herbs, fresh oregano and thyme complemented the stew's basic flavors. Seasoned with a healthy amount of salt and pepper, the broth had arrived. It was rich and tomatoey, garlicky, with strong herbal accents and a good dose of heat. Best of all, this seafood stew can be on the table in less than one hour.

Cioppino
SERVES 6 TO 8

Note that this stew comes together rather quickly, so be sure to have all the ingredients prepped and ready to go before you begin cooking. Serve with crusty bread or Garlic Toasts (page 138).

1	cup dry white wine or dry vermouth
¾	cup water
24	littleneck clams (about 2¼ pounds), scrubbed (see the illustration on page 158)
24	mussels (about 12 ounces), scrubbed and debearded if necessary (see the illustration on page 177)
6	tablespoons extra-virgin olive oil
2	tablespoons unsalted butter
1	medium onion, chopped medium
6	medium garlic cloves, minced or pressed through a garlic press (about 2 tablespoons)
1	teaspoon minced fresh thyme leaves or ¼ teaspoon dried
1	teaspoon minced fresh oregano leaves or ¼ teaspoon dried
½	teaspoon red pepper flakes
2	tablespoons unbleached all-purpose flour
1	(8-ounce) bottle clam juice
1	(28-ounce) can whole tomatoes, tomatoes chopped medium and juice reserved
1	bay leaf
1	pound large sea scallops (10 to 12 scallops), tendons removed (see the illustration at right)
1	pound large shrimp (31 to 40 per pound), peeled and deveined (see the illustration on page 169)
	Salt and ground black pepper

1. Bring the wine and water to a boil in a large Dutch oven. Add the clams, cover, and cook for 3 minutes. Stir in the mussels, cover, and cook until the clams and mussels have just begun to open, 2 to 4 minutes longer. As the clams and mussels open, transfer them to a large bowl. Discard any unopened clams or mussels.

2. Measure out and reserve 2½ cups of the steaming liquid, avoiding any gritty sediment that has settled on the bottom of the pot. (You should have about 2½ cups of broth; if not, add water.)

3. In a clean Dutch oven, heat the oil and butter over medium heat until the butter has melted. Add the onion and cook until softened, 5 to 7 minutes. Stir in the garlic, thyme, oregano, and red pepper flakes and cook until fragrant, about 30 seconds. Stir in the flour and cook for 1 minute.

4. Gradually whisk in the reserved steaming liquid and bottled clam juice, smoothing out any lumps. Stir in the tomatoes with their juice and bay leaf and bring to a boil. Reduce to a gentle simmer and cook until thickened and the flavors meld, about 20 minutes.

5. Stir in the scallops and continue to simmer gently until they are nearly cooked through, about 3 minutes. Stir in the shrimp and sprinkle the cooked clams and mussels over the top. Cover and continue to simmer gently until the shrimp are bright pink and the scallops are milky white, 1 to 2 minutes. Season with salt and pepper to taste and serve in wide, shallow bowls.

REMOVING TENDONS FROM SCALLOPS

The small, rough-textured, crescent-shaped tendon that attaches the scallop to the shell will toughen when cooked. Use your fingers to peel the tendon away from the side of each scallop before cooking.

SPANISH SHELLFISH STEW

LESS WELL-KNOWN THAN SAN FRANCISCO'S cioppino and France's bouillabaisse is Spain's version of shellfish stew, *zarzuela*. Chock-full of shellfish like lobsters, clams, and mussels, this tomato-based stew is seasoned with saffron and paprika and thickened with a *picada*, a flavorful mixture of ground almonds, bread crumbs, and olive oil. Unlike most fish stews, zarzuela contains no fish stock or clam juice—instead the shellfish release their rich liquors into the pot as they cook. The shells, too, serve to fortify the flavorful broth. We liked the sound of this popular Spanish dish and set about creating our own version.

We gathered together several recipes for zarzuela and started cooking. Following Spanish tradition, most recipes begin with a *sofrito* of onions, garlic, and red bell peppers, cooked until softened. Next paprika, saffron, red pepper flakes, and bay leaves are added to create a rich foundation. Tomatoes and dry white wine are then added to the pot to form the liquid base of the broth. Fresh tomatoes are available for such a brief time during the year that we immediately reached for canned. We looked at both whole and diced tomatoes. Although we had to chop the whole tomatoes, their flavor and texture in this stew were preferable to canned diced tomatoes. Some recipes also include brandy in addition to white wine. After making the broth with and without, tasters favored the depth of flavor that brandy lent to the dish. With our broth and flavoring settled, it was now time to turn our attention to the shellfish.

Typically, the dish includes langostinos (large, fresh prawns), shrimp, scallops, mussels, and clams. After some discussion, we decided to omit hard-to-find prawns from the master recipe. Later we'd develop a variation with lobster as a stand-in for prawns. Looking at the shellfish remaining, we focused on building flavor. Knowing that shells contribute significant flavor to dishes, and given that we had decided to peel our shrimp before adding them to the stew (for easier eating), we thought we'd use the shrimp shells to enrich the broth's flavor. We sautéed the shells in a touch of olive oil and then steeped them in the wine. We chose to do this at the outset of cooking, so the shells would have plenty of time to infuse the wine. A quick strain of the wine to remove the shells and we had a terrific flavor boost for our broth.

The final challenge was producing a stew with perfectly cooked shellfish. Since each of the different shellfish was a different size, requiring a different cooking time, we knew we'd have to stagger the time when we added each variety. After some trial and error, we determined that the clams should be added to the stew first, followed by the mussels and scallops, and finally the shrimp. A picada is stirred into the shellfish stew at the end to add both body and flavor. Most picadas contain ground almonds and fried bread ground into crumbs. We found that fried bread (which required a significant amount of oil) turned our stew greasy. Instead we toasted fresh bread crumbs with a little olive oil. We tossed in the almonds with the bread crumbs so they, too, toasted, intensifying their flavor. Stirring the picada into the shellfish stew once the shellfish was cooked thickened the broth perfectly, and its rich, mellow flavor rounded out the bold stew. All that was left to do was sprinkle the dish with a handful of chopped fresh parsley and a squeeze of lemon for a bright, fresh finish to this Spanish favorite.

CLEANING MUSSELS

Mussels often contain a weedy beard protruding from the crack between the two shells. It's fairly small and can be difficult to tug out of place. To remove it easily, trap the beard between the side of a small paring knife and your thumb and pull to remove it. The flat surface of the knife gives you some leverage to remove the pesky beard.

Spanish Shellfish Stew
SERVES 4 TO 6

The picada gives this stew body and rich flavor; do not omit it.

¼ cup olive oil

8 ounces large shrimp (31 to 40 per pound), peeled and deveined, shells reserved

1½ cups dry white wine or dry vermouth

1 medium onion, minced

1 red bell pepper, stemmed, seeded, and chopped fine

3 medium garlic cloves, minced or pressed through a garlic press (about 1 tablespoon)

1 teaspoon paprika

¼ teaspoon saffron threads, crumbled

⅛ teaspoon red pepper flakes

2 tablespoons brandy

1 (28-ounce) can whole tomatoes, tomatoes chopped medium and juice reserved

2 bay leaves

16 littleneck clams (about 1½ pounds), scrubbed (see the illustration on page 158)

16 mussels (about 8 ounces), scrubbed and debearded if necessary (see the illustration on page 177)

12 ounces large sea scallops (about 8 scallops), tendons removed (see the illustration on page 176)

1 recipe Picada

1 tablespoon minced fresh parsley leaves

Salt and ground black pepper

Lemon wedges, for serving

1. Heat 1 tablespoon of the oil in a medium saucepan over medium heat until shimmering. Add the reserved shrimp shells and cook until pink, about 5 minutes. Off the heat, stir in the wine, cover, and let steep until ready to use.

2. Heat the remaining 3 tablespoons oil in a large Dutch oven over medium-high heat until shimmering. Add the onion and bell pepper and cook until the vegetables are softened and lightly browned, 8 to 10 minutes. Stir in the garlic, paprika, saffron, and red pepper flakes and cook until fragrant, about 30 seconds. Stir in the brandy and simmer for 30 seconds. Stir in the tomatoes with their juice and bay leaves and cook until slightly thickened, 5 to 7 minutes.

3. Strain the wine mixture into the Dutch oven, pressing on the shrimp shells to extract as much liquid as possible. Continue to simmer until the flavors have melded, 3 to 5 minutes. (The broth can be refrigerated in an airtight container for up to 1 day. Return to a simmer before continuing.)

4. Add the clams, cover, and cook for 4 minutes. Add the mussels and scallops, cover, and continue to cook until most of the clams have opened, about 3 minutes longer. Add the peeled shrimp, cover, and continue to cook until the shrimp are bright pink, the scallops are milky white, and the clams and mussels have opened, 1 to 2 minutes longer.

Picada
MAKES ABOUT 1 CUP

Chopped or whole unsalted almonds can be substituted for the slivered almonds; however, they may require longer processing times.

¼ cup slivered almonds (see note)

2 slices high-quality white sandwich bread, torn into quarters

2 tablespoons extra-virgin olive oil

⅛ teaspoon salt

Pinch ground black pepper

Adjust an oven rack to the middle position and heat the oven to 375 degrees. Pulse the nuts in a food processor to fine crumbs, about 15 pulses. Add the bread, olive oil, salt, and pepper and continue to pulse the bread to coarse crumbs, about 10 pulses. Spread the mixture evenly over a rimmed baking sheet and toast, stirring often, until golden brown, about 10 minutes. Let cool. (The picada can be stored in an airtight container for up to 2 days.)

5. Off the heat, remove the bay leaves and any unopened clams and mussels. Stir in the picada and parsley and season with salt and pepper to taste. Serve in wide, shallow bowls with the lemon wedges.

➤ VARIATION

Spanish Shellfish Stew with Lobster

In Spain, this stew is often made with langostinos, or prawns. Fresh prawns are difficult to find stateside, so we chose to use lobster instead.

Follow the recipe for Spanish Shellfish Stew, reducing the amount of clams and mussels to 12 each. Stir 8 ounces cooked lobster meat, cut into ½-inch pieces, into the stew with the picada in step 5; cover, and let heat through, about 1 minute, before serving.

MEDITERRANEAN CALAMARI STEW

STEWED CALAMARI WITH TOMATOES, GARLIC, and white wine is a classic Mediterranean dish. Unlike fried calamari, which cooks in minutes, this dish relies on low heat and a relatively long simmering time to produce moist, tender pieces of squid in a sweet, garlicky tomato sauce. And while we love the crunchy richness of fried calamari, this stewed preparation puts the calamari front and center—no deep-fried coating to mask its sweet, subtle flavor.

The ingredients for this dish are few, so we wanted to maximize the flavor of each. We decided to approach this stew's preparation as we would any other—by browning the squid to build a fond. But instead of developing a golden brown exterior, the squid merely released liquid and steamed. Changing tack, we coated the squid in flour to encourage browning, but this resulted in gummy calamari. Flummoxed, we abandoned the browning technique and instead looked to build our stew's flavor in other ways.

We started by cooking onions until tender and sweet and then, since garlic is typically a star ingredient in this dish, we added a generous eight cloves. The resulting dish had a nice garlicky punch, but tasters felt it needed more depth of flavor. Reviewing a stack of recipes we found in our research, we noticed that several included celery with the aromatics. Tasters loved the added freshness and clean, vegetal flavor the celery brought to this stew.

Next, we added some dry white wine to our aromatics and settled on a generous ½ cup. We added it directly to the sautéed onion mixture and allowed it to reduce slightly. According to our research, squid can take anywhere from 30 to 50 minutes to become tender when gently simmered, so once we added the squid and some diced tomatoes to our pot, we began testing the squid for doneness at the 30-minute mark and every five minutes thereafter. It wasn't until it hit the 45-minute mark that the squid started to become tender enough for our liking. But when left to simmer for much longer, the squid became tough and rubbery; we realized there is about a 10-minute window for the squid to reach its ideal texture. With our basic technique in place, we turned to examining the tomatoes.

We'd used canned diced tomatoes initially, but decided to compare them to canned pureed and canned whole tomatoes. We immediately ruled out pureed tomatoes, which lacked the fresh flavor we wanted. The canned diced tomatoes were an improvement, but there wasn't enough time for the tomato pieces to sufficiently break down, leaving us with a watery stew. We had the best luck with canned whole tomatoes, which not only gave the stew a fresh tomato flavor, but broke down just enough to thicken the stew while still remaining a distinct component.

We wanted this squid stew to serve as a main course, either on its own or tossed with pasta, so we knew with 2 pounds of squid we'd need a generous amount of tomatoes to balance the flavors and provide enough for a main course dinner. We settled on three 28-ounce cans of whole tomatoes. Because the tomatoes tended to lose their fresh flavor the longer they cooked, we added them to the pot after the squid had simmered for 15 minutes. Green olives and capers lent a briny element that tasters appreciated and ¼ teaspoon of red pepper flakes provided just the right amount of heat. Finished with chopped parsley and a drizzle of extra-virgin olive oil, this stew perfectly showcased the flavor of the calamari.

Mediterranean Calamari Stew with Garlic and Tomatoes

SERVES 4 TO 6

If you cannot find pitted green olives, substitute pimento-stuffed green olives; if the olives are particularly salty, give them a rinse. This brothy stew is often served with polenta or pasta for a hearty meal or, for a lighter meal, with Garlic Toasts (page 138).

¼	cup extra-virgin olive oil, plus extra for serving
2	medium onions, minced
2	celery ribs, sliced thin
8	medium garlic cloves, minced or pressed through a garlic press (about 8 teaspoons)
¼	teaspoon red pepper flakes
½	cup dry white wine or dry vermouth
2	pounds fresh or thawed frozen squid, bodies cut into 1-inch-wide rings and tentacles cut in half
	Salt and ground black pepper
3	(28-ounce) cans whole tomatoes, drained and chopped coarse
⅓	cup pitted Greek green olives, chopped coarse
1	tablespoon capers, rinsed
3	tablespoons minced fresh parsley leaves

1. Heat the oil in a large Dutch oven over medium-high heat until shimmering. Add the onions and celery and cook until softened, 5 to 7 minutes. Stir in the garlic and red pepper flakes and cook until fragrant, about 30 seconds. Stir in the wine, scraping up any browned bits, and cook until nearly evaporated, about 1 minute.

2. Pat the squid dry with paper towels and season with salt and pepper. Stir the squid into the pot, cover, and gently simmer until it has released its liquid, about 15 minutes. Stir in the tomatoes, olives, and capers, cover, and continue to cook until the squid is very tender, 30 to 35 minutes.

3. Off the heat, stir in the parsley and season with salt and pepper to taste. Drizzle individual portions with extra-virgin olive oil before serving.

BRAZILIAN FISH STEW WITH COCONUT MILK

BRAZIL IS HOME TO A HOST OF CELEBRATED fish stews. Of these traditional offerings, none is more beloved and respected than *moqueca* (pronounced moh-KEH-kah), a mix of local white fish, tomatoes, onions, cilantro, and coconut milk. Cooked in a thick, covered pot made of black clay and mangrove tree sap, moqueca is undeniably Brazilian and deeply satisfying. While there are countless variations on moqueca, two regions lay claim to the stew's origin: Bahia in the northeast of Brazil and Espirito Santo in the south. *Moqueca baiana* (from Bahia) is a decidedly earthy, spicy rendition that employs the liberal use of an unrefined, pulpy palm oil called dendê and adds sliced peppers to the aromatic mix. Hailing from Espirito Santo, *moqueca capixaba* eschews dendê in favor of olive oil and offers a cleaner, more nuanced expression of the sea. After a visit to a local Brazilian restaurant, where we were fortunate enough to try both styles side by side, we knew we wanted to develop an authentic recipe for the lighter moqueca capixaba. Without a clay pot or easy access to traditional ingredients, we had our work cut out for us in bringing this Brazilian national treasure stateside.

Traditional moqueca capixaba starts with heating a clay pot (the size of which depends upon the number of diners) over an open flame. Olive oil is then added along with a generous amount of chopped onion, tomato, and cilantro. Once these aromatics become slightly softened, firm white fish is added, followed by another layer of onion, tomato, and cilantro. The pot is then covered with a hot clay lid and allowed to stew and bubble away until the fish is just cooked through. When the lid is removed, the flaky white fish is sitting in a substantial broth of its own juice, infused with the heady aroma of cilantro and onion. A splash of coconut milk is then added and allowed to briefly simmer and meld with the fish broth. Brought to the table with white rice and a thick hot pepper sauce, this stew can be transcendent. Unfortunately, as we found while researching recipes, it can also be cloyingly sweet, harsh-tasting, and even bland. Vowing to create a stew worthy of moqueca's reputation, we ordered some fish and headed into the kitchen.

In Brazil, the fish of choice for moqueca is a type of sand perch. Favored for its firm, mild white flesh, the fish releases considerable juice as it cooks, eliminating the need to add broth to the moqueca pot. While we have plenty of firm white fish available to us, none of the species we tested released nearly enough juice to make a moqueca of the proper consistency. Resigned to the fact that we would need to add some liquid to the pot, we chose our fish based on taste and texture alone. Haddock, cod, halibut, striped bass, and hake all received high marks, gently flaking in tender pieces as they cooked. In the end, haddock won for its slightly superior texture and sweeter flavor. From prior testing, we knew that larger pieces of fish are less likely to dissolve into tiny flakes when cooked in liquid. Thus we cut the fillets into large, palm-size pieces (about 3 to 4 inches each). By the time they were cooked through, the fillets had separated into hearty chunks that tasters liked. With the fish component settled, we started to build our moqueca.

Without a local source for black clay pots, we looked around the kitchen for an alternative that would deliver a comparable kind of even heat and settled on a Dutch oven. Usually crafted from thick, enameled cast iron, Dutch ovens absorb and conduct heat in much the same way as a thick clay pot—albeit slightly faster. To our new moqueca vessel we added a splash of olive oil and a generous amount of chopped tomatoes, onion, and cilantro leaves. Once softened and fragrant, we added our seasoned fish fillets and another layer of this same aromatic mix. To compensate for the lack of moisture in our native fish, we added a couple cups of water, brought everything to a simmer, and threw on the lid. After about 5 minutes of gentle simmering, we removed the lid, added a can of coconut milk, and let the flavors blend while the fish cooked through. While the aroma of this stew had tasters' mouths watering, the flavor and consistency left much to be desired. The broth, which was overly sweet and creamy, featured little fish flavor. In addition, the stew was pockmarked with bites of raw-tasting onion that overpowered the flavor of tomato and cilantro. We decided to tackle the broth issues first.

The 2 cups of water were providing ample cooking liquid for the fish, but, unfortunately, little else. It was clear that we needed a more flavorful replacement. Our Fish Stock (page 20) seemed like a good place to begin and indeed produced a deep, balanced bowl of stew. Perhaps if we were buying a whole haddock and breaking the fish down ourselves, it might make sense to simmer our own broth for this stew. However, given that we only needed 2 cups of liquid, and that this stew takes minutes to cook, preparing fish broth was out of the question. Searching for a quicker way to infuse our moqueca with briny depth, we looked to bottled clam juice. Substituting 1 cup clam juice for 1 cup of the water was good, but switching to all clam juice was even better. We then looked at scaling back the coconut milk. While the recipes we had consulted suggested using at least a full can of the creamy stuff, this had produced a heavy, one-note stew. To find the right balance, we started with just ¼ cup of coconut milk and slowly added more until tasters were pleased. At ¾ cup, the resulting broth was slightly sweet and rich, but not creamy, offering subtle, supporting flavor. With our broth in order, we targeted the tomato, onion, and cilantro.

Often seen as simply supporting characters that should dissolve into the background, aromatics take center stage in moqueca. Chopped coarse and added in two stages, they provide depth of flavor and freshness, as well as contrasting textures. To correct the raw bits of onion that tasters complained about, we minced the onion. Cut this way, the onions softened just enough to provide freshness, without a harsh finish. To bump up the cilantro flavor, we took a page from many South American cuisines and chopped both the leaves and stems together. Cut this way, the cilantro provided great flavor and even better texture. Tasters preferred the freshness of raw cilantro, so we reserved the second addition to finish the soup. Finally, we addressed the accompaniments.

Along with white rice, moqueca is often served with a creamy, vinegary pepper sauce made from native malagueta peppers packed in olive oil. Unable to find malagueta or any peppers packed in olive oil at our market, we looked to other options. With a wide range of hot peppers preserved in vinegar available to us, it made sense to start there. We pureed vinegar-preserved jalapeños, banana peppers, and hot cherry peppers (stemmed and seeded) with olive oil and salt. Tasters unanimously preferred the batch made with hot cherry peppers for its robust pepper flavor and heat. To balance the vinegar and spice, we added a little onion and sugar to the mix. Dolloped onto a serving of moqueca and rice, our creamy pepper sauce was the crowning jewel on this robust dish. Sans clay pot or Brazilian heritage, we had managed to create an inspired, authentic-tasting version of one of the world's truly great fish stews.

Brazilian Fish Stew with Coconut Milk

SERVES 6 TO 8

Pickled hot cherry peppers are usually sold jarred, next to the pickles or jarred roasted red peppers at the supermarket. Serve with steamed white rice.

PEPPER SAUCE

4	pickled hot cherry peppers (about 3 ounces), stemmed, seeded, and chopped coarse
½	cup coarsely chopped onion
¼	cup olive oil
⅛	teaspoon sugar
	Salt

STEW

2	tablespoons olive oil
1¼	pounds plum tomatoes (about 6 medium), cored and cut into ½-inch pieces
2	medium onions, minced
1	cup coarsely chopped fresh cilantro leaves and stems
3	pounds skinless haddock fillets (¾ to 1 inch thick), cut into 3- to 4-inch pieces
	Salt and ground black pepper
2	(8-ounce) bottles clam juice
¾	cup coconut milk

1. FOR THE PEPPER SAUCE: Process all the ingredients together in a food processor until smooth. Season with salt to taste and set aside.

2. FOR THE STEW: Heat the oil in a large Dutch oven over medium-high heat until shimmering. Add half of the tomatoes, half of the onions, and ½ cup of the cilantro and cook until the vegetables are softened, 5 to 7 minutes.

3. Pat the fish dry with paper towels and season with salt and pepper. Place the fish on top of the softened vegetables and sprinkle the remaining tomatoes and onions over the top. Add the clam juice and bring to a gentle simmer. Cover and simmer gently, stirring gently a few times, until the fish is almost cooked through, about 4 minutes.

4. Add the coconut milk and continue to simmer gently until the fish is just cooked through, 1 to 2 minutes. Sprinkle with the remaining ½ cup cilantro and season with salt and pepper to taste. Serve, passing the pepper sauce separately.

➤ VARIATION

Brazilian Fish and Shrimp Stew with Coconut Milk

Follow the recipe for Brazilian Fish Stew with Coconut Milk, reducing the amount of haddock to 2 pounds. Add 8 ounces large shrimp (31 to 40 per pound), peeled and deveined (see the illustration on page 169), to the stew with the coconut milk in step 4.

ROASTED RED PEPPER SOUP WITH SMOKED PAPRIKA AND CILANTRO CREAM **PAGE 124**

OLD-FASHIONED CHICKEN NOODLE SOUP **PAGE 26**

SPANISH-STYLE MEATBALL SOUP WITH SAFFRON **PAGE 50**

PORK STEW WITH HOMINY, TOMATOES, AND CHIPOTLES **PAGE 236**

BEEF BURGUNDY **PAGE 225**

SPANISH SHELLFISH STEW **PAGE 178**

LOBSTER AND CORN CHOWDER **PAGE 166**

189

VIETNAMESE RICE NOODLE SOUP WITH BEEF **PAGE 82**

THAI-STYLE CHICKEN CURRY **PAGE 290**

INDIAN-STYLE VEGETABLE CURRY WITH CILANTRO-MINT CHUTNEY **PAGE 284**

192

ITALIAN VEGETABLE STEW **PAGE 245**

HARVEST PUMPKIN SOUP   **PAGE 321**

CHILI CON CARNE **PAGE 262**

BLACK BEAN CHILI **PAGE 276**

TORTELLINI MINESTRONE **PAGE 322**

PROVENÇAL VEGETABLE SOUP **PAGE 99**

9

CHICKEN STEWS

CHICKEN STEWS

Classic Chicken Stew

WHEN WE THINK OF CHICKEN STEW, WE imagine tender, moist chunks of chicken, accompanied by potatoes, carrots, and peas, all enveloped in a glossy, flavorful, thick sauce—the kind of supper our grandmothers would slave over when we were kids. Now that we're adults, we think a bowl of chicken stew should be every bit as hearty and comforting, but it shouldn't require a whole day spent in the kitchen. There had to be a quicker, but just as flavorful, way.

Researching chicken stew, we uncovered a variety of recipes with a range of complexity. Some started with a whole chicken that was cut up, browned, and then simmered in water to make broth. The liquid was then strained and the meat was removed from the bones before composing the rest of the stew. The results were pretty tasty, but this seemed like an excessive amount of work (and time). On the other end of the spectrum were recipes that simply poached cubed, boneless, skinless breasts and some vegetables in a quick "sauce" made of canned soup. These versions tasted like bad cafeteria food. We knew more simmering time would be needed to develop the rich flavor we were after. We decided to go for the middle ground.

Given our experience with stews, and having prepared a number of research recipes, we suspected the method would go something like this: brown the meat, remove the meat from the pan, build a sauce with the fond (the browned bits left from the chicken) and aromatics (onion and garlic), deglaze the pan with broth, and return the chicken along with vegetables to simmer in the flavorful broth until tender. Seeing as a whole chicken provided so much flavor, we started there. We cut a chicken into small pieces, browned it, made a simple sauce (we could refine the flavors later), and simmered away. But we quickly encountered several problems. The breasts cooked through more quickly than the thighs and drumsticks and became dried out, bland, and stringy—a far cry from the tender pieces of stew meat we had envisioned. But the dark meat, the thighs and drumsticks, produced wonderfully tender chunks of meat—perfect for stew.

We made the stew again using whole chicken legs, but this time it was clear that tasters preferred the meatier thighs to the drumsticks. However, they found the bones undesirable (and unattractive) in the finished stew. To remedy this, we tried removing the meat from the bones at the end of cooking and shredding it into large pieces. This made great-tasting stew, but fussing with the meat and bones was time-consuming and messy. Maybe we could save time by getting rid of the bones altogether and using boneless thighs that we cut into small pieces prior to cooking. This was a win-win situation: tasters thought the stew tasted just as good and we liked the easy, streamlined process.

Now we could refine the cooking method. Chicken stew, we were finding, was best when it was gently simmered, which is easiest to do in a low oven. On the stovetop, the cooking time varied and even though we set the flame at the same heat level every time, the heat transfer was not uniform, leading to burnt pots. Stewing in a 300-degree oven was much more reliable, producing a predictably even, consistent level of heat. After 30 minutes in the oven, the thighs were cooked through and no longer pink. Unfortunately, they were not as tender as we wanted. After gradually increasing the cooking time, we ended up keeping the dish in the oven for about an hour. At this point, the meat was exceedingly tender and flavorful. During the longer stay in the oven the heat breaks down the connective tissue in the thighs, much as it does in a pot roast, yielding more tender meat. (White meat, on the other hand, contains little connective tissue, so there's no benefit to cooking it longer—in fact, cooking white meat longer will result in drier, rubbery meat.)

Finally we could consider the other flavors and ingredients in our stew. Peas, carrots, and potatoes are classic additions, and tasters gave each one a thumbs-up. Some white wine, added to the sauce, contributed an acidic note to an otherwise hearty flavor profile, and a bit of fresh thyme added depth. With a sprinkling of fresh parsley at the end, we had our ideal comfort food—a hearty, satisfying stew that didn't take all day to make.

So pleased were we with our classic chicken stew recipe that we decided to explore other flavor combinations. Leeks were a great complement to the chicken stew; we paired them with bright saffron. Root vegetables, other than potatoes, also work well in hearty stews, so we chose to add parsnips and celery root to the carrots already in the pot for another variation. Spinach and red bell peppers made for a colorful stew; tasters preferred the creaminess of white beans to starchy potatoes in this variation. Lastly, for those wanting a spicier dish, we paired jalapeños and chipotle chiles in adobo sauce with hominy and fresh cilantro for a hearty chicken stew with Southwestern flavors.

Classic Chicken Stew

SERVES 6 TO 8

Do not substitute boneless, skinless chicken breasts for the thighs in this recipe or the meat will taste very dry.

3	pounds boneless, skinless chicken thighs (about 12 thighs), trimmed and cut into 1-inch pieces
	Salt and ground black pepper
3	tablespoons vegetable oil
2	medium onions, minced
4	medium garlic cloves, minced or pressed through a garlic press (about 4 teaspoons)
1	teaspoon minced fresh thyme leaves or ¼ teaspoon dried
¼	cup unbleached all-purpose flour
½	cup dry white wine
3½	cups low-sodium chicken broth
1½	pounds red potatoes (4 to 5 medium), scrubbed and cut into ¾-inch chunks
1	pound carrots (about 6 medium), peeled and sliced ½ inch thick
2	bay leaves
1	cup frozen peas
¼	cup minced fresh parsley leaves

1. Adjust an oven rack to the lower-middle position and heat the oven to 300 degrees. Pat the chicken dry with paper towels and season with salt and pepper.

2. Heat 1 tablespoon of the oil in a large Dutch oven over medium-high heat until just smoking. Add half of the chicken and brown lightly, 6 to 8 minutes; transfer to a medium bowl. Repeat with 1 tablespoon more oil and the remaining chicken and transfer to the bowl.

3. Add the remaining 1 tablespoon oil to the pot and heat over medium heat until shimmering. Add the onions and ¼ teaspoon salt and cook until softened, 5 to 7 minutes. Stir in the garlic and thyme and cook until fragrant, about 30 seconds. Stir in the flour and cook for 1 minute. Stir in the wine, scraping up any browned bits.

4. Gradually whisk in the broth, smoothing out any lumps. Stir in the potatoes, carrots, bay leaves, and browned chicken with any accumulated juice and bring to a simmer. Cover, place the pot in the oven, and cook until the chicken is very tender, 50 to 60 minutes.

5. Remove the pot from the oven and remove the bay leaves. Stir in the peas, cover, and let stand for 5 minutes. Stir in the parsley and season with salt and pepper to taste before serving.

➤ VARIATIONS

Classic Chicken Stew with Leeks and Saffron

Follow the recipe for Classic Chicken Stew, substituting 4 medium leeks, white and light green parts only, halved lengthwise, sliced ½ inch thick, and rinsed thoroughly (about 6 cups) (see the illustrations on page 103), for the onions. Add ¼ teaspoon saffron threads, crumbled, to the pot with the garlic and thyme in step 3.

Classic Chicken Stew with Winter Root Vegetables

Turnips, rutabagas, or parsley root can be substituted for the carrots, celery root, or parsnips if desired.

Follow the recipe for Classic Chicken Stew, omitting the peas and reducing the amount of potatoes and carrots to 8 ounces each. Add 8 ounces celery root, peeled and cut into ¾-inch chunks, and 3 parsnips, peeled and sliced ½ inch thick, to the pot with the potatoes and carrots in step 4.

Classic Chicken Stew with Red Peppers, White Beans, and Spinach

Follow the recipe for Classic Chicken Stew, omitting the potatoes and peas and reducing the amount of carrots to 8 ounces. Add 2 red bell peppers, stemmed, seeded, and cut into 1-inch pieces, to the pot with the carrots in step 4. After removing the bay leaves from the stew in step 5, mash 1 (15-ounce) can cannellini beans, drained and rinsed, with about ⅓ cup of the stew liquid in a medium bowl until smooth, then add back to the pot. Stir in 1 (15-ounce) can more cannellini beans, drained and rinsed, and 4 ounces baby spinach (about 4 cups) and let stand for 5 minutes before adding the parsley.

Classic Chicken Stew with Hominy and Chipotle

For more heat, include the jalapeño seeds and ribs when mincing.

Follow the recipe for Classic Chicken Stew, omitting the potatoes. Add 2 jalapeño chiles, stemmed, seeded, and minced, and 1 tablespoon minced chipotle chile in adobo to the pot with the garlic in step 3. Substitute 2 (15-ounce) cans white or yellow hominy, drained and rinsed, for the peas and ¼ cup minced fresh cilantro leaves for the parsley.

Old-Fashioned Chicken and Dumplings

DESPITE AMERICA'S ONGOING LOVE AFFAIR with comfort food, chicken and dumplings, unlike its baked cousin, chicken pot pie, hasn't made a comeback. After making several dozen batches of this dish, we think we know why. It has to do with the dumplings—as tricky as it can be to make pie pastry or biscuits for pot pie, dumplings are far more temperamental. With pot pie, dry oven heat and a rich sauce camouflage minor flaws in biscuits or pastry, whereas moist, steamy heat highlights gummy, leaden dumplings. But the idea of this classic one-pot meal is immensely appealing—light yet substantial, tender yet durable dumplings accompanying a rich, hearty sauce of chicken and vegetables. We were determined to uncover the secret.

In different parts of the country, dumplings come in different shapes. They may be rolled thin and cut into strips, rolled thick and stamped out like biscuits, or simply dropped into the stew in rounds. Most flour-based dumplings are made of flour and salt, plus one or more of the following: butter, eggs, milk, and baking powder. Depending on the ingredient list, dumplings are usually mixed in one of three ways. The most common is biscuit- or pastry-style, in which cold butter is cut into the dry ingredients, then cold milk and/or eggs are stirred in just until mixed. Other dumplings are made by simply mixing wet into dry ingredients. Many of the eggier dumplings are made by adding flour to hot water and butter, then whisking in the eggs one at a time.

Working with our Classic Chicken Stew (page 202) as the base, we spent a full day making batch after batch of dumplings using some combination of these ingredients and mixing methods. By the end of the day, after sampling dumplings that ranged from tough and chewy to fragile and disintegrated, we finally found a method for producing light and fluffy dumplings that held up beautifully during cooking. To make these dumplings, we cut butter into a mix of flour, baking powder, and salt. Then, instead of adding cold liquid to the dry ingredients, we added warm liquid to the flour-butter mixture. This type of dumpling is a success because warm liquids, unlike cold ones, expand and set the starch in the flour, keeping it from absorbing too much of the cooking liquid. We even took the process a step further—instead of cutting the butter into the flour, we simply melted it and mixed it into the dry ingredients with the warm liquid. These were the firm yet tender dumplings we were looking for and, better yet, they were easy to make.

Although we were pretty sure that dumplings made with vegetable shortening wouldn't taste as good as those made with butter, we tasted them side by side in a test. Those made with butter tasted rich and were far superior. The shortening dumplings tasted flat, like cooked flour and chicken broth. The liquids were simple. Dumplings made with chicken broth tasted too similar to the stewing liquid. Those made with water were dull. Because buttermilk tends to separate and even curdle when heated, we ruled it out. Whole milk dumplings were best—they were tender and the flavor was rich.

With the dough resolved, we tested the formula by shaping it. After fussing with a rolling pin, biscuit cutters, and the like, we decided that the simpler route of dropping spoonfuls of dough into the stew actually yielded better-textured dumplings.

We then turned our attention to the stew. Following the method of our Classic Chicken Stew, we browned boneless, skinless chicken thighs, sautéed the aromatics, built the sauce, stirred in the vegetables, and moved the whole pot into the oven until the chicken was done. When it came out of the oven, we brought the stew to a gentle simmer on the stovetop, dropped the dumplings on top, covered the pot, and waited patiently. In about 15 minutes, the dumplings were plump and ready to be devoured. However, after just a few tests, we found some modifications to our working recipe were in order.

With the hearty dumplings in place, the potatoes from our chicken stew recipe made the dish too starchy, so we omitted them. We also used fewer carrots and less onion and added celery to make the dish more traditional. The garlic now seemed out of place with the more delicate sauce flavor, and tasters preferred the fragrant, fruity flavor of dry sherry to that of white wine. We found the stew in our chicken and dumplings needed slightly more sauce in order to accommodate all of the dumplings, so we increased the amount of broth by almost a cup and the flour by about a tablespoon. With these adjustments, the consistency of the sauce was just right, not too thick and not too thin.

With our tender dumplings floating in a rich and deeply flavorful sauce, we finally had a hearty and satisfying chicken stew with dumplings—a great American comfort food classic.

Old-Fashioned Chicken and Dumplings
SERVES 6 TO 8

Do not substitute boneless, skinless chicken breasts for the thighs in this recipe or the meat will taste very dry. Also, do not use low-fat or nonfat milk in the dumplings. The uncooked dumpling dough doesn't hold very well, so be sure to mix it just before cooking.

STEW

3	pounds boneless, skinless chicken thighs (about 12 thighs), trimmed and cut into 1-inch pieces
	Salt and ground black pepper
2	tablespoons vegetable oil
3	tablespoons unsalted butter
2	celery ribs, sliced ¼ inch thick
I	medium onion, minced
I	teaspoon minced fresh thyme leaves or ¼ teaspoon dried
⅓	cup unbleached all-purpose flour
¼	cup dry sherry
4¼	cups low-sodium chicken broth

MAKING DUMPLINGS

1. Gather a golf-ball-size portion of the dumpling batter onto a soupspoon, then push the dumpling into the stew using a second spoon.

2. Cover the stew with the dumplings, leaving about ¼ inch of space around each dumpling to allow room to expand. Cover the pot and simmer gently for about 15 to 18 minutes.

3. When fully cooked, the dumplings will have doubled in size.

4   carrots, peeled and sliced ¼ inch thick

2   bay leaves

I   cup frozen peas

3   tablespoons minced fresh parsley leaves

DUMPLINGS

2   cups (10 ounces) unbleached
    all-purpose flour

I   tablespoon baking powder

I   teaspoon salt

I   cup whole milk (see note)

3   tablespoons unsalted butter

1. FOR THE STEW: Adjust an oven rack to the lower-middle position and heat the oven to 300 degrees. Pat the chicken dry with paper towels and season with salt and pepper.

2. Heat 1 tablespoon of the oil in a large Dutch oven over medium-high heat until just smoking. Add half of the chicken and brown lightly, 6 to 8 minutes; transfer to a medium bowl. Repeat with the remaining 1 tablespoon oil and the remaining chicken and transfer to the bowl.

3. Add the butter to the pot and melt over medium heat. Add the celery, onion, and ¼ teaspoon salt and cook until the vegetables are softened, 5 to 7 minutes. Stir in the thyme and cook until fragrant, about 30 seconds. Stir in the flour and cook for 1 minute. Slowly whisk in the sherry, scraping up any browned bits.

4. Gradually whisk in the broth, smoothing out any lumps. Stir in the carrots, bay leaves, and browned chicken with any accumulated juice and bring to a simmer. Cover, place the pot in the oven, and cook until the chicken is very tender, 50 to 60 minutes.

5. Remove the pot from the oven and remove the bay leaves. Stir in the peas and parsley and season with salt and pepper to taste. (The stew can be refrigerated for up to 3 days; reheat over medium-low heat, adjusting the consistency with additional broth as needed, before continuing.)

6. FOR THE DUMPLINGS: Whisk the flour, baking powder, and salt together in a large bowl. Microwave the milk and butter in a microwave-safe bowl until the mixture is warm (do not overheat), about 1 minute. Whisk the warm milk mixture to melt the butter, then stir into the flour mixture with a wooden spoon until just incorporated and smooth.

7. Return the stew to a simmer. Following the illustrations on page 204, drop golf-ball-size dumplings into the stew, leaving about ¼ inch of space around each dumpling (you should have about 18 dumplings). Cover, reduce to a gentle simmer, and cook until the dumplings have doubled in size, 15 to 18 minutes. Serve.

CAJUN CHICKEN STEW

CASTING ABOUT FOR ANOTHER TAKE ON OUR classic chicken stew, we turned to the Deep South for inspiration. Louisiana's Cajun-style cooking is rustic and satisfying, and we thought it ideal for a spicy, chunky chicken stew. We imagined a highly seasoned, heady stew with sausage, fresh corn, the classic combination of green peppers, onions, and celery, and tender pieces of chicken.

One of the potential problems we foresaw with this stew was the sausage. Its flavor could easily overwhelm the chicken and corn, so our stew would have to be carefully balanced. Maximizing the flavor of the corn was another concern— we wanted real corn flavor to permeate the sauce and we weren't sure how many ears we would have to shuck to impart any real flavor. The level of spiciness and heat was important, too; we wanted it potent, but not so dominating that the other flavors were overshadowed.

We began with our preferred method for chicken stew as a jumping-off point. We browned bite-size pieces of boneless thigh meat first to develop flavor, then removed them from the pot while we sautéed aromatics and built a simple sauce of flour and chicken broth. Before adding the aromatics to the pot however, we decided to sauté a few slices of bacon first to render its fat. Pork is often used in Cajun cuisine, so bacon seemed a natural inclusion. We cooked the stew in a low (300-degree) oven for about an hour until the chicken was tender. Sadly, tasters were disappointed—the resulting stew tasted too smoky. We decided to forgo the bacon and move on to the sausage.

Andouille sausage, which is spicy and smoked, is commonly used in Cajun cookery to add heat and meatiness to dishes. For our stew, we decided to slice some andouille into half-moons, brown it, and stir the pieces into the stew. While tasters liked the meaty flavor it imparted, they felt it added too much of its intense dry spice flavor and dominated the stew. We decided to give kielbasa a try, as it has a milder flavor. We found the kielbasa lent a similar meatiness and hint of smokiness to the stew.

As for aromatics, we turned to the traditional Cajun combination of onions, bell peppers, and celery. We opted to use red bell peppers instead of green, as they contributed both color and sweetness to the dish. In addition to garlic, we also added a bit of thyme for a more fragrant sauce.

Now it was time to figure out how to get the most corn flavor in our stew. We started with three ears of corn; the kernels imparted a nice, light sweet corn flavor and some texture. But tasters demanded more. First, we worked our way up to six ears—now there were bites of corn in every spoonful. Next, we followed the flavor extraction method from our Corn Chowder (page 109) and scraped the cobs with the back of a butter knife to release the corn milk and pulp after cutting off the kernels. This step boosted the corn flavor significantly. The finished stew had sweet, corny flavor throughout, and tasters were pleased. As an added bonus, the natural starch from the corn pulp also helped to thicken the stew slightly, so that only a small amount of flour was needed.

With the stew nearly complete we tested different amounts of heat. Cayenne pepper was preferred for the lasting, pungent warmth it imparted. We started with ⅛ teaspoon but ultimately ¼ teaspoon was ideal.

The stew was bold, spicy, and full of flavor. A final sprinkling of fresh cilantro and a few dashes of hot sauce countered the dish's richness, bringing our Cajun-style stew into balance.

Cajun Chicken, Sausage, and Corn Stew

SERVES 6 TO 8

Do not substitute boneless, skinless chicken breasts for the thighs in this recipe or the meat will taste very dry. The flavor of this stew depends on using fresh corn; do not substitute frozen or canned corn. Serve with Simple Rice Pilaf (page 286) and hot sauce.

2	pounds boneless, skinless chicken thighs (about 8 thighs), trimmed and cut into 1-inch pieces
	Salt and ground black pepper
3	tablespoons vegetable oil
1	pound kielbasa sausage, sliced ¼ inch thick
2	medium onions, minced
2	red bell peppers, stemmed, seeded, and cut into ½-inch pieces
2	celery ribs, chopped fine
4	medium garlic cloves, minced or pressed through a garlic press (about 4 teaspoons)
1	teaspoon minced fresh thyme leaves or ¼ teaspoon dried
¼	teaspoon cayenne pepper
2	tablespoons unbleached all-purpose flour
6	ears corn, husks and silk removed, kernels cut off the cobs, and cobs scraped clean of pulp (see the illustrations on page 108)
2½	cups low-sodium chicken broth
2	bay leaves
¼	cup minced fresh cilantro leaves

1. Adjust an oven rack to the lower-middle position and heat the oven to 300 degrees. Pat the chicken dry with paper towels and season with salt and pepper.

2. Heat 1 tablespoon of the oil in a large Dutch oven over medium-high heat until just smoking. Add half of the chicken and brown lightly, 6 to 8 minutes; transfer to a medium bowl. Repeat with 1 tablespoon more oil and the remaining chicken and transfer to the bowl.

3. Add the remaining 1 tablespoon oil to the pot and return to medium heat until shimmering. Add the kielbasa and brown lightly, about 2 minutes.

Stir in the onions, bell peppers, celery, and ¼ teaspoon salt and cook until the vegetables are softened, 8 to 10 minutes.

4. Stir in the garlic, thyme, and cayenne and cook until fragrant, about 30 seconds. Stir in the flour and cook, stirring constantly, for 1 minute. Stir in the corn kernels and pulp.

5. Gradually stir in the broth, scraping up any browned bits and smoothing out any lumps. Add the bay leaves and browned chicken with any accumulated juice and bring to a simmer. Cover, place the pot in the oven, and cook until the chicken is very tender, 50 to 60 minutes.

6. Remove the pot from the oven and remove the bay leaves. Stir in the cilantro and season with salt and pepper to taste before serving.

CHICKEN CACCIATORE

CACCIATORE, WHICH MEANS "HUNTER-STYLE" in Italian, originally referred to a simple method of cooking fresh-killed game. Game hen or rabbit was sautéed along with wild mushrooms, onions, and other foraged vegetables, then braised with wine or broth. Unfortunately, when applied to chicken and translated by American cooks, cacciatore mutated into a generic pasty "red sauce" dish, often featuring sauces that were greasy and overly sweet along with dry, overcooked chicken. We thought it was time for a resurrection. We knew there was a really good version of this dish to be found, and we were determined to discover it.

From the beginning, we knew that we wanted a sauce that was just substantial enough to cling to the chicken; we didn't want the chicken to be swimming in broth, nor did we want the sauce to be reminiscent of Spackle. Another thing we wanted was a streamlined cooking method; utilizing boneless, skinless thighs, our favorite cut of meat for chicken stew, would be a step in the right direction.

We began with our simple method for preparing chicken stew. We cut boneless thighs into small pieces and browned them before sautéing onion and garlic. Next, we added flour, then chicken broth, and, finally, our browned chicken (which we

had set aside while making the sauce) and a good amount of sliced white mushrooms before transferring the stew to the slow, even heat of the oven. The results were unfortunate. The mushrooms tasted washed out and though the sauce had some mushroom flavor, it was weak and watered down. Clearly, we had to find a way to concentrate the mushroom flavor and get rid of the excess moisture the mushrooms were exuding.

We decided to revisit a two-pronged method we've relied on in the past—first cooking the mushrooms, covered, so they would soften and release their juice, and then uncovering the pot so the mushrooms could brown. This method worked well, and we found we could add the onions to cook at the same time. The resulting stew had deep, concentrated mushroom flavor and the sauce was no longer watery.

With the moisture problem solved, we moved on to test different types of mushrooms. So far, we'd been using white mushrooms, the supermarket staple, which provided decent mushroom flavor, but we wondered if we could do better. Cremini mushrooms offered a fuller mushroom flavor that tasters preferred (although you can substitute white mushrooms if necessary). The flavor was on the right track now but tasters wanted more texture. We thought hearty portobello mushrooms might just do the trick. These have substantial flavor and a meatier, firmer texture than cremini. In the end, we found equal parts of both varieties provided the substantial texture our tasters wanted. As for flavor, we turned to dried porcini, which have an intense, heady flavor and aroma. Tasters were unanimous—they loved the dried porcini for the woody dimension they added. Our triple-mushroom punch had worked—we now had big, hearty chunks of mushrooms throughout, along with rich, meaty flavor.

We now looked to incorporate the supporting ingredients, including the tomatoes. Fresh tomatoes were out of the question, as they were obliterated after an hour in the oven. Canned diced tomatoes fared better; they held their shape (thus avoiding an unfortunate "red sauce" effect) and had a concentrated, sweet flavor. Deglazing the pan with a bit of red wine added bold flavor and unlocked all the flavor in the fond (browned bits) on the bottom of the pan. A tablespoon of sherry vinegar worked to add some brightness to the stew at the end of cooking. For an herbal note, instead of reaching for a number of herbs (which our hearty stew definitely needed), we took a shortcut and used herbes de Provence, a dried spice mixture that combines several different herbs, including basil, fennel, thyme, and sage. While not traditional in Italian cooking, herbes de Provence added a pleasing aroma and rounded out the mushroom flavor in the stew.

We thought our chicken stew was finished until one taster commented that a fresh grating of Parmesan cheese on top might be a nice addition. But rather than having a few random bites of nutty, salty Parmesan, we opted to simmer a sizeable chunk of its rind in the stew while it cooked. This technique imparted a wonderful aroma and flavor, rounding out the stew and leaving tasters clamoring for seconds of our hearty, mushroom-laden chicken stew.

Chicken Cacciatore

SERVES 6 TO 8

Do not substitute boneless, skinless chicken breasts for the thighs in this recipe or the meat will taste very dry. White mushrooms can be substituted for the cremini mushrooms if necessary. Parmesan rind is added for flavor, but it can be replaced with a 2-inch chunk of Parmesan cheese. Serve with Creamy Polenta (page 232) or buttered noodles.

3	pounds boneless, skinless chicken thighs (about 12 thighs), trimmed and cut into 1-inch pieces
	Salt and ground black pepper
3	tablespoons olive oil
12	ounces portobello caps (about 3 medium), wiped clean and cut into ¾-inch pieces
12	ounces cremini mushrooms, wiped clean, trimmed, and halved if small, quartered if large (see note)
2	medium onions, minced
½	ounce dried porcini mushrooms, rinsed and minced

4	medium garlic cloves, minced or pressed through a garlic press (about 4 teaspoons)
1½	teaspoons herbes de Provence
2	tablespoons unbleached all-purpose flour
⅓	cup dry red wine
2½	cups low-sodium chicken broth
1	(14.5-ounce) can diced tomatoes, drained
1	(5-inch-long) piece Parmesan cheese rind (see note)
2	bay leaves
¼	cup minced fresh parsley leaves
1	tablespoon sherry vinegar

1. Adjust an oven rack to the lower-middle position and heat the oven to 300 degrees. Pat the chicken dry with paper towels and season with salt and pepper.

2. Heat 1 tablespoon of the oil in a large Dutch oven over medium-high heat until just smoking. Add half of the chicken and brown lightly, 6 to 8 minutes; transfer to a medium bowl. Repeat with 1 tablespoon more oil and the remaining chicken and transfer to the bowl.

3. Add the remaining 1 tablespoon oil to the pot and return to medium heat until shimmering. Add the portobellos, cremini, onions, porcini, and ¼ teaspoon salt, cover, and cook until the mushrooms have released their liquid and the onion has softened, about 5 minutes. Uncover and continue to cook until the mushrooms are dry and browned, 10 to 15 minutes.

4. Stir in the garlic and herbes de Provence and cook until fragrant, about 30 seconds. Stir in the flour and cook for 1 minute. Stir in the wine, scraping up any browned bits.

5. Gradually stir in the broth, smoothing out any lumps. Add the tomatoes, Parmesan rind, bay leaves, and browned chicken with any accumulated juice and bring to a simmer. Cover, place the pot in the oven, and cook until the chicken is very tender, 50 to 60 minutes.

6. Remove the pot from the oven, remove the bay leaves, and remove the Parmesan rind (scraping off any cheese that has melted and adding it back to the pot). Stir in the parsley and vinegar and season with salt and pepper to taste before serving.

CHICKEN PROVENÇAL

WHEN DONE RIGHT, CHICKEN PROVENÇAL represents the best of simple French cooking: tender, moist pieces of chicken are slowly simmered with an aromatic, garlicky tomato sauce and a sprinkling of nutty niçoise olives. But order it in a restaurant and the results are often disappointing, the flavor dull and muddy and the sauce thin and practically nonexistent. We knew such a simple dish shouldn't be so difficult to prepare.

Starting out, we assessed our basic approach to chicken stew. In the test kitchen, we like using boneless chicken thighs, which stay moist and tender even when cooked for long periods of time. Readily available, boneless thighs are also easy to prepare, and cutting them into small pieces in advance saves us the extra step of having to shred bone-in pieces of meat after cooking. After browning the meat in the pot, we were left with a flavorful fond (browned bits), which we could use to develop our sauce.

Moving on to the sauce, we sautéed a couple of onions and a few cloves of garlic before adding flour and a few cups of chicken broth. We knew we wanted the sauce to be garlicky and tomatoey without veering into pasta sauce territory. We considered both chopped fresh tomatoes and canned diced tomatoes. To test them, we made two stews, one with the fresh tomatoes and one with the canned. After about an hour in the oven—the time required to get our chicken moist and tender— the fresh tomatoes had broken down too much into a sauce best served with spaghetti. The canned diced tomatoes fared much better, retaining their shape and providing sweet flavor. To concentrate the tomato flavor even further, we added a bit of tomato paste. Up until now we had been using three cloves of garlic, but we wanted the sauce to have a more pungent flavor. We increased the amount of garlic one clove at a time, eventually settling on a hefty six cloves.

In keeping with the theme of our stew, we added niçoise olives to the pot. Unfortunately, cooking them with the chicken was a flop; they all but disintegrated and their flavor was muted by the end of cooking. We tried stirring whole pitted olives into the pot before serving; while this made for an attractive presentation, the olives were overpowering in such big bites, so we decided to chop them up before stirring them in, which ensured more even flavor distribution.

When we were researching recipes, we found a handful that included mushrooms. After a few tests, we found we liked the earthiness and meatiness contributed by white mushrooms. To make sure they didn't release liquid into the stew and throw off the consistency of our sauce, we cooked them, covered, with the onions, then uncovered them and browned them for deeper flavor and to drive off any remaining moisture. To enhance the savory, meaty flavor of the stew even more, we added some minced anchovy. Commonly used in Mediterranean cuisine, anchovies contribute depth to dishes without tasting overtly fishy.

Tasters were pleased with the stew, but asked for another component to make it more substantial. White beans were a logical choice, given that they are common in French cuisine. We liked the consistency of the stew as it was, so we decided to use canned beans and stir them in at the end to prevent them from breaking down and thickening the sauce further. Stirring them in off the heat and letting them warm through for a few minutes before serving was ideal.

Our stew was now hearty and satisfying, but the flavor needed some last-minute adjustments. We found that a small amount of white wine, simmered in the sauce, reinforced the brightness of the tomatoes. And just a teaspoon of herbes de Provence, a highly fragrant mixture made up of dried basil, fennel seed, lavender, marjoram, rosemary, sage, summer savory, and thyme, gave the stew a heady, herbal lift.

For a final punch in flavor, we stirred in a small amount of lemon zest, a common and, as it turned out, welcome addition. With a sprinkling of fresh parsley, our French-inspired chicken stew was now complete.

Herbs 101

Both fresh herbs and dried herbs are widely available, but sometimes convenience—and what you already have on hand in your pantry—plays a factor when deciding what to use. However, not all fresh and dried herbs are interchangeable. Here's a guide to what to use based on the application.

WHICH IS MORE POTENT?

Depending on the variety, fresh herb leaves are 80 to 90 percent water. With drying, water is lost and, consequently, so are weight and volume. The volatile essential oils that give an herb its characteristic flavor and aroma are left closer to the surface, where they easily evaporate, leaving the herb without much flavor or aroma.

There is sometimes the misconception that dried herbs are less potent than fresh. However, because of the aforementioned water loss, the opposite is true. Ounce for ounce, dried herbs are more potent than fresh. Recommended substitution ratios range from 1 part dried to 2, 3, or even 4 parts fresh. Because the freshness of a dried herb has such a big impact on its potency, bear in mind that these recommendations are very rough guidelines at best. To complicate matters further, the fineness or coarseness of a dried herb can affect substitution amounts. (For example, dried sage is available in three forms: ground, "rubbed" leaves that appear finely chopped, and coarsely crumbled leaves, each of which has different levels of potency.)

TASTING FRESH AND DRIED HERBS

Dried herbs are more convenient to use than fresh because they require no more prep than a twist of the lid. They're also a lot less expensive than fresh, and until recently they were more readily available. While we've generally held the bias that fresh is better than dried, we recently decided to look into the matter more thoroughly. We purchased fresh and dried versions of basil, chives, dill, oregano, parsley, rosemary, sage (in coarsely crumbled, rubbed, and ground forms), tarragon, and thyme. Then we cooked our way through 24 recipes (including sauces, braises, and stews), making each with fresh and dried herbs and comparing differences in flavor. Most of the time, tasters preferred fresh herbs over dried and commented that the dried herbs tasted "dusty" and "stale," while fresh herbs tasted "clean" and "bright." Many of the subtleties and nuances of fresh herbs seemed to be lost with drying.

However, there are some instances in which some dried herbs worked fine, especially soups and stews, which have fairly long cooking times (20 minutes plus) and a good amount of moisture. Chili, for example, was better when made with a dried herb (oregano) than with fresh. Dried sage and thyme also fared reasonably well in some applications. Those herbs that we unofficially classify as delicate (basil, chives, dill, parsley, and tarragon) seemed to have lost most of their flavor when dried; we preferred fresh forms of these herbs. Here are our detailed assessments of these herbs.

BASIL

There are many varieties of basil, but sweet basil is most commonly used in this country and is the type sold in dried form. The flavors of sweet basil contain hints of anise, mint, and clove. Dried basil is sold in a flaky, chopped form and it lacks the complex flavor of fresh. It elicited comments such as "stale" and "dead" when used to make stuffed tomatoes and a tomato sauce for pasta.

DRIED: Avoid using dried basil in any application.

FRESH: Fresh leaves bruise and discolor easily; shred or chop fresh basil just before using. For freshest flavor, add near the end of cooking.

CHIVES

Chives are appreciated for their mild allium flavor as well as for their emerald-green color and appearance when snipped. The delicate flavor of chives pairs well with seafood and eggs. Dried chives, however, look and taste dull and they have a fibrous, papery texture. They performed especially poorly in a sour cream dip and in a vinaigrette.

DRIED: Avoid using dried chives in any application.

FRESH: Fresh chives cannot withstand cooking. For best flavor and appearance, add fresh chives just before serving.

DILL

Remarkably, dried dill keeps some of the vibrant color of feathery fresh dill, but the similarities end there. The flavor is lost with drying and what's left is a stale, dusty flavor and aroma. Dried dill was nearly tasteless in a smoked salmon dip as well as with buttered steamed new potatoes.

DRIED: Avoid using dried dill in any application.

FRESH: Fresh dill cannot withstand cooking. For best flavor and appearance, add fresh dill at the end of cooking.

OREGANO

Warm, earthy, robust oregano has a distinct flavor and fragrance. Used in place of fresh, dried oregano made a quick-cooked tomato pasta sauce taste like pizzeria sauce. However, dried oregano does have its place, particularly in chili, where its assertive flavor held its own in a mix of other spices and seasonings. In contrast, the sweetness of fresh oregano was lost in chili.

DRIED: Dried oregano is acceptable for use in long-cooked soups and stews if fresh is not available. Because of its intensity, dried oregano works best in recipes where other flavors are abundant, as in chili. Otherwise, its flavor can be overpowering.

FRESH: Substituting fresh oregano for dried will result in a more subdued flavor.

PARSLEY

Parsley is used as a garnish as often as it is used as an herb, adding freshness, a generic herbaceousness, and, of course, color to dishes of all kinds. Both flat-leaf (or Italian) and curly parsley are widely available. In recipes where the flavor of parsley is an essential component, the stronger, grassier flavor of flat-leaf parsley is preferred. Dried parsley or parsley flakes have no flavor or freshness and a dull appearance.

DRIED: Avoid using dried parsley in any application.

FRESH: For the best flavor and appearance, add chopped fresh parsley leaves near the end of cooking. Fresh parsley stems can be used to flavor stocks and broths.

ROSEMARY

Rosemary has a warm, piney, honeyed flavor that is a particularly good match with lamb and beef. Long, slow braising gave the tough, brittle, pine-needlelike leaves of dried rosemary time to soften, but its muted flavor was just this side of acceptable, lacking the complexity of fresh. In a marinade and a quick-cooked sauce, the texture of dried rosemary was unpalatable and the flavor medicinal and harshly resinous.

DRIED: Avoid using dried rosemary in any application.

FRESH: The flavor of fresh rosemary mellows with long cooking; if a bright, pungent flavor is desired, add fresh rosemary near the end of cooking.

ARE YOUR DRIED HERBS FRESH?

We recommend replacement of dried herbs after about 12 months. If you are questioning the age and freshness of an open jar, crumble a small amount between your fingers and take a whiff. If it releases a lively aroma, it's good to use. If it doesn't, it's best to get a new jar. If the fragrance is present but relatively mild, consider using more than you normally would. To track the ages of the dried herbs stored in your pantry or spice drawer, write the purchase date on an adhesive dot and place the dot on the lid. That way, you'll know when your herbs need to be replaced.

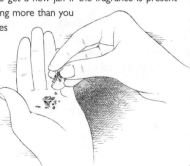

SAGE

Earthy, musky sage is often matched with poultry and pork. It is available dried in three forms: ground, rubbed (finely chopped), and coarsely crumbled. Note that crumbled is more potent. Dried sage was acceptable in a cornbread and sausage stuffing where other flavors were plentiful. In a pan sauce, however, it failed to match the complexity and fullness of flavor of fresh and tasted stale and dull.

DRIED: Dried sage is acceptable for use in long-cooked soups and stews if fresh is not available.

FRESH: Use fresh sage in any recipe where the flavor of sage is at the fore.

TARRAGON

With a sweet licorice-like flavor and fragrance, tarragon is well suited to seafood, chicken, and eggs. Dried tarragon is sold in a flaky, chopped form; a licorice-like aroma may be present in dried tarragon, but most of the nuances and flavor of fresh are absent. In both a vinaigrette and a quick-cooked pan sauce, dried tarragon tasted dusty and stale.

DRIED: Avoid using dried tarragon in any application.

FRESH: For freshest flavor and aroma, add fresh tarragon near the end of cooking.

THYME

The hearty, spicy, woodsy flavor and aroma of thyme is welcome in almost any dish, including soups, stews, and preparations with meats, poultry, and mushrooms. In a long, slow braise, dried thyme provided an underpinning of flavor, but it lacked the vibrant character of fresh. In a marinade and pan sauce, dried thyme couldn't match the round, deep flavor of fresh.

DRIED: Dried thyme is acceptable for use in long-cooked soups and stews if fresh is not available. Avoid using dried thyme in marinades and quick-cooked applications.

FRESH: Fresh thyme can withstand long cooking, but its flavor mellows slightly; if a pungent, assertive flavor is desired, add more fresh thyme near the end of cooking.

Chicken Provençal

SERVES 6 TO 8

Do not substitute boneless, skinless chicken breasts for the thighs in this recipe or the meat will taste very dry.

3	pounds boneless, skinless chicken thighs (about 12 thighs), trimmed and cut into 1-inch pieces
	Salt and ground black pepper
3	tablespoons olive oil
1	pound white mushrooms, wiped clean, trimmed, and halved if small, quartered if large
2	medium onions, minced
6	medium garlic cloves, minced or pressed through a garlic press (about 2 tablespoons)
1	anchovy fillet, rinsed and minced (about ½ teaspoon)
1	teaspoon herbes de Provence
⅛	teaspoon cayenne pepper
2	tablespoons unbleached all-purpose flour
2	tablespoons tomato paste
⅓	cup dry white wine
2½	cups low-sodium chicken broth
1	(14.5-ounce) can diced tomatoes, drained
2	bay leaves
1	(15-ounce) can cannellini beans, drained and rinsed
½	cup pitted niçoise olives, chopped coarse
¼	cup minced fresh parsley leaves
½	teaspoon grated zest from 1 lemon

1. Adjust an oven rack to the lower-middle position and heat the oven to 300 degrees. Pat the chicken dry with paper towels and season with salt and pepper.

2. Heat 1 tablespoon of the oil in a large Dutch oven over medium-high heat until just smoking. Add half of the chicken and brown lightly, 6 to 8 minutes; transfer to a medium bowl. Repeat with 1 tablespoon more oil and the remaining chicken and transfer to the bowl.

3. Add the remaining 1 tablespoon oil to the pot and return to medium heat until shimmering. Add the mushrooms, onions, and ¼ teaspoon salt, cover, and cook until the mushrooms have released their liquid and the onions have softened, about 5 minutes. Uncover and continue to cook until the mushrooms are dry and browned, about 10 minutes.

4. Stir in the garlic, anchovy, herbes de Provence, and cayenne and cook until fragrant, about 30 seconds. Stir in the flour and tomato paste and cook for 1 minute. Slowly stir in the wine, scraping up any browned bits.

5. Gradually stir in the broth, smoothing out any lumps. Stir in the tomatoes, bay leaves, and browned chicken with any accumulated juice and bring to a simmer. Cover, place the pot in the oven, and cook until the chicken is very tender, 50 to 60 minutes.

6. Remove the pot from the oven and remove the bay leaves. Stir in the beans and olives, cover, and let stand for 5 minutes. Stir in the parsley and lemon zest and season with salt and pepper to taste before serving.

PITTING OLIVES

Removing the pits from olives by hand is not an easy job. We found the following method to be the most expedient: Cover a cutting board with a clean kitchen towel and spread the olives on top, spacing them about 1 inch apart. Place a second clean towel over the olives. Using a mallet, pound all the olives firmly for 10 to 15 seconds, being careful not to split the pits. Remove the top towel and, using your fingers, press the pit out of each olive.

CHICKEN BOUILLABAISSE

WE LOVE THE INTENSE GARLICKY FENNEL, orange, and saffron flavors of bouillabaisse, the Provençal fish stew. Served with crusty bread and a hefty dollop of rouille (a spicy, garlicky, bread-thickened mayonnaise), it's one of the world's greatest stews. Many cooks have adapted this recipe as a humble, homey chicken dinner: chicken bouillabaisse—and now it was our turn to come up with our own version. We wanted tender chunks of chicken in a stew infused with robust Provençal flavors.

The chicken was our starting point. For perfectly tender, moist chicken, we reached for boneless, skinless thighs, which we had determined would provide tender chunks of meat. After cutting the meat into small pieces and browning them, we set them aside and turned our attention to the other ingredients.

We began with traditional bouillabaisse aromatics—a head of fennel, one leek, an onion, and a whole head of garlic sweated in olive oil. Since all of these aromatics turn sweet as they cook, tasters found the end result rather cloying, and we needed to make some cuts. Fennel was a must since it provided the traditional anise backbone. The garlic could be dramatically reduced however. Cutting the amount down to a mere four cloves—sautéed briefly after the other vegetables had softened—provided ample garlicky flavor while dialing back on sweetness. To tone down the sweetness further, we omitted the onion in one test and found that tasters actually preferred the dish made with milder, less-sweet leeks alone. As is traditional, we also sautéed earthy saffron with the garlic for flavor and color. (A mere ¼ teaspoon of the world's most expensive spice was all that was needed.) A small amount of cayenne punched up the flavor even more.

We had yet to determine what to use for the cooking liquid. With all the other flavorings contributing complexity to the stew, we were pleased to find that store-bought broth worked well, as the nuances of homemade chicken broth were lost. But the broth could certainly use some enhancement. To give the store-bought broth more body and a long-simmered flavor, we added some flour and tomato paste to the pot before adding the broth. Orange zest is typically stirred into the mix near the end of cooking but we found it worked best to add it at the same time as the broth to allow it to give up more of its flavor. Tasters also preferred the pastis, a licorice-flavored liqueur that's commonly included in bouillabaisse, added at the start of the simmer, which burned off more of its alcoholic taste, leaving only the essence of licorice behind.

As for additional ingredients, traditional white wine and tomatoes were both givens. A half-cup of wine brought just the right brightness, while drained canned diced tomatoes were the best way to ensure consistently good tomato flavor year-round. At this point, we thought the pot could use a starchy element, so we added two Yukon Gold potatoes, cut into small chunks, which enhanced the body of the broth and also absorbed some of its rich flavors.

With the broth in order, we whipped up a robust, tangy rouille spiked with saffron. With a spoonful or two stirred right into our soup bowls, and a few hunks of garlicky toast ready and waiting to be dipped into the sauce, we were ready to dig in. Empty bowls indicated our success in creating a hearty braised chicken dish with all the best in traditional bouillabaisse flavors.

Chicken Bouillabaisse

SERVES 6 TO 8

Do not substitute boneless, skinless chicken breasts for the thighs in this recipe or the meat will taste very dry.

3   pounds boneless, skinless chicken thighs (about 12 thighs), trimmed and cut into 1-inch pieces
    Salt and ground black pepper
3   tablespoons olive oil, plus extra as needed
1   large leek, white and light green parts only, halved lengthwise, sliced thin, and rinsed thoroughly (see the illustrations on page 103)

1 small fennel bulb (about 9 ounces),
   trimmed of stalks, cored, and sliced thin
   (see the illustrations on page 27)

4 medium garlic cloves, minced or pressed
   through a garlic press (about 4 teaspoons)

¼ teaspoon saffron threads, crumbled

⅛ teaspoon cayenne pepper

3 tablespoons unbleached all-purpose flour

1 tablespoon tomato paste

½ cup dry white wine

3 cups low-sodium chicken broth

¼ cup pastis, Pernod, or ouzo

1 (14.5-ounce) can diced tomatoes, drained

12 ounces Yukon Gold potatoes (about 2 small),
   scrubbed and cut into ¾-inch chunks

1 (3-inch long) strip zest from 1 orange (see
   the illustration on page 148), trimmed
   of white pith

1 tablespoon minced fresh tarragon or
   parsley leaves

1 recipe Garlic Toasts (page 138)

1 recipe Saffron Rouille

1. Adjust an oven rack to the lower-middle position and heat the oven to 300 degrees. Pat the chicken dry with paper towels and season with salt and pepper.

2. Heat 1 tablespoon of the oil in a large Dutch oven over medium-high heat until just smoking. Add half of the chicken and brown lightly, 6 to 8 minutes; transfer to a medium bowl. Repeat with 1 tablespoon more oil and the remaining chicken, and transfer to the bowl.

3. Add the remaining 1 tablespoon oil to the pot and return to medium heat until shimmering. Add the leek, fennel, and ¼ teaspoon salt and cook until the vegetables are softened, 5 to 7 minutes.

4. Stir in the garlic, saffron, and cayenne and cook until fragrant, about 30 seconds. Stir in the flour and tomato paste and cook for 1 minute. Slowly whisk in the wine, scraping up any browned bits.

5. Gradually whisk in the broth and pastis, smoothing out any lumps. Stir in the tomatoes, potatoes, orange zest, and browned chicken with

any accumulated juice and bring to a simmer. Cover, place the pot in the oven, and cook until the chicken is very tender, 50 to 60 minutes.

6. Remove the pot from the oven and remove the zest. Stir in the tarragon, season with salt and pepper to taste, and serve with the Garlic Toasts and Saffron Rouille.

Saffron Rouille

MAKES ABOUT ¾ CUP

Be sure to use a high-quality olive oil in this recipe; for information on our winning brand, see page 149.

4½ teaspoons water

⅛ teaspoon saffron threads, crumbled

1 slice high-quality white sandwich bread,
   crusts removed, torn into 1-inch pieces

2 teaspoons juice from 1 lemon

1 large egg yolk

1 teaspoon Dijon mustard

1 small garlic clove, minced or
   pressed through a garlic press
   (about ½ teaspoon)
   Pinch cayenne pepper

¼ cup vegetable oil

¼ cup extra-virgin olive oil
   Salt and ground black pepper

1. Microwave the water and saffron together in a medium bowl on high until steaming, about 10 seconds, then set aside for 5 minutes to let the saffron bloom. Stir in the bread and lemon juice, let the bread soften for 5 minutes, then mash to a smooth paste.

2. Whisk in the egg yolk, mustard, garlic, and cayenne until smooth, about 15 seconds. Whisking constantly, slowly drizzle in the oils until a smooth mayonnaise-like consistency is reached. Season with salt and pepper to taste and serve. (The rouille can be refrigerated in an airtight container for up 2 days.)

CHICKEN PAPRIKASH

WHILE MOST AMERICAN COOKS RELY ON paprika to add a splash of color to deviled eggs, in Hungary paprika is used in a variety of dishes not only for its showy red hue but also for the rich, full flavor it contributes. Chicken paprikash is one such dish. In this Hungarian classic, chicken, onions, and paprika come together in a vibrant red sauce made rich and velvety with sour cream. We wanted to make this Hungarian specialty into a saucy stew and add more vegetables so it was a heartier dish.

Although we suspected sweet paprika would take our stew in the direction we wanted, we decided to leave no stone unturned and started by testing all three types of paprika—sweet, hot, and smoked. Following our established method for making chicken stew, we browned pieces of bone-less chicken thighs in oil, then set the meat aside while we sautéed some onion and garlic. We then made three separate stews, each using a different type of paprika. After cooking the paprika with the aromatics to mellow its raw flavor, we stirred in flour and some chicken broth before returning the chicken to the pot and transferring the stew to a 300-degree oven to gently simmer until the meat was tender (maintaining the temperature is easier to do in the oven than on the stovetop). Tasters were unanimous—sweet paprika was the favorite, preferred for the floral, fruity quality it imparted. Not surprisingly, the stew made with hot paprika was too spicy and slightly bitter, and the one made with smoked paprika was incredibly smoky. Although we had used just 2 tablespoons of paprika per stew, smoked paprika truly is quite potent and we found in retests that even smaller amounts dominated the stew in an unpleasant fashion.

While 2 tablespoons of sweet paprika contributed ample presence, tasters felt the stew could handle more. We decided to increase the amount of paprika in the sauce by tablespoon increments, in search of a sweet, mellow flavor that permeated the dish without being overpowering. At ¼ cup, tasters were satisfied.

Continuing to refine the underlying flavor profile, we decided to eliminate the garlic, as its flavor here seemed too harsh and out of place with the mellow notes now gracing the dish. We added a little marjoram when we added the paprika; the herb's delicate sweetness worked well with the paprika. To deglaze the pot and loosen the flavorful browned bits at the bottom, we stirred in some white wine before adding the broth; the wine added a pleasant acidity that tasters liked.

Moving on to additional components that would make the stew heartier, we thought of bell peppers, which would amplify the sweet, peppery flavor of the dish. We tried softening two minced peppers with the onion at the start of cooking, but by the time the stew had finished cooking, these bits had completely softened and lost their flavor. In our next test, we cut the pieces larger and added them with the broth instead. Now the peppers were slightly softened but they had maintained their subtle flavor and presence. Tasters insisted their spoonfuls of stew could hold more pepper, so we doubled the amount and found that two red and two green bell peppers provided nice sweet and vegetal tones to the dish.

Looking for other ways to make our stew more substantial and build more complex flavor, we thought carrots would be a nice fit. Their sweetness complemented the paprika and they contributed both texture and color to the dish. Thinking tomato paste might deepen the stew's flavor and provide a hint of acidity, we added 2 tablespoons to the sautéed onions and paprika. This test was a flop—the flavors and color were now muddied and dull. Looking for other ways to add some acidity to balance the sauce, we thought of canned diced tomatoes; these held their texture after cooking and provided the missing acidity.

Our paprikash was close to finished now but we still needed to add the sour cream, which would make the sauce rich and creamy. Since sour cream will break if stirred directly into a hot liquid, it had to be tempered first (by stirring a little of the hot broth into it). We tried different amounts of sour cream, ranging from 1 cup, which was too rich, down to ¼ cup, which was too lean. Ultimately, tasters preferred ⅓ cup sour cream, which rounded out the stew's flavor and contributed the right amount of body. Since the sour cream was subduing the paprika flavor, we decided to try stirring some of the paprika into the sour cream. We found that reserving a single tablespoon of paprika for the creamy finish was perfect, adding an intense hit of sweet flavor. A little minced parsley sprinkled over the top brightened the stew's flavor even more.

Chicken Paprikash
SERVES 6 TO 8

Do not substitute boneless, skinless chicken breasts for the thighs in this recipe or the meat will taste very dry. Paprika is essential to this recipe, so it's best to use a fresh container; do not substitute hot or smoked Spanish paprika for the sweet paprika. Serve with boiled potatoes or buttered egg noodles.

3	pounds boneless, skinless chicken thighs (about 12 thighs), trimmed and cut into 1-inch pieces
	Salt and ground black pepper
3	tablespoons vegetable oil
2	medium onions, minced
¼	cup sweet paprika (see note)
1	teaspoon minced fresh marjoram leaves or ¼ teaspoon dried
3	tablespoons unbleached all-purpose flour
⅓	cup dry white wine
2½	cups low-sodium chicken broth
3	carrots, peeled and sliced ½ inch thick
2	red bell peppers, stemmed, seeded, and cut into 1-inch pieces
2	green bell peppers, stemmed, seeded, and cut into 1-inch pieces
1	(14.5-ounce) can diced tomatoes, drained
⅓	cup sour cream
¼	cup minced fresh parsley leaves

1. Adjust an oven rack to the lower-middle position and heat the oven to 300 degrees. Pat the chicken dry with paper towels and season with salt and pepper.

2. Heat 1 tablespoon of the oil in a large Dutch oven over medium-high heat until just smoking. Add half of the chicken and brown lightly, 6 to 8 minutes; transfer to a medium bowl. Repeat with 1 tablespoon more oil and the remaining chicken and transfer to the bowl.

3. Add the remaining 1 tablespoon oil to the pot and return to medium heat until shimmering. Add the onions and ¼ teaspoon salt and cook until softened, 5 to 7 minutes. Stir in 3 tablespoons of the paprika and marjoram and cook until fragrant, about 30 seconds. Stir in the flour and cook for 1 minute. Slowly whisk in the wine, scraping up any browned bits.

4. Gradually whisk in the broth, smoothing out any lumps. Add the carrots, red and green bell peppers, tomatoes, and browned chicken with any accumulated juice and bring to a simmer. Cover, place the pot in the oven, and cook until the chicken is very tender, 50 to 60 minutes.

5. Remove the pot from the oven. Whisk the remaining 1 tablespoon paprika and ½ cup of the hot stew liquid into the sour cream to temper, then stir the sour cream mixture into the pot. Stir in the parsley and season with salt and pepper to taste before serving.

INGREDIENTS: Sweet Paprika

Some cooks think of paprika as merely a coloring agent. But the best versions of this sweet Hungarian spice (made from a different variety of red pepper than hot or smoked paprika) pack a punch that goes beyond pigment. We sampled six brands, two from the supermarket and four ordered online. Our findings? It pays to mail-order your paprika—the supermarket brands had little flavor and even less aroma.

THE BEST PAPRIKA
The Spice House Hungarian Sweet Paprika outshone the competition with the complexity of its "earthy," "fruity" flavors and "toasty" aroma, making the slight inconvenience of mail-ordering it well worthwhile.

SPICE HOUSE

10

HEARTY MEAT STEWS AND BRAISES

Hearty Meat Stews and Braises

Hearty Beef Stew

BEEF STEW SHOULD BE RICH AND SATISFYING, with fall-apart meat and tender vegetables draped in a thick, velvety sauce. Unfortunately, many recipes for beef stew result in tough, dry meat and a watery, bland sauce. In addition, the classic vegetables—potatoes, carrots, and peas—often become mushy and flavorless during the long simmer. We wanted to develop a foolproof recipe for beef stew that would always turn out tender meat, a sauce that had great flavor and a rich, smooth consistency, and perfectly cooked vegetables that were easy to pierce with a fork but didn't fall apart.

The basic process for building beef stew involves first browning the meat, then using the leftover browned bits as a base for building the sauce along with aromatics like onion and garlic as well as a little flour for thickening. The meat is then cooked in the sauce with vegetables and flavorings until it's tender (and the sauce is thick and rich). Given our familiarity with the stew-making process, we knew it would need little revision—it was already fairly streamlined and sensible. The questions we did have revolved around the nitty-gritty. What cut of meat would have the most flavor and be incredibly tender after a long simmer? Would we need to take any extra steps to ensure the sauce was full of deep, rich flavor? Also, would we have to add the vegetables at different times so they didn't deteriorate and turn to mush by the time the meat was tender? We decided to start with the starring ingredient—the beef.

First, we had to determine the ideal cut of beef for our stew. We browned and cooked 12 different cuts of beef, then got out a fistful of forks. The biggest disappointment came from the packages labeled "stew meat," because they contained misshapen and small bits of meat along with scraps from various parts of the animal—basically, the butcher's leftovers. We needed to handpick the beef for consistent results. Chuck proved to be our cut of choice—flavorful, tender, and juicy with a moderate price tag. The names given to different cuts of chuck vary, but the most commonly used names for retail chuck cuts include boneless chuck eye roasts, cross rib roasts, blade steaks and roasts,

shoulder steaks and roasts, and arm steaks and roasts. We particularly like chuck eye roast, but all chuck cuts work well when trimmed and braised.

Now we could move on to building the sauce in which the meat would braise. We found that the development of a fond (the dark, flavorful bits left over from browning the meat) was essential to infusing our sauce with deep, meaty flavor. We began by sautéing onion, garlic, and thyme in some vegetable oil, letting the aromatics mingle with these browned bits. As for the liquid, we tried water, wine, homemade beef broth, store-bought beef broth, store-bought chicken broth, and combinations of these liquids. Water made the stews taste, well, watery. Stew made with homemade beef broth tasted great, but we decided that beef stew has plenty of other hearty ingredients to give it flavor and therefore doesn't require the extra step of making homemade broth. Using all store-bought beef broth was a little overpowering, but cutting it with some chicken broth balanced the flavors nicely. A modest amount of wine was also a welcome addition, contributing some acidity and flavor.

Our braising liquid had substantial meatiness at this point, but we felt it could use a slightly deeper flavor. We've long known that ingredients rich in glutamates—a class of amino acids that give meat its savory taste—can enhance the flavor of a dish. Tomatoes are one such ingredient. We experimented with various canned tomato products, finally landing on tomato paste; a small amount lent just the right background note. Along with the tomato paste, we stirred in a bit of flour for thickening. Now we could add the browned meat back to the pot and let it stew away.

After a little testing, we learned that the temperature of the stewing liquid during cooking was crucial. We found it essential to keep the temperature of the liquid below boiling (212 degrees Fahrenheit), as boiled meat turns tough and the exterior of the meat becomes especially dry. Keeping the liquid at a simmer allows the internal temperature of the meat to rise slowly. By the time the meat is fork-tender, much of the connective tissue will have turned to gelatin. The gelatin, in turn, helps to thicken the stewing liquid. Simmering the stew in the oven—rather than on the stovetop—gave us the most consistent results. We found that putting a covered Dutch oven in a 325-degree oven ensured that the temperature of the stewing liquid remained below the boiling point, at about 200 degrees. (The oven must be kept at a temperature higher than 200 degrees because ovens are not completely efficient in transferring heat; a cooking temperature of 325 degrees recognizes that some heat will be lost as it penetrates through the pot and into the stew.) After a couple hours, our beef emerged from the oven tender and juicy.

Next, it was on to the vegetables. We opted to use frozen peas for their wide availability and reliable flavor; we found they tasted best when stirred in just a few minutes before serving. They heated through quickly and retained their bright green color. The carrots and potatoes, on the other hand, weren't so simple and required further testing. We ultimately determined that they should both be added halfway through the stew's cooking time so they would retain some texture. For the spuds, we went with low-starch red potatoes, which held their shape better than other varieties.

While our method was a little more involved than just throwing everything in the pot and simmering, it was still easy and streamlined, and the fresh-flavored results—punched up with a good helping of minced parsley stirred in at the end—were well worth the effort.

With our classic stew mastered, we couldn't help but picture a version with a heartier vegetable selection. Tasters favored the addition of earthy parsnips, meaty mushrooms, and bitter kale in this stew. To make sure they all retained their flavor and texture in the finished dish, we staggered their addition to the pot and browned the mushroom (a single portobello), which helped to concentrate its flavor and enrich the base of the stew. Given tasters' appreciation of the mushroom's meatiness, we also developed an Asian-inspired variation featuring shiitake mushrooms; earthy cabbage and water chestnuts contributed additional texture. Soy sauce, scallions, and ginger enhanced the flavor profile of this exotic spin on our beef stew.

Hearty Beef Stew
SERVES 6

A $7 to $10 bottle of medium-bodied red table wine made from a blend of grapes, such as Côtes du Rhône, will work well here.

1	(3½- to 4-pound) boneless beef chuck eye roast, trimmed and cut into 1½-inch pieces (see the illustrations on page 221)
	Salt and ground black pepper
3	tablespoons vegetable oil
2	medium onions, minced
3	medium garlic cloves, minced or pressed through a garlic press (about 1 tablespoon)
1	tablespoon minced fresh thyme leaves or 1 teaspoon dried
3	tablespoons unbleached all-purpose flour
1	tablespoon tomato paste
1	cup dry red wine (see note)
1¼	cups low-sodium chicken broth
1¼	cups beef broth
2	bay leaves
1½	pounds red potatoes (about 5 medium), scrubbed and cut into 1-inch chunks
1	pound carrots (about 6 medium), peeled and sliced 1 inch thick
1	cup frozen peas
¼	cup minced fresh parsley leaves

1. Adjust an oven rack to the lower-middle position and heat the oven to 325 degrees. Pat the beef dry with paper towels and season with salt and pepper.

2. Heat 1 tablespoon of the oil in a large Dutch oven over medium-high heat until just smoking. Add half of the meat and brown well on all sides, 7 to 10 minutes; transfer to a medium bowl. Repeat with 1 tablespoon more oil and the remaining beef and transfer to the bowl.

3. Add the remaining 1 tablespoon oil to the pot and heat over medium heat until shimmering. Add the onions and ¼ teaspoon salt and cook until softened, 5 to 7 minutes. Stir in the garlic and thyme and cook until fragrant, about 30 seconds. Stir in the flour and tomato paste and cook for 1 minute.

4. Slowly whisk in the wine, scraping up any browned bits. Gradually whisk in the chicken broth and beef broth, smoothing out any lumps. Stir in the bay leaves and browned meat with any accumulated juice and bring to a simmer. Cover, place the pot in the oven, and cook for 1 hour.

5. Stir in the potatoes and carrots and continue to cook in the oven, covered, until the meat is tender, 1 to 1½ hours longer.

6. Remove the stew from the oven and remove the bay leaves. Stir in the peas, cover, and let stand for 5 minutes. Stir in the parsley and season with salt and pepper to taste before serving.

➤ VARIATIONS

Hearty Beef Stew with Parsnips, Kale, and Mushrooms

A $7 to $10 bottle of medium-bodied red table wine made from a blend of grapes, such as Côtes du Rhône, will work well here.

1 (3½- to 4-pound) boneless beef chuck eye roast, trimmed and cut into 1½-inch pieces (see the illustrations below)
Salt and ground black pepper

3 tablespoons vegetable oil

2 medium onions, minced

1 medium portobello mushroom cap (about 4 ounces), wiped clean and cut into ½-inch pieces

3 medium garlic cloves, minced or pressed through a garlic press (about 1 tablespoon)

1 tablespoon minced fresh thyme leaves or 1 teaspoon dried

3 tablespoons unbleached all-purpose flour

1 tablespoon tomato paste

1 cup dry red wine (see note)

1¼ cups low-sodium chicken broth

1¼ cups beef broth

2 bay leaves

12 ounces red potatoes (2 to 3 medium), scrubbed and cut into 1-inch chunks

4 carrots, peeled and sliced 1 inch thick

3 parsnips, peeled, halved lengthwise, and sliced 1 inch thick

½ bunch kale (about ½ pound), stemmed, leaves chopped into ½-inch pieces (see the illustrations on page 56)

1. Adjust an oven rack to the lower-middle position and heat the oven to 325 degrees. Pat the beef dry with paper towels and season with salt and pepper.

CUTTING BEEF STEW MEAT

There's no guarantee that packaged stew meat is going to be cut into regularly shaped, even-sized pieces or be from the same cut of beef, which is why we choose to cut it ourselves. We like to use a beef chuck eye roast, but any boneless beef roast from the chuck will work. The trick is not to cut the pieces of meat too small while trimming away the fat—the fat will render into the stew and be easy to skim off later. That said, don't be surprised if you have a good amount of trim—count on roughly ½ pound trim for every 4 pounds of meat.

1. Pull apart the roast at its major seams (delineated by lines of fat and silver skin); use a knife as necessary.

2. With a sharp, thin-tipped knife, trim off the excess fat and silver skin.

3. Cut the meat into pieces as directed in specific recipes.

2. Heat 1 tablespoon of the oil in a large Dutch oven over medium-high heat until just smoking. Add half of the meat and brown well on all sides, 7 to 10 minutes; transfer to a medium bowl. Repeat with 1 tablespoon more oil and the remaining beef and transfer to the bowl.

3. Add the remaining 1 tablespoon oil to the pot and heat over medium heat until shimmering. Add the onions, mushroom, and ¼ teaspoon salt and cook until the vegetables are softened, 5 to 7 minutes. Stir in the garlic and thyme and cook until fragrant, about 30 seconds. Stir in the flour and tomato paste and cook for 1 minute.

4. Slowly whisk in the wine, scraping up any browned bits. Gradually whisk in the chicken broth and beef broth, smoothing out any lumps. Stir in the bay leaves and browned meat with any accumulated juice and bring to a simmer. Cover, place the pot in the oven, and cook for 1 hour.

5. Stir in the potatoes, carrots, and parsnips and continue to cook in the oven, covered, until the meat is mostly tender, 45 to 75 minutes.

6. Stir in the kale and continue to cook in the oven, covered, until the kale is softened, about 15 minutes longer. Remove the stew from the oven and remove the bay leaves. Season with salt and pepper to taste and serve.

Asian Beef Stew with Cabbage and Water Chestnuts

The soy sauce is a salty addition to this stew, so season the stew meat and finished stew carefully. Chinese rice cooking wine, also known as Shaoxing, can be found in Asian markets or the international foods aisle of large supermarkets. Serve with Simple Rice Pilaf (page 286).

1	(3½- to 4-pound) boneless beef chuck eye roast, trimmed and cut into 1½-inch pieces (see the illustrations on page 221)
	Salt and ground black pepper
3	tablespoons vegetable oil
12	ounces shiitake mushrooms, wiped clean, stemmed, and sliced ¼ inch thick
6	scallions, white and green parts separated, whites minced and greens sliced thin
6	medium garlic cloves, minced or pressed through a garlic press (about 2 tablespoons)
3	tablespoons minced or grated fresh ginger (see the illustrations on page 89)
2	tablespoons unbleached all-purpose flour
1	cup Chinese rice cooking wine or dry sherry (see note)
1	cup water
¾	cup low-sodium chicken broth
¾	cup beef broth
⅓	cup soy sauce
1	pound green cabbage (½ medium head), cored and cut into 1½-inch pieces
2	(8-ounce) cans sliced water chestnuts, drained

1. Adjust an oven rack to the lower-middle position and heat the oven to 325 degrees. Pat the beef dry with paper towels and season with salt and pepper.

2. Heat 1 tablespoon of the oil in a large Dutch oven over medium-high heat until just smoking. Add half of the meat and brown well on all sides, 7 to 10 minutes; transfer to a medium bowl. Repeat with 1 tablespoon more oil and the remaining beef and transfer to the bowl.

3. Add the remaining 1 tablespoon oil to the pot and place over medium heat until shimmering. Add the mushrooms and cook until softened and beginning to brown, 5 to 7 minutes. Stir in the scallion whites, garlic, and ginger and cook until fragrant, about 30 seconds. Stir in the flour and cook for 1 minute.

4. Slowly whisk in the wine, scraping up any browned bits. Gradually whisk in the water, chicken broth, beef broth, and soy sauce, smoothing out any lumps. Stir in the browned meat with any accumulated juice and bring to a simmer. Cover, place the pot in the oven, and cook until the meat is mostly tender, 1¾ to 2¼ hours.

5. Stir in the cabbage and continue to cook in the oven, covered, until the cabbage is wilted, about 15 minutes longer. Remove the stew from the oven. Stir in the water chestnuts and let stand for 5 minutes. Stir in the scallion greens and season with salt and pepper to taste before serving.

BEEF CARBONNADE

A BASIC BEEF STEW CAN BE ALTERED IN dozens of ways, usually by adding more ingredients to the pot. But can you go the other way and strip beef stew down to its bare bones (or, to be more precise, to its beef)? If you trade the carrots, peas, and potatoes for a mess of onions and add a good dose of beer as part of the braising liquid, you've created a simple Belgian beef stew called *carbonnade à la flamande*. In this stew, the heartiness of the beef melds with the soft sweetness of sliced onions in a lightly thickened broth that is rich, deep, and satisfying, with the malty flavor of beer.

We started by working with the method from our Hearty Beef Stew (page 220): Brown cubed chuck eye roast and set aside, sauté onions in the empty pot, stir in flour for body, add broth, return the beef to the pot, and simmer the stew in the oven. With the basics in place, we now had to figure out the particulars—the best way to cook the onions, the right type of beer, and what additional flavors (if any) we wanted.

Onions—and lots of them—go into a traditional carbonnade. We found that 2 pounds of onions was just the right amount for a stew serving six. After testing white, red, and yellow onions in the stew, we decided that thinly sliced yellow onions tasted best in carbonnade. We sliced them with the grain, from pole to pole; when sliced the opposite way, against the grain, the onions became stringy when cooked. To deepen the gentle sweetness of the onions, we tried adding a bit of brown sugar, a traditional ingredient in carbonnade, but tasters found it made the onions too sweet. We then thought to add a spoonful of tomato paste while sautéing the onions, a trick we had used in other recipes to add a subtle sweetness and deepen flavor—and it did the same thing here.

An essential component of Belgian cuisine is beer, Belgium's national drink. Belgians routinely pour beer into dishes at times when other cooks might uncork a bottle of wine. Cooking with wine is fairly straightforward; most reasonable choices work just fine in a stew. Cooking with beer is a different story. Beers of the lighter persuasion lacked potency and resulted in a pale, watery-tasting stew. We tried a number of dark beers and found that

moderately dark ales, very dark ales, and stouts made the richest and best-tasting carbonnades. A few of our favorites were Chimay (a Trappist ale from Belgium), Newcastle Brown Ale, and Anchor Steam (this beer cannot technically be classified as an ale).

While the braising liquid for carbonnade is typically beer, broth is sometimes added. We made carbonnades with beer as the only liquid, but they lacked backbone and were sometimes overwhelmingly bitter, depending on the type of beer used. A combination of beef broth and chicken broth, which helped to round out the flavor profile, added along with the beer was a hit. Fresh thyme and

---

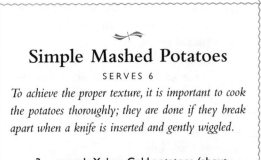

Simple Mashed Potatoes

SERVES 6

To achieve the proper texture, it is important to cook the potatoes thoroughly; they are done if they break apart when a knife is inserted and gently wiggled.

3	pounds Yukon Gold potatoes (about 6 medium), peeled, sliced ¾ inch thick, rinsed well, and drained
	Salt and ground black pepper
12	tablespoons (1½ sticks) unsalted butter, melted
1½	cups half-and-half, warmed

1. Place the potatoes and 1 tablespoon salt in a large saucepan, fill the pot with cold water, and bring to a boil. Reduce to a simmer and cook until the potatoes are tender, 18 to 20 minutes.

2. Drain the potatoes, then return immediately to the saucepan on the still-hot burner. Using a potato masher, mash the potatoes until a few small lumps remain. Gently fold in the melted butter, followed by 1 cup of the warm half-and-half. Add the remaining ½ cup half-and-half as needed to adjust the consistency, season with salt and pepper to taste, and serve.

ground nutmeg were natural additions and cider vinegar perked things up with sweet-and-sour tones. With the right cut of beef, plenty of yellow onions, and a rich, dark beer, we made the simplest of all stews, carbonnade, come to life.

Beef Carbonnade

SERVES 6

The traditional copper-colored Belgian ale works best in this stew. If you can't find one, choose another dark or amber-colored ale of your liking. Serve with buttered egg noodles or Simple Mashed Potatoes (page 223).

1	(3½- to 4-pound) boneless beef chuck eye roast, trimmed and cut into 1½-inch pieces (see the illustrations on page 221)
	Salt and ground black pepper
3	tablespoons vegetable oil
4	ounces (about 4 slices) bacon, chopped fine
2	pounds onions (about 4 medium), halved and sliced pole to pole into ¼-inch-thick pieces (see the illustration on page 105)
2	medium garlic cloves, minced or pressed through a garlic press (about 2 teaspoons)
1	tablespoon minced fresh thyme leaves or 1 teaspoon dried
⅛	teaspoon ground nutmeg
3	tablespoons unbleached all-purpose flour
1	tablespoon tomato paste
¾	cup low-sodium chicken broth
¾	cup beef broth
2	cups beer (see note)
2	bay leaves
1	tablespoon cider vinegar

1. Adjust an oven rack to the lower-middle position and heat the oven to 325 degrees. Pat the beef dry with paper towels and season with salt and pepper.

2. Heat 1 tablespoon of the oil in a large Dutch oven over medium-high heat until just smoking. Add half of the meat and brown well on all sides, 7 to 10 minutes; transfer to a medium bowl. Repeat with 1 tablespoon more oil and the remaining beef and transfer to the bowl.

3. Add the bacon to the pot and cook over medium heat until rendered and crisp, 5 to 7 minutes. Stir in the remaining 1 tablespoon oil, onions, and ¼ teaspoon salt and cook until softened, 5 to 7 minutes. Stir in the garlic, thyme, and nutmeg and cook until fragrant, about 30 seconds. Stir in the flour and tomato paste and cook for 1 minute.

4. Slowly whisk in the chicken broth and beef broth, scraping up any browned bits and smoothing out any lumps. Stir in the beer, bay leaves, vinegar, and browned meat with any accumulated juice and bring to a simmer. Cover the pot partially (leaving about 1 inch of the pot open), place the pot in the oven, and cook until the meat is tender and the sauce is thickened and glossy, 2 to 2½ hours, stirring well after 1 hour.

5. Remove the stew from the oven and remove the bay leaves. Season with salt and pepper to taste and serve.

BEEF BURGUNDY

WHILE WE LOVE TRADITIONAL BEEF STEW, overflowing with homey chunks of potatoes and carrots, we're also quite enamored with its upper-class cousin, beef Burgundy. Beef Burgundy is a refined, complexly flavored stew made up of chunks of tender beef coated in an herby, wine-laced sauce brimming with earthy mushrooms and elegant pearl onions. Like most classic French recipes, this one is not for the faint of heart—most recipes have multiple components and mile-long ingredient lists. We wanted to find a way to make this classic stew more accessible for today's home cooks.

After testing a few recipes, we quickly made a couple of important observations. First, marinating the beef overnight in the red wine and herbs that will later go into the stew—a common recommendation in recipes—was a time-consuming step that did not improve the flavor of the cooked meat. Second, the braising liquid requires straining to rid it of bits of aromatic vegetables and herbs so that it may become a silky sauce. We found that bundling these ingredients in cheesecloth to form an aromatic bouquet made it possible to extract them in one easy step. The aromatics cannot be sautéed when bundled in cheesecloth, but we were happy to discover that this did not affect the flavor of the finished stew. For good measure, we used generous amounts of chopped onions, carrots, and garlic, as well as dried mushrooms, parsley, thyme, and bay leaves, to create a balanced mélange of vegetal and meaty flavors. Finally, salt pork is classically served in the stew as a "garnish" but while most tasters enjoyed the flavor it contributed, they objected to the fatty pieces now dotting the dish. Instead of fishing out pieces of pork fat before serving, we sautéed the salt pork (to render its fat) and added it to the bouquet.

We knew from our Hearty Beef Stew (page 220) that chuck eye roast would be the best cut to use, as it would provide the most flavorful, tender bites of meat. Because the beef in beef Burgundy is cut into chunks larger than is found in other beef stews (2-inch chunks rather than 1½-inch chunks), we found it necessary to take extra care to trim off as much fat as possible; larger pieces of beef also mean larger, more detectable bites of undesirable fat.

With our simpler method and the meat under control we turned our focus to one of the main components of the dish: the wine. Beef Burgundy does not exist without a healthy dose of it and anything less than a whole bottle left the sauce lacking and unremarkable. After numerous experiments, we had determined that a Burgundy, or at least a decent Pinot Noir, is indeed the wine of choice. Though most recipes indicate that all of the wine should be added at the outset, we found that saving just a bit of the wine to add at the very end vastly improved the sauce, brightening its flavor and giving it resonance.

Focusing finally on the requisite mushroom and pearl onion garnish, we noted that it was impossible to cook these vegetables in the stew alongside the beef because they turned mushy. The convenience of already peeled frozen pearl onions was too great to ignore, and a brisk simmer in a separate pan with some water, butter, and sugar was all they needed to take on some flavor and life. Giving the mushrooms a quick sauté also worked well and created glazed beauties that were ready to grace the stew, along with a sprinkling of fresh parsley. Once we added

the final flourish, a little brandy for richness and warmth, we finally had a delicious beef Burgundy that didn't leave us out of breath.

Beef Burgundy

SERVES 6

If not enough fat is rendered from the salt pork for browning the meat, add vegetable oil. Serve with boiled potatoes, Simple Mashed Potatoes (page 223), or buttered egg noodles.

AROMATIC BOUQUET

4	ounces salt pork, cut into ¼-inch-thick matchsticks
2	medium onions, chopped coarse
2	carrots, peeled and chopped coarse
I	medium garlic head, cloves separated and crushed
10	sprigs fresh parsley, torn into pieces
6	sprigs fresh thyme
2	bay leaves, crumbled
½	ounce dried porcini mushrooms, rinsed

STEW

I	(3½- to 4-pound) boneless beef chuck eye roast, trimmed and cut into 2-inch pieces (see the illustrations on page 221) Salt and ground black pepper
3	tablespoons unsalted butter, cut into 3 pieces
⅓	cup unbleached all-purpose flour
I	tablespoon tomato paste
I	(750-milliliter) bottle red Burgundy or Pinot Noir
I½	cups low-sodium chicken broth
I¼	cups beef broth
3	tablespoons minced fresh parsley leaves
2	tablespoons brandy

GARNISH

8	ounces frozen pearl onions (about 2 cups)
½	cup water
2	tablespoons unsalted butter, cut into 2 pieces
I	tablespoon sugar
I	pound white mushrooms, wiped clean, trimmed, and halved if small or quartered if large

1. FOR THE AROMATIC BOUQUET: Cook the salt pork in a large Dutch oven over medium heat until lightly browned and crisp, about 12 minutes. With a slotted spoon, transfer the salt pork to a plate. Pour off and reserve the fat (you should have 2 tablespoons). Following the illustrations below, assemble the salt pork and remaining bouquet ingredients in a double-layer cheesecloth pouch and tie securely with kitchen twine.

2. FOR THE STEW: Adjust an oven rack to the lower-middle position and heat the oven to 325 degrees. Pat the beef dry with paper towels and season with salt and pepper. Heat 1 tablespoon of the rendered pork fat in a large Dutch oven over medium-high heat until just smoking. Add half of the meat and brown well on all sides, 7 to 10 minutes; transfer to a medium bowl. Repeat with 1 tablespoon more pork fat and the remaining beef and transfer to the bowl.

MAKING THE AROMATIC BOUQUET

1. Lay a double layer of cheesecloth (14 inches square) in a medium bowl. Place the designated ingredients in the cheesecloth-lined bowl.

2. Gather together the edges of the cheesecloth and fasten them securely with kitchen twine. Trim any excess cheesecloth with scissors if necessary.

3. Add the butter to the pot and melt over medium heat. Stir in the flour and tomato paste and cook for 1 minute. Gradually whisk in all but 2 tablespoons of the wine, scraping up any browned bits. Gradually whisk in the chicken broth and beef broth, smoothing out any lumps.

4. Stir in the browned meat with any accumulated juice, submerge the aromatic bouquet in the liquid, and bring to a simmer. Cover, place the pot in the oven, and cook until the meat is tender, 2½ to 3 hours, stirring well after 1½ hours.

5. FOR THE GARNISH: Bring the pearl onions, water, butter, and sugar to a boil in a 12-inch nonstick skillet. Reduce to a simmer, cover, and cook until the onions are fully thawed and tender, 5 to 8 minutes. Uncover, increase to a boil, and cook until all the liquid evaporates, 3 to 4 minutes. Stir in the mushrooms and cook, stirring occasionally, until the vegetables are browned and glazed, 10 to 15 minutes. Set aside off the heat.

6. Remove the stew from the oven and remove the aromatic bouquet. Stir in the onion-mushroom garnish, cover, and let stand for 5 minutes. Stir in the remaining 2 tablespoons red wine, parsley, and brandy and season with salt and pepper to taste before serving.

DAUBE PROVENÇAL

DAUBE PROVENÇAL, ALSO KNOWN AS DAUBE *Niçoise,* is a beef stew from the city of Nice that makes the most of ingredients typical of the region. These ingredients include olives, tomatoes, oranges, mushrooms, anchovies, garlic, and red wine—each of which contributes to the stew's sunny flavor. With our basic beef stew method established, we looked to expand our repertoire and add this lesser-known French stew to our collection of hearty stews.

Scanning a number of research recipes, we noted that several called for browning the beef in olive oil rather than vegetable oil or rendered pork fat (which both have a higher smoke point, making them ideal for browning). Testing the difference between these fats in our daube, we found that we too liked the flavor of olive oil here (but we kept an eye on the pot to make sure it didn't scorch). As with our Beef Burgundy (page 225), we cut our chuck roast into more substantial and more rustic 2-inch chunks.

With our meat browned, we could begin looking at the other elements of our stew. Tasters loved the earthiness contributed by dried porcini. Niçoise olives lent a briny and authentic local flavor and tomatoes (canned, so we could make this hearty stew in the dead of winter) brought brightness and texture. Orange peel contributed a subtle floral element, while herbs, particularly thyme and bay leaves, are a natural addition in anything from Provence. Four garlic cloves, sliced thin and added straight to the cooking liquid, imbued the whole dish with their aroma.

Things were going well, but tasters weren't enthusiastic about every authentic ingredient we tried. When we broached the subject of anchovies, some tasters claimed that these pungent fish have no place in beef stew. When we made our stew without the anchovies, though, tasters complained that the stew lacked depth of flavor. Over the next couple of days, we quietly added the anchovies back in one at a time and stopped at three fillets, at which point tasters praised the rich, earthy flavors of the dish and noticed a complexity that had been missing without them. (They never knew the secret.)

Pig's trotters, a standard ingredient in many older recipes, contribute body to the sauce in the form of gelatin and flavor from the pork meat and fat. But the protests against a foot in the stew were too much, and this time we caved in. We substituted salt pork, a salt-cured cut from the pig's belly, and adjusted the amount of salt in the stew to accommodate it. The salt pork, like the anchovies, added a richness of flavor that was unmistakably absent when it was not included. We added it in a single piece that we removed and discarded just before serving, once the pork had given up its flavor to the stew.

As with beef Burgundy, red wine is also a key ingredient in daube Provençal. Our working recipe contained a half bottle, but the flavor was

barely permeating the stew. Could we add more? Conservatively, we began adding more wine, being careful not to sacrifice the integrity of the other flavors. In the end, we discovered that this stew was bold enough to allow for an entire bottle. The wine (we like Cabernet Sauvignon, but Côtes du Rhône and Zinfandel work well too) gave the sauce rich, round flavors and a velvety texture.

With tender and flavorful beef, and all the bright and briny flavors of Provence in line, our stew was an ideal rendition of a French classic.

Daube Provençal

SERVES 6

There are many salty ingredients in this stew, so season it carefully. We tie the salt pork with twine in order to make it easy to identify after cooking; otherwise, it looks exactly like a piece of stew meat. Cabernet Sauvignon is our favorite wine for this recipe, but Côtes du Rhône and Zinfandel also work. Kalamata olives can be substituted for the niçoise olives.

1	(3½- to 4-pound) boneless beef chuck eye roast, trimmed and cut into 2-inch pieces (see the illustrations on page 221) Salt and ground black pepper
3	tablespoons olive oil
2	medium onions, halved and sliced ⅛ inch thick
¾	ounce dried porcini mushrooms, rinsed and minced
1	tablespoon minced fresh thyme leaves or 1 teaspoon dried
⅓	cup unbleached all-purpose flour
2	tablespoons tomato paste
1	(750-milliliter) bottle dry red wine (see note)
1	cup water
¾	cup low-sodium chicken broth
¾	cup beef broth
5	ounces salt pork, rind removed, tied tightly with butcher's twine
4	(3-inch-long) strips zest from 1 orange (see the illustration on page 148), trimmed of white pith and cut into thin matchsticks

1   cup pitted niçoise olives (see the illustration on page 212), patted dry and chopped coarse

4   medium garlic cloves, peeled and sliced thin

3   medium anchovy fillets, rinsed and minced

2   bay leaves

1   pound carrots (about 6 medium), peeled and sliced 1 inch thick

1   (14.5-ounce) can whole peeled tomatoes, drained and cut into ½-inch pieces

2   tablespoons minced fresh parsley leaves

1. Adjust an oven rack to the lower-middle position and heat the oven to 325 degrees. Pat the beef dry with paper towels and season with salt and pepper.

2. Heat 1 tablespoon of the oil in a large Dutch oven over medium-high heat until just smoking. Add half of the meat and brown well on all sides, 7 to 10 minutes; transfer to a medium bowl. Repeat with 1 tablespoon more oil and the remaining beef and transfer to the bowl.

3. Add the remaining 1 tablespoon oil to the pot and heat over medium heat until shimmering. Add the onions, mushrooms, thyme, and ¼ teaspoon salt and cook until softened, 5 to 7 minutes. Stir in the flour and tomato paste and cook for 1 minute. Slowly whisk in the wine, scraping up any browned bits.

4. Gradually whisk in the water, chicken broth, and beef broth, smoothing out any lumps. Stir in the salt pork, orange zest, half of the olives, garlic, anchovies, bay leaves, and browned meat with any accumulated juice and bring to a simmer. Cover the pot partially (leaving about 1 inch of the pot open), place the pot in the oven, and cook for 1½ hours.

5. Stir in the carrots and continue to cook in the oven, partially covered, until the meat is tender and the sauce is thickened and glossy, 1 to 1½ hours longer.

6. Remove the stew from the oven and remove the salt pork and bay leaves. Stir in the tomatoes and remaining olives, cover, and let stand for 5 minutes. Stir in the parsley and season with salt and pepper to taste before serving.

HUNGARIAN GOULASH

THOUGH YOU'D NEVER GUESS IT FROM THE gussied-up versions served in this country, traditional Hungarian goulash is the simplest of stews, calling for little more than beef, onions, and paprika. Sour cream has no place in the pot, nor do mushrooms, green peppers, or most herbs. Instead, the best goulash features the simple heartiness of beef melded with the sweetness of long-cooked onions. But the real revelation is the paprika. Instead of being a mere accent, its fruity, almost chocolaty flavors infuse the meat and help transform the braising liquid into a rich, thick sauce. Ignoring the countless recipes with endless ingredient lists, we set out to bring a humble but delicious beef stew back to its roots.

The Hungarian herdsmen who developed this campfire stew used tough cuts of meat such as shin (a cross section from the front leg that includes both bone and meat), cooking it for hours over a low fire until tender. While many modern recipes still call for shin, it is not widely available in this country. Instead, we reached for chuck eye roast, the test kitchen favorite for beef stew, and cut it into sizable chunks (about 1½ inches).

As for the paprika, tasters affirmed that the traditional sweet kind was best, preferring its floral, fruity qualities to the spiciness of hot paprika or the overwhelming smoky flavor of smoked paprika. Fresh, high-quality paprika is a must, but to achieve the desired level of intensity, some recipes call for as much as ½ cup per 3 pounds of meat. However, because this stew is nothing more than meat, onions, and sauce, we found that once we reached 3 tablespoons of paprika, the spice began contributing a gritty, dusty texture that stood out against the simple ingredients.

To eliminate the grittiness, we tried steeping the paprika in beef broth and then straining it through a coffee filter. This captured plenty of paprika flavor without a trace of its texture, but straining took nearly 30 minutes—a deal breaker. After consulting with chefs at a few Hungarian restaurants, we were turned on to a new idea: paprika cream, a condiment our sources said was as common in

Hungarian cooking as the dried spice. We couldn't find it locally, so we ordered it online. "Paprika cream" turned out to be a deep red paste, packaged in a metal tube, that contained ground paprika camouflaged in a puree of red bell peppers. When we added it to our stew, it created vibrant paprika flavor without any offensive grittiness.

This convenience product was great, but we didn't want to have to hunt it down every time we made goulash. Why not create our own paprika cream? We began with a jar of roasted red peppers (their tender texture was better for our purposes than fresh). We drained the peppers and pureed them in a food processor along with the paprika. To better approximate the lively yet concentrated flavors of the cream from the tube, we also added a couple of tablespoons of tomato paste and a little vinegar. Bingo! We were able to add up to ⅓ cup paprika without any resulting grittiness.

Up to now we had also been following the standard stew protocol: Sear the meat in batches, cook aromatics (in this case, just onions), return the beef to the pot along with broth and other ingredients, and cook until the meat is tender. But once we introduced the paprika paste into the mix, we found that the flavor of the seared meat competed with the paprika's brightness. Referring back to the hundreds of goulash recipes we had gathered in our research, we found an interesting trend: Many did not sear the meat. Instead, the onions went into the pot first to soften, followed by the paprika and meat, and then the whole thing was left to cook. That's it. There is no browning of the meat, and no additional liquids are ever added.

Intrigued, but dubious that this method would work, we cooked the onions briefly in oil, added the paprika paste and raw meat, and placed the covered pot in the oven. (We have found that the gentle, steady heat of a low oven provides better results for stew than the stove.) Sure enough, the onions and meat provided enough liquid to stew the meat. As we cooked batch after batch using this no-sear method, we noticed something peculiar: The meat above the liquid actually browned during cooking. In effect, we were developing similar (though not quite as intense) flavors as if we had seared the beef. Toward the end of cooking, after

the meat browned, we added a little broth to thin out the stewing liquid and make it more sauce-like.

In keeping with authentic goulash, the only vegetables in the pot were onions. But in deference to our American tasters, who wanted at least a few vegetables in their stew, we incorporated carrots into the mix, finding that we also appreciated the sweetness and textural contrast they provided. And even through sour cream is not traditional, some tasters did like to dollop it on top of their bowl before eating. Even with these slight adulterations, our Hungarian goulash was the real deal: a simple dish of tender braised beef packed with paprika flavor.

Hungarian Goulash

SERVES 6

Paprika is vital to this recipe, so it's best to use a fresh container; do not substitute hot or smoked paprika for the sweet paprika. See page 216 for information on our winning brand of paprika. A Dutch oven with a tight-fitting lid is crucial to the success of this dish, since there is not much braising liquid; if necessary, place a sheet of foil over the pot before adding the lid to ensure a tight seal. Serve with sour cream and buttered egg noodles.

1	(3½- to 4-pound) boneless beef chuck eye roast, trimmed and cut into 1½-inch pieces (see the illustrations on page 221)
	Salt and ground black pepper
1	(12-ounce) jar roasted red peppers, drained and rinsed (about 1 cup)
⅓	cup sweet paprika (see note)
2	tablespoons tomato paste
1	tablespoon white vinegar
3	pounds onions (about 6 medium), minced
2	tablespoons vegetable oil
4	carrots, peeled and sliced 1 inch thick
1	bay leaf
1	cup beef broth, warmed

1. Adjust an oven rack to the lower-middle position and heat the oven to 325 degrees. Pat the beef dry with paper towels, season with salt and pepper, and set aside. Process the roasted red peppers, paprika, tomato paste, and 2 teaspoons of

the vinegar in a food processor until smooth, 1 to 2 minutes, scraping down the sides of the bowl as needed.

2. Combine the onions, oil, and 1 teaspoon salt in a large Dutch oven, cover, and cook, stirring occasionally, until the onions soften but have not yet begun to brown, 8 to 10 minutes. (If the onions begin to brown, reduce the heat to medium-low and stir in 1 tablespoon water.)

3. Stir in the processed roasted pepper mixture and continue to cook, uncovered, until the onions begin to stick to the bottom of the pan, about 2 minutes. Stir in the beef, carrots, and bay leaf until well coated. Using a rubber spatula, carefully scrape down the sides of the pot. Cover, place the pot in the oven, and cook, stirring every 30 minutes, until the meat is mostly tender and the surface of the liquid is ½ inch below the top of the meat, 2 to 2½ hours.

4. Stir in the beef broth until the surface of the liquid measures ¼ inch from the top of the meat (the beef should not be fully submerged). Continue to cook in the oven, covered, until the meat is tender, about 30 minutes longer.

5. Remove the stew from the oven and remove the bay leaf. Defat the braising liquid (see page 18; if necessary, return the defatted liquid to the pot and reheat). Stir in the remaining 1 teaspoon vinegar. Season with salt and pepper to taste and serve.

OSSO BUCO

THE ITALIAN CLASSIC, OSSO BUCO, IS A complexly flavored dish composed of simple ingredients: veal shanks, aromatics (onions, carrots, and celery, all sautéed), and liquids (a blend of wine, stock, and tomatoes). The shank is a robust cut of meat and the bone adds tremendous flavor to the stewing liquid in this braise. The resulting dish yields extraordinarily tender meat in a velvety, rich sauce. Our goals for this dish were as follows—we wanted to perfect the cooking technique, while extracting the most flavor from its core ingredients.

Most recipes we reviewed called for shanks from the upper portion of the hind leg, cut into pieces between 1 and 1½ inches thick. We found that purchasing shanks is tricky, even when they are special-ordered. From one market, we received perfectly butchered shanks, which were ideal except for the weight. Each shank weighed between 12 and 16 ounces—too large for individual servings. Part of the charm of osso buco is receiving an individual shank as a portion. At another market, the shanks were in the ideal weight range, but the butchering job was less than perfect. In the same package, shanks varied from 1 to 2½ inches thick and were occasionally cut on an extreme bias, making tying difficult and searing uneven. The first step, then, is to shop carefully. We found a thickness of 1½ inches and a weight of 8 ounces ideal and each shank should have two nicely cut flat sides to facilitate browning.

Preparing the meat for braising was the first step. Most recipes called for tying the shanks. Though this step seemed excessive at first, we did find that tying a piece of kitchen twine around the thickest part of each shank prevented the meat from falling apart and made for a more attractive presentation.

After seasoning the shanks with salt and pepper and then searing them to get a nice golden brown crust, we turned our attention to the braising liquid. Braising, by design, is a relatively inexact cooking method because the rate at which the liquid reduces can vary greatly. Some of the initial recipes we tried yielded far too much liquid, which was thin in flavor and texture. In other cases, the liquid nearly evaporated by the time the meat was tender. We knew that only slow, gentle heat would turn the braising liquid into a moderate amount of flavorful, rich sauce. We found that the easiest method worked best: natural reduction in the oven. Cracking the lid on the Dutch oven ensured that the liquid reduced as the osso buco cooked, giving the sauce the right consistency. We also found stirring a little flour into the aromatics helped to promote the proper body in the final braising liquid.

The braising liquid traditionally begins with beef broth to which wine (we liked white) and tomatoes are added. Because the braising liquid absorbs flavor from the rich juice of the shanks, we felt that the nuances of homemade beef broth would be lost and turned to store-bought broth. In an early test, tasters found the beef broth on its own to be too potent. Instead, we found an even combination of store-bought chicken broth and beef broth worked best to create the balanced meaty flavor we were looking for. Three cups of broth seemed to be the right amount, and to enrich the flavor we used a hefty amount of diced onion, carrot, and celery. Tasters liked the large amount of garlic in one recipe, so we minced about six cloves and added them to the pot prior to the broth. We rounded out the flavors with some tomato paste and a couple of bay leaves.

A few recipes called for an entire bottle of wine, but when we tried this amount it completely overpowered the other flavors. We scaled the wine back to a single cup and were happy with the results. As for the tomatoes, we chose reliable canned diced tomatoes and added them with the broth.

We still needed to determine the ideal braising time. Several sources suggested cooking osso buco almost to the consistency of pulled pork. While meat cooked this way tasted good, we were after a more elegant presentation. We wanted compact meat firmly attached to the bone, so we cooked the meat until it was just fork-tender but still clinging to the bone, which took two hours.

Just before serving, osso buco is sprinkled with gremolata, a mixture of minced garlic, parsley, and

lemon or orange zest. We tested both kinds of zest, but tasters favored the more delicate citrus flavor in the version with orange zest. In some recipes, the gremolata is used as a garnish, and in others it is added to the pot just before serving. We liked the flavor contributed by both additions, so we stirred half of the gremolata into the pot and let the braise stand for a few minutes so that the flavors of the garlic, orange, and parsley permeated the dish. Then we sprinkled the remaining gremolata on individual servings for a bright finish.

Osso Buco

SERVES 6

The vegetables in the braising liquid do not get strained out before serving, so be mindful to cut them into tidy-looking pieces. Osso buco is traditionally served with risotto, although Creamy Polenta (page 232) and Simple Mashed Potatoes (page 223) are also good options.

OSSO BUCO

6	(8- to 10-ounce) veal shanks, 1½ inches thick, tied (see the illustration at left)
	Salt and ground black pepper
3	tablespoons vegetable oil
2	medium onions, chopped medium
2	carrots, peeled and chopped medium
2	celery ribs, chopped medium
6	medium garlic cloves, minced or pressed through a garlic press (about 2 tablespoons)
2	tablespoons unbleached all-purpose flour
2	tablespoons tomato paste
1	cup dry white wine
1½	cups low-sodium chicken broth
1½	cups beef broth
1	(14.5-ounce) can diced tomatoes, drained
2	bay leaves

GREMOLATA

¼	cup minced fresh parsley leaves
3	medium garlic cloves, minced or pressed through a garlic press (about 1 tablespoon)
2	teaspoons grated zest from 1 orange

TYING VEAL SHANKS

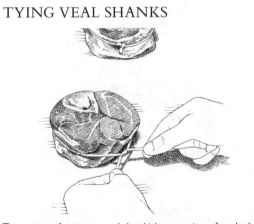

Tie a piece of twine around the thickest portion of each shank before browning to keep the meat attached to the bone while the shanks simmer.

1. **FOR THE OSSO BUCO:** Adjust an oven rack to the lower-middle position and heat the oven to 325 degrees. Pat the shanks dry with paper towels and season with salt and pepper.

2. Heat 1 tablespoon of the oil in a large Dutch oven over medium-high heat until just smoking. Add half of the shanks and brown well on all sides, 7 to 10 minutes; transfer to a large bowl. Repeat with 1 tablespoon more oil and the remaining shanks and transfer to the bowl.

3. Add the remaining 1 tablespoon oil to the pot and place over medium heat until shimmering. Add the onions, carrots, celery, and ¼ teaspoon salt and cook until the vegetables are softened, 7 to 10 minutes. Stir in the garlic and cook until fragrant, about 30 seconds. Stir in the flour and tomato paste and cook for 1 minute. Slowly whisk in the wine, scraping up any browned bits, and cook until nearly evaporated, about 5 minutes.

4. Gradually whisk in the chicken broth and beef broth, smoothing out any lumps. Stir in the tomatoes and bay leaves. Nestle the browned shanks into the pot with any accumulated juice and bring to a simmer. Cover the pot partially (leaving about 1 inch of the pot open), place the pot in the oven, and cook until the meat is very tender and a fork poked into it meets little resistance, but is not falling off the bone, about 2 hours, turning each shank over after 1 hour.

5. Remove the pot from the oven. Transfer the shanks to a large platter, remove the twine, and tent loosely with aluminum foil while finishing the sauce. Defat the braising liquid (see page 18; if necessary, return the defatted liquid to the pot and reheat).

6. **FOR THE GREMOLATA:** Combine all the gremolata ingredients in a small bowl.

7. Off the heat, stir half of the gremolata into the sauce and let stand for 5 minutes. Season the sauce with salt and pepper to taste. Place the veal shanks in individual serving bowls, ladle some of the sauce over each shank, and sprinkle with the remaining gremolata before serving.

Creamy Polenta

SERVES 6

This recipe uses traditional dried polenta (coarse-ground cornmeal); do not substitute instant polenta. If you do not have a heavy-bottomed saucepan, you may want to use a flame tamer (see the illustration below) to help maintain a gentle simmer.

6	cups water
	Salt and ground black pepper
1½	cups polenta (see note)
3	tablespoons unsalted butter

1. Bring the water to a boil in a heavy-bottomed 4-quart saucepan. Stir in 1½ teaspoons salt, then very slowly pour the polenta into the boiling liquid while stirring constantly in a circular motion with a wooden spoon.

2. Reduce to a gentle simmer and cook the polenta, stirring often and making sure to scrape the bottom and corners of the pot clean, until the polenta has lost its raw cornmeal taste and becomes soft and smooth, 20 to 30 minutes. Stir in the butter, season with salt and pepper to taste, and serve immediately.

MAKING A FLAME TAMER

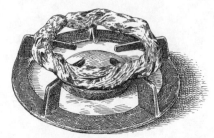

A flame tamer is a metal disk that can be fitted over a burner (electric or gas) to reduce the heat transfer. This device is especially useful when trying to keep a pot at the barest simmer. If you don't own a flame tamer, you can fashion one: Take a long sheet of aluminum foil and shape it into a 1-inch-thick ring that will fit on your burner. Make sure that the ring is an even thickness so that a pot will rest flat on it.

Braised Short Ribs

SHORT RIBS ARE MAKING A COMEBACK. THEY used to be passed over in the supermarket meat case, viewed as rather intimidating hunks of meat and bone. But nowadays braised ribs are on every restaurant menu, and increasingly in home kitchens—and with good reason. Braising makes them yielding, tender, and succulent. Douse them with the rich, velvety sauce from the braise and they are as satisfying as beef stew, but with a bit more panache.

Whichever way you cut it, short ribs are just what their name says they are: short ribs cut from any part along the length of the cow's ribs. They can come from the lower belly section or higher up toward the back, from the shoulder (or chuck) area, or the forward midsection. They can be cut English-style (a length of wide, flat rib bone, to which a plate of fatty meat is attached) or flanken-style (a long, continuous piece of meat that includes two or three segments of rib bone). But no matter what, they're always fatty. Of course, this is also what make them so deeply flavorful.

Our first challenge was to get them to give up their fat. The first step in most braises is browning the meat. Browning adds color and flavor, but in the case of short ribs it also presents an opportunity to render some of the fat. We browned the ribs on all sides, then carefully poured off the fat that rendered. From there we cooked them in a simple combination of beef broth, chicken broth, and red wine. The resulting ribs were good, and the combination of broths provided a well-rounded but meaty flavor and the wine gave the sauce the bold, potent background we were after, but there were still a few issues to work out.

Like most braises, short ribs need aromatic vegetables. A basic mirepoix of onions, carrots, and celery made a world of difference, but with the big, bold flavors of beef and red wine, we felt this braise needed more. A handful of minced garlic helped and we found nine cloves just right for this braise. A modest amount of fresh herbs, including thyme and rosemary, boosted the flavor of the meat and a couple of bay leaves rounded out the aromatics. Finally, tasters thought bacon added some welcome smokiness, which we further enhanced by cooking the aromatics right in the bacon fat.

The braising liquids required only a cursory investigation. We tested varying amounts of chicken broth, beef broth, and red wine, eventually settling on 2 cups of each broth and a full bottle of wine. This might seem like a lot of wine, but for a bold, rich sauce that stood up to the meaty ribs, nothing less would do. Stepping up the quality of the wine—from a cheap sell to a good, solid wine worthy of drinking—improved the sauce dramatically. It now had the complexity and resonance that we were seeking. Finally, we added some diced tomatoes and tomato paste to sweeten the braise and intensify the flavors.

If the braising liquid were to transform itself into the sauce we were after, it would need some thickening. As with our Osso Buco (page 231), we found that adding just a little flour to the braise helped. But since we had a lot more liquid in the pot with the ribs than we did with the veal shanks, we'd need to take things even further. To that end, we found it necessary to reduce the braising liquid for almost 10 minutes after the meat was cooked. Now we had a silky sauce that cloaked the ribs gracefully. Also, we found it very important to defat the braising liquid because as browned short ribs braise, they continue to release good amounts of fat. Straining the spent vegetables from the liquid before finishing the sauce also helped the sauce to look every bit as refined as it tasted.

Short Ribs Braised in Red Wine and Bacon

SERVES 6

This recipe works with either English-style or flanken-style short ribs. A $7 to $10 bottle of medium-bodied red table wine made from a blend of grapes, such as a Côtes du Rhône, will work well here. Once cooked, the ribs can sit in the finished sauce to stay warm for up to an hour before serving.

6   pounds bone-in short ribs, trimmed of
      excess fat and silver skin (see note)
      Salt and ground black pepper
2   tablespoons vegetable oil
6   ounces (about 6 slices) bacon, chopped fine
3   medium onions, chopped medium

2   carrots, peeled and chopped medium

1   celery rib, chopped medium

9   medium garlic cloves, minced or pressed
    through a garlic press (about 3 tablespoons)

1   tablespoon minced fresh rosemary or
    ¾ teaspoon dried

1   tablespoon minced fresh thyme leaves or
    1 teaspoon dried

¼   cup unbleached all-purpose flour

1   tablespoon tomato paste

1   (750-milliliter) bottle dry red wine (see note)

2   cups low-sodium chicken broth

2   cups beef broth

1   (14.5-ounce) can diced tomatoes

3   bay leaves

6   tablespoons minced fresh parsley leaves

1. Adjust an oven rack to the lower-middle position and heat the oven to 325 degrees. Pat the ribs dry with paper towels and season with salt and pepper.

2. Heat 1 tablespoon of the oil in a large Dutch oven over medium-high heat until just smoking. Add half of the ribs and brown well on all sides, 7 to 10 minutes; transfer to a large plate. Repeat with the remaining 1 tablespoon oil and remaining ribs and transfer to the plate.

3. Pour off all of the fat left in the pot, add the bacon, and cook over medium heat until rendered and crisp, 5 to 7 minutes. Stir in the onions, carrots, celery, and ¼ teaspoon salt and cook until softened, 7 to 10 minutes. Stir in the garlic, rosemary, and thyme and cook until fragrant, about 30 seconds. Stir in the flour and tomato paste and cook for 1 minute. Slowly whisk in the wine, scraping up any browned bits.

4. Gradually whisk in the chicken broth and beef broth, smoothing out any lumps. Stir in the tomatoes with their juice and the bay leaves. Nestle the browned ribs into the pot, bone side up, with any accumulated juice, and bring to a simmer. Cover, place the pot in the oven, and cook until the meat is very tender and a fork poked into it meets little resistance, 2½ to 3 hours, turning each rib over after 1 hour.

5. Remove the pot from the oven. Transfer the ribs to a large plate, discarding any loose bones that have fallen away from the meat, and tent loosely with foil while finishing the sauce. Strain the braising liquid through a fine-mesh strainer, discarding the solids, then defat the liquid (see page 18).

6. Return the braising liquid to the pot and simmer over medium-high heat until thickened and saucy, 5 to 10 minutes. Off the heat, season with salt and pepper to taste, then return the ribs to the sauce to warm through. Sprinkle individual portions with parsley before serving.

➤ VARIATION

Porter-Braised Short Ribs

Follow the recipe for Short Ribs Braised in Red Wine and Bacon, omitting the tomato paste and rosemary. Substitute 3 cups porter beer for the red wine and whisk 2 tablespoons Dijon mustard and 2 teaspoons Worcestershire sauce into the pot with the beer in step 3.

PORK STEW

THOUGH LESS COMMON HERE IN THE UNITED States, pork stews are popular in many parts of the world. One of our favorites is a dish from France that combines braised pork with carrots, prunes, brandy, and a touch of cream. The pork is fall-apart tender, its flavor enhanced by the sweetness of the carrots and the prunes, yet savory with a broth and cream sauce—a luxurious blend of flavors and textures. We wanted a rich, satisfying pork stew with a careful balance of savory and sweet.

We already knew from our experience with stewing beef that the shoulder, or chuck, is the best cut for braising, and so we assumed that pork shoulder would also make the best, most flavorful pork stew. To test this proposition, we stewed various cuts of pork from both the shoulder and loin, including several kinds of chops. The shoulder cuts were indeed far superior to those from the loin. Like beef chuck, pork shoulder has enough fat to keep the meat tender and juicy during the long cooking process.

But which cut from the shoulder works best? Pork shoulder is called Boston butt or Boston shoulder in most markets. The picnic roast also comes from the shoulder, but includes the skin and bone, which means more prep work. As with beef, we recommend buying a boneless roast and cutting it into pieces yourself. Once the pork was cut up and seasoned with salt and pepper, we browned it to enhance its flavor. After setting aside the meat, we added leeks to the pot, to soften; they contributed a sweet, aromatic backdrop and kept with the French flavors of the dish.

With the cut of meat and the choice of aromatic settled, we moved on to the braising liquid. We needed a full 5 cups of liquid to properly braise the pork and provide ample liquid for the stew. Brandy would be the defining flavor of our braising liquid, complemented by chicken broth for a savory element and cream for richness. We knew this would require a careful balancing act. Starting with 1 cup of brandy (enough to generously deglaze the pan and add a distinct flavor without taking over), we added 2 cups each of the chicken broth and cream. But this was too heavy. And because this stew requires a significant amount of time in the oven, the sweetness of the cream was also now a bit cloying, which in turn dulled the flavor of the brandy. (Like our beef stews, this pork stew is started on the stovetop, but the bulk of the cooking happens in the oven for gentle, all-encompassing heat.) The obvious fix was to decrease the amount of cream (to 1 cup) and increase the amount of chicken broth (to 3 cups). This was an improvement, but the cream still had that overly sweet, "cooked" flavor. Holding the cream and adding it at the end of cooking worked best: the cream retained its fresh flavor without overpowering the other ingredients.

We already knew prunes and carrots would play an integral role in our stew, but we thought another vegetable might further round out the flavors. We settled on fennel—with its subtle anise notes, it perfectly complemented the other flavors of the stew. Combined with the cream, brandy, and pork, it was a hit. Because fennel and carrots cook at a much faster pace than pork, we added them halfway through cooking so they could coast to the finish line together. The prunes were best added at the very end of cooking to prevent them from breaking down and disintegrating into the stew. Freshly minced tarragon, as well as some lemon juice, added a welcome complexity to the finished dish.

With our French-inspired pork stew perfected, we set out to take this dish in a totally different direction and created a variation that featured hominy, tomatoes, and chipotle chile in adobo sauce. Minced cilantro and lime juice completed this Mexican-inspired stew.

Pork Stew with Brandy, Fennel, and Prunes
SERVES 6

Boneless pork butt roast is often labeled as boneless Boston butt in the supermarket. While 1 cup of brandy may seem like a lot for this recipe, we recommend using an inexpensive brand and not skimping on the amount; it provides just the right balance of flavors. Don't substitute dried tarragon for the fresh.

1	(3½- to 4-pound) boneless pork butt roast, trimmed and cut into 1½-inch pieces (see note)
	Salt and ground black pepper
3	tablespoons vegetable oil
1	large leek, white and light green parts only, halved lengthwise, sliced ¼ inch thick, and rinsed thoroughly (see the illustrations on page 103)
3	medium garlic cloves, minced or pressed through a garlic press (about 1 tablespoon)
3	tablespoons unbleached all-purpose flour
1	cup brandy (see note)
3	cups low-sodium chicken broth
2	bay leaves
1	pound carrots (about 6 medium), peeled and sliced 1 inch thick
1	large fennel bulb (about 1 pound), trimmed of stalks, cored, and cut into ½-inch-thick strips (see the illustrations on page 27)
1	cup heavy cream
1	cup prunes, halved
2	tablespoons minced fresh tarragon leaves
1	tablespoon juice from 1 lemon

1. Adjust an oven rack to the lower-middle position and heat the oven to 325 degrees. Pat the pork dry with paper towels and season with salt and pepper.

2. Heat 1 tablespoon of the oil in a large Dutch oven over medium-high heat until just smoking. Add half of the pork and brown well on all sides, 7 to 10 minutes; transfer to a medium bowl. Repeat with 1 tablespoon more oil and the remaining pork and transfer to the bowl.

3. Add the remaining 1 tablespoon oil to the pot and place over medium heat until shimmering. Add the leek and ¼ teaspoon salt and cook until wilted and lightly browned, 5 to 7 minutes. Stir in the garlic and cook until fragrant, about 30 seconds. Stir in the flour and cook for 1 minute.

4. Slowly whisk in the brandy, scraping up any browned bits. Gradually whisk in the chicken broth, smoothing out any lumps. Stir in the bay leaves and browned pork with any accumulated juice and bring to a simmer. Cover, place the pot in the oven, and cook for 1 hour.

5. Stir in the carrots and fennel and continue to cook in the oven, covered, until the meat is tender, about 1 hour longer.

6. Remove the stew from the oven and remove the bay leaves. Stir in the cream and prunes, cover, and let stand for 5 minutes. Stir in the tarragon and lemon juice and season with salt and pepper to taste before serving.

➤ VARIATION

Pork Stew with Hominy, Tomatoes, and Chipotles

Boneless pork butt roast is often labeled as boneless Boston butt in the supermarket. While 1 cup of sherry may seem like a lot for this recipe, we recommend using an inexpensive brand and not skimping on the amount; it provides just the right balance of flavors.

1	(3½- to 4-pound) boneless pork butt roast, trimmed and cut into 1½-inch pieces (see note) Salt and ground black pepper
3	tablespoons vegetable oil
1	medium onion, minced
3	medium garlic cloves, minced or pressed through a garlic press (about 1 tablespoon)
2	teaspoons chili powder
2	teaspoons minced chipotle chile in adobo sauce
½	teaspoon dried oregano
3	tablespoons unbleached all-purpose flour
1	cup dry sherry (see note)
3	cups low-sodium chicken broth
1	(14.5-ounce) can diced tomatoes, drained
2	bay leaves
1	pound carrots (about 6 medium), peeled and sliced 1 inch thick
2	(14-ounce) cans white or yellow hominy, drained and rinsed
2	tablespoons minced fresh cilantro leaves
1	tablespoon juice from 1 lime

1. Adjust an oven rack to the lower-middle position and heat the oven to 325 degrees. Pat the pork dry with paper towels and season with salt and pepper.

2. Heat 1 tablespoon of the oil in a large Dutch oven over medium-high heat until just smoking. Add half of the pork and brown well on all sides, 7 to 10 minutes; transfer to a medium bowl. Repeat with 1 tablespoon more oil and the remaining pork and transfer to the bowl.

3. Add the remaining 1 tablespoon oil to the pot and place over medium heat until shimmering. Add the onion and ¼ teaspoon salt and cook until softened, 5 to 7 minutes. Stir in the garlic, chili powder, chipotles, and oregano and cook until fragrant, about 30 seconds. Stir in the flour and cook for 1 minute.

4. Slowly whisk in the sherry, scraping up any browned bits. Gradually whisk in the chicken broth, smoothing out any lumps. Stir in the tomatoes, bay leaves, and browned pork with any accumulated juice and bring to a simmer. Cover, place the pot in the oven, and cook for 1 hour.

5. Stir in the carrots and hominy and continue to cook in the oven, covered, until the meat is tender, about 1 hour longer.

6. Remove the stew from the oven and remove the bay leaves. Stir in the cilantro and lime juice and season with salt and pepper to taste before serving.

Brazilian Black Bean and Pork Stew

FEIJOADA IS A BRAZILIAN BLACK BEAN AND pork stew that has become so popular it is now considered one of Brazil's national dishes. Espousing the humble attitude of old-world frugality, feijoada originally used up every last bit of the pig, including the feet, ears, tail, and snout—nothing was off-limits. But not only do authentic recipes require a lot of pork, they also require a lot of time and can quickly become a daunting project. We sought a modern, streamlined interpretation of feijoada, using the basic flavor elements—creamy beans and smoky, tender pork—for a hearty but not ho-hum stew.

Typical recipes for this stew call for cooking the beans and meat on the stovetop for hours and hours, adjusting the heat as needed to maintain the proper simmer. While these recipes tried to take into account the various cooking times of all the contents of the pot, the result was often overcooked meat, mushy beans, and too much liquid. Luckily, we had a leg up on these recipes from the outset; previous testing had shown us that cooking in the low, slow heat of the oven results in optimally cooked stews. These stews boast tender meat and creamy beans, but they require a lot less attention. We decided to pursue this modus operandi, starting with the beans, then layering in the other elements of this stew.

Usually we prefer to soak beans in a saltwater solution (or brine them) prior to cooking, as this step softens the tough bean skins and evens out the cooking time, so that fewer beans burst open. But, as with our Black Bean Soup (page 142), a few broken beans wouldn't be a bad thing in this dish; we wanted a somewhat thickened stew and a portion of burst beans would only contribute to our desired texture. After two hours in the oven, our beans were perfectly tender. The addition of sautéed onion and garlic complemented the earthy flavor of the beans, while some chili powder, cumin, and coriander added fragrance. We also found that adding a small amount of baking soda to the beans and water at the beginning of cooking produced a darker, more appealing color. Now

that we had achieved properly cooked and flavorful beans, we focused on selecting the meat.

From the beginning, we decided that although many authentic recipes call for a random assortment of pork products (pig ears, tails, and feet), we wanted to use ingredients that were easy both to find and to cook. With these cuts of meat crossed off our list, we took a look at what was left: pork butt, slab bacon, spareribs, pork loins, and numerous varieties of sausages, ham hocks, and salt pork. We ultimately chose a combination of pork products that maintained some tradition, but that could easily be found and seemed more approachable to cook. We went with a ham hock for smoky flavor, chunks of pork butt for big, meaty bites, and pieces of linguiça, the Portuguese pork sausage, for its potent, garlicky bite.

The challenge now was to figure out how to layer the meat in with the beans so the flavors melded while getting all the elements of the stew to cook at the right rate. We wanted chunks of pork that were juicy and tender rather than tough and desiccated, and sausage that was moist rather than dried out.

From our earlier experience with pork stews, we knew that it would take about the same amount of time to cook in the oven as the beans, though the sausage wouldn't take nearly as long. With that in mind, we began by browning the pork, which we'd cut into 1½-inch pieces, and cooking the aromatics, then adding the beans and cooking liquid (with so many other flavors in the pot, water was the best choice), and finally placing the pot in the oven. After an hour, we stirred in the sausage and allowed the stew to finish cooking. Tasting our first batch, we found that while the beans and pork were cooked properly after two hours in the oven, the sausage was still drying out. After a few more tests we found that 30 minutes was plenty of time for the sausage to cook and still remain juicy, so we adjusted our timing and added it to the stew later on.

Now that the cooking method and time were settled, we had a new problem on our hands. We noticed that once all the pork and sausage were in the pot, real estate was at a premium. The ham hock, used to add depth and smoky flavor, was now crowding the pot. Could we get the same flavor using chopped bacon rather than the large ham hock? Tasters agreed that although the bacon resulted in a slightly stronger flavor, it got the job done and enabled us to comfortably fit all the meat and beans in the pot.

We had finally arrived at a flavorful yet streamlined black bean and pork stew. The beans were rich and creamy and the pork was tender and juicy. With an easy-to-make fresh Brazilian hot sauce ready and waiting to be spooned over the top, our hearty stew had the fresh, zesty finish it needed.

Brazilian Black Bean and Pork Stew

SERVES 6

Boneless pork butt roast is often labeled as boneless Boston butt in the supermarket. The baking soda added to the beans helps preserve their dark hue; without it, the beans will turn a muddy, grayish color. Be sure to serve this stew with the hot sauce; it adds important flavor. For more heat, include the jalapeño seeds and ribs when mincing.

STEW

- I (3½- to 4-pound) boneless pork butt roast, trimmed and cut into 1½-inch pieces (see note)
  Salt and ground black pepper
- 3 tablespoons vegetable oil
- 4 ounces (about 4 slices) bacon, chopped fine
- I medium onion, minced
- 4 medium garlic cloves, minced or pressed through a garlic press (about 4 teaspoons)
- I tablespoon chili powder
- I teaspoon ground cumin
- I teaspoon ground coriander
- 7 cups water
- I pound dried black beans, picked over and rinsed
- 2 bay leaves
- ⅛ teaspoon baking soda (see note)
- I pound linguiça sausage, cut into ½-inch pieces

HOT SAUCE

- 2 firm, ripe tomatoes, cored, seeded, and chopped fine
- I medium onion, minced
- I small green bell pepper, stemmed, seeded, and chopped fine
- I jalapeño chile, stemmed, seeded, and minced (see note)
- ⅓ cup white wine vinegar
- 3 tablespoons extra-virgin olive oil
- I tablespoon minced fresh cilantro leaves
- ½ teaspoon salt

1. Adjust an oven rack to the lower-middle position and heat the oven to 325 degrees. Pat the pork dry with paper towels and season with salt and pepper.

2. Heat 1 tablespoon of the oil in a large Dutch oven over medium-high heat until just smoking. Add half of the pork and brown well on all sides, 7 to 10 minutes; transfer to a medium bowl. Repeat with 1 tablespoon more oil and the remaining pork and transfer to the bowl.

3. Add the bacon to the pot and cook over medium heat until rendered and crisp, 5 to 7 minutes. Stir in the remaining 1 tablespoon oil, onion, and ¼ teaspoon salt and cook until the onion is softened, 5 to 7 minutes. Stir in the garlic, chili powder, cumin, and coriander and cook until fragrant, about 30 seconds.

4. Stir in the water, beans, bay leaves, ¼ teaspoon salt, baking soda, and browned pork with any accumulated juice and bring to a simmer. Cover, place the pot in the oven, and cook for 1½ hours.

5. Stir in the linguiça and continue to cook in the oven, covered, until the meat and beans are fully tender, about 30 minutes longer.

6. FOR THE HOT SAUCE: Meanwhile, combine all the ingredients in a medium bowl and let stand at room temperature until the flavors meld, about 30 minutes. (The hot sauce can be refrigerated in an airtight container for up to 2 days.)

7. Remove the stew from the oven and remove the bay leaves. Season with salt and pepper to taste and serve with the hot sauce.

11

VEGETABLE STEWS

Vegetable Stews

Hearty Vegetable Stew

VEGETABLE STEWS CAN BE A HARD SELL because they often taste one-dimensional, much like a pan of sautéed vegetables with broth added. We wanted a hearty vegetable stew, one that could be as soul satisfying in the dead of winter as a beef stew. To get there, we'd need to figure out the best way to build flavor (minus the meat) and determine just which combination of vegetables work best together.

To start, we worked on developing a great base of flavor. We selected a number of aromatics—onion, carrot, celery, and bell pepper—and sautéed them until they were well browned to coax out their natural sweetness. The addition of garlic, thyme, and tomato paste added further depth and a little flour added to the pot would help thicken our stew once the liquid was added. At this point, a little bit of flavorful fond had built up, so we deglazed the pot with wine, which picked up the browned bits and added complexity at the same time. We tried red wine first, but it overpowered the vegetables. White wine proved to be a much better choice. We tested a few different amounts and found that just a half-cup did the trick, adding brightness, a slight acidity, and depth all at once. After the wine reduced, we were ready to add the liquid components.

We began our testing with vegetable broth and water. Vegetable broth alone can be overly sweet and since our stew would include a number of vegetables (which are also naturally sweet) we found that cutting the broth with water was necessary. Ultimately, a ratio of nearly equal parts vegetable broth and water (3 cups and 2½ cups, respectively) proved best.

Now for the real hurdle: What vegetables should be featured in our stew? In many recipes, root vegetables are a major component, not just for their earthy flavor but also because their starch acts as a thickener and gives the stew a rich, velvety consistency. We selected a variety of root vegetables and worked our way through them.

Carrots made the stew taste too sweet (and we were already using them for an aromatic), turnips proved to be slightly bitter, and sweet potatoes fell apart during cooking. In the end, tasters preferred red potatoes, parsnips, and celery root. The red potatoes and celery root held their shape after the long simmering time and added some heartiness, and the parsnips contributed sweet yet earthy flavor. The size we cut these vegetables proved to be key—too small and they disappeared into the stew, too large and they didn't cook through. In the end, 1-inch pieces were just right.

In addition to the root vegetables, we also wanted to include greens for contrast. Tasters liked both kale and spinach, but the real winner was Swiss chard, which tastes earthy but still somewhat delicate. We utilized both the stems and leaves, sautéing the stems with the aromatics and the leaves toward the end of the cooking to ensure they didn't disintegrate. However, in spite of our best attempts, the stew was still falling short.

In most stews, meat helps provide balance. But since we were after a vegetarian stew, that wasn't an alternative here. Mushrooms are a common addition to stews (vegetarian or not), as they are meaty and rich. We decided to give them a shot here. We tried portobellos first, but even with just one small mushroom in the pot, its bold, earthy flavor dominated in a way that tasters disliked. We found that white button mushrooms, the supermarket standard, worked much better. To intensify their flavor and rid them of excess liquid that could water down our stew, we sautéed them first until they released their juice and then browned them. This, combined with our aromatics, created an especially rich, flavorful fond.

Tasters approved of our mushroom-enriched vegetable stew, but were now begging for a touch of freshness and acidity. Summery zucchini added with the chard leaves at the end of cooking contrasted nicely with the long-cooked vegetables and a splash of lemon juice and a sprinkle of minced parsley perked up the stew's flavors. At last, we had a vegetable stew that was undeniably hearty (we had managed to squeeze in a whopping 10 vegetables) and full of flavor.

Hearty Ten-Vegetable Stew

SERVES 6 TO 8

Kale greens or curly-leaf spinach, stemmed and sliced ½ inch thick, can be substituted for the chard leaves (omit the stems); the kale may require up to 5 minutes of additional simmering time in step 5 to become tender.

2	tablespoons vegetable oil
1	pound white mushrooms, wiped clean, trimmed, and sliced thin
	Salt and ground black pepper
½	large bunch Swiss chard (about 8 ounces), stems and leaves separated, stems chopped fine, and leaves sliced ½ inch thick (see the illustrations on page 56)
2	medium onions, minced
1	celery rib, cut into ½-inch pieces
1	carrot, peeled and cut into 1-inch pieces
1	red bell pepper, stemmed, seeded, and cut into ½-inch pieces
6	medium garlic cloves, minced or pressed through a garlic press (about 2 tablespoons)
2	teaspoons minced fresh thyme leaves or ¾ teaspoon dried
2	tablespoons unbleached all-purpose flour
1	tablespoon tomato paste
½	cup dry white wine
3	cups vegetable broth
2½	cups water
8	ounces red potatoes (about 2 medium), scrubbed and cut into 1-inch pieces
2	parsnips, peeled and cut into 1-inch pieces
8	ounces celery root, peeled and cut into 1-inch pieces
2	bay leaves
1	medium zucchini (about 8 ounces), halved lengthwise, seeded, and cut into ½-inch pieces
¼	cup minced fresh parsley leaves
1	tablespoon juice from 1 lemon

1. Heat 1 tablespoon of the oil in a large Dutch oven over medium heat until shimmering. Add the mushrooms and ¼ teaspoon salt, cover, and cook until the mushrooms have released their liquid, about 5 minutes. Uncover and continue to cook until the mushrooms are dry and browned, 5 to 10 minutes.

2. Stir in the remaining 1 tablespoon oil, chard stems, onions, celery, carrot, and bell pepper and cook until the vegetables are well browned, 7 to 10 minutes.

3. Stir in the garlic and thyme and cook until fragrant, about 30 seconds. Stir in the flour and tomato paste and cook for 1 minute. Stir in the wine, scraping up the browned bits, and cook until nearly evaporated, about 1 minute.

4. Stir in the broth, water, potatoes, parsnips, celery root, and bay leaves and bring to a boil. Reduce to a gentle simmer, cover the pot partially (leaving about 1 inch of the pot open), and cook until the stew is thickened and the vegetables are tender, about 1 hour.

5. Stir in the zucchini and chard leaves and continue to simmer until they are just tender, 5 to 10 minutes. Off the heat, remove and discard the bay leaves and stir in the parsley and lemon juice. Season with salt and pepper to taste and serve.

Potatoes 101

Think all potatoes are the same? Think again. Until recently, most markets sold potatoes under generic names, such as "baking potato" or "boiling potato," which helped shoppers choose the right potato for each recipe. But now many markets sell potatoes by varietal name, such as Yukon Gold and Red Creamer. So how do you use these potatoes? We find that potato varieties can be divided into three major categories based on texture.

POTATO VARIETIES

DRY, FLOURY POTATOES

WHAT YOU NEED TO KNOW: Also known as "baking" potatoes, this group contains more total starch (20 percent to 22 percent) and amylose than other categories, giving these varieties a dry, mealy texture.

HOW TO USE THEM: These are a good choice when you want to thicken a stew or soup but not if you want distinct chunks of potatoes. Also great for baking and frying, and especially good for mashing, because they can drink up butter and cream.

COMMON VARIETIES:
Russet, Russet Burbank, Idaho

"IN-BETWEEN" POTATOES

WHAT YOU NEED TO KNOW: These potatoes contain less total starch (18 percent to 20 percent) and amylose than dry, floury potatoes but more total starch and amylose than firm, waxy potatoes. Although they are "in-between" potatoes, their texture is more mealy than firm, putting them closer to dry, floury potatoes.

HOW TO USE THEM: They can be mashed or baked and they can be used in soups and salads but won't be quite as firm as waxy potatoes.

COMMON VARIETIES:
Yukon Gold, Yellow Finn, Purple Peruvian, Kennebec, Katahdin

FIRM, WAXY POTATOES

WHAT YOU NEED TO KNOW: Also known as "boiling" potatoes, these contain a relatively low amount of total starch (16 percent to 18 percent) and very little amylose, which means they have a firm, smooth, waxy texture. Freshly dug potatoes, which are often called "new" potatoes, fall into this group.

HOW TO USE THEM: Perfect when you want the potatoes to hold their shape, as with potato salad and some soups and stews; also a good choice when roasting or boiling.

COMMON VARIETIES:
Red Bliss, French Fingerling, Red Creamer, White Rose

SCRUBBING POTATOES

Recipes in which the potatoes are not peeled usually instruct the cook to "scrub" the potatoes. Here's a quick and easy way to get the job done. Buy a rough-textured bathing or exfoliating bath glove and dedicate it for use in the kitchen. The glove cleans away dirt but is relatively gentle and won't scrub away the potato skin.

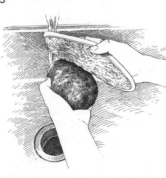

TIPS FOR BUYING AND STORING POTATOES

BUYING

Look for firm specimens that are free of green spots, sprouts, cracks, and other blemishes. We generally prefer to buy loose potatoes, so we can see what we are getting. Stay away from potatoes in plastic bags, which can act like greenhouses and cause potatoes to sprout, soften, and rot.

STORING

If stored under unsuitable heat and light conditions, potatoes will germinate and grow. To avoid this, keep potatoes in a cool, dark, dry place. Although some experts warn that refrigerating potatoes can dramatically increase the sugar level, we've never encountered this problem in the test kitchen. Store potatoes in a paper (not plastic) bag and away from onions, which give off gases that will hasten sprouting. Most varieties should keep for several months. The exception is new potatoes—because of their thinner skins, they will keep no more than one month.

ITALIAN VEGETABLE STEW

SIMILAR TO FRANCE'S RATATOUILLE, ITALY'S classic vegetable stew, known as *giambotta,* turns a bounty of summer vegetables into a comforting, filling mélange of fresh flavors and satisfying textures—in theory. In practice, most recipes result in characterless bowls of stewed vegetables. Add off-season vegetables to the mix, and you get a veggie stew with all the freshness and flavor of canned soup. Determined to create a satisfying bowl of this Italian-inspired dish, any time of year, we compiled some recipes and started cooking.

True to its simple roots, most recipes call for layering the vegetables in a large pot, covering them with broth and/or water, sprinkling seasonings over the top, and letting everything stew until tender. But even when we generously garnished our bowls with chopped fresh basil and grated Italian cheese, the stew that resulted tasted bland and had zero texture. Given the number of high-moisture vegetables in the pot—zucchini, tomatoes, bell peppers, and eggplant are the traditional mix—it came as little surprise that the resulting stew was watery and insipid. Some recipes tried to remedy this deluge of flavorlessness by salting the vegetables before adding them to the pot. While these recipes were slightly better, they took twice as long to prepare, and sometimes turned out too salty. If we wanted to turn out a rich-tasting bowl of Italian vegetable stew that still had some bite to it, it was clear that we would have to find a way to rid our vegetables of excess moisture so we could keep all their bright, fresh flavor in the pot.

We began by selecting the tomatoes, as they would provide the underlying flavor profile of our stew. Being that one of our goals was to prepare this stew year-round, we needed to consider the canned options. Packed at the height of ripeness, canned tomatoes offer consistently good tomato flavor. We tested tomato puree, crushed tomatoes, diced tomatoes, and whole tomatoes. While tomato puree and crushed tomatoes produced soupy stews, both diced and whole tomatoes delivered decent results after half an hour of gentle simmering. In the end, tasters preferred the taste and texture of whole tomatoes chopped into smaller pieces. Yet, even with a large can of tomatoes in the pot, tasters felt the stew lacked real tomato punch. We found that three simple steps amplified the tomato flavor significantly. First, we sautéed the chopped tomatoes to bring out their flavor and achieve some caramelization. Second, we added a tablespoon of tomato paste to the sautéed tomatoes for more concentrated flavor. Third, we reserved the juice the tomatoes had been packed in and added it to the pot later on with vegetable broth (we decided to nix the water as a simmering liquid, as we were trying to rid the pot of excess water, not add more). We partially covered the pot so the broth and tomato juice would achieve a thickened consistency. At last, we had the deep tomato flavor we were looking for. Pleased with our base, we concentrated on the eggplant and zucchini.

We figured first we'd nail down the cooking times. By adding the eggplant and zucchini (cut into substantial 1-inch chunks) when we added the broth and tomato juice and removing a sample of each at intervals, we were able to pinpoint the range in which they were done. Between 35 and 40 minutes, tasters found the zucchini to be tender yet slightly firm and the eggplant tender and creamy. Unfortunately, an old problem had reared its ugly head again. Although our vegetables were properly cooked, they tasted washed out and dull, and our stew had become slightly brothy and watery.

We knew the best way to reduce extra liquid in the pot and develop rich flavor in our vegetables was to use dry heat. We decided to treat the eggplant and zucchini as we would meat or chicken—we browned each vegetable in olive oil at the start of cooking. This technique not only boosted the flavor of both veggies and drove off excess moisture, but it also provided some browned bits on the bottom of the pot (also called fond), which lent serious richness to the stew. To compensate for the browning, we cut a few minutes from the simmering time. Now we could focus on the stew's remaining elements.

Since the tomatoes, eggplant, and zucchini had required such careful handling, we expected the same of the red bell pepper. To our surprise and delight, tasters were pleased when we simply sautéed it (with an onion) to form the aromatic base. Added this early, it softened and melded with the flavors of the stew. Next, we examined options for the stew's starchy component. While a handful of recipes called for pasta, the majority relied on potatoes for starchiness. Tasters quickly approved of this path, pleased with the character and heartiness provided by some spuds. We ruled out russet potatoes, which absorbed the stew's richness but crumbled into a mess. Tasters preferred Yukon Gold potatoes, which held their shape but also sopped up the stew's deep flavors.

Finally, we added fresh oregano and garlic to the mix and finished our bowls with grated Pecorino Romano and a drizzle of extra-virgin olive oil. Whether prepared in the dead of winter or at the height of summer, this satisfying stew provides full, rich flavor and big bites of tender vegetables.

Italian Vegetable Stew

SERVES 6

Do not peel the eggplant as the skin helps it hold together during cooking. Serve with Creamy Polenta (page 232) or Classic Garlic Bread (page 248).

¼   cup extra-virgin olive oil, plus extra for serving

1   medium eggplant (about 1 pound), cut into 1-inch cubes (see note)

2   medium zucchini (about 1 pound), halved lengthwise, seeded, and cut into 1-inch pieces

2   tablespoons unsalted butter

1   (28-ounce) can whole tomatoes, tomatoes chopped medium and juice reserved

1   medium onion, minced

1   red bell pepper, stemmed, seeded, and chopped coarse

1   tablespoon tomato paste

4   medium garlic cloves, minced or pressed through a garlic press (about 4 teaspoons)

1   teaspoon minced fresh oregano leaves or ¼ teaspoon dried

3   cups vegetable broth

1   pound Yukon Gold potatoes (about 2 medium), peeled and cut into ½-inch pieces

2   tablespoons chopped fresh basil leaves Salt and ground black pepper Grated Pecorino Romano cheese, for serving

1. Heat 2 tablespoons of the oil in a large Dutch oven over medium-high heat until shimmering. Brown the eggplant lightly on all sides, 5 to 7 minutes, then transfer to a medium bowl. Repeat with the remaining 2 tablespoons oil and zucchini and transfer to the bowl.

2. Melt the butter in the Dutch oven over medium heat. Add the tomatoes, onion, bell pepper, and tomato paste and cook until dry and beginning to brown, 11 to 13 minutes.

3. Stir in the garlic and oregano and cook until fragrant, about 30 seconds. Stir in the broth, scraping up any browned bits. Stir in the potatoes and reserved tomato juice and bring to a boil.

4. Gently stir in the browned eggplant and zucchini, cover the pot partially (leaving about 1 inch of the pot open), and simmer gently until the vegetables are tender and the stew has thickened, 25 to 35 minutes. Off the heat, stir in the basil and season with salt and pepper to taste. Drizzle individual bowls with additional olive oil, sprinkle with the Pecorino, and serve.

MUSHROOM RAGOÛT

TYPICALLY, A *RAGOÛT* IS MADE WITH MEAT OR poultry; mushroom ragoût, however, is a rich, well-seasoned stew made with a variety of mushrooms. Mushroom ragoût is luxurious in texture with a hearty, deep brown color. Although we could imagine how wonderful this dish would be if prepared with an assortment of exotic wild mushrooms, we wanted our recipe to include only more commonly available varieties. We also wanted our version to be vegetarian, so we would need to find a way to amplify the mushrooms' rich, meaty flavor.

We began our tests with the mushrooms. We wanted our ragoût to include mushrooms that offered variety in flavor, texture, and appearance. To start, we focused on portobello, cremini, white, shiitake, and oyster mushrooms because they are typically found fresh in many supermarkets. Cremini are baby portobellos and testing revealed that including both portobellos and cremini was unnecessary for flavor. We opted for portobellos since they are meatier in texture and can be cut into thick, hearty slices. We also chose to include white mushrooms. While their flavor pales in comparison to portobellos, sautéing does give the mushrooms more bite. And at such a low price point, white mushrooms added a lot of heft to our ragoût without breaking the bank. Shiitakes (sliced caps only because the stems are tough) offered a savory, earthy flavor to the mix.

Oyster mushrooms are much more delicate than the other mushroom types. Light beige and almost trumpet-shaped with ruffled edges, oyster mushrooms may have acquired their name from their elusive briny flavor. Tasters loved the addition of oyster mushrooms in the ragoût. Their flavor contributed complementary and contrasting mushroom tones, but it was their appearance that won accolades. Their light color deepens when they are cooked, but their ruffled edges hold up, giving the ragoût an exotic look. Since we wanted the shape and ruffled edges of these mushrooms to stand out from the crowd, we chose not to slice them thin but rather to cut them into large pieces.

Porcini mushrooms are rarely found fresh in this country, but they are available dried. They are treasured throughout Italy and France for their smoky, pungent, and earthy flavor. Tasters loved the ragoûts in which dried porcini were included. Because they are so potent, we needed a mere ½ ounce of this ingredient.

With our mushrooms chosen, we turned our attention to the aromatics. We tried carrot, celery, and onion, but the carrot and celery looked out of place in this stew, and their flavors and textures took away from the mushrooms rather than enhancing them. We then performed a number of tests focusing on alliums. We tried regular onions, shallots, garlic, and leeks. The leeks were too delicate in flavor and texture and shallots turned out to be too subtle as well. Onions, however, stood up nicely to the assortment of assertive mushroom flavors. Garlic added a pungent note and depth.

While we usually use olive oil or vegetable oil to sauté aromatics for stews, butter is the traditional fat used in ragoût. We tried both and found that tasters preferred butter for the richness it provided; it also helped thicken the liquid in the stew. For the liquid, we relied on vegetable broth; its sweetness balanced the earthiness of the mushrooms.

Most mushroom stews also contain wine to cut through the richness. We found that white wine didn't have enough heft to brighten the flavors. Red wine was too strong and sharp. Next we tried dry Madeira and dry sherry. These fortified wines are often found in mushroom ragoûts, and testing showed us why. They are stronger in flavor than white wine but not as overpowering as red wine.

Many mushroom ragoût recipes include tomatoes for brightness. We tried both canned whole tomatoes, which we chopped, and tomato paste. The tomato paste dulled both the flavor and color of our stew, so we stuck with the canned tomatoes, which added some color and freshness.

With our main ingredients in hand, we began testing cooking methods. We found that browning brings out the flavors of the mushrooms, with one exception. The oyster mushrooms were too delicate to be sautéed for more than a minute or two. We decided to add them with the garlic, after the other mushrooms were browned. As for herbs, we turned to parsley, sage, and thyme. The parsley was used to add brightness to the stew just before serving. The sage and thyme, both sturdy and potent, went into the pot with the garlic and oyster mushrooms.

Some sources indicate that mushroom ragoût is done once the liquid is added, but we found that cooking the mushrooms in the stew for about 20 minutes improves their texture and concentrates their flavor. After this time, though, our ragoût was still somewhat thin; to thicken it, we stirred in a few additional tablespoons of butter. This extra butter, added at the end of cooking, enriched the flavor, thickened the texture, and gave the liquid a bit of a glossy shine. For a finishing touch, we stirred in some balsamic vinegar; its rich, sweet, but sharp flavor balanced the deep tones of the mushrooms.

INGREDIENTS: Balsamic Vinegar

Traditional balsamic vinegar takes a minimum of 12 years to make and costs an astonishing $60 per ounce. We were happy to discover that you don't need to spend a fortune for this ingredient or book a flight to Italy to handpick one; we found a great balsamic at our local supermarket. Tasters thought Lucini Gran Riserva Balsamico most closely resembled a traditional balsamic vinegar with its balance of sweet and tart and its viscosity. And at $2 an ounce, it won't break the bank.

**THE BEST
BALSAMIC VINEGAR**
Tasters like the "sweet, nuanced flavor" of this tart and sweet balsamic vinegar.

LUCINI

Mushroom Ragoût
SERVES 4 TO 6
Serve with Creamy Polenta (page 232) or Classic Garlic Bread (page 248).

5	tablespoons unsalted butter
2	medium onions, minced
½	ounce dried porcini mushrooms, rinsed and minced
	Salt and ground black pepper
1	pound portobello caps (about 4 medium), wiped clean, halved, and sliced ½ inch thick
10	ounces white mushrooms, wiped clean, trimmed, and halved if small, quartered if large
4	ounces shiitake mushrooms, wiped clean, stemmed, and sliced ¼ inch thick
4	ounces oyster mushrooms, wiped clean, trimmed, and halved if small, quartered if large
3	medium garlic cloves, minced or pressed through a garlic press (about 1 tablespoon)
1	teaspoon minced fresh sage leaves or ¼ teaspoon dried
1	teaspoon minced fresh thyme leaves or ¼ teaspoon dried
¼	cup dry Madeira or dry sherry
3	cups vegetable broth
1	(14.5-ounce) can whole tomatoes, tomatoes chopped medium and juice reserved
2	tablespoons minced fresh parsley leaves
1½	teaspoons balsamic vinegar

1. Melt 2 tablespoons of the butter in a large Dutch oven over medium heat. Add the onions, porcini mushrooms, and ¼ teaspoon salt and cook until softened and lightly browned, 8 to 10 minutes.

2. Stir in the portobello, white, and shiitake mushrooms, cover, and cook until the mushrooms have released their liquid, 8 to 10 minutes. Uncover and continue to cook until dry and a dark, thick fond forms on the bottom of the pot, 10 to 15 minutes.

3. Stir in the oyster mushrooms, garlic, sage, and thyme and cook until fragrant, about 30 seconds. Stir in the Madeira, scraping up any browned bits, and cook until almost completely evaporated, about 1 minute.

4. Stir in the broth and tomatoes with their juice and bring to a boil. Reduce to a gentle simmer, cover the pot partially (leaving about 1 inch of the pot open), and cook until slightly thickened and the flavors meld, 20 to 25 minutes.

5. Off the heat, stir in the remaining 3 tablespoons butter, parsley, and vinegar. Season with salt and pepper to taste and serve.

➤ VARIATION

Mushroom Ragoût with Farro
Farro is a grain that can be found alongside other grains or near the pasta in specialty or gourmet markets.

Follow the recipe for Mushroom Ragoût, increasing the amount of vegetable broth to 5 cups and adding 1 cup farro to the pot with the broth and tomatoes in step 4.

Classic Garlic Bread
SERVES 6 TO 8
This garlic bread is best served piping hot.

- 9   medium garlic cloves, unpeeled
- 6   tablespoons (¾ stick) unsalted butter, softened
- 2   tablespoons grated Parmesan cheese
  Salt and ground black pepper
- I   loaf high-quality Italian bread (about I pound), halved lengthwise

1. Adjust an oven rack to the middle position and heat the oven to 500 degrees. Toast the garlic cloves in a small skillet over medium heat, stirring occasionally, until fragrant and golden, about 8 minutes. When cool enough to handle, peel the cloves and mince or press through a garlic press. Combine the garlic, butter, Parmesan, ½ teaspoon salt, and ⅛ teaspoon pepper in a small bowl.

2. Place the loaf halves, cut side up, on a baking sheet and spread evenly with the garlic-butter mixture. Bake until golden brown, 8 to 10 minutes, rotating the sheet halfway through baking. Cut into 2-inch slices and serve.

QUINOA AND VEGETABLE STEW

IN COUNTRIES ALONG THE ANDEAN highlands, quinoa plays a starring role in many dishes. Among them is a quinoa stew with vegetables including potatoes and corn. While some recipes include meat, many rely solely on the quinoa for protein. Unfortunately, most of the authentic recipes call for obscure ingredients, such as annatto powder or Peruvian varieties of potatoes and corn. We decided to make our own version of this unique stew for the American table, but aimed to keep the ingredient list easy to navigate.

In our research, we learned that although recipes might have varied ingredient lists, they all followed the same basic cooking method. First, a mix of cumin, coriander, and annatto powder was cooked in oil (bloomed) until fragrant. Next, onion, garlic, green pepper, and tomato were added and sautéed to form the background notes. Broth, water, or a combination of the two was then stirred into the pot, as were the native potatoes and giant kernels of Andean corn. When these were almost tender, quinoa was added and allowed to simmer until cooked through. Garnished with diced avocado, cilantro, and salty queso fresco, the authentic stews were hearty, delicious, and filling. Following this method, we set about creating our own, accessible version.

After cooking a few of the recipes with annatto powder, we were able to identify its flavor and understand its overall contribution to the stew. Ground from the red pulp found inside achiote seeds (which are from the annatto tree), annatto powder is used extensively in South American and Caribbean cooking. We found its flavor to be slightly sweet and earthy, with just a hint of peppery bitterness. Although its flavor can be somewhat subtle, the color it lends to foods is anything but. Just a teaspoon or two was enough to turn a pot of our stew a rich shade of crimson. After examining our notes, we quickly realized that annatto powder has a flavor profile and color similar to that of sweet paprika. To test whether we could substitute readily available paprika for hard-to-find annatto, we bloomed a few tablespoons of each in vegetable oil. Tasting them side by side, we had a difficult time telling the difference. Once they were mixed into the stew, any slight discrepancies disappeared completely. To round out the spice profile, we added cumin and coriander until the flavor was balanced and rich. To prevent our spices from burning (which happened in many of the recipes we tested), we added them to the pot only after we had sautéed our aromatics.

For our aromatics, we first tried onion, green bell pepper, tomato, and garlic. This combination was perfectly fine, but tasters complained about the texture and flavor of the pepper, which turned army green and flavorless by the time the stew was done. Red bell pepper, on the other hand, remained sweet and fire-engine red. Tasters also wanted more tomato presence in the stew. Instead of loading up the pot with tomatoes at the outset, we set them aside and stirred them in toward the end of cooking so they could warm through. Now they provided a welcome burst of freshness and clean tomato flavor. After adding a few cups of vegetable broth (which united the varying elements of the stew and was more flavorful than water alone or in combination) to the softened aromatics, we had to make a decision about the other vegetables that would give our stew its South American feel.

Given that Peru is thought to be the birthplace of the potato, it came as little surprise that most authentic recipes included the spud. Yet while we generally have access to only a few types of potatoes, Peruvians cultivate literally thousands of varieties. We ordered and tasted a range of these specialty spuds to sample in our stew so we could find a reasonable substitution. While their brilliant colors (red, pink, and even blue) were anything but pedestrian, we found their texture to be similar to that of domestic red potatoes.

Another unique vegetable that showed up in many recipes was giant Andean corn. Dense, chewy, and nutty, Andean corn is worlds away from the domestic sweet corn we are used to eating. We ordered some frozen Andean corn online so we could try it in our stew. Though the chewy kernels were certainly unique, tasters almost unanimously preferred the sweeter stew made with native corn.

Finally, to round out our vegetable selection and add some green to the pot, we stirred in some frozen peas. Happy with our vegetables, we focused on the quinoa.

Having cooked quinoa before, we knew it could go from crunchy to mushy almost instantly. Wary of overcooking the quinoa, we added it after the potatoes had softened. After about 10 minutes, we were rewarded with firm yet cushy bites of quinoa. While the quinoa still had some texture to it, we now found that the broth lacked body. One colleague suggested stretching the cooking time of the quinoa as far as we could go—just a few extra minutes would help it release additional starch into the stew without causing the quinoa to soften too much. After a few more minutes of gentle simmering, the quinoa offered a slight chew, and had also given up sufficient starch so the broth now had substantial body.

All that was needed now was a flurry of garnishes. We liked the traditional combination of salty quesco fresco (feta cheese makes a good substitute), creamy avocado, and citrusy cilantro. Our quinoa stew was the best of both worlds: a humble ode to its authentic roots and a streamlined yet flavorful offering for modern-day tastes.

Quinoa and Vegetable Stew with Avocado and Cilantro

SERVES 6 TO 8

This stew tends to thicken as it sits; add additional warm vegetable broth as needed before serving to loosen. Be sure to rinse the quinoa to remove its bitter coating (known as saponin). Do not omit the queso fresco or feta, avocado, and cilantro; these garnishes are important to the flavor of the stew.

2	tablespoons vegetable oil
I	medium onion, chopped medium
I	red bell pepper, stemmed, seeded, and cut into ½-inch pieces
5	medium garlic cloves, minced or pressed through a garlic press (about 5 teaspoons)
I	tablespoon paprika
2	teaspoons ground coriander
I½	teaspoons ground cumin
6	cups vegetable broth
I	pound red potatoes (about 3 medium), scrubbed and cut into ½-inch pieces
I	cup quinoa, rinsed (see the illustration at right)
I	cup fresh or frozen corn
2	medium tomatoes (about I2 ounces), cored and chopped coarse
I	cup frozen peas
	Salt and ground black pepper
8	ounces queso fresco or feta cheese, crumbled
I	medium, ripe avocado, pitted, peeled, and diced (see the illustrations on pages 44 and 46)
½	cup minced fresh cilantro leaves

1. Heat the oil in a large Dutch oven over medium heat until shimmering. Add the onion and bell pepper and cook until softened, 5 to 7 minutes. Stir in the garlic, paprika, coriander, and cumin and cook until fragrant, about 30 seconds. Stir in the broth and potatoes and bring to a boil. Reduce to a gentle simmer and cook for 10 minutes.

2. Stir in the quinoa and continue to simmer for 8 minutes. Stir in the corn and continue to simmer until the potatoes and quinoa are just tender, 5 to 7 minutes. Stir in the tomatoes and peas and let them heat through, about 2 minutes.

3. Off the heat, season with salt and pepper to taste. Sprinkle individual bowls with the queso fresco, avocado, and cilantro before serving.

➤ VARIATION

Quinoa and Vegetable Stew with Eggs, Avocado, and Cilantro

Serving this stew with a cooked egg on top is a common practice in Peru.

Follow the recipe for Quinoa and Vegetable Stew with Avocado and Cilantro, cracking 6 large eggs evenly over the top of the stew after removing it from the heat and seasoning with salt and pepper in step 3; cover and let the eggs poach off the heat until the whites have set but the yolks are still soft, about 4 minutes. To serve, carefully scoop the cooked egg and stew from the pot with a large spoon, then garnish individual bowls with the queso fresco, avocado, and cilantro.

RINSING GRAINS OR RICE

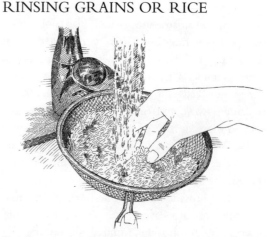

Place the grain or rice in a fine-mesh strainer and rinse under cool water until the water runs clear, occasionally stirring the grains around lightly with your hand. Set the strainer over a bowl and let drain until needed.

CALLALOO

THERE'S MORE TO CARIBBEAN CUISINE THAN the stereotypical rice and beans and roasted meats. We were recently introduced to callaloo, a lively, pesto-green stew that's both creamy and spicy, with a rich, coconutty broth, studded with leafy greens and other vegetables. While you might think the name comes from a children's rhyme, it actually refers to the main ingredient, callaloo leaves, which come from a few different varieties of leafy green plants grown throughout this region. The earthy, citrusy greens of these plants are transformed into a velvety stew, most often enriched with salt pork, hot chiles, onion, garlic, thyme, and coconut milk.

Given its popularity across a wide range of cultures and nations, variations on callaloo abound. We found some recipes that made tweaks to the standard list of ingredients, while others called upon unique garnishes like okra, pumpkin, crab, or conch. While we never shy away from recreating authentic dishes that require hard-to-find ingredients, developing a recipe for callaloo felt especially challenging given that its main ingredient is very rarely available stateside. However, the appeal of this stew was undeniable. We aimed to translate the real McCoy into a close-to-authentic, manageable version of callaloo that we could enjoy anytime—not just on our next vacation.

As with many rustic stews, most versions of callaloo don't rely on a laundry list of ingredients, but rather a thoughtful selection of a few key elements. With just a handful of flavors in the pot, it was necessary to choose all of our ingredients carefully. We began with the foundation of the stew, and tested both salt pork—the traditional choice—and bacon, rendered until crisp. Tasters strongly preferred the texture and hint of smoke that bacon provided. Given that callaloo was originally cooked over an open fire, which would have imparted a smoky flavor, we felt this was a step in the right direction.

Next, we looked to our aromatics. While most recipes called for either onion or scallions, a few suggested using both. We gave it a try, sautéing both until softened, before building the stew. To our surprise, the addition of scallions noticeably boosted the stew's flavor. Garlic and fresh thyme also appeared in a number of recipes. We added moderate amounts of both, working our way up to the right amounts (four cloves and a teaspoon of thyme).

We were at the point where most recipes added heat and spice to the pot, most commonly in the form of Scotch bonnet chiles. Intriguingly, some recipes just threw the chile in whole, let it simmer in the pot, and then removed it before blending the stew until creamy. We weren't sure how much heat—if any—this method would pack. As it turned out, not much. The resulting stew was mild, with just a bit of chile flavor. Abandoning the traditional "steep and remove" technique, we seeded and minced a single pepper before cooking it with the other aromatics. This method provided subtle but persistent heat. With a rich aromatic base, we turned our attention to the cooking liquid.

One test confirmed that callaloo made with all coconut milk was too sweet and one-dimensional. Another liquid would be necessary to balance the flavor and sweetness and provide enough broth to cook the vegetables. Water, not surprisingly, diluted the flavors; vegetable broth wasn't much better. The broth's natural sweetness only served to exacerbate that of the coconut milk. Chicken broth, however, showed promise. After much testing, we found that a 3–1 ratio (approximately) of chicken broth to coconut milk produced a balanced, rich-tasting, creamy broth. It was time to make a decision about the greens.

Unless you grow them in your own garden, it's highly unlikely that you have access to any of the Caribbean greens traditionally used for callaloo. While we found many recipes calling for spinach as a substitute, these stews tasted overly vegetal, and the cooked spinach clumped together in an unappetizing manner. Looking for an alternative that would better replicate the earthy, slightly citrusy notes of callaloo leaves, we tested collard greens, kale, and Swiss chard. The collards and kale provided the earthy flavor we wanted but, even when cooked for extended periods of time, never quite softened to the creamy texture we were after. In the end, Swiss chard leaves proved the best option, offering hearty, earthy flavor, a hint of citrus, and a more delicate texture. (We opted to discard the stems, as they didn't cook down enough to meld seamlessly into the background the way the onions and scallions did.) Now that our stew had great flavor and the right greens in place, we set about achieving the right consistency.

Once fully cooked, the stew is usually "blended" using a simple tool that's basically a wooden dowel with wire rings attached to the bottom. This swizzle stick, as it is called, is vigorously spun between two hands to create a rustic blending effect. This technique chops some of the softened greens to a pulp, lending the stew a thicker consistency and bright green color, while leaving most of the leaves and garnishes in larger pieces. Wishing to replicate this effect, we decided to puree a small portion of the stew, then stir it back in. Now we had the perfect balance of thickened, creamy broth with tender leaves suspended throughout. With a great stew on our hands, we took one last look at the other ingredients found in authentic recipes.

Out of the long list of callaloo recipes we prepared, those containing tender chunks of pumpkin were among our favorites. Since pumpkins can be difficult to find unless it's October, we switched to readily available butternut squash, which provided comparable texture and sweetness. We cut the butternut squash into ½-inch pieces and added it to the pot just after we sautéed the aromatics; after about 15 minutes of simmering, it was perfectly tender. Only a few pieces of the cooked squash ended up being pureed, which meant that most of the chunks stayed intact and provided some textural interest in the finished stew. Okra also appeared in a number of recipes. This ingredient, however, was nixed quickly, as it resulted in a viscous broth that tasters disliked. Finally, we tested a range of seafood, from traditional crab and conch to local cod and even scallops. While none of these additions were bad, tasters whole-heartedly preferred the simple, clean combination of greens and squash. As a final addition, a handful of recipes

called for a few dashes of angostura bitters, an aromatic alcohol infused with herbs and citrus. While not a must, the bitters nicely countered the sweet flavors of the stew.

Caribbean-Style Swiss Chard and Butternut Squash Stew
SERVES 4 TO 6

For more heat, include the chile seeds and ribs when mincing. See page 121 for more information on pureeing soup. Serve with Simple Rice Pilaf (page 286).

- 4 ounces (about 4 slices) bacon, chopped fine
- 2 medium onions, minced
- 4 scallions, minced
- 1 Scotch bonnet or habanero chile, stemmed, seeded, and minced (see note)
- 4 medium garlic cloves, minced or pressed through a garlic press (about 4 teaspoons)
- 1 teaspoon minced fresh thyme leaves or ¼ teaspoon dried
- 3½ cups low-sodium chicken broth
- 1 pound butternut, delicata, or carnival squash, peeled and cut into ½-inch pieces (see the illustrations on page 112)
- 1 large bunch Swiss chard (about 1 pound), stemmed, leaves sliced ½ inch thick (see the illustrations on page 56)
- 1 cup coconut milk
  Salt
  Angostura bitters (optional)

1. Cook the bacon in a large Dutch oven over medium heat until crisp and rendered, 5 to 7 minutes. Stir in the onions and scallions and cook until softened, 5 to 7 minutes. Stir in the chile, garlic, and thyme and cook until fragrant, about 30 seconds.

2. Stir in the broth and squash, scraping up any browned bits, and bring to a boil. Reduce to a gentle simmer and cook for 10 minutes. Stir in the chard leaves and continue to simmer until the vegetables are tender, 5 to 10 minutes. Stir in the coconut milk and bring to a brief simmer.

3. Puree 1 cup of the stew until smooth, then return to the pot. Season with salt and bitters (if using) and serve.

North African Vegetable Stew

TOO OFTEN, VEGETABLE STEWS LACK THE depth, complexity, and richness of their meat-laden counterparts. But that's not true of stews that are inspired by North African cuisine. The combination of heady, potent spices and hearty, filling vegetables and beans is one that rarely leaves diners hungry. We set out to create a rich-tasting, satisfying vegetable stew in the manner of Moroccan and Tunisian cookery, one that featured a spicy, tomatoey base studded with a balanced selection of leafy and hearty vegetables, meaty beans, and bites of pasta.

We started by testing a number of vegetable stews to determine what we liked best. While they varied widely, almost all delivered on their promise of unique, deep flavors, and satisfying textures. Unfortunately, along with great flavor came the difficulty of finding ingredients, such as *harissa* and *ras el hanout*. In addition, many stews required soaking a variety of dried beans or making fresh pasta. We decided to start with our established method for stews (sautéing aromatics and spices, adding broth and cooking vegetables, beans, or pasta, and finishing with flavorful garnishes) and choose appropriate substitutions along the way. We started at the heart of North African cuisine—the spices.

Our favorite stews contained an exotic spice blend called ras el hanout. Meaning "head of the shop," ras el hanout is a proprietary blend of a spice seller's top spices. Although ras el hanout can vary considerably from store to store, it often includes cinnamon, paprika, nutmeg, cardamom, cumin, and coriander. Given its relative obscurity stateside, and the fact that when you do find it, there's no way to know how long it has been on the shelves, we decided to make our own. To test a few different blends, we cobbled together a working recipe for our stew. First, we softened onion in olive oil, then added a test batch of ras el hanout and a few cloves of garlic. Next, we stirred in a little flour to add body and thickness. Once the

spices became fragrant and the flour had lost its raw flavor, we stirred in vegetable broth and simmered the mixture for 20 minutes. Using this method, we tested and tasted a dozen different combinations of spices—some containing every traditional spice and others featuring just a few. Tasters overwhelmingly preferred mixes that contained a modest list of spices, as these produced a cleaner-tasting broth. In the end, cumin, paprika, coriander, and cinnamon proved the winners, offering a warm, complex array of flavors. We tested ratios of these spices until everyone was happy. Next, we tackled the "meat" of our stew.

The recipes we tested contained a large mix of vegetables, beans, and pastas. Our favorites, unfortunately, contained the most labor-intensive ingredients, including dried chickpeas and dried butter beans (lima beans), fresh pasta, and a laundry list of vegetables. As with our ras el hanout, we set about paring this list down. First, we addressed the vegetables. Since our stew would also feature beans and pasta, we limited the number of vegetables in the pot. Tomatoes were a given, and for a hearty green, we settled on Swiss chard. We also liked the sweetness contributed by a couple of carrots. We chose to sauté the chopped chard stems with the onion and add the greens towards the end of cooking in order to obtain the best flavor and texture from both. The carrots we liked cut into ½-inch pieces, as they retained some bite and didn't disintegrate into the stew. While tasters appreciated the texture of the carrots and chard, they didn't care for chunks of tomato in the final stew. Wishing to the keep the tomato flavor, but ditch the chunks, we tried switching to tomato paste. By stirring in a full 2 tablespoons of paste before adding the broth, we got just the rich tomato flavor we were after. Next, we set about determining the best way to incorporate the beans and pasta.

Beans play an important role in North African vegetable stews, as they provide much of the protein and hearty texture associated with meat. The most traditional stews we tasted featured both chickpeas and butter beans, which offered a balance of bite, earthiness, and creaminess. With convenience in mind, we settled on canned chickpeas and canned butter beans, now available in many supermarkets (but if you cannot find canned butter beans, you can substitute frozen baby lima beans).

While handmade pasta may be de rigueur in North African cooking, it's a bit more work than we had in mind. We opted for convenience again, looking to dried pasta and experimenting with shapes and sizes. Most of the traditional stews we tasted featured thin, short noodles, but tasters found them difficult to scoop up with a spoon. Instead, they liked smaller, shorter shapes, especially ditalini. With a hearty vegetable and bean stew on the stove, we focused on one last challenging ingredient.

Harissa, like ras el hanout, is a ubiquitous North African ingredient. It's essentially a spicy paste of ground chiles, cumin, coriander, garlic, and olive oil. We knew from our Spicy Moroccan-Style Chicken and Lentil Soup (page 43) that heat levels vary among different brands of harissa, so we decided to make our own. We spooned our harissa into the stew until tasters were satisfied with both heat and spice levels, reserving the rest for diners to add to their bowls. A final shower of parsley provided a dose of freshness to our boldly flavored North African stew.

North African Vegetable and Bean Stew

SERVES 6 TO 8

You can substitute 1 (10-ounce) bag frozen baby lima beans for the butter beans. Also, you can substitute store-bought harissa if you wish, but be aware that spiciness can vary greatly by brand.

1	tablespoon extra-virgin olive oil
1	medium onion, minced
½	large bunch Swiss chard (about 8 ounces), stems and leaves separated, stems chopped fine, and leaves sliced ½ inch thick (see the illustrations on page 56)
4	medium garlic cloves, minced or pressed through a garlic press (about 4 teaspoons)
1	teaspoon ground cumin
½	teaspoon sweet paprika
½	teaspoon ground coriander
¼	teaspoon ground cinnamon
2	tablespoons tomato paste
2	tablespoons unbleached all-purpose flour
7	cups vegetable broth
2	carrots, peeled and cut into ½-inch pieces
1	(15-ounce) can chickpeas, drained and rinsed
1	(15-ounce) can butter beans, drained and rinsed (see note)
½	cup ditalini pasta
⅓	cup minced fresh parsley leaves
1	recipe Harissa (page 43) (see note)
	Salt and ground black pepper

1. Heat the oil in a large Dutch oven over medium heat until shimmering. Add the onion and chard stems and cook until softened, 5 to 7 minutes. Stir in the garlic, cumin, paprika, coriander, and cinnamon and cook until fragrant, about 30 seconds. Stir in the tomato paste and flour and cook for 1 minute.

2. Stir in the broth and carrots and bring to a boil. Reduce to a gentle simmer and cook for 10 minutes. Stir in the chard leaves, chickpeas, butter beans, and pasta and continue to simmer until the vegetables and pasta are tender, 10 to 15 minutes longer.

3. Off the heat, stir in the parsley and ¼ cup of the harissa. Season with salt and pepper to taste and serve, passing the remaining harissa separately.

12
CHILIS

CHILIS

Classic Beef Chili

LIKE POLITICS, CHILI SPARKS HEATED DEBATES. Some purists insist that a chili that contains beans or tomatoes is just not chili. Others claim that homemade chili powder is essential or that ground meat is taboo. But there is one kind of chili that almost every American has eaten (or even made) at one time or another. It's the kind of chili you liked as a kid and still see being served at Super Bowl parties. Made with ground meat, tomatoes, beans, and chili powder, this thick, fairly smooth chili is spiced but not spicy, and while it won't guarantee impassioned arguments, it will please everyone.

Although this simple chili should come together easily, it should not taste as if it did. The flavors should be rich and balanced, the texture thick and hearty. Unfortunately, many "basic" recipes yield a pot of underspiced, underflavored chili reminiscent of Sloppy Joes. Our goal was to develop a no-fuss chili that tasted far better than the sum of its parts.

Most of the recipes for this simple chili begin by sautéing onions and garlic. Tasters liked a red bell pepper added to these aromatics but rejected other options, including green bell pepper, celery, and carrots. After this first step, things became less clear. The most pressing concerns were the spices (how much and what kind) and the meat (how much ground beef and whether or not to add another meat). There were also the cooking liquid (what kind, if any) and the proportions of tomatoes and beans to consider.

Our first experiments with these ingredients followed a formula we had seen in many recipes: 2 pounds ground beef, 3 tablespoons chili powder, 2 teaspoons ground cumin, and 1 teaspoon each red pepper flakes and dried oregano. Most recipes add the spices after the beef has been browned, but we have usually found that ground spices develop a deeper flavor when they come into direct contact with the hot cooking oil (also called blooming). To see if these results would apply to chili, we made one pot of chili in which the spices were toasted and one pot in which they weren't. The

batch made with untoasted spices tasted weak. The batch made with toasted spices was far better, with bold spice flavor. To prevent the spices from burning, we added them to the pot after we sautéed the aromatics.

Although we didn't want a chili with killer heat, we did want real warmth and depth of flavor. Commercial chili powder is typically 80 percent ground dried red chiles, with the rest a mix of garlic powder, onion powder, oregano, ground cumin, and salt. To boost flavor, we increased the amount of chili powder from 3 to 4 tablespoons, added more cumin and oregano, and tossed in some cayenne for heat. We tried some more exotic spices, including cinnamon (which was deemed "awful"), allspice (which seemed "out of place"), and coriander (which added some "gentle warmth"). Only the coriander became part of our working recipe.

It was now time to consider the meat. Two pounds of ground beef seemed ideal when paired with two 15-ounce cans of beans. Tests using 90 percent, 85 percent, and 80 percent lean ground beef showed that there is such a thing as too much fat. Pools of orange oil floated to the top of the chili made with ground chuck (80 percent lean beef). At the other end of the spectrum, the chili made with 90 percent lean beef was a tad bland—not bad, but not as full-flavored as the chili made with 85 percent lean beef, which was our final choice.

We wondered if another type of meat should be used in place of some of the ground beef. After trying batches of chili made with ground pork, diced pork loin, and sausage removed from its casing and crumbled, tasters preferred the hearty flavor and texture of an all-beef chili.

Next we tried adding various liquids to our chili. Some of us have always made chili with beer and been satisfied with the results. But when we tried beer, we were surprised to find that it subdued that great beefy flavor. We then tried batches made with water (too watery), chicken broth (too chickeny and dull), beef broth (too tinny), wine (too acidic), and no liquid at all except for that in the tomatoes. This no-liquid chili was beefy-tasting and by far the best.

Tomatoes were definitely going into the pot, but we had yet to decide on the type and amount. We first tried two small (14.5-ounce) cans of diced tomatoes, which were clearly not enough. What's more, the tomatoes were too chunky and they were floating in a thin sauce. We tried two 28-ounce cans of diced tomatoes, pureeing the contents of one can in the blender to thicken the sauce. Although the chunkiness was reduced, the sauce was still watery. Next we paired one can of tomato puree with one can of diced tomatoes and, without exception, tasters preferred the thicker consistency. Though we usually don't like the slightly cooked flavor of tomato puree, we decided that this recipe needed the body it provided. In any case, after the long simmering time, any such flavor was hard to detect.

We tried cooking the chili with the lid on, with the lid off, and with the lid on in the beginning and off at the end. The chili cooked with the lid on was too soupy, that cooked with the lid off too dense. Keeping the lid on for half of the cooking time and then removing it was ideal—the consistency was rich but not too thick. Almost two hours of gentle simmering was sufficient to meld the flavors; shorter cooking times yielded chili that was soupy or bland—or both.

Most recipes add the beans toward the end of cooking, the idea being to let them heat through without causing them to fall apart. But this method often makes for very bland beans floating in a sea of highly flavorful chili. After testing several options, we found it best to add the beans with the tomatoes. The more time the beans spent in the pot, the better they tasted and we found that they held their shape just fine, especially dark red kidney beans, black beans, and pinto beans (the other common choice for chili, light red kidney beans, tends to break down more).

It was now time to try some of those offbeat additions to the pot that other cooks swear by, including cocoa powder, ground coffee beans, mushrooms, and lima beans. Our conclusion? Each of these ingredients was either weird tasting or too subtle to make much difference. A sprinkling of garnishes was all our chili needed—tasters liked any combination of cilantro, scallions, onion, avocado, cheese, and sour cream, as well as a squeeze of fresh lime juice.

Satisfied that we'd created a basic chili good enough to silence any debate, we had some fun with variations using bacon, Moroccan spices, Southwestern flavors, and turkey instead of beef. For the turkey recipes, though, we found we had to treat the meat differently. Since the meat simmers with the beans and vegetables for almost two hours, it breaks down dramatically—looking more like a fine meat sauce, like Bolognese, than thick, hearty chili. By adding half of the meat to the cooked vegetables and the other half after the chili

INGREDIENTS: Chili Powder

While there are numerous applications for chili powder, its most common use is in chili. Considering that most chili recipes rely so heavily on chili powder (ours uses a whopping ¼ cup), we thought it was necessary to gather up as many brands as possible to find the one that made the best chili. To focus on the flavor of the chili powder, we made a bare-bones version of our chili and rated each chili powder for aroma, depth of flavor, and level of spiciness. Tasters concluded that Spice Islands Chili Powder was the clear winner. This well-known supermarket brand was noted by one taster as having "a big flavor that stands out from the others."

THE BEST CHILI POWDER
Spice Islands Chili Powder is our favorite chili powder, with its perfect balance of chili flavor and spiciness.

SPICE ISLANDS

had simmered for an hour, we were able to create the perfect balance of flavor while at the same time keeping some of the meat in larger pieces. We found that when adding the second pound of meat to the chili, it is important to add the turkey in small pieces to the simmering chili. This prevents the meat from cooking in long strands. Because turkey has a milder flavor than beef, we created two lively turkey chili variations—one using the bright, tangy flavors of tequila and lime and another that packs a hot and spicy punch with habaneros and chipotle chiles.

Classic Beef Chili

SERVES 6 TO 8

Serve with Sweet and Easy Cornbread (page 260), lime wedges, minced fresh cilantro, sliced scallions, minced onion, diced avocado, shredded cheddar or Monterey Jack cheese, and/or sour cream.

¼	cup chili powder
1	tablespoon ground cumin
2	teaspoons ground coriander
1	teaspoon red pepper flakes
1	teaspoon dried oregano
½	teaspoon cayenne pepper
	Salt and ground black pepper
2	tablespoons vegetable oil
2	medium onions, minced
1	red bell pepper, stemmed, seeded, and cut into ½-inch pieces
6	medium garlic cloves, minced or pressed through a garlic press (about 2 tablespoons)
2	pounds 85 percent lean ground beef
2	(15-ounce) cans dark red kidney beans, drained and rinsed
1	(28-ounce) can diced tomatoes
1	(28-ounce) can tomato puree
	Water, as needed

1. Combine the chili powder, cumin, coriander, red pepper flakes, oregano, cayenne, and 1 teaspoon salt in a small bowl and set aside.

2. Heat the oil in a large Dutch oven over medium heat until shimmering. Add the onions and bell pepper and cook until softened, 8 to 10 minutes. Stir in the garlic and cook until fragrant, about 30 seconds. Stir in the spice mixture and cook, stirring constantly, until fragrant, about 1 minute (do not let the spices burn).

3. Stir in half of the beef, increase the heat to medium-high, and cook, breaking up the meat with a wooden spoon, until no longer pink, 3 to 5 minutes. Repeat with the remaining beef. Stir in the beans, diced tomatoes with their juice, and tomato puree and bring to a simmer. Cover, reduce to a gentle simmer, and cook, stirring occasionally, for 1 hour.

4. Uncover and continue to simmer gently until the beef is tender and the sauce is dark, rich, and slightly thickened, about 45 minutes longer. (If at any time the chili begins to stick to the bottom of the pot or looks too thick, stir in water as needed.) Season with salt and pepper to taste before serving.

VARIATIONS

Beef Chili with Bacon and Pinto Beans

Follow the recipe for Classic Beef Chili, reducing the amount of salt to ½ teaspoon in step 1. Substitute 8 ounces (about 8 slices) bacon, cut into ½-inch pieces, for the vegetable oil; cook the bacon over medium heat until crisp and rendered, 5 to 7 minutes. Pour off all but 2 tablespoons of the bacon fat (leaving the bacon in the pot), then add the onions and bell pepper and cook as directed in step 2. Substitute 2 (15-ounce) cans pinto beans, drained and rinsed, for the kidney beans.

Beef Chili with Moroccan Spices and Chickpeas

Serve with minced fresh cilantro, sliced scallions, minced onion, and/or sour cream.

Follow the recipe for Classic Beef Chili, omitting the chili powder and red pepper flakes. Add 4 teaspoons sweet paprika, 1 tablespoon ground ginger, and ½ teaspoon ground cinnamon to the spice mixture in step 1. Substitute 2 (15-ounce)

Sweet and Easy Cornbread

SERVES 6 TO 8

The slightly sweet flavor of this cornbread tastes great with chili. Don't use stone-ground or whole-grain cornmeal here, or the bread will taste dry and tough.

1½	cups (7½ ounces) unbleached all-purpose flour
1	cup (5 ounces) yellow cornmeal (see note)
2	teaspoons baking powder
¾	teaspoon salt
¼	teaspoon baking soda
1	cup buttermilk
¾	cup fresh corn or frozen corn, thawed
¼	cup packed (1¾ ounces) light brown sugar
2	large eggs
8	tablespoons (1 stick) unsalted butter, melted and cooled

1. Adjust an oven rack to the middle position and heat the oven to 400 degrees. Grease an 8-inch square baking dish. Whisk the flour, cornmeal, baking powder, salt, and baking soda together in a medium bowl.

2. Process the buttermilk, corn, and sugar in a food processor until combined, about 5 seconds. Add the eggs and continue to process until well combined (some corn lumps will remain), about 5 seconds. Fold the buttermilk mixture into the flour mixture with a rubber spatula. Fold in the melted butter until just incorporated (do not overmix).

3. Scrape the batter into the prepared pan and smooth the top. Bake until golden brown and a toothpick inserted into the center comes out clean, 25 to 35 minutes, rotating the pan halfway through baking.

4. Let the cornbread cool in the pan for 10 minutes, then turn out onto a wire rack and let cool for 20 minutes before serving.

cans chickpeas, drained and rinsed, for the kidney beans. Add 1 cup raisins (if desired) to the pot with the beans and tomatoes in step 3. Stir in 1 teaspoon grated zest and 1 tablespoon juice from 1 lemon before serving.

Southwestern Chili with Chipotle, Black Beans, and Corn

Follow the recipe for Classic Beef Chili, omitting the red pepper flakes and cayenne pepper. Add 1 tablespoon minced chipotle chile in adobo sauce to the spice mixture in step 1. Substitute 1 (15-ounce) can black beans, drained and rinsed, for both cans of kidney beans. After the chili has thickened in step 4, stir in 2 cups frozen corn kernels and continue to simmer until heated through, about 2 minutes. Stir in 1 to 2 more tablespoons minced chipotle chile in adobo sauce to taste before serving.

Classic Turkey Chili

Do not use ground turkey breast here (also labeled 99 percent fat free) or the meat will be very dry. The technique for adding the ground turkey to the pot is a little different and makes the ground turkey appear crumbled, like ground beef; otherwise, the turkey will have a stringy appearance.

Follow the recipe for Classic Beef Chili, substituting 2 pounds 93 percent lean ground turkey for the beef; add only 1 pound of the ground turkey in step 3. Add the remaining 1 pound of turkey, pinched in teaspoon-size pieces (see the illustration on page 261), to the chili after uncovering it in step 4. Continue to cook as directed.

Tequila-Lime Turkey Chili

Do not use ground turkey breast here (also labeled 99 percent fat free) or the meat will be very dry. The tequila adds a noticeable zing to this chili.

Follow the recipe for Classic Beef Chili, substituting 2 (15-ounce) cans pinto beans, drained and rinsed, for the kidney beans and 2 pounds 93 percent lean ground turkey for the beef; add only 1 pound of the ground turkey in step 3. Add the remaining 1 pound of turkey, pinched in teaspoon-size pieces (see the illustration on page 261), ¼ cup tequila, and 1 tablespoon honey to the chili

GETTING THE RIGHT TEXTURE FROM GROUND TURKEY

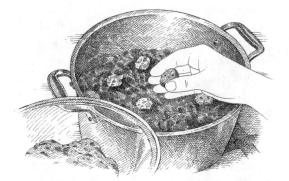

Pack the meat together in a ball, then pinch off teaspoon-size pieces of meat and stir them into the chili. This technique makes the ground turkey appear crumbled, like ground beef, rather than stringy.

after uncovering it in step 4; continue to cook as directed. Stir in 2 tablespoons more tequila and 1 teaspoon grated zest and 2 tablespoons juice from 1 lime before serving.

Smoky-Spicy Turkey Chili

Do not use ground turkey breast here (also labeled 99 percent fat free) or the meat will be very dry. Chipotle chiles give this chili a smoky flavor and habaneros lend a spicy kick. To make the chili even spicier, include the habanero seeds and ribs when mincing; to make it milder, use less habanero.

Follow the recipe for Classic Beef Chili, omitting the red pepper flakes and cayenne. Add 2 habanero chiles, stemmed, seeded, and minced, and 2 tablespoons minced chipotle chile in adobo sauce to the spice mixture in step 1. Substitute 2 pounds 93 percent lean ground turkey for the beef; add only 1 pound of the ground turkey in step 3. Add 1 tablespoon light brown sugar to the pot with the beans in step 3. Add the remaining 1 pound of turkey, pinched in teaspoon-size pieces (see the illustration above), to the chili after uncovering it in step 4. Continue to cook as directed. Serve with sliced pickled banana peppers, chopped fine.

CHILI CON CARNE

CHILI CON CARNE IS A STRICTLY TEXAN chili that consists primarily of beef and chiles—no tomatoes, onions, or beans to be found. And after much research on this type of chili, we had our work cut out for us: We wanted a chili that would be hearty, heavy on the meat, and spicy but not overwhelmingly hot. It should have a creamy consistency somewhere between soup and stew, and its flavors should be balanced so that no single spice or seasoning stands out or competes with the chiles or beef.

Because chiles are the heart of chili con carne, we started there and considered the wide variety of chiles available. After much testing and tasting, we settled on a combination of ancho and New Mexico for the dried chiles (for more information on dried chiles, see page 270), with a few jalapeños added for their fresh flavor and bite. Chili made with toasted and ground whole dried chiles tasted noticeably fuller and warmer than those made with chili powder. And because this chili would be mostly meat and spices, with few additional ingredients, taking the extra time to toast and grind the chiles was well worth the effort. The two main toasting methods are oven and skillet and, after trying both, we went with the oven simply because it required less attention and effort than skillet toasting. The chiles will puff in the oven, become fragrant, and dry out sufficiently after five to six minutes. Because chiles can take on a distinctly bitter flavor if toasted too long, we made sure to remove them from the oven promptly—six minutes in a 350-degree oven was enough to develop their flavor. With the chiles toasted, all we had to do was grind them using a spice grinder. (However, if you can't find these chiles, chili powder can be substituted.)

There was little agreement in the recipes we had collected as to whether the ground chile powders should be toasted further. After running several tests, we found that sautéing the ground chiles—we could include the other spices we decided upon later—for just a minute was the key to unlocking their rich, deep flavor.

Moving on to the meat, chuck is a common choice, and a cut that we find flavorful, tender, and juicy. Most of the recipes we looked at specified that the meat should be cut into ½-inch cubes; however, we found that larger 1½-inch chunks gave the chili a satisfying heartiness. In addition, cutting a chuck roast into larger chunks was much faster and easier than breaking it down into fussy ½-inch pieces.

Next we set out to determine the best type, or types, of liquid for the chili. Our research indicated that the main contenders were water, chicken broth, beef broth, beer, black coffee, and red wine. We tried each one on its own, as well as in a variety of combinations. The surprise result was that we liked plain water best simply because it didn't compete with the beef or chiles.

Although we typically simmer ground meat chilis on the stove, chili con carne is essentially a stew and it seemed appropriate to cook it in the oven, our preferred method for cooking stews because the gentle, consistent heat of the oven guarantees evenly cooked meat. To be sure, we pitted the stovetop and oven against each other and found that cooking the chili covered in a 325-degree oven gave us the best results, ensuring fork-tender beef every time.

Though common in other chili recipes, tomatoes and onions are left out of Texas chili. Including these two ingredients may break with tradition, but we found both to be essential. The acidity of the tomato and the sweetness of the onion, both used in small amounts, add interest and dimension to the chili. The batches we tested without them were decidedly dull. After experimenting with various tomato products, we settled on one small can of tomato sauce—its texture didn't interfere with that of our smooth chili sauce. Five cloves of fresh garlic were also a welcome addition, as were some cumin and a little oregano.

Of the other "secret" ingredients we came across, we found only two to be essential. Some bacon lent the chili a subtly sweet, smoky essence that tasters appreciated and a bit of brown sugar

contributed some necessary sweetness. The rest, though, fell by the wayside. Coke, unsweetened chocolate, and peanut butter were just a few of the random ingredients that didn't make the cut.

Chili con carne typically employs a thickener to tighten the sauce and make it smoother. Masa harina (a flour ground from corn treated with lime or calcium oxide) is the most traditional choice, but we wanted to find a more accessible ingredient. Flour worked well as a thickener in some of our other beef stews, so we followed the same path. Just a few tablespoons, added to the pot with the ground chiles, gave the sauce the appropriately glossy, clingy consistency.

All our chili needed now was a sprinkling of garnishes for color and freshness—such as diced avocado, onion, minced cilantro, and shredded cheese—and we had a meal that was simple yet utterly satisfying.

Chili con Carne
SERVES 6

If given the choice, we prefer to use whole dried chiles, rather than commercially ground chili powder, in this recipe. For more heat, include the jalapeño seeds and ribs when mincing. We've found that this chili is easy to over-season, so be careful when adding salt to the pot. Serve with minced fresh cilantro, sliced scallions, minced onion, diced avocado, shredded cheddar or Monterey Jack cheese, and/or sour cream.

3	ancho chiles (about ¾ ounce), toasted and ground (see page 270) or 3 tablespoons ancho chili powder
3	New Mexico chiles (about ¾ ounce), toasted and ground (see page 270) or 3 tablespoons New Mexican chili powder
3	tablespoons unbleached all-purpose flour
I	tablespoon ground cumin
2	teaspoons dried oregano
6	ounces (about 6 slices) bacon, cut into ¼-inch pieces
I	(3½- to 4-pound) boneless beef chuck eye roast, trimmed and cut into 1½-inch pieces (see the illustrations on page 221)

1   medium onion, minced

4   jalapeño chiles, stemmed, seeded, and
     minced (see note)

5   medium garlic cloves, minced or pressed
     through a garlic press (about 5 teaspoons)
     Vegetable oil, as needed

4   cups water

1   (8-ounce) can tomato sauce

1   tablespoon light brown sugar

2   tablespoons juice from 1 lime
     Salt and ground black pepper

1. Adjust an oven rack to the lower-middle position and heat the oven to 325 degrees. Combine the toasted and ground chiles, flour, cumin, and oregano in a small bowl and set aside.

2. Cook the bacon in a large Dutch oven over medium-low heat until crisp and rendered, 5 to 7 minutes. Using a slotted spoon, transfer the bacon to a paper towel–lined plate. Pour off and reserve the bacon fat in a small bowl.

3. Pat the beef dry with paper towels. Add 1 tablespoon of the bacon fat to the pot and heat over medium-high heat until just smoking. Add half of the meat and brown well on all sides, 7 to 10 minutes; transfer to a medium bowl. Repeat with 1 tablespoon more bacon fat and the remaining beef and transfer to the bowl.

4. Add 1 tablespoon more bacon fat to the pot and heat over medium heat until shimmering. Add the onion and cook until softened, 5 to 7 minutes. Stir in the jalapeños and garlic and cook until fragrant, about 30 seconds. Stir in 1 tablespoon more bacon fat (or oil, if necessary) and the spice mixture and cook, stirring constantly, until fragrant, about 1 minute (do not let the spices burn).

5. Stir in the water and tomato sauce, scraping up any browned bits. Stir in the sugar, crisp bacon, and browned beef with any accumulated juice and bring to a simmer. Cover, place the pot in the oven, and cook until the beef is tender and the sauce is thickened, about 2 hours, stirring halfway through cooking.

6. Remove the chili from the oven, stir in the lime juice, and season with salt and pepper to taste before serving.

WHITE CHICKEN CHILI

WHITE CHICKEN CHILI IS A FRESHER, LIGHTER cousin of the thick red chili most Americans know and love. While its origins date back to the health and Southwestern crazes of the 1980s, white chicken chili has since shown up in a number of Midwestern family cookbooks and has become a regular on the chili cook-off circuit. Its appeal is not surprising. First, because the recipe uses chicken rather than beef, many folks appreciate it for being a healthier alternative. Second, because there are no tomatoes to mask the other flavors, the chiles, herbs, and spices take center stage. Unlike red chili, which uses any combination of dried chiles, chili powders, and cayenne pepper, white chicken chili gets its backbone from fresh green chiles—which contribute vibrant flavor and spiciness.

The ingredients in white chicken chili are fairly consistent: diced or ground chicken, green chiles (usually fresh but sometimes canned or pickled), onions, white beans, garlic, spices, and chicken broth. But most of the recipes we tried were too watery and bland, bearing a closer resemblance to chicken and bean soup than actual chili. While the floating bits of mushy beans and overcooked chicken were hard to overlook, the chiles themselves were often barely noticeable. But amid all these bad recipes, we saw the possibility of creating something great—a rich, stew-like chili with moist, tender chicken, perfectly cooked beans, and a complex flavor profile.

The basic procedure for making white chicken chili is fairly simple. Most recipes start by browning the chicken. Next, the browned chicken is set aside and the chiles, onion, garlic, and spices are sautéed in the same pot. Finally, the chicken is added back in along with chicken broth and white beans and simmered until the chicken has cooked through.

Starting with the chicken, we found that ground chicken was moist but had a chewy, spongy texture and an unattractive crumbly appearance so we ruled it out. The choice between white and dark meat chicken parts was a close call. Chicken thighs tasted richer and meatier, but they tended to compete with the fresh flavors of the chiles and seasonings. Boneless, skinless chicken breasts were attractive but lent little flavor to the broth. We had better luck with bone-in, skin-on breasts. We browned the pieces first to help develop fond (the flavorful bits on the bottom of the pot) and render fat, which we saved to sauté the aromatics.

We were ready to move on to the main order of business: the chiles. Some recipes rely solely on canned or jarred green chiles. While offering convenience, these chiles resulted in a chili that tasted slightly vinegary. That left us with several widely available fresh chiles to choose from: poblanos, Anaheims, banana peppers, Italian peppers, jalapeños, and serranos. Banana peppers and Italian peppers were dull and uninspiring. Extremely hot serranos were also out. We hoped to find a one-size-fits-all chile but discovered that more than one variety was necessary to provide the complexity and modest heat we were looking for. A trio of poblanos, Anaheims, and jalapeños did just that, with each chile bringing its own inimitable characteristics to the table.

We briefly sautéed the chopped chiles along with diced onions, garlic, and spices over relatively high heat before adding the broth, beans, and chicken. This technique yielded chiles that didn't soften much and had a flat, vegetal flavor. Roasting softened the chiles but provided an unwanted smokiness that muddied the dish. We found our solution in two easy steps. First, before sautéing, we briefly chopped the chiles in a food processor until they resembled chunky salsa; this helped to release all of their liquid, aroma, and flavor. Second, when we sautéed the chiles and onions, we lowered the heat and covered the pot. In 10 minutes, the chiles and onions were softened and the flavors of the garlic and spices were nicely bloomed. For the spices, tasters liked the standard cumin but preferred aromatic coriander to the more commonly used dried oregano.

At this point, we were ready to deal with the chicken. We poached the chicken breasts until they were just done (about 20 minutes) and set them aside while the base continued to cook; once they were cool enough to handle, we could shred the meat and add it back to the pot. As for the beans, we opted for simplicity and stirred two cans of cannellini beans into the pot.

While the flavor of our chili was good, we still had the wateriness issue to contend with. We thought back to a number of our bean soups, in which we pureed or mashed some of the cooked beans, then stirred them back into the soup in order to thicken the broth. We didn't see any reason why that wouldn't work here. Mashing some beans directly in the pot was an easy fix, but it didn't do anything for the flavor of the chili. What if we processed the beans with some of the sautéed chiles and onions? In our next test, we reserved some of the sautéed mixture and processed it with a cup of the beans and a cup of the broth. Not only did our chili have a nicely thickened consistency but now it also had a persistent chile flavor that was present in every spoonful.

With a host of complex Southwestern flavors, interesting textures, and filling but not heavy ingredients, this white chicken chili was on par to become every bit as popular as its meaty red cousin.

White Chicken Chili
SERVES 6 TO 8

For more heat, include the jalapeño seeds and ribs. If you can't find Anaheim chiles, add an additional poblano and an additional jalapeño to the chili. Serve with sour cream, tortilla chips, and lime wedges.

2	medium onions, chopped coarse
2	jalapeño chiles, stemmed, seeded, and chopped coarse, plus 1 jalapeño chile, stemmed, seeded, and minced (see note)
3	poblano chiles, stemmed, seeded, and chopped coarse (see note) (see page 271)
3	Anaheim chiles, stemmed, seeded, and chopped coarse (see note) (see page 271)
3	pounds bone-in, split chicken breasts (about 4 breasts), trimmed
	Salt and ground black pepper

2 tablespoons vegetable oil

6 medium garlic cloves, minced or pressed through a garlic press (about 2 tablespoons)

1 tablespoon ground cumin

1½ teaspoons ground coriander

2 (15-ounce) cans cannellini beans, drained and rinsed

4 cups low-sodium chicken broth

¼ cup minced fresh cilantro leaves

4 scallions, sliced thin

3 tablespoons juice from 2 limes

1. Pulse the onions and chopped jalapeños together in a food processor to the consistency of chunky salsa, about 12 pulses. Transfer the mixture to a medium bowl. Pulse the poblano and Anaheim chiles together in the food processor to the consistency of chunky salsa, about 12 pulses, then transfer to the bowl.

2. Pat the chicken dry with paper towels and season with salt and pepper. Heat 1 tablespoon of the oil in a large Dutch oven over medium-high heat until just smoking. Brown half of the chicken on both sides, 7 to 10 minutes, then transfer to a plate. Repeat with the remaining 1 tablespoon oil and remaining chicken; transfer to the plate.

3. Pour off all but 2 tablespoons of the fat left in the pot. Add the processed chile-onion mixture, garlic, cumin, coriander, and 1 teaspoon salt, cover, and cook over medium heat until the vegetables are softened, 8 to 10 minutes.

4. Remove the pot from the heat and transfer 1 cup of the cooked vegetables to the food processor. Add 1 cup of the beans and 1 cup of the broth to the food processor. Puree the mixture until smooth, about 20 seconds, then return it to the pot.

5. Stir in the remaining 3 cups broth, scraping up any browned bits. Add the browned chicken with any accumulated juice and bring to a simmer. Cover, reduce to a gentle simmer, and cook until the chicken registers 160 to 165 degrees on an instant-read thermometer, about 20 minutes.

6. Remove the chicken from the pot, let cool slightly, then shred the meat into bite-size pieces (see the illustration on page 43), discarding the skin and bones. Meanwhile, stir the remaining beans into the pot and continue to simmer until the beans are heated through and the chili has thickened slightly, about 10 minutes.

7. Stir the shredded chicken into the chili and let it heat through, about 2 minutes. Stir the minced jalapeño, cilantro, scallions, and lime juice into the chili. Season with salt and pepper to taste before serving.

CHICKEN MOLE

LIKE CHILIS, MOLES DERIVE THEIR COMPLEX flavor from dried chiles and spices. In its native country, Mexico, rich-tasting mole is often paired with mild-mannered chicken and served in tortillas or ladled over white rice—both ideal canvases for mole to display its character. An authentic mole has intricate layers of flavor—besides chiles and spices, moles can include nuts, fruit, and chocolate— but these exotic flavors come with a price: an extensive list of ingredients and a notoriously long and complicated cooking method. Our goal was to transform chicken mole into a chili that was easy to make and easy to serve, but that still offered all the deep, nuanced flavor of an authentic mole.

We began by testing several recipes uncovered in our research, and after three days of shopping, we finally found all of the ingredients to start cooking. All of the moles we tried tasted a bit different from one another—some were sweeter, others were a bit spicy, and a few had a thicker consistency—but they all featured deep, rich, exotic flavors and took far too long to prepare. Moles are generally made by cooking each ingredient (garlic, nuts, chiles, etc.) individually, typically by frying in an ample quantity of oil. This step acts to toast each item, to bring it to its peak of flavor. Next, all the ingredients are combined in a large pot with broth or water and simmered. The mixture is then pureed smooth and returned to the pot to continue cooking until the flavors meld. Depending on the mole and the number of ingredients, this could take as long as three hours. While the basic method seemed workable, we automatically nixed toasting the nuts, chiles, etc., separately, as this seemed too fussy; the only ingredient in the mole we felt deserved this attention were the dried chiles, which required heat to release their flavor and aroma. With a rough recipe cobbled together, we decided to test the variables.

Dried chiles are a key ingredient in mole so we thought it would be an appropriate place for us to start. Most authentic mole recipes call for several different types of chiles, such as guajillos, pasillas, anchos, and chipotles (for more information on dried chiles, see page 270), but these chiles are meant to add flavor only, and are in no way intended to bring heat to the sauce. We sought out and tested all of these chiles in various sauces and were pleased to find that we could come up with a delicious chili using just two of the most common: anchos and chipotles. Two ancho chiles laid down a full, mild, base of chile flavor while just half a chipotle added a more intense chile flavor and a hint of heat and smokiness. Since canned chipotles in adobo are a test kitchen pantry staple (and are more convenient and readily available than dried chiles), we were curious how they would compare to the dried chipotles. We tested them side by side and noted little difference. With only one type of dried chile to purchase, our shopping list was already looking more manageable.

Next, we moved on to the nut and seed components of mole. Most recipes call for some combination of toasted almonds, pumpkin seeds, peanuts, and sesame seeds. We tested sauces made with each seed and nut on its own to determine their individual flavors, then came up with our own favorite combination. In the end, we liked the rich, creamy flavors of toasted almonds and sesame seeds, but not so much the overpowering flavor of peanuts or pumpkin seeds. Most recipes call for finely ground almonds, but we didn't like their gritty texture in the otherwise smooth puree; straining the sauce was an option, but we were looking to simplify the recipe, not add more steps. Rather, we solved

this problem by substituting almond butter for the ground almonds and were pleasantly surprised to find that the butter also gave the sauce a luxurious, velvety texture. We also thought to try peanut butter, since it's more readily available, but its noticeable flavor stood out in the sauce.

Up to now we had been using semisweet chocolate in the sauce, but wondered if different chocolate types, including authentic Mexican chocolate, might make a difference. After testing various amounts of chocolate, we determined that 1 ounce was just enough to add flavor without overpowering the sauce. We pitted cocoa powder, unsweetened, semisweet, bittersweet, and Mexican chocolate against one another. (Mexican chocolate contains cinnamon and sometimes almonds and vanilla.) Only the unsweetened chocolate and cocoa powder stood out as tasting bitter, while the semisweet, bittersweet, and Mexican chocolates all worked well. A touch of sugar balanced the bitterness of the chocolate (we liked the complex flavor of dark brown sugar).

Our mole-inspired chili had begun to come together, but it was still missing some of the complexity of the more elaborate recipes. Two dried spices, cinnamon and cloves, and some raisins were a step in the right direction. Replacing the water with chicken broth and adding a can of diced tomatoes helped round out the flavor (the tomatoes also deepened the color). These additions were a huge improvement, but the sauce needed more resonance. Hesitant to lengthen our shopping list, we decided to revisit our cooking method, hoping to coax more flavor from our existing ingredients.

We had dismissed the technique of cooking each ingredient separately, but since we were sautéing the onions and garlic anyway, why not sauté the chiles, chocolate, and spices too? Instead of throwing everything (dry and liquid ingredients) into the pot together, we tried incorporating the ingredients in stages. We started by sautéing the dried anchos in plenty of oil (to preventing burning) until they were dark red and toasted. We then stirred in the sesame seeds and cooked them until they were golden. Minced onion went in next (the moisture ensured the chiles and seeds didn't burn). Once the onion was softened we added the raisins, chocolate, almond butter, garlic, chipotles, and dried spices. As the heat drove off the excess moisture the mixture cooked down, becoming bubbly, rich, and deeply fragrant. We then added the broth and tomatoes.

This technique of sautéing the ingredients in stages only took a few extra minutes but proved to be just the boost the sauce needed, drawing out the flavor of the ingredients and intensifying it significantly. We were also able to skip the step of toasting the dried ancho chiles in the oven. We simply ripped the untoasted chiles into small pieces, discarding the seeds and stems before sautéing. Later, when brought to a simmer with the broth, the chiles rehydrated and became soft, blending into a smooth sauce when pureed.

With our recipe nearly complete, it was time to turn our attention to incorporating the chicken, which we planned to shred after it was cooked for easy serving. After trying a variety of bone-in chicken pieces, tasters thought the deeper flavor and tenderness of dark meat—in particular the meaty thighs—was better suited to the assertive sauce than mild breast meat. We browned the thighs on both sides before setting them aside and building the sauce. Although we removed the skin at this point (tasters complained of soggy skin and excess grease in the final dish), browning the thighs with the skin on produced flavorful browned bits on the bottom of the pot as well as rendered fat to sauté the mole ingredients (as opposed to the vegetable oil we'd been using).

Finally, we worked out the details of cooking. We saw no reason that the mole couldn't simmer and develop flavor at the same time as the chicken cooked, so after returning the pureed sauce to the pot, we nestled in the browned thighs, making sure to cover them completely with the sauce. Although it is traditionally simmered on the stove, we found that cooking our mole in a 325-degree oven was much more reliable, guaranteeing a predictably even, consistent level of heat and ensuring that the chocolate-thickened mole didn't burn on the bottom of the pot. As for cooking time, 1¼ hours produced a chili that was deep and flavorful, and by this time the thighs were so tender it only took a few minutes to pull the meat off the bones and stir it back into the sauce. After a sprinkling of sesame seeds and scallions, our mole-style chili was complete—glossy, dark, and rich, the perfect foil to a stack of hot corn tortillas or a bowl of steamed white rice.

Chicken Mole Chili
SERVES 6 TO 8

Ground ancho powder can be substituted for the whole ancho chiles; add 2 tablespoons ground ancho powder to the raisin-chocolate mixture in step 1 and skip the ancho toasting instructions in step 3. See page 121 for more information on pureeing. Serve with Simple Rice Pilaf (page 286) or warm corn tortillas (see page 269).

¼	cup raisins
¼	cup almond butter
I	ounce bittersweet, semisweet, or Mexican chocolate, broken into pieces
2	medium garlic cloves, minced or pressed through a garlic press (about 2 teaspoons)
I	teaspoon minced chipotle chile in adobo sauce
½	teaspoon ground cinnamon
⅛	teaspoon ground cloves
4	pounds bone-in, skin-on chicken thighs (about 11 thighs), trimmed Salt and ground black pepper
2	tablespoons vegetable oil
2	ancho chiles (about ½ ounce), stemmed, seeded, and broken into small pieces (see note) (see page 270)
2	tablespoons sesame seeds, plus extra for serving
I	medium onion, minced
2	cups low-sodium chicken broth
I	(14.5-ounce) can diced tomatoes
I	teaspoon dark brown sugar, plus extra to taste
2	scallions, sliced thin

1. Adjust an oven rack to the lower-middle position and heat the oven to 325 degrees. Combine the raisins, almond butter, chocolate, garlic, chipotles, cinnamon, and cloves in a small bowl and set aside. Pat the chicken dry with paper towels and season with salt and pepper.

2. Heat 1 tablespoon of the oil in a large Dutch oven over medium-high heat. Brown half of the chicken well on both sides, 10 to 15 minutes; transfer to a plate. Repeat with the remaining 1 tablespoon oil and remaining chicken; transfer to the plate. Remove and discard the chicken skin.

3. Pour off all but 2 tablespoons of the fat left in the pot, add the ancho chiles, and cook over medium heat, stirring constantly, until they are dark red and toasted, about 5 minutes. Stir in 2 tablespoons of the sesame seeds and cook until golden, about 1 minute. Stir in the onion and cook until just softened, about 2 minutes.

4. Stir in the raisin-chocolate mixture and cook, stirring constantly, until the chocolate is melted and bubbly, 1 to 2 minutes (do not let the chocolate burn). Stir in the broth, scraping up any browned bits.

5. Stir in the diced tomatoes with their juice and 1 teaspoon of the sugar and bring to a simmer. Puree the sauce until smooth, then return to the pot and season with salt, pepper, and additional sugar to taste.

6. Nestle the browned chicken with any accumulated juice into the pot, spoon the sauce over the chicken, and bring to a simmer. Cover the pot, transfer to the oven, and cook until chicken is very tender, 1 to 1¼ hours.

7. Remove the chicken from the pot, let cool slightly, then shred the meat into bite-size pieces (see the illustration on page 43), discarding the bones. Whisk the sauce to re-emulsify, then stir in the shredded chicken and reheat gently over low heat, 1 to 2 minutes. Serve, sprinkling individual portions with scallions and additional sesame seeds.

INGREDIENTS: Diced Tomatoes

Unlike most kinds of canned produce, which pale in comparison to their fresh counterparts, a great can of diced tomatoes offers flavor almost every bit as intense as ripe in-season fruit. For this reason it's one of the most important staples we stock in our pantry. We rely on diced tomatoes for everything from tomato sauce to chili to soups and stews. But supermarket shelves are teeming with different brands of diced tomatoes. To make sense of the selection, we gathered 16 widely available styles and brands and tasted them plain and in tomato sauce, rating them on tomato flavor, saltiness, sweetness, texture, and overall appeal.

To our surprise, nearly half of the brands fell short. The lowest-rated tomatoes were flat-out awful, eliciting complaints like "mushy, gruel-like texture" and "rubbery and sour." We found that various factors, such as geography and additives, played into whether a sample rated highly. Our top-ranked tomatoes were grown in California, source of most of the world's tomatoes, where the dry, hot growing season develops sweet, complex flavor; the bottom-ranked brands came from the Midwest and Pennsylvania. We tasted tomatoes that were too sweet or too acidic (from not enough or too much citric acid) or bland from lack of salt. Tasters overwhelmingly favored those brands with more salt. In fact, the tomatoes with the least salt—125 mg per serving compared to 310 mg in the top-rated brand—ranked last. In the end, one can stood out from the pack. Hunt's Diced Tomatoes were our tasters' favorite, praised for being "fresh" and "bright," with a "sweet-tart" flavor and "juicy," "firm, crisp-tender chunks."

THE BEST
DICED TOMATOES

Tasters chose this brand over all others, praising the tomatoes for their "fresh," "bright" flavor.

HUNT'S

CARNE ADOVADA

NOT AS WELL KNOWN AS TEXAS'S CHILI CON Carne (page 262), but no less delicious, is New Mexico's *carne adovada*, which literally translates to "marinated meat." Like many New Mexican dishes, it stars local chiles. Meltingly tender chunks of pork butt are braised in an intense, richly flavored red chile sauce with hints of oregano, onion, and garlic. It's at once smoky yet bright, spicy yet sweet. Most recipes we found in our research toast and grind nearly two dozen dried New Mexico chiles (commonly Anaheims). We typically don't mind taking this extra step, but sometimes we yearn for an easier method. Our goal was clear. We wanted a streamlined route to this regional favorite—one that didn't require toasting and grinding dried chiles, but still delivered complexity and subtle heat.

We began by reaching for a jar of chili powder, which we felt would provide a solid baseline of warmth and depth; store-bought chili powder is mostly ground dried red chiles, with the rest a mix of garlic powder, onion powder, oregano, ground cumin, and salt. First we cubed and browned a boneless pork butt in oil before setting it aside. (Large, 1½-inch chunks gave the dish a rustic feel.) After softening some onion and garlic in the fat and fond (flavorful browned bits left from browning the pork), we added ⅓ cup chili powder, about the same amount our research recipes use of freshly roasted and ground dried New Mexico chiles. Then we stirred in some chicken broth, pureed the mixture, and added back the reserved meat to cook through. As with our meaty stews, we found that cooking in the oven, as opposed to the stovetop, ensured that the meat cooked evenly. After two hours, the meat was tender and the sauce was an attractive rust-red, but the dish tasted utterly flat, and the meat juices had made the sauce runny.

Chili powder alone wasn't cutting it, so for some smoky depth, we turned to a test kitchen pantry staple, canned chipotle chiles in adobo sauce. We tried various quantities before deciding that a tablespoon brought the right amount of complexity and heat. In addition to being spicy, dried chiles also boast a rich, fruity side. Wondering how to replicate the fruity quality of dried chiles, it occurred to us that we could use actual fruit. Since the flavor of chiles is sometimes described as raisiny, we hoped raisins might supply that nuance, but tasters rejected the dried fruit in the sauce. We tried soaking the raisins in hot water to soften them, then made a puree and stirred it in. Tasters liked the subtle flavor it contributed. To replicate the slightly bitter quality of freshly ground dried chiles, we tried stirring in cocoa powder or unsweetened chocolate. In carne adovada, however, they tasted out of place. A colleague suggested we soak the raisins in coffee instead of water; indeed, some coffee brought the flavors into robust, bittersweet balance.

For final touches, we stirred in flour with the spices, which nicely thickened the sauce. Tasters couldn't detect the small amount of oregano—a must in carne adovada—in the chili powder, so we reinforced it with an additional teaspoon. At the end we stirred in lime juice, lime zest, and cilantro to brighten the earthy dish. While these aren't traditional, our tasters felt the dish benefited from their addition. At last, using easy-to-find ingredients, we'd developed a streamlined version of carne adovada that delivers authentic flavor.

WARMING TORTILLAS

Our preferred way to warm tortillas is over the open flame of a gas burner. This technique gives them a nice roasted flavor. However, you can also toast them in a skillet one at a time over medium-high heat until soft and speckled with brown spots (20 to 30 seconds per side), or warm them in the microwave. To microwave, simply stack tortillas on a plate, cover with microwave-safe plastic wrap, and microwave on high power until warm and soft, 1 to 2 minutes. Once warmed, keep the tortillas wrapped in aluminum foil or a kitchen towel until ready to use or they will dry out. If your tortillas are very dry, pat each with a little water before warming.

To warm tortillas over the open flame of a gas burner, place each tortilla directly on the cooking grate over a medium flame. Heat until slightly charred around edges, 15 to 30 seconds per side.

Chiles 101

Chiles, both dried and fresh, are common ingredients used the world over, with unique flavors that range from mild and fresh to acidic and spicy to rich and deeply toasted. Some chiles are used for their spicy heat, while others with a more mild flavor are used to provide subtle background notes. You should use caution when working with chiles because the compound that makes them taste spicy, called capsaicin, can easily be rubbed off onto your hands (and then onto whatever you touch), causing a mild to very strong burning sensation. We recommend wearing disposable latex gloves and washing your hands thoroughly with soap and water when done handling chiles. As an added precaution, your cutting board and knife should be washed to prevent transferring the chiles' heat to other foods.

DRIED CHILES

Although the availability of dried peppers is somewhat regional, you should be able to find at least a few options at most specialty or gourmet markets. When buying dried chiles, look for ones that are glossy and slightly pliable and avoid those that look overly dry and brittle. When cooking with dried chiles, we've found it important to toast them first in order to bring out their latent flavors. For most recipes, we like to toast the chiles in the oven, then grind them into a powder using a spice grinder. The resulting chile powder can then be used as you would any store-bought chile powder; however, it will have a fresher and more complex flavor (as in our Chili con Carne on page 262). An alternative to this toast-and-grind method is to break the dried chile into small pieces, then toast them right in the pot before building your soup, stew, or chili, as we do in our Chicken Mole Chili (page 267).

CHILE	APPEARANCE AND FLAVOR	HEAT	SUBSTITUTIONS
New Mexico	Smooth, shiny, brick-red skin, with a crisp, slightly acidic, earthy flavor	Mild	Ancho
Ancho (dried poblano pepper)	Dark mahogany red with wrinkly skin and a sweet, raisiny flavor	Mild-Medium	New Mexico, Pasilla
Pasilla (dried chilaca chile)	Long, wrinkled, purplish to dark brown, with a rich, smoky flavor	Mild-Medium	Ancho, Guajillo
Guajillo	Shiny, dark red skin with a complex, tangy, slightly smoky flavor	Medium	Pasilla, Ancho
Chipotle (smoked jalapeño pepper, dried or canned in adobo sauce)	Brick-red to brown, with a smoky, chocolate flavor	Hot	Guajillo
De Arbol	Small and red, usually sold with the stem attached, with a bright, spicy flavor	Very Hot	Thai
Thai	Small and red with a very spicy flavor	Very Hot	De Arbol

TOASTING DRIED CHILES

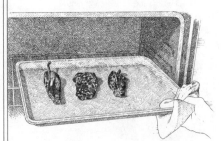

1. Clean the chiles of any visible dirt with a damp paper towel, then lay them on a baking sheet and toast in a 350-degree oven until fragrant and puffed, about 6 minutes.

2. Let the chiles cool then, wearing gloves to protect your skin, break open the chiles and brush out the seeds. (The seeds can be reserved to add extra heat to dishes.) Remove the stems.

3. Using a spice grinder, grind the toasted, stemmed chiles to a fine powder, adding the seeds as desired to increase the heat level in the dish. To help the chiles grind evenly, we find it helpful to pick up the spice grinder and shake it gently during grinding.

FRESH CHILES

When shopping for fresh chiles, look for those with bright colors and tight, unblemished skin. Note that much of the heat in a chile lies in the seeds and ribs; you can omit the seeds or add them to a dish as desired to help control the spice levels. We sometimes add some of the seeds with the chiles and reserve the remaining seeds to adjust spiciness just before serving.

CHILE		APPEARANCE AND FLAVOR	HEAT	SUBSTITUTIONS
Anaheim		Large, yellow-green to red in color, with a tangy, mild flavor	Mild	Poblano, Bell Pepper
Poblano		Thick-skinned, green to reddish-brown in color, with a crisp bell pepper flavor	Mild-Medium	Anaheim, Bell Pepper
Jalapeño		Small, green or red in color, with a spicy, bright, grassy flavor	Medium	Serrano
Serrano		Small, dark green, with a flavor similar to that of jalapeños but spicier	Hot	Jalapeño
Thai		Small, red or green, with a bright, very spicy flavor	Very Hot	Habanero, Serrano, Jalapeño
Habanero		Small, heart-shaped, orange to red in color with a very spicy, citrusy flavor	Very Hot	Thai, Serrano, Jalapeño

SEEDING FRESH CHILES

Using a knife to remove the seeds and ribs from a hot chile pepper takes a very steady hand. Fortunately, there is a safer and equally effective alternative.

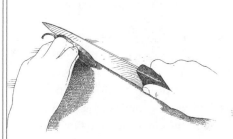

1. Cut the pepper in half lengthwise with a knife.

2. Starting opposite the stem end, run the edge of a small melon baller scoop down the inside of the pepper, scraping up the seeds and ribs.

3. Cut off the core with the scoop.

Carne Adovada

SERVES 6

Boneless pork butt roast is often labeled as boneless Boston butt in the supermarket. You can substitute 1½ teaspoons ground espresso powder dissolved in ½ cup boiling water for the brewed coffee if desired. See page 121 for more information on pureeing. Serve with Simple Rice Pilaf (page 286) or warm corn tortillas (see page 269).

½	cup brewed coffee, hot (see note)
¼	cup raisins
⅓	cup chili powder
3	tablespoons unbleached all-purpose flour
1	teaspoon dried oregano
1	(3½- to 4-pound) boneless pork butt roast, trimmed and cut into 1½-inch pieces (see note)
	Salt and ground black pepper
3	tablespoons vegetable oil
2	medium onions, minced
6	medium garlic cloves, minced or pressed through a garlic press (about 2 tablespoons)
1	tablespoon minced chipotle chile in adobo sauce
2	cups low-sodium chicken broth
1	cup water
¼	cup minced fresh cilantro leaves
1	teaspoon grated zest and 1 tablespoon juice from 1 lime

1. Adjust an oven rack to the lower-middle position and heat the oven to 325 degrees. Combine the hot coffee and raisins in a small bowl, cover, and let sit until the raisins are plump, about 5 minutes. Combine the chili powder, flour, and oregano in a small bowl. Pat the pork dry with paper towels and season with salt and pepper.

2. Heat 1 tablespoon of the oil in a large Dutch oven over medium-high heat until just smoking. Add half of the pork and brown well on all sides, 7 to 10 minutes; transfer to a medium bowl. Repeat with 1 tablespoon more oil and the remaining pork and transfer to the bowl.

3. Pour off all but 2 tablespoons of the fat left in the pot, add the onions, and cook over medium heat until softened, 5 to 7 minutes. Stir in the garlic and chipotles and cook until fragrant, about 30 seconds. Stir in the spice mixture and remaining 1 tablespoon oil and cook, stirring constantly, until fragrant, about 1 minute (do not let the spices burn). Stir in the broth, water, and raisin-coffee mixture, scraping up any browned bits.

4. Puree the sauce until smooth, then return to the pot. Stir in the browned pork with any accumulated juice and bring to a simmer. Cover, place the pot in the oven, and cook until the pork is tender and the sauce is thickened, about 2 hours, stirring halfway through cooking.

5. Remove the pot from the oven and stir in the cilantro, lime zest, and lime juice. Season with salt and pepper to taste and serve.

CHILI VERDE WITH PORK AND HOMINY

POZOLE IS THE MEXICAN NAME FOR BOTH hominy (dried field corn kernels treated with lime and boiled until tender but still chewy) and the stew made with hominy and pork. While this dish is made throughout Mexico in several distinct incarnations, we thought the appeal of *pozole verde* (green pozole), which is chock-full of bright, fresh chiles and tomatillos (the tangy little tomato-like fruits common in Mexican cuisine), was undeniable. We hoped to translate this stew into a bold, bright chili that could be made in less time and in a more streamlined fashion than authentic pozole, which requires hours of simmering and old-world tools, such as a *comal* (a cast-iron pan), to prepare the chiles and tomatillos.

We started with the chili basics: choice of meat and cooking method. Traditional recipes start with a pork shoulder roast, which is simmered for hours before it's shredded and returned to the pot. In order to save time and get a jump start on deep flavor, we took a cue from our recipe for Carne Adovada: we cut the roast into sizable (about 1½-inch) pieces that we browned, then set aside while we built the chili in the fond, or flavorful browned bits, left behind in the pot. As for cooking method, we knew that two hours in a moderate,

325-degree oven would produce moist, tender, evenly cooked meat.

With the pork ready to go, we addressed the chiles and tomatillos, which are traditionally roasted in a cast-iron pan known as a *comal* and then ground to a puree using a mortar and pestle before being added to the pot. For the chiles, we tested the usual suspects: poblanos, serranos, and jalapeños. Tasters preferred the poblanos, which have a mild to moderate heat and a deep herbal flavor that is more complex than the straightforward grassy taste of jalapeños or serranos. As for the tomatillos, we decided to use fresh for the bright, tangy flavor they would impart. (That said, fresh tomatillos can be difficult to locate, so canned can be substituted.) Now we had to figure out the best way to bring out the flavors of these two key ingredients.

Traditional recipes dry-roast whole tomatillos and chiles on the stovetop until soft and charred; this method works to impart smokiness and concentrate flavor. Modern recipes skip the roasting, relying on sautéing, high-heat oven-roasting, or broiling to achieve the same effect—and then ditch the mortar and pestle in favor of a blender or food processor. We began with the most authentic method for roasting—using the stovetop and a cast-iron pan. While this method wasn't incredibly difficult, it did require closely monitoring the chiles and tomatillos, as cooking them just a few seconds too long made both unusable. Also, we found that the blackened skins on the tomatillos had good flavor, but the chile skins tasted bitter and needed to be removed. Looking for an easier and more hands-off method, we tried sautéing and oven-roasting; both were quickly eliminated from consideration, as neither one added enough char to create the smokiness we were looking for. Broiling seemed much more promising, especially when we tossed everything with a little oil to promote charring. The tomatillos could be broiled whole, but we found that the poblanos weren't developing even color. Ultimately, we found that cutting them in half and broiling them skin side up helped them blacken more evenly. One taste, and we knew that we'd hit the jackpot: Broiling brought a sweet richness to the poblanos and tempered the tartness of the tomatillos.

We now had to puree the tomatillos and chiles. A mortar and pestle is the tool preferred in more authentic recipes, but we wanted an easier, quicker option. A quick whir in the blender made a puree that was too smooth; a few pulses in the food processor better approximated the coarse, rustic texture produced by a mortar and pestle.

Next, it was time to decide on the liquid and other seasonings. We tested using water on its own and water cut with chicken broth. Although the chili made with water alone tasted fine, the version made with both water and broth was far superior, adding depth of flavor. In addition to a base of sautéed onion and garlic, oregano and cumin provided an earthy backbone. A pinch of cloves and cinnamon, plus two bay leaves, added complexity and enhanced the floral notes. To balance the acidity of the tomatillos, we stirred in some sugar.

With the chili's flavor balanced and the pork on its way to being fall-apart tender, we could now consider the other starring ingredient—the hominy. There were two options: freshly rehydrated hominy, which takes hours to prepare, or canned hominy, which we simply had to drain and rinse. We prepared a batch of chili using each and gathered tasters. The chili made with freshly cooked hominy was superb, but the chili with canned hominy was also very good. The hominy was chewy (as hominy should be) and relatively sweet, so we decided it was well worth using canned to save a significant amount of prep time.

Canned hominy comes in white and yellow varieties, depending on the type of field corn used. In our tests, we found that both types are fine. Flavor isn't much of an issue, as both are sweet and "corny" tasting. We determined that adding the canned hominy at the beginning of cooking allows it to soak up some of the flavorful broth as well as infuse the chili with corn flavor. Additionally, the starch from the hominy naturally thickened the chili, making it unnecessary to add flour.

Finally, fresh lime juice and a generous handful of minced cilantro emphasized the fresh, clean flavor of this Mexican-inspired chili. Our recipe turned out to be remarkably simple—less than an hour of hands-on work—and delivered a uniquely bright but still rich chili with all the hallmark flavors of an authentic pozole verde.

Chili Verde with Pork and Hominy

SERVES 6

Boneless pork butt roast is often labeled as boneless Boston butt in the supermarket. The outer husk of a fresh tomatillo should be dry, the tomatillo itself should be bright green, with a fresh, fruity smell. You can substitute three (11-ounce) cans of tomatillos, drained, rinsed, and patted dry, for the fresh tomatillos; broil as directed in step 1. You can substitute 4 large jalapeño chiles, stemmed, seeds and ribs removed, for the poblanos if necessary.

1½	pounds tomatillos (16 to 20 medium), husks and stems removed, rinsed well, dried, and halved if larger than 2 inches in diameter (see note)
3	poblano chiles, halved lengthwise, stemmed, and seeded (see note) (see page 271)
3	tablespoons vegetable oil
4	medium garlic cloves, minced or pressed through a garlic press (about 4 teaspoons)
2	teaspoons sugar
1	teaspoon dried oregano
1	teaspoon ground cumin
	Pinch ground cloves
	Pinch ground cinnamon
	Salt and ground black pepper
1	(3½- to 4-pound) boneless pork butt roast, trimmed and cut into 1½-inch pieces
1	medium onion, chopped medium
2½	cups low-sodium chicken broth
1	cup water
2	(15-ounce) cans white or yellow hominy, drained and rinsed
2	bay leaves
¼	cup minced fresh cilantro leaves
1	tablespoon juice from 1 lime

1. Position an oven rack 6 inches from the broiler element and heat the broiler. Line a rimmed baking sheet with foil. Toss the tomatillos and poblanos with 1 tablespoon of the oil. Arrange the tomatillos, cut side down if halved, and poblanos, skin side up, on the prepared baking sheet. Broil until the vegetables blacken and begin to soften, 5 to 10 minutes, rotating the pan halfway through broiling.

2. Remove the tomatillos and poblanos from the oven, let cool slightly, then remove the skins from the poblanos (leave the tomatillo skins intact). Transfer the vegetables with any accumulated juice to a food processor and pulse until the mixture is almost smooth, about 10 pulses; set aside.

3. Adjust an oven rack to the lower-middle position and heat the oven to 325 degrees. Combine the garlic, sugar, oregano, cumin, cloves, cinnamon, 1 teaspoon salt, and ½ teaspoon pepper in a small bowl. Pat the pork dry with paper towels and season with salt and pepper.

4. Heat 1 tablespoon more oil in a large Dutch oven over medium-high heat until just smoking. Add half of the meat and brown well on all sides, 7 to 10 minutes; transfer to a medium bowl. Repeat with the remaining 1 tablespoon oil and remaining pork and transfer to the bowl.

5. Pour off all but 1 tablespoon of the fat left in the pot, add the onion, and cook over medium heat until softened, 5 to 7 minutes. Stir in the garlic-spice mixture and cook, stirring constantly, until fragrant, about 1 minute (do not let the spices burn). Stir in the processed tomatillo-poblano mixture, broth, and water, scraping up any browned bits.

6. Stir in the pork with any accumulated juice, hominy, and bay leaves and bring to a simmer. Cover, place the pot in the oven, and cook until the pork is tender and the sauce is thickened, about 2 hours, stirring halfway through cooking.

7. Remove the pot from the oven and remove the bay leaves. Stir in the cilantro and lime juice, season with salt and pepper to taste, and serve.

BLACK BEAN CHILI

BLACK BEAN CHILI IS THE VEGETARIAN'S answer to hearty, satisfying chili, but so often it can turn out dull and unremarkable. Most versions we've come across over the years either taste like warmed black beans straight from the can or they take a kitchen-sink philosophy and include a hodgepodge of vegetables. We wanted a chili that was primarily about the beans, which should be creamy, tender, and well seasoned. It should have enough complexity and depth to hold your interest for a whole bowl; although not meaty, it needed to taste rich and satisfying. With these goals in mind, we headed into the test kitchen.

Since beans were to be the core of our chili, that's where we started testing. The first question was what type to use: canned or dried. While we typically use canned beans in chilis, a test pitting canned beans against dried beans made it clear that, in this case, dried beans—with their superior texture and flavor—were the only way to go. Usually we prefer to soak beans in a saltwater solution (or brine them) prior to cooking, as this step softens the tough bean skins and evens out the cooking time, so that fewer beans burst open. But, as with our Black Bean Soup (page 142), a few broken beans wouldn't be a bad thing in this dish; we wanted a thick chili and a portion of burst beans would only contribute to our desired texture.

When it comes to chilis and stews where even cooking is crucial, we usually favor the oven for its uniform, consistent heat. The same held true here. After testing a range of temperatures from 250 to 400 degrees, we determined that 325 worked best. Higher temperatures caused too vigorous a simmer and burst every single bean, while lower temperatures meant too long a cooking time.

When cooking unbrined beans, it's particularly important to use a flavorful liquid to ensure well-seasoned interiors. In this case, we found a combination of equal parts vegetable broth and water gave the beans a flavorful backbone. We also wanted to include tomatoes, a traditional ingredient that lends brightness and acidity to chili. After testing fresh chopped tomatoes, canned diced tomatoes, and canned crushed tomatoes, tasters preferred the smooth texture of the crushed tomatoes. One 28-ounce can, combined with the single pound of beans we were working with, provided a solid tomato base without treading into marinara territory. Since acidic ingredients can toughen beans by preventing their cells from absorbing water, we added the tomatoes to the pot halfway through cooking. A small amount of baking soda, stirred in at the beginning of cooking, ensured that our beans stayed dark and didn't turn gray or drab.

Confident that we had solved our bean cooking method, we looked for ways to boost the meaty flavor of the chili. Looking for something that would complement but not overwhelm the black beans, we hit on mushrooms, known for their high level of glutamates, a class of amino acids that give meat its savory taste. We made three batches of beans, adding a different sliced mushroom to each; we tried white, cremini, and portobello mushrooms. While tasters found that the portobellos' bold, earthy flavor dominated the chili, the cremini and white mushrooms were praised for complementing the beans with their meaty texture and rich flavor. Since it was a tie between the two, we opted to go with the more readily available white mushrooms.

To further ensure that the mushrooms played a supporting role to the beans, we chopped them fine, then sautéed them with some onion to drive off moisture and create a flavorful fond on the bottom of the pot. The chopped pieces of mushroom were now hard to identify as mushrooms given the rich, dark color of the chili, but they still provided plenty of flavor, texture, and body. An additional test determined that pulsing the mushrooms in the food processor produced the same results as chopping by hand, but took a fraction of the time.

As for aromatics and spices, in addition to onion, we stirred in a generous quantity of garlic, chili powder, and a couple of bay leaves. Whole cumin seeds and minced chipotle added depth and smokiness. So far, so good, but something was missing. Looking for another way to deepen the flavor of the chili, we reviewed existing recipes for black bean chili again, hoping for inspiration. We noticed a few called for mustard seeds. It seemed a bit odd for chili, but we were curious and gave it a shot, adding a few tablespoons with the other aromatics. We found that the chili now had an appealing pungency and an additional level of complexity that tasters immediately noticed but couldn't identify. We eventually settled on 1 table-spoon of mustard seeds (more than this, and the chili took on a bitter taste) rounded out with a tablespoon of brown sugar. To enhance the flavor of the mustard seeds, we employed the technique of "blooming," a common test kitchen practice for bringing out the flavor of dried spices by briefly sautéing them. Sautéing the seeds in oil proved to be a minor disaster, causing them to pop out of the pot. Toasting them in a dry pan, along with the cumin seeds, achieved the same goal but with less drama.

Finally, for some textural contrast and a bit of sweetness, we added two red bell peppers, cut into ½-inch pieces; stirring them in with the tomatoes preserved their color and texture. With a spritz of lime and a sprinkling of minced cilantro, this rich, hearty chili was so satisfying, no one missed the meat.

Black Bean Chili

SERVES 6 TO 8

We strongly prefer the texture and flavor of mustard seeds and cumin seeds in this chili; however, ground cumin and dry mustard can be substituted—add ½ teaspoon ground cumin and/or ½ teaspoon dry mustard to the pot with the chili powder in step 3. Serve with sour cream, shred-ded cheddar or Monterey Jack cheese, chopped tomatoes, and/or minced onion.

I	pound white mushrooms, wiped clean, trimmed, and broken into rough pieces
I	tablespoon mustard seeds (see note)
2	teaspoons cumin seeds (see note)
3	tablespoons vegetable oil
I	medium onion, chopped medium
9	medium garlic cloves, minced or pressed through a garlic press (about 3 tablespoons)
I	tablespoon minced chipotle chile in adobo sauce

3	tablespoons chili powder
2½	cups vegetable broth
2½	cups water, plus extra as needed
I	pound dried black beans, picked over and rinsed
I	tablespoon light brown sugar
⅛	teaspoon baking soda
2	bay leaves
I	(28-ounce) can crushed tomatoes
2	red bell peppers, stemmed, seeded, and cut into ½-inch pieces
½	cup minced fresh cilantro leaves
	Salt and ground black pepper
	Lime wedges, for serving

1. Adjust an oven rack to the lower-middle position and heat the oven to 325 degrees. Pulse the mushrooms in a food processor until uniformly coarsely chopped, about 10 pulses; set aside.

2. Toast the mustard seeds and cumin seeds in a large Dutch oven over medium heat, stirring constantly, until fragrant, about 1 minute. Stir in the oil, onion, and processed mushrooms, cover, and cook until the vegetables have released their liquid, about 5 minutes. Uncover and continue to cook until the vegetables are dry and browned, 5 to 10 minutes.

3. Stir in the garlic and chipotles and cook until fragrant, about 30 seconds. Stir in the chili powder and cook, stirring constantly, until fragrant, about 1 minute (do not let it burn). Stir in the broth, water, beans, sugar, baking soda, and bay leaves and bring to a simmer, skimming any impurities that rise to the surface. Cover, place the pot in the oven, and cook for 1 hour.

4. Stir in the crushed tomatoes and bell peppers, cover, and continue to cook in the oven until the beans are fully tender, about 1 hour longer. (If at any time the chili begins to stick to the bottom of the pot or look too thick, stir in additional water as needed.)

5. Remove the pot from the oven and remove the bay leaves. Stir in the cilantro, season with salt and pepper to taste, and serve with the lime wedges.

13

CURRIES AND TAGINES

CURRIES AND TAGINES

INDIAN-STYLE CHICKEN CURRY

THE TERM "CURRY" IS DERIVED FROM THE Tamil word *kari*, which simply means sauce or gravy. We tend to think of curry as a spiced yellow-colored meat and vegetable stew typically served over rice. But a curry can be most any type of stew, and as a result there are hundreds, perhaps thousands, of ways to make curry. They can come from any number of countries, although India is probably the country that people associate most with curry. We wanted to develop a recipe for an Indian-style yellow curry and set out to discover what separates good curry from bad curry. The mild, neutral flavor of chicken (commonly the choice of meat in curries) would be a good match for our boldly flavored curry sauce, but we'd have to make sure the tender meat stayed moist during the cooking process. And while we wanted an authentic-tasting curry, we didn't want it to consist of exotic, hard-to-find ingredients; we hoped to find a way to use supermarket staples.

As we quickly found out, there are many variables when making curry, including the types of spices used and whether they are whole or ground, the amounts of the aromatics, whether or not the meat is seared, and whether the curry contains some form of dairy (such as yogurt) or coconut milk.

While some curries are made with exotic whole and ground spices (fenugreek, asafetida, dried rose petals, and so on), we decided to limit ourselves to everyday ground spices such as cumin, cloves, cardamom, cinnamon, and coriander. Our testing dragged on for days, and it was hard to reach a consensus in the test kitchen. Frankly, most of the homemade spice mixtures we tried were fine.

We had been reluctant to use store-bought curry powder, assuming its flavor would be inferior to a homemade blend, but it seemed worth a try. We were surprised to find that tasters liked the store-bought curry powder nearly as well as a homemade mixture made with seven spices. It turns out that store-bought curry powder contains some of the exotic spices we had dismissed at the outset. As long as we used enough, our recipe had

good flavor. We cooked the curry powder in oil (a process known as blooming) to develop its flavors and infuse the cooking oil. This simple step took just a few seconds and turned commercial curry powder into a flavor powerhouse.

Finally, we experimented with garam masala, a spice blend often sprinkled onto Indian dishes before serving. Like curry powder, garam masala varies in ingredients but it usually includes warm spices such as black pepper, cinnamon, coriander, and cardamom (its name means "hot spice blend" in Hindi). Following our success with the curry powder, we decided to buy a jar of commercial garam masala. But when we added a few pinches to the cooked curry, the result was raw and harsh-tasting. What if we bloomed the garam masala along with the curry powder? Sure enough, the garam masala mellowed into a second wave of flavor that helped the curry reach an even more layered complexity.

With our flavor base of spices in place, we moved on to the aromatics. Garlic and ginger are an integral part of all curries (and of Indian cuisine in general) and we found that using a healthy amount of both was crucial to a well-rounded curry flavor. A little fresh minced jalapeño also boosted the flavor and added some heat. Many of the curries we tested included some form of tomato product, be it fresh chopped tomatoes, tomato sauce, or tomato paste. We tried each of these on their own and in combination with one another. Fresh tomatoes by themselves added the acidity the curry needed, but didn't offer a very deep flavor. Tomato sauce had an assertive tinny taste. Tomato paste supplied a sweet, roasted flavor when cooked with the onions. A combination of fresh tomatoes and tomato paste worked best. We added the tomato paste to the onions along with the garlic and ginger and stirred the fresh tomatoes in just before serving to preserve their texture.

As the curry was beginning to come together, we investigated whether it was essential to sear the chicken before it simmered in the sauce—some recipes we found did this, while others did not. We decided to use bone-in chicken pieces with the skin on and sear them, as this helped to contribute flavor to the sauce. Furthermore, we liked having the choice of white or dark meat (though you can certainly use all one or the other). Not surprisingly, the breasts cooked in a third of the time as the thighs, so we would have to stagger the cooking. Once the base curry sauce was simmering and ready for the chicken, we added only the thighs and cooked them for 40 minutes. At that point we added the breast meat and cooked the entire dish for an additional 20 minutes. All the meat was perfectly cooked at the same time.

As for the liquid component of the sauce, we were surprised to find that water did a fine job. We tried chicken broth, but given the complexity of our curry spices, we found that it was unnecessary (as well as untraditional). Most authentic curry recipes we researched also stir in yogurt or coconut milk with the water. Though we had trouble with both yogurt and coconut milk at the beginning of our testing, we found that if we added one of them at the end of cooking (to prevent curdling) and used less of it (so it didn't overwhelm the other flavors) it was the perfect finish to our curry. We slightly preferred the flavor of coconut milk, but yogurt makes for a lighter, yet still flavorful, sauce.

Finished with some green peas, a handful of minced cilantro, and a little butter to round out the sauce, our chicken curry boasted all the exotic flavor and aroma of authentic Indian cuisine.

INGREDIENTS: Curry Powder

Though blends can vary dramatically, curry powders come in two basic styles—mild or sweet and a hotter version called Madras. The former combines as many as 20 different ground spices, herbs, and seeds. Tasters sampled six curry powders, mixed into rice pilaf and in our vegetable curry. The winner was Penzeys Sweet Curry Powder, though Durkee Curry Powder came in a close second.

THE BEST CURRY POWDER

Neither too sweet nor too hot, this blend sets the standard with its "user-friendly balance" of "sweet" and "earthy" notes.

PENZEYS

Indian-Style Chicken Curry
SERVES 4 TO 6

For more heat, include the jalapeño seeds and ribs when mincing. If using both chicken breasts and thighs/drumsticks, we recommend cutting the breast pieces in half so that each serving can include both white and dark meat. We prefer the richer flavor of regular coconut milk here; however, light coconut milk can be substituted. For an even lighter curry, substitute ½ cup plain whole milk yogurt for the coconut milk; mix the yogurt with ¼ cup of the hot sauce to temper, then stir it into the curry off the heat just before serving. Serve with Simple Rice Pilaf (page 286) and Onion Relish (page 282) or Cilantro-Mint Chutney (page 282).

4	pounds bone-in, skin-on chicken pieces (split breasts cut in half, drumsticks, and/or thighs), trimmed (see note)
	Salt and ground black pepper
2	tablespoons vegetable oil, plus extra as needed
2	tablespoons curry powder
1	teaspoon garam masala
2	medium onions, minced
6	medium garlic cloves, minced or pressed through a garlic press (about 2 tablespoons)
1	jalapeño chile, stemmed, seeded, and minced (see note)
1	tablespoon minced or grated fresh ginger (see the illustrations on page 89)
1	tablespoon tomato paste
1	cup water
2	plum tomatoes, cored, seeded, and chopped fine
½	cup frozen peas
½	cup coconut milk (see note)
2	tablespoons unsalted butter
¼	cup minced fresh cilantro leaves

1. Pat the chicken dry with paper towels and season with salt and pepper. Heat 1 tablespoon of the oil in a large Dutch oven over medium-high heat until just smoking. Add half of the chicken

and cook until browned on both sides, 7 to 10 minutes. Transfer the chicken to a large plate. Repeat with the remaining 1 tablespoon oil and remaining chicken; transfer to the plate. (If using thighs and/or drumsticks, remove and discard the skin.)

2. Pour off all but 2 tablespoons of the fat left in the pot (or add more oil if necessary). Add the curry powder and garam masala and cook over medium heat until fragrant, about 10 seconds. Stir in the onions and ¼ teaspoon salt and cook until softened, 5 to 7 minutes. Stir in the garlic, chile, ginger, and tomato paste and cook until fragrant, about 30 seconds.

3. Gradually stir in the water, scraping up any browned bits. Nestle the browned chicken with any accumulated juice into the pot and bring to a simmer.

4. Cover, reduce to a gentle simmer, and cook until the chicken is fully cooked and tender, about 1 hour for the thighs and drumsticks (175 degrees on an instant-read thermometer) or 20 minutes for the breasts (160 to 165 degrees on an instant-read thermometer), turning the pieces over halfway through cooking. (If using both types of chicken, simmer the thighs and drumsticks for 40 minutes before adding the breasts.)

5. Transfer the chicken to a serving platter, tent loosely with foil, and let rest while finishing the sauce. Defat the braising liquid (see page 18; if necessary, return the defatted liquid to the pot and reheat).

6. Stir in the tomatoes, peas, coconut milk, and butter and simmer gently until the butter is melted and the vegetables are heated through, 1 to 2 minutes. Off the heat, stir in the cilantro and season with salt and pepper to taste. Spoon the sauce over the chicken and serve.

➤ VARIATIONS
Indian-Style Chicken Curry with Sweet Potatoes and Cauliflower
Follow the recipe for Indian-Style Chicken Curry, omitting the tomatoes and peas. Add 12 ounces sweet potato (about 1 medium), peeled and cut into 1-inch chunks, to the pot during the last

PREPARING CAULIFLOWER

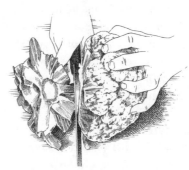

1. Start by pulling off the outer leaves and trimming off the stem near the base of the head.

2. Turn the cauliflower upside down so the stem is facing up. Using a sharp knife, cut around the core to remove it.

3. Using the tip of a chef's knife, separate the florets from the inner stem.

4. Cut the florets in half, or in quarters if necessary, so that individual pieces are the size specified in the recipe.

20 minutes of cooking in step 4 (with the breast pieces, if using). Stir ½ medium head cauliflower, trimmed, cored, and cut into 1-inch florets (about 4 cups) (see the illustrations on page 281), into the pot with the coconut milk and butter in step 6; cover and simmer until the cauliflower is tender, 10 to 12 minutes.

Indian-Style Chicken Curry with Red Potatoes and Green Beans

Follow the recipe for Indian-Style Chicken Curry, omitting the tomatoes and peas. Add 12 ounces red potatoes (2 to 3 medium), scrubbed and cut into ½-inch chunks, to the pot during the last 20 minutes of cooking in step 4 (with the breast pieces, if using). Stir 8 ounces green beans, trimmed and cut into 1-inch lengths, into the pot with the coconut milk and butter in step 6; cover and simmer until the beans are tender, 10 to 12 minutes.

INDIAN-STYLE VEGETABLE CURRY

IN INDIA, VEGETABLE-BASED CURRIES ARE every bit as popular as those that contain poultry or meat. But vegetable curries can be complicated affairs, with lengthy ingredient lists and fussy techniques meant to compensate for the lack of meat. We wanted something simpler—a curry we could make on a weeknight in less than an hour. We imagined a satisfying curry with robust spices, amplified vegetable flavors, and a clean and balanced sauce.

Though some curries are made with homemade spice blends or obscure spices, we knew from our chicken curry (see page 280) that store-bought curry powder and garam masala would contribute ample complexity and depth of flavor—if treated properly. We began with the same amounts that we used in our chicken curry, 2 tablespoons curry powder and 1 teaspoon garam masala, which we

---

ACCOMPANIMENTS FOR INDIAN-STYLE CURRY

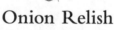

Onion Relish

MAKES ABOUT I CUP

If using a regular yellow onion, increase the amount of sugar to 1 teaspoon.

I	medium Vidalia onion, minced (see note)
I	tablespoon juice from I lime
½	teaspoon sweet paprika
½	teaspoon sugar
⅛	teaspoon salt
	Pinch cayenne pepper

Mix all the ingredients together in a medium bowl. (The relish can be refrigerated in an airtight container for 1 day.)

Cilantro-Mint Chutney

MAKES ABOUT I CUP

We prefer the richer flavor of whole milk yogurt here; however, low-fat yogurt or nonfat yogurt can be substituted.

2	cups packed fresh cilantro leaves
I	cup packed fresh mint leaves
⅓	cup plain whole milk yogurt
¼	cup minced onion
I	tablespoon juice from I lime
I½	teaspoons sugar
½	teaspoon ground cumin
¼	teaspoon salt

Process all the ingredients together in a food processor until smooth, about 20 seconds, scraping down the sides of the bowl as needed. (The chutney can be refrigerated in an airtight container for up to 1 day.)

bloomed in oil. Unfortunately, tasters complained that the flavor of the curry dominated the flavor of the vegetables, while the garam masala was barely noticeable—it seemed that the sweet, vegetal tones of our meatless curry needed more warm spice notes (from the garam masala) and less bold, potent notes (from the curry). Ultimately, after numerous tests, we found that 4 teaspoons of curry powder and 1½ teaspoons of garam masala ensured a curry with well-rounded flavor.

With the spices settled, we turned to the rest of our flavor base. Sautéed onion added depth and body, as did equal amounts of garlic and ginger. A spoonful of tomato paste contributed sweetness, and minced fresh serrano chile provided some heat.

Now we considered other ingredients that would add heartiness and make our vegetable curry substantial and filling. Potatoes were a given, but beans, especially chickpeas, were also common in Indian cuisine. We found that for the chickpeas, a single can was sufficient; it didn't make sense to cook dried chickpeas for our simple vegetable curry. After testing different types of potatoes, tasters ultimately preferred red potatoes (with the skins left on), which maintained their shape in the finished dish. Cauliflower and peas are also a classic pairing in curries; we saw no reason to break with tradition, and stirred in half a head of cauliflower before adding the liquid, and some frozen peas toward the end of the cooking time. While the combination of textures in our curry was good, the vegetables themselves were a bit bland.

In most meat or chicken stews and in our chicken curry, we begin by browning the meat, which leads to the development of a flavorful fond (browned bits) on the bottom of the pan; these browned bits then permeate the cooking liquid, leading to a richly flavored sauce. We wondered if treating some of our vegetables in a similar fashion would work the same way. We started with the onions; instead of sautéing them, we browned them for about 10 minutes, which enabled a fond to form and exponentially increased flavor. However, the bulk of our vegetables were still lacking in flavor. Next, we tried browning the potatoes with the onions. This unconventional move was an unqualified success, substantially boosting the flavor

INGREDIENTS: Coconut Milk

Coconut milk is not the thin liquid found inside the coconut itself; that is called coconut water. Coconut milk is a product made by steeping equal parts shredded coconut meat and either warm milk or water. The meat is pressed or mashed to release as much liquid as possible, the mixture is strained, and the result is coconut milk.

We tasted seven nationally available brands (five regular and two light) in curry, Thai Chicken Soup (page 85), coconut rice, and coconut pudding. Among the five regular brands, tasters gravitated to those with more solid cream at the top of the can (most cans recommend shaking before opening to redistribute the solids). These brands also had a much stronger coconut flavor. In the soup and curry, tasters preferred Chaokoh because of its exceptionally low sugar content (less than 1 gram per ⅓ cup). By comparison, brands with more than twice as much sugar tasted "saccharine." In the sweet recipes, tasters gave velvety Ka-Me top votes for its "fruity" and "complex" flavor. In these recipes, the extra sugar was an advantage. The light coconut milks we tasted were not nearly as creamy—a serious flaw in desserts but less so in soup. Of the two light brands tasted, we preferred the richer flavor of A Taste of Thai.

THE BEST COCONUT MILK

Chaokoh, with its superior smooth texture, is our favorite coconut milk for curry and soup.

CHAOKOH

of the potatoes and creating additional fond that deepened the flavor of the dish.

We wondered if any of the other vegetables would benefit from special treatment. An Indian cooking method we researched called *bhuna* involves sautéing the spices and main ingredients together to enhance and meld flavors. We tried this technique with the cauliflower and, sure enough, it developed a richer, more complex flavor. (Eggplant and green beans also took well to this method and so became a variation.)

Lastly, we tweaked the liquid in the sauce. Up until now we had been using water, which is the traditional choice; also, it allows the other flavors in the dish to shine through. However, tasters commented that the sauce could use more body and a brighter flavor. Tomato paste added a nice sweetness and hint of acidity, so we tested additional tomato products that might further our cause. It turned out that canned diced tomatoes offered assertive flavor and more acidity to the dish. We decided to process them briefly in a food processor so that they would smoothly integrate into the sauce.

Finishing the dish with coconut milk unified the flavors of the sauce. In the end, we had managed to create a quick vegetable curry that was so satisfying and hearty, even the meat lovers in the test kitchen were asking for seconds.

Indian-Style Vegetable Curry with Potatoes and Cauliflower

SERVES 4 TO 6

For more heat, include the chile seeds and ribs when mincing. We prefer the richer flavor of regular coconut milk here; however, light coconut milk can be substituted. For an even lighter curry, substitute ½ cup plain whole milk yogurt for the coconut milk; mix the yogurt with ¼ cup of the hot sauce to temper, then stir it into the curry off the heat just before serving. Serve with Simple Rice Pilaf (page 286) and Onion Relish (page 282) or Cilantro-Mint Chutney (page 282).

1	(14.5-ounce) can diced tomatoes
3	tablespoons vegetable oil
4	teaspoons curry powder
1½	teaspoons garam masala
2	medium onions, minced
12	ounces red potatoes (2 to 3 medium), scrubbed and cut into ½-inch chunks
	Salt and ground black pepper
3	medium garlic cloves, minced or pressed through a garlic press (about 1 tablespoon)
1	serrano chile, stemmed, seeded, and minced (see note)
1	tablespoon minced or grated fresh ginger (see the illustrations on page 89)
1	tablespoon tomato paste
½	medium head cauliflower, trimmed, cored, and cut into 1-inch florets (about 4 cups) (see the illustrations on page 281)

1½	cups water
1	(15-ounce) can chickpeas, drained and rinsed
1½	cups frozen peas
½	cup coconut milk (see note)
¼	cup minced fresh cilantro leaves

1. Pulse the diced tomatoes with their juice in a food processor until nearly smooth with ¼-inch pieces visible, about 3 pulses; set aside.

2. Heat the oil in a large Dutch oven over medium-high heat until shimmering. Add the curry powder and garam masala and cook until fragrant, about 10 seconds. Stir in the onions, potatoes, and ¼ teaspoon salt and cook, stirring occasionally, until the onions are browned and the potatoes are golden brown at the edges, about 10 minutes.

3. Reduce the heat to medium. Stir in the garlic, chile, ginger, and tomato paste and cook until fragrant, about 30 seconds. Add the cauliflower and cook, stirring constantly, until the florets are coated with the spices, about 2 minutes.

4. Gradually stir in the water, scraping up any browned bits. Stir in the chickpeas and processed tomatoes and bring to a simmer. Cover, reduce to a gentle simmer, and cook until the vegetables are tender, 20 to 25 minutes.

5. Uncover, stir in the peas and coconut milk, and continue to cook until the peas are heated through, 1 to 2 minutes. Off the heat, stir in the cilantro, season with salt and pepper to taste, and serve.

➤ VARIATION

Indian-Style Vegetable Curry with Sweet Potatoes and Eggplant

Follow the recipe for Indian-Style Vegetable Curry with Potatoes and Cauliflower, omitting the peas and substituting 12 ounces sweet potato (about 1 medium), peeled and cut into 1-inch chunks, for the red potatoes. Substitute 8 ounces green beans, trimmed and cut into 1-inch lengths, and 1 medium eggplant (about 1 pound), cut into ½-inch pieces, for the cauliflower.

PORK VINDALOO

VINDALOO IS A COMPLEX, SPICY DISH THAT originated in Goa, a region on India's western coast. Because Goa was once a Portuguese colony, much of the local cuisine incorporates Indian and Portuguese ingredients and techniques. In fact, the word vindaloo comes from the Portuguese words for wine vinegar (*vinho*) and garlic (*alhos*). In addition to these two ingredients, vindaloo gets its warm, pungent flavor from a mixture of spices (such as cumin and cardamom), chiles (usually in the form of cayenne and paprika), tomatoes, and mustard seeds. As for the main ingredient, although there are versions made with other types of meat (such as lamb and chicken), vindaloo is most often made with pork.

A well-prepared vindaloo features tender meat in a thick, reddish-orange sauce with a delicately balanced flavor. The heat of the chiles is tamed by the sweetness of the aromatic spices and the acidity of the tomatoes and vinegar. Onions and garlic add pungency, while the mustard seeds lend their unique flavor and crunch. Though some vindaloos can be mouth-searingly hot, we preferred to create a dish with softer flavors—focusing more on the deep blend of spices and not on excessive heat level.

Most vindaloo recipes we tested were pretty good but we noticed two recurring problems—tough and/or dry meat and muddied flavors. We decided to start with the meat component in this dish and then focus on the flavoring options.

Given our experience preparing pork stews, we figured that pork shoulder would make the best vindaloo, as it has enough fat to keep the meat tender and juicy during the long cooking process. Pork shoulder is often called Boston butt or Boston shoulder in markets. The picnic roast also comes from the shoulder. For vindaloo, a boneless Boston butt is your best option because there is less waste. (You can use a picnic roast, but the bone, skin, and thick layer of fat will need to be discarded.) As with our other meat and pork stews, we opted to purchase a boneless roast and cut it into pieces ourselves. When we purchased precut pork labeled

"stew meat," the results were disappointing. The pieces were irregularly sized and seemed to have come from several parts of the animal. The resulting stew had pieces that were dry and overcooked. After cutting our roast into 1½-inch chunks, we browned it to enhance its flavor and that of the stewing liquid. We left a little room in the pot between the pieces of meat and cooked them for at least seven minutes to get each pork cube well browned.

Spices are the cornerstone of this stew. We used a classic combination of sweet and hot spices and found that we got the best flavor from small amounts of many spices, rather than larger amounts of fewer spices. For chile flavor, we used sweet paprika and cayenne. To give the stew its characteristic earthy qualities, we added cumin, along with sweet, aromatic cardamom and cloves. Mustard seeds, a spice used frequently in the cooking of South India, added pungency. Bay leaves rounded out the flavor of this stew and a sprinkling of cilantro just before serving lent the final fresh note.

Our next area of concern was the stewing liquid. Most traditional recipes simply use water. The theory is that water is a neutral medium that allows the flavors of the meat and spices to come through as clearly as possible. We wondered, though, if chicken broth would add richness and body to the stewing liquid. We prepared two batches—one with water, the other with chicken broth. Tasters felt that the chicken broth added complexity and fullness without calling attention to itself.

A hallmark of pork vindaloo is its interplay of sweet and sour flavors. Two tablespoons of red wine vinegar and 1 teaspoon of sugar provided the right balance. In order to give it time to soften and mix with the other flavors, we added the vinegar at the beginning of cooking. For further acidity, canned diced tomatoes, with their juice, were far less work than fresh tomatoes (which needed to be peeled and seeded) and performed admirably in taste tests.

Pleased with the pork vindaloo recipe we had created we turned our attention to developing variations with lamb and chicken. Substituting a boneless lamb shoulder roast (of equal weight) for the pork shoulder worked well. The lamb cooked in the same amount of time as the pork, and the complex spices in the sauce balanced its slightly gamey taste. Chicken, with its mild flavor, was also a nice match for the spices in the vindaloo. Tasters preferred the richer, more tender dark meat (we used boneless thighs), which cooked in about half the time as the pork and lamb. Our Indian pork stew had lent itself to two additional recipes that were just as flavorful and just as easy.

Simple Rice Pilaf

SERVES 4

This recipe works with regular long-grain, basmati, and jasmine rice. Be sure to rinse the rice until the water runs clear. A nonstick saucepan is crucial to prevent the wet rice from sticking to the pot; for the most evenly cooked rice, be sure to use a wide-bottomed saucepan with a tight-fitting lid.

3	tablespoons unsalted butter
½	cup minced onion
	Salt and ground black pepper
1½	cups long-grain white rice (see note), rinsed (see the illustration on page 250)
2½	cups boiling water

1. Melt the butter in a large nonstick saucepan over medium heat. Add the onion and 1 teaspoon salt and cook until softened, 5 to 7 minutes.

2. Stir in the rinsed rice and cook until the edges begin to turn translucent, about 3 minutes. Stir in the boiling water and return to a boil. Reduce to a low simmer, cover, and cook until all the water is absorbed, 16 to 18 minutes.

3. Remove the pot from the heat. Lay a clean kitchen towel over the saucepan, underneath the lid, and let stand for 10 minutes. Fluff the rice with a fork, season with salt and pepper to taste, and serve.

Pork Vindaloo

SERVES 6

Boneless pork butt roast is often labeled as boneless Boston butt in the supermarket. Serve with Simple Rice Pilaf.

1	(3½- to 4-pound) boneless pork butt roast, trimmed and cut into 1½-inch pieces (see note)
	Salt and ground black pepper
3	tablespoons vegetable oil
3	medium onions, minced
8	medium garlic cloves, minced or pressed through a garlic press (about 8 teaspoons)
1	tablespoon sweet paprika
¾	teaspoon ground cumin
½	teaspoon ground cardamom
¼	teaspoon cayenne pepper
¼	teaspoon ground cloves
3	tablespoons unbleached all-purpose flour
1½	cups low-sodium chicken broth
1	(14.5-ounce) can diced tomatoes
2	tablespoons red wine vinegar
1	tablespoon mustard seeds
2	bay leaves
1	teaspoon sugar
¼	cup minced fresh cilantro leaves

1. Adjust an oven rack to the lower-middle position and heat the oven to 325 degrees. Pat the pork dry with paper towels and season with salt and pepper. Heat 1 tablespoon of the oil in a large Dutch oven over medium-high heat until just smoking. Add half of the pork and brown well on all sides, 7 to 10 minutes; transfer to a medium bowl. Repeat with 1 tablespoon more oil and the remaining pork; transfer to the bowl.

2. Add the remaining 1 tablespoon oil to the pot and return to medium heat until shimmering. Add the onions and ¼ teaspoon salt and cook, stirring occasionally, until softened, 5 to 7 minutes. Stir in the garlic, paprika, cumin, cardamom, cayenne, and cloves and cook until fragrant, about 30 seconds. Stir in the flour and cook for 1 minute.

3. Gradually whisk in the broth, scraping up any browned bits and smoothing out any lumps. Stir

in the tomatoes with their juice, vinegar, mustard seeds, bay leaves, sugar, and browned pork with any accumulated juice and bring to a simmer. Cover, place the pot in the oven, and cook until the meat is tender, about 2 hours.

4. Remove the stew from the oven and remove the bay leaves. Stir in the cilantro, season with salt and pepper to taste, and serve.

➤ VARIATIONS

Lamb Vindaloo
Follow the recipe for Pork Vindaloo, substituting 1 (3½- to 4-pound) boneless lamb shoulder roast, trimmed and cut into 1½-inch pieces, for the pork; brown and cook the meat as directed.

Chicken Vindaloo
Follow the recipe for Pork Vindaloo, substituting 3 pounds boneless chicken thighs (about 12 thighs), trimmed and cut into 1½-inch pieces, for the pork; brown and cook the chicken as directed, reducing the oven time to 1 hour in step 3.

INGREDIENTS: Basmati Rice

Prized for its nutty flavor and perfume-like aroma, basmati rice is eaten worldwide in pilafs and as an accompaniment to curries. Most Indian-grown rice comes from the Himalaya foothills, where the snow-flooded soil and humid climate offer ideal growing conditions. Choosing among the multitude of boxes, bags, and burlap sacks available today on supermarket shelves can be confusing. To find a truly great grain, we steamed seven brands, five from India and two domestic options. Matched against Indian imports, domestic brands Lundberg and Della suffered. They were less aromatic and the grains didn't elongate as much. Their overall texture was mushy, too. While all of the imported brands were acceptable, tasters overwhelmingly chose the longest sample—Tilda—as their favorite.

THE BEST BASMATI RICE
Indian-grown Tilda Pure Basmati Rice was tasters' top choice. It was praised for its "beautiful long grains," "slightly nutty" flavor, and "strong aroma."

TILDA

THAI-STYLE CURRY

WHILE INDIAN CURRIES MIGHT RELY ON A simple mix of dried spices for potent, aromatic flavor, Thai curries depend on a paste, usually consisting of garlic, ginger, shallots, lemon grass, kaffir lime leaves, shrimp paste, and chiles, for flavor. These curry pastes can be quite involved, requiring a good amount of time (up to an hour of preparation) and a well-stocked pantry (or refrigerator). The good news is that the curries themselves come together rather quickly and simmer gently for a short amount of time. Like Indian curries, they frequently contain coconut milk, which not only blends and carries flavors but also forms the base of the sauce. We set out to simplify the curry paste and create a streamlined Thai curry recipe that could be easily adapted to allow different types of meat and seafood to take center stage.

In many recipes, curry paste is only used in small amounts so store-bought paste is a good option, but here it is the backbone of the dish and the difference in flavor is well worth the time and effort to prepare it from scratch. We set out to explore the two most common types of Thai curries: green curry and red curry. We wanted to understand the basic structure of these dishes and figure out ways to make them—and all their hard-to-find ingredients—accessible to the American home cook. In doing so, we would need to find substitutes for some ingredients, such as kaffir lime leaves and shrimp paste, which are not readily available in most American supermarkets.

Our work was divided into three neat areas: developing recipes for the pastes; cooking the pastes to draw out their flavor; and incorporating the protein into the curry. We started with the pastes.

Thai curry pastes are intensely flavored. They are used in stir-fries, soups, and sauces as well as curries. Traditionally, ingredients are pounded together in a mortar and pestle to form a smooth paste. Since this process can take up to an hour and requires a tool most American cooks don't own, we wanted to develop paste recipes that could be assembled by other means. We tested a blender and a food processor, but the lack of liquid in the curry paste presented a problem. The solution was to add some liquid. Once the liquid was added (we'd have to settle on the choice of liquid later), the blender became our preferred paste maker.

Focusing first on green curry, we noted that fresh green Thai chiles are the basis for most green curry pastes. These tiny chiles are less than an inch long and offer an intriguing balance of heat and floral flavors. They can be difficult to find so we tested several substitutions and found that serranos and jalapeños are the best candidates.

Shallots, garlic, and ginger are constants in most curry pastes. After testing various ratios, we concluded that green curry paste was best with high amounts of garlic and a few shallots, as well as a generous dose of ginger, to achieve the right balance of flavors.

Toasted and ground coriander seeds, as well as fresh coriander root, are other common additions to curry pastes. We found that cilantro leaves (the name commonly used for the leaves of the coriander plant) are too moist and floral to use as a substitute for the roots but that cilantro stems are fine. The stems are fairly dry and have a pungent, earthy flavor that's similar to the roots.

Lemon grass is an essential ingredient in Thai curry and we were happy to discover that it is relatively easy to find. We did find a substitute for galangal, a rhizome related to ginger that's both peppery and sour: A combination of fresh ginger and lime juice added the necessary hot and sour notes in this instance. We found that adding the lime juice directly to the finished curry rather than to the curry paste best preserves its flavor.

Kaffir lime leaves have a clean, floral flavor, which many tasters compare to lemon verbena. We found that lime zest approximates this flavor.

Shrimp paste—a puree of salted, fermented shrimp and other seasonings—adds a salty, fishy note to Thai curry pastes. Since this ingredient is very hard to find, we searched for substitutes. Anchovy paste was a reasonable solution, but adding fish sauce directly to the curry is traditional and adds the same kind of subtle fishy flavor (see page 74 for more information on fish sauce), so we opted to use it instead, adding it to the pan later on.

With our green curry paste ingredients in order, we turned our attention to the red curry paste.

Red curry paste relies on a similar assortment of ingredients as green curry paste, although dried red Thai chiles, rather than fresh, are used. (Though dried red Thai chiles are traditional, de árbol chiles work well too.) The dried chiles are usually soaked in hot water until softened, but we found that we could get more flavor out of the chiles if we toasted them and then tossed them in the blender dry (they rehydrate with the moisture in the blender). The pastes made with dried chiles alone seemed thin, so we relied on a mixture of toasted dried chiles and fresh red jalapeños. This combination provided a more satisfying combination of flavor and body.

We were now satisfied with the base flavors for our green and red curry pastes, but we needed to identify the liquid component that would help our ingredients come together to form a paste. In our research, coconut milk and oil were two of the more common options. We added each one to a blender with the other curry ingredients to determine which would form the smoothest paste. The coconut milk subdued the potent flavors of the curry paste. The oil, on the other hand, didn't compete with the curry flavors, and it made for a smooth paste. But we had to use a fair amount of it in order to achieve that smooth texture. By adding some water, however, we were able to reduce the amount of oil to 2 tablespoons, resulting in a less greasy sauce. The flavors of the curry now came through strong and clear.

We moved on to the other components of the dish—the meat and vegetables. We decided to use chicken for our master recipe and offer beef and shrimp as variations. Common additions for vegetables include pea eggplant, breadfruit, bamboo shoots, young jackfruit, banana blossoms, and pumpkin tendrils. All except the bamboo shoots were difficult to find. We had noted that it wasn't unusual to have a curry with only protein, especially with such a hefty amount of herbs that would be added later on. Indeed, tasters liked the simplicity of a chicken-only curry.

With the meat decided upon, we looked at the cooking method. The best option was to add water to the paste mixture (along with a little fish sauce and brown sugar) after it cooked and poach

HOMEMADE THAI CURRY PASTE

MAKING A CURRY PASTE IS AN IMPORTANT FIRST STEP WHEN MAKING ANY NUMBER OF authentic Thai dishes, including Thai curry. You can find store-bought Thai curry pastes at the supermarket, but we only like to use them in small amounts to add extra flavor to a sauce or soup (as in our Thai Chicken Soup, page 85). When making an actual Thai curry, these store-bought curry pastes fall flat. Luckily, making a homemade Thai curry paste is a snap; it requires only a blender and most of the ingredients can be found at a well-stocked supermarket. Our green curry paste has a fresh, spicy, and slightly floral flavor, while our red curry paste tastes deeper, smokier, and slightly hotter.

Thai Green Curry Paste

MAKES ENOUGH FOR I RECIPE THAI CURRY

We strongly prefer the flavor of Thai chiles here; however, serrano and jalapeño chiles are decent substitutes. For more heat, include the chile seeds and ribs when mincing.

⅓ cup water
3   medium shallots, peeled and quartered
12 fresh green Thai, serrano, or jalapeño chiles, stemmed, seeded, and minced (see note)
8   medium garlic cloves, peeled
2   stalks lemon grass, bottom 5 inches only, minced (see the illustrations on page 85)
2   tablespoons minced cilantro stems
2   tablespoons grated zest from 2 limes
2   tablespoons vegetable oil
1   tablespoon minced or grated fresh ginger (see the illustrations on page 89)
2   teaspoons ground coriander
1   teaspoon ground cumin
1   teaspoon salt

Process all the ingredients together in a blender to a fine paste, about 3 minutes, scraping down the sides of the blender as needed. (The curry paste can be refrigerated in an airtight container for up to 1 day.)

Thai Red Curry Paste

MAKES ENOUGH FOR I RECIPE THAI CURRY

If you can't find fresh red jalapeño chiles, you can substitute green jalapeños but the color of the sauce will turn slightly muddy. For more heat, include the jalapeño seeds and ribs when mincing.

8   dried red chiles, such as Thai or de árbol, toasted and ground (see page 270)
⅓ cup water
4   medium shallots, peeled and quartered
6   medium garlic cloves, peeled
2   stalks lemon grass, bottom 5 inches only, minced (see the illustrations on page 85)
1   red jalapeño chile, stemmed, seeded, and minced (see note)
2   tablespoons minced cilantro stems
2   tablespoons vegetable oil
1   tablespoon grated zest from 1 lime
2   teaspoons ground coriander
1   teaspoon ground cumin
1   teaspoon salt
1   teaspoon minced or grated fresh ginger (see the illustrations on page 89)
1   teaspoon tomato paste

Process all the ingredients together in a blender to a fine paste, about 3 minutes, scraping down the sides of the blender as needed. (The curry paste can be refrigerated in an airtight container for up to 1 day.)

the meat in the liquid. For our chicken curry, we opted for boneless, skinless chicken breasts, which worked well with the light, bright sauce. We tested cutting the chicken in different shapes, but tasters unanimously preferred shredded chicken. This was simple enough to achieve; we removed the chicken once it was fully cooked and then shredded it when it was cool enough to handle. Then we returned the chicken to the sauce, finishing it with coconut milk for a luxuriously smooth texture. For our beef variation, we found blade steak to be the best option—it lends itself well to the cooking method and remains tender and flavorful. Shrimp is a quick and easy substitute for both the chicken and beef, requiring just a few minutes of simmering time to cook through.

Once the curry was finished, a final garnish of fresh Thai basil, cilantro, and lime juice completed the dish. Our Thai curries were both saucy and hot, and perfectly complemented by a scoop of rice pilaf.

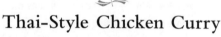

Thai-Style Chicken Curry

SERVES 4

We like to use large chicken breasts here because they fit more easily into the skillet. If your chicken breasts are smaller, try to fit them in the pan in a single layer; smaller chicken breasts will have a shorter cooking time. If you can't find Thai basil leaves, substitute regular basil. Serve with Simple Rice Pilaf (page 286).

I	recipe Thai Green Curry Paste or Thai Red Curry Paste (page 289)
I¼	cups water
2	tablespoons fish sauce (see page 74)
I	tablespoon light brown sugar
I½	pounds boneless, skinless chicken breasts (about 4 breasts), trimmed
I	(14-ounce) can coconut milk
½	cup loosely packed fresh Thai basil leaves (see note)
½	cup loosely packed fresh cilantro leaves
2	tablespoons juice from I lime

1. Cook the curry paste in a 12-inch nonstick skillet over medium-high heat, stirring often, until the paste begins to sizzle and no longer smells raw, about 2 minutes. Stir in the water, fish sauce, and sugar and bring to a simmer.

2. Add the chicken and return to a simmer. Flip the chicken over, cover, and cook until the chicken registers 160 to 165 degrees on an instant-read thermometer, 15 to 20 minutes.

3. Remove the chicken from the pan, let cool slightly, then shred the meat into bite-size pieces (see the illustration on page 43). Meanwhile, stir the coconut milk into the skillet, return the sauce to a simmer, and cook until the sauce is thick and creamy, about 8 minutes.

4. Return the shredded chicken to the skillet and let it heat through, about 2 minutes. Off the heat, stir in the basil, cilantro, and lime juice and serve.

➤ VARIATIONS

Thai-Style Beef Curry

To make slicing the steak easier, freeze it for 15 minutes.

Follow the recipe for Thai-Style Chicken Curry, substituting 1½ pounds blade steak, trimmed (see the illustrations on page 291), and sliced lengthwise into ½-inch-thick pieces, for the chicken. Increase the amount of water to 2 cups and simmer the beef as directed in step 2 until tender, about 40 minutes. When the beef is tender, add the coconut milk and continue to simmer and thicken the sauce as directed in step 3.

Thai-Style Shrimp Curry

Follow the recipe for Thai-Style Chicken Curry, omitting the chicken. Add the coconut milk to the skillet with the water, fish sauce, and sugar in step 1; simmer the sauce, uncovered, until thick and creamy, about 10 minutes. Stir in 1 pound medium shrimp (40 to 50 per pound), peeled and deveined (see the illustration on page 169), and continue to simmer until the shrimp are fully cooked, about 5 minutes. When the shrimp are cooked, remove the skillet from the heat, stir in the basil, cilantro, and lime juice and serve.

TRIMMING BLADE STEAKS

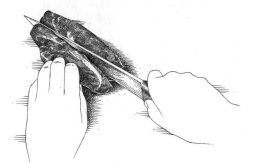

1. Halve each steak lengthwise, leaving the gristle on one half.

2. Cut away the gristle from the half to which it is still attached.

CHICKEN TAGINE

TAGINES ARE A NORTH AFRICAN SPECIALTY— exotically spiced, assertively flavored stews that are slow-cooked in earthenware vessels of the same name. They can include all manner of meats, vegetables, and fruit, but we set our sights on a tagine that included moist, tender chicken, complemented by richly flavored figs and fragrant honey.

While we love tagine, it's not a dish we ever thought was suited for American home cooking. Why? The few traditional recipes we had seen required time-consuming, labor-intensive cooking methods, a special pot (the tagine), and hard-to-find ingredients. We're usually game for a day in the kitchen or a hunt for exotica, but isn't tagine, at its most elemental level, just stew?

A little research proved that we weren't the first to take a stab at making tagine more accessible. While most of the recipes we tried lacked the

depth of an authentic tagine, they did hold promise, proving that a Western cooking method (braising in a Dutch oven) was a serviceable substitution for stewing for hours in a tagine. We also discovered that the flavors we associated with Moroccan cooking weren't necessarily "exotic" or hard to come by—they were a strategic blending of ingredients we already had in our cupboard.

Almost all of the recipes we collected for chicken tagine specified a whole chicken, broken into pieces, and we soon found out why. Batches made entirely with white meat lacked the depth and character of those made with both dark and white. But when we cooked the white and dark meat the same way—simmered partially submerged in broth—the white meat turned dry and stringy.

Noting that the dark meat—drumsticks and thighs—takes roughly one hour of simmering time to become tender, we found that the breasts (cut in half for easier serving) took only 20 minutes. Giving the dark meat a 40-minute head start in the pot took care of the different cooking times and ensured that all of the chicken was perfectly cooked and ready at the same time.

A couple of carrots, a couple of onions, and several minced garlic cloves rounded out the basic flavors of the stew, and we finally felt ready to tackle the defining ingredients: spices, figs, and honey. Many recipes called for a spice blend called *ras el hanout*, which translates loosely as "head of the shop" and is a proprietary blend of a spice seller's top spices (we've seen blends that contained up to 30 spices). We experimented with a broad range of spices until we landed on a blend that was short on ingredients but long on flavor. Cumin and ginger lent depth, cinnamon brought warmth that tempered a little cayenne heat, and coriander boosted the stew's lemon flavor (which we had yet to finalize). Paprika added sweetness but, perhaps more important, colored the broth a deep, attractive red. Thoroughly blooming the spices in hot oil brought out the full depth of their flavors.

Finding the right fig proved harder than we anticipated. Sweet, fresh, juicy figs were the obvious choice for the stew, but they are seasonal and thus a rarity at our local markets. Other options included various dried figs, and, after tasting several varieties in the tagine, we concluded that Turkish figs were our favorite type. Stirring them in just before serving helped them retain their flavor and texture.

The lemon flavor in authentic tagines comes from preserved lemon, a long-cured Moroccan condiment that's hard to find outside of specialty stores. "Quick" preserved lemons can be produced at home in a few days, but we wanted to keep our recipe as simple as possible. Part tart citrus, part pickled brine, traditional preserved lemon has a unique flavor that's tough to imitate. So we chose not to try; instead, we aimed for a rich citrus backbone in the dish. We added two broad ribbons of lemon zest along with the onions to the pot; the high heat coaxed out the zest's oils and mellowed them. Adding a few tablespoons of lemon juice just before serving reinforced the bright flavor.

For the honey, we found that adding a tablespoon with the broth rounded out the flavors of the spices and citrus. Minced cilantro leaves freshened the flavors of the stew at the end, but we felt it still lacked a certain spark. A last-minute addition of raw garlic (mashed to a paste), grated lemon zest, and a second spoonful of honey seemed to clinch it, as the sharpness and sweetness brought out the best in each of the stew's components.

With a streamlined yet authentically flavored chicken tagine in our repertoire, we looked to create a lamb tagine with boldly flavored ingredients that would stand up to this rich meat. Right away, we decided to swap the figs and honey for sweet dried apricots and briny olives. Boneless lamb shoulder provided tender, succulent bites in the finished stew. As for the olives, big, green Moroccan olives were the obvious choice, but they were hard to find at our local supermarkets; Greek "cracked" olives, however, tasted great and were easy to find. Stirring in the olives and chopped dried apricots at the end of the simmering time ensured that they retained their flavor and texture. Served over couscous, our tagines provide all the bold and exotic flavors of North African cuisine.

Chicken Tagine with Dried Figs and Honey
SERVES 4 TO 6

If using both chicken breasts and thighs/drumsticks, we recommend cutting the breast pieces in half so that each serving can include both white and dark meat. We prefer the soft texture of Turkish or Calimyrna figs; however, Mission figs can be substituted. Serve with Simple Couscous (page 295).

4	pounds bone-in, skin-on chicken pieces (split breasts cut in half, drumsticks, and/or thighs), trimmed (see note) Salt and ground black pepper
2	tablespoons olive oil, plus extra as needed
2	medium onions, halved and sliced pole to pole into ¼-inch-thick pieces (see the illustration on page 105)
2	(2-inch-long) strips zest from 1 lemon (see the illustration on page 148), trimmed of white pith
4	medium garlic cloves, minced or pressed through a garlic press (about 4 teaspoons), plus 1 medium garlic clove, mashed to a fine paste (see the illustrations on page 102)
1¼	teaspoons sweet paprika
½	teaspoon ground cumin
¼	teaspoon ground ginger
¼	teaspoon ground coriander
¼	teaspoon ground cinnamon
⅛	teaspoon cayenne pepper
2	cups low-sodium chicken broth
2	carrots, peeled and sliced ½ inch thick
2	tablespoons honey
1	cup dried Turkish or Calimyrna figs, stemmed and quartered (see note) (see the illustration on page 294)
½	teaspoon grated zest and 3 tablespoons juice from 1 lemon
2	tablespoons minced fresh cilantro leaves

1. Pat the chicken dry with paper towels and season with salt and pepper. Heat 1 tablespoon of the oil in a large Dutch oven over medium-high heat until just smoking. Add half of the chicken and cook until browned on both sides, 7 to 10 minutes. Transfer the chicken to a large plate. Repeat with the remaining 1 tablespoon oil and remaining chicken; transfer to the plate. (If using thighs and/or drumsticks, remove and discard the skin.)

2. Pour off all but 1 tablespoon of the fat left in the pot (or add more oil if necessary). Add the onions, lemon zest strips, and ¼ teaspoon salt and cook over medium heat until the onions are softened, 5 to 7 minutes. Stir in the minced garlic, paprika, cumin, ginger, coriander, cinnamon, and cayenne and cook until fragrant, about 30 seconds.

3. Gradually stir in the broth, scraping up any browned bits. Stir in the carrots and 1 tablespoon of the honey. Nestle the browned chicken with any accumulated juice into the pot and bring to a simmer.

4. Cover, reduce to a gentle simmer, and cook until the chicken is fully cooked and tender, about 1 hour for the thighs and drumsticks (175 degrees on an instant-read thermometer) or 20 minutes for the breasts (160 to 165 degrees on an instant-read thermometer), turning the pieces over halfway through cooking. (If using both types of chicken, simmer the thighs and drumsticks for 40 minutes before adding the breasts.)

5. Transfer the chicken to a serving platter, tent loosely with foil, and let rest while finishing the sauce. Remove the lemon zest strips, then defat the braising liquid (see page 18; if necessary, return the defatted liquid to the pot and reheat).

6. Stir in the figs and simmer gently until the figs are heated through, about 5 minutes. Off the heat, stir in the garlic paste, remaining 1 tablespoon honey, grated lemon zest and juice, and cilantro. Season the sauce with salt and pepper to taste, spoon the sauce over the chicken, and serve.

> VARIATION

Lamb Tagine with Dried Apricots and Olives
SERVES 6

If you cannot find pitted Greek green olives, substitute pimento-stuffed green olives; if the olives are particularly salty, be sure to rinse them. A variety of dried fruits, including pitted prunes, dark raisins, golden raisins, or currants, can be substituted for the apricots. Serve with Simple Couscous (page 295).

1	(3½- to 4-pound) boneless lamb shoulder roast, trimmed and cut into 1½-inch pieces
	Salt and ground black pepper
3	tablespoons olive oil
3	medium onions, halved and sliced pole to pole into ¼-inch-thick pieces (see the illustration on page 105)
4	(2-inch-long) strips zest from 1 lemon (see the illustration on page 148), trimmed of white pith
8	medium garlic cloves, minced or pressed through a garlic press (about 8 teaspoons), plus 2 medium garlic cloves, mashed to a fine paste (see the illustrations on page 102)
2½	teaspoons sweet paprika
1	teaspoon ground cumin
½	teaspoon ground ginger
½	teaspoon ground coriander
½	teaspoon ground cinnamon
¼	teaspoon cayenne pepper
¼	cup unbleached all-purpose flour
4	cups low-sodium chicken broth
2	tablespoons honey
1	pound carrots (about 6 medium), peeled and sliced 1 inch thick
2	cups pitted Greek green olives, halved
1	cup dried apricots, chopped medium (see the illustration on page 294)
¼	cup minced fresh cilantro leaves
¼	cup juice from 2 lemons
½	teaspoon grated zest from 1 lemon

1. Adjust an oven rack to the lower-middle position and heat the oven to 325 degrees. Pat the meat dry with paper towels and season with salt and pepper. Heat 1 tablespoon of the oil in a large Dutch oven over medium-high heat until just smoking. Add half of the lamb and brown well on all sides, 7 to 10 minutes; transfer to a medium bowl. Repeat with 1 tablespoon more oil and the remaining lamb; transfer to the bowl.

2. Add the remaining 1 tablespoon oil to the pot and return to medium heat until shimmering. Add the onions, lemon zest strips, and ¼ teaspoon salt and cook over medium heat until the onions are softened, 5 to 7 minutes. Stir in the minced garlic, paprika, cumin, ginger, coriander, cinnamon, and cayenne and cook until fragrant, about 30 seconds. Stir in the flour and cook for 1 minute.

3. Slowly whisk in the broth, scraping up any browned bits and smoothing out any lumps. Stir in the honey and browned lamb with any accumulated juice and bring to a simmer. Cover, place the pot in the oven, and cook for 1 hour.

4. Stir in the carrots and continue to cook in the oven, covered, until the meat is tender, 1 to 1½ hours longer.

5. Remove the tagine from the oven and remove the lemon zest strips. Stir in the olives and apricots, cover, and let stand off the heat for 5 minutes. Stir in the garlic paste, cilantro, lemon juice, and grated lemon zest. Season with salt and pepper to taste and serve.

CHOPPING DRIED FRUIT

Dried fruit, like apricots, dates, or figs, very often sticks to the knife when you try to chop it. To avoid this problem, coat the blade with a thin film of vegetable cooking spray just before you begin chopping any dried fruit. The chopped fruit won't cling to the blade, and the knife will stay relatively clean.

VEGETABLE TAGINE

VEGETABLE TAGINES AREN'T AS WELL KNOWN as meat tagines, but they're no less delicious. We wanted a tagine with a hearty mix of vegetables that could hold their own in a meat-free tagine. The intense, earthy flavor of artichokes, a popular Mediterranean vegetable, came to mind first. We also liked the idea of chickpeas, another mainstay of Mediterranean cooking, as they could contribute additional heartiness and a rich, nutty flavor. We envisioned a stew overflowing with big, rich chunks of artichokes and tender chickpeas, enlivened with pungent garlic, warm spices, briny olives, and tangy lemon. Since vegetables cook quickly, this tagine would make a speedy, but flavorful weeknight supper.

Starting with the artichokes, we decided to consider all the available options: fresh, frozen, jarred, and canned. Fresh artichokes were quickly scratched off the list. Though they tasted great, fresh artichokes were just too time-consuming to prepare. Canned artichokes were too watery no matter how well we drained them or how long we browned them, and so were also eliminated. Jarred artichokes, which are packed in vinaigrette, seemed like a possibility, as the flavors of the marinade might complement the traditional tagine herbs and spices. We couldn't have been more wrong—the marinade dominated our tagine, even when we thoroughly rinsed the artichokes. We moved on to frozen artichokes. After thawing them and draining off the excess liquid, we patted them dry then sautéed them to drive off any remaining moisture that was still clinging to them. Deep golden brown in color, with an intense, earthy flavor, the frozen variety was our winner.

With the choice of artichokes settled we moved on to building the rest of the stew. For the chickpeas, we opted to use canned in keeping with our speedy theme. Two cans provided ample heartiness in our tagine, and we found that all we had to do was simmer them in the sauce. For more substance and a stronger vegetable presence, we added two bell peppers, cut into matchsticks, which made for an elegant presentation. Tasters preferred the sweet flavor of red or yellow bell peppers over the more overtly vegetal green peppers.

At this point, we referred back to our chicken tagine (see page 292) to help us narrow down the aromatics, cooking liquid, and spices. An onion was essential; its pungency mellowed into a sweet, subtle flavor when cooked. As for the garlic, eight cloves offered the ideal amount of headiness and depth. For the liquid component, we used a few cups of store-bought vegetable broth to keep with our vegetable theme. Thickened with just 2 tablespoons of flour, the broth was the perfect consistency to coat the vegetables. Two spoonfuls of honey, stirred in with the broth, maintained the balance of sweet and savory we were after.

The lemon flavor in authentic tagines comes from preserved lemons, which are difficult to find and impossible to make at home in a reasonable amount of time. However, we found that sautéing several strips of lemon zest contributed similar flavor to our tagine. Though we finished our meat tagines with lemon juice, we found it stood out too much in our vegetable stew. Grated lemon zest, on the other hand, imparted bright lemon flavor, but not acidity. For the olives we tried several kinds of green and black Mediterranean olives, and tasters preferred the more subdued flavor of kalamata olives. They weren't too salty or too briny, and they merged easily with the other components.

As for the spices, cumin, coriander, ginger, and cinnamon gave us the complexity and warmth we were seeking. Paprika gave the stew sweetness and a deep, exotic red hue, while cayenne provided some heat. Tasters wanted more pronounced sweetness however, so we decided to incorporate some dried fruits. Dates, figs, and apricots offered interesting flavor but ultimately we liked the look and subdued sweetness of golden raisins the best.

Our stew was close to finished, but tasted a little lean. Looking for ways to enrich it, we landed on yogurt and stirred ½ cup plain whole milk yogurt into the pot. This was good, but plain whole milk Greek yogurt, with its fuller, richer flavor, was even better. To prevent the yogurt from curdling, we spooned a portion of the tagine's liquid into the yogurt to gently warm it through, then stirred the mixture back into the pot (a process called tempering).

At last, we had a vegetable tagine that tasted every bit as bright and exotic as its meat-laden counterparts—and was just as satisfying.

Simple Couscous

SERVES 4 TO 6

Use regular fine-grain couscous here. Large-grain couscous, often labeled Israeli-style, takes longer to cook and won't work in this recipe.

4	tablespoons (½ stick) unsalted butter
2	cups couscous
½	cup minced onion
	Salt and ground black pepper
2	cups water
1¾	cups low-sodium chicken broth
1½	teaspoons juice from 1 lemon

1. Melt 2 tablespoons of the butter in a 12-inch skillet over medium-high heat. Add the couscous and cook, stirring frequently, until some grains begin to brown, about 3 minutes. Transfer the couscous to a large heatproof bowl.

2. Melt the remaining 2 tablespoons butter in the skillet over medium heat. Add the onion and ¾ teaspoon salt and cook until softened, 5 to 7 minutes. Stir in the water and broth and bring to a boil.

3. Pour the boiling liquid over the toasted couscous, cover tightly with plastic wrap, and let sit until the couscous is tender, about 12 minutes. Remove the plastic wrap, fluff the couscous with a fork, and gently stir in the lemon juice. Season with salt and pepper to taste and serve.

Artichoke, Pepper, and Chichkpea Tagine

SERVES 4 TO 6

To thaw the frozen artichokes quickly, microwave them on high, covered, for 3 to 5 minutes. Frozen artichokes are generally packaged already quartered; if yours are not, cut the artichoke hearts into quarters before using. Serve with Simple Couscous (page 295). While we prefer the richer, fuller flavor of whole milk Greek yogurt, regular plain whole milk yogurt can be substituted; note that the sauce will be slightly thinner.

¼   cup extra-virgin olive oil, plus extra
     for serving

2   (9-ounce) boxes frozen artichokes, thawed
     and patted dry (see note)

2   yellow or red bell peppers, stemmed, seeded,
     and cut into matchsticks

1   medium onion, halved and sliced ¼ inch thick

4   (2-inch-long) strips zest from 1 lemon
     (see the illustration on page 148), trimmed of
     white pith

6   medium garlic cloves, minced or pressed
     through a garlic press (about 2 tablespoons),
     plus 2 medium garlic cloves, mashed to a fine
     paste (see the illustrations on page 102)

1   tablespoon sweet paprika

½   teaspoon ground cumin

¼   teaspoon ground ginger

¼   teaspoon ground coriander

¼   teaspoon ground cinnamon

⅛   teaspoon cayenne pepper

2   tablespoons unbleached all-purpose flour

3   cups low-sodium vegetable broth

2   (15-ounce) cans chickpeas, drained and
     rinsed

½   cup pitted kalamata olives, halved

½   cup golden raisins

2   tablespoons honey

½   cup plain whole milk Greek yogurt (see note)

½   cup minced fresh cilantro leaves

1   teaspoon grated zest from 1 lemon
     Salt and ground black pepper

1. Heat 1 tablespoon of the oil in a large Dutch oven over medium heat until shimmering. Add the artichokes and cook until golden brown, 5 to 7 minutes. Transfer to a medium bowl.

2. Add 1 tablespoon more oil to the pot and return to medium heat until shimmering. Stir in the bell peppers, onion, and lemon zest strips and cook until the vegetables are softened and lightly browned, 5 to 7 minutes. Stir in the minced garlic, paprika, cumin, ginger, coriander, cinnamon, and cayenne and cook until fragrant, about 30 seconds. Stir in the flour and cook for 1 minute.

3. Gradually whisk in the broth, scraping up any browned bits and smoothing out any lumps. Stir in the browned artichokes, chickpeas, olives, raisins, and honey and bring to a simmer. Cover, reduce to a gentle simmer, and cook until the vegetables are tender, about 15 minutes.

4. Off the heat, remove the lemon zest strips. Stir ¼ cup of the hot liquid into the yogurt to temper, then stir the yogurt mixture into the pot. Stir in the remaining 2 tablespoons oil, garlic paste, cilantro, and lemon zest. Season with salt and pepper to taste and drizzle lightly with additional olive oil before serving.

14
SLOW-COOKER FAVORITES

Slow-Cooker Favorites

Slow-Cooker Chicken Broth

GIVEN THAT CHICKEN BROTH IS TRADITIONALLY simmered low and slow to draw out maximum flavor from meat and bones, this task seemed well suited for the slow cooker. Our goal in creating a recipe for slow-cooker chicken broth was to create a broth with as much unadulterated chicken flavor as possible—with as little effort as possible.

We started with the most common technique for making broth: the simmering method. We placed all the ingredients (chicken, vegetables, aromatics, and water) in our slow cooker, simmered everything for hours, then strained and defatted the broth. We tested a tremendous number of ingredients—everything from thyme and parsley to carrots and parsnips—and found that we preferred broth with fewer ingredients, as it had a much purer flavor. Onions, garlic, and salt complemented the flavor of the chicken; everything else was a distraction.

As for the chicken itself, we tried making broth with a whole cut-up chicken, including whole legs and wings, as well as the more traditional neck and back. While a whole chicken yielded a fairly decent broth, cutting it up took more time than we anticipated, especially given that we were trying to streamline the process, and we also thought some of the parts weren't necessary. We tried using specific parts next. Chicken legs and necks both made good broth, but tasters slightly preferred the flavor of broth made with backs or wings. However, while chicken backs might be inexpensive, they can be difficult to find. Chicken wings were clearly the best choice, producing a refined and full-flavored broth.

We made a number of batches of broth and tasted the various batches at different intervals. It was clear that more time yields a better broth—but only up to a point. About eight hours on low or up to five hours on high was optimal. After that, however, we could not taste any improvement; the meat and bones were spent, having given up all their flavor.

Sometimes when making stocks and broths, we find it necessary to skim off the foamy gray matter that floats to the top of the pot during cooking. However, we found no benefits from skimming our broth made from chicken wings in the slow cooker. Because the broth never comes to a strong boil, the foam that accumulates on top is minimal; disturbing it halfway through cooking only reincorporates it into the broth. However, we did find it important to defat the broth at the end of cooking in order to prevent the final product from being greasy.

Now that our ingredient list and technique were established, we decided to give making a broth with roasted chicken a try. Roasted-chicken broth, a great base for sauces and gravies, gets its depth of flavor from roasted chicken and aromatics. This turned out to be a relatively simple departure from our master recipe. Tossing the chicken wings and onion in a roasting pan, we roasted them in a 450-degree oven until they were golden brown. From here we added everything to the slow cooker and let it go. The resulting broth was dark in color and had a pleasant caramelized-onion flavor. With a minimum of active time in the kitchen, we had made two robustly flavored broths ready to go into our next soup, stew, or sauce or to be frozen for future use.

SMASHING GARLIC

Smash the garlic cloves with the side of a large chef's knife and discard the loosened skin.

Slow-Cooker Chicken Broth

MAKES ABOUT 12 CUPS

This recipe does not produce much chicken meat, and any meat left over after straining the broth will be very dry and flavorless; it should not be eaten.

  3 pounds chicken wings
12 cups water
  1 medium onion, chopped medium
  3 medium garlic cloves, smashed and peeled
     (see the illustration on page 299)
  1 teaspoon salt

1. Combine all the ingredients in the slow cooker. Cover and cook on low until the broth is rich and deeply flavored, 8 to 9 hours. (Alternatively, cover and cook on high for 4 to 5 hours.)

2. Strain the broth through a fine-mesh strainer, then defat the broth (see page 18). (The broth can be refrigerated in an airtight container for up to 4 days or frozen for up to 1 month; see page 5 for more information on freezing broth.)

VARIATION

Slow-Cooker Roasted-Chicken Broth

This broth has a deeper flavor and color that is well suited to stews, gravies, and sauces.

Follow the recipe for Slow-Cooker Chicken Broth, roasting the chicken wings and onion together in a large nonstick roasting pan on the lower-middle rack of a 450-degree oven until golden brown, about 40 minutes. Transfer the roasted chicken wings and onion to the slow cooker, add the remaining ingredients, and continue to cook as directed.

SLOW-COOKER CHICKEN NOODLE SOUP

RECIPES FOR SLOW-COOKER CHICKEN NOODLE soup abound. In theory, it should work—you should be able to combine chicken, vegetables, noodles, and water in a slow cooker and come back half a day later to find that time and low heat have worked together to render a rich broth and tender meat. The reality, however, is not so ideal. We made a handful of recipes, and they were all watery, bland, and lacking in chicken flavor. To make matters worse, the meat was tough and flavorless and the noodles were flabby and waterlogged. We were going to have to build our recipe from the ground up.

With our goal established—soup with rich chicken flavor, tender vegetables and noodles, and big bites of succulent meat—we decided to start our testing by choosing the type of chicken. While we tend to rely on chicken thighs over breasts in slow-cooked dishes because thighs are less likely to dry out, we realize that many people enjoy both dark meat and white meat in their chicken noodle soup and decided to include both in ours. Initial testing showed us that bone-in chicken pieces were the best choice, as the bones helped to keep the chicken moist during the long cooking time. Once the meat was cooked, we would simply need to shred it and then add it back to the soup before serving.

With the chicken settled on, we began to consider how to prepare it for the slow cooker. Many slow-cooker chicken soup recipes call for browning the chicken before adding it to the slow cooker. While this helps develop a deeper flavor, we wondered if we could avoid the extra work. To find out if this step was indeed necessary, we set up a side-by-side test of browned versus unbrowned chicken to see which would prevail with tasters. Using bone-in, skin-on thighs as well as a breast, we seared a batch in a skillet, then nestled the pieces in the slow cooker along with chicken broth and sautéed aromatics. The other batch went into the slow cooker cold with the cooking liquid and aromatics. As it turned out, tasters favored the flavor of the soup made with seared chicken. Working with a covered slow cooker, we did not have the benefit of evaporation to reduce and intensify the broth as we would on the stovetop. Since bold chicken flavor was the focal point of this soup, the additional flavor achieved by browning the chicken pieces helped to enrich the broth and compensate for the absence of evaporation.

Our final tests with the chicken focused on the timing. Chicken is notorious for drying out with extended cooking, even in the moist environment of a slow cooker. After several tests, we found that the optimal cooking time and temperature was four to six hours on low. Any longer and the chicken took on a rubbery texture, and cooking the chicken on high for half that time turned out inconsistent results and negated using a slow cooker in the first place.

We were now ready to turn our attention to finishing the soup base. We knew our slow-cooker chicken soup would benefit from a wide range of aromatics; we thought sautéed carrots, celery, and onion worked best. To this mixture we also decided to add tomato paste—to encourage browning and add depth of flavor—as well as some garlic, thyme, and red pepper flakes for further savory notes. To deglaze the skillet, we used some of the broth, scraping up the browned bits (the fond) from the skillet. Transferring the mixture to the slow cooker, we then stirred in the remaining chicken broth and some bay leaves before adding the chicken thighs and breast. After four hours, we shredded the chicken and returned it to the slow cooker along with some peas for good measure (we would focus on including the noodles later). Tasting the results, we were impressed with the flavor of the soup, but

found there were issues remaining with the texture of the chicken breast—even under our optimal time and temperature, tasters were still noticing the meat beginning to dry out.

We needed to find a way to further protect the chicken breast from the extended time in the slow cooker. Skipping the browning of the chicken breast (which accelerated the cooking process) and resting it on top of—instead of in—the soup worked okay, but parts of the breast still ended up turning dry. Taking our idea a step further, we discovered that if we wrapped the chicken breast in foil to insulate it from the heat before resting it on top of the soup, the breast cooked perfectly in the same amount of time as the thighs. Now when we served up our soup, tasters couldn't get enough of the tender, juicy meat.

The noodles were the last element that we needed to investigate. Egg noodles are the obvious choice for a traditional chicken noodle soup; we assumed all we'd have to do was stir in the uncooked noodles several minutes before serving time. When we put this theory to the test, however, the egg noodles softened slightly but never really cooked through; they merely tasted raw and mushy. We realized that the soup wasn't hot enough (especially since it was cooked on low) to actually cook the egg noodles, which require a constant simmer in order to cook properly. To fix this, we simply boiled the egg noodles in a separate pot, then stirred them into the soup, along with a pinch of fresh parsley for a bright, fresh touch.

With a successful, rich-tasting chicken noodle soup recipe at the ready, we created a variation using a few well-chosen Asian ingredients. Soy sauce, star anise, and ginger contributed to our exotic spin on this American classic. We swapped the egg noodles for ramen noodles, which we were able to cook directly in the slow cooker, and added shredded napa cabbage and carrots for some crunch and texture.

Slow-Cooker
Chicken Noodle Soup

SERVES 8

Do not cook this soup on high power or the chicken will become tough. Also, do not try to cook the noodles right in the soup in the slow cooker or they will taste mushy and raw.

1½	pounds bone-in, skin-on chicken thighs (4 to 5 thighs), trimmed
	Salt and ground black pepper
1	tablespoon vegetable oil
3	carrots, peeled and cut into ½-inch pieces
2	celery ribs, cut into ½-inch pieces
1	medium onion, minced
3	medium garlic cloves, minced or pressed through a garlic press (about 1 tablespoon)
1	tablespoon tomato paste
2	teaspoons minced fresh thyme leaves or ½ teaspoon dried
⅛	teaspoon red pepper flakes
8	cups low-sodium chicken broth
2	bay leaves
1	(10- to 12-ounce) bone-in, skin-on split chicken breast, trimmed
½	cup frozen peas
1	cup (1½ ounces) wide egg noodles
2	tablespoons minced fresh parsley leaves

1. Pat the chicken thighs dry with paper towels and season with salt and pepper. Heat the oil in a 12-inch skillet over medium-high heat until just smoking. Brown the chicken thighs well on both sides, 7 to 10 minutes; transfer to a plate, let cool slightly, then remove and discard the skin.

2. Pour off all but 1 tablespoon of the fat left in the pan. Add the carrots, celery, and onion and cook over medium heat until softened, 7 to 10 minutes. Stir in the garlic, tomato paste, thyme, and red pepper flakes and cook until fragrant, about 30 seconds. Stir in 1 cup of the chicken broth, scraping up any browned bits, then transfer to the slow cooker.

3. Stir the remaining 7 cups broth, bay leaves, and browned chicken with any accumulated juice into the slow cooker. Season the chicken breast with salt and pepper, wrap it in a foil packet, and lay the packet on top of the soup, following the illustrations on page 303. Cover and cook on low until the chicken is tender, 4 to 6 hours.

4. Remove the foil packet, open it carefully (watch for steam), and transfer the chicken breast to a cutting board. Transfer the chicken thighs to the cutting board. Let all of the chicken cool slightly, then shred it into bite-size pieces (see the illustration on page 43), discarding the skin and bones. Meanwhile, let the soup settle for 5 minutes, then remove as much fat as possible from the surface using a large spoon. Discard the bay leaves and stir in the shredded chicken and peas.

5. Bring 2 quarts water to a boil in a large saucepan. Add 1½ teaspoons salt and the noodles and cook, stirring often, until tender. Drain the noodles, stir them into the soup, and let the soup sit until everything is heated through, 2 to 5 minutes. Stir in the parsley, season with salt and pepper to taste, and serve.

➤ VARIATION

Slow-Cooker Asian-Style Chicken Noodle Soup

Do not cook this soup on high power or the chicken will become tough. Be sure to use low-sodium soy sauce or the soup may taste overly salty.

1½	pounds bone-in, skin-on chicken thighs (4 to 5 thighs), trimmed
	Salt and ground black pepper
1	tablespoon vegetable oil
1	medium onion, minced
3	medium garlic cloves, minced or pressed through a garlic press (about 1 tablespoon)
1	tablespoon tomato paste
⅛	teaspoon red pepper flakes
8	cups low-sodium chicken broth
3	tablespoons low-sodium soy sauce
2	tablespoons sugar

2   star anise pods

1   (10- to 12-ounce) bone-in, skin-on split
    chicken breast, trimmed

8   ounces napa cabbage (½ medium head),
    shredded (about 4 cups) (see the illustrations
    on page 61)

2   (3-ounce) packages ramen noodles,
    flavoring packets discarded

2   carrots, shredded

2   scallions, sliced thin on the bias
    (see the illustration on page 73)

1   tablespoon minced or grated fresh ginger
    (see the illustrations on page 89)

1. Pat the chicken thighs dry with paper towels and season with salt and pepper. Heat the oil in a 12-inch skillet over medium-high heat until just smoking. Brown the chicken thighs well on both sides, 7 to 10 minutes; transfer to a plate, let cool slightly, then remove and discard the skin.

2. Pour off all but 1 tablespoon of the fat left in the pan. Add the onion and cook over medium heat until softened, 5 to 7 minutes. Stir in the garlic, tomato paste, and red pepper flakes and cook until fragrant, about 30 seconds. Stir in 1 cup of the chicken broth, scraping up any browned bits, then transfer to the slow cooker.

3. Stir the remaining 7 cups broth, soy sauce, sugar, star anise, and browned chicken with any accumulated juice into the slow cooker. Season the chicken breast with salt and pepper, wrap it in a foil packet, and lay the packet on top of the soup, following the illustrations at right. Cover and cook on low until the chicken is tender, 4 to 6 hours.

4. Remove the foil packet, open it carefully (watch for steam), and transfer the chicken breast to a cutting board. Transfer the chicken thighs to the cutting board. Let all of the chicken cool slightly, then shred it into bite-size pieces (see the illustration on page 43), discarding the skin and bones. Meanwhile, let the soup settle for 5 minutes, then

remove as much fat as possible from the surface using a large spoon.

5. Discard the star anise and stir in the cabbage, noodles, and carrots. Cover and cook on high until the noodles and carrots are tender, 5 to 10 minutes. Stir in the shredded chicken, scallions, and ginger, season with salt and pepper to taste, and serve.

MAKING A FOIL PACKET

Depending on the recipe, the cooking time, and how the vegetables are cut, it is sometimes necessary to wrap vegetables in an aluminum foil packet to keep them from overcooking. The packet helps keep them out of the cooking liquid and slows down their cooking, protecting their flavors from fading. We also sometimes place chicken in a foil packet to prevent the meat from drying out.

1. Place the vegetables or chicken pieces on one side of a large piece of foil. Fold the foil over, shaping it into a packet that will fit into your slow cooker, then crimp to seal the edges.

2. Place the foil packet directly on top of the soup or stew, pressing gently as needed to make it fit inside the cooker.

Slow Cooking 101

The low, moist heat of the slow cooker makes it ideal for the long, hands-off cooking of soups, stews, and chilis. But learning how to extract maximum flavor from recipes in the slow cooker has taken some effort and lots of testing. Over the years we've learned a few things. First, all slow cookers are not created equal, which is why these recipes have a range of cooking times. The key when it comes to timing is to get to know your slow cooker and whether it runs slow (and low) or fast (and hot). And second, a little advance prep can go a long way in building a flavorful base for a soup or stew. It is a rare recipe where raw ingredients can simply be dumped into a slow cooker with good results. Here are a few things we've learned that will help you turn out rich and flavorful soups and stews in your slow cooker.

KNOW YOUR SLOW COOKER

Through years of slow-cooker recipe development, we've learned that not all slow cookers are the same—some run hot (and fast) while others run cool (and slow). And since all slow-cooker recipes come with a time range, knowing how your individual slow cooker runs will be helpful in determining which end of the range will likely yield the best results. We have done all of our testing using our winning slow cooker (see below), but if you are using a different brand you might find that you need slightly altered cooking times. One quick way to determine how hot or cool your cooker runs is to perform a simple water test. Place 4 quarts of room temperature water in your slow cooker, cover it, and cook on either high or low for six hours, then measure the temperature of the water. Ideally, the water should register between 195 and 205 degrees on an instant-read thermometer. If your cooker runs hotter or cooler, be ready to check the food for doneness either earlier or later than our recipes indicate. Also, we've found that some cookers run hot or cool on just one of the settings (either low or high), so consider checking both if you find you are having problems.

PREP-AHEAD TIPS

Our slow-cooker recipes require a bit of prep work before the ingredients can be added to the slow cooker. Here are some things you can do up to a day in advance to streamline your prep:

1. Sauté the aromatics as described (in step 1 and/or 2 of most recipes), then transfer them to an airtight container and refrigerate.
2. Peel and cut any vegetables as directed (except potatoes, which discolor after being cut) and refrigerate.
3. While you can't brown meat ahead (because doing so is unsafe), you can trim and cut the meat as directed. Refrigerate the meat separately in an airtight container.

THE BEST SLOW COOKER

After testing a number of slow cookers, we found our favorite in the Crock-Pot Touchscreen Slow Cooker ($129.99), which has a 6.5-quart capacity. It had the best control panel, which was simple to set and clearly indicated that the cooker has been programmed. It has a clear glass lid, so it's easy to see the food as it cooks. Also, the insert has handles, which makes it easy to remove the insert from the cooker.

CROCK-POT

TIPS FOR SUCCESS

PUMP UP THE AROMATICS

To keep the flavor of slow-cooker recipes from being washed out, we use a hefty amount of onions and other aromatics to build a flavor base. You need more aromatics, spices, and herbs in a slow-cooker recipe than one made on the stovetop because the long cooking time and moist heat dulls their impact. Also, seasoning at the end of cooking with fresh herbs will brighten the flavor of the final dish.

SAUTÉ YOUR AROMATICS

While many slow-cooker recipes recommend simply dumping the raw aromatics into the slow cooker before cooking, we have found that this technique results in a flat-tasting dish (not to mention crunchy onions). Instead we like to sauté aromatics, often with a little tomato paste to encourage browning, before simmering. This simple step maximizes their flavors, resulting in a more deeply flavored dish.

TRIM AWAY EXCESS FAT

During the extended cooking time in the slow cooker, beef and chicken can release a large amount of fat. Trimming and removing excess fat and skin from meat and poultry before adding them to the slow cooker reduces the amount of fat that can be rendered and prevents the dish from becoming greasy. And once the dish has finished cooking, it's also helpful to skim any residual fat off the surface with a large spoon.

KEEP THE LID ON

Slow cookers rely on their lids to retain heat and moisture and maintain their cooking temperature. After placing the lid on the slow cooker to begin cooking, we have found that it is important to avoid lifting the lid until the cooking time is finished—doing so can release heat and extend the cooking time significantly.

SLOW-COOKER CHICKEN STEW

WE HAVE PLENTY OF EXPERIENCE COOKING chicken stew in the oven, but we wondered if this hearty stew could be successfully replicated in a slow cooker. Our goal was a chicken stew that could be easily prepared and left to cook on its own but, at the end of the day, still boasted bites of juicy chicken and tender vegetables draped in a velvety sauce.

Starting with the meat, we quickly settled on chicken thighs, which we knew would remain moist and tender over the long cooking time. In addition, we found that the richer flavor of dark meat paired well with the heartier flavors and thicker sauce of a stew. We chose bone-in thighs; the bone helps to keep the meat from drying out, while also contributing deeper flavor to the dish. As with our Slow-Cooker Chicken Noodle Soup (page 302), we found that browning the thighs first was necessary; this led to the development of a rich, flavorful fond on the bottom of the pan that could be used to sauté the aromatics. Removing the skin after browning the chicken ensured that the sauce didn't become greasy after simmering for hours.

Moving on to the aromatics, we found that two onions and a few garlic cloves provided the right background notes. To these basic aromatics, we added thyme, bay leaves, and tomato paste; we found that the tomato paste added some depth to our slow-cooked sauce. A half-cup of dry white wine worked to deglaze the pan and pull up all the rich browned bits; we then transferred these flavorful bits, along with our sautéed aromatics, to the slow cooker. We stirred in chicken broth, then added the potatoes, carrots, and browned chicken. After four hours, we got out our forks. The results were mixed. The good news was that the chicken was tender; the bad news, however, was that the sauce was watery and the potatoes were mushy and blown out.

We decided to focus on the consistency of the sauce first, before moving on to fix the texture of the potatoes. Many slow cooker stew recipes turn to a slurry (a starch stirred together with liquid) of either flour or cornstarch, which has to be stirred in at the end of the cooking time. While both of these options worked to thicken the sauce, they imparted a starchy taste and required extra cooking time to thicken the liquid. We found a substitute, however, in instant tapioca; this ingredient was ideal because it thickened the sauce without making it gloppy or contributing any off-flavors.

Now we had to find a way to prevent the potatoes from disintegrating as they simmered away for hours in the slow cooker. Leaving them in large pieces worked, but now they were too large to eat comfortably. We decided to wrap the potatoes (and carrots for good measure) in a foil packet to insulate them, then we placed the packet on top of the chicken in the slow cooker (and out of the cooking liquid). When we opened the packet and poured the tender vegetables and their juices back into the stew at the end of cooking, the results were amazing—both the carrots and potatoes were tender and creamy, but not too soft. After shredding the chicken and stirring it back into the pot, we found that all our stew needed was a bit of green—peas and minced parsley did the trick— and it was a homey chicken stew that was just as flavorful as it was fuss-free.

Slow-Cooker Chicken Stew
SERVES 6 TO 8

Do not cook this stew on high power or the chicken will become tough.

4   pounds bone-in, skin-on chicken thighs (10 to 12 thighs), trimmed
   Salt and ground black pepper
3   tablespoons vegetable oil
2   medium onions, minced
3   medium garlic cloves, minced or pressed through a garlic press (about 1 tablespoon)
1   tablespoon tomato paste
2   teaspoon minced fresh thyme leaves or ½ teaspoon dried
½   cup dry white wine
3½   cups low-sodium chicken broth

3   tablespoons Minute tapioca

2   bay leaves

1½   pounds red potatoes (4 to 5 medium),
     scrubbed and cut into ½-inch pieces

1   pound carrots (about 6 medium), peeled and
     cut into ½-inch pieces

1   cup frozen peas

¼   cup minced fresh parsley leaves

1. Pat the chicken dry with paper towels and season with salt and pepper. Heat 1 tablespoon of the oil in a 12-inch skillet over medium-high heat until just smoking. Add half of the chicken and brown well on both sides, 7 to 10 minutes; transfer the chicken to a medium bowl. Repeat with 1 tablespoon more oil and the remaining chicken; transfer to the bowl. Let the chicken cool slightly, then remove and discard the skin.

2. Pour off all but 2 tablespoons of the fat left in the pan. Add the onions and cook over medium heat until softened, 5 to 7 minutes. Stir in the garlic, tomato paste, and thyme and cook until fragrant, about 30 seconds. Stir in the wine, scraping up any browned bits, then transfer to the slow cooker.

3. Stir the broth, tapioca, and bay leaves into the slow cooker. Nestle the browned chicken with any accumulated juice into the slow cooker. Toss the potatoes and carrots with the remaining 1 tablespoon oil and season with salt and pepper. Following the illustrations on page 303, wrap the vegetables in a foil packet and lay the packet on top of the stew. Cover and cook on low until the chicken is tender, 4 to 6 hours.

4. Transfer the vegetable packet to a plate. Transfer the chicken to a cutting board, let it cool slightly, then shred it into bite-size pieces (see the illustration on page 43), discarding the bones. Meanwhile, let the stew settle for 5 minutes, then remove as much fat as possible from the surface using a large spoon.

5. Discard the bay leaves and stir in the shredded chicken and peas. Carefully open the vegetable packet (watch for steam) and stir the vegetables with any accumulated juices into the stew. Let the stew sit until everything is heated through, 2 to 5 minutes. Stir in the parsley, season with salt and pepper to taste, and serve.

➤ VARIATION

Slow-Cooker Moroccan-Style Chicken Stew with Chickpeas and Apricots

Do not cook this stew on high power or the chicken will become tough. Adding the apricots in two batches, at the beginning of cooking and at the end of cooking, ensures that their flavor permeates the sauce and that some pieces retain their texture in the finished stew.

4   pounds bone-in, skin-on chicken thighs
     (10 to 12 thighs), trimmed
     Salt and ground black pepper

2   tablespoons vegetable oil

2   medium onions, minced

3   medium garlic cloves, minced or pressed
     through a garlic press (about 1 tablespoon)

1   tablespoon tomato paste

1½   teaspoons sweet paprika

½   teaspoon ground cardamom

¼   teaspoon cayenne pepper

½   cup dry white wine

3½   cups low-sodium chicken broth

2   (15-ounce) cans chickpeas, drained and rinsed

1   cup dried apricots, chopped medium
     (see the illustration on page 294)

3   tablespoons Minute tapioca

2   bay leaves

1   cinnamon stick

2   tablespoons minced fresh cilantro leaves
     Light brown sugar

1. Pat the chicken dry with paper towels and season with salt and pepper. Heat 1 tablespoon of the oil in a 12-inch skillet over medium-high heat until just smoking. Add half of the chicken and brown well on both sides, 5 to 8 minutes; transfer the chicken to a medium bowl. Repeat with the remaining 1 tablespoon oil and the remaining chicken; transfer to the bowl. Let the chicken cool slightly, then remove and discard the skin.

2. Pour off all but 2 tablespoons of the fat left in the pan. Add the onions, garlic, tomato paste, paprika, cardamom, ½ teaspoon salt, and cayenne and cook, stirring often, until the onions are softened and lightly browned, 8 to 10 minutes. Stir in the wine, scraping up any browned bits, then transfer to the slow cooker.

3. Stir the chicken broth, chickpeas, half of the apricots, tapioca, bay leaves, and cinnamon stick into the slow cooker. Nestle the browned chicken with any accumulated juice into the slow cooker. Cover and cook on low until the chicken is tender, 4 to 6 hours.

4. Transfer the chicken to a cutting board, let it cool slightly, then shred it into bite-size pieces (see the illustration on page 43), discarding the bones. Meanwhile, let the stew settle for 5 minutes, then remove as much fat as possible from the surface using a large spoon.

5. Remove the bay leaves and cinnamon stick and stir in the shredded chicken and remaining apricots. Let the stew sit until everything is heated though, 2 to 5 minutes. Stir in the cilantro, season with salt, pepper, and brown sugar to taste, and serve.

SLOW-COOKER CASSOULET

UNLIKE A SIMPLE CHICKEN OR BEEF STEW, which require just one type of meat, cassoulet contains a host of meats, all of which meld together into one rich and hearty meal. While this classic French peasant dish—which also comprises tender beans and a buttery bread crumb topping—can be replicated easily at restaurants, the time investment required usually takes this dish out of the realm of casual weeknight fare. With that in mind, we thought this was the perfect opportunity to create a slow-cooker version of cassoulet. We wanted pork, chicken, and sausage to be the dominant forces in this stew, surrounded by soft, creamy beans stewed for hours in a flavorful broth. Looking to develop a foolproof recipe that would streamline this classic stew and turn out perfectly cooked meat and beans every time, we headed into the test kitchen.

Our first question was about the type of dried beans to use. Given the fact that the legume would be spending hours in the slow cooker, we knew that it had to be a hearty, sturdy variety. We tested navy, cannellini, and great Northern beans. The great Northern beans won out; they delivered

the creamy texture we wanted and were slightly sturdier than the other two varieties, holding their own for the duration of cooking. An overnight soak in salt water gave them a head start on slowly absorbing the moisture they needed to cook evenly. It also served to ensure that the beans would not split open and disintegrate during the long cooking process.

Our next step was to choose the proper cuts of meat. Our experience with chicken stews has taught us that chicken thighs tend to remain moist and tender when cooked for long periods of time, so we decided to include them in our cassoulet. Choosing the pork, however, was a bit more challenging.

Looking for a cut of pork that would be moist, tender, and flavorful, we started with bone-in pork shoulder. We boned, trimmed, and cubed a pork shoulder, a process that took quite a bit of time. While the meat in this stew was tender, the preparation time that was involved sent us in search of a speedier alternative. Pork butt seemed a good choice for its high fat content, but it too required a substantial amount of butchering that seemed to go against the fact that our goal was a streamlined slow-cooker stew. We eventually settled on bone-in country-style pork ribs. These are also available boneless, but we found that the bone added more flavor to the stew and helped the meat remain moist.

We tested two methods of preparing the thighs and ribs prior to adding them to the slow cooker: browned and unbrowned. While browning adds deeper flavor to stews and braises, it also took more time than we liked, given that each cut had to be browned in batches. Luckily, we found that sautéing the aromatics with a dollop of tomato paste encouraged browning and caramelization in the pan, which worked to replace the flavorful browned bits that would have been left behind from browning the meat. Also, sautéing a hefty amount of garlic (6 cloves) amped up the flavor of our cassoulet. Deglazing the skillet with white wine (which tasters preferred over red) worked to pick up the browned bits; the addition of wine to the sauce also helped the other individual flavors shine through. Chicken broth (used in place of water) and a single can of diced tomatoes helped liven up the sauce.

Our cassoulet was coming together nicely, but we still had trouble figuring out the cooking time. Usually, meat stews require nine to 11 hours on low in order for the meat to become tender, while chicken can only handle four to six hours on low before overcooking and becoming dry. Meeting in the middle (cooking for about six to eight hours) worked fine. This was just enough time to make the country-style pork ribs tender, and we were able to protect the chicken thighs by wrapping them in a foil packet so that they could withstand the extra cooking time.

The last important component in question was the sausage. We tested Italian sausage, chorizo, and kielbasa and preferred the last one for two reasons. Not only did it contribute a smoky flavor to the stew, but it also seemed to retain its flavor throughout the cooking process. The others ended up as rubbery, flavorless chunks of meat by the end of the long cooking time.

After topping individual portions with a simple toasted bread crumb topping, we were pleased with our streamlined cassoulet; it was every bit as hearty and flavorful as the traditional French renditions— but it was infinitely easier to prepare.

Slow-Cooker Cassoulet
SERVES 6 TO 8

Do not cook this stew on high power or the chicken will become tough. Serve with Garlic Toasts (page 138).

2	tablespoons vegetable oil
2	medium onions, minced
6	medium garlic cloves, minced or pressed through a garlic press (about 2 tablespoons)
1	tablespoon minced fresh thyme or 1 teaspoon dried
1	tablespoon tomato paste
½	cup white wine
3½	cups low-sodium chicken broth
1	pound dried great Northern beans, picked over, salt-soaked (see page 145), and rinsed
1	(14.5-ounce) can diced tomatoes, drained
8	ounces kielbasa, sliced 1 inch thick
2	bay leaves
2	pounds bone-in country-style pork ribs Salt and ground black pepper
2	pounds bone-in chicken thighs (5 to 6 thighs), skin removed and trimmed
2	slices high-quality white sandwich bread, torn into pieces
2	tablespoons unsalted butter, melted
2	tablespoons minced fresh parsley leaves

1. Heat the oil in a 12-inch skillet over medium-high heat until shimmering. Add the onions, garlic, thyme, and tomato paste and cook, stirring often, until the onions are softened and lightly browned, 8 to 10 minutes. Stir in the wine, scraping up any browned bits, then transfer to the slow cooker.

2. Stir the chicken broth, beans, tomatoes, kielbasa, and bay leaves into the slow cooker. Season the pork with salt and pepper, then nestle it into the slow cooker. Season the chicken with salt and pepper, wrap it in a foil packet, and lay the packet on top of the stew, following the illustrations on page 303. Cover and cook on low until the pork is tender, 6 to 8 hours.

3. Meanwhile, pulse the bread, melted butter, ⅛ teaspoon salt, and ⅛ teaspoon pepper in a food processor until the bread is coarsely ground, about 8 pulses. Transfer the crumbs to a 12-inch skillet and toast over medium-high heat, stirring often, until brown and dry, about 5 minutes; set aside.

4. Remove the foil packet, open it carefully (watch for steam), and transfer the chicken to a cutting board. Let the chicken cool slightly, then shred it into bite-size pieces (see the illustration on page 43), discarding the bones. Meanwhile, let the stew settle for 5 minutes, then remove as much fat as possible from the surface using a large spoon.

5. Remove the bay leaves and stir in the shredded chicken. Let the stew sit until everything is heated through, 2 to 5 minutes. Stir in the parsley and season with salt and pepper to taste. Serve, sprinkling individual portions with the toasted bread crumbs.

SLOW-COOKER BEEF STEW

RECIPES FOR SLOW-COOKER BEEF STEW ARE divided into two types. In one, the meat, vegetables, and seasoning are simply dumped into a pot and left to their own devices. Effortless, yes. But flavorful? We'd have to say no. The second type of stew, the one in which the meat is browned before it goes into the slow cooker, is the more flavorful stew. Here the foundation for flavor is built on the browned bits left behind (the fond), which are the backbone of the stew's sauce. But this browning, which needs to be done in batches so the meat doesn't steam, can take a good chunk of time, adding precious minutes to the time it takes the hurried cook to prep the recipe and leave for work. In developing a recipe for slow-cooker beef stew, we wanted to find a way to maximize flavor, while minimizing both prep time and labor.

We knew that in order to successfully justify jettisoning the browning step, we needed to come up with a flavor replacement for the fond. We tried an array of "browning sauces," like Gravy Master and Kitchen Bouquet, as well as bouillon cubes and different combinations of beef and chicken broth. After extensive testing, we landed on a winning solution. We used a combination of soy sauce (its salty elements reinforced the beefy flavor and added color) and tomato paste, which we browned with the onions before adding them to the slow cooker. This step created additional flavor notes and also took care of the problem with throwing onions into the slow cooker raw, which tasters agreed made the stew taste vegetal.

There were, however, still those in the test kitchen who were having a hard time coming to grips with this unconventional, unbrowned approach to a full-flavored stew. To make sure that everyone was on board with our new technique, we conducted a blind taste test of three stews, side by side: browned beef stew, unbrowned beef stew with no flavor replacement, and unbrowned beef stew with our fond replacement of sautéed aromatics, tomato paste, and soy sauce. Unaware of the different methods used, the majority of tasters favored the third stew. We were happy that taste buds, rather than preconceived notions, settled the controversy. Our third stew was rich and full-bodied, and we were pleased with how much time we had saved. Knowing that our test cooks are a tough crowd to please, we were satisfied that we had landed on a reliable way to save valuable prep time, without sacrificing flavor.

Satisfied with our faux fond, we moved on to address one troubling issue that resulted from not browning: greasiness. Because browning helps to render fat and we were now not browning, our stew had a grease slick on top. Up until now, we had been using a chuck eye roast that we trimmed and cut into 1½-inch pieces. Wondering if leaner roasts would solve our problem, we tested five stews made with different cuts of beef: top round, bottom round, eye round, rump roast, and top sirloin. After all that work, it turned out that none were as flavorful and tender as the chuck eye roast. All of the others were too lean, resulting in flavorless, dry meat. We decided that we didn't mind using a spoon to skim a bit of grease from the stew if that was what it would take to get maximum flavor, so we returned to the chuck eye roast.

The next dilemma was how to thicken our stew. While many slow-cooker recipes turn to a slurry (a starch stirred together with liquid) of either flour or cornstarch, we knew from previous testing that this would only lead to a stew that tasted starchy. Instant tapioca, stirred in at the onset of cooking, was a better choice. The stew was now thick without being tacky, there was no raw, starchy aftertaste, and it required no last-minute fussing.

Moving on, we wanted to find a way to perk up the vegetables that seemed to suffer dramatically in the slow cooker. Stealing a trick we had learned with our Slow-Cooker Chicken Stew (page 305), we insulated the potatoes and carrots by wrapping them in a foil packet. Then we placed the packet on top of the beef in the slow cooker. It may have looked a bit odd, but when we opened the packet and poured the tender vegetables and their juice back into the stew at the end of cooking, the results were amazing. The carrots were both perfectly cooked and the potatoes were intact. Finally, we had a slow-cooker beef stew that was easy to make and tasted great.

Slow-Cooker Beef Stew

SERVES 6 TO 8

Be sure to use low-sodium soy sauce or the stew may taste overly salty. Feel free to add a pound of parsnips, peeled and cut into 1-inch pieces, to the foil packet along with the carrots and potatoes.

3	tablespoons vegetable oil
3	medium onions, minced
¼	cup tomato paste
6	medium garlic cloves, minced or pressed through a garlic press (about 2 tablespoons)
I	tablespoon minced fresh thyme leaves or 1 teaspoon dried
1½	cups low-sodium chicken broth
1½	cups beef broth
¼	cup low-sodium soy sauce (see note)
2	tablespoons Minute tapioca
2	bay leaves
I	(5-pound) boneless beef chuck eye roast, trimmed and cut into 1½-inch pieces (see the illustrations on page 221) Salt and ground black pepper
1½	pounds red potatoes (about 5 medium), scrubbed and cut into 1-inch chunks
I	pound carrots (about 6 medium), peeled and sliced 1 inch thick
2	cups frozen peas

1. Heat 2 tablespoons of the oil in a 12-inch skillet over medium-high heat until shimmering. Add the onions, tomato paste, garlic, and thyme and cook, stirring often, until the onions are softened and lightly browned, 8 to 10 minutes. Stir in the chicken broth, scraping up any browned bits, then transfer to the slow cooker.

2. Stir the beef broth, soy sauce, tapioca, and bay leaves into the slow cooker. Season the beef with salt and pepper, then nestle into the slow cooker. Toss the potatoes and carrots with the remaining 1 tablespoon oil and season with salt and pepper. Following the illustrations on page 303, wrap the vegetables in a foil packet and lay the packet on top of the stew. Cover and cook on low until the meat

is tender, 9 to 11 hours. (Alternatively, cover and cook on high for 5 to 7 hours.)

3. Transfer the vegetable packet to a plate. Let the stew settle for 5 minutes, then remove as much fat as possible from the surface using a large spoon.

4. Discard the bay leaves and stir in the peas. Carefully open the vegetable packet (watch for steam) and stir the vegetables with any accumulated juices into the stew. Let the stew sit until everything is heated through, 2 to 5 minutes. Season with salt and pepper to taste and serve.

➤ VARIATION

Slow-Cooker Beef Burgundy

Be sure to use low-sodium soy sauce or the stew may taste overly salty. We prefer to use Pinot Noir in this recipe, but any $7 to $10 bottle of medium-bodied red table wine made from a blend of grapes, such as a Côtes du Rhône, will work. Regular bacon can be substituted for the thick-cut bacon.

STEW

8	ounces (about 6 slices) thick-cut bacon, cut into ¼-inch pieces
3	medium onions, minced
I	medium carrot, peeled and chopped fine
¼	cup tomato paste
6	medium garlic cloves, minced or pressed through a garlic press (about 2 tablespoons)
I	tablespoon minced fresh thyme leaves or 1 teaspoon dried
I	(750-milliliter) bottle Pinot Noir (see note)
I	cup low-sodium chicken broth
¼	cup low-sodium soy sauce (see note)
2	tablespoons Minute tapioca
2	bay leaves
I	(5-pound) boneless beef chuck eye roast, trimmed and cut into 1½-inch pieces (see the illustrations on page 221) Salt and ground black pepper

GARNISH

8	ounces frozen pearl onions (about 2 cups)
½	cup water
3	tablespoons unsalted butter

2 teaspoons sugar

10 ounces cremini mushrooms,
wiped clean, trimmed, and halved
if small or quartered if large
Salt and ground black pepper

1. FOR THE STEW: Cook the bacon in a 12-inch skillet over medium heat until crisp, about 8 minutes. Transfer the bacon to a paper towel–lined plate, leaving the fat in the skillet, and refrigerate until needed.

2. Pour off all but 2 tablespoons of the bacon fat left in the pan. Add the onions, carrot, tomato paste, garlic, and thyme and cook over medium-high heat, stirring often, until the vegetables are softened and lightly browned, 8 to 10 minutes. Stir in the wine, scraping up any browned bits, and simmer until the mixture measures about 3 cups, 10 to 12 minutes; transfer to the slow cooker.

3. Stir the chicken broth, soy sauce, tapioca, and bay leaves into the slow cooker. Season the beef with salt and pepper and nestle into the slow cooker. Cover and cook on low until the meat is tender, 9 to 11 hours. (Alternatively, cover and cook on high for 5 to 7 hours.)

4. FOR THE GARNISH: About 30 minutes before serving, bring the frozen pearl onions, water, butter, and sugar to a boil in a 12-inch skillet over medium-high heat. Cover, reduce to a simmer, and cook until the onions are fully thawed and tender, 5 to 8 minutes.

5. Uncover, increase the heat to medium-high, and cook until all the liquid evaporates, 3 to 4 minutes. Stir in the mushrooms and ¼ teaspoon salt and continue to cook until the vegetables are browned and glazed, 10 to 12 minutes. Off the heat, season with salt and pepper to taste and set aside.

6. Before serving, let the stew settle for 5 minutes, then remove as much fat as possible from the surface using a large spoon. Remove the bay leaves, stir in the onion-mushroom garnish, and season with salt and pepper to taste. Let the stew sit until everything is heated through, 2 to 5 minutes. Reheat the bacon in the microwave on high power until heated through and crisp, about 30 seconds. Serve the stew, sprinkling individual portions with bacon.

SLOW-COOKER CHILI CON CARNE

IF YOU'RE FROM TEXAS, CHILI MEANS ONE thing: Hearty chunks of beef simmered with dried chiles in water or broth—no tomatoes or beans in sight. Although many authentic recipes for this type of chili, also called chili con carne, demand a mix of dried chiles in place of supermarket chili powder, we were hoping to find an easier way to infuse our chili with rich, deep flavor and heat. This Lone Star State classic seemed like a natural for the slow cooker—hours of simmering would render the meat incredibly tender, and a streamlined ingredient list would keep the process fairly straightforward.

Since chili con carne is all about the meat, that's where we started. We opted to use chuck eye roast; it's a cut that we find flavorful, tender, and juicy, and it takes just 10 minutes to trim the meat and cut it into large pieces. To save on prep time, we decided not to brown the meat but instead sautéed aromatics and tomato paste to develop rich flavor. We knew from our Slow-Cooker Beef Stew (page 310) that we could augment the flavor with soy sauce, which adds depth and meatiness; although this ingredient was a tad unconventional for chili, we found that it worked just fine.

As for the aromatics and spices, we found that tasters enjoyed the sweetness provided by sautéed onions, even though they were not standard in most traditional recipes. A hefty amount of garlic—eight cloves—provided a punch of flavor. As for the spices, dried chiles are the authentic choice, but for a simple slow-cooker chili, the work involved in toasting and seeding them seemed excessive. Instead we utilized the test kitchen's technique for blooming spices in hot oil to help enhance the flavor of store-bought chili powder. Added to the skillet with the onions, the chili powder contributed ample fragrance. We also enjoyed the addition of a little cumin and dried oregano.

At this point the flavors were nearly there, but the chili still needed a bit more complexity. We thought of the deep, smoky flavor of chipotles (smoked jalapeño peppers), which are available dried or canned in adobo sauce. After trying both, we settled on the flavor of those packed in adobo sauce, which is made of tomato sauce, vinegar, and a blend of other spices.

We were now ready to look more closely at the liquid component of the chili. Up until this point we had been using water, as most recipes suggested, though we were eager to see the effects of substituting a more flavorful broth. Beef broth overwhelmed the already meaty flavor of the chili and vegetable broth made the chili taste too sweet. Chicken broth, however, was a great success, enriching the chili without making its presence known.

While testing broths we also found most tasters requested the addition of (gasp) tomatoes. With several options available, we tried diced tomatoes, tomato puree, and crushed tomatoes; the tomato puree beat out the others, contributing acidity and flavor, and blending into the chili the best out of the tomato products. However, now that we had

added the tomato puree, our chili was thinner than we liked. Unable to rely on evaporation to thicken the chili due to the covered slow cooker, we felt the use of a thickener was the next best solution. Flour and cornstarch both made the chili taste starchy, but tapioca gave our chili just the right texture without contributing any off-flavors.

The chili was almost complete, but some tasters were left wondering about beans. While research confirmed that real chili con carne doesn't include beans, we liked the creaminess that they brought to the dish and their starch helped balance the spices. We tested stirring them in at the beginning of the cooking time as well as during the last half hour of cooking and found that the beans held up well and had the best flavor when we added them at the onset of cooking.

With some dark brown sugar stirred in for a hint of sweetness, our slow-cooked chili con carne

Cheddar Cheese Bread

MAKES ONE 8-INCH LOAF

Be sure to grate the Parmesan on the large holes of a box grater; it adds a nice texture and prevents the cheese from burning. Do not substitute finely grated or pregrated Parmesan. The texture of the bread improves as it cools, so resist the urge to slice the loaf while it is piping hot.

3	ounces Parmesan cheese, grated on the large holes of a box grater (1 cup)
2½	cups (12½ ounces) unbleached all-purpose flour
1	tablespoon baking powder
1	teaspoon salt
⅛	teaspoon cayenne pepper
⅛	teaspoon ground black pepper
4	ounces extra-sharp cheddar cheese, cut into ½-inch cubes (1 cup)
1	cup whole milk
½	cup sour cream
3	tablespoons unsalted butter, melted and cooled
1	large egg

1. Adjust an oven rack to the middle position and heat the oven to 350 degrees. Grease an 8½ by 4½-inch loaf pan, then sprinkle ½ cup of the Parmesan evenly over the bottom of the pan.

2. Whisk the flour, baking powder, salt, cayenne, and black pepper together in a large bowl. Stir in the cheddar, breaking up any clumps, until it is coated with the flour mixture. In a medium bowl, whisk the milk, sour cream, melted butter, and egg together until smooth. Gently fold the milk mixture into the flour mixture with a rubber spatula until just combined (do not overmix). The batter will be heavy and thick.

3. Scrape the batter into the prepared pan and smooth the top. Sprinkle the remaining ½ cup Parmesan evenly over the top. Bake until golden brown and a toothpick inserted into the center comes out with just a few crumbs attached, 45 to 50 minutes, rotating the pan halfway through baking.

4. Let the loaf cool in the pan for 10 minutes, then turn out onto a wire rack and let cool 1 hour before serving.

was finally complete. While our version may not have been considered completely authentic in some circles, judging by the smiles on our tasters' faces, that was just fine.

Slow-Cooker Chili con Carne
SERVES 6 TO 8

For a milder chili, use the smaller amount of chipotles; for a spicier chili, use the full 4 tablespoons. Be sure to use low-sodium soy sauce or the chili may taste overly salty. Serve with lime wedges, minced fresh cilantro, minced onion, diced avocado, shredded cheddar or Monterey Jack cheese, and/or sour cream. Serve with Cheddar Cheese Bread (page 312).

2	tablespoons vegetable oil
3	medium onions, minced
8	medium garlic cloves, minced or pressed through a garlic press (about 8 teaspoons)
¼	cup chili powder
¼	cup tomato paste
2	tablespoons ground cumin
1	teaspoon dried oregano
	Salt and ground black pepper
1	(28-ounce) can tomato puree
2	(15-ounce) cans dark red kidney beans, drained and rinsed
2	cups low-sodium chicken broth
¼	cup Minute tapioca
2–4	tablespoons minced chipotle chile in adobo sauce (see note)
3	tablespoons low-sodium soy sauce (see note)
2	tablespoons dark brown sugar, plus extra as needed
1	(5-pound) boneless beef chuck eye roast, trimmed and cut into 1½-inch pieces (see the illustrations on page 221)

1. Heat the oil in a 12-inch nonstick skillet over medium heat-high until shimmering. Add the onions, garlic, chili powder, tomato paste, cumin, oregano, and ¼ teaspoon salt and cook, stirring often, until the onions are softened and lightly browned, 8 to 10 minutes. Stir in the tomato puree, scraping up any browned bits, then transfer to the slow cooker.

2. Stir the beans, broth, tapioca, chipotles, soy sauce, and brown sugar into the slow cooker. Season the beef with salt and pepper and nestle into the slow cooker. Cover and cook on low until the meat is tender and the chili is flavorful, 9 to 11 hours. (Alternatively, cover and cook on high for 5 to 7 hours.)

3. Let the chili settle for 5 minutes, then remove as much fat as possible from the surface using a large spoon. Season with salt, pepper, and brown sugar to taste and serve.

SLOW-COOKER WHITE CHICKEN CHILI

WHITE CHICKEN CHILI IS A SIMPLE YET flavorful dish of shredded chicken and white beans. It's spiked with vibrant, spicy green chiles and earthy warm spices, then finished with a shower of fresh cilantro. We figured it would make a good candidate for the slow cooker: The chicken would cook gradually and flavor the broth, the beans would turn creamy, and the chiles would lace the dish with heat.

Many recipes for slow-cooker white chicken chili follow a basic method of dumping the chicken, beans, canned green chiles, onions, garlic, spices, and liquid (either water or broth) into the slow cooker and letting the mixture simmer for hours. This hands-off approach has ease in its favor, but after trying several of these recipes, we found it doesn't have much else. These chilis had a consistency more like soup and by the end of cooking, the dish had no chile flavor (or any flavor at all) no matter how potent the spices were at the beginning. We wanted to keep the streamlined approach, but the resulting chili had to be rich and thick, with hearty, spicy flavor. Clearly, we had our work cut out for us.

We began by selecting the cut of chicken. Dark meat tends to match the heartier flavor profile and consistency of chili better than white meat, so we chose bone-in, skin-on chicken thighs. We knew thighs would remain moist and tender during the hours of simmering. To prevent too much fat from being released into the cooking liquid, we removed the skin before setting the chicken in the slow cooker.

Next, it was time to build the base of our chili. We began by sautéing onions, garlic, chiles, and spices before putting them in the slow cooker. Canned green chiles were squishy, rubbery, and had zero heat—and that was before they had cooked for hours. Fresh jalapeños improved the stew considerably. Cumin and coriander were standard in most recipes and we decided to follow suit—trying to incorporate additional earthy spices like cinnamon or cayenne only posed a distraction for tasters. As for the cooking liquid, we tested water and store-bought chicken broth, which were both common. Although the water was fine, the broth was superior, adding not only depth of flavor but body to the chili.

With a strong foundation in place (so strong, in fact, that we could skip browning the chicken for extra flavor), we were ready to add the beans. Cannellini beans were a popular choice; we tested both canned and dried beans. In the end, we found that canned cannellini beans worked best. Even after we soaked the dried beans, they remained undercooked after the four hours the chili was in the slow cooker; the canned beans, on the other hand, emerged tender but kept their shape.

Tasting our chili at this stage in development, we found the flavor was much improved, but the texture remained problematic—our chili was watery and thin. We knew that the slow cooker wasn't allowing for any evaporation, so we cut back on the chicken broth (from four cups to three) and upped the amount of beans (from two cans to three). The chili was now less soupy, but it still wasn't thick enough to please all of our tasters.

Looking once more at the recipes we unearthed in our research, we found that some suggested adding hominy—dried corn kernels without the hull and germ. We wondered if maybe a can of hominy would soak up some of the extra liquid in the chili. While the hominy added rich flavor, it didn't do anything for the texture of the dish. Would pureeing it help? We processed a can of hominy with some chicken broth, then stirred the mixture into the pot. As we had hoped, the pureed hominy

made for a velvety-smooth chili base with a hearty note of toasted corn.

To finish, we stirred in some cilantro and were about to add a squeeze of lime when we spied a jar of pickled jalapeños. We chopped a few tablespoons and stirred them in instead. Now our chili had just the right kick and sweetness.

Slow-Cooker
White Chicken Chili
SERVES 6 TO 8

Do not cook this chili on high power or the chicken will become tough. For more heat, include the jalapeño seeds and ribs when mincing. Serve with lime wedges, minced fresh cilantro, and/or sour cream.

2	tablespoons vegetable oil
2	medium onions, minced
4	jalapeño chiles, stemmed, seeded, and minced (see note)
6	medium garlic cloves, minced or pressed through a garlic press (about 2 tablespoons)
4	teaspoons ground cumin
2	teaspoons ground coriander
3	cups low-sodium chicken broth
I	(15-ounce) can white or yellow hominy, drained and rinsed
	Salt and ground black pepper
3	(15-ounce) cans cannellini beans, drained and rinsed
3	pounds bone-in chicken thighs (8 to 10 thighs), skin removed and trimmed
2	tablespoons minced jarred pickled jalapeños
¼	cup minced fresh cilantro leaves

1. Heat the oil in a 12-inch skillet over medium-high heat until shimmering. Add the onions, jalapeños, garlic, cumin, and coriander and cook, stirring often, until the onions are softened and lightly browned, 8 to 10 minutes. Stir in 1 cup of the chicken broth, scraping up any browned bits, then transfer to the slow cooker.

2. Puree the hominy, remaining 2 cups chicken broth, and ½ teaspoon salt in a blender until smooth, 1 to 2 minutes. Stir the pureed hominy

mixture and beans into the slow cooker. Season the chicken with salt and pepper and nestle into the slow cooker. Cover and cook on low until the chicken is tender, 4 to 6 hours.

3. Transfer the chicken to a cutting board, let it cool slightly, then shred it into bite-size pieces (see the illustration on page 43), discarding the bones. Let the chili settle for 5 minutes, then remove as much fat as possible from the surface using a large spoon.

4. Stir in the shredded chicken and pickled jalapeños. Let the chili sit until everything is heated through, 2 to 5 minutes. Stir in the cilantro, season with salt and pepper to taste, and serve.

SLOW-COOKER BLACK BEAN CHILI

GOOD BLACK BEAN CHILI IS ROBUST, HEARTY, and earthy-tasting, with creamy beans and a jet-black hue that provides the perfect backdrop for a colorful array of garnishes. Most black bean chilis we've sampled, however, are not so good—their flavor is dull and washed-out, and their color a drab and murky gray. Add the moist cooking environment of the slow cooker to the mix, and things don't improve much. But we thought the appeal of a hands-off black bean chili was undeniable, and resolved to spend some time up front to infuse our chili with as much flavor as possible. We set out to create a black bean chili that we could walk away from for part of the day, but it had to be rich and full-flavored when we returned.

Before we could focus on the flavor profile, we began with our beans, looking for the best way to prepare them. Usually we prefer to soak beans in a saltwater solution prior to cooking. This softens the tough bean skins and prevents the beans from bursting during cooking. However, we wanted a thick, rich chili and some burst beans would only contribute to our desired consistency. We opted to skip the soaking.

Moving on to the liquid component of our chili, we knew it had to be flavorful to ensure well-seasoned beans. Because we were working with a slow cooker, we knew using a flavorful liquid was even more important, as there would be no opportunity for the liquid to reduce and concentrate in flavor. We tested various amounts of chicken broth and water and settled on equal amounts; tasters felt the chili made with chicken broth alone was too chickeny in flavor. For 1 pound of beans, we found 2½ cups of each was sufficient. To prevent the cooked beans from losing their attractive, dark shade, we stirred in a small amount of baking soda at the beginning of cooking; this resulted in dark, earthy-colored beans.

Now we could focus on developing the flavor profile. We began by sautéing two onions, some garlic, and chili powder. Two red bell peppers brought a pleasant sweetness to the dish, while two jalapeños added a spicy, bright undertone. Cumin supplied some sweetness and warmth and oregano added depth. To bring out the flavors of the spices, we sautéed them with the vegetables.

The chili was coming together nicely, but tasters felt its flavor would be greatly improved by the addition of some meat. We tested cooking the beans with smoked ham hocks, bacon, and ham. Each of the three gave the beans a slightly different flavor; the ham hock provided a smooth background taste, while the bacon and ham produced chili with a more assertive and salty flavor. But after 10 hours in the slow cooker, the bacon was slimy and bloated. Ultimately, we went with the ham hocks, which contributed both rich, smoky flavor and bites of meat.

Through testing we also found that tasters appreciated some chunks of tomatoes in the chili; they contributed a necessary brightness that was noticeably missing. After testing fresh chopped tomatoes and canned whole tomatoes (which we cut into chunks), tasters preferred the texture and concentrated flavor of canned whole tomatoes. Because acidic ingredients can toughen beans by preventing cells from absorbing water, and we were using a large can of tomatoes, we decided to add them to the pot at the end of cooking.

After 10 hours in the slow cooker, our chili was boldly flavored, but it was a bit thin. We tried two methods for thickening the chili. For the first test, we pureed some beans in a blender and stirred the puree back into the chili. For the second test, we used a potato masher to smash some of the beans in a separate bowl, then returned the smashed beans back to the slow cooker. In the end, tasters were pleased with the rustic look and texture of the latter method—mashing some of the beans in a bowl. The broth was now nicely thickened, with whole beans suspended throughout.

Finished with minced cilantro for color and freshness, our slow-cooker black bean chili was richly flavored and utterly satisfying—and practically effortless.

Slow-Cooker Black Bean Chili
SERVES 6 TO 8

For more heat, include the jalapeño seeds and ribs when mincing. Serve with lime wedges, minced onion, diced avocado, shredded cheddar or Monterey Jack cheese, and/or sour cream.

I	tablespoon vegetable oil
2	medium onions, minced
2	red bell peppers, stemmed, seeded, and chopped fine
2	jalapeño chiles, stemmed, seeded, and minced (see note)
3	tablespoons chili powder
5	medium garlic cloves, minced or pressed through a garlic press (about 5 teaspoons)
I	tablespoon ground cumin
I	tablespoon dried oregano
2½	cups low-sodium chicken broth
2½	cups water

I	pound dried black beans, picked over and rinsed
	Salt and ground black pepper
2	bay leaves
⅛	teaspoon baking soda
2	smoked ham hocks, rinsed
I	(28-ounce) can whole tomatoes, drained and cut into ½-inch pieces
2	tablespoons minced fresh cilantro leaves

1. Heat the oil in a 12-inch skillet over medium-high heat until shimmering. Add the onions, bell peppers, jalapeños, chili powder, garlic, cumin, and oregano and cook, stirring often, until the vegetables are softened and lightly browned, 8 to 10 minutes. Stir in 1 cup of the chicken broth, scraping up any browned bits, then transfer to the slow cooker.

2. Stir the remaining 1½ cups chicken broth, water, beans, 2 teaspoons salt, bay leaves, and baking soda into the slow cooker, then nestle in the ham hocks. Cover and cook on low until the beans are tender, 9 to 11 hours. (Alternatively, cover and cook on high for 5 to 7 hours.)

3. Transfer the ham hocks to a cutting board, let them cool slightly, then shred the meat into bite-size pieces, discarding the skin and bones. Let the chili settle for 5 minutes, then remove as much fat as possible from the surface using a large spoon.

4. Remove the bay leaves. Transfer 1 cup of the cooked beans to a bowl and mash with a potato masher or fork until smooth. Stir the mashed beans, shredded ham, and tomatoes into the chili. Let the chili sit until everything is heated through, 2 to 5 minutes. Stir in the cilantro, season with salt and pepper to taste, and serve.

15

SPEEDY SOUPS

SPEEDY SOUPS

Lemony Chicken and Rice Soup

SERVES 4 TO 6

Egg yolks give this quick soup, based on the Greek classic avgolemono, *a rich, silky texture. Be careful not to overcook the chicken in step 3 or it will taste dry. Also, be sure to heat the soup very gently after adding the egg yolks in step 5 or they may curdle.*

1   pound boneless, skinless chicken breasts (about 3 breasts), trimmed
     Salt and ground black pepper
1   tablespoon vegetable oil
2   carrots, peeled and sliced ¼ inch thick
1   medium onion, minced
1   teaspoon minced fresh thyme leaves or ¼ teaspoon dried
6   cups low-sodium chicken broth
½   cup long-grain white rice
6   (3-inch-long) strips zest from 1 lemon (see the illustration on page 148), trimmed of white pith
2   tablespoons minced fresh parsley leaves
4   large egg yolks
2   tablespoons juice from 1 lemon

1. Pat the chicken dry with paper towels and season with salt and pepper. Heat the oil in a large Dutch oven over medium-high heat until just smoking. Brown the chicken lightly on both sides, about 5 minutes; transfer to a plate.

2. Add the carrots and onion to the fat left in the pot and cook over medium heat until softened, 5 to 7 minutes. Stir in the thyme and cook until fragrant, about 30 seconds. Stir in the broth, rice, and lemon zest strips, scraping up any browned bits, and bring to a boil.

3. Add the browned chicken, cover, and simmer gently until the chicken registers 160 to 165 degrees on an instant-read thermometer, about 10 minutes. Remove the chicken from the pot, let it cool slightly, then shred it into bite-size pieces (see the illustration on page 43).

4. Return the soup to a simmer, cover, and continue to cook until the rice is tender, about 10 minutes. Remove the lemon zest strips and stir in the shredded chicken and parsley.

5. Whisk the egg yolks and lemon juice together in a bowl. Stir a few tablespoons of the hot soup into the yolk mixture to temper, then whisk the yolk mixture into the pot. Continue to cook the soup gently over low heat, whisking constantly, until it thickens slightly, about 1 minute; remove immediately from the heat. Season with salt and pepper to taste and serve.

Asian Chicken Noodle Soup

SERVES 4 TO 6

Ginger, soy sauce, and ramen noodles put an Asian-inspired spin on traditional chicken noodle soup. Be careful not to overcook the chicken in step 3 or it will taste dry.

1   pound boneless, skinless chicken breasts (about 3 breasts), trimmed
     Salt and ground black pepper
1   tablespoon vegetable oil
1   medium onion, minced
1   tablespoon minced or grated fresh ginger (see the illustrations on page 89)
2   medium garlic cloves, minced or pressed through a garlic press (about 2 teaspoons)
6   cups low-sodium chicken broth
2   tablespoons dry sherry
2   tablespoons soy sauce
1   pound bok choy (1 small head), greens sliced thin and stalks chopped medium (see the illustrations on page 56)
1   (3-ounce) package ramen noodles, flavoring packet discarded
2   scallions, sliced thin

1. Pat the chicken dry with paper towels and season with salt and pepper. Heat the oil in a large Dutch oven over medium-high heat until just smoking. Brown the chicken lightly on both sides, about 5 minutes; transfer to a plate.

2. Add the onion to the fat left in the pot; cook over medium heat until softened, 5 to 7 minutes. Stir in the ginger and garlic and cook until fragrant, about 30 seconds. Stir in the broth, sherry, and soy sauce, scraping up any browned bits, and bring to a boil.

3. Add the browned chicken, cover, and simmer gently until the chicken registers 160 to

165 degrees on an instant-read thermometer, about 10 minutes. Remove the chicken from the pot, let it cool slightly, then shred it into bite-size pieces (see the illustration on page 43).

4. Return the soup to a simmer, stir in the bok choy and noodles, and cook until the noodles are tender, about 3 minutes. Stir in the shredded chicken and scallions, season with salt and pepper to taste, and serve.

Fast Tortilla Soup

SERVES 4 TO 6

Our speedy version of the Mexican classic relies on a base of sautéed chipotle chiles, garlic, and tomato paste to develop potent flavor in minutes. Be careful not to overcook the chicken in step 3 or it will taste dry.

1	pound boneless, skinless chicken breasts (about 3 breasts), trimmed
	Salt and ground black pepper
1	tablespoon vegetable oil
1	medium onion, minced
1	tablespoon minced chipotle chile in adobo sauce
2	teaspoons tomato paste
2	medium garlic cloves, minced or pressed through a garlic press (about 2 teaspoons)
6	cups low-sodium chicken broth
2	tablespoons juice from 1 lime
4	ounces tortilla chips, crushed into large pieces (about 4 cups)
3	plum tomatoes, cored and cut into ½-inch pieces
1	medium, ripe avocado, pitted, peeled, and diced (see the illustrations on pages 44 and 46)
½	cup fresh cilantro leaves

1. Pat the chicken dry with paper towels and season with salt and pepper. Heat the oil in a large Dutch oven over medium-high heat until just smoking. Brown the chicken lightly on both sides, about 5 minutes; transfer to a plate.

2. Add the onion to the fat left in the pot and cook over medium heat until softened, 5 to 7 minutes. Stir in the chipotles, tomato paste, and garlic

and cook until fragrant, about 30 seconds. Stir in the broth, scraping up any browned bits, and bring to a boil.

3. Add the browned chicken, cover, and simmer gently until the chicken registers 160 to 165 degrees on an instant-read thermometer, about 10 minutes. Remove the chicken from the pot, let it cool slightly, then shred it into bite-size pieces (see the illustration on page 43).

4. Return the soup to a simmer, cover, and continue to cook until the flavors have melded, 5 to 10 minutes. Stir in the lime juice and season with salt and pepper to taste. Divide the shredded chicken, tortilla chips, tomatoes, and avocado among individual bowls. Ladle the hot soup into the bowls, sprinkle with the cilantro, and serve.

Quick Clam Chowder

SERVES 6 TO 8

The flour is key to achieving the right consistency, and it also ensures that the soup won't curdle or separate. We prefer the creamy texture of Yukon Gold potatoes in this chowder; however, red potatoes will also work. Be careful not to overcook the clams in step 3 or they will taste rubbery.

4	ounces (about 4 slices) bacon, chopped fine
1	medium onion, minced
2	medium garlic cloves, minced or pressed through a garlic press (about 2 teaspoons)
⅓	cup unbleached all-purpose flour
4	(6.5-ounce) cans minced clams, drained and juice reserved
3	(8-ounce) bottles clam juice
1½	pounds Yukon Gold potatoes (about 3 medium), peeled and cut into ½-inch pieces
1	teaspoon minced fresh thyme leaves or ¼ teaspoon dried
2	bay leaves
1	cup heavy cream
2	tablespoons minced fresh parsley leaves
	Salt and ground black pepper

1. Cook the bacon in a large Dutch oven over medium heat until rendered and crisp, 5 to 7 minutes. Stir in the onion and cook until softened, 5 to

7 minutes. Stir in the garlic and cook until fragrant, about 30 seconds. Stir in the flour and cook for 1 minute.

2. Gradually whisk in the reserved clam juice and bottled clam juice, scraping up any browned bits and smoothing out any lumps. Stir in the potatoes, thyme, and bay leaves and bring to a boil. Reduce to a simmer and cook until the potatoes are tender, 20 to 25 minutes.

3. Stir in the drained clams and cream and continue to simmer gently until the clams are heated through, about 2 minutes. Remove the bay leaves and stir in the parsley. Season with salt and pepper to taste and serve.

Harvest Pumpkin Soup

SERVES 4 TO 6

Using canned pumpkin shaves off significant prep and cooking time in this warm-spiced, slightly sweet soup. Be sure to buy pure canned pumpkin, not pumpkin pie filling, which has sugar and spices added. Crumbled blue cheese and toasted, chopped walnuts make nice garnishes to this soup. See page 121 for more information on pureeing soup.

2	tablespoons unsalted butter
1	medium onion, minced
2	medium garlic cloves, minced or pressed through a garlic press (about 2 teaspoons)
½	teaspoon ground cumin
½	teaspoon ground coriander
¼	teaspoon ground nutmeg
3	cups low-sodium chicken broth, plus extra as needed
2	cups water
1	(15-ounce) can pure pumpkin (see note)
¼	cup maple syrup
½	cup half-and-half
	Salt and ground black pepper

1. Melt the butter in a large Dutch oven over medium heat. Add the onion and cook until softened, 5 to 7 minutes. Stir in the garlic, cumin, coriander, and nutmeg and cook until fragrant, about 30 seconds.

2. Stir in the broth, water, pumpkin, and maple syrup, scraping up any browned bits, and bring to a

boil. Reduce to a simmer and cook until the flavors have melded, about 15 minutes.

3. Working in batches, puree the soup until smooth, 1 to 2 minutes. Return the soup to a clean pot.

4. Stir in the half-and-half and additional broth as needed to adjust the soup's consistency. Heat the soup gently over low heat until hot (do not boil). Season with salt and pepper to taste and serve.

Eleventh-Hour Butternut Squash Soup

SERVES 6

Using precut butternut squash saves time (and effort) in this recipe, but you can cut up your own squash, if desired (see the illustrations on page 129). Browning the squash first, before building the soup, adds great flavor in just minutes. Crumbled blue cheese and toasted, chopped walnuts make nice garnishes to this soup. See page 121 for more information on pureeing soup.

2	tablespoons vegetable oil
2	pounds peeled, seeded butternut squash, cut into 1- to 2-inch chunks (see note)
1	medium onion, minced
2	medium garlic cloves, minced or pressed through a garlic press (about 2 teaspoons)
1	tablespoon minced fresh sage or 1 teaspoon dried
4	cups low-sodium chicken broth, plus extra as needed
½	cup water
2	bay leaves
¼	cup half-and-half
2	tablespoons minced fresh parsley leaves
	Salt and ground black pepper

1. Heat 1 tablespoon of the oil in a large Dutch oven over medium heat until shimmering. Add the squash and cook until lightly browned, 8 to 10 minutes. Transfer to a bowl.

2. Add the remaining 1 tablespoon oil to the pot and place over medium heat until shimmering. Add the onion and cook until softened, 5 to 7 minutes. Stir in the garlic and sage and cook until fragrant, about 30 seconds.

3. Stir in the broth and water, scraping up any browned bits. Stir in the bay leaves and browned squash and bring to a boil. Cover, reduce to a simmer, and cook until the squash is tender, about 15 minutes.

4. Remove the bay leaves. Working in batches, puree the soup until smooth, 1 to 2 minutes. Return the soup to a clean pot.

5. Stir in the half-and-half and additional broth as needed to adjust the soup's consistency. Heat the soup gently over low heat until hot (do not boil). Stir in the parsley, season with salt and pepper to taste, and serve.

Baby Carrot Bisque

SERVES 4 TO 6

Fuss-free baby carrots help you pull off this soup in short order. Using both vegetable broth and chicken broth provides a balanced sweet and savory flavor profile. If your carrots are particularly large, they may require a longer simmering time in step 2 to become tender. Crumbled goat cheese and toasted, slivered almonds make nice garnishes to this soup. See page 121 for more information on pureeing soup.

I	tablespoon vegetable oil
I½	pounds baby carrots
I	medium onion, minced
2	medium garlic cloves, minced or pressed through a garlic press (about 2 teaspoons)
I	teaspoon minced fresh thyme leaves or ¼ teaspoon dried
½	teaspoon ground coriander
2½	cups low-sodium chicken broth, plus extra as needed
2½	cups vegetable broth
2	bay leaves
½	cup half-and-half
	Salt and ground black pepper
I	tablespoon minced fresh chives

1. Heat the oil in a large Dutch oven over medium heat until shimmering. Add the carrots and onion and cook until the onion is softened, 5 to 7 minutes. Stir in the garlic, thyme, and coriander and cook until fragrant, about 30 seconds.

2. Stir in the chicken broth, vegetable broth, and bay leaves, scraping up any browned bits, and bring to a boil. Cover, reduce to a simmer, and cook until the carrots are tender, about 20 minutes.

3. Remove the bay leaves. Working in batches, puree the soup until smooth, 1 to 2 minutes. Return the soup to a clean pot.

4. Stir in the half-and-half and additional chicken broth as needed to adjust the soup's consistency. Heat the soup gently over low heat until hot (do not boil). Season with salt and pepper to taste and serve, sprinkling individual portions with the chives.

Tortellini Minestrone

SERVES 4 TO 6

A few convenience products—V8 juice, pesto, and fresh tortellini—pack this simple minestrone with loads of flavor. Bacon infuses the soup with an underlying richness, while zucchini provides color and freshness. Be sure to use fresh tortellini in this soup; frozen or dried tortellini will require different cooking times and additional cooking liquid. We prefer the flavor of fresh pesto, found in the refrigerator section of the supermarket; do not use jarred pesto. Any small white canned beans will work well here.

2	ounces (about 2 slices) bacon, chopped fine
2	carrots, peeled and cut into ½-inch pieces
I	medium onion, minced
3	medium garlic cloves, minced or pressed through a garlic press (about I tablespoon)
I	tablespoon minced fresh oregano leaves or I teaspoon dried
3½	cups low-sodium chicken broth
2½	cups V8 vegetable juice
I	(15-ounce) can cannellini beans, drained and rinsed (see note)
I	(9-ounce) package fresh cheese tortellini (see note)
I	medium zucchini (about 8 ounces), halved lengthwise, seeded, and cut into ½-inch pieces
	Salt and ground black pepper
½	cup prepared pesto (see note)
	Grated Parmesan cheese, for serving

1. Cook the bacon in a large Dutch oven over medium heat until rendered and crisp, 5 to 7 minutes. Stir in the carrots and onion and cook until softened, 5 to 7 minutes. Stir in the garlic and oregano and cook until fragrant, about 30 seconds.

2. Stir in the broth, scraping up any browned bits. Stir in the vegetable juice and beans and bring to a boil. Reduce to a simmer and cook until the beans have heated through, about 10 minutes.

3. Stir in the tortellini and zucchini and continue to simmer until they are tender, 5 to 7 minutes.

4. Season with salt and pepper to taste. Dollop individual portions with the pesto and sprinkle with the Parmesan before serving.

Tomato Florentine Soup

SERVES 4 TO 6

For long-cooked flavor in little time, we sauté canned tomatoes with brown sugar and tomato paste; the brown sugar adds sweetness and facilitates caramelization, and the tomato paste brings depth and richness. A small amount of flour gives this tomato and spinach soup some body and prevents it from becoming watery. If you use larger pasta, it may require a longer simmering time in step 3.

2 tablespoons unsalted butter

3 (14.5-ounce) cans diced tomatoes, drained and juice reserved

1 medium onion, minced

1 tablespoon tomato paste

1 tablespoon light brown sugar

3 medium garlic cloves, minced or pressed through a garlic press (about 1 tablespoon)

2 tablespoons unbleached all-purpose flour

5 cups low-sodium chicken broth

1 cup small pasta, such as ditalini, tubettini, or small elbows (see note)

2 bay leaves

10 ounces baby spinach (about 10 cups)

Salt and ground black pepper

Grated Parmesan cheese, for serving

1. Melt the butter in a large Dutch oven over high heat. Add the tomatoes, onion, tomato paste, and sugar and cook until the tomatoes are dry and beginning to brown, 11 to 13 minutes.

2. Stir in the garlic and cook until fragrant, about 30 seconds. Stir in the flour and cook for 1 minute.

3. Gradually whisk in the broth and reserved tomato juice, scraping up any browned bits and smoothing out any lumps. Stir in the pasta and bay leaves and bring to a boil. Reduce to a simmer and cook until the pasta is tender, 10 to 12 minutes.

4. Remove the bay leaves. Stir in the spinach and continue to simmer until wilted, about 3 minutes. Season with salt and pepper to taste and serve with the Parmesan.

Easy Black Bean Soup

SERVES 4 TO 6

Pureeing a portion of the beans gives this soup body, and sliced chorizo adds meaty richness to this satisfying soup.

4 (15-ounce) cans black beans, drained and rinsed

3 cups low-sodium chicken broth

2 tablespoons vegetable oil

6 ounces chorizo, halved lengthwise and sliced ¼ inch thick

1 medium onion, minced

1 red bell pepper, stemmed, seeded, and chopped fine

6 medium garlic cloves, minced or pressed through a garlic press (about 2 tablespoons)

1 tablespoon minced fresh oregano leaves or 1 teaspoon dried

½ teaspoon ground cumin

½ teaspoon cayenne pepper

½ cup minced fresh cilantro leaves

Salt and ground black pepper

Hot sauce

Lime wedges, for serving

1. Puree 2 cups of the beans with 1 cup of the broth in a blender until smooth; set aside.

2. Heat 1 tablespoon of the oil in a large Dutch oven over medium heat until just smoking. Brown the chorizo well on both sides, about 5 minutes, then transfer to a paper towel–lined plate.

3. Add the remaining 1 tablespoon oil to the pot and place over medium heat until shimmering.

Add the onion and bell pepper and cook until softened, 5 to 7 minutes. Stir in the garlic, oregano, cumin, and cayenne and cook until fragrant, about 30 seconds.

4. Stir in the remaining 2 cups broth, scraping up any browned bits. Stir in the remaining beans, pureed beans, and browned chorizo and bring to a boil. Reduce to a simmer and cook until the flavors have melded, about 10 minutes.

5. Stir in the cilantro and season with salt, pepper, and hot sauce to taste. Serve with the lime wedges.

Pantry White Bean Soup with Rosemary

SERVES 4 TO 6

Steeping the rosemary sprig for 10 minutes infuses this soup with deep flavor and aroma quickly, and the resulting rich broth rids the beans of any "canned" flavor. The croutons are stirred into the soup before serving; don't skip this step because they add important flavor and texture and help thicken the broth.

4	ounces (about 4 slices) bacon, chopped fine
I	medium onion, minced
I	tablespoon extra-virgin olive oil, plus extra for serving
4	medium garlic cloves, minced or pressed through a garlic press (about 4 teaspoons)
4	cups low-sodium chicken broth
3	(15-ounce) cans navy beans, drained and rinsed
2	bay leaves
I	sprig fresh rosemary
I	recipe Butter Croutons (page 116)
I	large tomato, cored, seeded, and cut into ½-inch pieces
	Salt and ground black pepper
	Balsamic vinegar, for serving

1. Cook the bacon in a large Dutch oven over medium heat until rendered and crisp, 5 to 7 minutes. Stir in the onion and oil and cook until softened, 5 to 7 minutes. Stir in the garlic and cook until fragrant, about 30 seconds.

2. Stir in the broth, scraping up any browned bits. Stir in the beans and bay leaves, bring to a simmer, and cook until the flavors have melded, about 10 minutes.

3. Off the heat, submerge the rosemary in the soup, cover, and let stand until fragrant, about 10 minutes.

4. Discard the rosemary and bay leaves. Stir in the croutons and tomato and season with salt and pepper to taste. Serve, drizzling individual portions with vinegar and additional olive oil.

Vegetarian Bean Chili

SERVES 4

The combination of beans and corn make this meat-free chili a hearty meal. You can use any type of canned beans in this chili; we like to use two varieties, such as pinto and black beans for contrast in flavor and appearance. To make the chili spicier, add extra chipotle chiles. Serve with lime wedges, minced fresh cilantro, sliced scallions, minced onion, diced avocado, shredded cheddar or Monterey Jack cheese, and/or sour cream.

2	tablespoons vegetable oil
I	medium onion, minced
3	tablespoons chili powder
2	teaspoons ground cumin
3	medium garlic cloves, minced or pressed through a garlic press (about I tablespoon)
I	(28-ounce) can crushed tomatoes
2	(15-ounce) cans beans, drained and rinsed
2	teaspoons minced chipotle chile in adobo sauce
I½	cups frozen corn
2	tablespoons minced fresh cilantro leaves
	Salt and ground black pepper

1. Heat the oil in a large Dutch oven over medium-high heat until shimmering. Add the onion and cook until softened, 5 to 7 minutes. Stir in the chili powder, cumin, and garlic and cook until fragrant, about 30 seconds.

2. Stir in the tomatoes, scraping up any browned bits. Stir in the beans and chipotles and bring to a boil. Reduce to a simmer and cook until slightly thickened and the flavors have melded, about 15 minutes.

3. Stir in the corn and cook until heated through, about 2 minutes. Stir in the cilantro, season with salt and pepper to taste, and serve.

Quick Pork and Hominy Chili

SERVES 4 TO 6

You can find canned tomatillos and canned hominy alongside other Latin American ingredients at the supermarket. For more heat, include the jalapeño seeds and ribs when mincing. Serve with chopped tomato and shredded cheddar or Monterey Jack cheese.

1	(28-ounce) can tomatillos, drained
1	tablespoon vegetable oil
1	medium onion, minced
2	poblano chiles, stemmed, seeded, and chopped medium
1	jalapeño chile, stemmed, seeded, and minced (see note)
2	medium garlic cloves, minced or pressed through a garlic press (about 2 teaspoons)
1	teaspoon cumin
½	teaspoon cayenne pepper
1	pound ground pork
1	tablespoon unbleached all-purpose flour
2½	cups low-sodium chicken broth
1	(15-ounce) can white or yellow hominy, drained and rinsed
2	tablespoons minced fresh cilantro leaves
	Salt and ground black pepper

1. In a large bowl, mash the drained tomatillos to a chunky consistency with a potato masher; set aside.

2. Heat the oil in a large Dutch oven over medium-high heat until shimmering. Add the onion, poblanos, and jalapeño and cook until softened, 5 to 7 minutes. Stir in the garlic, cumin, and cayenne and cook until fragrant, about 30 seconds.

3. Stir in the ground pork and cook, breaking up the meat with a wooden spoon, until no longer pink, about 4 minutes. Stir in the flour and cook for 1 minute.

4. Stir in the broth, scraping up any browned bits. Stir in the mashed tomatillos and hominy and bring to a boil. Reduce to a simmer and cook until the flavors have melded, about 15 minutes.

5. Stir in the cilantro, season with salt and pepper to taste, and serve.

Sirloin Steak and Potato Stew

SERVES 4 TO 6

Anchovy and soy sauce, ingredients not usually found in beef stew, add layers of flavor without drawing attention to themselves. Be careful not to overcook the beef in step 4 or it will taste dry.

2	pounds sirloin steak tips, trimmed and cut into ½-inch pieces
	Salt and ground black pepper
2	tablespoons vegetable oil
3	carrots, peeled and sliced ¼ inch thick
1	medium onion, minced
3	medium garlic cloves, minced or pressed through a garlic press (about 1 tablespoon)
1	tablespoon tomato paste
1	anchovy fillet, rinsed and minced
¼	cup unbleached all-purpose flour
½	cup dry red wine
3	cups beef broth
1	large Yukon Gold potato (about 12 ounces), peeled and cut into ½-inch pieces
1½	teaspoons minced fresh thyme leaves or ½ teaspoon dried
2	bay leaves
½	cup frozen peas
2	teaspoons soy sauce

1. Pat the beef dry with paper towels and season with salt and pepper. Heat 1 tablespoon of the oil in a large Dutch oven over medium-high heat until just smoking. Add half of the beef and cook, stirring occasionally, until well browned, 5 to 7 minutes; transfer to a medium bowl. Repeat with the remaining 1 tablespoon oil and the remaining beef; transfer to the bowl.

2. Add the carrots and onion to the fat left in the pot and cook over medium heat until softened,

5 to 7 minutes. Stir in the garlic, tomato paste, and anchovy and cook until fragrant, about 30 seconds.

3. Stir in the flour and cook for 1 minute. Gradually whisk in the wine, scraping up any browned bits and smoothing out any lumps. Stir in the broth, potato, thyme, and bay leaves and bring to a boil. Cover, reduce to a simmer, and cook until the carrots and potato are tender, about 15 minutes.

4. Remove the bay leaves. Stir in the browned beef, peas, and soy sauce and continue to cook until everything is heated through, about 2 minutes (do not overcook the beef); remove from the heat. Season with salt and pepper to taste and serve.

Beef Stroganoff Stew
SERVES 4 TO 6

Cooking the egg noodles directly in the stew's sauce stream-lines this classic dish. Sirloin steak tips can be substituted for the tenderloin if necessary. White mushrooms can be substituted for the cremini mushrooms. Be careful not to overcook the beef in step 4 or it will taste dry.

12   ounces beef tenderloin, sliced in half lengthwise, then sliced crosswise into ¼-inch pieces (see note)
     Salt and ground black pepper
2   tablespoons vegetable oil
1   pound cremini mushrooms, wiped clean, trimmed, and sliced thin (see note)
1   medium onion, minced
1   tablespoon unbleached all-purpose flour
2   teaspoons tomato paste
½   cup dry white wine
4   cups beef broth
4   cups (6 ounces) wide egg noodles
1   tablespoon spicy brown mustard
½   cup sour cream
1   tablespoon minced fresh parsley leaves

1. Pat the beef dry with paper towels and season with salt and pepper. Heat 1 tablespoon of the oil in a large Dutch oven over medium-high heat until just smoking. Add half of the beef and cook, stirring occasionally, until well browned, 5 to 7 minutes; transfer to a medium bowl. Repeat with the remaining 1 tablespoon oil and remaining beef; transfer to the bowl.

2. Add the mushrooms and onion to the fat left in the pot. Cover and cook over medium heat until the mushrooms release their liquid, 8 to 10 minutes. Uncover, increase the heat to high, and cook until the liquid has evaporated and the mushrooms begin to brown, about 4 minutes.

3. Stir in the flour and tomato paste and cook for 1 minute. Gradually whisk in the wine, scraping up any browned bits and smoothing out any lumps. Stir in the broth, noodles, and mustard and continue to simmer until the noodles are tender, 10 to 15 minutes.

4. Whisk a few tablespoons of the hot liquid into the sour cream to temper, then stir the sour cream mixture into the pot. Add the browned beef and continue to cook gently over low heat until everything is heated through, about 2 minutes (do not overcook the beef); remove from the heat. Stir in the parsley, season with salt and pepper to taste, and serve.

16

BIG-BATCH FAVORITES

Big-Batch Favorites

Big-batch cooking isn't simply a matter of doubling or tripling a recipe's ingredient list. For instance, triple a beef stew recipe and suddenly you're working with almost 10 pounds of meat, which can be awkward to manage and can throw off your browning and cooking times (and requires a different cooking vessel). In addition, not all ingredients need to be doubled or tripled. Here's what we learned about big-batch cooking while developing the recipes in this chapter.

Brown Just Half of the Meat

For our beef and pork stews, we found that it wasn't necessary to brown all of the meat, which would take as long as 45 minutes for several batches. Instead, we browned only half of the meat, developing great flavor in a fraction of the time. Deglazing the pot or skillet later and adding that rich liquid to the simmering stew ensured that we didn't lose any flavor by skimping on the browning.

Don't Double or Triple Everything

When scaling recipes up, it isn't always necessary to increase all ingredients proportionally. For instance, we tripled the meat in our Big-Batch Beef Burgundy, but when we tripled the sodium-rich ingredients like salt pork, chicken broth, and beef broth, the stew was unpalatably salty, so we merely doubled these in order to keep the flavor of the dish in balance.

Brown in a Dutch Oven, Cook in a Roasting Pan

We usually cook our stews in the oven for the most consistent results, and we usually use a Dutch oven. But to cook larger batches of stew, the Dutch oven is too small. We still needed the Dutch oven for browning the meat, but we found that a turkey-size roasting pan was the best option for cooking the stew in the oven since its large surface area allowed the large volume to cook more evenly. Also, the roasting pan makes it easier to maneuver a big batch of stew in and out of the hot oven.

Allow Time for Cooling

If you're making the recipe ahead of time, be sure to allow adequate time for cooling prior to refrigerating it. A big pot of hot stew or chili will cause your refrigerator temperature to rise significantly, putting other food at risk of spoiling. For this reason, we recommend cooling soups, stews, and chilis for 45 minutes before refrigerating.

Take Your Time Reheating

When reheating big-batch dishes, it is important to do so slowly (our recipes generally take 1½ to 2 hours to reheat) and gently over medium-low heat, stirring frequently. Vigorous simmering can cause the meat to toughen and the vegetables to overcook.

Big-Batch Creole-Style Gumbo

SERVES 18 TO 20

Fish sauce, an ingredient not usually found in gumbo, lends depth and complexity to the stew; do not omit it. To prevent the gumbo from tasting overly salty, be sure to use low-sodium chicken broth. The roux cooking time in step 2 may be longer depending on the type of pot you use; the color of the finished roux should be that of an old, dark copper penny. The pot of gumbo will be heavy—up to 25 pounds—so use caution when handling. Serve with rice. To read more about Creole-Style Gumbo, see page 170.

1½	cups plus 2 tablespoons unbleached all-purpose flour
1	cup vegetable oil
2	medium onions, minced
2	green bell peppers, stemmed, seeded, and chopped fine
2	celery ribs, chopped fine
9	medium garlic cloves, minced or pressed through a garlic press (about 3 tablespoons)
2	teaspoons minced fresh thyme leaves or ½ teaspoon dried
½	teaspoon cayenne pepper
1	(28-ounce) can diced tomatoes, drained
7½	cups low-sodium chicken broth
½	cup fish sauce (see note)
4	pounds boneless, skinless chicken thighs (about 16 thighs), trimmed and cut into 1-inch pieces
1	pound andouille sausage, halved lengthwise and sliced thin
1	pound frozen sliced okra, thawed
4	pounds extra-large shrimp (21 to 25 per pound), peeled and deveined (see the illustration on page 169)
	Salt and ground black pepper

1. Adjust an oven rack to the lowest position and heat the oven to 350 degrees. Toast 1½ cups of the flour in a large Dutch oven over medium heat, stirring constantly, until it just begins to brown, about 5 minutes.

2. Off the heat, whisk in the oil until smooth. Cover the pot, transfer it to the oven, and cook until the mixture is deep brown and fragrant, about

1 hour. Remove the pot from the oven, whisk the roux to combine, and let cool slightly. Very carefully scrape the roux (it will be scalding hot) into a 12-quart stockpot.

3. Stir the onions, bell peppers, and celery into the hot roux and cook over medium heat, stirring often, until the vegetables are softened, about 10 minutes. Stir in the garlic, thyme, and cayenne and cook until fragrant, about 1 minute. Stir in the remaining 2 tablespoons flour and cook for 1 minute. Stir in the tomatoes and cook until they look dry, about 1 minute. Gradually stir in the broth and fish sauce, scraping up any browned bits and smoothing out any lumps.

4. Stir in the chicken and bring to a boil. Cover, reduce to a gentle simmer, and cook until the chicken is tender, about 30 minutes.

5. Stir in the sausage and okra and continue to simmer, uncovered, until heated through, about 5 minutes. Stir in the shrimp and continue to simmer until they are just cooked through, 3 to 5 minutes (do not overcook the shrimp). Season with salt and pepper to taste and serve.

TO MAKE AHEAD

Follow the recipe for Big-Batch Creole-Style Gumbo through step 2, then let the roux cool completely. Transfer the roux to an airtight container and refrigerate for up to 1 week. Return the roux to a 12-quart stockpot and reheat over medium-high heat, whisking often, until very hot, before continuing with step 3. Alternatively, make the stew through step 4, then let cool for 45 minutes; transfer the stew to an airtight container and refrigerate for up to 2 days. To serve, remove any fat that has collected on top and return the stew to a 12-quart stockpot. Cover and bring to a simmer over medium-low heat, stirring occasionally, about 1½ hours. Add water as needed to adjust the stew's consistency and continue with step 5 as directed.

Big-Batch Chicken Stew with Mushrooms, Parsnips, and Sage
SERVES 18 TO 20

You can substitute white mushrooms for the cremini. To prevent the stew from tasting overly salty, be sure to use low-sodium chicken broth and do not season the chicken before browning. If the drippings begin to scorch when browning the chicken in step 2, deglaze the skillet with some of the wine and add the drippings to the stockpot. Be careful not to overcook the chicken breasts in step 5 or they will taste dry. The pot of stew will be heavy—up to 25 pounds—so use caution when handling. Serve with rice or mashed potatoes.

8	tablespoons (1 stick) unsalted butter
3	medium onions, minced
12	medium garlic cloves, minced or pressed through a garlic press (about ¼ cup)
1	ounce dried porcini mushrooms, rinsed and minced
¼	cup minced fresh sage leaves
1	tablespoon minced fresh thyme leaves or 2 teaspoons dried
1¼	cups unbleached all-purpose flour
12	cups low-sodium chicken broth
3	bay leaves
4½	pounds boneless, skinless chicken thighs (about 18 thighs), trimmed and cut into 1-inch pieces
3	tablespoons vegetable oil
2	pounds portobello caps (about 8 medium), wiped clean and cut into 1-inch pieces
2	pounds cremini mushrooms, wiped clean, trimmed, and halved if small, quartered if large (see note)
1	cup dry white wine
2	pounds parsnips (about 12 medium), peeled and cut into ¾-inch pieces
1	pound carrots (about 6 medium), peeled and sliced ½ inch thick

4½ pounds boneless, skinless chicken breasts (about 12 breasts), trimmed, cut in half lengthwise, then sliced crosswise into ½-inch-thick pieces (see the illustrations below)

Salt and ground black pepper

1. Melt 5 tablespoons of the butter in a 12-quart stockpot over medium heat. Add the onions and cook until softened and lightly browned, 8 to 10 minutes. Stir in the garlic, porcini mushrooms, 2 tablespoons of the sage, and thyme and cook until fragrant, about 1 minute. Stir in the flour and cook for 1 minute. Gradually whisk in the broth, smoothing out any lumps. Stir in the bay leaves, bring to a simmer, then remove the pot from the heat.

2. Pat the chicken thighs dry with paper towels. Heat 1 tablespoon of the oil in a 12-inch nonstick skillet over medium-high heat until just smoking. Add one-third of the chicken thighs and brown lightly, 6 to 8 minutes; transfer to the stockpot. Repeat with the remaining 2 tablespoons oil and remaining chicken thighs in two batches; transfer to the stockpot.

3. Melt 1 tablespoon more butter in the skillet over medium-high heat. Add the portobello mushrooms, cover, and cook until they have released their liquid, about 5 minutes. Uncover and continue to cook until the mushrooms are dry and browned, 5 to 10 minutes; transfer to the stockpot. Repeat with the remaining 2 tablespoons butter and cremini mushrooms in two batches; transfer to the stockpot.

4. Add the wine to the skillet, scraping up any browned bits, bring to a simmer, then transfer to the stockpot. Stir the parsnips and carrots into the stockpot and bring to a boil. Cover, reduce to a gentle simmer, and cook for 15 minutes.

5. Stir in the chicken breasts and continue to simmer, uncovered, until the breast meat is just cooked through, the vegetables are tender, and the sauce has thickened slightly, 10 to 15 minutes (do not overcook the chicken).

6. Remove from the heat. Remove the bay leaves, stir in the remaining 2 tablespoons sage, and season with salt and pepper to taste. Cover and let sit for 5 minutes before serving.

TO MAKE AHEAD
Follow the recipe for Big-Batch Chicken Stew with Mushrooms, Parsnips, and Sage through step 4, then let cool for 45 minutes; transfer the stew to an airtight container and refrigerate for up to 2 days. To serve, remove any fat that has collected on top and return the stew to a 12-quart stockpot. Cover, bring to a simmer over medium-low heat, and cook, stirring occasionally, about 1½ hours. Add water as needed to adjust the stew's consistency and continue with step 5 as directed.

CUTTING CHICKEN BREASTS FOR STEW

1. Slice each breast in half lengthwise.

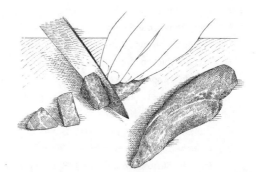

2. Then slice the halved breast crosswise into ½-inch-thick pieces.

Big-Batch Chicken Tagine with Dried Apricots

SERVES 18 TO 20

If you cannot find pitted Greek green olives, substitute pimento-stuffed green olives; if the olives are particularly salty, be sure to rinse them. A variety of dried fruits, including pitted prunes, dark raisins, golden raisins, or currants, can be substituted for the apricots. To prevent the stew from tasting overly salty, be sure to use low-sodium chicken broth and do not season the chicken before browning. If the drippings begin to scorch when browning the chicken in step 2, deglaze the skillet with some of the broth and add the drippings to the stockpot. Be careful not to overcook the chicken breasts in step 5 or they will taste dry. The pot of tagine will be heavy—up to 25 pounds—so use caution when handling. Serve with couscous.

6	tablespoons olive oil
4	large onions, halved and sliced pole to pole into ¼-inch-thick pieces (see the illustration on page 105)
4½	pounds boneless, skinless chicken thighs (about 18 thighs), trimmed and cut into 1-inch pieces
21	medium garlic cloves, minced or pressed through a garlic press (about 7 tablespoons), plus 5 medium garlic cloves, mashed to a fine paste (see the illustrations on page 102)
2½	tablespoons sweet paprika
2½	teaspoons ground cumin
1½	teaspoons ground ginger
1½	teaspoons ground coriander
1½	teaspoons ground cinnamon
¾	teaspoon cayenne pepper
¼	cup unbleached all-purpose flour
12	cups low-sodium chicken broth
3	pounds carrots (about 18 medium), peeled and sliced ½ inch thick
6	tablespoons honey, plus extra as needed
10	(2-inch-long) strips zest from 3 lemons (see the illustration on page 148), trimmed of white pith
4½	pounds boneless, skinless chicken breasts (about 12 breasts), trimmed, cut in half lengthwise, then sliced crosswise into ½-inch-thick pieces (see the illustrations on page 331)
6	cups pitted Greek green olives (see the illustration on page 212), halved (see note)
3	cups dried apricots, chopped coarse (see the illustration on page 294)
⅓	cup juice from 2 lemons, plus extra as needed
1½	teaspoons grated zest from 1 lemon Salt and ground black pepper
½	cup minced fresh cilantro leaves

1. Heat 3 tablespoons of the oil in a 12-quart stockpot over medium heat until shimmering. Add the onions and cook until softened and browned at the edges, 10 to 13 minutes. Remove the pot from the heat.

2. Pat the chicken thighs dry with paper towels. Heat 1 tablespoon more oil in a 12-inch nonstick skillet over medium-high heat until just smoking. Add one-third of the chicken thighs and brown lightly, 6 to 8 minutes; transfer to the stockpot. Repeat with the remaining 2 tablespoons oil and remaining chicken thighs in two batches; transfer to the stockpot.

3. Add the minced garlic, paprika, cumin, ginger, coriander, cinnamon, and cayenne to the fat left in the skillet and cook over medium heat until fragrant, about 1 minute. Stir in the flour and cook for 1 minute. Gradually whisk in 2 cups of the broth, scraping up any browned bits and smoothing out any lumps. Bring to a simmer, then transfer to the stockpot.

4. Stir the remaining 10 cups broth, carrots, honey, and lemon zest strips into the stockpot and bring to a boil. Cover, reduce to a gentle simmer, and cook for 15 minutes.

5. Stir in the chicken breasts, olives, and apricots and continue to simmer, uncovered, until the breast meat is just cooked through, the carrots are tender, and the sauce has thickened slightly, 10 to 15 minutes (do not overcook the chicken).

6. Off the heat, remove the lemon zest strips. Combine the lemon juice, grated lemon zest, and mashed garlic together in a bowl, then stir into the stew. Cover and let sit for 5 minutes. Season with salt, pepper, additional honey, and additional lemon juice to taste. Stir in the cilantro and serve.

TO MAKE AHEAD

Follow the recipe for Big-Batch Chicken Tagine with Dried Apricots through step 4; let cool for 45 minutes. Transfer to an airtight container and refrigerate for up to 2 days. To serve, remove any fat that has collected on top and return the stew to a 12-quart stockpot. Cover and bring to a simmer over medium-low heat, stirring occasionally, about 1½ hours. Add water as needed to adjust the stew's consistency and continue with step 5 as directed.

Big-Batch Hearty Beef Stew

SERVES 18 TO 20

You will need a turkey-size roasting pan that measures about 18 by 13 inches with 4-inch-high sides for this recipe; alternatively, you can use 2 disposable aluminum roasting pans with these same dimensions, one nested inside the other and supported by a baking sheet. A $7 to $10 bottle of medium-bodied red table wine made from a blend of grapes, such as a Côtes du Rhône, will work well here. If the drippings begin to scorch when browning the meat in step 2, deglaze the pot with some of the wine and add the drippings to the roasting pan. The pan of stew will be heavy—up to 25 pounds—so use caution when handling. Serve with boiled potatoes, mashed potatoes, or buttered egg noodles. To read more about Hearty Beef Stew, see page 219.

2½	pound carrots (about 15 medium), peeled and sliced 1 inch thick
4	bay leaves
10	pounds boneless beef chuck eye roast, trimmed and cut into 1½-inch pieces (see the illustrations on page 221)
3	tablespoons vegetable oil
6	tablespoons (¾ stick) unsalted butter
5	medium onions, chopped medium
7	medium garlic cloves, minced or pressed through a garlic press (about 7 teaspoons)
2	tablespoons minced fresh thyme leaves or 2 teaspoons dried
1¼	cups unbleached all-purpose flour
3	tablespoons tomato paste
2½	cups dry red wine (see note)
2¾	cups low-sodium chicken broth
2¾	cups beef broth
3¾	pounds red potatoes (about 11 medium), scrubbed and cut into 1-inch chunks
2¼	cups frozen peas
½	cup minced fresh parsley leaves
	Salt and ground black pepper

1. Adjust an oven rack to the lower-middle position and heat the oven to 325 degrees. Place the carrots, bay leaves, and half of the meat in a large roasting pan (see note); set aside.

2. Pat the remaining meat dry with paper towels. Heat 1 tablespoon of the oil in a large Dutch oven over medium-high heat until just smoking. Add one-third of the meat and brown well on all sides, 7 to 10 minutes; transfer to the roasting pan. Repeat with the remaining 2 tablespoons oil and the remaining meat in two batches; transfer to the roasting pan.

3. Add the butter to the pot and melt over medium heat. Add the onions and cook until softened, 10 to 13 minutes. Stir in the garlic and thyme and cook until fragrant, about 30 seconds. Stir in the flour and tomato paste and cook for 1 minute. Gradually whisk in the wine, scraping up any browned bits and smoothing out any lumps. Gradually whisk in the chicken broth and beef broth and bring to a boil. Pour the mixture into the roasting pan and stir to combine.

4. Cover the pan tightly with aluminum foil. Place the pan in the oven and cook for 2 hours.

5. Stir in the potatoes and continue to cook in the oven, covered, until the meat is tender and the sauce is thickened, 2 to 2½ hours longer.

6. Remove the stew from the oven and remove the bay leaves. Stir in the peas, cover, and let sit for

10 minutes. Stir in the parsley, season with salt and pepper to taste, and serve.

TO MAKE AHEAD

Follow the recipe for Big-Batch Hearty Beef Stew through step 5, then let cool for 45 minutes. Cover the roasting pan tightly with foil and refrigerate the stew for up to 2 days. (We think storing and reheating the stew in the roasting pan is best because it minimizes handling so the tender pieces of meat stay intact. If tight on space, you can transfer the stew to an airtight container; return it to the roasting pan before continuing.) To serve, remove any fat that has collected on top and re-cover the pan tightly with foil. Reheat the stew in a 425-degree oven until hot, 2 to 2½ hours. Add water as needed to adjust the stew's consistency and continue with step 6 as directed.

Big-Batch Daube Provençal

SERVES 18 TO 20

You will need a turkey-size roasting pan that measures about 18 by 13 inches with 4-inch-high sides for this recipe; alternatively, you can use 2 disposable aluminum roasting pans with these same dimensions, one nested inside the other and supported by a baking sheet. We tie the salt pork with twine in order to make it easy to identify after cooking; otherwise, it looks exactly like a piece of stew meat. You can substitute 8 ounces of bacon for the salt pork; add the raw bacon strips to the roasting pan and remove before serving. Cabernet Sauvignon is our favorite wine for this recipe, but Côtes du Rhône and Zinfandel also work. If niçoise olives are not available, kalamata olives can be substituted. If the drippings begin to scorch when browning the meat in step 2, deglaze the pot with some of the wine and add the drippings to the roasting pan. The pan of stew will be heavy— up to 25 pounds—so use caution when handling. Serve with polenta, buttered egg noodles, or boiled potatoes. To read more about Daube Provençal, see page 226.

3	pounds carrots (about 18 medium), peeled and sliced 1 inch thick
2	(4-ounce) pieces salt pork, rind removed, tied tightly with kitchen twine

10	(3-inch-long) strips zest from 2 oranges (see the illustration on page 148), trimmed of white pith and cut into thin matchsticks
10	medium garlic cloves, peeled and sliced thin
8	anchovy fillets, rinsed and minced (about 4 teaspoons)
12	sprigs fresh thyme, tied together with kitchen twine
4	bay leaves
10	pounds boneless beef chuck eye roast, trimmed and cut into 2-inch pieces (see the illustrations on page 221)
2¼	cups pitted niçoise olives (see the illustration on page 212), patted dry and chopped coarse
½	cup plus 2 tablespoons olive oil
5	medium onions, halved and sliced pole to pole into ⅛-inch-thick pieces (see the illustration on page 105)
1½	ounces dried porcini mushrooms, rinsed and minced
1⅔	cups unbleached all-purpose flour
6	tablespoons tomato paste
2	(750-milliliter) bottles dry red wine (6¼ cups)
2½	cups low-sodium chicken broth
2½	cups beef broth
3	(14.5-ounce) cans whole peeled tomatoes, drained and chopped into ½-inch pieces
½	cup minced fresh parsley leaves
	Salt and ground black pepper

1. Adjust an oven rack to the lower-middle position and heat the oven to 325 degrees. Place the carrots, salt pork, orange zest strips, garlic, anchovies, thyme bundle, bay leaves, half of the meat, and half of the olives in a large roasting pan (see note); set aside.

2. Pat the remaining meat dry with paper towels. Heat 1 tablespoon of the oil in a large Dutch oven over medium-high heat until just smoking. Add one-third of the meat and brown well on all sides, 7 to 10 minutes; transfer to the roasting pan. Repeat with 2 tablespoons more oil and the remaining meat in two batches; transfer to the roasting pan.

3. Add the remaining 7 tablespoons oil to the pot and heat over medium heat until shimmering. Add the onions and mushrooms and cook until softened, 10 to 13 minutes. Stir in the flour and tomato paste and cook for 1 minute. Gradually whisk in the wine, scraping up any browned bits and smoothing out any lumps. Gradually whisk in the chicken broth and beef broth and bring to a boil. Pour the mixture into the roasting pan and stir to combine.

4. Cover the pan tightly with aluminum foil. Place the roasting pan in the oven and cook until the meat is tender and the sauce is thickened and glossy, 3¼ to 3¾ hours.

5. Remove the stew from the oven and remove the salt pork, thyme bundle, and bay leaves. Stir in the tomatoes and remaining olives, cover, and let sit for 10 minutes. Stir in the parsley, season with salt and pepper to taste, and serve.

TO MAKE AHEAD

Follow the recipe for Big-Batch Daube Provençal through step 4, then let cool for 45 minutes. Cover the roasting pan tightly with foil and refrigerate the stew for up to 2 days. (We think storing and reheating the stew in the roasting pan is best because it minimizes handling so the tender pieces of meat stay intact. If tight on space, you can transfer the stew to an airtight container; return it to the roasting pan before continuing.) To serve, remove any fat that has collected on top and re-cover the pan tightly with foil. Reheat the stew in a 425-degree oven until hot, 1½ to 2 hours. Add water as needed to adjust the stew's consistency and continue with step 5 as directed.

Big-Batch Beef Burgundy

SERVES 18 TO 20

You will need a turkey-size roasting pan that measures about 18 by 13 inches with 4-inch-high sides for this recipe; alternatively, you can use 2 disposable aluminum roasting pans with these same dimensions, one nested inside the other and supported by a baking sheet. You can substitute 8 ounces of bacon for the salt pork; if not enough fat is rendered from the salt pork or bacon for browning the meat, add vegetable oil. If the drippings begin to scorch

when browning the meat in step 3, deglaze the pot with some of the wine and add the drippings to the roasting pan. The pan of stew will be heavy—up to 25 pounds—so use caution when handling. Serve with boiled potatoes, mashed potatoes, or buttered egg noodles. To read more about Beef Burgundy, see page 224.

AROMATIC BOUQUET

8 ounces salt pork, cut into ¼-inch-thick matchsticks (see note)
3 medium onions, chopped coarse
3 medium carrots, peeled and chopped coarse
3 medium garlic heads, cloves separated and crushed
15 sprigs fresh parsley, torn into pieces
12 sprigs fresh thyme
4 bay leaves, crumbled
1 ounce dried porcini mushrooms, rinsed

STEW

10 pounds boneless beef chuck eye roast, trimmed and cut into 2-inch pieces (see the illustrations on page 221)
8 tablespoons (1 stick) unsalted butter
1⅔ cups unbleached all-purpose flour
3 tablespoons tomato paste
2 (750-milliliter) bottles red Burgundy or Pinot Noir (about 6¼ cups)
2½ cups low-sodium chicken broth
2½ cups beef broth

GARNISH

4 tablespoons (½ stick) unsalted butter
2¼ pounds white mushrooms, wiped clean, trimmed, and halved if small or quartered if large
Salt and ground black pepper
20 ounces frozen pearl onions (about 5 cups)
1 cup water
3 tablespoons sugar
¼ cup brandy
½ cup minced fresh parsley leaves

1. FOR THE AROMATIC BOUQUET: Cook the salt pork in a large Dutch oven over medium heat until lightly browned and crisp, about 12 minutes. With a slotted spoon, transfer the salt pork to a

plate. Pour off and reserve the fat. Following the illustrations on page 226, assemble the salt pork and remaining bouquet ingredients in a double-layer cheesecloth pouch and tie securely with kitchen twine; set aside.

2. FOR THE STEW: Adjust an oven rack to the lower-middle position and heat the oven to 325 degrees. Place half of the meat in a large roasting pan (see note); set aside.

3. Pat the remaining meat dry with paper towels. Heat 1 tablespoon of the rendered pork fat in a large Dutch oven over medium-high heat until just smoking. Add one-third of the meat and brown well on all sides, 7 to 10 minutes; transfer to the roasting pan. Repeat with 2 tablespoons more pork fat and the remaining meat in two batches; transfer to the roasting pan.

4. Add the butter to the pot and melt over medium-low heat. Stir in the flour and tomato paste and cook for 1 minute. Gradually whisk in 6 cups of the wine, scraping up any browned bits and smoothing out any lumps. Gradually whisk in the chicken broth and beef broth and bring to a boil. Pour the mixture into the roasting pan and stir to combine.

5. Nestle the bouquet into the pan, then cover the pan tightly with aluminum foil. Place the roasting pan in the oven and cook until the meat is tender and the sauce is thickened and glossy, 3¼ to 3¾ hours.

6. FOR THE GARNISH: Meanwhile, melt 1 tablespoon of the butter in a 12-inch nonstick skillet over medium heat. Add half of the mushrooms and ¼ teaspoon salt, cover, and cook until the mushrooms have released their liquid, about 5 minutes. Uncover and cook until the mushrooms are dry and browned, 5 to 10 minutes. Transfer to a large bowl, cover, and set aside. Repeat with 1 tablespoon more butter, ¼ teaspoon salt, and the remaining mushrooms; transfer to the bowl.

7. Add the pearl onions, water, sugar, remaining 2 tablespoons butter, and ½ teaspoon salt to the skillet and bring to a boil over high heat. Cover, reduce to medium-low heat, and simmer, shaking the pan occasionally, until the onions are tender, about 10 minutes. Uncover, increase the heat to high, and simmer until all the liquid evaporates and the onions are browned, about 10 minutes. Transfer the onion mixture to the bowl with the mushrooms, season with salt and pepper to taste, and set aside.

8. Remove the stew from the oven and remove the aromatic bouquet. Stir in the mushroom-onion garnish, remaining ¼ cup wine, and brandy. Season with salt and pepper to taste, cover, and let sit for 10 minutes. Stir in the parsley and serve.

TO MAKE AHEAD

Follow the recipe for Big-Batch Beef Burgundy through step 5, remove the bouquet, then let the stew cool for 45 minutes. Cover the roasting pan tightly with foil and refrigerate the stew for up to 2 days. (We think storing and reheating the stew in the roasting pan is best because it minimizes handling so the tender pieces of meat stay intact. If tight on space, you can transfer the stew to an airtight container; return it to the roasting pan before continuing.) The garnish can be cooked through step 7, transferred to an airtight container, and refrigerated for up 2 days; reheat gently in the microwave until warm before using. To serve, remove any fat that has collected on top of the stew and re-cover the pan tightly with foil. Reheat the stew in a 425-degree oven until hot, 1½ to 2 hours. Add water as needed to adjust the stew's consistency and continue with step 8 as directed.

Big-Batch Pork Stew with Brandy, Fennel, and Prunes
SERVES 18 TO 20

You will need a turkey-size roasting pan that measures about 18 by 13 inches with 4-inch high sides for this recipe; alternatively, you can use 2 disposable aluminum roasting pans with these same dimensions, one nested inside the other and supported by a baking sheet. Boneless pork butt roast is often labeled Boston butt in the supermarket. While 2 cups of brandy may seem like a lot for this recipe, we recommend using an inexpensive brand and not skimping on the amount; it provides just the right balance of flavors. If the drippings begin to scorch when browning the meat in step 2, deglaze the pot with some of the broth and add the drippings to the roasting pan. To prevent the stew from tasting overly salty, be sure to use low-sodium chicken broth and season to taste only before serving. The pan of stew will be heavy—up to 25 pounds—so use caution when handling. Serve with buttered egg noodles or rice. To read more about Pork Stew with Brandy, Fennel, and Prunes, see page 234.

4	bay leaves
10	pounds boneless pork butt roast, trimmed and cut into 1½-inch pieces
5	tablespoons vegetable oil
3	large leeks, white and light green parts only, halved lengthwise, sliced ¼ inch thick, and rinsed thoroughly (about 4½ cups) (see the illustrations on page 103)
9	medium garlic cloves, minced or pressed through a garlic press (about 3 tablespoons)
9	tablespoons unbleached all-purpose flour
2	cups brandy (see note)
9	cups low-sodium chicken broth
3	pounds carrots (about 18 medium), peeled and sliced 1 inch thick
3	large fennel bulbs (about 3 pounds), trimmed of stalks, cored, and cut into ½-inch-thick strips (see the illustrations on page 27)
3	cups heavy cream, warmed
3	cups prunes, halved
¼	cup minced fresh tarragon leaves
¼	cup minced fresh parsley leaves
3	tablespoons juice from 1 lemon
	Salt and ground black pepper

1. Adjust an oven rack to the lower-middle position and heat the oven to 325 degrees. Place the bay leaves and half of the meat in a large roasting pan (see note); set aside.

2. Pat the remaining meat dry with paper towels. Heat 1 tablespoon of the oil in a large Dutch oven over medium-high heat until just smoking. Add one-third of the meat and brown well on all sides, 7 to 10 minutes; transfer to the roasting pan. Repeat with 2 tablespoons more oil and the remaining meat in two batches; transfer to the roasting pan.

3. Add the remaining 2 tablespoons oil to the pot and heat over medium heat until shimmering. Add the leeks and cook until wilted and lightly browned, 8 to 10 minutes. Stir in the garlic and cook until fragrant, about 30 seconds. Stir in the

flour and cook for 1 minute. Slowly whisk in the brandy, scraping up any browned bits and smoothing out any lumps. Gradually whisk in the broth and bring to a boil. Pour the mixture into the roasting pan and stir to combine.

4. Cover the pan tightly with aluminum foil. Place the roasting pan in the oven and cook for 1½ hours.

5. Stir in the carrots and fennel and continue to cook in the oven, covered, until the meat is tender and the sauce is thickened, 1 to 1½ hours longer.

6. Remove the stew from the oven and remove the bay leaves. Stir in the cream and prunes, cover, and let sit for 10 minutes. Stir in the tarragon, parsley, and lemon juice, season with salt and pepper to taste, and serve.

TO MAKE AHEAD

Follow the recipe for Big-Batch Pork Stew with Brandy, Fennel, and Prunes through step 5, then let cool for 45 minutes. Cover the roasting pan tightly with foil and refrigerate the stew for up to 2 days. (We think storing and reheating the stew in the roasting pan is best because it minimizes handling so the tender pieces of meat stay intact. If tight on space, you can transfer the stew to an airtight container; return it to the roasting pan before continuing.) To serve, remove any fat that has collected on top and re-cover the pan tightly with foil. Reheat the stew in a 425-degree oven until hot, 1½ to 2 hours. Add water as needed to adjust the stew's consistency and continue with step 6 as directed.

Big-Batch Classic Beef Chili

SERVES 18 TO 20

The pot of chili will be heavy—up to 25 pounds—so use caution when handling. Serve with lime wedges, diced fresh tomatoes, diced avocado, sliced scallions, chopped red onion, minced cilantro, sour cream, and/or shredded Monterey Jack or cheddar cheese. To read more about Classic Beef Chili, see page 257.

⅔	cup chili powder
2½	tablespoons ground cumin
1½	tablespoons ground coriander

2½ teaspoons dried oregano

2 teaspoons red pepper flakes

¾ teaspoon cayenne pepper

Salt and ground black pepper

¼ cup vegetable oil

5 medium onions, minced

2 red bell peppers, stemmed, seeded, and cut into ½-inch pieces

15 medium garlic cloves, minced or pressed through a garlic press (about 5 tablespoons)

5 pounds 85 percent lean ground beef

3 (28-ounce) cans tomato puree

5 (15-ounce) cans dark red kidney beans, drained and rinsed

2 (28-ounce) cans diced tomatoes

Water, as needed

1. Combine the chili powder, cumin, coriander, oregano, red pepper flakes, cayenne, and 1 teaspoon salt in a small bowl; set aside.

2. Heat the oil in a 12-quart stockpot over medium heat until shimmering. Add the onions and bell peppers and cook until softened, 18 to 20 minutes. Stir in the garlic and spice mixture and cook, stirring constantly, until fragrant, about 2 minutes (do not let the spices burn).

3. Increase the heat to medium-high. Stir in the beef, 1 pound at a time, and cook, breaking up the meat with a wooden spoon, until no longer pink, 3 to 5 minutes per pound. Stir in the tomato puree, beans, and diced tomatoes with their juice and bring to a simmer. Cover, reduce to a gentle simmer, and cook, stirring occasionally, for 1 hour.

4. Uncover and continue to simmer gently until the beef is tender and the sauce is dark, rich, and slightly thickened, about 2 hours longer. (If at any time the chili begins to stick to the bottom of the pot or looks too thick, stir in water as needed.) Season with salt and pepper to taste before serving.

TO MAKE AHEAD

Follow the recipe for Big-Batch Classic Beef Chili completely through step 4, then let cool for 45 minutes; transfer the chili to an airtight container and refrigerate for up to 2 days. To serve, remove any fat that has collected on top and return the chili to a 12-quart stockpot. Cover and bring to a simmer over medium-low heat, stirring occasionally, about 1½ hours. Add additional water as needed to adjust the chili's consistency and season with salt and pepper to taste before serving.

Big-Batch Chili con Carne
SERVES 18 TO 20

You will need a turkey-size roasting pan that measures about 18 by 13 inches with 4-inch-high sides for this recipe; alternatively, you can use 2 disposable aluminum roasting pans with these same dimensions, one nested inside the other and supported by a baking sheet. For more heat, include the jalapeño seeds and ribs when mincing. If not enough fat is rendered from the bacon for browning the meat, add vegetable oil. If the drippings begin to scorch when browning the meat in step 3, deglaze the pot with some of the water and add the drippings to the roasting pan. The pan of chili will be heavy—up to 25 pounds— so use caution when handling. Serve with minced fresh cilantro, sliced scallions, minced onion, diced avocado, shredded cheddar or Monterey Jack cheese, and/or sour cream. To read more about Chili con Carne, see page 261.

12 pounds boneless beef chuck eye roast, trimmed and cut into 1½-inch pieces (see the illustrations on page 221)

1 cup unbleached all-purpose flour

7 ancho chiles (about 1¾ ounces), toasted and ground (see page 270) or 7 tablespoons ancho chili powder

7 New Mexico chiles (about 1¾ ounces), toasted and ground (see page 270) or 7 tablespoons New Mexico chili powder

2½ tablespoons ground cumin

5 teaspoons dried oregano

14 ounces (about 14 slices) bacon, minced

3 medium onions, minced

10 jalapeño chiles, stemmed, seeded, and minced (see note)

12 medium garlic cloves, minced or pressed through a garlic press (about ¼ cup)

8 cups water, plus extra as needed

1 (15-ounce) can tomato sauce

2½ tablespoons light brown sugar, plus extra as needed

5 tablespoons juice from 3 limes
¼ cup minced chipotle chile in adobo sauce,
plus extra as needed
Salt and ground black pepper

1. Adjust an oven rack to the lower-middle position and heat the oven to 325 degrees. Place half of the meat in a large roasting pan (see note); set aside. Combine the flour, ground chiles, cumin, and oregano in a small bowl; set aside.

2. Cook the bacon in a large Dutch oven over medium heat until rendered and crisp, about 12 minutes. Using a slotted spoon, transfer the bacon to a paper towel–lined plate and refrigerate until needed. Pour off and reserve the bacon fat in a small bowl.

3. Pat the remaining meat dry with paper towels. Heat 1 tablespoon of the rendered bacon fat in a large Dutch oven over medium-high heat until just smoking. Add one-third of the meat and brown well on all sides, 7 to 10 minutes; transfer to the roasting pan. Repeat with 2 tablespoons more bacon fat and the remaining meat in two batches; transfer to the roasting pan.

4. Add 2 tablespoons more bacon fat to the pot and heat over medium heat until shimmering. Add the onions and cook until softened, 8 to 10 minutes. Stir in the jalapeños and garlic and cook until fragrant, about 1 minute. Stir in the spice mixture and ¼ cup more bacon fat and cook, stirring constantly, until fragrant, about 1 minute.

5. Gradually whisk in the water, scraping up any browned bits and smoothing out any lumps. Gradually whisk in the tomato sauce and sugar and bring to a boil. Pour the mixture into the roasting pan.

6. Stir the contents of the roasting pan to combine, then cover the pan tightly with aluminum foil. Place the roasting pan in the oven and cook until the meat is tender and the sauce is thickened, 4 to 4½ hours.

7. Remove the chili from the oven. Stir in the lime juice and chipotles and adjust the sauce consistency with additional water as needed. Season with salt, pepper, additional sugar, and additional chipotles to taste, cover, and let sit for 10 minutes. Reheat the bacon in the microwave on high power

until heated through and crisp, about 30 seconds. Serve, sprinkling individual portions with the crisp bacon.

TO MAKE AHEAD

Follow the recipe for Big-Batch Chili con Carne through step 6, then let cool for 45 minutes. Cover the roasting pan tightly with foil and refrigerate the chili for up to 2 days. (We think storing and reheating the chili in the roasting pan is best because it minimizes handling so the tender pieces of meat stay intact. If tight on space, you can transfer the chili to an airtight container; return it to the roasting pan before continuing.) To serve, remove any fat that has collected on top and re-cover the pan tightly with foil. Reheat the chili in a 425-degree oven until hot, 1½ to 2 hours. Add additional water as needed to adjust the chili's consistency and continue with step 7 as directed.

Big-Batch White Chicken Chili
SERVES 18 TO 20

If Anaheim chiles cannot be found, substitute an additional 3 poblanos and 2 jalapeños. For more heat, include the jalapeño seeds and ribs when mincing. If the drippings begin to scorch when browning the chicken in step 1, deglaze the skillet with some of the broth and reserve the drippings; add them to the stockpot in step 5. To prevent the chili from tasting overly salty, be sure to use low-sodium chicken broth and do not season the chicken before browning. The pot of chili will be heavy—up to 25 pounds—so use caution when handling. Serve with sour cream, tortilla chips, and lime wedges. To read more about White Chicken Chili, see page 263.

7½ pounds bone-in, skin-on split chicken breasts (about 10 breasts)
5 tablespoons vegetable oil
9 cups low-sodium chicken broth
5 medium onions, chopped coarse
7 poblano chiles, stemmed, seeded, and chopped coarse (see note) (see page 271)
7 Anaheim chiles, stemmed, seeded, and chopped coarse (see note) (see page 271)

4   jalapeño chiles, stemmed, seeded, and
     chopped coarse, plus 1 jalapeño chile,
     stemmed, seeded, and minced (see note)

12   medium garlic cloves, minced or pressed
     through a garlic press (about ¼ cup)

2   tablespoons ground cumin

2   teaspoons ground coriander
     Salt and ground black pepper

4   (15-ounce) cans cannellini beans, drained and
     rinsed

⅔   cup minced fresh cilantro leaves

10   scallions, sliced thin

7   tablespoons juice from 4 limes

2   tablespoons minced fresh oregano leaves

1. Pat the chicken dry with paper towels. Heat 1 tablespoon of the oil in a 12-inch skillet over medium-high heat until just smoking. Brown one-third of the chicken on both sides, 7 to 10 minutes; transfer to a large bowl. Repeat with 2 tablespoons more oil and the remaining chicken in two batches; transfer to the bowl and remove all the skin. Add 1 cup of the broth to the skillet, scraping up any browned bits, and bring to a simmer; transfer the drippings to a bowl and reserve.

2. Meanwhile, toss the onions, poblano chiles, Anaheim chiles, and chopped jalapeños together in a large bowl. Process the vegetables, in four batches, in a food processor to the consistency of chunky salsa, about 12 pulses.

3. Heat the remaining 2 tablespoons oil in a 12-quart stockpot over medium heat until shimmering. Add the processed vegetable mixture, garlic, cumin, coriander, and 1 teaspoon salt and cook until the vegetables are softened, about 20 minutes.

4. Return 2½ cups of the cooked vegetables to the food processor. Add 2½ cups of the beans and

2½ cups more broth to the food processor. Puree the mixture until smooth, about 20 seconds, then return it to the pot.

5. Stir the remaining 5½ cups broth, reserved drippings, and browned chicken with any accumulated juice into the pot and bring to a simmer. Cover, reduce to a gentle simmer, and cook until the chicken registers 160 to 165 degrees on an instant-read thermometer, about 30 minutes.

6. Remove the chicken from the pot, let cool slightly, then shred the meat into bite-size pieces (see the illustration on page 43), discarding the bones. Meanwhile, stir the remaining beans into the pot and continue to simmer, uncovered, until the beans are heated through and the chili has thickened slightly, about 30 minutes.

7. Remove the chili from the heat. Stir the shredded chicken into the chili, cover, and let sit for 10 minutes. Stir the remaining minced jalapeño, cilantro, scallions, lime juice, and oregano into the chili. Season with salt and pepper to taste and serve.

TO MAKE AHEAD

Follow the recipe for Big-Batch White Chicken Chili through step 6, then let cool for 45 minutes; transfer the chili and shredded chicken to separate airtight containers and refrigerate for up to 2 days. To serve, remove any fat that has collected on top of the chili and return to a 12-quart stockpot. Cover and bring to a simmer over medium-low heat, stirring occasionally, about 1½ hours. Add water as needed to adjust the chili's consistency, stir in the shredded chicken, and continue heating, 5 to 10 minutes longer, until the chicken is heated through. Continue with step 7 as directed.

INDEX

A NOTE ON CONVERSIONS

SOME SAY COOKING IS A SCIENCE AND AN ART. We would say that geography has a hand in it, too. Flour milled in the United Kingdom and elsewhere will feel and taste different from flour milled in the United States. So, while we cannot promise that the loaf of bread you bake in Canada or England will taste the same as a loaf baked in the States, we can offer guidelines for converting weights and measures. We also recommend that you rely on your instincts when making our recipes. Refer to the visual cues provided. If the bread dough hasn't "come together in a ball," as described, you may need to add more flour—even if the recipe doesn't tell you so. You be the judge.

The recipes in this book were developed using standard U.S. measures following U.S. government guidelines. The charts below offer equivalents for U.S., metric, and Imperial (U.K.) measures. All conversions are approximate and have been rounded up or down to the nearest whole number. For example:

EXAMPLE:

1 teaspoon = 4.9292 milliliters, rounded up to 5 milliliters

1 ounce = 28.3495 grams, rounded down to 28 grams

Volume Conversions

U.S.	METRIC
1 teaspoon	5 milliliters
2 teaspoons	10 milliliters
1 tablespoon	15 milliliters
2 tablespoons	30 milliliters
¼ cup	59 milliliters
⅓ cup	79 milliliters
½ cup	118 milliliters
¾ cup	177 milliliters
1 cup	237 milliliters
1¼ cups	296 milliliters
1½ cups	355 milliliters
2 cups	473 milliliters
2½ cups	592 milliliters
3 cups	710 milliliters
4 cups (1 quart)	0.946 liter
1.06 quarts	1 liter
4 quarts (1 gallon)	3.8 liters

Weight Conversions

OUNCES	GRAMS
½	14
¾	21
1	28
1½	43
2	57
2½	71
3	85
3½	99
4	113
4½	128
5	142
6	170
7	198
8	227
9	255
10	283
12	340
16 (1 pound)	454

Conversions for Ingredients Commonly Used in Baking

Baking is an exacting science. Because measuring by weight is far more accurate than measuring by volume, and thus more likely to achieve reliable results, in our recipes we provide ounce measures in addition to cup measures for many ingredients. Refer to the chart below to convert these measures into grams.

INGREDIENT	OUNCES	GRAMS
Flour		
1 cup all-purpose flour*	5	142
1 cup whole wheat flour	5½	156
Sugar		
1 cup granulated (white) sugar	7	198
1 cup packed brown sugar (light or dark)	7	198
1 cup confectioners' sugar	4	113
Cocoa Powder		
1 cup cocoa powder	3	85
Butter†		
4 tablespoons (½ stick, or ¼ cup)	2	57
8 tablespoons (1 stick, or ½ cup)	4	113
16 tablespoons (2 sticks, or 1 cup)	8	227

* U.S. all-purpose flour, the most frequently used flour in this book, does not contain leaveners, as some European flours do. These leavened flours are called self-rising or self-raising. If you are using self-rising flour, take this into consideration before adding leavening to a recipe.

† In the United States, butter is sold both salted and unsalted. We generally recommend unsalted butter. If you are using salted butter, take this into consideration before adding salt to a recipe.

Oven Temperatures

FAHRENHEIT	CELSIUS	GAS MARK (IMPERIAL)
225	105	¼
250	120	½
275	130	1
300	150	2
325	165	3
350	180	4
375	190	5
400	200	6
425	220	7
450	230	8
475	245	9

Converting Temperatures from an Instant-Read Thermometer

We include doneness temperatures in many of our recipes, such as those for poultry, meat, and bread. We recommend an instant-read thermometer for the job. Refer to the table above to convert Fahrenheit degrees to Celsius. Or, for temperatures not represented in the chart, use this simple formula:

Subtract 32 degrees from the Fahrenheit reading, then divide the result by 1.8 to find the Celsius reading.

EXAMPLE:

"Roast until the thickest part of a chicken thigh registers 175 degrees on an instant-read thermometer." To convert:

$175°F - 32 = 143$

$143 \div 1.8 = 79°C$ (rounded down from 79.44)